The ILLUSTRATED
BOOK of TREES

0 11557 02811 9

The ILLUSTRATED BOOK of TREES

Revised and Updated

THE COMPREHENSIVE FIELD GUIDE TO MORE THAN 250 TREES OF EASTERN NORTH AMERICA

William Carey Grimm

revised by John Kartesz

STACKPOLE
BOOKS

To my friend and fellow nature lover Johnny Lewis

Copyright © 2002 by Stackpole Books

Published by
STACKPOLE BOOKS
5067 Ritter Road
Mechanicsburg, PA 17055
www.stackpolebooks.com

First edition

10 9 8 7 6 5 4 3 2

Printed in the United States of America

Illustrations by the author
Cover design by Caroline Stover

Cataloging-in-Publication Data is on file with the Library of Congress.

ISBN-10: 0-8117-2811-0
ISBN-13: 978-0-8117-2811-9

Contents

Species of Trees

Preface

Over the past four decades, *The Illustrated Book of Trees* by William Carey Grimm has helped advance the public's awareness of trees of eastern North America and has also served as a comprehensive field and laboratory guide for tree identification. Understandably, over the decades, numerous new facts about trees and new insights into tree taxonomy, nomenclature, and phytogeography have surfaced. To keep the book current as a definitive work on eastern trees, a new edition needed to be published.

In preparing this new edition, I wanted to keep the text as simplified as possible, yet provide a high degree of scientific accuracy. Some 270 trees are treated within this work, including all of our native trees plus numerous introductions that have become established as part of our naturalized tree flora. The geographic scope of this work includes all of the U.S. states east of the Mississippi River (except for areas in southern Florida) plus all of the provinces of eastern Canada. A most significant change in this edition is the expansion of the species descriptions, making them more uniform in structure, and arranging them into an abbreviated or telegraphic style. Also new is the development of a diagnostic character box for the purpose of providing rapid identification of species. Other changes include the expansion and revision of the dichotomous keys to include both the native and introduced species, along with the addition of many new illustrations, with modification of existing ones to reflect the most significant diagnostic characters useful in identification. Additionally, the text itself has been expanded to include helpful suggestions for separating species with similar morphologies, plus numerous factual novelties.

I hope that the publication of this new edition of *The Illustrated Book of Trees* will encourage the general public's long-established interest in eastern trees and that this classic will continue to serve as a trusted source of identification for these species found in our forest, parks, and woodlots.

John T. Kartesz

The Study of Trees

The serious student of trees should first become familiar with their general structure. In this book an attempt has been made to eliminate as much of the technical language of botany as possible, and the relatively few terms that have been employed for the sake of convenience should not prove too difficult for anyone to master. Identifications, in most instances, have been based on characters that are evident for long periods of time; principally on leaves and fruits in summer identifications and twig and bark characteristics in winter identifications. The accompanying plates have been planned to show the leaves, twigs, fruits, and detailed characteristics of the buds. In some instances, particularly where the flowers are conspicuous, drawings of the flowers have also been included.

Trees are, of course, woody plants, but so are the so-called shrubs. We often recognize a tree as being larger than a shrub, and usually think of trees as having a solitary stem or trunk. Actually the differences between trees and shrubs are purely relative ones. There is no real line of demarcation between trees and shrubs. The gray birch, for instance, often has several stems in a clump, and it could, therefore, just as logically be called a large shrub as a tree. In this book you will find many species that are described as being either shrubs or small trees. Frequently a species will be merely shrubby in one portion of its range and be quite large and treelike somewhere else. The great-laurel and the mountain-laurel are usually only shrubs in the mountains of Pennsylvania, yet they grow to be nearly 40 feet in height and assume treelike proportions in the Great Smoky Mountains of North Carolina and Tennessee. In a work on trees it is often doubtful just which borderline species should be included and which ones should be omitted. Many species very properly belong both in a work on trees and also in one on shrubs. For some of the more shrubby tree species, refer to *The Illustrated Book of Wildflowers and Shrubs* (Stackpole 1993).

How Trees Grow

Trees, like all other green plants, are able to make their own foods out of raw materials derived from the soil and from the air. The roots serve the very important function of anchoring the trees to the earth; the very youngest portions of the roots also absorb water and dissolved mineral nutrients from the soil. The water passes upward through the *sapwood*, the lighter-colored outer wood in the trunks and larger branches of the tree, and finally reaches the leaves. The leaves of the tree are, in a sense, food factories. It is within the leaves that sugars and starches are made from water and nutrients from the soil and from the gas carbon dioxide, which is derived from the air. The machines utilized in this process of food-making, or *photosynthesis*, are microscopic bodies called *chloroplasts*, which are green because they contain a green pigment known as *chlorophyll*. The energy necessary to run this food-making machinery comes from the sunlight. Much more water passes into the leaves than is actually needed in the food-making and other life processes, so the leaves pass off this excess water into the atmosphere in the form of an invisible vapor. Oxygen, another important waste product of food making, also is returned to the air.

The food materials that are manufactured within the leaves of the tree must be transported to all the growing parts of the tree, even to the very tips of the roots. The sap containing this food material is distributed through the inner bark of the branches, trunks, and roots. Thus if a tree is girdled, or the layer of inner bark is completely severed throughout the circumference of its trunk, the tree will not die immediately, but it will gradually starve to death because the food materials made within the leaves cannot be transported to its roots.

Nearly everyone at some time has observed the *annual rings*, or rings of growth, in some sawed-off tree trunk. Between the innermost layer of the bark and the outermost layer of the wood there is a very thin layer of actively growing cells called the *cambium layer*. It is within this layer that

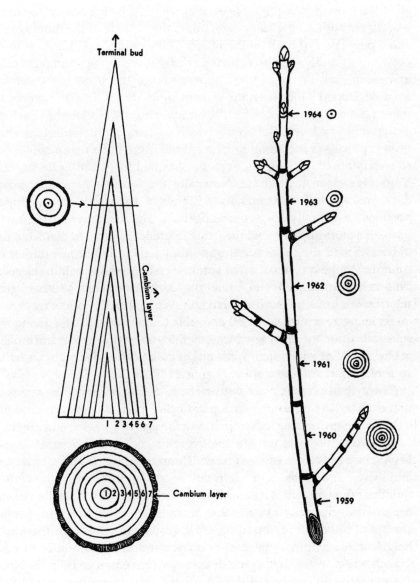

HOW A TREE GROWS

all of the growth in diameter takes place. Each growing season the cambium layer adds a new layer of wood on the outside of the older wood, and a new layer of bark on the inside of the older bark. Because trees grow most rapidly soon after their growth begins in the spring, the cells of the *spring wood* are larger and thinner walled than those in the *summer wood* developed later, when the growth slows down. The differences in these cells are responsible for the annual rings. Catastrophes such as extreme heavy freezes or ice storms may temporarily interfere with growth processes and result in false annual rings, but a reasonably accurate estimate of the tree's age can be obtained by counting the annual rings very close to its base. Naturally the number of annual rings decreases when the count is made higher on the trunk, for the upper portions are actually not as old as the base. The diagram on page 3 will make this more apparent. As the trunk or branches grow in diameter, the older layers of the sapwood die, and they generally become darker in color due to the accumulation of various waste products within the cells. This darker interior portion, called the *heartwood*, merely serves to give the trunk or branch structural strength. We have seen hollow trees that go on living year after year. They are able to do so because the living tissue is all within the outer few inches of the trunks; unless they are broken off by a violent wind, such trees might go on living for many years in spite of the fact that the trunks are entirely hollow.

Growth also takes place within the *buds* that occur on the younger branches, or *twigs*. Contrary to popular belief, buds do not appear on the twigs in the spring; they develop during the growing season and are fully developed before autumn. The buds contain rudimentary branches and leaves, or in some cases flowers, which are simply modified branches and leaves. They remain in a dormant condition throughout the winter months. When growth is resumed in the spring, some of the buds expand rapidly, due primarily to the intake of water. It is then that most people say that the trees are "budding." All growth in length, in the tree's height, in the lengthening of its branches, and in the formation of new branches takes place in the growth tissues, which emanate from the buds. A spike driven into the trunk of a tree six feet above the ground will always be six feet above the ground, but it will gradually be buried within the expanding layers of wood laid down by the tree's cambium layer.

Tree Identification

SUMMER CHARACTERISTICS
Leaves

The leaves of trees are used much in making summer identifications. Unlike flowers or fruits, leaves or leaflike structures are present on all living trees during the summer months, and are available for study for a comparatively long period of time. Small trees often do not have the characteristic bark of older specimens, but they do have leaves by which they may be identified. In attempting to identify any tree by its leaves, or leaflike structures, care should be taken to procure *normal or typical leaves at all times.* As a rule, the leaves found on sprout growth are seldom characteristic of the species, and in many cases may prove to be very confusing. Such leaves are frequently much larger than normal leaves, often differing markedly in shape and other characteristics. The keys and the descriptions in this book are all based on normal leaves and other normal characteristics. Do not collect the first specimen you find. Look carefully at the tree, or preferably several trees; then select a branch that has average-looking or normal leaves.

On pages 6 and 7 an attempt has been made to illustrate most of the important characteristics that are used for the identification of trees by means of their leaves. There are other important things such as leaf texture, the presence or absence of hairiness, or pubescence, the color, and the odor or taste. These characteristics cannot be illustrated, but such characteristics are often mentioned in both the keys and the text.

The leaves of firs, larches, pines, and spruces are long, narrow, and needlelike; in fact, they are commonly referred to simply as *needles.* In the case of the larches and the pines the needles are arranged in clusters or bundles, usually with a sheath about the base of the cluster. The needles of the firs and the spruces are arranged singly along the branchlets or twigs. The leaves of the hemlock and of the balsam fir are also narrow, but they are distinctly flattened and have almost parallel margins. Such

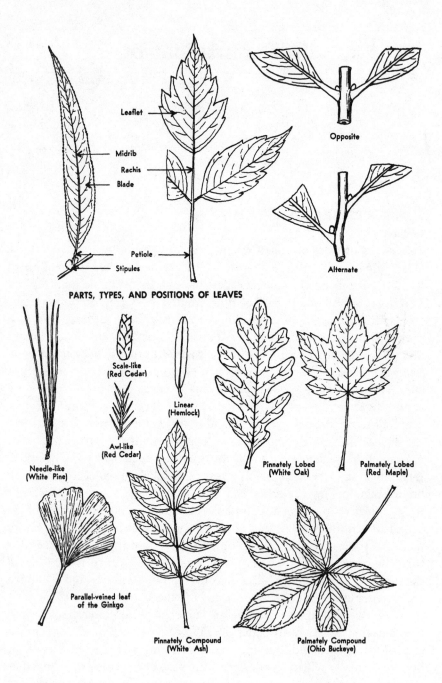

Leaflet

Midrib

Rachis

Blade

Petiole

Stipules

Opposite

Alternate

PARTS, TYPES, AND POSITIONS OF LEAVES

Scale-like
(Red Cedar)

Awl-like
(Red Cedar)

Linear
(Hemlock)

Needle-like
(White Pine)

Pinnately Lobed
(White Oak)

Palmately Lobed
(Red Maple)

Parallel-veined leaf
of the Ginkgo

Pinnately Compound
(White Ash)

Palmately Compound
(Ohio Buckeye)

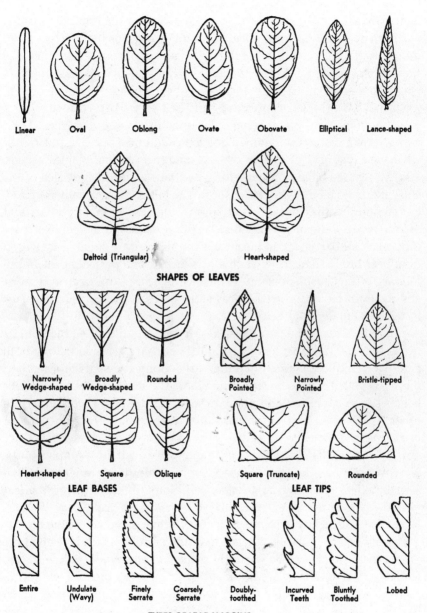

Linear   **Oval**   **Oblong**   **Ovate**   **Obovate**   **Elliptical**   **Lance-shaped**

Deltoid (Triangular)   Heart-shaped

SHAPES OF LEAVES

Narrowly
Wedge-shaped   Broadly
Wedge-shaped   Rounded   Broadly
Pointed   Narrowly
Pointed   Bristle-tipped

Heart-shaped   Square   Oblique   Square (Truncate)   Rounded

LEAF BASES   **LEAF TIPS**

Entire   Undulate
(Wavy)   Finely
Serrate   Coarsely
Serrate   Doubly-
toothed   Incurved
Teeth   Bluntly
Toothed   Lobed

TYPES OF LEAF MARGINS

leaves are said to be *linear*. If one were to examine the branchlets of the northern or Atlantic white-cedars, it would be obvious that the leaves are quite small and *scalelike*, with their edges overlapping each other like the shingles on a roof. The red-cedar also has scalelike leaves, which are closely pressed against the branchlets, but on the more vigorous growth the leaves are awl-like, or spreading, stiff, and very sharp-pointed.

The majority of our trees are classified as *broad-leaved* trees. Their leaves have a distinctly flattened portion called the *blade*. They also usually have a distinct leafstalk, or *petiole*. Some trees such as maples, aspens, and basswoods have relatively long petioles, while the petioles of the elms and most birches are rather short. The petioles are usually rounded, but sometimes they are grooved, and in the case of most poplars and aspens they are distinctly flattened. At the very base of the petioles there is often a pair of *stipules*. In most trees the stipules are small or they soon disappear, but in some instances they are leaflike and persistent. Such stipules are often conspicuous on certain willows, the American sycamore, and the tuliptree. The paired thorns at the bases of the leaves of the black locust are actually modified stipules.

In many leaves the petiole is extended through the leaf blade to its tip as the *midrib*. Conspicuous primary veins are arranged along both sides of this midrib, much like the barbs along the shaft of a feather; these leaves are said to be *pinnately veined*. The leaves of oaks, chestnuts, beeches, elms, birches, and many other trees are pinnately veined. In other leaves several primary veins appear to radiate from the summit of the petiole, like the spread fingers of one's hand; these leaves are described as *palmately veined*. Our maples are excellent examples of the latter type. When the leaf blade appears as a single piece without divisions, the leaf is known as a *simple* leaf. Sometimes, however, the leaf blade is divided into smaller leaflike sections that are called *leaflets*. Such leaves are said to be *compound*. In locusts, sumacs, and ashes, the leaflets are arranged along the prolongation of the petiole, which is termed the *rachis*; they are said to be *pinnately compound* or *pinnate*, and with two leaflets at the apex they are termed *even-pinnate*. If a pinnate leaf terminates in a solitary terminal leaflet, it is termed *odd-pinnate*. Some leaves, like those of the buckeyes, in which the leaflets radiate from the summit of the petiole, are known as *palmately compound*. The leaflets of compound leaves are often mistaken for leaves. In the case of a true leaf a bud is formed in the axil of the leaf, which is in the upper angle that it makes with the twig, a bud is never formed in the axil of a leaflet. Additionally, true leaves will commonly have a stipule at the base of the blade; however, leaflets have stipules at their bases.

Leaves are arranged in a definite manner on the twigs. The large majority of our trees have *alternate* leaves, which means the leaves are arranged singly and alternately along the twigs or branchlets. Some trees have the leaves arranged in pairs, one leaf directly across or on the opposite side of the twig from the other. Such leaves are classified as *opposite*. The maples and the ashes have opposite leaves. The point on the twig where the leaves are attached is spoken of as the *node*. Thus alternate leaves occur one at each node, while opposite leaves occur two at each node. Sometimes, as in the catalpas, there are three leaves at a node; in this arrangement leaves are termed *whorled*.

Shapes of leaves must, of course, be taken into consideration in making identifications. In some instances the shapes of the leaves are so unique that they may be readily identified by shape alone, such as the leaves of the tuliptree and the sweet-gum. The common shapes of leaves and the terms that are used in describing them are shown on page 7. This same page also illustrates the various types of leaf tips, leaf bases, and leaf margins.

The student of trees should become familiarized with the more common terms applied to leaves, for they are quite convenient as well as necessary in an accurate description. Many leaves have teeth on their margins. They may be so fine as to be almost obscure, or they may be very large and conspicuous. Often these teeth on the leaf margins are forwardly pointed and sharp, resembling the teeth on a saw; this type of margin is defined as *serrate*, versus teeth that are not forwardly pointed and resemble the canine teeth in your mouth, which are defined as *dentate*. In some cases the larger teeth have smaller teeth on them; then the margins are said to be *double-serrate* or *doubly toothed*. Not infrequently the teeth may be blunt, and sometimes they end in bristle-tips. Some leaves have deep indentations that may extend halfway or more to the midribs. Such leaves are said to be *lobed*. The projecting portions of these leaves are spoken of as the *lobes*, while the deep indentations that separate them are called the *sinuses*. The pattern of lobing follows the pattern of venation. Most of our oaks have *pinnately lobed* leaves, while those of the maples are *palmately lobed*. Leaves that have neither teeth nor lobes on their margins are known as *entire*.

Flowers

A few of our trees have complete, showy flowers, as, for example, the apples, the locusts, and the magnolias. The majority of our trees, however, have relatively inconspicuous flowers. A *complete flower* is one that has all four sets of floral organs: a *calyx*, which is composed of the *sepals*; a *corolla*, composed of the *petals; stamens;* and in the center, one or more *pistils.* The principal function of the sepals is to protect the other organs when the flower is in the bud stage. The corolla is generally the showy part of the flower, often attracting insects at flowering time. Only the stamens and the pistils are absolutely essential in the reproductive process, as they constitute the sexual elements of the flower. The stamens are the male element, producing the male germ cells or *pollen* within the *anthers,* which are often borne on slender stalks called the *filaments.* The pistil is the female organ, commonly consisting of three parts: the *ovary* at the base, which contains the *ovules,* or egg cells; the *stigma,* which receives the pollen; and the *style,* which connects the stigma and the ovary. A flower that contains both of these sexual elements, stamens and pistils, is known as a *perfect flower.* The majority of our trees have *imperfect* or unisexual flowers, the stamens and pistils occurring in separate flowers and very often on separate trees. Flowers that contain only stamens are called *staminate flowers;* those that contain only pistils are *pistillate flowers.* The portion of a flower to which the various organs are attached is called the *receptacle.*

In order to produce fruits and seeds it is absolutely essential that the pollen from the staminate flowers reaches the stigmas of the pistillate ones. This transfer of the pollen is known as *pollination.* Insects, particularly the bees, are a highly efficient agency for transferring the pollen from one flower to another. *Insect pollination* is the most certain and economical method of pollination, but it involves the necessity of attracting insect visitors to the flowers; consequently, those flowers that are insect-pollinated generally secrete *nectar,* the sweet fluid from which bees make their honey. Such flowers advertise the fact that nectar is present by having showy corollas or by broadcasting enticing odors, or often by using a combination of both. One need only stand beneath a flowering tuliptree or basswood and listen to the all-pervading hum of bees to realize just how effectively alluring such flowers can be.

In spite of the fact that *wind pollination* entails many risks and is extremely wasteful of pollen, the majority of our native trees depend entirely upon this method of pollination. To assure any degree of success, the pollen must be produced in prodigious quantities, and then the tree must depend upon the mercies of the winds to carry it to its intended destination. Of course wind pollination entails no necessity for showiness, nor the production of alluring odors or nectar. In fact, the simpler the flower structure the better. For this reason, most wind-pollinated tree flowers are stripped to the bare essentials, and most persons would not

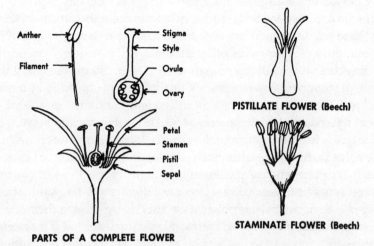

Anther
Filament

Stigma
Style
Ovule
Ovary

PISTILLATE FLOWER (Beech)

Petal
Stamen
Pistil
Sepal

STAMINATE FLOWER (Beech)

PARTS OF A COMPLETE FLOWER

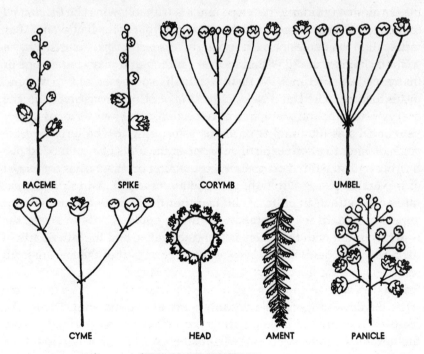

RACEME   SPIKE   CORYMB   UMBEL

CYME   HEAD   AMENT   PANICLE

TYPES OF INFLORESCENCES

recognize many of them as flowers at all. Inasmuch as foliage would interfere materially with the wind-borne pollen reaching the stigmas of the pistillate flowers, the flowers are usually produced early in the spring before the leaves appear or at least before they are fully developed.

The flowers, like the buds, which will provide for the future growth of leafy branches, are sometimes formed on trees long before the flowering season. On the winter twigs of birches one will note long, cylindrical, scaly objects that we call *aments,* or *catkins.* These catkins are really well-developed staminate flowers. Each of the flowers is subtended by a rather large *bract,* which is in reality a modified leaf. Similarly, on the winter twigs of the red maple there are clusters of buds that contain flowers, giving the tree a running start on the spring season. Sometimes flowers are borne solitary, but more often they are borne in some kind of clusters. These flower clusters are spoken of as *inflorescences.* Some of the more common types of these inflorescences are illustrated diagrammatically on page 10, along with the terms that are used in describing them.

Flowers differ markedly in their general structure, and our system of plant classification is based largely on this fact. The pistil is the portion of the flower that ordinarily develops into the fruit following the *fertilization* of the *egg cell* within the ovule by a *sperm cell* from the pollen grain. After fertilization the ovules develop into *seeds.* A *simple pistil* is one that has a solitary chamber or *cell* within its ovary, although it may contain one or many seeds. Sometimes the pistil is actually composed of two or more pistils that are united, and we call this kind of pistil a *compound pistil.* The ovary of a compound pistil, in a cross section, will show as many chambers or cells as the number of pistils composing it. The term *carpel* is applied either to a simple pistil or to one of the units of a compound pistil. Thus a pistil with five carpels is a compound pistil, which is composed of five united pistils. Often the styles of a compound pistil will be separate and distinct, in spite of the fact that the ovaries are united and appear as one. In some instances, as in the apple and its relatives, the ovary is united with the receptacle and the calyx, and the latter parts of the flower also develop and become an integral part of the mature fruit.

Fruits

After the flowering season, the fruits begin to develop on the trees. The fruits are usually available for study for a much longer period than are the flowers. In some species the fruits mature in the autumn, but they persist on the trees throughout part or all of the winter season. Even in those cases of fruits dropping from the trees, one may often find rem-

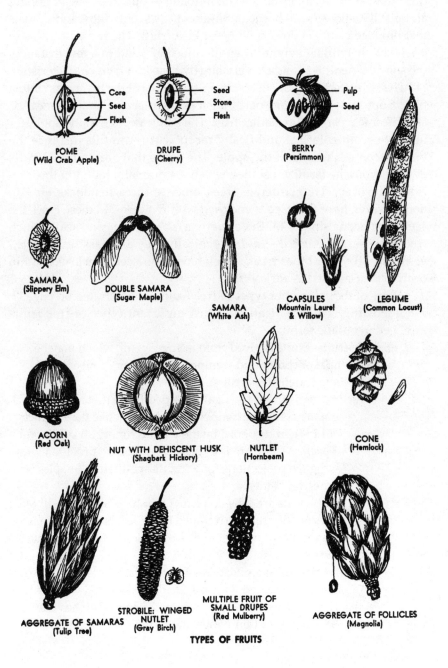

POME
(Wild Crab Apple)

Core
Seed
Flesh

DRUPE
(Cherry)

Seed
Stone
Flesh

BERRY
(Persimmon)

Pulp
Seed

SAMARA
(Slippery Elm)

DOUBLE SAMARA
(Sugar Maple)

SAMARA
(White Ash)

CAPSULES
(Mountain Laurel
& Willow)

LEGUME
(Common Locust)

ACORN
(Red Oak)

NUT WITH DEHISCENT HUSK
(Shagbark Hickory)

NUTLET
(Hornbeam)

CONE
(Hemlock)

AGGREGATE OF SAMARAS
(Tulip Tree)

STROBILE: WINGED
NUTLET
(Gray Birch)

MULTIPLE FRUIT OF
SMALL DRUPES
(Red Mulberry)

AGGREGATE OF FOLLICLES
(Magnolia)

TYPES OF FRUITS

nants of them on the ground. Of course not all trees bear fruits, and some species do not produce fruits until they are many years old, or at least not until they attain a rather large size. In many of our trees the staminate and pistillate flowers are borne on different trees; only those individuals that produce pistillate flowers will ever bear fruits. The fruits of trees are often very helpful in arriving at an identification, and in a few instances the specific identifications are very largely based on fruit characteristics.

Following fertilization, the ovary of the pistil begins to develop into a fruit. Sometimes accessory parts, such as the receptacle and the calyx, also become a part of the mature fruit. The edible portion of the apple, for instance, is an enlarged and fleshy receptacle, for in this instance the pistil becomes the core of the apple. The seeds that are found in fruits develop from the fertilized ovules, which are normally found in the interior of the ovary. The coniferous trees, pines, spruces, hemlocks, etc., do not, however, have their seeds enclosed within ovaries. In these cases the seeds are borne simply on the upper surfaces of the cone scales; such trees are said to be *naked-seeded*. Botanically they are classified as *gymnosperms;* all of our other trees, which have their seeds enclosed within ovaries, are classified as *angiosperms.*

Many of the commoner types of tree fruits are illustrated on page 13. The following is a classification of the important types of tree fruits arranged in outline form.

   I. Simple fruits: Fruits derived from a single pistil, which may be either simple or compound (composed of two or more carpels).

      1. Dry and indehiscent fruits:

         a. *Achenes.* These are small 1-seeded fruits that are wingless but are commonly supplied with plumelike hairs, which aid in their dispersal by the winds (American sycamore).

         b. *Samaras.* These are 1-seeded fruits that are provided with winglike projections for wind dissemination (maples, ashes, and elms).

         c. *Nuts.* Nuts are 1-seeded fruits that have a hard shell. Most nuts are entirely surrounded by a husk or bur that may or may not split open at maturity (walnuts, hickories, chestnuts, beeches).

         d. *Acorns.* This specific type of nut is characteristic of the oaks. The nut is seated within a *cup* that is covered with scales.

         e. *Nutlets.* These are diminutive nuts. In the birches they have a pair of thin wings that aid in dissemination by the wind. In the hophornbeam the nutlets are enclosed within a bladderlike or baglike bract.

2. Dry and dehiscent fruits:
   a. *Legumes.* Pods that result from a simple pistil. At maturity they split completely into two halves (black locust, honey-locust, redbud).
   b. *Follicles.* These are podlike fruits that also result from a simple pistil, but at maturity they split down only one side (magnolias).
   c. *Capsules.* Podlike fruits that result from a compound pistil. At maturity they split into two or more parts that correspond to the number of carpels of which they are composed (willows, mountain-laurel, great-laurel).
3. Fleshy fruits:
   a. *Pomes.* Fruits that are derived from a compound pistil surrounded by, and united with, the enlarged calyx and the receptacle. The latter forms the fleshy portion of the fruit; the former forms the "core," which contains the seeds (apples, service-berries, mountain-ashes).
   b. *Drupes.* Commonly known as "stone fruits." The inner portion of the ovary, which contains the seed, is hard and bony. The outer portion is fleshy and often very juicy (cherries, plums, nanny-berry).
   c. *Berries.* Fruits that are fleshy or pulpy throughout, with the seeds embedded within the fleshy portion (common persimmon, common pawpaw).

II. Compound fruits: These fruits are derived from a number of separate pistils.
   a. *Aggregate fruits.* Fruits that result from separate pistils, which were borne in the same flower. The cone-shaped fruit clusters of the tuliptree are aggregations of samara-like fruits. Those of the magnolias are aggregations of follicles.
   b. *Multiple fruits.* These fruits result from the pistils of several flowers. The ball-like heads of the sycamore are composed of numerous achenes. The "berries" of the red mulberry are actually composed of many small drupes. The *strobili* or conelike fruits of the birch are also multiple fruits.

WINTER CHARACTERISTICS

The leaves of most trees are shed annually, at some time during the autumn. We say that the leaves of such trees are *deciduous*, and often refer to such trees as *deciduous trees*. Most of our common broad-leaved trees, or *hardwoods*, have deciduous leaves. A few, like the rhododendron and the mountain-laurel, retain their leaves for two or more years and are known as *evergreens*. Most *coniferous* or cone-bearing trees, such as pines, hemlocks, and spruces, are also evergreens. The coniferous trees are also known as *softwoods*.

Twigs

The smallest branchlets of trees are commonly known as the *twigs*. Twigs afford perhaps the best means of identifying trees in the winter season. They vary widely in such important characteristics as size, shape, color, and general appearance. The twigs of some trees, like the black locust and the Osage-orange, are armed with prickles or thorns. Those of the stag-horn sumac are coated with a dense, velvety hair. The twigs of the stag-horn sumac, the buckeye, and the Kentucky coffeetree are stout, while those of the birch, the American hornbeam, and the willow are very slender. The twigs of some trees are more or less hairy, while others may be decidedly glabrous or even lustrous.

When the leaves fall, they leave scars on the twigs, which we know as the *leaf scars*. Naturally the position of these scars corresponds to the position of the leaves. Trees like maples, ashes, and buckeyes, which have opposite leaves, will have opposite leaf scars; those that have alternate leaves, like birches, oaks, and willows, will have alternately arranged leaf scars. The tubes, or *fibrovascular bundles*, which served to conduct water into the leaves and food materials from the leaves back into the branches, are ruptured when the leaf falls. The broken ends of these fibrovascular bundles, in many cases, are very distinctly seen within the leaf scars, and they are known as the *bundle scars*. Some trees have but a solitary bundle scar within each of the leaf scars, but the majority of our trees have three or more bundle scars within each of the leaf scars. When they are numerous, the bundle scars may be scattered throughout the leaf scars; but often they are arranged in definite groups, in curved lines, or in a circle. The number and the arrangement of these bundle scars is often important in making winter identifications. The leaf scars also show considerable variation from one genus to another, and sometimes vary in the different species of a single genus. They vary not only in size but also in shape: round, semiround, crescent-shaped, 3-lobed, heart-

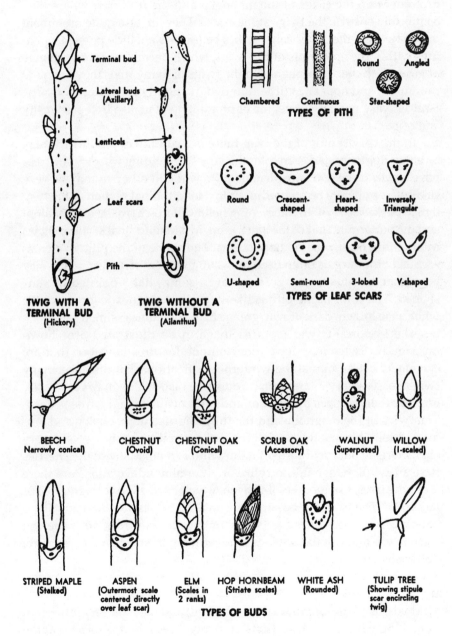

Terminal bud

Lateral buds
(Axillary)

Lenticels

Leaf scars

Pith

**TWIG WITH A
TERMINAL BUD
(Hickory)**

**TWIG WITHOUT A
TERMINAL BUD
(Ailanthus)**

Round   Angled

Star-shaped

TYPES OF PITH

Chambered   Continuous

Round   Crescent-
shaped   Heart-
shaped   Inversely
Triangular

U-shaped   Semi-round   3-lobed   V-shaped

TYPES OF LEAF SCARS

**BEECH
Narrowly conical)**

**CHESTNUT
(Ovoid)**

**CHESTNUT OAK
(Conical)**

**SCRUB OAK
(Accessory)**

**WALNUT
(Superposed)**

**WILLOW
(1-scaled)**

**STRIPED MAPLE
(Stalked)**

**ASPEN
(Outermost scale
centered directly
over leaf scar)**

**ELM
(Scales in
2 ranks)**

**HOP HORNBEAM
(Striate scales)**

**WHITE ASH
(Rounded)**

**TULIP TREE
(Showing stipule
scar encircling
twig)**

TYPES OF BUDS

shaped, etc. As a rule the larger twigs have the largest and most prominent leaf scars.

Twigs are also often marked by the *stipule scars,* scars that are made by the stipules at the bases of the leaf petioles. These stipule scars are very prominent on the twigs of the magnolia and the tuliptree, where they completely encircle the twigs at the nodes. They are also quite prominent on the twigs of the American Beech. The *lenticels* are little porelike openings within the epidermis of the twigs, which permit the interexchange of gases with the atmosphere. On the twigs of many trees they are quite prominent and appear as little rounded or slightly elongated dots. The lenticels vary not only in degree of prominence, but also in their density and color.

In the very center of the twig there is a column of *pith,* which may be either lighter or darker in color than the surrounding wood. Some trees have a very large and conspicuous pith, while in others it may be very small. The pith may be *continuous,* or in a longitudinal section of the twig it may be *chambered,* with intervening hollow places, as in the black walnut and the butternut. That of the black gum, in a longitudinal section, shows intervening hard, woody diaphragms. The shape of the pith, in a cross section of the twig, is often used in making winter identifications; it may be rounded, angled, triangular, or even somewhat 5-pointed or star-shaped. The color of the pith is likewise often diagnostic for it may be white, pale brown, dark brown, greenish, or sometimes salmon pink.

The important twig features that can be illustrated are shown on page 17. Twigs may have other unique features however, that are extremely useful in making winter identifications. For instance, many twigs possess very characteristic odors or tastes. One may very easily identify the sassafras by its odor and taste even when the tree is dead. The twigs of the magnolia and the tuliptree also have a spicy and aromatic odor. Those of the black birch and the yellow birch possess a very characteristic odor and taste of oil of wintergreen. Many of the cherries have an awful, pungent, cherrylike or bitter almondlike odor. And there are some trees, like the tree-of-heaven, which have a very disagreeable or fetid odor. The twigs of the slippery elm and the basswood are mucilaginous when chewed. As one gets acquainted with our trees, he or she will learn to use many of these things in identifying them when the leaves are not available.

Buds

The buds, of course, are located on the twigs, and they are very important in making winter identifications. In many trees a bud is formed at the very tip of the season's growth, thus terminating the growth for the season. Such buds are referred to as the *terminal buds*. There is but one terminal bud, and in most trees it is usually larger than the other buds on the twig. Other buds are formed along the sides of the twigs, and we usually refer to them as the *lateral buds*. These buds usually occur solitary in the axils of the leaves, or in the upper angle that the leaf makes with the twig; they are also known as *axillary buds* for that reason. In a few species more than one bud occurs at each *node*, or place where a leaf was attached to the twig; we call these buds *accessory buds*. In the red maple and the silver maple additional buds occur on each side of many of the true axillary buds. In some other trees, like the black walnut and the butternut, other buds occur on the twigs above the true axillary buds; they are said to be superposed, being termed *superposed buds*.

Most buds are covered with one or more *bud scales*, which are in reality modified leaves. Their function is to protect the delicate growing point within the bud from drying out, or from mechanical injury that may result from too sudden changes in the temperature of the air. The number of scales, and particularly the number of visible scales, varies with the different kinds of trees. Such characteristics as the number of scales on the buds and their arrangement, color, etc., are very useful in winter identification. A few of our native trees have buds that are not covered with scales at all; they are said to have *naked buds*. Additional protection to the growing point within the buds is sometimes present in the form of hairs, or coatings of waterproof gums or resins.

The twigs of many trees do not develop true terminal buds at all. Growth in such species is more or less indefinite. It finally slows down, however, and the tip of the growth dies and is sloughed off just above one of the lateral or axillary buds, leaving a little scar at the tip. Thus the topmost lateral bud assumes the position of the terminal bud, but it is usually not any larger than the other buds beneath it. Sometimes this bud is called a *false terminal bud*. Excellent examples of this kind are found on the twigs of the stag-horn sumac, the elm, and the basswood.

Buds that contain rudimentary stems and leaves are usually called the *leaf buds*, while those that contain only partially developed flowers are called the *flower buds*. The accessory buds of the red maple and the silver maple are flower buds. The large terminal buds on the twigs of the sassafras, and the flattened, biscuitlike terminal buds found on many of the twigs of the flowering dogwood, are likewise flower buds. The twigs of a few trees, like the birch and the Eastern hop-hornbeam, have partially developed staminate flowers on the twigs all winter in the form of aments, or catkins.

Buds vary greatly in size, shape, color, etc. The buds of some trees are rather minute, while others have very large and conspicuous buds. Those of the black locust, the honey-locust, and a few other species are embedded within the twigs, and they are scarcely recognizable as buds at all. The cigar-shaped buds of the American beech are so long, slender, and sharp-pointed that they are unmistakable for those of any other tree. The buds of the striped maple and the mountain maple, as well as the alders, are evidently stalked. Most of the common types of buds are illustrated on page 17.

Bark

The bark of trees has a protective function, covering the trunks and the branches of the tree. Many trees can be readily identified at any season of the year by bark characteristics alone. The bark of trees varies in color and general appearance, not only among the various species but often on the same tree. Often the color of the younger trunks and branches, as well as the appearance of their bark, will be much different from that of the older trunks. Yet most trees have some outstanding characteristic, as far as their bark is concerned, which enables those familiar with them to base their identification on bark characteristics alone. Even the novice can identify the American sycamore by the strikingly mottled appearance of the bark of its branches; or the American beech by the persistent smoothness of its light gray trunk; or the shag-bark hickory by the shaggy appearance of its trunk, from which the bark exfoliates in long, loose plates. Cherries and birches have very conspicuous, horizontally elongated lenticels on the bark of their trunks and branches.

Some trees never develop a thick bark, while in others the bark may attain a thickness of several inches. As trees grow, they normally shed the outer layers of bark. The bark of the yellow birch and the paper birch peels off in very thin filmlike, or papery, layers. In most trees the bark sooner or later develops cracks called *fissures*, or *furrows*, which separate the more elevated portions called *ridges*. These furrows and ridges assume various patterns that are often so distinctive that the identification of the tree may be safely based upon them. In some trees the ridges of the bark are broken into distinct blocks forming the alligator bark, which may be seen on the flowering dogwood, the black gum, and the common persimmon.

KEY BASED ON SUMMER CHARACTERISTICS

Pines/needles (handwritten)

Page

1. Leaves linear, needlelike, scalelike, or awl-like, <³⁄₁₆ inch wide. (2)
1a. Leaves with a flat blade, >³⁄₁₆ inch wide. (12)
2. Leaves opposite or whorled, not tightly clustered from a common base, evergreen. (3)
2a. Leaves alternate, generally scattered or sometimes in tight clusters from a common base along the branch, deciduous or evergreen. (6)
3. Leaves linear, mostly >1 inch long, supported by short petiolelike structures; apex bristle-tipped. . . . .
. . . . .FLORIDA-NUTMEG *(Torreya taxifolia)*   174
3a. Leaves scalelike or awl-like (or if linear without a bristle-tip), <1 inch long; without petiolelike base. (4)
4. Leaves both scalelike and awl-like; fruits bluish and berrylike. . . .
. . . . .EASTERN RED-CEDAR *(Juniperus virginiana)*   171
4a. Leaves all scalelike; fruit a small, dry cone. (5)
5. Branchlets flattened; scale leaves usually >⅛ inch long; cones egg-shaped with thin scales. . . . .
. . . . .NORTHERN WHITE-CEDAR *(Thuja occidentalis)*   169
5a. Branchlets not flattened; scale leaves much smaller; cones roundish and with shield-shaped scales. . . . .
. . . . .ATLANTIC WHITE-CEDAR *(Chamaecyparis thyoides)*   166
6. Leaves mostly densely clustered from a common base with 2 to many leaves per cluster. (7)
6a. Leaves scattered individually along the stems, not at all clustered. (8)
7. Leaves 2–5 per cluster, evergreen, basally enclosed by a conspicuous membranous sheath. . . . . PINES *(Pinus)*   132
7a. Leaves >5 per cluster, deciduous, lacking a basal sheath. . . . .
. . . . .AMERICAN LARCH *(Larix laricina)*   120
8. Leaves small, <¹⁄₁₆ inch long; flowering plants producing small pinkish flowers. . . . . .SALT-CEDAR *(Tamarix ramosissima)*   385
8a. Leaves larger, >¹⁄₁₆ inch long; nonflowering plants. (9)
9. Leaves deciduous, arranged featherlike on deciduous branchlets; cones globose. . . . .
. . . . .BALD-CYPRESS AND POND-CYPRESS *(Taxodium)*   163
9a. Leaves evergreen, not at all featherlike, branchlets not deciduous; cones egg-shaped to cylindrical. (10)

Page

Page

56. Pith diaphragmmed, bark vertically striped; hairs on leaves
stellate; fruits 2- or 4-winged; flowers white, showy, petals 4. . . . . .
. . . . SILVERBELLS *(Halesia)*   503
56a. Pith continuous, bark not vertically striped; hairs on leaves not
stellate; fruits unwinged; flowers without the above combination.
(57)
57. Leaf margins conspicuously long ciliate, nearly entire, leaf tip
strongly acuminate; leaves 2-ranked; flowers large and showy
(not discussed in text). . . . .
. . . . . . SILKY-CAMELLIA AND MOUNTAIN-CAMELLIA *(Stewartia spp.)*
57a. Leaf margins eciliate, entire or not; leaves more than 2-ranked;
flowers small, not showy. (58)
58. Most leaves not more than twice as long as wide; branchlets very
slender and zigzag; leaf scars with 1 bundle-scar. . . . .
. . . . TREE SPARKLE-BERRY *(Vaccinium arboreum)*   431
58a. Most leaves 2–4 times as long as wide; branchlets moderate and
not zigzag; leaf scars with 3 bundle-scars. (59)
59. Buds naked and densely hairy, terminal bud present; leaves large,
2–6 inches long, 1–2 inches wide; leaf blades with conspicuously
straight and parallel veins; fruit a fleshy drupe; petals 5. . . . .
. . . . CAROLINA FALSE BUCKTHORN *(Frangula caroliniana)*   567
59a. Buds with a solitary, glabrous, or hairy scale, terminal bud lacking; leaves mostly narrower, shorter or both; leaf blades without
conspicuously straight and parallel veins; fruit a dry capsule;
petals absent. . . . . WILLOWS *(Salix)*   404
60. Leaf margins with simple teeth. (61)
60a. Leaf margins doubly serrate. (68)
61. Leaves lopsided or asymmetrical at the base. (62)
61a. Leaves symmetrical or nearly so at the base. (64)
62. Leaves conspicuously and strongly heart-shaped at base, nearly
as long as broad. . . . . AMERICAN BASSWOOD *(Tilia americana)*   378
62a. Leaves not heart-shaped at base; clearly longer than broad. (63)
63. Leaves with 3 prominent veins arising from the summit of the
leaf stalk; pith at nodes chambered; bark commonly warty or
corky-ridged, but otherwise smooth; fruit a fleshy drupe, but not
burlike. . . . . HACKBERRIES *(Celtis)*   228
63a. Leaves merely with one prominent midrib; pith not chambered
at nodes; bark rough and furrowed, but without warts or corky
ridges; fruit a dry, burlike drupe. . . . . PLANERTREE *(Planera aquatica)*   226

Page

64. Leaves often arranged in clusters on short lateral spurs; hairs
    often black. . . . . .HOLLIES *(Ilex)*   552

64a. Leaves never as above. (65)

65. Branchlets with chambered pith; leaves with small branched hairs
    on the lower surface; bole or main stem often vertically striped. . .
    . . . . .SILVERBELLS *(Halesia)*   503

65a. Branchlets with continuous pith; leaves otherwise; bole striped or
    not. (66)

66. Most leaves >2 inches wide, broadly oval or heart-shaped to
    triangular, often hairy beneath; bole not vertically striped. . . . . . .
    . . . . .POPLARS *(Populus)*   388

66a. Most leaves <2 inches wide, oval or obovate, usually glabrous
    beneath at maturity, or merely with scattered hairs; bole vertically
    striped. (67)

67. Leaf blades basally long-tapered, conspicuously clustered on
    branch tips; flowers solitary, large, 2½ to 3⅓ inches across, with
    numerous, conspicuous, yellow stamens at the centers; plants
    known originally only from the Altamaha River, in Georgia, now
    thought to be extirpated in the wild. . . . .
    . . . . .FRANKLINTREE *(Franklinia alatamaha)*   374

67a. Leaf blades cordate to rounded, not long-tapered basally, nor
    conspicuously clustered on branch tips; flowers numerous and
    smaller, without a yellow cluster of stamens at the centers; plants
    from various locations. . . . . .SERVICE-BERRIES *(Amelanchier)*   492

68. Leaves asymmetrical at the base. . . . . .ELMS *(Ulmus)*   216

68a. Leaves symmetrical at the base. (69)

69. Mature leaves glabrous above, hairs in axils of veins below, lateral
    veins of the leaves extending into the marginal teeth without
    forking; fruits enveloped by the base of 3-lobed, leaflike bracts;
    bark very tight, fluted or musclelike; bud scales not vertically
    striate. . . . . .AMERICAN HORNBEAM *(Carpinus caroliniana)*   368

69a. Mature leaves with some hairs above and hairy throughout below,
    lateral veins forking within the margin of the leaf; fruits enclosed
    in baglike bracts arranged in hoplike clusters; bark loose and
    flaking; bud scale minutely vertically striate. . . . .
    . . . . .EASTERN HOP-HORNBEAM *(Ostrya virginiana)*   370

70. Young twigs and leaf undersurfaces covered with scurfy scales
    and brown dots. . . . . .RUSSIAN-OLIVE *(Elaeagnus angustifolia)*   531

70a. Young twigs and leaf undersurfaces lacking scurfy scales and
    brown dots. (71)

Page

Page

92. Petioles and branches with milky sap if broken; introduced tree.
...........................CHINESE TALLOWTREE (*Triadica sebifera*)   565

92a. Petioles and branches lacking milky sap if broken; plants native or introduced. (93)

93. Leaves with veins curving and strongly paralleling the leaf margins. ....ALTERNATE-LEAF DOGWOOD (*Cornus alternifolia*)   540

93a. Leaves otherwise. (94)

94. First-year branches conspicuously winged or strongly 4-angled below the nodes. ....CRAPE-MYRTLE (*Lagerstroemia indica*)   534

94a. First-year branches rounded below nodes. (95)

95. Leaf scars with but 1 bundle-scar. (96)

95a. Leaf scars with 3 or more bundle-scars. (101)

96. Leaves strongly mucronate; blades long-hairy beneath; plants restricted to Georgia and adjoining South Carolina (not discussed in text). .......................GEORGIAPLUME (*Elliottia racemosa*)

96a. Leaves not mucronate; blades not long-hairy beneath; plants of various locations. (97)

97. Leaves 2-ranked, margins conspicuously long ciliate, apex long acuminate; flowers large and showy; plants mostly shrubby (not discussed in text). ....
......SILKY-CAMELLIA AND MOUNTAIN-CAMELLIA (*Stewartia spp.*)

97a. Leaves more than 2-ranked, margins and apex various; flowers small, not showy; plants shrubby or not. (98)

98. Leaves 1½ inches or more wide, long-acuminately pointed at the tip; leaf blades with irregularly placed dark spots below; petioles >½ inch long; large tree. ....
......................COMMON PERSIMMON (*Diospyros virginiana*)   500

98a. Leaves narrower, short-pointed or rounded at the tip; leaf blades not black spotted below; petioles shorter; short, shrubby trees or shrubs. (99)

99. Leaves less than twice as long as wide, deciduous, membranous, margins minutely toothed; branchlets very slender and zigzag; fruit a black berry. ....TREE SPARKLE-BERRY (*Vaccinium arboreum*)   431

99a. Leaves 2 or more times as long as wide, leathery, evergreen or persisting, margins completely entire; branchlets and fruits otherwise. (100)

100. Most leaves <2 inches long, with a tiny but conspicuous apical notch. ....BUCKWHEAT-TREE (*Cliftonia monophylla*)   419

100a. Most leaves >2 inches long, without an apical notch. ....
....SWAMP TITI (*Cyrilla racemiflora*)   421

Page

101. Branchlets with a pleasant fruity odor and resinous sap; leaves mostly rounded or notched apically. . . . .
. . . . .AMERICAN SMOKETREE (*Cotinus obovatus*)   606

101a. Branchlets and leaves otherwise. (102)

102. Pith of the branchlets with transverse woody partitions. . . . .
. . . . .BLACK GUM AND TUPELOS (*Nyssa*)   543

102a. Pith of the branchlets otherwise. (103)

103. Buds with a solitary scale; branches extremely narrow at tips. . . . .
. . . . .WILLOWS (*Salix*)   404

103a. Buds with 2 or more scales; branches moderate thick to thick at tips. (104)

104. Leaves bristle-pointed at the tip; branchlets with a small, 5-angled pith. . . . . .OAKS (*Quercus*)   282

104a. Leaves merely long-pointed at the tip; branchlets with a large, round white pith. . . . . .CORKWOOD (*Leitneria floridana*)   243

105. Plants armed with thorns, spines, or prickles. (106)

105a. Plants unarmed. (110)

106. Leaflet margins entire; short and broad-based; spines paired at the nodes, thorns lacking. (107)

106a. Leaflet margins toothed; thorns or spines present. (108)

107. Leaves bipinnately compound; spines narrow at base and quite long, to 2 inches; barely reaching our area in Louisiana. . . . .
. . . . .HONEY MESQUITE (*Prosopis glandulosa*)   512

107a. Leaves 1-pinnately compound; spines broad at base and short, <1 inch long; plants throughout our range. . . . .
. . . . .BLACK LOCUST (*Robinia pseudoacacia*)   527

108. Leaflets <1½ inches long; branchlets moderately stout; thorns often branched. . . . .
. . . . .HONEY-LOCUST AND WATER-LOCUST (*Gleditsia*)   516

108a. Leaflets longer; branchlets exceptionally stout with short prickles or broad-based spines. (109)

109. Branchlets ¾ inch or more thick, with scattered spines or prickles and some in rows beneath the leaf stalks; most leaves 2 feet or more long, divided into a number of leaflets, not aromatic. . . . .
. . . . .DEVIL'S-WALKINGSTICK (*Aralia spinosa*)   626

109a. Branchlets more slender, with broad-based scattered and axillary spines; most leaves <1½ feet long, merely pinnate, aromatic. . . . . .
. . . . .HERCULES'–CLUB (*Zanthoxylum clava-herculis*)   622

110. Leaflets entire or with a few large teeth at base only. (111)

110a. Leaflets regularly and prominently toothed. (118)

Page

121. Branchlets with chambered pith; twigs easily broken by hand;
      fruit husk indehiscent; nut surface rugose. .....WALNUTS *(Juglans)*   245

121a. Branchlets with continuous pith; twigs extremely difficult to
      break by hand; fruit husk splitting into segments; nut surface not
      rugose. . . . . .HICKORIES *(Carya)*   250

122. Leaves simple. (123)

122a. Leaves compound. (133)

123. Leaves with multiple primary veins from base. (124)

123a. Leaves with a single, primary, basal vein. (127)

124. Twigs of previous year hollow except at nodes and occasionally
      elsewhere within the twig; flowers blue; fruits oval-shaped
      capsules. . . . . .PRINCESSTREE *(Paulownia tomentosa)*   650

124a. Twigs of previous year with continuous pith; flowers not blue;
      fruits not oval-shaped capsules. (125)

125. Twigs of current year densely hairy, with milky sap; fruits fleshy.
      . . . . .PAPER-MULBERRY *(Broussonetia papyrifera)*   236

125a. Twigs of current year glabrous or nearly so, with or without milky
      sap; fruits dry. (126)

126. All leaf blades opposite, palm-shaped, conspicuously 3- to 7-lobed
      (rarely unlobed), 2–7 inches long, margins entire or toothed; fruit,
      a winged samara. . . . . .MAPLES *(Acer)* 83 580

126a. Leaves often whorled or opposite, heart-shaped, unlobed or not
      conspicuously lobed, margins entire, 4–12 inches long; fruit an
      elongated, wingless capsule. . . . . .CATALPAS *(Catalpa)*   653

127. Leaf margin entire and unlobed. (128)

127a. Leaf margin toothed or lobed. (132)

128. Leaves evergreen, leathery in texture. (129)

128a. Leaves deciduous, not leathery. (130)

129. Leaf blades finely hairy below, upper surface minutely glandular-
      dotted; fruit a flattened, dry capsule; plants restricted to coastal
      Florida. . . . . .BLACK MANGROVE *(Avicennia germinans)*   629

129a. Leaf blades glabrous below, upper surface not minutely glandular-
      dotted; fruit a fleshy drupe; plants throughout much of the
      Southeast. .DEVILWOOD *(Osmanthus americanus)*   632

130. Leaves with the veins curving conspicuously and tending to
      parallel the leaf margins; leaf margins eciliate and twigs lacking
      conspicuous warty lenticels. . . . . .DOGWOODS *(Cornus)* 89 537

130a. Leaf veins otherwise; margins either ciliate or twigs with con-
      spicuous warty lenticels. (131)

KEY BASED ON WINTER CHARACTERISTICS

7. Leaves and twigs with a characteristic unpleasant or noticeably pleasant odor when bruised. (8)

7a. Leaves and twigs otherwise. (13)

8. Leaves and stems strongly aromatic with a pleasant camphor odor, dorsal surface of blades with conspicuous yellow callosities within principal vein angle. . . . .
. . . . .CAMPHORTREE (*Cinnamomum camphora*) 201

8a. Leaves without a camphor odor, dorsal surface not as above. (9)

9. Leaves with yellow resin dots beneath; catkinlike buds often present on the twigs. . . . . . . .SOUTHERN BAYBERRY (*Morella cerifera*) 271

9a. Leaves and twigs otherwise. (10)

10. Leaf blades glandular-dotted beneath; petioles reddish; plants mostly shrubby (not discussed in text). . . . .
. . . . .FLORIDA ANISETREE (*Illicium floridanum*)

10a. Leaf blades not glandular-dotted beneath; petioles not reddish; plants treelike. (11)

11. Twigs ringed at the nodes by stipule scars. . . . .
. . . . .MAGNOLIAS (*Magnolia*) 177

11a. Twigs otherwise. (12)

12. Leaves entire, with a pleasant spicy odor; bundle-scar solitary. . . .
. . . . .BAYS (*Persea*) 203

12a. Leaves often with a few teeth, with fetid, cherrylike odor; bundle-scars 3. . . . . .CHERRIES (*Prunus*) 434

13. Twigs zigzag, <⅛ inch in diameter; leaf apex with a noticeable mucro, margins with minute, nearly microscopic teeth throughout; mostly small trees or tall shrubs. . . . .
. . . . .TREE SPARKLE-BERRY (*Vaccinium arboreum*) 431

13a. The combination of characters not as above. (14)

14. Leaf margins toothed or lobed. (15)

14a. Leaf margins entire. (17)

15. Leaves tending to be clustered toward the tips of the twigs; buds scaled. . . . . .OAKS (*Quercus*) 282

15a. Leaves more distantly and evenly spaced along twigs; buds scaled or naked. (16)

16. Most leaves >3 inches long; twigs somewhat clubby; buds naked.
. . . . .LOBLOLLY-BAY (*Gordonia lasianthus*) 375

16a. Most leaves <3 inches long; twigs slender; buds with 1 or more scales. . . . . .HOLLIES (*Ilex*) 552

Page

36. Twigs with leaf scars crowded on short lateral spurs; buds rusty-
     woolly, not imbedded in the bark. . . . . .BULLIES *(Sideroxylon)*   496

36a. Twigs without lateral spurs; buds glabrous, brown, partially
     sunken in the bark. . . . . .OSAGE-ORANGE *(Maclura pomifera)*   234

37. Spines or prickles broad-based, mostly ½ inch or less long. (38)

37a. Thorns not noticeably broad-based, often >½ inch long. (39)

38. Twigs noticeably and conspicuously aromatic if broken; thorns
     scattered, becoming elevated on corky cushions; a southeastern
     coastal plain species. . . . .
     .HERCULES'-CLUB *(Zanthoxylum clava-herculis)*   622

38a. Twigs not noticeably and conspicuously aromatic; thorns in pairs
     at the nodes, becoming buried within the bark; a species found
     throughout our area. . . . . .BLACK LOCUST *(Robinia pseudoacacia)*   527

39. Bud scales sticky with elongated tips; barely reaching our area in
     Louisiana. . . . . .HONEY MESQUITE *(Prosopis glandulosa)*   512

39a. Buds not as above; bud scales not sticky; plants found throughout
     much of our area. (40)

40. Buds prominent, several-scaled, roundish-ovoid, often red; thorns
     simple, 1–2 inches long. . . . . .HAWTHORNS *(Crataegus)*   481

40a. Buds sunken in the bark or hidden by the leaf scars; thorns often
     branched and several inches long. . . . .
     . . . . .HONEY-LOCUST AND WATER-LOCUST *(Gleditsia)*   516

41. Terminal bud absent. . . . . .PLUMS *(Prunus)*   434

41a. Terminal bud present. . . . . .APPLES *(Malus)*   469

42. Twigs with a characteristic odor if broken, pleasant or foul. (43)

42a. Twigs otherwise. (53)

43. Twigs ringed at the nodes by stipule-scars. (44)

43a. Twigs otherwise. (45)

44. Terminal bud flattened, somewhat 2-edged, 2-scaled, resembling
     a duck's bill. .TULIPTREE *(Liriodendron tulipifera)*   191

44a. Terminal bud not flattened, with a solitary scale. . . . .
     . . . . .MAGNOLIAS *(Magnolia)*   177

45. Bark with conspicuous horizontally elongated lenticels. (46)

45a. Bark lacking conspicuous horizontally elongated lenticels. (47)

46. Broken twigs with an oil of wintergreen odor and taste; bud
     scales 2 or 3; catkins commonly present. . . . . .BIRCHES *(Betula)*   354

46a. Broken twigs with a cherrylike or disagreeable bitter almond
     odor and taste; bud scales about 5, catkins never present. . . . .
     . . . . .CHERRIES *(Prunus)*   434

Page

Page

88. Outer or lower bud scale centered directly above the leaf scar;
pith uniform and continuous. ....ASPENS AND POPLARS *(Populus)*   388

88a. Outer bud scale not so centered; pith with transverse woody
partitions....................BLACK GUM AND TUPELOS *(Nyssa)*   543

89. Twigs moderate to very thick and clubby. (90)

89a. Twigs thin, not at all clubby. (91)

90. Branches with short but conspicuous white, vertical stripes
throughout..........................SILKTREE *(Albizia julibrissin)*   510

90a. Branches lacking white vertical stripes..........................
...................................CHINA-BERRY *(Melia azedarach)*   619

91. Leaf scars minutely fringed on the upper margin; twigs
noticeably zigzag, pith continuous, often with fine red streaks;
buds not triangular...........EASTERN REDBUD *(Cercis canadensis)*   514

91a. Leaf scars otherwise; twigs not noticeably zigzag, pith continuous
or chambered at the nodes, not reddish streaked; buds triangular.
(92)

92. Bark and branches often with corky or warty outgrowths; pith
finely chambered at the nodes; pseudoterminal bud conspicu-
ously cocked; native species. ....HACKBERRIES *(Celtis)*   228

92a. Bark and branches without corky outgrowths; pith continuous at
nodes; pseudoterminal bud not conspicuously cocked; introduced
species. ....CHINESE TALLOWTREE *(Triadica sebifera)*   565

93. Broken twigs with milky sap.....................................
........................PAPER-MULBERRY *(Broussonetia papyrifera)*   236

93a. Broken twigs without milky sap. (94)

94. Terminal bud absent; leaf scars half-round. (95)

94a. Terminal bud present; leaf scars otherwise. (96)

95. Twigs rather zigzag, mucilaginous if chewed; pith round and
white; buds appearing to be hooded with one scale atop a second.
..........................AMERICAN BASSWOOD *(Tilia americana)*   378

95a. Twigs rather straight, not mucilaginous; pith star-shaped or
5-angled; buds with >2 scales, not one atop another. ....
....CHESTNUTS *(Castanea)*   276

96. Leaf scars narrowly crescent-shaped; buds usually sticky. ....
....MOUNTAIN-ASHES *(Sorbus)*   477

96a. Leaf scars more or less heart-shaped; circular or 3-lobed; buds
otherwise. (97)

KEY TO THE PINES *(Pinus)*

Page

12. Needles 1½–3½ inches long; branches exceptionally tough and pliable; branchlets very stout; cones 2¼–4 inches long, the scales armed with a stout hooked prickle, mature cones not curved, not pointing forward on branches. ....
.............................TABLE MOUNTAIN PINE *(P. pungens)*   160

12a. Needles usually < 1½ inches long; branches brittle, often snapping when bent; branchlets slender; cones <2 inches long, the scales unarmed, mature cones noticeably curved and pointing forward on branches. ....JACK PINE *(P. banksiana)*   150

13. Most needles 10 inches or more long, drooping backward conspicuously on branches due to their large size; buds silvery-white, bud scales prominently fimbriate; cones mostly >6 inches long. ...
.....................................LONG-LEAF PINE *(P. palustris)*   140

13a. Most needles <8 inches long, not drooping backward on branches; buds brownish or ashy, not as above; cones mostly <6 inches long. (14)

14. Most needles 5 to nearly 8 inches long. (15)

14a. Most needles not over 5 inches long. (16)

15. Needles yellow-green, in clusters of 3s; cones 2–3 inches long; trunks usually with small, tufted branches. ....
....POND PINE *(P. serotina)*   146

15a. Needles dark yellow, in clusters of 2s or 3s; cones 3–6 inches long; trunks otherwise. (17)

16. Needles in clusters of 3s; sheaths of needle clusters ½ inch or more long; cones mostly perpendicular to branch, sessile, dull, light reddish-brown to brown, the scales armed with a stout prickle................................LOBLOLLY PINE *(P. taeda)*   144

16a. Needles in clusters of 2s or 3s on the same tree; sheaths of needle clusters shorter; cones often forward or backward pointed on branch, with a short but conspicuous stalk, lustrous, chocolate-brown, the scales armed with a short and slender prickle. ....
....SLASH PINE *(P. elliottii)*   142

17. Needles slender, straight, flexible, bluish-green; cones longer than broad, cone-scales tipped with a weak prickle. ....
...................................SHORT-LEAF PINE *(P. echinata)*   155

17a. Needles stout, twisted, stiff, yellowish-green; cones as long as broad, cone-scales tipped with a stout prickle. ....
....PITCH PINE *(P. rigida)*   148

KEY TO THE SPRUCES *(Picea)*

Page

1. Branches pendulous; cones very large, 4–8 inches long, cone-scales wedge-shaped apically; branchlets glabrous; introduced species. . . . . .NORWAY SPRUCE *(P. abies)* 123
1a. Branches spreading horizontally or ascending; cones smaller, <3¼ inches long, cone-scales rounded apically; branchlets glabrous or hairy; native species. (2)
2. Branchlets completely glabrous, glaucous; needles often ill-scented when crushed, sharply pointed. . . . .
. . . . .WHITE SPRUCE *(P. glauca)* 130
2a. Branchlets finely hairy, not glaucous; needles pleasantly scented when crushed, sharply pointed or blunt. (3)
3. Cone 1–2 inches long, deciduous after one season, cone-scales with entire margins; needles ⅜ inch or more long, appressed to twig, dark, shiny, yellowish-green, leaf-cushions of twigs laterally rounded, intervening grooves V-shaped. . . .RED SPRUCE *(P. rubens)* 125
3a. Cone ½–1¼ (1½) inches long, persisting for several to many seasons, cone-scales with jagged margins; needles ⅜ inch or less long, often divergent from twig, waxy, dark, dull bluish-green; leaf-cushions of twigs flattened, intervening grooves closed. . . . . .
. . . . .BLACK SPRUCE *(P. mariana)* 128

KEY TO THE HEMLOCKS *(Tsuga)*

1. Leaves about ½ inch long, extending only laterally (in one plane) from the branchlets, margins minutely toothed; cones ½–¾ inch long, cone-scale margins about as long as wide. . . . .
. . . . .EASTERN HEMLOCK *(T. canadensis)* 116
1a. Leaves up to ¾ inch long, extending in all directions from the branchlets, margins entire; cones 1–1½ inches long, cone-scale longer than wide. . . . . .CAROLINA HEMLOCK *(T. caroliniana)* 118

KEY TO THE BALSAM FIRS *(Abies)*

1. Cone bracts not extending beyond the cone-scales or scarcely so.
. . . . .BALSAM FIR *(A. balsamea)* 112
1a. Cone bracts projecting well beyond the scales and reflexed. . . . . . .
. . . . .FRASER FIR *(A. fraseri)* 115

KEY TO THE BALD-CYPRESS AND POND-CYPRESS
(Taxodium)

Page

1. Deciduous branchlets ascending, leaves awl-shaped, appearing to be spirally arranged. . . . . .POND-CYPRESS (T. ascendens) 165
1a. Deciduous branchlets spreading laterally from the larger twigs, leaves more spreading, linear, flat, featherlike, arranged on twigs in one plane. . . . . .BALD-CYPRESS (T. distichum) 163

KEY TO THE PALMETTOS (Sabal)

1. Leaves >3 feet wide, with conspicuous threadlike marginal fibers; trunks >8 feet in height. . . . . .CABBAGE PALMETTO (S. palmetto) 668
1a. Leaves <3 feet wide, lacking threadlike marginal fibers; trunks <8 feet in height. . . . . .DWARF PALMETTO (S. minor) 670

KEYS TO THE ASPENS AND POPLARS (Populus)

Summer Key

1. Leaf blades with a thick feltlike layer of white to silver hairs below, often obscuring entirely the lower surface at maturity, prominently 3- to 5-lobed; buds and shoots densely white or silvery-hairy . . . . .WHITE POPLAR (P. alba) 388
1a. Leaf blades without the feltlike layer of hairs below, undersurface never obscured by hairs at maturity, unlobed; leaf buds and shoots not covered with dense white or silvery hairs. (2)
2. Petioles conspicuously flattened laterally, not grooved above. (3)
2a. Petioles not flattened laterally, grooved above. (6)
3. Leaves nearly round in outline, mostly <2½ inches broad, the margins very finely and irregularly toothed. . . . .
. . . . .QUAKING ASPEN (P. tremuloides) 390
3a. Leaves mostly ovoid, triangular, or diamond-shaped in outline, mostly >2½ inches broad, the margins more coarsely and regularly toothed. (4)

Winter Key

Page

5.   Buds small, <½ inch long, lustrous, slightly resinous, but not
     fragrant. (6)
5a. Buds large, >⅔ inch long, resinous, fragrant. ....
     ....BALSAM POPLAR *(P. balsamifera)*   395
6.   Bud scale margins scarious; plants of higher elevation, mostly in
     the mountains...................QUAKING ASPEN *(P. tremuloides)*   390
6a. Bud scale margins not scarious; plants of swamp forests.........
     ....SWAMP COTTONWOOD *(P. heterophylla)*   402

KEYS TO THE WILLOWS *(Salix)*

Summer Key

1.   Branches long-pendulous; fruits small, ³⁄₁₆ to ¼ inch long. ....
     ....WEEPING WILLOW *(S. x pendulina and S. x sepulcralis)*   413
1a. Branches not long-pendulous, fruits generally larger. (2)
2.   Leaves more or less hairy on both surfaces, tomentose below .....
     ....GRAY WILLOW *(S. bebbiana)*   413
2a. Leaves glabrous, at least on the upper surface, not tomentose
     below at maturity. (3)
3.   Leaves not glaucous beneath. (4)
3a. Leaves glaucous beneath (or rarely, thinly so in black willow). (5)
4.   Leaves very narrow, mostly <⅝ inch wide; petioles without
     glands at the summit. ....BLACK WILLOW *(S. nigra)*   405
4a. Leaves oblong-lanceolate, mostly >⅝ inch wide; petioles with
     prominent glands near the summit... .SHINING WILLOW *(S. lucida)*   409
5.   Leaf margin entire or crenate. ....PUSSY WILLOW *(S. discolor)*   416
5a. Leaf margin serrulate or serrate. (6)
6.   Leaves green and lustrous on both surfaces. ....
     ....BLACK WILLOW *(S. nigra)*   405
6a. Leaves distinctly paler or whitened below. (7)
7.   Leaf blades glabrous beneath; bud apex obtuse, bud scale margins
     fused; trees 35 to 85 feet high; stamens 2. ....
     ....CRACK WILLOW *(S. fragilis)*   411
7a. Leaf blades hairy beneath along midrib; bud apex acute, bud
     scale margins free and overlapping; shrubs or trees <35 feet high;
     stamens 4 or more. ....CAROLINA WILLOW *(S. caroliniana)*   407

Winter Key

KEYS TO THE WALNUTS (*Juglans*)

Summer Key

Winter Key

KEYS TO THE HICKORIES (*Carya*)

Summer Key

Page

8. Most leaves with 5–7 leaflets; terminal buds ⅛–⅜ inch long;
    plants are shrubby trees; restricted to central Florida. . . . .
    . . . . .SCRUB HICKORY *(C. floridana)*   269

8a. Most leaves with 7–9 leaflets; terminal buds ³⁄₁₆–⁷⁄₁₆ inch long;
    plants treelike; of various locations. (9)

9. Leaflets narrowly lanceolate, pale with minute, silvery scales
    beneath, not falcate; nut thin-shelled, not winged along suture. . .
    . . . . .SAND HICKORY *(C. pallida)*   266

9a. Leaflets broadly lanceolate or oblong, with minute white to
    brownish scales and often silky hairs beneath, clearly falcate; nut
    very thick-shelled, winged along suture. . . . .
    . . . . .NUTMEG HICKORY *(C. myristiciformis)*   258

10. Leaflets usually 5, rarely 7, with densely ciliate margins and tufts
    of hairs near the tips of the marginal teeth, often becoming quite
    glabrous beneath. (11)

10a. Leaflets usually 7, rarely 9, margins not densely ciliate, hair tufts
    often lacking, rather densely hairy or felted beneath. (12)

11. Leaflets ovate or obovate; most husked fruits >1½ inches long. . . .
    . . . . .SHAG-BARK HICKORY *(C. ovata)*   259

11a. Leaflets lanceolate or oblanceolate; most husked fruits <1½
    inches long. . . . .
    . . . . . . .SOUTHERN SHAG-BARK HICKORY *(C. carolinae-septentrionalis)*   261

12. Bark shaggy; leaves >12 inches long, only slightly aromatic when
    crushed; shoots and petioles not densely hairy; terminal bud very
    elongate, ¾–1¼ inches long, with persistent scales remaining
    until spring; fruit husk ⅓–½ inch thick. . . . .
    . . . . .SHELL-BARK HICKORY *(C. laciniosa)*   261

12a. Bark not shaggy, leaves <12 inches long, very aromatic when
    crushed; shoots and petioles densely hairy; terminal bud smaller,
    ½–¾ inch long, with outer scales soon deciduous; fruit husk
    ⅛–¼ inch thick. . . . . .MOCKERNUT HICKORY *(C. alba)*   264

Winter Key

1. Bud scales valvate with one (rarely a few) pairs of scales, the
    edges of which meet, but do not overlap, or buds appearing
    naked; fruit husks winged along sutures near middle of fruit. (2)

1a. Bud scales imbricate with 6 or more overlapping scales; fruit
    husks not winged or only very slightly so. (5)

Page

2. Buds bright sulfur yellow, appearing naked. . . . .
. . . . .BITTER-NUT HICKORY *(C. cordiformis)*   256

2a. Buds not bright sulfur yellow, mostly yellowish to yellow-brown
to buff, appearing scaled. (3)

3. Twigs glabrous; buds golden-brown, or pale silvery-brown to buff.
. . . . .NUTMEG HICKORY *(C. myristiciformis)*   258

3a. Twigs hairy, occasionally so only near apex; buds yellow to
yellow-brown, reddish-brown to dark gray. (4)

4. Twigs hairy only at apex; terminal bud ⅛–¼ inch long, buds
yellowish to yellow-brown to reddish-brown; pith dark chestnut-
brown; bark of bole light gray, scaly; fruit conspicuously flattened,
nut angled in cross-section, finely wrinkled on surface. . . . .
. . . . .WATER HICKORY *(C. aquatica)*   254

4a. Twigs hairy throughout; terminal bud about ½ inch long, buds
dark gray; pith light brown; bark on bole gray to brown, furrowed
or slightly scaly; fruit elongated, ovoid, nut round in cross-section,
smooth surfaced. . . . . .PECAN *(C. illinoinensis)*   251

5. Largest terminal bud usually ½ inch or more long; twigs stout. (6)

5a. Largest terminal bud <½ inch long; twigs moderate or fairly
slender. (9)

6. Outer bud scales early deciduous, exposing the silky inner scales;
largest terminal bud ½–¾ inch long; bark not shaggy toward
maturity; twigs 1 inch from terminal bud, generally >¼ inch in
diameter. . . . . .MOCKERNUT HICKORY *(C. alba)*   264

6a. Outer bud scales persistent; largest terminal buds ¾–1 inch long;
bark shaggy on maturing trees; twigs 1 inch from the terminal
bud, ³⁄₁₆–¼ inch in diameter. (7)

7. Terminal bud ¾ inch or more long; twigs buffy or orange-brown;
nuts pointed at both ends. . . . . .SHELL-BARK HICKORY *(C. laciniosa)*   261

7a. Terminal bud shorter; twigs grayish to reddish-brown; nuts
usually rounded at both ends. (8)

8. Buds light brown to gray; twigs mostly ¼ inch or more in
diameter. . . . . .SHAG-BARK HICKORY *(C. ovata)*   259

8a. Buds dark brown; twigs mostly ³⁄₁₆–¼ inch in diameter. . . . .
. . . . . . .SOUTHERN SHAG-BARK HICKORY *(C. carolinae-septentrionalis)*   261

9. Twigs and buds rusty-hairy. . . . . .BLACK HICKORY *(C. texana)*   270

9a. Twigs and buds other than rusty-hairy. (10)

KEYS TO THE BIRCHES (*Betula*)

Summer Key

1. Broken twigs and leaves with a distinct smell and taste of winter-green; leaves with 9–12 prominent veins per side, if fewer (3-6), then trees very rare, known only from southwestern Virginia. (2)

1a. Broken twigs and leaves lacking a smell and taste of wintergreen; leaves with 5–10 prominent veins per side. (4)

2a. Leaves not round in outline, veins 9-12 per side; plants of various localities. (3)

Winter Key

3. Twigs slightly hairy, yellowish-brown, dull, with a faint odor and taste of wintergreen when broken; buds broadly acute, lowest bud scale slightly hairy; bark yellow to yellowish-gray and peeling in thin papery layers; catkin scales ¼–½ inch long, finely hairy with ciliate margins, lateral lobes ascending. . . . .
. . . . .YELLOW BIRCH *(B. alleghaniensis)*

3a. Twigs glabrous, reddish-brown to blackish, lustrous, with a strong odor and taste of wintergreen when broken; buds sharply acute, lowest bud scale glabrous; bark reddish-brown, cherrylike, and not peeling; catkin scales ¼–⁵⁄₁₆ inch long, glabrous, lateral lobes divergent. . . . . .SWEET BIRCH *(B. lenta)*

4. Bark close-fitting, not peeling, with prominent triangular chevronlike blotches below each of the nonpendulous branches; native species, typically multistemmed. . . . .
. . . . .GRAY BIRCH *(B. populifolia)*

4a. Bark peeling, without prominent triangular chevronlike blotches below each of the branches, or if so, then an introduced species with long pendulous branches, and typically single-stemmed. (5)

5. Shoots glabrous or essentially so; buds shiny and resinous; introduced species. . . . . .EUROPEAN WHITE BIRCH *(B. pendula)*

5a. Shoots hairy, especially toward tips; buds nonresinous; native species. (6)

6. Bark light brown, pinkish to cinnamon-colored; fruiting catkins erect to nearly so. . . . . .RIVER BIRCH *(B. nigra)*

6a. Bark white, fruiting catkins drooping or spreading. . . . .
. . . . .PAPER BIRCH *(B. papyrifera)*

KEYS TO THE CHESTNUTS *(Castanea)*

Summer Key

1. Most leaves >5 inches long, glabrous beneath; petioles mostly <⅔ inch long. . . . . .AMERICAN CHESTNUT *(C. dentata)*

1a. Most leaves <5 inches long, whitish hairy beneath; petioles mostly >⅔ inch long, hairy beneath. . . . .
. . . . .ALLEGHENY-CHINKAPIN *(C. pumila)*

Winter Key

KEYS TO THE OAKS *(Quercus)*

Summer Key

Page

Winter Key

Page

20. Buds and twigs reddish-brown; buds with few to many long apical hairs, not angled in cross-section; twigs moderately stout; acorns up to 1 inch or more long. . . . .
. . . . .NORTHERN RED OAK *(Q. rubra)* 283

20a. Buds and twigs straw-colored; buds glabrous or slightly short-hairy, angled in cross-section; twigs slender; acorns smaller. . . . . .
. . . . .SHUMARD OAK *(Q. shumardii)* 292

21. Buds broad and rounded. (22)

21a. Buds ovoid but narrower, more or less pointed. (33)

22. Plants shrublike, thicket-forming; buds often more than one at a node. . . . . .DWARF CHINKAPIN OAK *(Q. prinoides)* 353

22a. Plants treelike, not thicket-forming; buds always solitary at nodes. (23)

23. Body of bud scales and twigs essentially glabrous. (24)

23a. Body of bud scales hairy; twigs hairy or not. (27)

24. Plants small trees of deep sands or pine barrens; bark rough, reddish-brown to gray. . . . . .SAND POST OAK *(Q. margarettae)* 336

24a. Plants various as to size and habitat; bark scaly, silver-gray. (25)

25. Small trees, often multistemmed from base; found on limestone bluffs and prairies along our southern coastal plain. . . . .
. . . . .BASTARD OAK *(Q. sinuata)* 331

25a. Large, single-trunked trees; found on moist to dry slopes to wetlands. (26)

26. Terminal buds ⅛–¼ inch long, reddish-brown; twigs reddish-green to gray, with a polished or pearly appearance; bark not peeling from branches; acorns sessile or short-stalked branches; plants of moist to dry forest slopes. . . . .
. . . . .WHITE OAK *(Q. alba)* 339

26a. Terminal buds 1/16–3/16 inch long, chestnut-brown; twigs reddish-brown to straw-colored, dull; bark exfoliating or peeling from branches; acorns long-stalked; plants mostly of swamp forests or wet uplands. . . . . .SWAMP WHITE OAK *(Q. bicolor)* 343

27. Twigs developing corky ridges. . . . . .BUR OAK *(Q. macrocarpa)* 331

27a. Twigs lacking corky ridges. (28)

28. Acorn nearly enclosed by cup; trunk base of mature trees buttressed. . . . . .OVERCUP OAK *(Q. lyrata)* 336

28a. Acorn and trunk not as above. (29)

29. Twigs mostly glabrous. (30)

29a. Twigs rough-hairy. (32)

Page

30. Twigs orange-brown; buds to ¼ inch long. . . . .
. . . . .CHINKAPIN OAK *(Q. muehlenbergii)*   349

30a. Twigs other than orange-brown; buds up to ⅛ inch long. (31)

31. Twigs not brittle at base; bark rough, reddish-brown to gray. . . . . .
. . . . .SAND POST OAK *(Q. margarettae)*   336

31a. Twigs brittle at base; bark scaly, silvery-gray. . . . .
. . . . .BLUFF OAK *(Q. austrina)*   341

32. First year twig cuticle not hidden by hairs. . . . .
. . . . .BOTTOM-LAND POST OAK *(Q. similis)*   329

32a. First year twig cuticle hidden by hairs. . . . . . .POST OAK *(Q. stellata)*   334

33. Branches with small, painfully sharp thornlike twigs. (34)

33a. Branches without painfully sharp thornlike twigs. (36)

34. Buds and twigs completely glabrous. . . . . .WILLOW OAK *(Q. phellos)*   313

34a. Buds and/or twigs hairy. (35)

35. Buds pale hairy above the middle, not angled; plants of wet
bottomlands. . . . . .PIN OAK *(Q. palustris)*   289

35a. Buds lustrous red-brown, angled; plants of dry, well-drained
upland soils. . . . . .NORTHERN PIN OAK *(Q. ellipsoidalis)*   291

36. Buds round in cross-section. (37)

36a. Buds angled in cross-section. (41)

37. Remnant leaves with unlobed margin or nearly so, lacking a
bristle-tip; twigs slightly hairy initially, becoming glabrous; plants
rare, restricted to the coastal plain of Georgia and adjacent South
Carolina. .OGLETHORPE OAK *(Q. oglethorpensis)*   342

37a. Remnant leaves not as above; twigs hairy or not; plants from
various locations. (38)

38. Bark gray, flaky; inner surface of acorn cup glabrous; twigs
orange-brown. . . . . .CHINKAPIN OAK *(Q. muehlenbergii)*   349

38a. Bark not gray and flaky; inner surface of acorn cup hairy; twigs
otherwise. (39)

39. Acorns 1 inch long or larger, hairy at apex only; bole of mature
trees bark striped with long, vertical lighter gray stripes. . . . .
. . . . .NORTHERN RED OAK *(Q. rubra)*   283

39a. Acorns <1 inch long, hairy below apex; bark of mature trees not
as above. (40)

40. Remnant leaves with 1 bristle per lobe, rarely 2. . . . .
. . . . .GEORGIA OAK *(Q. georgiana)*   297

40a. Remnant leaves with 2 or more bristles per lobe. . . . .
. . . . .TEXAS OAK *(Q. texana)*   297

Page

41. Buds and twigs completely glabrous. . . . .
. . . . .SHUMARD OAK (*Q. shumardii*)   292

41a. Buds and/or twigs hairy. (42)

42. Twigs glabrous; acorn with concentric grooves toward pointed tip.
. . . . .SCARLET OAK (*Q. coccinea*)   286

42a. Twigs hairy or glabrous; acorn lacking concentric grooves toward
tip. (43)

43. At least some evergreen leaves remaining until spring; buds
angled in cross-section; plants mostly shrubby. . . . .
. . . . .BLUEJACK OAK (*Q. incana*)   322

43a. Any deciduous leaves remaining on tree appearing brown by
mid-winter; buds angled in cross-section or not; plants as trees
or shrubs. (44)

44. Young twigs glabrous. (45)

44a. Young twigs at least somewhat hairy. (46)

45. Twigs greenish-brown; mostly northern, upland species. . . . .
. . . . .SHINGLE OAK (*Q. imbricaria*)   320

45a. Twigs red-brown; mostly southern, lowland species. . . . .
. . . . .WATER OAK (*Q. nigra*)   311

46. Small, northern, thicket-forming shrub; buds not >⅛ inch long,
often more than 1 per node. . . . . .BEAR OAK (*Q. ilicifolia*)   309

46a. Large tree; buds >⅛ inch long, 1 per node. (47)

47. Bark of mature trees broadly ridged, similar to that of the black
cherry. . . . . .CHERRY-BARK OAK (*Q. pagoda*)   303

47a. Bark of mature trees narrowly ridged, deeply fissured; plants of
drier slopes and ridges. . . . . .SOUTHERN RED OAK (*Q. falcata*)   301

Note: Many of the winter characteristics of oaks are variable, and
thus winter identification must be considered tentative.

KEYS TO THE ELMS *(Ulmus)*

Summer Key

1. Branches with corky or winglike projections. (2)
1a. Branches lacking such projections. (5)
2. Leaves mostly <2 inches long. (3)
2a. Leaves mostly >2 inches long. (4)

Winter Key

KEYS TO THE HACKBERRIES *(Celtis)*

Summer Key

Winter Key

KEYS TO THE MAGNOLIAS *(Magnolia)*

Summer Key

Page

1. Leaves extremely thick and leathery, very lustrous above, usually rusty-hairy beneath. . . . . .SOUTHERN MAGNOLIA *(M. grandiflora)*   180

1a. Leaves not extremely leathery, nor conspicuously lustrous above, or if somewhat leathery and lustrous, not rusty-hairy beneath. (2)

2. Leaves eared at base. (3)

2a. Leaves pointed to rounded at base, lacking ears. (6)

3. Leaves huge, 20 or more inches long, conspicuously crowded at branch tips. (4)

3a. Leaves shorter, scattered along the branches. (5)

4. Trunk usually twisted or crooked; stamens $^7/_{16}$–$^1/_2$ inch long; fruits subcylindrical to ovoid; hairs mostly confined to midrib on lower leaf surface; small tree known from the Florida Panhandle region only. . . . . .ASHE MAGNOLIA *(M. ashei)*   191

4a. Trunk straight, upright; stamens $^2/_3$–$^3/_4$ inch long; fruits subglobose to globose; hairs throughout lower leaf surface; large tree found throughout much of the Southeast. . . . .
. . . . .BIG-LEAF MAGNOLIA *(M. macrophylla)*   190

5. Leaves mostly 9–12 inches long; mountain species; stamens $^1/_3$–$^2/_3$ inch long; fruits $2^2/_3$–$4^1/_2$ inches long. . . . .
. . . . .FRASER MAGNOLIA *(M. fraseri)*   186

5a. Leaves mostly 5–9 inches long; coastal plain species; stamens $^1/_8$–$^1/_4$ inch long; fruits $1^1/_2$–$2^1/_2$ inches long. . . . .
. . . . .PYRAMID MAGNOLIA *(M. pyramidata)*   188

6. Leaves mostly 12–24 inches long; broadest above middle and gradually tapered to base, crowded at branch tips. . . . .
. . . . .UMBRELLA MAGNOLIA *(M. tripetala)*   184

6a. Leaves <12 inches long; broadly wedge-shaped to rounded at base, scattered along the branches. (7)

7. Leaves mostly >6 inches long. . . . . .CUCUMBER-TREE *(M. acuminata)*   177

7a. Leaves mostly <6 inches long. (8)

8. Leaves evergreen or persistent, broadest at or near the middle, usually strongly whitened beneath and lustrous above, aromatic; petals small, <2 inches long. . . . . .SWEET-BAY *(M. virginiana)*   182

8a. Leaves deciduous, broadest above the middle, not at all whitened beneath, dull above, nonaromatic; petals larger, mostly >2 inches long. . . . . .CUCUMBER-TREE *(M. acuminata)*   177

Winter Key

KEYS TO THE APPLES AND CRABAPPLES *(Malus)*

Summer Key

1. Leaves permanently hairy beneath; sepals hairy externally. (2)
1a. Leaves glabrous beneath at maturity; sepals glabrous externally. (3)

Note: The prairie crabapple may be identified in winter by its persistently hairy and often thorny twigs, but it is nearly impossible
to distinguish the sweet crabapple from the southern crabapple by
winter characteristics.

KEYS TO THE SERVICE-BERRIES *(Amelanchier)*

Summer Key

Winter Key

KEYS TO THE PEACHES, PLUMS, AND CHERRIES
(Prunus)

Summer Key

Winter Key

KEY TO THE HONEY-LOCUST AND WATER-LOCUST
(Gleditsia)

KEYS TO THE SUMACS *(Rhus)*

Summer Key

KEYS TO THE HOLLIES *(Ilex)*

Summer Key

Winter Key

KEYS TO THE MAPLES *(Acer)*

Summer Key

Page

1. Leaves pinnately compound. . . . . . . .ASH-LEAF MAPLE *(A. negundo)*   603

1a. Leaves simple. (2)

2. Broken petioles, twigs and buds with milky sap. . . . .
. . . . .NORWAY MAPLE *(A. platanoides)*   581

2a. Broken petioles, twigs and buds with clear sap. (3)

3. Leaves deeply 5-lobed, sinuses cut mostly below mid-leaf, the
terminal lobe with conspicuously outward-sloping sides; branch-
lets ill-scented. . . . . .SILVER MAPLE *(A. saccharinum)*   597

3a. Leaves shallowly to moderately 3- to 5-lobed, sinuses cut to about
the middle of the leaf blade, the terminal lobe with parallel or
inward-sloping sides; branchlets not ill-scented. (4)

4. Leaf margins lobed but otherwise entire, or with a few coarse and
irregular teeth. (5)

4a. Leaf margins lobed and also regularly serrate-toothed. (8)

5. Leaves glabrous or nearly so beneath, the lobes with scattered but
sharply pointed teeth. . . . . .SUGAR MAPLE *(A. saccharum)*   587

5a. Leaves more or less hairy beneath; the lobes entire or merely
wavy-toothed. (6)

6. Leaf blades 4–6 inches long, usually 3-lobed with drooping sides;
prominent stipules often present; a tree primarily of the glaciated
areas of the north. . . . . .BLACK MAPLE *(A. nigrum)*   594

6a. Leaf blades shorter, 3- to 5-lobed; stipules not usually prominent;
a lowland, southern tree species. (7)

7. Leaves with long and narrowly pointed, acute lobes, yellow-green
and hairy beneath; bark smooth and chalky-white to light gray. . .
. . . . .CHALK MAPLE *(A. leucoderme)*   594

7a. Leaves with short and broadly triangular, obtuse lobes, light pale
green to blue-green or gray-green, tawny-hairy beneath; bark
gray and furrowed. . . . . .FLORIDA MAPLE *(A. barbatum)*   590

8. Leaves green above but conspicuously whitened or bluish-green
beneath; buds sessile with >2 bud scales. (9)

8a. Leaves green above and beneath; buds conspicuously stalked,
with 2 opposing bud scales. (12)

Winter Key

Page

10. Buds red to greenish-purple, appressed, exuding a white sap
when cut, terminal bud solitary; edge of leaf scars meeting
around twig; mature bark dark gray, ridged, not shedding; fruits
always in pairs. ....NORWAY MAPLE *(A. platanoides)*   581
10a. Buds green, occasionally pink, with dark marks, spreading, not
exuding white sap when cut, terminal bud often appearing
double; edge of leaf scars not meeting around twig; mature bark
pinkish-brown, mottled, scaly, and shedding; fruits occasionally
in groups of 3. ....SYCAMORE MAPLE *(A. pseudoplatanus)*   592

KEYS TO THE BUCKEYES *(Aesculus)*

Summer Key

1. Leaflets mostly 7–9 sessile or with extremely short stalks; flowers
white, spotted with yellow and purple, upper petal claw shorter
than calyx, stamens much exserted; buds sticky; fruits spiny. ....
..........................HORSE-CHESTNUT *(A. hippocastanum)*   569
1a. Leaflets mostly 5, stalked; flower colors various, upper petal claw
mostly longer than calyx; buds not sticky; fruits spiny, warty, or
smooth; stamens various. (2)
2. Petals white, stamens 3–4 times longer than petals; inflorescence
narrow, 8–20 inches long; an understory shrub or small tree;
native to Georgia and Alabama only. ....
..........................BOTTLEBRUSH BUCKEYE *(A. parviflora)*   572
2a. Petals yellow to red; stamens not more than twice as long as
petals; inflorescence broad, 4–10 inches long; trees or shrubs from
various locations. (3)
3. Twigs with a disagreeable odor when broken; fruits with a prickly
husk; petals nearly equal in length, pale yellow to green-yellow;
stamens nearly twice as long as petals. ....
....OHIO BUCKEYE *(A. glabra)*   572
3a. Twigs lacking a disagreeable odor when broken; fruits with a
smooth husk; petals unequal in length with the upper pair
appearing larger and narrower, yellow to red; stamens shorter or
only slightly longer than upper petal. (4)

Winter Key

KEYS TO THE BLACK GUM AND TUPELOS (Nyssa)

Summer Key

Page

1. Leaves mostly >2½ inches broad and 6 inches long, abundantly hairy below, the margins often with a few, irregular coarse teeth. . . . . .WATER TUPELO *(N. aquatica)*   547

1a. Leaves mostly <2½ inches broad and 5 inches long, thinly hairy below mostly along the veins and midrib or glabrous, margins nearly always entire, rarely with a few teeth. (2)

2. Leaf apices bluntly pointed or rounded; branchlets hairy; fruits about 1 inch long, red, short-stalked, the stone thinly winged; trees usually with several crooked trunks. . . . .
. . . . .OGEECHEE TUPELO *(N. ogeche)*   549

2a. Leaf apices rather sharply pointed; branchlets glabrous; fruits about ½ inch long, black to dark blue, long-stalked, the stone indistinctly ribbed or with prominent sharp ridges; trees usually with a single straight trunk. (3)

3. Leaves oval to obovate, mostly 1–3 inches wide, 2–6 inches long, apex acute to acuminate; fruits 2–6 together on stalk. . . . .
. . . . .BLACK GUM *(N. sylvatica)*   543

3a. Leaves narrower, usually ½–1½ inches wide, 1½–4 inches long, apex obtuse; fruits mostly paired on stalk, occasionally solitary. . . . . .SWAMP TUPELO *(N. biflora)*   547

Winter Key

1. Twigs about ¼ inch in diameter; terminal buds about ⅛ inch long, roundish. (2)

1a. Twigs more slender; terminal buds to about ¼ inch long, ovoid, pointed. (3)

2. Mature twigs glabrous, dark red or reddish-brown; terminal bud glabrous or only slightly hairy, usually straight with 3 or more visible scales; leaf scars nearly round; fruits purple; single trunked tree. . . . . .WATER TUPELO *(N. aquatica)*   547

2a. Mature twigs hairy, light greenish-brown to reddish-brown; terminal bud densely hairy, often cocked to one side, with 2–3 visible scales; leaf scars broadly crescent-shaped to triangular; fruits red; multitrunked tree. . . . . . .OGEECHEE TUPELO *(N. ogeche)*   549

KEYS TO THE DOGWOODS *(Cornus)*

Summer Key

Winter Key

KEY TO THE BULLIES *(Sideroxylon)*

KEYS TO THE ASHES *(Fraxinus)*

Summer Key

Winter Key

Page

1. Twigs 4-angled or 4-winged. . . . . .BLUE ASH (*F. quadrangulata*) 637
1a. Twigs otherwise. (2)
2. Leaf scars U-shaped or deeply notched on the upper margin. (3)
2a. Leaf scars without such a notch on the upper margin. (4)
3. Outermost terminal bud scales appearing apically flattened; twigs usually more or less woolly; leaf scars without a deep V-shaped notch; northern swamp or bog tree. . . . .PUMPKIN ASH (*F. profunda*) 641
3a. Outermost terminal bud scales apically pointed; twigs usually glabrous but sometimes hairy; leaf scars with a deep V-shaped notch; trees of rich soils. . . . . .WHITE ASH (*F. americana*) 638
4. Buds blackish; terminal bud ¼ inch or more long and pointed at the tip. . . . . .BLACK ASH (*F. nigra*) 647
4a. Buds brown or rusty; terminal bud shorter and blunt. (5)
5. Outermost pairs of terminal bud scales apically pointed; twigs grayish or ashy, sometimes hairy. . . . . .GREEN ASH (*F. pennsylvanica*) 643
5a. Outermost pairs of terminal bud scales appearing apically flattened; twigs light brown or orange-brown. . . . .
. . . . .CAROLINA ASH (*F. caroliniana*) 645

KEYS TO THE CATALPAS (*Catalpa*)

Summer Key

1. Most leaves 4–8 inches long, ill-scented if crushed, thin textured, apices abruptly short-pointed; flowers small, but numerous per inflorescence, corolla ¾–1⅔ inches wide, conspicuously yellow-spotted, lower lobe not notched; fruits ⅓–½ inch thick; bark scaly.
. . . . .SOUTHERN CATALPA (*C. bignonioides*) 653
1a. Most leaves 8–12 inches long, not ill-scented if crushed, thick textured, apices long-pointed; flowers large, but few per inflorescence, corolla >1⅔ inches wide, not conspicuously yellow-spotted, lower lobe notched; fruits nearly ⅔ inch thick; bark furrowed. . . .
. . . . .NORTHERN CATALPA (*C. speciosa*) 656

Winter Key

KEYS TO THE ARROW-WOODS AND BLACKHAWS
(Viburnum)

Summary Key

Summer Key

Winter Key

KEYS TO THE MULBERRIES (*Morus*)

Summer Key

Winter Key

KEY TO THE RHODODENDRONS (*Rhododendron*)

KEYS TO THE SYCAMORES AND PLANETREES (*Platanus*)

Summer Key

Page

1. Fruiting ball 1 per stalk; inner bark where exposed white; leaves shallowly 3- to 5-lobed, lobes shorter than broad; native species. . . . . .AMERICAN SYCAMORE (*P. occidentalis*)   206

1a. Fruiting ball 2 or more per stalk; inner bark where exposed greenish-white to green-yellow or brown; introduced species. (2)

2. Inner bark where exposed greenish-yellow; leaves 2- to 5-lobed (usually 3), the middle lobe as long or slightly longer than broad; fruiting balls 2 (rarely 3) per stalk, each 1 inch across. . . . . .LONDON PLANETREE (*P. hybrida*)   209

2a. Inner bark greenish-white to grayish; leaves deeply 5- to 7-lobed (rarely 3), lobes longer than broad; fruiting balls 2–6 per stalk, each 1 inch or less across. . . . . . .ORIENTAL PLANETREE (*P. orientalis*)   209

Winter Key

1. Inner bark when exposed greenish-yellow; fruiting balls 2 (rarely 3) per stalk. .LONDON PLANETREE (*P. hybrida*)   209

1a. Inner bark when exposed white to greenish-white to grayish. (2)

2. Fruiting balls 1 per stalk. . . . .AMERICAN SYCAMORE (*P. occidentalis*)   206

2a. Fruiting balls 2 to 6 per stalk. . . . . .ORIENTAL PLANETREE (*P. orientalis*)   209

KEYS TO THE MOUNTAIN-ASHES (*Sorbus*)

Summer Key

1. Peduncles, pedicels, leaf rachises, leaves on both surfaces, and petioles, densely white-tomentose at anthesis; leaflets oblong, acute or obtuse, dull green above, paler and generally permanently hairy beneath; introduced species. . . . . .EUROPEAN MOUNTAIN-ASH (*S. aucuparia*)   481

1a. Peduncles, pedicels, leaf rachises and petioles glabrous or sparingly piose; leaflets glabrous or soon glabrate on the main veins, more or less persistently but sparingly pilose beneath; native species. (2)

Page

2. Leaflets bluish to gray-green, lateral leaflets oval or oblong, broadest near the middle, abruptly acute, 2–3½ inches long, rarely >3 times as long as wide, not lustrous, serrate to the middle or below. . . . . .NORTHERN MOUNTAIN-ASH *(S. decora)*   480

2a. Leaflets dull green, lateral leaflets lanceolate to oblong-lanceolate, broadest below the middle, tapering rather gradually to the acute or acuminate apex, 1–3¼ inches long, commonly >3 times as long as wide, more or less lustrous above, often serrate to the base. . . . .
. . . . .AMERICAN MOUNTAIN-ASH *(S. americana)*   477

Winter Key

1. Winter buds conspicuously white-hairy throughout, not at all or scarcely gummy; introduced species. . . . .
. . . . .EUROPEAN MOUNTAIN-ASH *(S. aucuparia)*   481

1a. Winter buds glabrous or slightly hairy, usually more or less ciliate, conspicuously gummy; native species. (2)

2. Winter buds with glabrous or sparingly pilose outer scales, the inner one ciliate with whitish or rusty hairs. . . . .
. . . . .NORTHERN MOUNTAIN-ASH *(S. decora)*   480

2a. Winter buds completely glabrous. . . . .
. . . . .AMERICAN MOUNTAIN-ASH *(S. americana)*   477

KEYS TO THE SILVERBELLS *(Halesia)*

Summer Key

1. Leaves broadly obovate to suborbicular; corolla lobes longer than tube; fruits with 2 lengthwise wings. . . . .
. . . . .TWO-WING SILVERBELL *(H. diptera)*   505

1a. Leaves elliptic, ovate to oblong; corolla lobes shorter than tube; fruits with 4 lengthwise wings. (2)

2. Corolla <½ inch long; fruits <1¼ inches long, tapered toward base. . . . . .CAROLINA SILVERBELL *(H. carolina)*   505

2a. Corolla >½ inch long; fruits 1¼–2 inches long, ellipsoid to obovoid. . . . . .MOUNTAIN SILVERBELL *(H. tetraptera)*   503

Winter Key

Distribution of Trees
in Eastern North America

When the first Europeans came to the shores of the New World, the greater part of eastern North America was covered with forest. It was a magnificent forest of huge trees, stretching virtually unbroken from the very shores of the Atlantic westward across the mountain range to the tallgrass prairies of the plains. Within this forest was a vast array of tree species, more than 200 different types. Some of them were familiar to Europeans because they were quite similar to the trees that grew in their homelands, but others were strange and entirely unlike any trees they had ever seen before. In all of the continent of Europe there were fewer kinds of trees than grew in the forests of eastern North America. Small wonder that such intrepid plantsmen as Andre Michaux and John Fraser were lured into the vast wilderness in search of plant treasures that might be introduced into the great gardens of the Old World.

It is a curious yet enigmatic fact that many of the trees, the shrubs, and the herbaceous plants that flourish in eastern North American forests are most closely related to species growing in faraway eastern Asia. Aeons ago, in the dim distant Cretaceous period of Earth's history, species of tuliptree (*Liriodendron*) were widely distributed throughout the northern hemisphere. The fossilized impressions of their leaves are found in the shales of both Europe and North America. Today, however, but two living species are known to science; one grows in our eastern forests and the other in central China. The nearest of kin to our magnolia (*Magnolia*), silverbell (*Halesia*), sassafras (*Sassafras*), fringetree (*Chionanthus*), and yellow-wood (*Cladrastis*) are also to be found in the eastern portion of Asia. No members of any of these tree genera are found natively in western North America, Europe, or anywhere else in the world save the eastern parts of North America and Asia. Why they should be found today in two such widely separated parts of the world is a question yet to be answered.

The forests of eastern North America are made up of a number of different associations of trees that are known as *forest types*. In 1940 the Committee on Forest Types of the Society of American Foresters recognized and defined 97 such forest types in the eastern United States. Those who are interested in a more detailed study of this subject are referred to the publication on *Forest Cover Types of the Eastern United States.* It is quite evident, even to the most casual observer, that forests are not all alike. Major differences are evident from north to south, from east to west, and, as we shall see later, with changing altitude.

Over most of eastern North America the deciduous, or hardwood, forest is dominant. It is not, of course, everywhere uniform, and I shall subsequently discuss some of the more important forest types. The ultimate type of forest that will cover the land (the *climax forest*) is determined by such factors as soil and climate. Whenever this climax type of forest is removed, the land is modified by a series of steps or stages, a process we know as plant *succession*. We can witness the slow return of climax forest types in abandoned fields and areas denuded by lumbering or fire. In some places the type of forest cover on the land is not the one that soil and climate would normally permit. Such a forest is known as a *subclimax forest*. Good examples are the white pine–hemlock forest once quite common in the northeastern United States, and the pine forests of the southeastern coastal plain.

The *northern coniferous forest* requires a cool, moist climate and is the prevailing forest type over much of eastern Canada and northern Maine. It extends southward at higher elevations into the Appalachians to the Great Smoky Mountains of North Carolina and Tennessee. The dominant trees are red spruce (*Picea rubens*), white spruce (*Picea glauca*), balsam fir (*Abies balsamea*), and American larch (*Larix laricina*) in the North; red spruce and Fraser fir (*Abies fraseri*) in the southern Appalachians and Great Smokies. At the northern end it occurs in the lowlands and even reaches the coast, but at the southern extremity of its range it is found only at elevations of around 5,000 feet or more.

At such altitudes the climate is comparable to that found in northern New England and southern Canada. The high mountains intercept the moisture-bearing winds and have an average annual precipitation of 70 inches or more. The highest midsummer temperature ever recorded at the summit of Mt. Mitchell (6,684 ft.), in North Carolina, was 81 on July 5, 1948.

The *northeastern pine forest* is most prevalent about the northern and western Great Lakes. Originally, at least, it was characterized by dense stands of Eastern white pine *(Pinus strobus)*, red pine *(Pinus resinosa)*, and jack pine *(Pinus banksiana)*.

The *northern hardwood-hemlock forest* extends from southern Canada and the Great Lakes region through New York and northern Pennsylvania to New England, then southward in the mountains to northern Georgia. Sugar maple *(Acer saccharum)*, red maple *(Acer rubrum)*, American beech *(Fagus grandifolia)*, yellow birch *(Betula alleghaniensis)*, eastern hemlock *(Tsuga canadensis)*, and eastern white pine *(Pinus strobus)* are the principal species, but associated with them are a variety of other hardwoods. Southward, in the coves of the southern Appalachians, the tuliptree *(Liriodendron tulipifera)*, yellow buckeye *(Aesculus flava)*, white oak *(Quercus alba)*, and northern red oak *(Quercus rubra)* are prominent members of this association.

The *southern hardwood forest* is the most extensive. It occurs over most of the area west of the Appalachians northward to the southern Great Lakes and over much of the Piedmont and coastal plain from Florida to New England, and also the drier slopes and ridges of the mountains. The dominant trees are the various species of oaks *(Quercus* sp.) and hickories *(Carya* sp.) The American chestnut *(Castanea dentata)* was formerly one of the most important trees. In many places the hardwoods are mixed with pines. This forest occupies drier and often more shallow soils than does the northern hardwood-hemlock forest. It is very variable and a number of associations are recognized: chestnut oak association, white oak association, scarlet oak–black oak association, and so on.

The *southeastern pine forest* is prevalent throughout the South Atlantic and Gulf Coastal Plains. It is characterized by a growth of long-leaf pine *(Pinus palustris)*, slash pine *(Pinus elliottii)*, and loblolly pine *(Pinus taeda)*. As pointed out previously, this forest is actually a subclimax one, which has been maintained throughout the centuries by recurrent fires. If fire were to be excluded for any great length of time, the pines would be succeeded by hardwood trees.

The *cypress-tupelo-sweetgum forest* is the forest type that occurs in the river swamps of the South Atlantic and Gulf Coastal Plains and of the Mississippi Valley bottomlands as far north as southern Illinois and Indiana. Bald-cypress *(Taxodium distichum)*, water tupelo *(Nyssa aquatica)*, and sweet-gum *(Liquidambar styraciflua)* are dominant trees, but there is an admixture of a number of other hardwoods including swamp chestnut oak *(Quercus michauxii)*, pumpkin ash *(Fraxinus profunda)*, sweet-bay *(Magnolia virginiana)*, and water hickory *(Carya aquatica)*.

Scientific Names and Their Meanings

Many persons look with horror at the scientific names that are given to trees, as well as all other living things, and wonder just why such names are necessary. They often ask why the common names are not sufficient. The answer to that question is, of course, that common names are not applied universally to the same species. For instance, the common name black oak has been applied not only to *Quercus velutina* but to at least a half dozen other oak species, and *Quercus velutina* in some places is known as the yellow oak rather than black oak. The name *Quercus velutina*, however, applies to that one particular species of oak and the name is universally known and accepted. No other oak, anywhere in the world, has that particular name.

Scientific names are always Latinized, yet one can readily see the similarity between many of these Latin names and their English counterparts: *pinus* and pine, *populus* and poplar, *larix* and larch, for example. Many scientific names have actually been adopted by us verbatim. We think nothing of talking about the rhododendron, the magnolia, and the viburnum, yet all of these are actually genera of scientific names. As a matter of fact, scientific names are little, if any, more difficult to learn than are the so-called common names.

The scientific names are based on what is known as the binominal system, which was put into broad practice by the Swedish botanist Linnaeus in 1753. Linnaeus is known as the father of modern taxonomic botany. Prior to his time there was no broadly accepted or uniform method of naming plants or any other living things.

The first part of the scientific name is known as the generic name and is always spelled with a capital letter. All oaks, for instance, are grouped together within the genus *Quercus*; all true pines, within the genus *Pinus*. The second part is known as the specific name (epithet), or the name of a particular species. Specific names are not generally capitalized and none is capitalized within the present work. Our eastern white pine is called

Pinus strobus, the northern red oak is *Quercus rubra,* and the tuliptree is *Liriodendron tulipifera.*

Following the scientific name of a plant (and indeed considered part of it) is the name of the person who described it. Usually, as is the case in the present book, this name is abbreviated; thus *Pinus strobus* L. means that Linnaeus first described our eastern white pine and gave it that particular scientific name. Let us take a look at the name of the eastern hemlock. It is written *Tsuga canadensis* (L.) Carr. When Linnaeus first described and named this tree he considered it to be a pine and called it *Pinus canadensis;* however, in following years it was determined that the hemlocks were not true pines, but only related members. In 1847, Endlicher proposed the name *Tsuga* for the hemlocks, and later Carriére transferred Linnaeus's *Pinus canadensis* to the new genus, where it has remained to this day.

Sometimes subcategories of species or infraspecific names of trees are recognized, e.g., *Nyssa sylvatica* var. *biflora* (Walt.) Sarg. In the year 1788, Thomas Walter described a new species of tupelo gum in his *Flora Caroliniana,* which he named *Nyssa biflora.* When that eminent authority on North American trees, Charles Sprague Sargent, published his monumental *Sylva of North America* in 1893, he decided that Walter's *Nyssa biflora* was merely a variety of the black gum, which Humphry Marshall described as *Nyssa sylvatica* in the year 1785. Thus, according to Sargent, *Nyssa biflora* became a variety of the latter species; however, today *Nyssa biflora* is considered to be a full species as it was described originally.

The scientific names of our trees have been derived from various sources. In many instances the generic names were simply adopted from the old Greek or Latin names: *Pinus* for the pines, *Acer* for the maples, *Quercus* for the oaks, etc. Sometimes scientific names signify some outstanding characteristic. The one for our sourwood is *Oxydendrum arboreum.* *Oxydendrum* is derived from two Greek words meaning sour and tree, a name suggested by the leaves of this tree, which actually do have a sour taste; in addition, its twigs do bear a disagreeable smell. *Zanthoxylum,* the generic name for the devil's walkingstick, is likewise derived from two Greek words that mean yellow and wood, and they aptly describe the yellow-colored wood of these trees. Generic, and sometimes specific names as well, are used to memorialize some person; thus the genus *Magnolia* was described by Linnaeus in memory of Pierre Magnol, a former director of the botanical garden at Montpellier, France. *Magnolia fraseri* of our southern Appalachian mountains was dedicated by Thomas Walter to John Fraser, the Scotch nurseryman who explored these mountains for plants and who first introduced this magnolia to Europe. Specific names may refer to a geographical area, often indicating where the original or type specimen was collected.

For those persons who may be interested in knowing about the derivations of the scientific names of our trees, the following lists of generic and specific names and their meanings have been included.

GENERIC NAMES

Abies—The classical Latin name of the European silver fir.

Acer—The classical Latin name of the maples from the Celtic meaning hard.

Aesculus—The ancient Latin name for an oak or other mast-bearing tree.

Ailanthus—From a Moluccan name meaning tree-of-heaven, referring to the height of the tree.

Albizia—Dedicated to Cavalier Filippo degl'Albizzi who introduced trees of the genus into Europe.

Amelanchier—From the French name of a related plant.

Aralia—From the French-Canadian name *aralie.*

Asimina—From the Native American name *assimin.*

Avicennia—Named for Avicenna of Bokhara (980–1036), a physician in the Orient.

Betula—The classical Latin name of the birches.

Broussonetia—Named for Auguste Broussonet (1761–1807), physician and naturalist of Montpellier, France.

Carpinus—The classical Latin name of the hornbeams.

Carya—From the Greek word meaning nut.

Castanea—The classical Latin name of the chestnuts, from the Greek *castana.*

Catalpa—From the Native American name.

Celtis—From the classical Latin name of a species of lotus.

Cercis—The classical Greek name for the Judas-tree.

Chamaecyparis—From the classical Greek meaning a ground cypress.

Chionanthus—From the Greek words meaning snow and flower.

Cinnamomum—The ancient name of the cinnamon tree, from the Hebrew *(quinnamon)* and the Greek *(kinnamomon).*

Cladrastis—From the Greek words meaning brittle and branch.

Cliftonia—Named for Francis Clifton, an 18th century English physician.

Cornus—From the Latin meaning a horn, referring to its hard wood.

Cotinus—From the Greek name for the wild olive.

Crataegus—From the classical Greek name of the hawthorns, meaning strength.

Cyrilla—Named for Domenico Cirillo (1734–99), Italian physician and botanist.

Diospyros—From the Greek words meaning Jove's grain.

Elaeagnus—The Greek name for the Chastetree *(Vitex agnus-castus);* the Elaiagnos of Theophrastus, referring to the willow of marshes *(helodes)* and the white seed masses *(hagnos).*

Fagus—The classical Latin name of the beech, from a Creek word meaning to eat.

Firmiana—Named for Count Karl Joseph von Firmian (1716–82), Austrian statesman and governor of Lombardy.

Frangula—the classical Latin *frangere,* to break; perhaps regarding the brittle branches.

Franklinia—Named for Benjamin Franklin (1706–90).

Fraxinus—The classical Latin name of the ashes.

Ginkgo—From the Chinese meaning silver fruit.

Gleditsia—Named for Johann Gottleib Gleditsch (1714–86), Director of the botanical garden at Berlin.

Gordonia—Named for James Gordon (1728–91), English nurseryman.

Halesia—Named for Stephen Hale (1677–1761), English clergyman and author of *Vegetable Staticks.*

Hamamelis—From the classical Greek, probably alluding to some plant producing flowers and fruits at the same time.

Ilex—The classical Latin name of the holly oak.

Juglans—The classical Latin name of the walnuts, meaning the nut of Jupiter.

Juniperus—The classical Latin name of the junipers.

Kalmia—Named for Peter Kalm (1716–79), Swedish botanist.

Lagerstroemia—Named for Magnus von Lagerstrom (1694–1759) of Gothenburg; friend of Linnaeus.

Larix—The classical Latin name of the European Larch.

Leitneria—Named for E. F. Leitner, German naturalist killed in Florida during the Seminole War.

Liquidambar—From the Latin words meaning liquid and amber, in reference to the fragrant gum.

Liriodendron—From the Greek words meaning lily and tree.

Maclura—Named for William McClure (1763–1840), American geologist.

Magnolia—Named for Pierre Magnol (1638–1715), director of the botanical garden at Montpellier, France.

Malus—The classical Latin name for the common apple.

Melia—A classical Greek name for the ash tree, transferred to this genus by Linnaeus.

Morus—The classical Latin name for the mulberry.

Myrica—The classical Latin name for the tamarisk, or another fragrant shrub; or perhaps from the Greek *myrizein,* to perfume.

Nyssa—From the name of a water nymph.

Osmanthus—From the Greek words meaning odor and flower.

Ostrya—From the Greek meaning a tree with very hard wood.

Oxydendrum—From the Greek words meaning sour and tree.

Paulownia—In honor of Anna Paulownia (1795–1865), daughter of Czar Paul I of Russia and princess of the Netherlands.

Persea—The ancient Greek name for some unidentified Egyptian tree.

Picea—An old Latin name for a pitchy pine.

Pinckneya—Named for Charles Coatesworth Pinckney (1746–1825), South Carolina statesman and Revolutionary War general who was interested in botany.

Pinus—The classical Latin name for pine trees.

Planera—Named for Johann Jacob Planer (1743–89), German botanist and professor of medicine at Erfurt.

Platanus—The classical Greek and Latin names for the Oriental planetree.

Populus—The classical Latin name of the poplars.

Prosopis—From Dioscorides as a name of a burdock.

Prunus—The classical Latin name of the plums.

Ptelea—From the Greek name of the elm.

Pyrus—From the Latin name of the common pear tree.

Quercus—The classical Latin name of the oaks.

Rhamnus—The ancient Greek name for the buckthorns.

Rhododendron—From the Greek words meaning rose and tree.

Rhus—The classical Greek and Latin names for the Sicilian sumac.

Robinia—Named for Jean Robin (1550–1629) and his son Vespasian (1579–1662), herbalists to the kings of France.

Sabal—Derivation unknown but probably of Native American origin.

Salix—The classical Latin name of the willows.

Sassafras—A Spanish name, perhaps of Native American origin.

Sapium—From the Latin name of a resinous pine or fir tree.

Sideroxylon—From the Greek meaning "iron" and "wood," referring to the hard wood of the genus.

Sophora—Latinized from the Arabic name *sufayra*, plants with pea-shaped flowers.

Sorbus—The classical Latin name of the European mountain-ash.

Symplocos—From the Greek meaning connected, referring to the stamens, which are united at the base.

Tamarix—Ancient Latin for a river, or perhaps a word of African or Hebrew origin.

Taxodium—From the Greek meaning like a yew.

Thuja—From the Greek name of a highly aromatic wood prized in ancient times for making furniture.

Tilia—The classical Latin name of the lindens.

Torreya—Named for John Torrey (1796–1873), distinguished North American botanist.

Toxicodendron—From the Greek meaning poison tree.

Triadica—From the Greek meaning "three," referring to calyx, ovary, and fruit.

Tsuga—The Japanese name for a hemlock tree.

Ulmus—The classical Latin name of the elms.

Vaccinium—The classical Latin name of an Old World species, probably the cowberry.

Vernicia—From the Latin "varnish," referring to the oily seeds.

Viburnum—The classical Latin name of the wayfaring-tree.

Zanthoxylum—From the Greek words meaning yellow and wood.

SPECIFIC NAMES

abies—the classical Latin name for the silver fir of Europe.

acuminata—acuminate; with narrowly pointed leaves.

affinis—nearly related.

alabamensis—of Alabama.

alata—winged; from the corky wings on the twigs.

alatamaha—named for the Altamaha River in Georgia.

alba—white.

albidum—whitish.

allegheniensis ⎫
alleghaniensis ⎭ — of the Allegheny Mountains.

alternifolia—with alternate leaves.

altissima—from the Latin meaning very tall.

americana—of America.

angustifolia—with narrow leaves.

aquatica—living or growing in water.

arborea—treelike.

arkansana—of Arkansas.

ashei—named for William Willard Ashe, pioneer forester and dendrologist of the United States Forest Service.

australis ⎫
austrina ⎭ —of the South.

azedarach—from the Persian meaning noble tree.

babylonica—of Babylon, the tree mistakenly thought to have been the willow under which exiled Jews sat down and wept (Psalms 137: 1–2).

balsamea—pertaining to balsam, a fragrant resin.

balsamifera—balsam bearing; with the odor of balsam.

banksiana—dedicated to Joseph Banks (1743–1820), President of the Royal Society of London.

barbatum—bearded.

bebbiana—dedicated to Michael Schuck Bebb (1833–95), American specialist on the willows.

bicolor—two-colored.

biflora—two-flowered.

bignonioides—like Bignonia.

biloba—from the Latin meaning two-lobed.

borbonia—an old generic name for Persea.

breviloba—short-lobed.

calleryana—named for the missionary Joseph Maxine Marie Callery (1810–62).

camphora—for camphor.

canadensis—of Canada.

carolina ⎫
caroliniana ⎭ —of the Carolinas.

cassine—old name for Ilex vomitoria.

cerasus—the classical Latin and the Greek name of the cherry.

cerifera—bearing wax.

chapmannii—dedicated to Alvan Wentworth Chapman (1809–99), author of Flora of the Southern United States.

cinerea—ashy.

clausa—closed, referring to cones remaining closed for some time before releasing their seeds.

clava-herculis—Hercules' club.

communis—from the Latin meaning common.

copallina—exuding a copal-like gum.

cordata—heart-shaped.

cordifolia—with heart-shaped leaves.

cordiformis—heart-shaped.

coronaria—for a crown or wreath.

crassifolia—thick-leaved.

crus-galli—like a cock's spur.

decidua—deciduous; with leaves shed the same year.

decora—showy or ornamental.

deltoides—deltoid or triangular.

dentata—toothed; with toothed margins on the leaves.

discolor—partly colored; with two or more different colors.

distichum—two-ranked; with the leaves in two rows.

drummondii—named for its discoverer, Thomas Drummond (1780–1835).

durandii—dedicated to Elias Magloire Durand (1794–1873), American botanist.

echinata—spiny or prickly.

elliottii—named for its discoverer, Stephen Elliott (1771–1830), banker and botanist and author of *Sketch Book of Botany of South Carolina and Georgia*.

ellipsoidalis—ellipsoidal, referring to the shape of the acorns.

falcata—sickle-shaped.

flabellata—fanlike.

fraseri—dedicated to John Fraser (1750–1811), Scotch nurseryman who explored the southern Appalachian Mountains for plants.

florida—flowering.

floridana—of Florida.

fragalis—fragile, referring to the brittle-based twigs.

georgiana—of Georgia.

geminata—paired or twin.

glabra—smooth; without hairs.

glabrata—becoming smooth.

glandulosa—bearing glands.

glauca—whitened with a powdery bloom.

grandidentata—large-toothed.

grandifolia—large-leaved; with large leaves.

hemisphaerica—half a sphere.

heterophylla—with various leaves or leaves of different size and shape.

hippocastanum—from the Latin words meaning horse and chestnut.

hortulana—referring to horticulture.

ilicifolia—with hollylike leaves.

illinoiensis—of Illinois.

imbricaria—overlapping, probably in reference to the use of the wood as shingles.

incana—hoary.

indica—of Intia.

ioensis—of Iowa.

julibrissin—from the native Persian name of the tree.

kentukea—of Kentucky.

laciniosa—full of flaps or folds, referring to the shaggy bark.

laevigata
laevis }—smooth.

lanuginosa—woolly.

laricina—like a larch.

lasianthus—hairy flowered.

latifolia—with broad leaves.

laurifolia—with laurel-like leaves.

lenta—flexible or tough.

lentago—an old name meaning flexible.

leucoderme—white-skinned, with a white bark.

lyrata—shaped like a lyre.

lucida—lustrous; shining.

lycioides—like *Lycium,* the wolfberry.

macrocarpa—large-fruited.

macrophylla—large-leaved.

mahaleb—from the Arabic name Mahhlab.

mariana
marilandica}—of Maryland.

margaretta—named for Margaret Henry Wilcox, later Mrs. W. W. Ashe.

marshallii—named for Humphry Marshall (1722–1801), American botanist.

maximum—largest.

michauxii—dedicated to François-André Michaux (1770–1855), French botanist who explored the southern Appalachians for plants.

minor—smaller.

monophylla—one-leaved.

monticola
montana}—of the mountains.

muhlenbergii—dedicated to Gotthilf Henry Ernst Muhlenberg (1753–1815), a minister and botanist of Pennsylvania.

munsoniana—dedicated to Thomas Volney Munson (1843–1913), American nurseryman.

myristiciformis—with the shape of the nutmeg, *Myristica.*

myrtifolia—with myrtlelike leaves.

negundo—from an old aboriginal name of a species of *Vitex.*

nigrum
nigra}—black

nutans—nodding.

nuttallii—dedicated to Thomas Nuttall (1786–1859), English-American botanist and ornithologist.

obovatum
obovatus}—obovate; with leaves inversely ovate.

occidentalis—referring to the western hemisphere.

octandra—with eight stamens.

odorata—fragrant.

ogeche—of the Ogeechee River, Georgia.

oglethorpensis—of Oglethorpe County, Georgia.

ovata—egg-shaped.

pagodifolia—with leaves like a pagoda.

pallida—pale.

palmetto—from the Spanish, palmito, meaning a small palm.

palustris—of swamps or wet places.

papyifera—paper bearing; with a papery bark.

parviflora—small-flowered.

pauciflora—few-flowered.

pavia—old generic name of the buckeye honoring Peter Paaw (died 1617) of Leyden.

pendula—long, drooping; referring to branches.

pensylvanicum
pennsylvanica}—of Pennsylvania.
pensylvanica

persica—from *Malum persicum* (apple-of-Persia), the Greek and Roman name for peach.

phellos—the ancient Greek name of the cork oak.

platanoides—from the Latin meaning like Platanu, the sycamore.

pomifera—bearing pomes, or apples.

populifolia—poplar-leaved.

prinoides—with leaves resembling those of the chestnut oak, *Quercus prinus.*

prinus—the classical Greek name of a Europe oak.

profunda—deep; referring to deep swamps.

prunifolium—with leaves resembling those of the plum tree.

pruniosa—frosty in appearance; with a bloom.

pseudoacacia—old generic name meaning false acacia.

pseudoplatanus—from the Latin meaning false and sycamore.

pubens ⎫ downy; with short and
pubescens ⎭ soft hairs.

pumila—dwarf; small.

punctata—dotted.

pungens—sharp-pointed.

pyramidata—pyramidal; shaped like a pyramid.

quadrangulata—four-angled.

racemiflora—with flowers in racemes.

resinosa—resinous.

rigida—stiff.

rubens—reddish.

rubra ⎫ —red.
rubrum ⎭

rufidulum—reddish or rusty.

saccharinum ⎫ sweet or sugary,
saccharum ⎭ referring to the sap.

sebiferum—from the Latin meaning bearing wax or tallow.

septentrionalis—northern.

serotina—late.

shumardii—dedicated to Benjamin Franklin Shumard (1820–69), State Geologist of Texas.

silicicola—growing in sand.

simplex—simple, not compound.

sinuata—wavy.

speciosa—showy.

spicatum—with flowers and fruits in spikes; spikelike.

stellata—star-shaped; with star-shaped hairs.

stricta—upright or stiff.

strobus—Latin word for pine cone.

styraciflua—old name for the genus *Liquidambar*, meaning styrax flowing.

subcordata—slightly heart-shaped.

subintegerrima—almost entire.

sylvatica—of the woods.

sylvestris—from the Latin, meaning of the forest.

taeda—ancient name of resinous pines.

taxifolia—of yew leaf.

tenax—tough.

tenuifolia—thin-leaved.

texana—of Texas.

thomasii—named for David Thomas (1776–1859), American civil engineer and horticulturist.

tinctoria—pertaining to dyes.

tomentosa—covered with matted or woolly hairs.

tremuloides—like *Populusus tremula*, the European aspen, from the Latin trembling.

triacanthos—three-horned.

tridens—in threes; with 3 lobes.

tripetala—with three petals.

tulipifera—old generic name meaning tulip bearing.

typhina—resembling the cattail, *Typha*, from the velvety twigs.

uber—fruitful.

umbellata—with flowers or fruits in umbels.

velutina—velvety.

vernix—varnish.

virginica ⎫ —of Virginia.
virginiana ⎭

vomitoria—causing vomiting.

MAIDENHAIR-TREE FAMILY—
GINKGOACEAE

The Maidenhair-Tree—Ginkgo

MAIDENHAIR-TREE   *Ginkgo biloba* **L.**

> The combination of small, deciduous, fan-shaped, and occasionally 2-lobed leaves on spur shoots is peculiar; thus, this species ought not be mistaken for any other tree.

Summer. *Leaves* 1 to 2 inches long, 1 to 3 inches wide, alternate, simple, deciduous, fan-shaped, occasionally 2-lobed; leathery, glabrous, and green on both sides, scalloped along the margins; with innumerable fine veins radiating out into the fanlike blades from the summits; produced in small clusters, turning yellow in the autumn; stubby lateral spurlike shoots, which are scattered spirally on the more vigorous shoots; petioles about as long as the leaf blades, slender. *Cones* catkinlike, ⅛ to ¼ inch long, short-stalked, male and female cones produced on separate trees in early spring, cone scales absent.

Winter. *Twigs* stout, glabrous, yellowish to grayish-brown; at first smooth, but the outer thin layer of bark soon exfoliates in threadlike strands; lateral spurlike shoots stubby; leaf scars thickly clustered, semi-ovate, with two bundle scars. *Buds* short, rounded, divergent from twig, chestnut brown. *Bark* on the older trunks, becoming thick, ashy gray, shallowly fissured with rather narrow and irregular longitudinal ridges.

———

The maidenhair-tree is often called so because its leaves closely resemble those of the maidenhair fern. It is sometimes referred to as a living fossil, for it is the sole survivor of a group of trees that once flour-

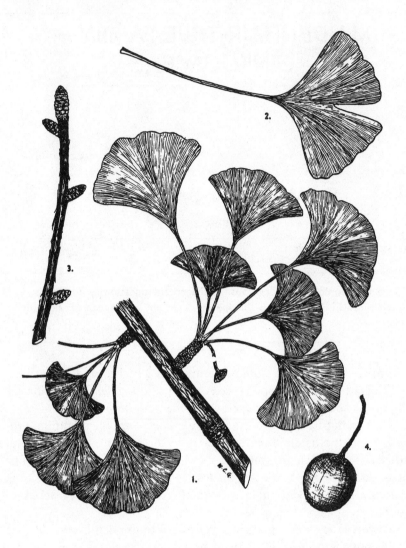

MAIDENHAIR-TREE

1. Branch with leaves.
2. Typical leaf.
3. Winter twig.
4. Fruit.

ished over a large part of the earth and have left the fossilized imprints of their leaves in the rocks of many lands. It remains questionable whether the maidenhair-tree has ever been found growing in a wild state, but it is believed to have originated in northern China. For untold centuries it has been grown in the temple gardens of China and Japan. It is believed to have been first planted in North America in 1754 by William Hamilton near Philadelphia.

The maidenhair-tree may attain a height of 50 to 80 feet and live for a thousand years. When young it has a slender pyramidal form with upright branches, but in age the branches spread, and it assumes a broader and more open crown. It has been widely planted in this country as a street and ornamental tree because its leaves turn bright yellow in the fall. It thrives on most moist and fairly fertile soils, is very tolerant of dust and city smoke, and is not usually damaged by storms, fungi, or insects. The staminate and pistillate flowers occur in the spring on separate trees and may take up to 45 years or more to develop. The reproductive structures are not often seen in this country because only the staminate trees are usually planted. These structures are plumlike in appearance with a thin flesh that has a rank smell resembling that of rancid butter; the pits are large, smooth, and silvery white. They are much esteemed by Oriental peoples, and the roasted pits are considered to be a delicacy. The name ginkgo comes from a Chinese word meaning "silver fruit" or "white nuts."

PINE FAMILY—PINACEAE

The Balsam Firs—Abies

The balsam firs have linear and flattened needles, which are stalkless and leave circular scars on the branchlets when they are shed after a period of several years. The needles are arranged spirally but occasionally appear to be 2-ranked (1-plane). The cones, which appear in the spring, are not often observed. Both staminate and pistillate cones occur on the same tree. The erect cones mature the first year, but instead of dropping from the tree intact like most other gymnosperms, the scales and attendant bracts drop, leaving the persistent spikelike axis. The cone scales are thin, rounded at the tip, and sometimes exceeded in length by the pointed tips of the bracts. Each scale usually bears a pair of small winged seeds.

Two species of balsam fir are native to eastern North America. In addition there is an intermediate form, *Abies x phanerolepis* (Fern.) Liu, which occurs throughout a considerable portion of the range of *Abies balsamea*. The balsam firs are valuable commercially for their wood, which goes into lumber and paper pulp; for the pitch, which is produced in the resin blisters on their trunks; and as Christmas trees. Some introduced species are highly prized as ornamental trees.

BALSAM FIR   *Abies balsamea* (L.) P. Mill.

> The resin blisters on the bark of our two native eastern firs and flat needles that fracture smoothly from the twig surface when shed and the erect cones are distinctive of the genus.

Leaves about ¾ inch long, narrowly linear, flattened, stalkless, fracturing smoothly from the twig, bases slightly narrowed, tips blunt or

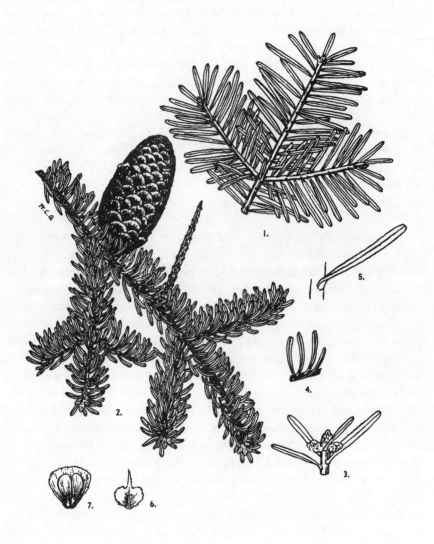

BALSAM FIR

1. Leafy branch from young tree.
2. Branch with cone and axis of cone from which scales have been shed.
3. Tip of branch with winter buds.
4. Portion of branch and leaves.
5. Single leaf.
6. Bract from cone.
7. Cone scale with seeds.

notched, dark green above, with two prominent whitish lines on their lower surfaces; on vigorous, young trees appearing 2-ranked and spreading horizontally; on the older trees tending to curve upward and more or less covering the upper sides of the twigs. *Cones* erect, 2 to 3 inches long, about 1 inch in diameter, cylindrical; cone scales dropping during the early fall through winter, leaving the characteristic erect central stalk (unique among native conifers). *Bark* grayish brown, smooth, covered to varying degrees with raised blisters containing a sticky, fragrant, liquid resin.

Comparison. This particular species is easily told from the Fraser fir by its northern distribution and by its cone bracts, which do not extend beyond the cone scales. Only in Virginia do the two species occur together naturally.

———

The balsam fir is a common and characteristic tree of the north country, but southward it occurs only along mountaintops or in cold swamps and bogs. The wood is light and soft, neither strong nor durable. It is occasionally utilized for lumber, but its principal uses are for making boxes and crates and as pulpwood. Although it is a hardy tree and handsome in its youth in its native habitats, it is not very desirable as an ornamental tree because it is short-lived and frequently loses all of its lower branches. It is also quite difficult to grow outside of its natural habitat. As a Christmas tree the balsam fir is most excellent, for it retains its fragrant and beautiful foliage quite well for some time after the tree is cut. The Canada balsam of commerce is derived from the blisters on the bark of the tree, the product coming principally from the fir forests of Canada. Canada balsam is used medicinally, as a glass cement in the preparation of optical instruments, and also in the making of microscope slides. The foliage is often used in the manufacture of balsam, or so-called "pine" pillows.

Several species of birds, including the ruffed grouse, are known to eat the seeds of the balsam fir. White-tailed deer frequently browse on the branchlets during the winter season, and the bark and branchlets are eaten to some extent by the varying hare. Swamps where balsam thickets occur are favorite winter yarding grounds of deer.

The balsam fir ranges from Labrador to Alberta; south to Pennsylvania, northern Minnesota, and northeastern Iowa; and southward along the Appalachian Mountains to Virginia.

FRASER FIR   *Abies fraseri* **(Pursh) Poir.**

This, the smaller southern counterpart of the northern balsam fir, is found at high elevations in the Appalachians from southeastern Virginia to western North Carolina, Tennessee, and northern Georgia. At one time it formed practically pure stands on the summit of Mt. Mitchell, as well as on several of the higher peaks in the Great Smoky Mountains National Park. However, like the red spruce, this species has suffered extensively from the effects of acid rain. The tree was named for its discoverer, the Scotch botanist John Fraser, who explored the southern Appalachians for plants during the latter part of the eighteenth century. It is also known as the southern balsam, or southern balsam fir, and it is the "she-balsam" of the southern mountaineer, so called because of the resin-filled blisters that are always present on the tree's trunk. To the mountaineer, the red spruce, which often associates with the fir but lacks blisters on its trunk, is the "he-balsam." The only obvious difference between the Fraser fir and the balsam fir lies in the cones of the two trees. Those of Fraser fir always have bracts projecting well beyond the cone scales and bending downward at their tips. The cones are also somewhat smaller, usually from 2 to 2½ inches long, and the whitish bands on the leaf undersurface are somewhat wider than those of the balsam fir.

The Hemlocks—Tsuga

The hemlocks are evergreen trees with a more or less pyramidal habit and with slender horizontal or drooping branches. Individuals can be told even at a distance by their very characteristic terminal branch (leader), which always droops. The linear and flattened leaves are apically notched, blunt, and attached to the branchlets by tiny woody stalks, which persist after the leaves fall, leaving the twigs with a rough texture. The leaves are arranged spirally on the branchlets but often appear to be 2-ranked (1-plane or featherlike) and remain for three years or more before being shed. The cones are small and often overlooked, with both staminate and pistillate types occurring on the same tree during the spring season. Hemlock cones mature in one season but they often remain over winter. They are very small, pendent, and have thin scales that bear a pair of small winged seeds.

The hemlocks are valuable commercially as a source of lumber and tannin-rich bark, which is used for tanning leather. Hemlocks are much used in ornamental planting. There is a fallacious notion that hemlock trees are poisonous. On the contrary, Native Americans and backwoodsmen often brewed a medicinal tea from the leafy branchlets. The poison hemlock from which the ancients brewed their well-known lethal tea is an entirely different plant, a member of the parsley family or *Apiaceae*.

EASTERN HEMLOCK   *Tsuga canadensis* (L.) Carr.

Eastern hemlock may be distinguished from other eastern native conifers by its slender twigs, tiny stalked, 2-ranked, flat, linear, dark green leaves, which have two longitudinal, narrow, whitish lines on their lower surfaces, and by the drooping terminal leader.

Leaves ½ inch long, flat, linear, dark green, margins minutely toothed, rounded or slightly notched apically, with two narrow, longitudinal whitish lines on their lower surfaces, each attached to a little woody stalk that persists on the twig after the leaf falls; appearing 2-ranked, but close examination reflects a row of smaller leaves along upper side of the twigs. *Cones* ½ to ¾ inch long, pendent, mature at the end of the first season, commonly persist on the twigs throughout the winter; scales thin, pale brown, about as long as wide. *Bark* varies from reddish brown to grayish brown, with long fissures separating rather broad-topped scaly ridges; inner bark cinnamon brown.

———

The eastern hemlock is the state tree of Pennsylvania. At maturity it is a large tree, often attaining a height of over 80 feet and a trunk diameter up to 3 feet. In the virgin forests, it commonly attained a height of over 100 feet and a trunk diameter of 4 feet. When growing in the open, the tree has a dense conical crown and the lateral branches may extend nearly to the ground; but when growing in dense stands, the trunks may be clear of branches for a height of 80 feet or more. The eastern hemlock thrives in cool, moist situations. It is frequently found along streams and the borders of swamps and bogs, or on steep northward-facing slopes. It is rather tolerant of shade but comparatively slow growing. Many of the larger trees found in the primeval forests of the land were more than four centuries old. In its natural habitat the eastern hemlock is commonly associated with the eastern white pine and various northern hardwoods, but occasionally it forms practically pure stands.

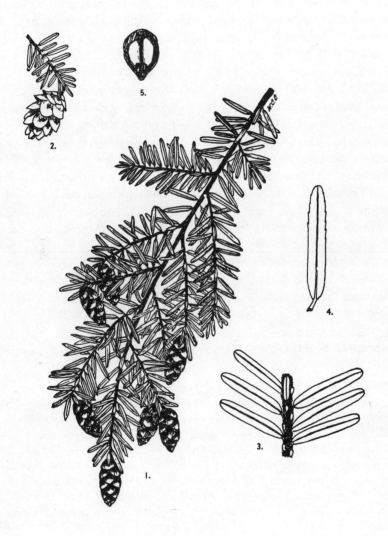

EASTERN HEMLOCK

1. Branch with closed cones.
2. Branch with open cone.
3. Portion of branch and leaves.
4. Leaf.
5. Cone scale with seeds.

In former years gigantic eastern hemlocks were often felled, stripped of their bark, and the huge trunks left to slowly decay in the forest. The eastern hemlock's bark, rich in tannic acid, was in great demand for tanning hides, but its wood for most purposes was quite inferior to that of the eastern white pine. The wood is hard, extremely brittle, and it is not durable; it's often referred to as "brash," because of its "ring shake" (separation between annual rings) and "star shake" (separation along radial lines). It is used today for rough lumber, building construction, boxes and crates, and as pulpwood. The eastern hemlock makes a very desirable shade or ornamental tree. It lends itself well to pruning, and it is sometimes used as a hedge plant. Thickets of young eastern hemlocks provide excellent winter cover for forest wildlife. Although deer often browse extensively on the foliage, it apparently has little or no actual nutritive value. The snowshoe hare or varying hare also feeds on eastern hemlock to some extent during the winter season. Red squirrels often cut the unripened cones to obtain the seeds, which are also eaten by bird species such as pine siskins, crossbills, and ruffed grouse.

The eastern hemlock ranges from Nova Scotia to eastern Minnesota, south to Maryland and Illinois, and southward along the Appalachian Mountains to Georgia and northern Alabama.

CAROLINA HEMLOCK   *Tsuga caroliniana* Engelm.

The Carolina hemlock is readily distinguished from the eastern hemlock by its more restricted distribution, smaller size, more bristly appearance of its branchlets, and its larger cones, which are twice the size of the eastern hemlock. Although the dark green leaves are similar to those of the eastern hemlock, they are somewhat longer, up to ¾ inch in length, with entire rather than minutely toothed margins, slightly notched apically and with two broad (rather than narrow) whitish lines below. Furthermore, the leaves are not 2-ranked as they are in the eastern hemlock, but rather stand out in all directions from the branchlets on more than 1 plane (more tail-like than featherlike) producing the bristly appearance. The pale brown cones range from 1 to 1½ inches in length and have longer and more oval-shaped scales than do the cones of the eastern hemlock.

The Carolina hemlock is considered by some to be the most beautiful of the North American conifers in cultivation. However, it is not a very common tree. It occurs here and there on dry slopes and rocky ridges of the southern Appalachians from southwestern Virginia to northern Geor-

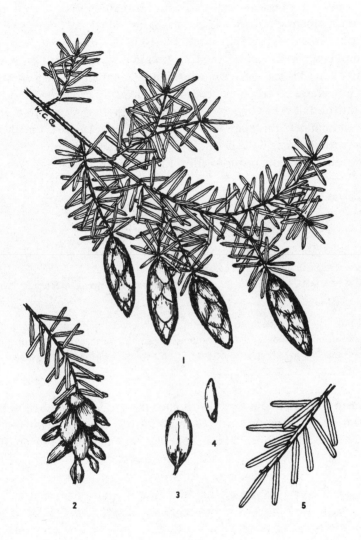

CAROLINA HEMLOCK

1. Branch with closed cones.   4. Seed.
2. Branch with open cone.   5. Leaves.
3. Detail of cone scale.

gia, usually at elevations between 2,000 and 4,000 feet. In some places, as on the walls of rocky gorges, it sometimes keeps company with the eastern hemlock. The tree was first discovered in 1837 by Dr. L. R. Gibbes, who found it growing on Table Rock Mountain in Pickens County, South Carolina, but it wasn't officially named until 1881. Although it produces no wood of commercial value, the Carolina hemlock has found its way into cultivation. It is typically a much smaller tree than the eastern hemlock but its pyramidal crown of spreading or slightly drooping branches is so beautiful that it has become a prized ornamental. Compared with the eastern hemlock, this species is far more difficult to grow in cultivation. Many individuals will succumb to heat, dryness, and other factors, which ordinarily do not appear to affect the eastern hemlock.

The Larches—Larix

AMERICAN LARCH   *Larix laricina* (Du Roi) K. Koch

One of our few native deciduous conifers, and the only one with clusters of very slender, numerous needles, produced on small spurs, as well as upright cones and scaly bark. This species ought not be confused with any other tree.

Summer. *Leaves* about ¾ to 1¼ inches long, deciduous, bright but pale green, very narrowly linear, 3-angled, soft, flexible, arranged in clusters of 10 to 30 on short, lateral, spurlike branches, not in rosettelike clusters but densely crowded on vigorous shoots or terminal branchlets, turning yellow in late September or early October.

Winter. *Leaves* all shed in the fall (unique among eastern native conifers except the bald- and pond-cypress species). *Cones* ½ to ¾ inch long, oblong ovoid, on short stalks, standing more or less erect on the twigs, maturing the first autumn, persisting on the branchlets throughout the winter, male and female cones produced on separate trees; scales about 10 to 20, thin, glabrous, light brown, rounded, with entire or slightly erose margins. *Twigs* slender, glabrous, pale orange brown, with numerous short, lateral, spurlike branches. *Bark* becoming roughened with small, thin, roundish, reddish brown scales.

———

AMERICAN LARCH

1. Branch with leaves and cones
   (summer).
2. Winter twig with cones.
3. Seed (enlarged).

The American larch is also known as the tamarack and as hackmatack. It is a tree of northern distribution, occurring northward as far as the limit of tree growth; at timberline, it develops a more shrubby appearance. In the southern portion of its range it is almost entirely confined to cold swamps and sphagnum bogs. While it sometimes attains a height of 60 feet or more, and a trunk diameter up to 2 feet, it very rarely attains such dimensions in the southern extremity of its range. The tree grows rather rapidly in its youth in the more favorable situations. It is very intolerant of shade and likely to be suppressed in competition with other trees.

The wood of the American larch is very heavy, hard, strong, and durable in contact with the soil. Its chief uses are for telephone poles, fence posts, railroad ties, and in shipbuilding. To a lesser extent it is used for interior finish and in cabinetmaking. The tree is seldom used for ornamental planting although it is quite attractive and adapted to grow in soils that are ordinarily too wet for most other trees. The American larch is not extensively utilized by wildlife. The white-tailed deer seems to only casually browse on it, and it is occasionally eaten by the porcupine and the snowshoe hare. The seeds are eaten by a few species of birds and by the red squirrel.

The American larch ranges from Labrador to Alaska, south to Minnesota and the region of the Great Lakes, to northern Pennsylvania, western Maryland and Preston County, West Virginia.

The European larch (*Larix decidua* P. Mill.), a tree adapted to much drier habitats, has larger needles, 1 to 1¼ inches long; more drooping branches; larger cones, ¾ to 1⅜ inches long, with hairy and more numerous (30 to 50) scales; a more red-brown plated bark pattern; and stouter, yellower twigs. It is occasionally planted in parks and other urban areas.

The Spruces—Picea

The spruces are evergreen trees of pyramidal habit. The leaves are arranged singly on the branchlets, each one being attached to a short, woody stalk that persists on the twig after the leaf falls. These little decurrent projections from the outer covering of the twig are known as sterigmata.

The ovoid or cylindrical cones of the spruces are pendent. They mature during the first season and either fall during the first winter or persist on the branches for one or more years. The cone scales are rather thin, and like those of other conifers, they bear a pair of winged seeds on their upper surfaces.

Three species of spruces are native to eastern North America: the red spruce *(P. rubens)*, white spruce *(P. glauca)*, and the black spruce *(P. mariana)*.

NORWAY SPRUCE   *Picea abies* (L.) Karst.

> The angled needles, pendent, glabrous branches, and long, relatively narrow, pendent, cigarlike cones are most distinctive.

Leaves about ¾ inch to nearly 1 to 2 inches long (somewhat larger than those of our native red spruce and black spruce), dark green, lustrous, 4-angled, with whitish lines, sharp-pointed, needlelike. *Cones* 4 to 8 inches long, cylindrical, straight; maturing during the first autumn, usually persisting on the trees throughout the first winter; cone scales thin, pointed, erose on the margins. *Twigs,* glabrous, on the older trees numerous pendent branchlets occurring on the lateral limbs. *Bark* on older trunks becoming roughened with rather thick, flaky, reddish brown scales.

Comparisons. The Norway spruce may be readily distinguished from our eastern native spruces by its very large cylindrical, cigarlike cones and glabrous, or nearly glabrous, orangish twigs that droop characteristically. Only the white spruce has equally glabrous twigs, but that species has much smaller cones and lacks the drooping branches.

Norway spruce is a native of central and northern Europe, where it is one of the most important timber trees and most common species of the genus. It was introduced into this country rather early as an ornamental tree, and in this respect it has found widespread favor. Large numbers of Norway spruce seedlings are now being used for reforestation purposes. It has also been planted for windbreaks, and in more recent years it has been cultivated extensively for Christmas tree purposes. Its large cones are also used frequently in Christmas decorations.

The Norway spruce grows well on a wide variety of soils and adapts itself to various climatic conditions. It grows rapidly and is very attrac-

NORWAY SPRUCE

1. Branch with closed cone.
2. Branch with open cone.
3. Seed.

tive, particularly in its youth, forming a broadly conical and dense crown with branches persisting nearly to the ground. Large specimens are often seen near old farmsteads and cemeteries.

RED SPRUCE   *Picea rubens* **Sarg.**

Fairly easily told by its 4-angled, sharp-pointed needles, pendent cones, hairy twigs, and smooth rather than ragged cone-scale margins.

Leaves ⅜ to ⅝ inch long, needlelike, lustrous with a lacquerlike finish, dark yellowish green, typically sharp-pointed and curved. *Cones* 1 to 2 inches long, oblong-ovate to cylindrical, dropping during their first winter as a rule; cone scales reddish brown, margin entire or nearly so. *Bark* becomes broken into irregular, thin, flaky, reddish brown scales; where newly exposed, light yellow to reddish brown (also see black spruce); often covered with grayish green lichens.

Comparisons. Red spruce, which is an upland tree, with a conical crown, is most frequently confused with the more lowland cylindrical-crowned black spruce, which it closely resembles. The former differs from the latter by having smooth rather than ragged cone-scale margins, and by having larger, nearly sessile, reddish brown to chocolate brown rather than gray- to purple-brown cones, which persist on the tree until autumn, or which may remain for one additional year, whereas the cones of black spruce have short scaly stalks and may persist on the tree for 20 to 30 years. Additionally, the longer lower branches of red spruce differ somewhat from the shorter lower branches of black spruce by appearing more horizontally layered (black spruce branches are more drooping) and then upturned toward their shiny, yellow-orange branch tips, while those of black spruce tend to droop more significantly immediately from the bole to the dull yellow-brown branch tip and then upturn gradually. The leaves also differ by being significantly curved and yellowish green in red spruce and straight or slightly curved and dull grayish green in black spruce. Moreover, the white lines on the needles of red spruce are light, while those in black spruce are more pronounced and the buds of red spruce differ from those of black spruce by being pointed, shiny, and reddish brown while those of black spruce are blunt, dull gray brown. The combination of characters should help to separate even the more difficult individuals.

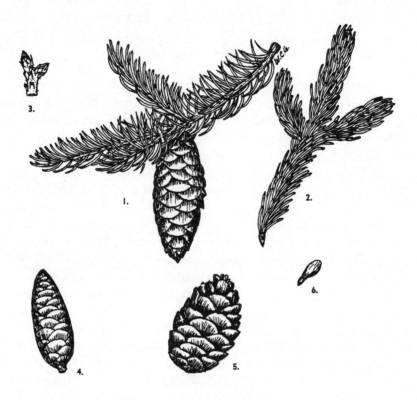

RED SPRUCE

1. Branch with closed cone.
2. Branch.
3. Buds.

4. Closed cone.
5. Open cone.
6. Seed.

The red spruce, our only spruce native to the Southeast, may attain a height of 40 to 80 feet, with a trunk diameter of 1 to 2 feet. It is typically a Canadian Zone tree, common in the maritime provinces of eastern Canada, but like the balsam fir, occurring southward only at higher elevations into the Appalachian Mountains. It prefers cold and moist situations with well-drained soils, but it frequently occurs along streams and about the borders of swamps and bogs. It is often common in very rocky areas. This spruce frequently occurs in mixed stands of northern hardwoods, eastern hemlock, and eastern white pine, although locally it may be found in practically pure stands. It grows slowly, and it may take two centuries to reach maturity. Although some fine stands of virgin red spruce may still be seen in the Great Smoky Mountains National Park and along the Blue Ridge Parkway north of Asheville, North Carolina, vast populations of this species have been destroyed due to the effects of acid rain. The southern mountaineer knew the red spruce as "he-balsam."

The red spruce is a very important source of wood for paper pulp. Its wood is light and soft, and most ideal for this purpose. It is used as construction lumber, in the making of boxes and crates, and for sounding boards of musical instruments. The smaller trees are commonly used for Christmas trees. The tender young growth, in the spring of the year, is sometimes used in making a beverage known as spruce beer. The seeds are eaten by such birds as the pine siskin and the crossbill, and by the red squirrel, which often cuts the unripened cones to procure the seeds within them. The trees, particularly when growing in close formation, provide excellent winter cover for wildlife, but a dearth of food results when the areas are too extensive. It is a handsome tree, particularly when growing in the open, where it develops a dense, pyramidal crown. However, it is seldom used for ornamental purposes because it demands a cool, moist climate and seldom succeeds out of its natural habitat.

The red spruce ranges from Nova Scotia to the valley of the St. Lawrence River, southward to northeastern Pennsylvania, and in the Appalachian Mountains from eastern West Virginia and western Maryland to northern Georgia.

BLACK SPRUCE   *Picea mariana* (P. Mill.) B. S. P.

It is often very difficult, if not impossible, to distinguish some specimens of black spruce and red spruce with any degree of certainty. Indeed, since they often hybridize, some authorities consider these plants to be merely variations of a single species. However, many trees clearly reflect the characteristics as defined here and in the preceding key.

Leaves usually ¼ to ⅜ inch long, needlelike, typically blunt-pointed, bluish green, more or less glaucous, particularly when young. *Cones* ½ to 1½ inch long, short ovoid to egg-shaped or occasionally nearly globular, characteristically persistent on the branches for several years; cone scales grayish brown, somewhat erose or with slightly toothed margins. *Bark* grayish brown, with thin and more or less appressed scales, olive green to yellowish green where newly exposed.

The black spruce, the second most widely distributed conifer tree in North America, is primarily a northern tree, extending north to the very limit of tree growth. In the far North it occurs on barren and stony slopes, but it makes its best growth on well-drained bottomlands. To the south it occurs almost exclusively in the swamps and bogs, where it is slow growing and barely attains a height of 20 to 30 feet and a trunk diameter of 6 to 10 inches. Along with the American larch *(Larix laricina)*, it often invades the bog mats surrounding lakes, or the cold sphagnum bogs, but it is often stunted and seldom attains a height of more than 10 to 15 feet. It is therefore often referred to as the swamp spruce or bog spruce.

Throughout most of its range the black spruce is of comparatively little commercial importance due to its small size. It often appears to be stunted and tightly cylindrical in shape with a deformed tip, largely due to terminal bud damage often caused by red squirrels. In the north it is utilized for paper pulp. Trees of this species are also often cut as Christmas trees. Like the red spruce, the twigs and leaves of the black spruce are sometimes used for making spruce beer. "Spruce gum," the resinous exudation of both the red spruce and the black spruce, is gathered in the North and used as a chewing gum.

The black spruce ranges from Labrador across the continent to the interior of Alaska, south to Saskatchewan, Manitoba, Minnesota, Michigan, and Pennsylvania, and along the Appalachian Mountains to Virginia.

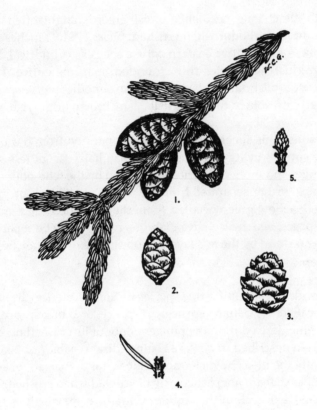

BLACK SPRUCE

1. Branch with closed cones.
2. Closed cone.
3. Open cone.
4. Leaf
5. Terminal bud.

WHITE SPRUCE   *Picea glauca* (Moench) Voss

> The completely glabrous twigs and elongated, pendent, cylindrical cones (1 ½ to 2 inches long), along with the fetid odor of the straight rather than curved needles are most distinct.

Leaves ½ to ¾ inch long, needlelike, bluish green, straight, often glaucous, with an unpleasant odor when crushed. *Cones* 1½ to 2 inches long (the largest cones of any native eastern spruce species), cylindrical, light reddish brown, lustrous; scales thin, rounded, margins entire. *Twigs* orange brown to purplish, shiny, glabrous (unlike our other native spruces, thus readily recognizable in the field). *Bark* ashy brown or grayish, thin, scaly.

Comparisons. This species can be easily separated from our other eastern native spruces by its glabrous rather than hairy twigs, less scaly bark, much longer and more cylindrical cones, and by the fetid odor of its needles. It can be further separated from the red spruce by its blue-green rather than dark yellow-green needles. From the introduced blue spruce and Norway spruce, which also have glabrous twigs, it can be separated by its shorter cones and by the less layered appearance of its branches.

———

The most widespread conifer tree species in North America, the white spruce is also called the Canada spruce, cat spruce, or skunk spruce, the latter names being derived from the pungent odor of its crushed needles. This odor is often described in books as being "disagreeable" or "skunk-like." Apparently the ill-scented characteristic is not universal, for some trees have needles that are not particularly ill-scented when crushed. This northern species is prevalent throughout Canada as far north as trees extend, where it becomes more stunted and shrubby, barely entering the United States along the northern border. It is a hardy species, sometimes planted as an ornamental tree, or for reforestation purposes, in the northern United States. In Canada it is the most important timber spruce and a leading source of pulpwood. The very narrow, pliable roots have been used by various North American Indian tribes for lacing their birch-bark canoes and in making various implements.

The range of the white spruce extends from Newfoundland and Labrador west to northwestern Alaska; south and east through the interior of Alaska to southern British Columbia, southern Manitoba, parts of

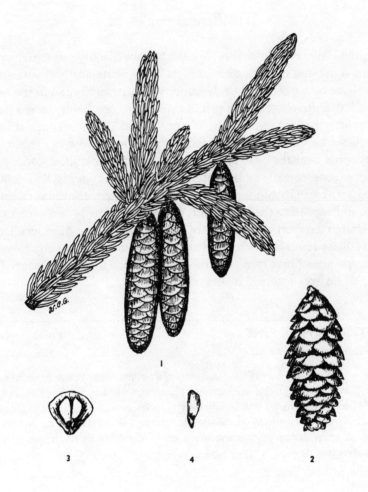

WHITE SPRUCE

1. Branch with leaves and closed cones.
2. Open cone.
3. Cone scale.
4. Seed.

Montana and Wyoming, the Black Hills of South Dakota, central portions of Minnesota and Michigan, northern New York, northwestern Massachusetts, and Maine.

The Pines—Pinus

The pines have needle-shaped leaves that are usually (all eastern ones) arranged in bundlelike clusters of from 2 to 5. Each cluster is surrounded at the base by a persistent or deciduous sheath, and borne in the axil of a small, deciduous, scalelike primary leaf. The needlelike leaves persist on the branches for two, three, or more years. The cones appear on the branches when growth is resumed in the spring. Clusters of staminate cones occur near the base of the new growth, the pistillate cones being scattered singly or in small clusters along the new shoots. Pollen is produced so abundantly that showers of sulphur cover automobiles and roads and as well as the soil within pine stands. The pollen is carried by the wind to the receptive stigmas of the pistillate cones. After fertilization the pistillate cones develop into woody-scaled cones. It usually takes two years, and sometimes three, for the cones to reach maturity. The seeds are winged and are dispersed by the wind.

EASTERN WHITE PINE   *Pinus strobus* L.

The white pine may be readily distinguished from the other native pines of eastern North America by its very slender, blue-green needles, arranged in clusters of 5, which at maturity lack basal sheaths; by its bark, which is not scaly as in many eastern pines; and by its slender, elongated (4–8 inches), and curved cones. Even at great distances, this species is easily identified by its unique layered branches that develop at right angles to the bole.

Needles 2½ to 5 inches long, very narrow, 5 per cluster, soft, flexible, bluish green; basal sheath lacking at maturity. *Cones* 4 to 8 inches long, narrowly cylindrical, usually slightly curved, maturing at the end of the second season, drooping, long-stalked, frequently exuding fragrant, gummy resin; cone scales rather thin, lacking prickles. *Bark* not scaly as in many other eastern pines, smooth, on the young trunks and branches

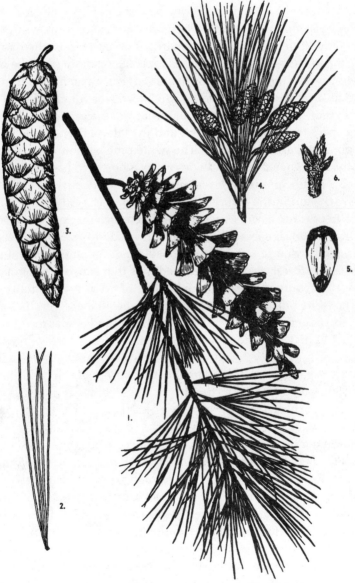

Wm. C. Grimm.

EASTERN WHITE PINE

1. Branch with leaves and open cone.
2. Cluster of leaves.
3. Closed cone.

4. Tip of branch with first year cones.
5. Cone scale with seeds.
6. Buds.

greenish brown, dark gray, shallowly fissured; on old trunks with broad and flat-topped longitudinal ridges.

———

King of the eastern pines, the white pine is not only one of our most magnificent forest trees, it is also the largest conifer in the Northeast. At maturity it commonly attains a height of 80 feet or more, with a trunk diameter of 2 to 3 feet. When growing in dense stands, the trunks are straight and clear of lateral branches for some distance from the ground. In the primeval forests of Pennsylvania, it was by no means unusual to find trees with trunk diameters of 4 to 5 feet, which were clear of lateral branches for a distance of nearly 100 feet from the ground. When grown in the open, the trunk often forks, and the lateral branches may persist well down toward the ground. The white pine is commonly associated with the eastern hemlock and with various northern hardwoods. Examples of this type of virgin forest may be seen today in the Cook Forest State Park, and in the Heart's Content tract in the Allegheny National Forest, in northwestern Pennsylvania. When such virgin forests were cut, the white pine was succeeded by the more shade-tolerant hardwoods and the eastern hemlock. It is highly probable that the stands of white pines in the virgin forest resulted from seedlings that started in old clearings, very likely in burned-over areas or in areas of extensive windfalls.

The white pine is one of our most valuable timber trees. Its soft, light wood warps and checks less than most timbers and is adapted to a variety of uses. It is in demand for general construction work, interior finish, cabinetmaking, and pattern making. As a shade or ornamental tree it has few peers among the pines. It is adaptable to a variety of soil conditions, and it makes rapid growth. Unfortunately it is susceptible to a fungus disease, the white pine blister rust (Cronartium ribicola), which has an alternate host in various wild currants and gooseberries (Ribes). The Indians are said to have used the inner bark of the white pine for food, and it has been used as an ingredient in cough remedies. Cottontail rabbits and snowshoe hares occasionally eat the bark of young trees, and porcupines may cause extensive damage by eating the bark. The cones are eagerly sought by red squirrels, which extract and eat the seeds. The seeds are eaten by such birds as the crossbills and the pine siskin. It is occasionally browsed by the white-tailed deer.

The range of the eastern white pine extends from Newfoundland to Manitoba, south through the northern United States to Pennsylvania, northern Ohio, and southeastern Iowa, and southward along the Appalachian Mountains to northern Georgia.

RED PINE   *Pinus resinosa* **Ait.**

> The needles of the red pine are unique among the eastern 2-needled pines in the peculiar manner by which they fracture completely when bent in two. This single character should separate the red pine from all other 2-needled species.

Needles 4 to 6 inches long, lustrous, slender, straight, soft, brittle, dark green, arranged in bundles of 2; sheaths persistent, elongated. *Cones* about 2 inches long, prickleless, nearly sessile, ovoid when closed, nearly spherical when open, standing at right angles to the branches, maturing at the end of the second season, usually not persisting on the branches beyond the following winter. *Twigs* reddish brown, roughened by the persistent leaf bases. *Bark* reddish brown, becoming roughened by shallow fissures, separating into broad, flat-topped, and scaly ridges on older trunks.

Comparisons. The red pine can hardly be confused with any of the other native pines, but it may be confused with the introduced Austrian pine. The latter, however, has somewhat stouter, less shiny, more sharply pointed and more pliable needles (which do not fracture completely when bent in two), with comparatively short basal sheaths. It also has short prickles on the cone scales and grayish to blackish bark. Moreover, the winter twigs of red pine are bright red, whereas those of Austrian pine are yellowish brown.

———

The red pine, so named because of the reddish appearance of its bark, is often referred to as the Norway pine. It is a native of North America, however, and not of Norway. The latter name is believed to have been given to the tree by some early explorer who confused it with a European species. The red pine is a large tree, often becoming 50 to 75 feet or more in height with a trunk diameter of 2 to 3 feet. It reaches its best development in the region of the upper Great Lakes. Red pine has been extensively used in reforestation projects throughout the North. It is characteristically a tree of light sandy soils, and it grows well on soils that are too poor for the white pine. During the first 60 or 70 years it makes very rapid growth, but thereafter the growth becomes much slower. Under natural conditions the red pine most often occurs as scattered trees, but locally it forms nearly pure stands in the Great Lakes states.

The wood of the red pine is light, hard, and very close-grained. It is not durable in contact with the soil without chemical treatment. It is used in building construction, for piling, masts, spars, boxes and crates, and also as pulpwood. Red pine is often used as an ornamental tree on account of its dark green tufts of foliage, and attractive broadly pyramidal or almost dome-shaped crown. In age, however, the crown becomes irregular, round-topped, and rather open.

The range of the red pine extends from Nova Scotia westward to Manitoba and south to Minnesota, Michigan, Pennsylvania, and Massachusetts.

AUSTRIAN PINE   *Pinus nigra* **Arnold**

Needles 3½ to 6 inches long, dark dull green, slender, stiff, arranged in bundles of 2, sheathes stout. *Cones* 2 to 3 inches long, 1 to 1¼ inches wide, stalkless, oblong, ovoid, standing more or less at a right angle to the branches; maturing at the end of the second season, usually persisting on the branches for several years; cone scales yellowish, lustrous, tips thickened, terminated by a short, bluntish spine. *Twigs* stout, brittle, yellowish brown at first but soon becoming dark, roughened by the persistent leaf bases. *Bark* on the older trunks dark grayish brown to blackish, coarsely and deeply fissured with irregular, scaly ridges.

Comparisons. This is a 2-needled pine with long, straight needles resembling those of the red pine, but much wider, coarser, and less lustrous green. Most important, they do not fracture when bent in half. The cones also differ by being spined at maturity and larger than those of the red pine. Additionally, the twigs are thicker than those of the red pine and much darker in color to nearly black. The red pine also has a more reddish brown bark on both the twigs and trunks.

This species is a European introduction commonly planted in parks and other urban settings. The dark green, salt-tolerant leaves are able to survive various air pollutants. The Austrian pine is planted extensively in North America and achieves heights of 60 to 70 feet.

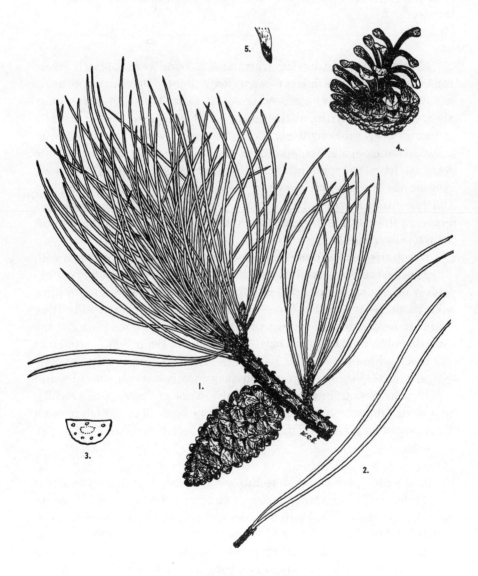

AUSTRIAN PINE

1. Branch with closed cone.
2. Cluster of leaves.
3. Cross-section of leaf.

4. Open cone.
5. Seed.

SCOTCH PINE   *Pinus sylvestris* **L.**

The most striking characteristic of the Scotch pine is its bright orange-red, flaky bark along its upper trunk and branches, its cones that point backwards along the branches, and its two slightly twisted, glaucous green needles and twisted cones.

Needles: 1½ to 3 inches long, arranged in bundles of 2, bluish green, rather stout, stiff, more or less twisted. *Twigs* slightly glaucous or not at all, smooth where needles have been removed. *Cones* 1¼ to 2½ inches long, short-stalked, occurring in clusters of 2 to 3, elliptic to oblong, usually pointing backward along the branches, narrowly ovoid when closed, with a somewhat elongated, tapered base, becoming broadly so or even quite roundish when open; mature at the end of the second season, soon shed; cone scales dull grayish brown, thickened at the tips, terminating in a sharp point, but without an actual prickle. *Bark* on upper trunk and branches flaky, bright orange red; on the lower trunk becoming grayish brown, quite rough.

Comparisons. The other 2-needled pines that might be confused with this species are the jack pine, which has shorter needles that are more widely diverging or V-shaped in appearance; the Table Mountain pine, with branches as tough as those of a hickory sapling (not at all brittle), and with heavily armed cones and coarser needles; the red pine and the Austrian pine, both of which have larger needles, twigs that are rough to the touch where the needles have been removed, and nearly flat cone bases; and the Virginia pine, which has conspicuous cone prickles and equally conspicuous bicolored cone scales. None of these species has the orange-red upper branches or the tapered cone bases of the Scotch pine. Of these 2-needled pines, only the Austrian and Scotch pines are introduced.

The Scotch pine is native to Europe and northern Asia, where it is one of the most important timber trees, often growing over 100 feet in height. It was introduced into this country quite early, around 1752, as an ornamental tree, later finding widespread usage in reforestation projects. Currently, it represents one of the most cultivated and widely distributed pines in the world. It grows rapidly during its youth, and is very tolerant of soil conditions, moisture, and climatic extremes. In North America, this is a small to medium-sized tree, commonly attaining a height of about 70 feet with a trunk diameter of 1½ to 3 feet, but it may reach a

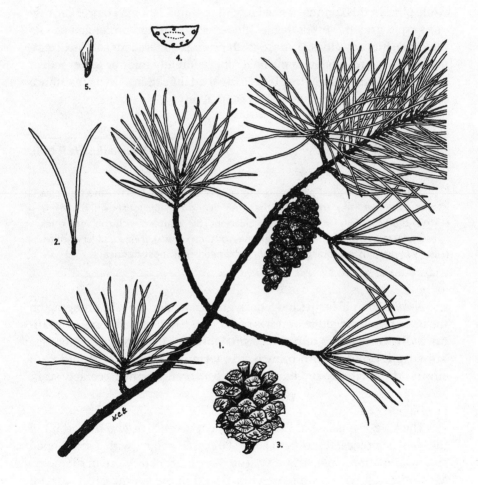

SCOTCH PINE

1. Branch with closed cone.
2. Cluster of leaves.
3. Open cone.
4. Cross-section of leaf.
5. Seed.

height of 100 feet. When grown in close stands, the trunks are generally straight and clean. Open-grown trees are usually crooked, with short trunks and irregular crowns, the lateral branches being more or less contorted and often drooping.

The wood of the Scotch pine is light, soft, easily split, and rather durable. Its utilization in Europe corresponds to our usage of the native white pine. In this country it is seldom of commercial importance. Because of its rapid growth, stiff branches, blue-green color, and prolonged needle retention, in many cities, young Scotch pines are offered for sale as Christmas trees. For reforestation purposes it is definitely inferior to our native pines. As an ornamental tree its principal qualifications are its resistance to city smoke, its hardiness, and its adaptability.

LONG-LEAF PINE   *Pinus palustris* P. Mill.

> Needles of the long-leaf pine are the longest of any of our North American pine species. In fact, they are so long that they droop conspicuously while hanging from the branches, facilitating identification. This, coupled with the very thick twigs, large cones (the largest of all our southern pines), fringed, silvery white-hairy bud scales, and bracts subtending the needles, is most distinct.

Needles 10 to 15 inches long, dark green, slender, flexible, drooping on the branches, arranged in bundles of 3. *Cones* 6 to 10 inches long, cylindrical, dull brown; scales tipped by a small prickle. *Twigs* very stout, orange brown, clustered toward branch tips, terminating in a large bud with silvery-white, fringed, spreading scales. *Bark* orange brown, coarsely scaly.

The long-leaf is one of the largest, most distinctive, and important of the southern pines. It grows to 80 to 100 feet in height, with a small open crown, and a tapering clean bole from 2 to 2½ feet or more in diameter. Magnificent forests of this pine flourished in the southeastern coastal plains in colonial times. It is claimed that many of the choicest stands were preempted by the king of England for the exclusive use of the Royal Navy. Such trees produced the very best grade of "southern yellow pine" lumber for general construction, flooring, shipbuilding, and other uses. It is one of the best producers of the resin from which naval stores—turpentine and rosin—are derived.

LONG-LEAF PINE

1. Cluster of leaves.
2. Branch with leaves and opened cone.
3. Seed.

Long-leaf has a growth habit unlike that of the other pines. It grows very little above ground during the first five or six years of its existence. During this time only a dense tuft of needles is seen above the surface, the so-called "grass stage" of its life cycle, while the plant is developing a long, strong taproot. At the end of this period growth in height increases rapidly for the next 40 to 50 years. In both natural stands and in cultivation, this species grows best in full sun. It is considered to represent one of the more fire-resistant pines of the Southeast.

The range of the long-leaf pine extends through the coastal plain from southeastern Virginia to central Florida and westward to eastern Texas.

A rapidly growing, but poorly formed natural hybrid (*Pinus* x *sondereggeri* H. H. Chapman) between this species and the loblolly pine can be found occasionally. Its morphology is intermediate between both of its parents, and its wood quality is inferior to both.

SLASH PINE   *Pinus elliottii* **Engelm.**

> The long-stalked (¾ to 1 inch), very lustrous, nearly varnished cones, relatively large needles in bundles of 2 to 3, and the orange brown to purplish brown bark, which peels off into thin, nearly papery layers, are most characteristic.

Needles 6 to 10 inches long, dark green, stiff, lustrous, arranged in bundles of 2 or 3, more commonly in 2s, tufted at the ends of the stout, orange-brown branchlets; basal sheath persistent, usually less than ½ inch long. *Cones* 3 to 7 inches long, ovoid, lustrous brown, on stalks ¾ to 1 inch long, with small, recurved prickles. *Buds* terminal, silvery brown, scaly with slender, loose tips; not silvery white as in the long-leaf pine. *Bark* orange brown to purplish brown, broken into large flat plates covered with thin, silvery-brown scales.

Comparisons. The leaves of the slash pine, which are more commonly found in 2s than 3s, are shorter and more lustrous than those of the long-leaf pine. The cones of the slash pine, which are initially forwardly pointed on the branch, but later recurved, help to separate it from the loblolly pine, which has cones that are nearly always found growing perpendicular to the branch. Also, the cones of the slash pine are usually somewhat larger, more lustrous brown, and with smaller, recurved prickles, which are less sharply pointed than those of the loblolly pine.

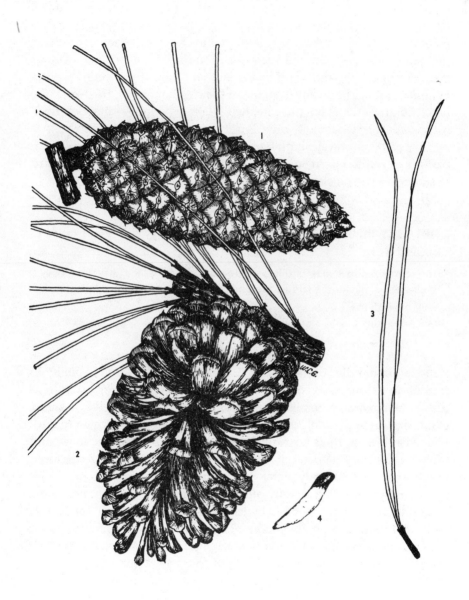

SLASH PINE

1. Unopened cone.
2. Branch with leaves and opened cone.
3. Cluster of leaves.
4. Seed.

The slash pine is a large tree, 80 to 100 feet in height with a round-topped crown and a clear trunk from 1½ to 2½ feet in diameter. It is a rapidly growing tree, of great importance in the production of naval stores as well as commercially valuable pulpwood and lumber. Its native habitat was in the semiswampy low grounds but it has been extensively planted in the lower South in reforestation projects. The hard resinous wood is not usually differentiated from that of the other "yellow" pines by lumbermen. The scientific name of the tree honors its discoverer, the noted South Carolina botanist Stephen Elliott, who in 1824 first described it as a variety of the loblolly pine. It is the state tree of Alabama.

The range of the slash pine originally extended through the coastal plain from southeastern South Carolina to central Florida and westward to southeastern Louisiana.

LOBLOLLY PINE   *Pinus taeda* L.

The southern distribution of this large tree, with its rather long needles mostly in clusters of 3, and the large cones, help to separate the loblolly pine from other eastern pines.

Needles 6 to 9 inches long, slender, yellowish green to grayish green, arranged in bundles of 3 or rarely 2; basal sheath persistent, usually ½ inch or more long. *Cones* 3 to 6 inches long, cylindrical ovoid, light reddish brown to brown, sessile or subsessile; scales thick, tipped by a sharp, stout, spreading prickle. *Twigs* moderately stout, reddish brown to dark yellowish brown. *Buds* terminal with reddish brown scales, loose and often reflexed tips. *Bark* on older trunks reddish brown, deeply fissured into irregular, broad, scaly plates.

Comparisons. The loblolly pine is very similar in appearance to the slash pine, but can be identified by its needles, mostly in 3s rather than 2s or 3s, and more terminally clustered, duller, and more spreading than those of the latter species. Also see the slash pine description for additional comparisons. It is also similar to the pitch pine, but that species has shorter needles.

The loblolly pine, named because of the "mud hole" or "mud puddle" habitat of this species, is also known as the old-field pine, a name derived from the tree's ability to rapidly invade abandoned fields. It is a large tree

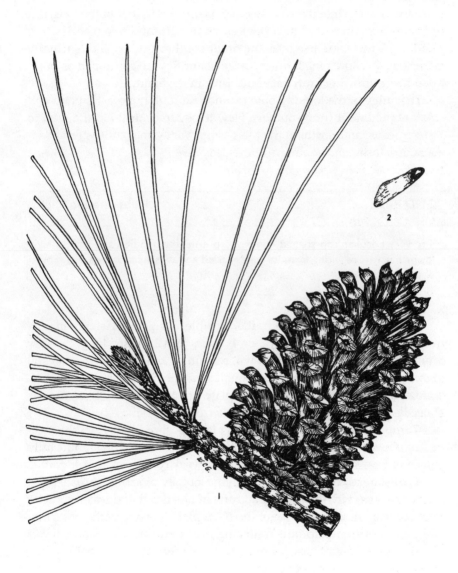

LOBLOLLY PINE

1. Branch with leaves and opened cone.   2. Seed.

from 80 to 100 feet or more in height with a large open crown and a clean bole, often 2 to 4 feet in diameter. The loblolly is one of the most rapidly growing, one of the largest, and the most commercially important of our southern pines. While its wood is rated as inferior to that of the long-leaf and short-leaf pines, it is, nevertheless, an important timber species. The wood finds the same usage as the other southern pines and is usually marketed as yellow pine lumber. Large quantities are consumed as pulpwood by the growing kraft paper industry in the South.

The range of the loblolly pine extends through the coastal plain and adjacent piedmont from southern New Jersey to central Florida west to eastern Texas; and north, in the Mississippi Valley, to southeastern Oklahoma, Arkansas, and southern Tennessee.

POND PINE   *Pinus serotina* Michx.

The very peculiar, top-shaped cones, 3- to 4-needle bundles, and irregularly formed crown, resulting from its very gnarled and twisted branches, are most distinct.

Needles 6 to 8 inches long, rather flexible, dark yellowish green, lustrous, arranged in bundles of 3 or 4. *Cones* 2 to 3 inches long, broadly ovoid, short and stocky, light brown, remain on the branches for several to many years; scales tipped with small weak prickles. *Bark* dark brown, divided into irregular, vertical, flaky plates; trunks often with small tufts of needles appearing to develop directly from the bole.

Comparisons. This wholly coastal plain species differs from the similar but more mountainous Table Mountain pine by having significantly longer, more conspicuously shiny needles, weak cone prickles, and flatter, more top-shaped cones. It differs from the loblolly pine by its broader and shorter cone and by the occasional tufts of needles that develop directly from the bole, similar to those of the pitch pine. It is one of the few pines that produces stump sprouts following fire or cutting and is unusual in that its cones remain closed for years, yet the seeds remain viable, often until fire forces the cones to open.

The pond pine is also known as the marsh pine or pocosin pine, the latter being a Native American name for pond or bog, referring to its

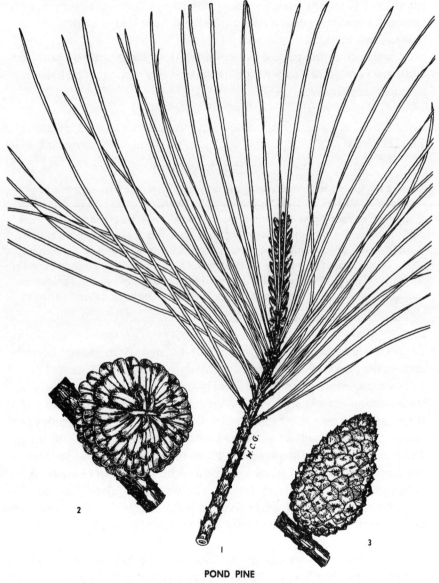

POND PINE

1. Branch with leaves.
2. Open cone.
3. Closed cone.

occurrence in swamps and low wet flats of the coastal plain. It attains a height of 75 feet or more with a trunk diameter of up to 2 feet. While the larger trees are frequently cut and marketed with the other pines as lumber, the tree's chief utilization now is in the form of pulpwood. Some experts have considered the tree to be a variety of the more upland pitch pine (*P. rigida* Mill.), a view not accepted here. The difference between the two trees is quite marked and their distributions are altogether discontinuous.

The range of the pond pine extends through the coastal plain from southern New Jersey to central Florida and Alabama. It is rare north of southeastern Virginia.

PITCH PINE   *Pinus rigida* P. Mill.

The pitch pine is easily told, being the only northern pine that regularly has its needles in clusters of 3. This is the only pine, with the exception of occasional individuals of pond pine or short-leaf pine, that has needles growing directly out of the bole, or out of the bark or large branches. This is especially true of trees grown in fire communities. The persistent dead branches create an undesirable, gnarled appearance of the tree, which along with the stiff, yellowish needles create a most accurate characterization. Moreover, the short, stiff, recurved prickle on the tip of the cone scale makes the very long persisting cone difficult to handle.

Needles 2 to 5 inches long, stout, stiff, twisted when viewed from the apex to the base, yellowish green, regularly in bundles of 3. *Cones* 1½ to 3 inches long, ovoid when closed, nearly spherical when open, nearly sessile, standing at right angles to the branches, maturing during autumn of the second season, often persisting on the branches for ten or more years; cone scales thickened at tips, armed with a short, stiff, recurved prickle. *Twigs* roughened by the persistent bases of the leaf clusters. *Bark* on the young trunks and on the branches broken into platelike reddish brown scales; on the older trunks becoming deeply and irregularly fissured with intervening flat-topped, scaly, reddish brown ridges; trunks often fire-scarred, with clusters of needles produced directly from the wood of the branches.

Comparisons. The shorter needles of this species and more inland and northern distribution help to separate it from the pond pine of the southeastern coastal plain.

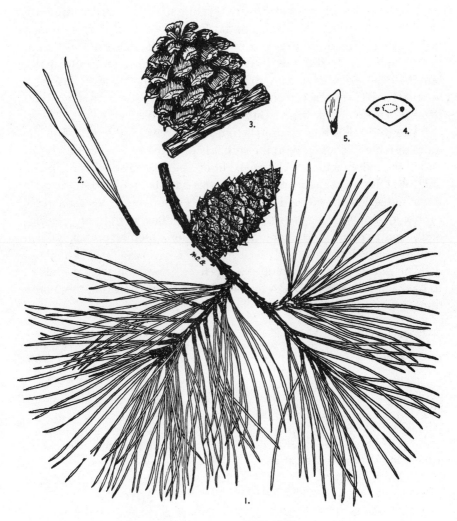

PITCH PINE

1. Branch with closed cone.
2. Cluster of leaves.
3. Open cone.
4. Cross-section of leaf.
5. Seed.

Pitch pine, referring to the significant high resin content of its wood, is also known locally as hard pine, jack pine, black pine, or yellow pine. It is characteristically a tree of dry, rocky ridges and cliffs, although it is sometimes found in swampy areas. While the pitch pine commonly occurs as a subordinate species in hardwood stands, it may assume a major role on the more exposed mountain ridges. It is quite resistant to fire and is often the only tree that is able to survive on repeatedly burned-over areas. In barren, dry, and sterile areas it seldom attains a very large size, very often remaining scrubby. Vigorous trees may attain heights of 40 to 60 feet, with trunk diameters of 1 to 2 feet.

The wood of the pitch pine is light, soft, weak, and brittle, but it is quite durable in contact with the soil. It is principally used as fuel wood and in the manufacture of charcoal, but occasionally also for mine props and rough lumber. Thousands of seedlings have been raised in the state forest nurseries for reforesting barren lands where more desirable trees cannot grow. Old trees are often quite picturesque, with their irregular and scraggy crowns, and their gnarled and often drooping branches laden with the persistent cones.

The range of the pitch pine extends from New Brunswick westward to Lake Ontario, south to Virginia and Tennessee, and along the mountains to Georgia.

JACK PINE   *Pinus banksiana* **Lamb.**

The very short needles of the jack pine, shorter than any other eastern native species, are also unique among the 2-needled pines, being conspicuous, widely diverging, or V-shaped in appearance. This, coupled with the short and conspicuously curved or lopsided cones, which are unarmed and forwardly pointed on the branches, is most distinctive.

Needles ⅓ to 1½ inches long, stout, stiff, straight, dark grayish green to dark yellowish green, arranged in bundles of 2, widely spreading, vase-shaped. *Cones* 1½ to 2 inches long, stalkless, oblong conical in shape, commonly curved like those of white pine, but much smaller, usually pointing forward along the branches, maturing during autumn of the second season, often remaining closed for a few years, and commonly persisting on the branches for ten or more years; cone scales thickened at tips, usually unarmed, occasionally with a very weak minute prickle. *Twigs* rather slen-

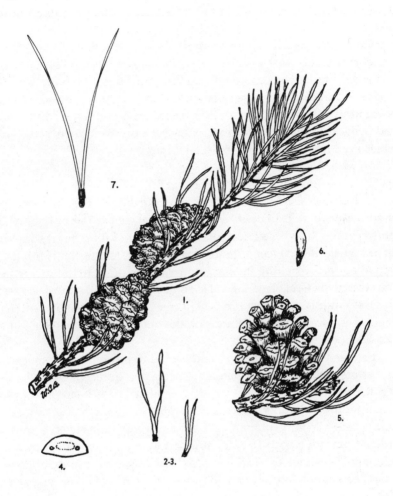

JACK PINE

1. Branch with closed cones.
2-3. Clusters of leaves.
4. Cross-section of leaf.

5. Open cone.
6. Seed.
7. Widely diverging needles.

der, purplish to reddish-brown, roughened by the persistent leaf bases. *Bark* dark reddish brown, shallowly fissured, with irregular, rounded, scaly ridges.

Comparisons. This species is most likely to be confused with the more southern Virginia pine, which has needles that are less widely spreading, and cones that are not curved. From the cultivated Scotch pine, it can be told by its larger, yellow-green rather than blue-green needles, by its cones being forwardly pointed rather than backwardly pointed on the branches, and by lacking the conspicuous orange bark on the branches and trunk, which are commonly found on Scotch pine.

———

Jack pine is also known as bank pine, northern scrub pine, gray pine, or spruce pine. It is an open-crowned, small tree, commonly only 20 to 30 feet in height with a trunk diameter of ¾ to 1 foot, but it sometimes attains a height of 60 feet or more in portions of its range. It is primarily a Canadian tree, reaching its maximum development in the region north and west of the Great Lakes. The jack pine in many respects closely resembles the Virginia pine. It is typically a tree of light sandy soils, often pioneering and forming pure stands on the burned-over forest lands in the North.

Formerly the jack pine was considered to be an inferior species, but its commercial importance has been increasing in recent years. Its wood is soft, light, brittle, and lacking in durability. It has been used to some extent for rough lumber, boxes, slack cooperage, mine props, fuel, and for railroad ties. Within comparatively recent years it has been extensively utilized for pulpwood. The jack pine grows well on even the poorest of soils, but it is rather short-lived, rarely reaching a maximum of 125 years. It has been planted for watershed protection and occasionally as an ornamental tree. The species plays an important role in providing unique resting sites for the rare Kirtland's warbler, a small sparrow-sized bird species that breeds in northern Michigan only.

The range of the jack pine extends from Nova Scotia northwest to the region of the Mackenzie River, southward through Canada to Minnesota, Wisconsin, northern Illinois, and Indiana; and in the east, south to northeastern New York and northern New England.

VIRGINIA PINE   *Pinus virginiana* **P. Mill.**

> The extremely numerous, dark-banded cones found on a single tree, coupled with the twisted, short needles in clusters of 2, and the purplish green, glaucous branches are most distinctive. The lower lateral branches often die yet remain on the tree for years, giving this pine a scrubby look.

Needles 1½ to 3 inches long, grayish green, stout, twisted, arranged in bundles of 2. *Twigs* glabrous, tough, flexible; young shoots purplish green and glaucous. *Cones* stalkless, narrowly egg-shaped when closed, ovoid when open, standing at nearly right angles to the branches, maturing at the end of the second season, persisting on the branches for several years; cone scales thin, tips slightly thickened and often deep purple or gray, with an extremely dark band on the interface (perhaps the darkest of any eastern species, with the possible exception of the sand pine and red pine), terminated by a small prickle. *Bark* dark brown, quite smooth on the younger trunks, eventually becoming shallowly fissured with rather small, flat, scaly plates.

Comparisons. When viewed from above, a significant portion of the inner surface tips of the cone scales of a fully open cone of the Virginia pine bear conspicuous dark, often deep purple or gray, bands, which help to separate it from other species with comparably sized cones. These bands are darker and wider than those of the short-leaf pine. The Virginia pine is most often confused with the jack pine, but see that species for distinguishing characters. The more upland Virginia pine can be separated from the more southern, coastal plain spruce pine and the sand pine. Also, the cone scales of the sand pine have stouter prickles than those of the Virginia pine. This species also differs from the shortleaf pine by having 3, rather than 2 or 3 needles per bundle, which are twisted rather than straight. The Virginia pine is also more scrubby in appearance than the straight-growing and more elegant short-leaf pine. The dark banded cone scale of Virginia pine represents perhaps the most pronounced of any of our eastern species, comparable only to that of the sand pine of the Southeast and the red pine of the Northeast.

Virginia pine is also known as scrub pine or Jersey pine. It is usually a small tree, often becoming 30 or 40 feet in height with a trunk diameter of 1 to 1½ feet, but occasionally somewhat larger. It is characteristically a

VIRGINIA PINE

1. Branch with closed cone.
2. Cluster of leaves.

3. Open cone.
4. Seed.

tree of dry rocky places, or of poor sandy soils. On many of the barren mountain ridges it commonly associates with the pitch pine. Virginia pine frequently invades worn-out and abandoned fields, and in such situations it often forms practically pure stands. Although reported to be tough and pliable by some workers, the branches are quite brittle and easily broken.

The wood of the Virginia pine is soft, coarse-grained, and usually knotty. It is seldom used for lumber, but it is used for mine props, railroad ties, and as fuel. In more recent years it has found a market as pulpwood. The Virginia pine is very seldom planted as an ornamental tree. In age it develops a rather flat-topped, open, and scraggy crown. The principal value of this tree lies in its ability to flourish on sterile and worn-out lands, thus providing some semblance of forest cover and preventing further erosion. In the Piedmont of the Southeast, this species and the short-leaf are the two prevalent pines.

SHORT-LEAF PINE   *Pinus echinata* P. Mill.

As the name infers, the 3- to 5-inch long, slender, straight needles in bundles of 2 or 3 of the short-leaf pine represent the shortest needles of any of the southern yellow pines. This, along with the whitish branches and very short, prickled cone scales, is most diagnostic.

Needles 3 to 5 inches long, straight, bluish green, slender, flexible, usually in bundles of 2, but occasionally 3 or very rarely 4. *Cones* 1½ to 2½ inches long, very short-stalked, conical when closed, egg-shaped when open, maturing at the end of the second season, often persisting on the branches for a few years; cone scales slightly thickened at tips, terminating in a more or less temporary prickle or small spine, inner extreme tip often conspicuously darker. *Twigs* rather stout, quite brittle, greenish to lavender, glaucous at first, soon becoming reddish brown and scaly. *Bark* on older trunks yellowish brown to cinnamon red, broken by deep furrows into irregular but somewhat rectangular, flat-topped, and scaly plates, often with at least some small, but conspicuous, resin pockets.

Comparisons. The interface of the cone scales is often conspicuously darker in color than the remainder of the scale, but usually less colorful than those of the Virginia pine. The bark on young branches of short-leaf pine tends to flake, but not so in similar species such as Virginia pine,

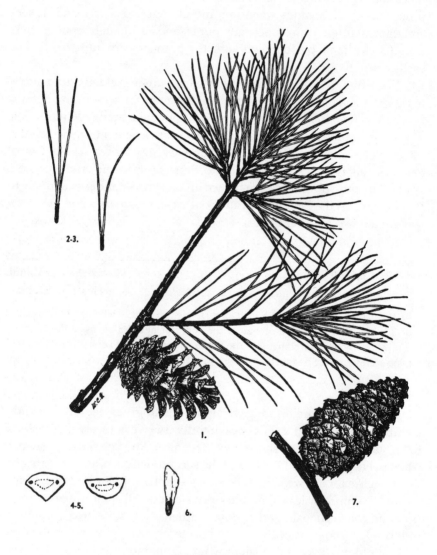

SHORT-LEAF PINE

1. Branch with open cone.
2-3. Clusters of leaves.
4-5. Cross-sections of leaves.

6. Seed.
7. Closed cone.

spruce pine, or sand pine. Also, the resin pockets in the bark, usually 2- rather than 3-needled bundles, straight rather than twisted needles, and less resinous buds will help to separate this species from the pitch pine and the pond pine.

———

Short-leaf pine is also known as yellow pine, oldfield pine, and rosemary pine. It attains a height of 80 to 100 feet or more, with a trunk diameter of 2 to 3 feet and occasionally 4 feet. This species is one of the four most commercially important southern yellow pine species, and is clearly the most widely distributed of the four. It prefers well-drained or dry, sandy to gravelly clay soils. Its maximum development is attained west of the Mississippi River. In the eastern states it commonly occurs in stands of hardwoods or as an associate of other species of pine.

The short-leaf pine drops its lowermost lateral branches quite early, even when growing in the open, producing a tall, clean, straight trunk. The crown is usually broadly rounded with long, slender, and somewhat drooping branches. The ability of young trees to sprout following injury or fire is unique. Loblolly pine alludes to its ability to seed itself into abandoned fields.

The yellowish wood of the short-leaf pine is moderately heavy, hard, and strong, with a very pronounced grain. It is one of the commercial timbers sold as "southern yellow pine" and is now commonly used in carpentry and general construction work. It is also used in the manufacture of furniture, agricultural machinery, boxes and crates, excelsior, and paper pulp.

The range of the short-leaf pine extends from southeastern New York and southern Pennsylvania to northern Florida, and west to Missouri, Oklahoma, and eastern Texas.

SPRUCE PINE   *Pinus glabra* Walt.

The exceptionally narrow needles in bundles of 2 of this coastal pine species, and very peculiar, sprucelike or oaklike bark are very distinctive. It can often be seen with a great abundance of cones. At a distance, this coastal pine species has a distinct resemblance to the eastern white pine.

Needles 1½ to 2½ inches long, 0.04 inch (1 mm) or less wide, slender, flexible, more or less twisted, dark green, arranged in bundles of 2. *Cones* 1¼ to 2½ inches long, often nearly round, reddish brown, lustrous; scales with minute prickles at the tips. *Twigs* slender, glabrous, flexible, purplish tinged. *Bark* on the younger trunks and branches gray, smooth; on older trunks furrowed, with flat, scaly ridges, and flat plates, resembling that of spruce or oak.

Comparisons. The cones of this species differ from those of the sand pine by having a much lighter and less pronounced band on the inner surface of the cone scales. The spruce pine also differs by occurring in intermixed hardwood forests on rich calcareous bottomlands, rather than on white, coastal sands along the Atlantic and Gulf coast beaches.

––––––––

The spruce pine, or walter pine, is a beautiful large tree found in the damp coastal intermixed hardwood forests on calcareous bottomlands of the southeastern states. Its beautiful form represents one of the most sought-after of our pine species for cultivation purposes. It occurs most often as a scattered tree, but occasionally forms nearly pure stands in local areas. It may attain a height of 80 to 90 feet, with a trunk diameter of 1½ to 2½ feet, but usually it is much smaller. As a timber tree it is of relatively minor importance but it is worthy of more extensive use as a shade or ornamental tree. The name of Walter pine honors the South Carolina botanist Thomas Walter, who published the first description of the tree in 1788 in his *Flora Caroliniana.*

The range of the spruce pine extends through the coastal plain from southeastern South Carolina to northern Florida and west to southeastern Louisiana.

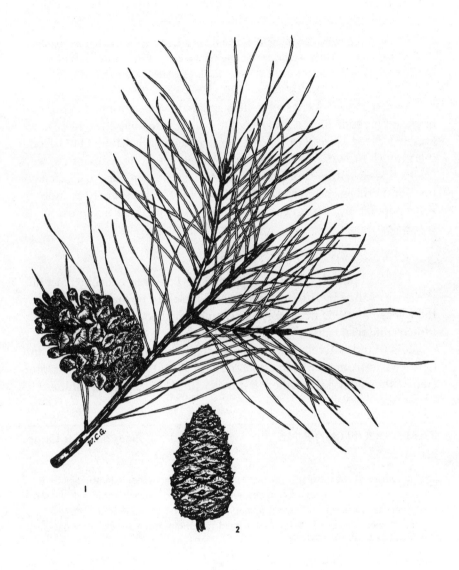

SPRUCE PINE

1. Branch with leaves and opened cone.   2. Closed cone.

SAND PINE   *Pinus clausa* (Chap. ex Engelm.) Vasey ex Sarg.

> The southern distribution along the Atlantic and Gulf coasts, needles in bundles of 2s, and unusual horizontal ridge on the spined cone scale are most distinct.

Needles 2 to 3¼ inches long, dark green, flexible, arranged in bundles of 2s. *Twigs* reddish brown to ashy brown, very flexible, straight or moderately twisted. *Cones* 2 to 3 inches long, reddish brown at first but becoming grayish brown, sessile, ovate when closed, oblong when open, with scales tipped with a short, but thickened, stout spine and conspicuous horizontal ridges; often remaining closed for several years to decades in some populations. *Bark* gray, comparatively smooth, thick and broken into plates.

———

The sand pine is a small to medium-sized tree rarely over 85 feet tall. It is easily killed by fire but soon reseeds itself in burned-over areas by the release of seeds from previously unopened cones. It is of relatively little commercial value except for pulpwood.

It is found natively in infertile white sands along the Atlantic and Gulf coasts from southern Alabama and Florida. It often forms pine stands on coastal ridges, where it grows with mixed oak communities.

TABLE MOUNTAIN PINE   *Pinus pungens* Lamb.

> This species is characterized by its very sharp, twisted needles in bundles of 2s, by its very flexible, tough branches, which are nearly unbreakable even when tied into knots, and by its heavily armed, curved-spine cones. Without gloves, the exceptionally sharp-spined cones are hard to handle, and are extremely difficult to remove from the branches.

Needles 1½ to 3½ inches long, dark green, stout, rigid, very sharp-pointed, somewhat twisted, arranged in bundles of 2. *Twigs* tough, very flexible, nearly unbreakable even when tied into knots. *Cones* quite distinctive, 2½ to 4 inches long, practically stalkless, broadly ovoid, thick, more massive than the short-needled pines, curved, often arranged in whorls of 3 or more on the stout branches; not opening for several years

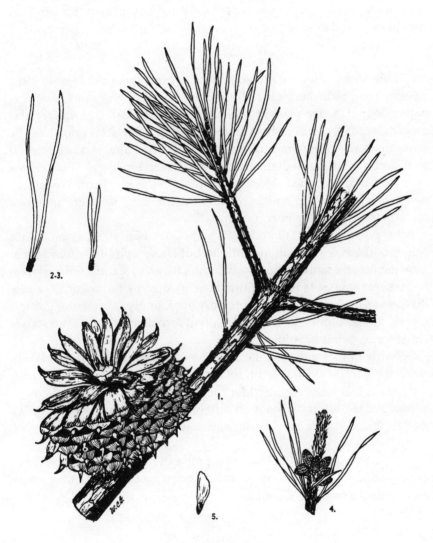

TABLE MOUNTAIN PINE

1. Branch with heavily armed, open cone.
2-3. Clusters of leaves.

4. Tip of branch with cluster of staminate flowers.
5. Seed.

following maturation, remaining on the branches for 20 or more years; scales thick and conspicuously keeled, terminated by large, stout, and strongly hooked sharp spines. *Bark* dark reddish brown, broken into irregular scaly plates.

———

Table Mountain pine is also known as bur pine, prickly cone pine, poverty pine, or hickory pine, the last due to its tough branches or perhaps due to its scaly, plated bark. It is usually a small tree of irregular growth, typically with a short trunk and long horizontal branches, the lowermost ones often gracefully drooping. It often attains a height of 30 to 40 feet, with a trunk diameter of 1 to 1½ feet. Dr. Joseph Illick cites a specimen that grew near Mont Alto, Franklin County, Pennsylvania, as being 73 feet in height and 23 inches in diameter. Specimens merely a few feet in height often bear cones.

It is typically a tree of poor soils and of dry, barren, rocky mountain ridges of the Appalachian Mountains, but Dr. Joseph Illick found them growing on an island in the Susquehanna River, in southern Pennsylvania, where their roots were continuously washed by the water. As a rule the Table Mountain pine is found scattered singly or in small groups, sometimes with pitch pines, but locally it forms practically pure stands along the Appalachian Mountains.

Owing to its small size, the Table Mountain pine is seldom of commercial value. Its wood is light, soft, coarse-grained, brittle, and invariably knotty. It is primarily used for fuel and for manufacturing charcoal, although it is occasionally sawed into lumber. The tree is an aggressive grower, and it may be used advantageously in controlling soil erosion on steep, barren slopes.

The range of the Table Mountain pine extends from southern Pennsylvania and New Jersey southward, principally along the Appalachian Mountains, to northern Georgia.

CYPRESS FAMILY—CUPPRESSACEAE

The Bald-Cypress
and the Pond-Cypress—Taxodium

Although currently restricted to eastern North America, the bald-cypress and the pond-cypress were historically much more widely distributed. Both the bald-cypress and the pond-cypress are characterized by their small, alternate, deciduous leaves that are basally decurrent, spirally arranged, linear, yellow green, and flat to awl-shaped. The leaves are of two basic types. Those of persistent branches project radially, while others on deciduous branches appear to be 2-ranked. The plants are monoecious with the male and female cones occurring on the same tree. The mature cones are woody, globose to subglobose, resinous, with 4 to 10, 4-angled, peltate scales, with slightly winged and 3-angled seeds. The buds are very small, round, and scaly; the pith is brown to tan. In flooded habitats both species produce unusually large buttressed bases, which may develop into peculiar kneelike projections as well.

BALD-CYPRESS   *Taxodium distichum* (L.) **L. C. Rich.**

> This is a large swamp tree of the South with a conspicuously swollen base, featherlike deciduous leaves, and fibrous, reddish brown bark, which peels off in thin, narrow strips.

Summer. *Leaves* ½ to ¾ inch long, flat, linear, featherlike arrangement in two rows (1-plane) on slender branchlets; dull, light green above, whitish below, shed in the fall. *Twigs* deciduous, light reddish brown; branchlets laterally spreading from larger twigs. *Cones* ¾ to 1 inch in diameter, nearly globular, 1 or 2 at end of twigs, composed of several

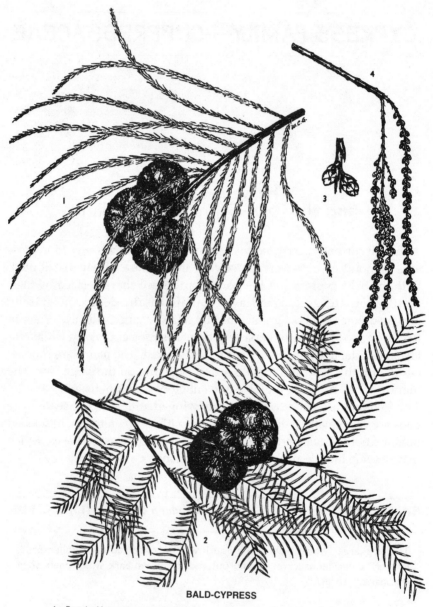

BALD-CYPRESS

1. Branch of form with appressed leaves (pondcypress).
2. Branch typical form with leaves and cones.
3. Detail of staminate flower bud.
4. Winter twig with staminate flower buds.

4-angled, shield-shaped, hard scales; seeds about ¼ inch long, small, brown, 3-angled.

Winter. *Staminate cones* catkinlike, often present, partly developed, in drooping clusters. *Twigs* light reddish brown, marked with small pits or scars left by the deciduous branchlets, showing no bundle scars, unlike true leaf scars. *Buds* small, roundish, scaly, noticeable. *Bark* fibrous, reddish brown, peels off in thin, narrow strips.

Comparisons. Aside from the differences pointed out by the key, the "knees" of the bald-cypress are more sharply pointed than those of the pond-cypress, and the branches are more upright.

———

The bald-cypress is also known as the swamp-cypress, southern-cypress, and tidewater red-cypress. It is the most characteristic and picturesque tree of the southern swamps and alluvial bottomlands. Young trees typically have pyramidal crowns, but older ones develop irregular, flat-topped crowns with long festoons of Spanish moss hanging from their branches. The tree often attains a height of 100 to 150 feet and trunk diameters of 3 to 6 feet or more. The wood is very durable, with wooden poles remaining intact for over 1,200 years without decay. The peculiar root system produces irregular conical structures called knees, which are thought to aid in the oxygen exchange to the root system. These knees are often used in making various novelties that are sold to tourists.

The bald-cypress is an important timber tree. Its wood is extremely durable and is used for siding, boats, greenhouse construction, tanks, boxes, crates, and railroad ties. It will grow very well on well-drained upland sites and makes a very handsome ornamental tree.

The bald-cypress may attain an age of 1,000 years or more and there is evidence that it once grew much farther north than at the present time. Wildman (1933) cites the excavation of a gigantic cypress stump in Philadelphia. Its present range extends through the coastal plain from southern Delaware to Florida west to southeastern Texas, and northward, in the Mississippi Valley, to southern Illinois and southwestern Indiana.

POND-CYPRESS *Taxodium ascendens* Brongn.

Leaves ⅛ to ⅝ inch long, slender, needle- to awl-shaped, spirally arranged within 1 plane, closely appressed. *Twigs* (branchlets) deciduous, mostly rigidly ascending, with appressed leaves. *Bark* prominently ridged, deeply furrowed, breaking into long vertical plates, occasionally spiraling upward.

Comparisons. The pond-cypress can be distinguished from the bald-cypress by its smaller size and by having its deciduous branchlets mostly rigidly ascending rather than spreading, with appressed, awl-shaped, or scalelike leaves, rather than flat leaves, that appear to be more appressed but multi-plane or spirally arranged (tail-like) rather than in 1 plane (feath-erlike) like the leaves of the bald-cypress. Trees with such characteristics occur commonly in ponds in flat pinelands, from southeastern Virginia to Florida and westward to Louisiana. However, on some individuals certain branches can be found with awl-like, appressed leaves, while other branches on the same individual can bear the more characteristic linear and spread-ing leaves of typical bald-cypress. The pond-cypress also has a noticeably thicker bark and stout and straight twigs that droop on younger plants.

———

Pond-cypress is a small to medium or even large-sized tree, rising to approximately 120 feet high. It is commonly found in wet, sandy depres-sions, shallow ponds, and swamps of flat woods and pine barrens. It occurs along the southeastern coastal plain from the dismal swamps in Virginia to Florida to Louisiana.

Some authorities consider this tree to represent a variety *(Taxodium distichum* var. *nutans* (Ait.) Sweet) of the previous species.

The Atlantic White-Cedar—Chamaecyparis

ATLANTIC WHITE-CEDAR   *Chamaecyparis thyoides* (L.) B.S.P.

> The dimorphic leaves, with one type being awl-shaped, occurring on seedlings and vigorous shoots, the other, more common type being scalelike and pro-ducing X patterns on the undersurfaces, along with the rounded cones of this coastal plain species are most distinct.

Leaves ¹⁄₁₆ to ⅛ inch long, rather minute, somewhat keeled, appearing 4-angled to the stem, dull bluish green, opposite, flattened, closely over-lapping and appressed, usually with a more or less prominent, glandular dot (pit), dimorphic: commonly scalelike and often glaucous with X pat-terns on the leaf undersurface, but awl-shaped on seedlings and vigorous

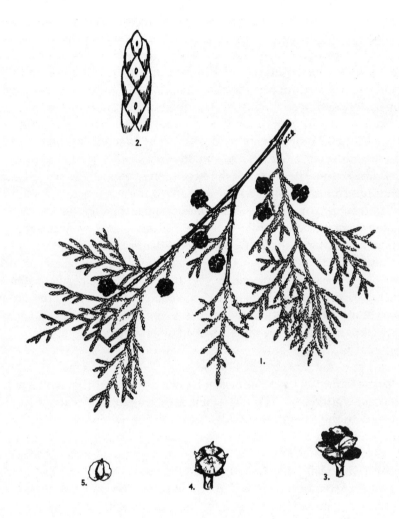

ATLANTIC WHITE-CEDAR

1. Branch with cones.
2. Portion of branch and leaves.
3. Open cone.
4. Closed cone.
5. Seed.

shoots. *Cones* about ¼ inch in diameter, spherical, knobby ball-shape, peculiar and distinctive; cone scales about 6, thickened, shield-shaped, joined to a central axis by stalks, with a small projection on the outer face of each scale, bluish purple and glaucous at first, turning brown later, remaining on tree until new cones develop fully. *Twigs* less distinctly fan-shaped and more roundish than the northern white-cedar, with mid-portion of the ultimate branchlets (including the clasping portion of leaves) being 0.04 inch (1 mm) wide. *Bark* ashy to reddish brown, rather thin, sloughing off in narrow and shreddy strips.

Comparison. The Atlantic white-cedar and the northern white-cedar are quite similar, except for the distinctly different cones and slightly wider branchlets of the latter. The cones of the former appear as smaller, globose, knobby balls, while those of the latter species appear more oblong. Furthermore the branches of the Atlantic white-cedar are not as profoundly flattened (less fan-shaped), and the leaves are narrower than those of the northern white-cedar. Also, the leaves of the northern white-cedar are larger and more yellow green compared with the blue-green leaves of the Atlantic white-cedar. The Atlantic white-cedar is a tree of the swamps and lowlands, rather than an upland plant.

———

The Atlantic white-cedar is also known as the southern white-cedar and coast white-cedar. It is a characteristic tree of freshwater swamps and bogs on the Atlantic and Gulf Coastal Plains. Extensive stands often occur on peat or muck soils overlying sand. It frequently forms pure stands on such sites following fire, developing into merchantable-sized timber in 75 to 100 years. Trees commonly attain a height of 30 to 50 feet with a trunk diameter of 1 to 2 feet, but often become 70 to 90 feet in height, with trunk diameters of 2 to 4 feet, under optimum conditions in the South. The trunk is straight and continuous with a narrow spirelike crown composed of short and slender, horizontal, or slightly ascending lateral branches.

The wood of the Atlantic white-cedar is light, soft, and slightly fragrant. It is not strong but it is very durable in contact with the soil. It is extensively used for building small boats and for siding, cooperage, shingles, railroad ties, posts, poles, and woodenware. The Atlantic white-cedar makes a very desirable ornamental tree and is often used in landscape work. It is the state tree of New Jersey.

The Atlantic white-cedar ranges along the Atlantic Coast from southern Maine to northern Florida, and westward along the Gulf Coast to Mississippi.

The Northern White-Cedar—Thuja

NORTHERN WHITE-CEDAR   *Thuja occidentalis* **L.**

> The small, erect, oblong cones, fibrous bark, glabrous, 4-ranked, opposite, straight, aromatic, scalelike leaves with conspicuous glandular dots or resin glands, and compressed branches appearing as though they were flattened with an iron are most distinctive.

Leaves ⅛ to ¼ inch long, opposite, 4-ranked, ovate, apically pointed or blunt, yellowish green, bronze in winter, entirely scalelike, overlapping, closely appressed to the twigs; lateral leaf pairs keeled, while the flat ones between them usually have a conspicuous glandular dot. *Cones* (fruits) ¼ to ½ inch long, oblong-ovoid to bell-shaped, small, short-stalked, erect, maturing during the first autumn, persisting through the winter; scales 6 to 12, thin, pale reddish brown. *Twigs* arranged in decidedly fan-shaped and flattened sprays in 1 plane, with the midportion of the ultimate branchlets (including the clasping portion of the leaves) about 0.06 to 0.08 inch (1.5 to 2 mm) wide. *Bark* thin, ashy to light reddish brown, shed in long, narrow, shredded strips.

Comparisons. Aside from the obvious cone differences, this species can be told from the similar Atlantic white-cedar by its somewhat thicker branchlets (0.06 inch [1.5 mm] versus 0.04 inch [1.0 mm] wide).

———

The northern white-cedar is commonly known as the arborvitae (meaning tree-of-life) and swamp-cedar. It has a densely pyramidal crown, and the lateral branches frequently are retained nearly to the base of the trunk. The trunks themselves commonly divide into 2 or more secondary stems. It may attain a height of 25 to 50 feet, and have a trunk diameter of 1 to 2 feet. The northern white-cedar is a tree of northern distribution, occurring in low swamps and along the banks of streams mostly on limestone soil, but also on shallow, dry limestone areas.

The wood of the northern white-cedar is light, soft, brittle, fragrant, and durable in contact with the soil. In the North, where it is a common tree, it is widely used for fence posts, rails, shingles, spools, boxes, canoes, and occasionally for construction lumber. Oil of cedar is distilled from the leaves and wood. Northern white-cedar is one of the most attractive of all our native evergreens, and the one most extensively used for ornamen-

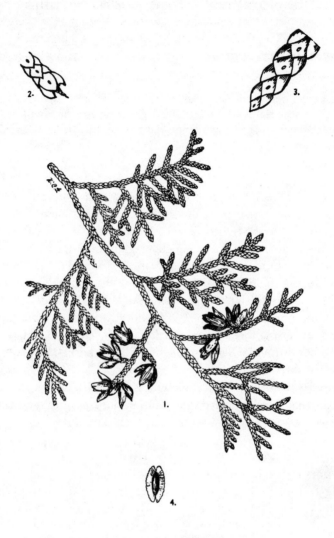

NORTHERN WHITE-CEDAR

1. Branch with open cones.   4. Seed.
2-3. Portions of branches with leaves
     (enlarged).

tal purposes. In the North, especially in areas of limestone, this species produces swamp thickets, which serve as valuable wintering grounds and nutritious browse for white-tailed deer. The snowshoe hare uses it for food also, and cottontail rabbits often feed on ornamental specimens during the winter season. The seeds are eaten by red squirrels, and by such birds as crossbills and pine siskins.

The range of the northern white-cedar extends from southern Labrador and Nova Scotia west to Manitoba; south to Massachusetts, New York, central Ohio, northern Indiana and Illinois, and Minnesota; and occasionally southward along the Appalachian Mountains to North Carolina and Tennessee. It has been planted extensively both as an ornamental tree and as a hedge in North America. This species has also been introduced into Europe, where it may represent the earliest North American introduction.

The Red-Cedars—Juniperus

EASTERN RED-CEDAR *Juniperus virginiana* L.

The slim, conical shape of this tree, the sharp, awl-shaped and scale-shaped leaves, the reddish brown, shreddy bark, and the blue, berrylike "cones" are most distinctive.

Leaves opposite (rarely whorled on young plants), 4-ranked, U-shaped in cross section, dark bluish green, usually but not always pitted on the back, persisting on the twigs for five or six years, dimorphic: one about ¹⁄₁₆ inch long, scalelike, ovate, short or blunt-tipped, closely appressed to the branchlets; the other, on younger trees and more vigorous shoots, ¼ to ½ inch long, narrow, sharply pointed, awl-like, loosely arranged and spreading. *Cones* about ¼ inch in diameter, with fleshy scales, closely resembling a berry, nearly globular, dark blue, glaucous, tasting sweet but resinous, maturing in two to three years. *Bark* thin, light reddish brown, exfoliates in long, narrow, shreddy strips.

Comparisons. Vegetatively, this species can be separated from both the Atlantic white-cedar and the northern white-cedar by its having at least some needlelike leaves rather than all scalelike leaves, and by its 4-angled, rather than flattened, spraylike branchlets.

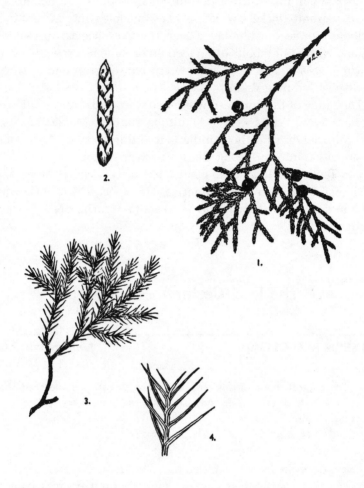

EASTERN RED-CEDAR

1. Branch with scale-like leaves and fruits.
2. Portion of branch with scale-like leaves.
3. Branch with awl-like leaves.
4. Portion of branch with awl-like leaves.

Eastern red-cedar is the most widespread of all of our native eastern conifers. It is also known as cedar, savin, and red juniper; the latter name being the most appropriate one, for the tree is really a juniper and not a true cedar. It is a medium-sized tree, usually 30 to 40 feet in height with a trunk diameter of 1 to 2 feet, although it occasionally attains a much larger size. Young trees characteristically have narrowly conical or columnar crowns, but in age the tree becomes rather irregular and round topped. The eastern red-cedar is typically a tree of dry and rocky soils. It is commonly found on limestone soils, or about limestone outcroppings on steep hillsides, and it frequently invades abandoned fields.

The soft, light, and fragrant wood of the red-cedar is durable in contact with the soil and is often used for fence posts. The heartwood is a dull red, contrasting with the nearly white and narrow sapwood. This wood is commonly employed in the manufacture of mothproof chests, for lead pencils, pails, furniture, and interior finish. Oil of cedar, used in polishes, medicines, and perfumes, is distilled from the leaves and wood. The red-cedar is one of the most desirable of our native evergreens for ornamental planting. It is slow growing but long lived.

The "cedar apples" often found on the twigs of the red-cedar are caused by a rust fungus, *Gymnosporangium juniperi-virginianae*, which has an alternate host in apple trees. It causes a leaf spot on apple leaves. Numerous species of wild birds feed on the berrylike fruits, particularly during the winter. The seeds pass unharmed through a bird's alimentary canal and are thus dispersed over the countryside.

The eastern red-cedar ranges from Nova Scotia south to northern Florida, and west to the Dakotas and Texas.

SOUTHERN RED-CEDAR

Juniperus virginiana var. *silicicola*
(Small) J. Silba

The southern red-cedar very closely resembles the eastern red-cedar, from which it is generally distinguished by its more slender, pendent or drooping branches, more rounded crown, and smaller fruits, which average about ⅛ inch in diameter. This expression occurs in or about the borders of coastal plain swamps and on sand dunes in the immediate vicinity of the coast, whereas the typical expression can also be found farther upland. Its range extends from southeastern North Carolina southward to central Florida, west to southern Mississippi, and also in southeastern Texas.

YEW FAMILY—TAXACEAE

The Florida-Nutmeg—Torreya

FLORIDA-NUTMEG   *Torreya taxifolia* **Arn.**

> The restricted distribution of northwestern Florida and southwestern Georgia; the 2-ranked, sharply pointed evergreen, needlelike leaves; and the twigs that emit a strongly disagreeable odor when crushed are distinctive.

Leaves 1 to 1½ inches long, ⅛ inch wide, opposite, simple, evergreen, linear, spirally arranged but appearing 2-ranked; rounded on the backs, lustrous above, occasionally falcate; silvery-white below with 2 stomatal lines paralleling the midvein; apices sharply pointed, bristle-tipped, bases tapered to short-stalked, dark green, yielding a fetid odor when crushed. *Cones* (aril) 1 to 1¼ inches long, fleshy, purplish, glaucous, ovoid, resembling an olive, containing a single seed, maturing at the end of the second year. *Twigs* with a disagreeable odor when crushed, bright green to reddish brown, hairy at first, becoming glabrous, branches whorled. *Bark* irregularly fissured and scaly, easily peeled, dark brown, tinged with orange.

The Florida-nutmeg, or stinking-cedar, is a small tree, 20 to 30 feet high, with a conical crown. It was discovered in 1833 by H. B. Croom and is a geographically restricted, rare species, known only from southwestern Georgia and adjacent Florida, occurring on limestone bluffs and ravines in the Apalachicola River region. Although seed germination is poor and individuals are susceptible to fungal root rot, it is a species that can do

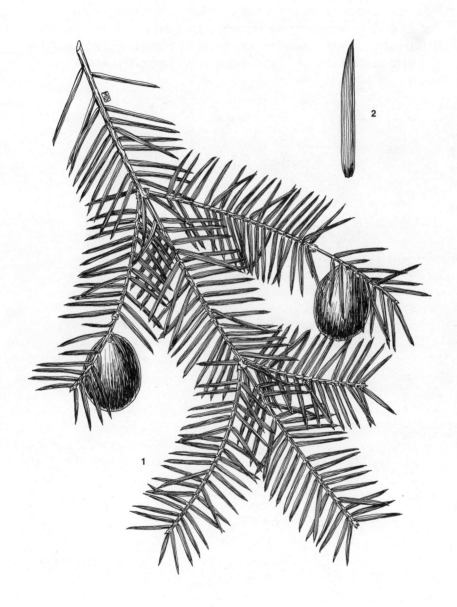

FLORIDA-NUTMEG

1. Branch with mature arils.   2. Detail of leaf.

well in cultivation and has been planted occasionally in some of our eastern states. One of its common names, stinking-cedar, comes from the fact that the crushed leaves and stems produce a strongly resinous odor offensive to some, especially over long exposures. The largest individual of this species in existence occurs in cultivation at the Biltmore Estate in western North Carolina.

MAGNOLIA FAMILY—MAGNOLIACEAE

The Magnolias—Magnolia

The leaves of the magnolias are alternate and simple with entire margins. They usually have a very prominent midrib, at least beneath, and are pinnately net-veined. The twigs are moderately stout to stout, usually quite glabrous, and conspicuously ringed at the nodes by the encircling stipule scars. The leaf scars are variable in shape but quite conspicuous, from nearly oval to crescent-shaped, with several bundle scars that are either scattered or arranged in a U-shaped line. The terminal buds are large, but the lateral ones are often very small and inconspicuous. They have a solitary outer scale, which is either glabrous or densely covered with silky hairs.

The flowers are usually quite showy and often fragrant. In our native species, flowering occurs after the leaves appear in late spring or early summer. The flowers are perfect, having 3 sepals, 6 or more petals arranged in series of 3, and numerous stamens and pistils. The fruits are a conelike aggregate of follicles that split open along one side at maturity, releasing the seeds on slender threads. The seeds have a thin, fleshy, scarlet-colored outer coat.

CUCUMBER-TREE　　　　　　　　　　*Magnolia acuminata* (L.) L.

> The large, round-based, deciduous leaves, which are paler green beneath than above, and the peculiar, cucumber-shaped, green terminal buds, along with the cucumber-shaped fruits, are most distinct.

Summer. *Leaves* 5 to 10 inches long, 3 to 6 inches wide, alternate, simple, deciduous, distributed in a scattered fashion along the twigs,

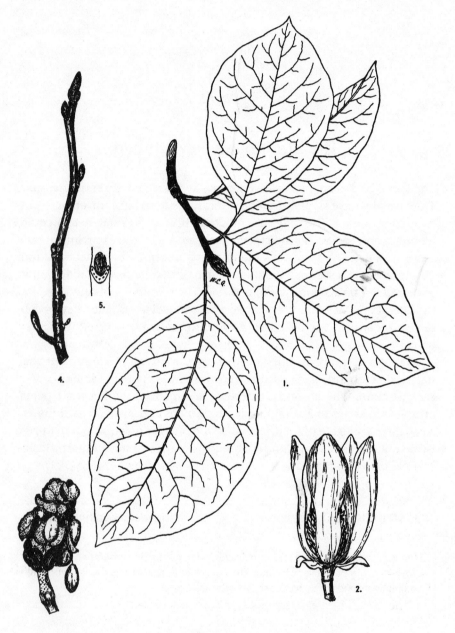

CUCUMBER-TREE

1. Branch with mature leaves.
2. Flower.
3. Fruit.
4. Winter twig.
5. Detail of bud and leaf scar.

broadly ovate, tips short-pointed, bases rounded or broadly wedge-shaped, margins entire but somewhat wavy; rather thin and membranous; upper surfaces light yellowish green; paler and usually finely hairy beneath; petioles short, rather stout, silky-hairy. *Flowers* 2 inches wide, perfect, bell-shaped, non-aromatic, solitary, at branch tips, appearing after leaves develop, very much resembling the leaves; petals 1½ to 3⅓ inches long, 6 per flower, fleshy, yellow green. *Fruits* in cones 2 to 3 inches long, in knobby clusters, green in early summer but turning red with the approach of fall, producing scarlet, fleshy seeds.

Winter. *Twigs* moderately stout, glabrous or slightly hairy, usually somewhat lustrous, with a spicy-aromatic odor, olive brown to pale reddish brown, with small, pale lenticels; stipule scars encircling the twigs at the nodes. Leaf scars narrowly crescent-shaped with 5- to 9-bundle scars. *Buds* large, pale greenish, densely covered with silvery-gray, silky hairs; terminal bud ½ to ¾ inch long, very much larger than the lateral buds, covered by single bud scale. *Bark* ashy brown, roughened by long furrows and narrow, scaly ridges.

The cucumber-tree, which is the most cold-hardy of our native magnolia species, is also known as the cucumber magnolia and mountain magnolia. It is a medium-sized to large tree, attaining a height of 60 to 90 feet and a trunk diameter of 2 to 4 feet. The slender branches are nearly horizontal below and shorter and ascending above, forming a broadly pyramidal crown. In the forest its trunk is straight, with a slight taper, and clear of lateral branches for some distance from the ground. It prefers deep, moist, and fertile soils, but is often found on rather rocky slopes. Seldom an abundant tree, it usually occurs as a scattered and minor associate in forests of oaks, beech-birch-maple, or northward into the mixed white pine and northern hardwood types.

The wood is light, soft, weak, brittle, close-grained, and durable. It is used for furniture, interior finish, siding, and woodenware. The cucumber-tree is very attractive, grows quite rapidly, and has many good qualities as a shade or ornamental tree. Ornamental magnolias of various kinds are often grafted on its roots. Its common name has been derived from the fancied resemblance of the fruits to cucumbers.

The cucumber-tree ranges from western New York and southern Ontario to northern Georgia and Florida, to Arkansas and Oklahoma.

The yellow cucumber-tree, or yellow-flowered magnolia (var. *subcordata* (Spach) Dandy) is a small tree attaining a height of about 25 feet, with a trunk up to about 10 inches in diameter, and with leaves 4 to 6 inches long, 3 to 4 inches wide, elliptic to oblong-obovate, with abruptly short-pointed tips, and broadly pointed to rounded bases. The flowers vary from canary yellow to orange, and the deep red, oblong clusters of fruits are seldom 1½ inches long. This tree was first described in 1803 by Andre Michaux, the French botanist who came to Charleston, South Carolina, in 1781, to collect New World plants for Louis XVI. For more than a century after Michaux collected and named the tree, it was known only in cultivation. Although it has more recently been rediscovered growing in a wild state, it is no longer recognized as a distinct taxon.

SOUTHERN MAGNOLIA   *Magnolia grandiflora* L.

> This magnolia is readily identified by its thick, leathery, wavy-margined evergreen leaves, which are bright lustrous green above and rust-colored beneath.

Leaves 5 to 9 inches long, 2 to 3 inches wide, thick, leathery, evergreen, oblong or elliptical, wavy-margined; upper surfaces bright lustrous green; lower surfaces paler and usually, but not always, densely rusty-hairy; petioles stout. *Twigs* also usually rusty-hairy. *Flowers* large, showy, aromatic, pure white, borne singly at branch end; petals 2 to 3 inches long, numbering 6 to 12. *Fruits* in cones 2½ to 4 inches long. *Bark* light brown or grayish brown, with small, thin scales.

Comparisons. The only other native evergreen magnolia in North America is the sweet-bay, which has smaller, narrower, and thinner leaves that are whitish or occasionally green rather than brown-hairy beneath (easy to observe in the wind) and less lustrous above, and has much smaller flowers.

The southern magnolia, which is also known as the evergreen magnolia or bull-bay, is one of the most striking and characteristic trees of the deep South. It grows naturally about the borders of the great coastal swamps, in hammocks, and along the banks of streams, but it has been extensively planted as a shade or ornamental tree as far inland as the foothills of the southern mountains. The tree attains a height of 60 to 90 feet or more with a trunk from 2 to 4 feet, or occasionally more, in diameter. In the open it develops an oblong to somewhat conical, dense, and symmetrical crown.

SOUTHERN MAGNOLIA

1. Branch with flower and mature
   leaves.
2. Fruit.
3. Terminal bud.
4. Mature leaf.

From late spring through the early summer the tree produces a succession of cup-shaped, white or creamy-white, lemon-scented flowers from 6 to 8 inches across. They are followed by ovoid, dull red, usually rusty-hairy fruit clusters from 3 to 4 inches in length. The southern magnolia is the principal source of magnolia lumber, which is used in the manufacture of furniture, boxes, sash, doors, veneer, and millwork. Most of it comes from the lower Mississippi Valley. It is the state tree of both Louisiana and Mississippi.

The range of the southern magnolia extends through the coastal plain from southeastern Virginia and North Carolina to central Florida west to eastern Texas.

SWEET-BAY   *Magnolia virginiana* L.

> The wonderfully aromatic leaves, which are usually distinctly glaucous beneath, and the showy, white, fragrant spring flowers of this species, which are the smallest of our native species, are most distinctive.

Summer. *Leaves* 3 to 5 inches long, 1 to 3 inches wide, alternate, evergreen or semievergreen, ovate to narrowly elliptical, tips bluntly pointed, bases wedge-shaped, margins entire; upper surfaces dark green, lustrous, except for the midrib; lower surfaces glabrous or nearly so, often conspicuously whitened. *Flowers* 2 or 3 inches in diameter, appearing in early summer, perfect, cup-shaped, creamy white, very fragrant; petals 1 to 2 inches long, numbering 8 to 12. *Fruits* in cones 1¼ to 2 inches long, oblong, glabrous, an aggregate of capsules, containing shiny crimson fleshy seeds.

Winter. *Leaves* often persisting well through the winter. *Twigs* rather slender, bright green during the first season but becoming reddish brown during the second, glabrous or nearly so. Leaf scars vary from semiovate to crescent-shaped, with several bundle scars arranged in a U-shaped line. *Buds* terminal, ¼ to ¾ inch long, greenish, covered with short, silvery gray, silky hairs; lateral buds very small, curved, inconspicuous. *Bark* light gray, quite glabrous.

Comparisons. Of our two evergreen magnolias, the sweet-bay differs from the southern magnolia by having much smaller leaves that are whitish or greenish rather than rusty beneath. The hairy undersurface of sweet-bay leaves and entire leaf margins help to separate this species from the loblolly-bay.

SWEET-BAY

1. Branch with leaves.
2. Leaf.
3. Flowering branch.
4. Fruit.
5. Detail of bud and leaf scar (enlarged).

The sweet-bay is also known as the sweetbay magnolia, laurel magnolia, or swamp magnolia. It is a small tree, rarely attaining a height of 20 feet, at least in the North, but it reaches much larger proportions in the South. Like the willow oak and the sweet-gum, the sweet-bay is characteristically a tree of the coastal plain swamps. In the southern part of its range the leaves are evergreen, but northward they are at least tardily deciduous.

The wood of the sweet-bay is similar to that of the cucumber-tree and other magnolias, but it is of relatively little commercial importance because of its small size. It is occasionally used for furniture, boxes, and venetian blinds. The tree is often planted ornamentally, and it is one of our most attractive native woody plants.

The sweet-bay ranges from southeastern Massachusetts southward in the Atlantic Coast states to Florida, and westward along the Gulf Coast to Louisiana and Texas.

UMBRELLA MAGNOLIA   *Magnolia tripetala* (L.) L.

The large, ill-scented flowers and the very large, thin or membranous, terminally clustered (like an umbrella) leaves of this tree, which are long-tapered at the base, along with the large, purple, glabrous buds, help to distinguish it from all other species of the genus.

Summer. *Leaves* 12 to 24 inches long, deciduous, thin or membranous, clustered at branch tips, obovate, tips short-pointed, base long-tapered, margins entire but often wavy; petioles short, stout. *Flowers* 4 to 5 inches high, white, ill-scented, cup-shaped; petals 3⅓ to 5 inches long, 6 to 9 per flower, light purple filaments. *Fruits* in cones 2½ to 4 inches long, ovoid oblong, glabrous.

Winter. *Twigs* stout, glabrous, but hairy near apex, lustrous, light brown to greenish brown, with spicy-aromatic odor, noticeably swollen at the base of each year's growth, as well as encircled by stipule scars. Leaf scars large, conspicuous, mainly clustered on the swollen parts of the twig, ovate, with several scattered bundle scars. *Buds,* terminal bud large, up to 2 inches long, conical, often curved, purplish, glaucous, covered with small pale dots; lateral buds very small, inconspicuous. *Bark* light gray, quite smooth, irregularly roughened with lumpy excrescences.

Comparisons. Only the big-leaf and Ashe magnolias produce leaves larger than the umbrella magnolia; however, their leaves are conspicuously

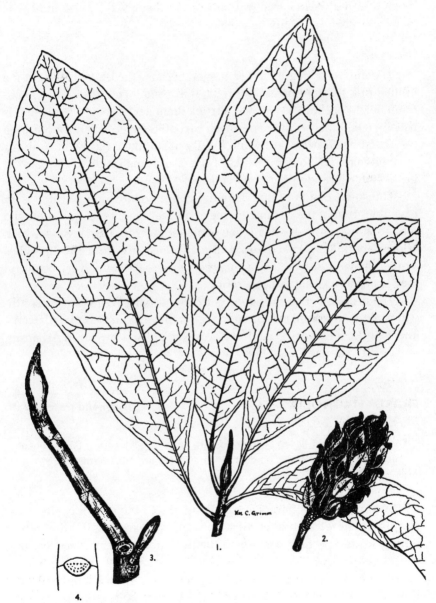

UMBRELLA MAGNOLIA

1. Branch with mature leaves.
2. Fruit.
3. Winter twig.
4. Leaf scar.

heart-shaped or eared rather than long-tapered basally. The flowers of the umbrella magnolia differ from those of the two former species by being ill-scented rather than fragrant. It can be separated from the cucumber-tree by its terminally clustered (rather than well-spaced) leaves, and by its glabrous rather than hairy terminal buds.

———————

The umbrella magnolia is so named because the leaves cluster at the branch tips, resembling an umbrella. It is a small tree attaining a maximum height of about 40 feet and a trunk diameter of about 1 foot, but it is usually much smaller in the northern part of its range. It is not a common tree, occurring rather rarely and locally in stands of hardwoods, and is most often found along the banks of rivers and small tributary streams. It prefers a fertile and rather moist soil.

The soft wood is of no particular commercial value, but it closely resembles that of the cucumber-tree and other magnolias. The umbrella magnolia makes a very attractive ornamental tree. The flowers, which appear about May, are creamy white and measure from 6 to 10 inches across. They are surrounded by the new leaves. Although very beautiful they have a rather unpleasant scent.

The umbrella magnolia ranges from southern Pennsylvania southward in the Appalachian Mountain region to northern Georgia, Alabama, and Florida, and west to central Kentucky and southwestern Arkansas, and north to Indiana and Ohio.

FRASER MAGNOLIA   *Magnolia fraseri* Walt.

> The yellow, fragrant flowers and deciduous, eared-based leaves of this mountain species, which are glabrous on their lower surfaces, are most distinctive.

Summer. *Leaves* 9 to 12 inches long, 5 to 7 inches wide, alternate, simple, clustered at branch tips, obovate or heart-shaped, tips rather bluntly acute to obtuse, bases prominently eared; upper surface lustrous, bright green, lower surface paler, glabrous; petioles 2 to 4 inches long. *Flowers* 8 to 10 inches wide, fragrant; petals 1/3 to 1/2 inch long, 6 to 9 per flower. *Fruits* in cones usually 2 2/3 to 4 inches long, glabrous, oblong, becoming bright red at maturity.

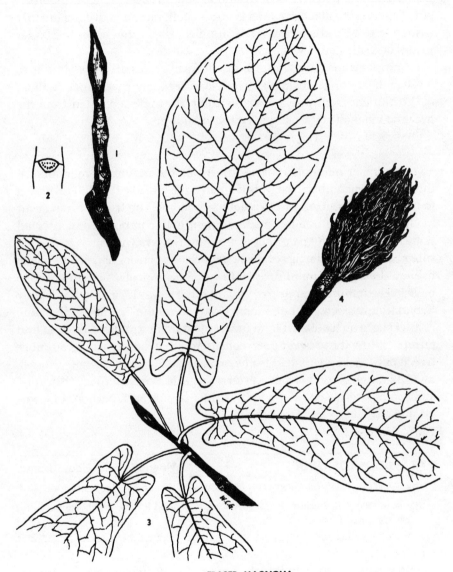

FRASER MAGNOLIA

1. Winter twig.
2. Detail of leaf-scar.
3. Branch with leaves.
4. Fruit.

Winter. *Twigs* moderately stout, dark reddish brown, glabrous, dotted with prominent lenticels. *Buds,* terminal bud 1 to 2 inches long, glabrous, purplish, may be glaucous; lateral buds small, placed above the broadly U-shaped or shield-shaped leaf scars. *Bark* dark brown, on the larger trunks becoming somewhat scaly.

Comparisons. The winter buds of this species are very similar to those of the umbrella magnolia. The leaves are somewhat similar to those of the big-leaf magnolia, but are smaller. It can be separated from the pyramid magnolia by its larger leaves and flowers.

———

The Fraser magnolia is also known as the mountain magnolia or the ear-leaf cucumber-tree. It is a small tree, usually from 30 to 40 feet in height, with a trunk 1 to 1½ feet in diameter. The trunks often occur in clumps and the tree has a spreading crown composed of contorted branches. In May, the pale yellow, fragrant flowers with an 8- to 12-inch spread are borne at the tips of the branchlets. The Fraser magnolia's native habitats are the cool, moist coves of the southern Appalachians. It seems to have been first discovered by William Bartram in 1775, in what is now Rabun County, Georgia, but Thomas Walter was the first to validly name it, after the Scotch botanist John Fraser, who first introduced the tree into Europe. While it has never been considered to be important as a timber tree, it does make a very handsome ornamental.

The range extends from western Virginia, southern West Virginia, and southeastern Kentucky southward to the northern portions of Georgia and Alabama.

PYRAMID MAGNOLIA   *Magnolia pyramidata* Bartr.

The southern distribution and large, rhombic-shaped leaves, which are basally eared, are most distinctive.

Summer. *Leaves* 5 to 9 inches long, 3 to 4 inches wide, alternate, deciduous, clustered near branch tips, clearly widest about or above the middle, blunt at apex, narrowed to an eared base, margins entire, bright green above, glabrous and green below. *Flowers* about 4 to 6 inches across, solitary at branch tips; petals 2 to 4½ inches long; stamens white to creamy white, 3/16 to ¼ inch long. *Fruits* 1½ to 2½ inches long, rose-colored clusters, seldom more than 2 inches long.

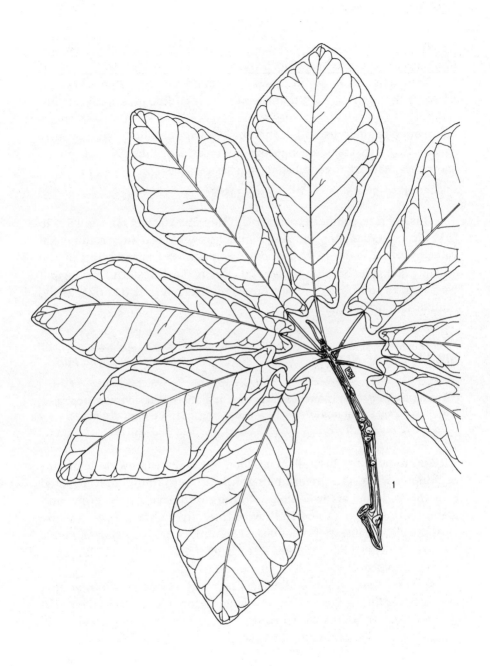

1

PYRAMID MAGNOLIA

1. Branch with cordate-based leaves and twig.

Winter. *Twigs* slender to moderately thick, dark reddish brown; terminal bud ¾ to 1 inch long. *Bark* brown.

Comparisons. Pyramid magnolia is similar to the larger-flowered Fraser magnolia; however, that species occurs in the mountains farther north. Pyramid magnolia is also similar to northern Florida's Ashe magnolia, but has glabrous, rather than hairy, twigs and buds, significantly smaller leaves that lack the glaucous undersurface of the Ashe magnolia, and petals that lack the reddish purple bases as well.

———

This is a rare, southern coastal plain tree, 35 to 60 feet high and 8⅛ to 24½ inches in diameter, with a pyramidal crown. It is of little commercial value. It grows in dense, rich woods on upland slopes and bluffs on the coastal plain from South Carolina to Georgia, northwestern Florida, and westward to southeastern Louisiana and Texas. It is also known as the southern cucumber-tree.

BIG-LEAF MAGNOLIA   *Magnolia macrophylla* **Michx.**

> The huge creamy-white flowers, each as large as a dinner plate, and huge, tropical-looking leaves, the largest leaves of any native magnolias, are most distinct.

Summer. *Leaves* 20 to 30 inches long, up to 12 inches wide, alternate, deciduous, huge, obovate or oblong, tips acute to rounded, contracted near the middle, narrowed below to the eared base, bright green and glabrous above, whitish beneath with fine, silvery hairs. *Flowers* white with purple, purple-spotted at base, fragrant, open, bell-shaped; petals 6⅛ to 8⅛ inches long; stamens ⅔ to ¾ inch long. *Fruits* subglobose to globose, pubescent.

Winter. *Twigs* stout, yellowish green, silvery-hairy when young, deciduous at the end of the first growing season. *Buds,* terminal bud 1½ to 2 inches long, coated with a white wool. *Bark* thin, light gray, smooth; on older trunks becoming minutely scaly.

———

The big-leaf or large-leaf magnolia is usually a small tree. It occasionally attains a height of about 50 feet and a trunk diameter of about a foot. The creamy-white flowers are often nearly 20 inches across, and give rise to globular, rosy-red clusters of fruits 2 to 3 inches long. It makes a handsome subject for ornamental planting. The tree occurs rather locally and rarely from Virginia and western North Carolina, central Kentucky, and southern Ohio southward to Georgia, northwestern Florida, Alabama, Mississippi, and Louisiana. Because of its unusual, spectacularly large flowers and leaves, this species has great potential for horticultural use. As with many magnolia species, however, it succumbs quickly in wet, poorly drained soil.

ASHE MAGNOLIA   *Magnolia ashei* **Weatherby**

> Its huge leaves with eared bases and large, white, fragrant flowers with reddish purple marks at their bases are most distinctive.

This shrub or small tree species is similar to the treelike big-leaf magnolia, but differs by having very crooked or gnarled trunks, shorter stamens (½ versus ⅔ to ¾ inch long), and flowering very early, during the second or third seasons, with some individuals producing flowers when only 4 inches high. It is a rare species known only in wooded slopes and bluffs in the Appalachicola region of northwestern Florida. It is much prized as an ornamental tree in the South and does well as far north as North Carolina and Virginia.

The Tuliptree—Liriodendron

TULIPTREE   *Liriodendron tulipifera* **L.**

> Most unique about this species is the unusual, palmately lobed and keystone-shaped leaf blade, which appears as though the tip was removed, along with the peculiar duck-bill–shaped winter buds and aromatic twigs.

Summer. *Leaves* alternate, simple, with an unusual square shape; lobes usually 4, occasionally 6 or more, base broad, with a broadly notched or indented summit; general outline suggests that of a keystone; blades

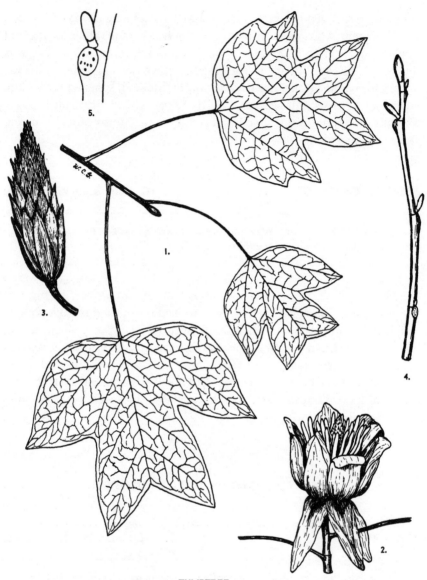

TULIPTREE

1. Branch with mature leaves.
2. Flower.
3. Fruit.

4. Winter twig.
5. Detail of bud and leaf scar.

4 to 6 inches across, about as long; very glabrous on both surfaces, dark green and lustrous above, paler and often slightly glaucous beneath; stipules large, ovate-shaped, often persistent on vigorous sprouts, ordinarily deciduous on the other twigs; petioles 3 to 6 inches long, glabrous, round, slender. *Flowers* magnolia-like or tuliplike, appearing after the leaves are developed in late May or June, with 3 sepals; petals number 6, greenish yellow with orange areas at their base.

Winter. *Fruits* (samara) 2 to 3 inches long, cone-shaped aggregate, usually persisting on the branches until individual samaras are in senescence, leaving the central stalk behind. *Twigs* moderately stout, olive brown to light reddish brown, very glabrous, usually quite lustrous, with a spicy aromatic odor, encircled by prominent stipule scars at the nodes. Leaf scars roundish, somewhat elevated, several bundle scars arranged in a circle. *Buds,* scales glabrous, greenish to reddish brown, glaucous; terminal bud ½ to ¾ inch long, oblong to narrowly ovate, 2-scaled, purplish-glaucous, white-spotted, duck-bill–shaped, flattened, more or less 2-edged; lateral buds much smaller, rather divergent. *Bark* on the younger trunks and branches quite smooth, light ashy gray, with very shallow, longitudinal, whitish deep furrows; on older trunks becoming very thick with deeply rounded, interlacing furrows and rather narrow, rounded ridges.

The tuliptree is also known as the yellow-poplar, tulip magnolia, tulip poplar, and whitewood. Actually it is not a poplar, but a member of the Magnolia Family. The fancied resemblance of the flowers to tulips has given the tree its common name of tuliptree. In the fall, the colorful yellow leaves add significantly to the autumn tapestry.

The tuliptree is one of the largest and finest of eastern American hardwoods. It commonly attains a height of 80 to 100 feet and a trunk diameter of 2 to 5 feet. Occasional specimens may be 150 feet or more in height, and have trunks 8 to 12 feet in diameter. In the forest it develops a straight and slightly tapering trunk that is clear of branches for a great distance from the ground. In the open the young trees have a pyramidal form, but the older trees develop rather shallow, broad, and open crowns. It prefers a deep, rich, moist soil, and although it is commonly found in bottomlands, it also occupies the rocky slopes of the mountains.

The wood is light, soft, brittle, weak, and is very easily worked. It is sold commercially as "yellow poplar" and used for furniture, interior finish, siding, shingles, musical instruments, toys and novelties, and various small articles. The bitter inner bark, particularly that of the roots, is sometimes used as a tonic and stimulant. Bees make quantities of honey from the flowers. The fruits provide some food for squirrels in the late fall and winter months, and white-tailed deer often browse on the twigs. The tuliptree makes a very desirable street, shade, or ornamental tree. The leaves turn to a bright orange-yellow in the fall.

The tuliptree ranges from Massachusetts to southern Michigan, south to northern Florida and Louisiana.

CUSTARD-APPLE FAMILY— ANNONACEAE

The Pawpaw—Asimina

COMMON PAWPAW *Asimina triloba* (L.) Dunal

> The large, deciduous, drooping leaves, which are broadest above the middle and have a rank odor, along with the large, bananalike fruit, and conspicuous chocolate-colored, flat, featherlike, naked buds are most distinctive.

Summer. *Leaves* 4 to 12 inches long, 2 to 4 inches wide, alternate, simple, deciduous, clustered apically, narrowly obovate, margins entire, with rank, green-pepperlike odor, tips short-pointed, gradually narrowed from above the middle to the pointed base; rather thin, conspicuously veiny and drooping; upper surfaces dark green, glabrous at maturity or with few appressed red hairs when young, paler and glabrous beneath or slightly hairy on the veins; petioles short, stout. *Flowers* ¾ to 2 inches wide, perfect, solitary, purplish or maroon, with strongly disagreeable odor, developing in the spring before or with the leaves on previous year's branches; petals 6, in 2 series. *Fruits* (berry) 3 to 5 inches long, 1 to 2 inches wide, resembling a stubby yellow banana, with thick brownish skin when ripe, becoming black when fully ripe in autumn; soft, sweet pulp containing several large, dark brown seeds.

Winter. *Twigs* rather slender, somewhat zigzag, aromatic, striate with whitish linear grooves, at first covered with rusty hairs but later becoming glabrous and olive-brown; pith diaphragmed or continuous, but occasionally chambered; leaf scars alternate, crescent-shaped or U-shaped, with usually 5 to 7 bundle scars. *Buds* naked, coated with chocolate-brown hairs; terminal bud ½ to ¾ inch long, narrow, elongated, often curved, somewhat flattened, resembling a chocolate feather; lateral buds about

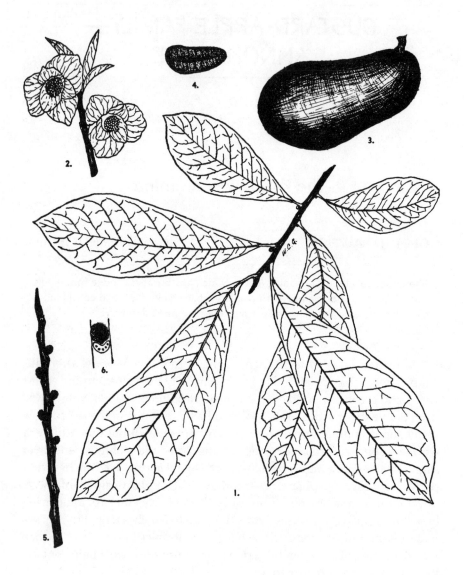

COMMON PAWPAW

1. Branch with mature leaves.
2. Flowering branch.
3. Fruit.
4. Seed.
5. Winter twig.
6. Detail of bud and leaf scar.

⅛ inch long, roundish, superposed, globose, stalked. *Bark* rather thin, quite smooth, brown, often blotched whitish.

Comparisons. The naked winter buds of this species are somewhat similar to those of the American witch-hazel, but differ by being chocolate rather than tan in color and more featherlike, rather than deer-footlike. The leaves are also somewhat similar to a deciduous magnolia or perhaps the black gum or the water tupelo, but those species have glabrous twigs and scaled, rather than naked, buds.

———

The common pawpaw is the only hardy member of the tropical custard-apple family, Annonaceae. It is a large shrub or small tree, sometimes attaining a height of nearly 40 feet with a trunk up to 1 foot in diameter. In the North, however, it seldom attains a height of more than 15 or 20 feet, and trunks are only a few inches in diameter. The plant has a singularly tropical appearance with its large and often drooping leaves. In the fall, it produces beautifully colored yellow foliage.

Pawpaws (from the Arawakan name of papaya) prefer to grow in moist and fertile situations. They are most commonly found in the stream valleys or on the lower slopes of the adjoining hills. Being very tolerant of shade, they are usually found in the understory of the forest, but they often occupy small clearings and roadsides where the sun filters through the crowns of the larger trees. The wood is of no commercial value, but the inner bark was valued historically in the production of cord and fish nets. The fruits are edible and nutritious, although many people do not relish their flavor. They are of two types: one with yellow flesh and an appealing taste, the other with whitish, nearly tasteless pulp. An alkaloid known as asiminine (for which the genus is named) is contained within the seeds, and it is reported that sensitive individuals who handle the fruits develop a dermatitis. The pawpaw is occasionally planted as an ornamental and it is indeed very attractive when in foliage, or when in flower in the early spring.

The common pawpaw ranges from southern New York southward to Florida and west to Nebraska and Texas.

LAUREL FAMILY—LAURACEAE

The Sassafras—Sassafras

SASSAFRAS   *Sassafras albidum* **(Nutt.) Nees.**

> Easily recognized by the spicy aromatic odor of its broken twigs and leaves when crushed, yellowish green branches and twigs, variably shaped, 0- to 3-lobed leaves, and by its very attractive, blue to black fruits on scarlet stalks.

Summer. *Leaves* 3 to 6 inches long, 2 to 4 inches wide, alternate, simple, deciduous, obovate to ovate, margins entire, 3 palmately veined, tips bluntly-pointed, bases wedge-shaped; glabrous and bright green above, paler and glabrous or slightly hairy beneath; variably shaped with three types found often on the same branch: unlobed, 3-lobed, and some that are 2-lobed and mitten-shaped; turning yellow and red in the autumn; petioles ½ to 1 inch long, slender, often reddish; stipules lacking. *Flowers* about ¼ inch wide, borne in loose terminal clusters, yellow to yellow-green, 6-parted perianth, corolla lacking; perfect, male and female flowers produced on separate trees. *Fruits* (drupe) ⅜ to ½ inch long, small, berrylike, dark blue, shiny, each borne in a cuplike structure, produced on a club-shaped, bright red stalk.

Winter. *Twigs* very brittle, stout, lustrous yellowish green or olive green, occasionally tinged with brown, very spicy and aromatic, often quite crooked or irregular in growth, pubescent to glabrous; leaf scars alternate, semiround, with a solitary dashlike bundle scar; stipule scars lacking. *Buds* ovoid, pointed, often slightly hairy, bright green, about the same color as the twig; terminal bud usually ⅓ to ⅗ inch long, scales 3 to 4, distinctly larger than the lateral buds, green. *Bark* on older trunks

SASSAFRAS

1. Branch with mature leaves.
2. Fruits.
3. Winter twig.
4. Details of bud and leaf scar.

becoming thick, reddish brown, with deep irregular fissures and flat-topped ridges, resembling a furlike texture, with frequent horizontal ax-mark cracks.

————

The sassafras is a small tree, often 20 to 40 feet in height with a trunk 1 to 2 feet in diameter. It reaches much larger size in the southern portion of its range. It usually has a comparatively short trunk, and the contorted branches form a flat-topped to rounded, rather open crown. It is a member of the laurel family, Lauraceae. (The plants that we usually call "laurels" are not laurels at all, being members of the heath family, Ericaceae.) Due to its many reported medicinal uses the sassafras is well known to country folk, and thus understandably represented one of the earliest North American trees to be introduced into Europe. It grows along the fencerows and the roadsides and often invades abandoned fields, preferring a sandy or stony, but fairly fertile soil.

The wood is soft, weak, brittle, coarse-grained, aromatic, and durable in contact with the soil. It is used for posts and furniture, and is sometimes marketed as ash or chestnut lumber. Although reported to be a carcinogen, sassafras tea, a great favorite in many rural areas, is brewed from the bark of the roots, which are dug in the early spring. The oil that is distilled from the bark is commonly used as a flavoring in candies, tobacco, and medicines, and is sometimes also used to perfume soaps. The young leaves and the pith of the branchlets are very mucilaginous, and when dried and powdered are used like gumbo to thicken soups. The berrylike fruits are extensively eaten by wild birds, including the bobwhite.

The sassafras ranges from Maine and Massachusetts to Michigan and Kansas, south to Florida and eastern Texas.

The Camphortree—Cinnamomum

CAMPHORTREE	*Cinnamomum camphora* (L.) J. Presl

> The small, fragrant, yellowish or greenish-white flowers and the evergreen leaves, which when crushed produce a distinct camphor odor, are most characteristic.

Summer. *Leaves* 2 to 5 inches long, alternate, simple, evergreen, leathery, lustrous, palmately veined with 3 major veins, elliptic to ovate, broadest at or below the middle; bright green and glabrous above, pale green and glaucous below; margins entire, wavy, achlorophyllus at edges; apices long-acuminate, bases cuneate to broadly rounded, leaves produce a strong camphor odor when crushed; petioles 1 to 3 inches or more. *Flowers* ⅛ inch long, tiny, fragrant, perfect, yellow to greenish-white, produced in clusters on the branches within the leaf axils in late spring. *Fruits* (berry) ⅓ to ½ inch wide, black, globose, with a spicy taste of camphor.

Winter. *Twigs* slender, glabrous, reddish or greenish, with the same camphor odor as the leaves and fruits. *Trunks* usually numerous.

The camphortree is a popular Asian ornamental, introduced into the deep South, where it is often used for shade. It is a 30- to 40-foot-high evergreen tree with a rounded crown. In some areas it is thoroughly naturalized, ranging from North Carolina westward to Texas. It spreads vegetatively by root suckering and by seeds passing through the digestive tracts of birds. This species can be seen growing in dry areas and along fencerows. Peculiar among most tree species is the camphortree's branching pattern, whereby new twigs are produced from the sides of existing branches rather than at the terminals. In Far Eastern Asia, the wood is used to repel insects and in cabinetmaking.

CAMPHORTREE

1. Branch with leaves (with wavy leaf margins) and fruits.

The Bays—Persea

RED BAY *Persea borbonia* (L.) Spreng.
SWAMP BAY *Persea palustris* (Raf.) Sarg.

> The alternate, evergreen leaves and twigs of these very similar species have a spicy aromatic odor similar to that of the sassafras.

Leaves 2 to 8 inches long, 1 to 2 inches wide, evergreen, elliptical to lanceolate, pointed at both ends, entire, revolute, aromatic; bright green and glabrous above, glabrous and grayish white beneath with short, tightly appressed pubescence (use lens) that lies parallel to the leaf surface in the red bay; more or less dense rusty-hairy beneath in the swamp bay, especially along the midrib and petiole, appearing gnarled or crooked rather than appressed; petioles about ½ inch long. *Flowers* small, 3/16 inch long, apetalous, perfect, inconspicuous, cream to white, developing in few-flowered panicles in the spring. *Fruits* (drupe) 3/8 to 5/8 inch long, dark blue or black, lustrous, ovoid; seated on a persistent calyx base; borne singly or in small clusters on axillary stalks, which are glabrous and ½ to 1 inch or less long in the red bay, and 1 to about 2½ inches long and rusty-hairy in the swamp bay. *Twigs* glabrous to slightly hairy with short hairs, light brown; leaf scar linear to elliptical with single bundle scar. *Buds,* terminal bud about ¼ inch long, naked, hairy. *Bark* reddish brown, divided by irregular fissures into flat, scaly ridges. The hairs on the undersurface of the leaves are most important in separating these two bay species.

Comparisons. The red bay differs from the swamp bay by occurring in more mesic maritime forests, well-drained hammocks, and coastal dunes, rather than wet, wooded sites. It also differs by having glabrous or short, straight, appressed-hairy (rather than long, often erect or contorted hairs) leaf undersurfaces, which lack the orangish or buff wax on the veins that is commonly found on the swamp bay; by having glabrous petioles and twigs; and by having shorter fruiting peduncles (½ to 1 versus 1 to 2 inches long). Both of these bays can be separated from the loblolly-bay by their aromatic, entire leaves versus the unscented and toothed leaf margins of the latter.

RED BAY

1. Fruiting branch.
2. Branch with mature leaves.
3. Detail of bud and leaf scar.

The red bay and the swamp bay are beautiful, small evergreen trees seldom more than 30 to 50 feet in height with a trunk diameter of 1 to 2 feet. They are common trees in the forests of the South Atlantic and Gulf Coastal Plains. They produce wood of relatively little commercial value but are used locally in cabinetmaking and for fine interior finish. The leaves make an excellent substitute for those of the true bay and have been used in the same manner for seasoning various foods, such as gumbo and meats, in the South.

The red bay is found in swamps close to the coast from North Carolina south to southern Florida and west to Texas. The more common and widespread swamp bay ranges throughout the coastal plain from Maryland and southern Delaware, to eastern Virginia south to Florida and west to Texas.

PLANETREE FAMILY—PLATANACEAE

The Sycamores and the Planetrees—Platanus

These are large trees with conspicuously exfoliating bark. The leaves are alternate, simple, deciduous, palmately lobed and veined. The petioles are hollow at their bases, enclosing the buds. The plants are monoecious and the green flowers are quite small, bracted, and in dense, spherical heads. Generally, the calyx and corolla are lacking, but there are usually 3 to 8 stamens with short filaments. The pistillate flowers have 2 to 9 distinct pistils and several staminodes. The unique achene-type fruits are contained within 1 to several spherical heads.

AMERICAN SYCAMORE   *Platanus occidentalis* **L.**

> Large individuals of this species are easily recognized, even at great distances, by their exfoliating or mottled bark, and massive, spreading branches. Its ball-like fruit clusters and large, maplelike leaves with 3 palmate veins also make it easy to identify. The winter twigs are easily recognized by the petiole scar completely surrounding the elongated buds.

Summer. *Leaves* 4 to 8 inches wide, alternate, simple, deciduous, broadly ovate to orbicular, somewhat maplelike in general appearance; lobes shallow, shorter than wide, 3 to 5, coarsely and wavy-toothed, tips acuminate-pointed, separated by very broad and usually shallow sinuses, terminal lobe shorter than wide; blades thin but firm, bright green and glabrous above, paler beneath, at first coated with flocculent, whitish hairs but eventually becoming glabrous or nearly so; petioles 1½ to 3 inches long, round, stout, usually hairy, with unusually swollen and hollow bases covering the bud; stipules large, leaflike; often persisting, particularly on the more vigorous growth. *Flowers* small, in dense globose

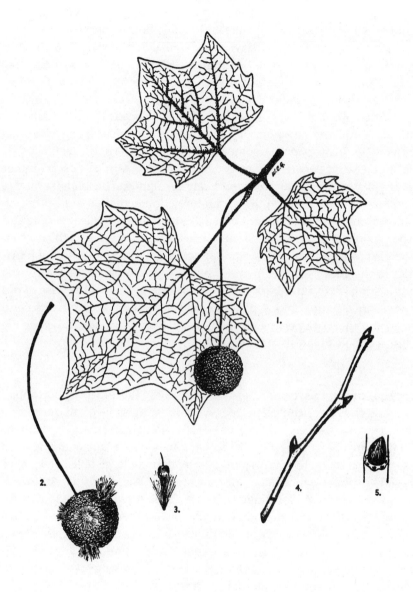

AMERICAN SYCAMORE

1. Branch with mature leaves and fruit.
2. Ball-like head of fruits.
3. An individual fruit (achene).

4. Winter twig.
5. Details of bud and leaf scar.

heads, appearing with the leaves, with 3 to 6 sepals and with an equal number of petals; unisexual, male and female flowers borne on the same tree; male flower head ¾ inch wide, red; female flower head 1 inch wide, somewhat larger than male head, green to reddish. *Fruits* in ball-like heads about 1 to 1¼ inches in diameter, usually borne solitary at the ends of slender, drooping stalks, 3 to 6 inches long.

Winter. *Fruits* (achene) produced in globose heads 1 inch in diameter, persisting through the winter. *Twigs* moderately slender, zigzag, yellowish brown to grayish, glabrous; somewhat swollen at the nodes, encircled by the stipule scars, decurrently ridged below the leaf scars; leaf scars rather narrow, margins wavy, almost completely surrounding the buds; several (5 to 9) bundle scars. *Buds* ¼ to ⅜ inch long, dome-shaped, dull-pointed, rather strongly divergent, light brown, hidden under the leaf petiole and exposed only after leaf abscission; covered with what appears to be a solitary visible scale, but scales number actually 3: inner one sticky-hairy, middle one sticky with resin, outer one shiny and usually red; terminal bud lacking. *Bark* outer bark dark brown, rather thick at the base of old trunks, broken into oblong platelike scales; on the younger trunks and branches, outer bark peeling off spontaneously in thin plates, exposing the whitish or pale greenish inner bark.

The American sycamore, also known as the buttonwood, buttonball tree, and the American planetree, is the most massive of all our native deciduous trees, exceeding all others in trunk diameter. Large specimens often attain a height of 100 to 175 feet and may have trunks ranging from 3 to 8 feet in diameter. Stumps from exceptionally large felled trees have served as square-dance floors in some areas of West Virginia. An exceptionally large one in Worthington, Indiana, measured 42.2 feet in circumference. Sycamore trunks usually divide low into several large secondary trunks, and the massive, spreading branches form a deep but rather open irregular crown. Hollow trunks are commonly found and were historically used for storage facilities for grain and for smoking meat. They also serve as excellent nesting sites for chimney swifts and other wildlife. The sycamore is characteristically a tree of the bottomlands, and to most of us it is closely associated with the banks of rivers and creeks. It attains its maximum development in the lower Ohio and Mississippi valleys. It is a shade-intolerant species and is very susceptible to fire as well as a fungal disease known as anthracnose. A similar disease, which is also destroying the flowering dogwood, can be especially prevalent during cool, wet springs, when it can kill young growth and weaken the tree, thus increasing its susceptibility to various secondary infections.

The wood is heavy, hard, tough, coarse-grained, and is difficult to work or split. It is used for furniture (both solid and veneer), interior finish, siding, musical instruments, boxes, and crates. At one time, practically all butcher blocks were made from the sycamore. While sometimes planted as a shade or street tree, it is much less commonly employed for such purposes than the London planetree.

The American sycamore ranges from Maine and Ontario south to northern Florida, west to the eastern portions of Nebraska, Kansas, and Texas.

The Oriental planetree (*P. orientalis* L.) from Asia differs from our native species by having a greenish white rather than white inner bark; 5–7 (versus 5) lobes, more deeply divided, which are longer than wide; and with much smaller fruiting heads (1 inch or less in diameter) occurring in clusters of 2 to 6.

LONDON PLANETREE   *Platanus hybrida* Brot.

The London planetree, a European species, supposedly arose from hybrid origin between the native American sycamore and the Oriental planetree (*Platanus orientalis* L.). The latter is very seldom seen in this country, although its name is very commonly misapplied to the London plane, which is very extensively planted as a street and shade tree.

The London planetree too closely resembles our native American sycamore in both leaf and bark characteristics to be readily distinguished from it. However, the terminal leaf lobe of the London planetree is as long or longer than wide. Also, the fruit heads are commonly borne in 2s or 3s per stalk, while those of the native American sycamore are usually solitary. The Oriental planetree regularly has 8 or more fruit heads to a common stalk. The London planetree also differs by exposing a greenish or yellow-brown inner bark and by having smaller leaves, which are less hairy with 2 to 5 (usually 3) lobes, with only the middle lobe being as long or longer than broad. Also, the bark of the London planetree tends to be more brown than white in patches where the bark has been removed.

The London planetree is not only popular but ideally adapted for street and shade tree purposes. It grows quite rapidly and is very tolerant of soil conditions and of city smoke. Its form is also somewhat more attractive than that of the native American sycamore.

WITCH-HAZEL FAMILY— HAMAMELIDACEAE

The Sweet-Gum—Liquidambar

SWEET-GUM   *Liquidambar styraciflua* **L.**

> The aromatic, star-shaped leaves, corky growth on the aromatic twigs and branches, shiny greenish buds, and spiny, globose Ping-Pong-ball–sized fruits are most distinct.

Summer. *Leaves* 6 to 8 inches wide, alternate, simple, deciduous, orbicular, distinctly star-shaped, base cordate, quite pleasantly fragrant when crushed; lobes usually 5, or more rarely 7, tapering, pointed, palmately veined, margins finely serrate-toothed; upper surfaces bright green and glabrous, paler and glabrous beneath except for small hair tufts in the principal vein axils; leaf blades 4 to 7 inches in diameter; petioles 3 to 5 inches long, slender, rounded. *Flowers* tiny, apetalous, unisexual, male and female flowers borne on the same tree in headlike clusters; staminate flowers green, borne in terminal racemes on compact, erect stalks; pistillate flowers axillary, borne in rounded clusters on long, slender, pendulous stalks. *Fruits* (capsule) 1 to 1½ inches in diameter, brown, hard, woody, borne in ball-like heads, pendent on long and slender stalks, persisting throughout the winter; composed of numerous, sharp-pointed capsules that give a spiny appearance, with 2 to 3 winged seeds within each.

Winter. *Twigs* moderately stout, often slightly angled, stellate in cross sections, usually greenish to yellowish brown to reddish brown, glabrous, lustrous, aromatic; becoming grayish and developing several parallel corky ridges during the second season; leaf scars crescent-shaped to broadly heart-shaped, with 3 conspicuous bundle scars; stipule scars present. *Buds* ovoid, pointed, with about 6 lustrous, reddish brown scales;

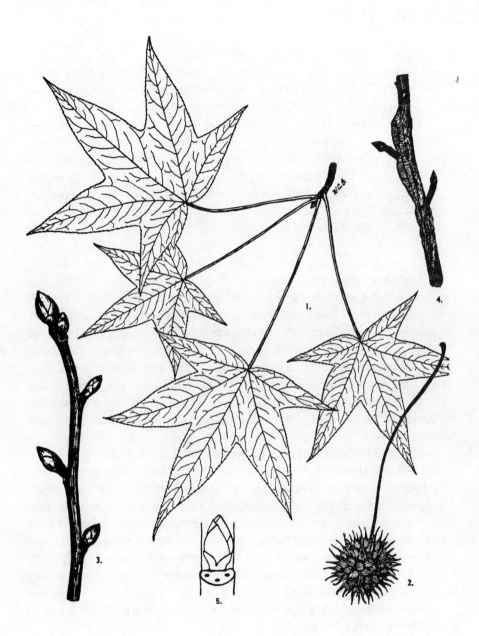

SWEET-GUM

1. Branch with mature leaves.
2. Fruit.
3. Winter twig.

4. Second year winter twig with corky ridges.
5. Details of bud and leaf scar.

pleasantly fragrant when crushed; terminal bud ¼ to ¾ inch long; ovoid, with several yellowish to brown, brightly shiny scales; lateral buds divergent, slightly smaller. *Bark* becoming rather thick on the trunks, grayish brown, roughened by deep furrows and rather narrow scaly ridges.

Comparisons. The fruits of this species are similar to those of the American sycamore, but are somewhat larger, with fewer individual fruits per cluster. The winter twigs could perhaps be confused with some of the winged elms, but the elms lack true terminal buds (present in the sweet-gum); also, the pseudo-terminal buds, which are present in the elms, are conspicuously cocked or bent, which is not the case in the true terminal bud of the sweet-gum.

The sweet-gum, also known as red-gum, star-leaf gum, bilsted, and alligator wood, is a large tree becoming 60 to 80 or more feet in height, with a trunk from 2 to 4 feet in diameter. In the open it develops a very symmetric pyramidal crown, and spreading or almost horizontal branches that persist rather low on the tapering trunk. When growing in the forests the trunks are straight and clean, with a rather small, lofty crown. The sweet-gum is most typically a tree of the coastal plain swamps and wet river bottoms, but it often grows on fairly moist and fertile upland soils. It is one of the most important timber trees in the southeastern United States.

The wood is heavy, hard, and close-grained, but not strong. Lumbermen classify the whitish sapwood as sapgum and the reddish brown heartwood as redgum lumber. It is used extensively for furniture, cabinet-making, interior finish, boxes, crates, slack barrels, novelties, and woodenware. A gum, also called sweetgum, liquidambar, or storax, which exudes from injuries, is often chewed by children and is also used in perfumes and drugs. The sweet-gum is sometimes planted as a shade or ornamental tree, being very beautiful in both form and foliage. The leaves turn a deep purplish red in the autumn.

The sweet-gum ranges from Connecticut to southern Illinois, south to Florida and eastern Texas.

The Witch-Hazels—Hamamelis

AMERICAN WITCH-HAZEL   *Hamamelis virginiana* L.

> Last of our tree species to flower in the fall (September to December!), this species is easily identified by its yellow, straplike petals, wavy-margined leaves, which are conspicuously asymmetrical at the base, conspicuous, deer-foot–shaped buds, and sprawling habit.

Summer. *Leaves* 2½ to 6 inches long, 1½ to 4 inches wide, alternate, simple, deciduous, 2-ranked, ovate or obovate, tips pointed to rounded, bases obliquely rounded or somewhat heart-shaped, margins coarsely wavy-toothed; upper surfaces dark green and glabrous, the lower surfaces paler and often rough-hairy along the veins and midrib; petioles short. *Flowers* perfect, fragrant, appearing in the fall, produced as 2 to 3 per cluster; petals yellow, 4, straplike, twisted or contorted. *Fruits* (capsule) about ½ inch long, elliptic or urn-shaped, bunched into 2s or 3s, brown, hairy, woody, with a persistent 4-lobed calyx at its base, containing a pair of lustrous black seeds, which are ejected forcibly from the fruits, and accompanied by a fairly audible snapping sound.

Winter. *Twigs* slender, more or less zigzag, grayish olive to tawny, with scattered rusty hairs, rough in texture; leaf scars half-round to somewhat 3-lobed, showing 3 bundle scars; pith continuous. *Buds,* terminal bud ½ to ¾ inch long, naked, stalked, flattened, resembling the foot of a deer, curved, yellow-rusty-hairy; lateral buds similar but smaller, more than one per leaf scar.

The American witch-hazel is a large, often multistemmed shrub or a small tree, occasionally 20 to 30 feet in height with a trunk up to 1 foot in diameter. It occurs in moist woodlands and along the banks of streams from the coast to the mountains, but is much more common in the uplands.

The bright yellow flowers with narrow, wavy petals open in the late fall, generally after the yellow autumn leaves have been shed. About the same time, the capsules, which have developed from flowers of the previous fall, suddenly snap open and shoot their seeds a considerable distance from the plant. Some mystical significance has been attached to the

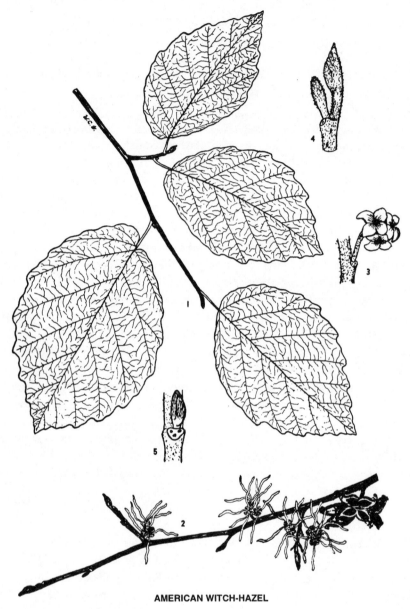

AMERICAN WITCH-HAZEL

1. Branch with leaves.
2. Twig and flowers and fruits.
3. Detail of flower cluster after petals fall.
4. Detail of deer-foot-shaped winter bud.
5. Detail of winter bud.

boughs of the witch-hazel, and they have been employed by credulous persons as divining rods to locate water or deposits of precious ores and minerals within the earth. The inner bark contains astringent properties, and the commercial extract of the American witch-hazel is derived from it through distillation processes.

The range of the witch-hazel extends from Nova Scotia to southern Quebec and southeastern Minnesota southward to central Florida and eastern Texas.

A second species, the Ozark witch-hazel (*H. vernalis* Sarg.), is a more shrubby species restricted to Missouri, Arkansas, Oklahoma, and Texas. It differs by producing somewhat orangish, rather than yellow flowers, with slightly smaller petals, from January to April.

ELM FAMILY—ULMACEAE

The Elms—Ulmus

The leaves of the elms are alternate, simple, commonly asymmetrical at their bases, prominently pinnately veined and arranged in 2 ranks along the branchlets. The twigs are slender, often somewhat zigzag, and have a round pith in cross section. The leaf scars are semicircular, somewhat raised, and usually have 3 conspicuous bundle scars. There is no terminal bud, but the pseudo-terminal one is conspicuously cocked to one side. The lateral buds are of medium size and have several scales arranged in 2 vertical series or ranks. Flower buds are conspicuously larger than those that will develop into leafy branchlets.

Our northern elms produce their flowers in the early spring, before the leaves appear; but some of the southern species flower in the fall. The mostly wind-pollinated flowers are perfect, containing both stamens and pistils, and are borne in clusters along the twigs of the previous season. The fruits commonly mature and are shed before the leaves are fully developed. There is a central seed cavity, containing one seed, which is surrounded by a thin, membranous, or papery, wing that is frequently notched at the tip. The seeds are disseminated by the wind.

The Dutch elm disease, caused by the fungus *Ceratocystis ulmi,* was first discovered in this country in 1930, and in spite of all efforts to eradicate it the disease has appeared in various parts of the eastern United States. It is a potentially very dangerous and fatal disease to which all of our native elms are highly susceptible. It attacks the living tree and continues to grow as a saprophyte in its tissues after the tree's death. Bark beetles are instrumental in spreading the disease. The symptoms are a wilting or yellowing of the leaves on one or several branches. Other common wilt diseases cause similar symptoms, but all ornamental elms that show such symptoms should have the immediate attention of a reliable tree surgeon.

AMERICAN ELM   *Ulmus americana* L.

> The light-dark, cross-sectional color pattern of the bark and ciliate-margined fruits of this characteristically vase-shaped tree are most diagnostic.

Summer. *Leaves* 3 to 5 inches long, 1 to 3 inches wide, alternate, simple, deciduous, ovate, obovate to oblong, usually broadest about the middle, tips taper-pointed, bases strongly unsymmetrical or lopsided, margins coarsely and sharply double-serrate; upper surfaces dark green, lustrous, usually glabrous but occasionally roughish with no more than 2 to 3 forked veins per leaf; paler and hairy beneath but not conspicuously roughened; petioles short, stout. *Flowers* ½ inch long, perfect, red green, red, or yellow green, fasciculate, developing in early spring before the leaves. *Fruits* (samara) ¼ to ½ inch long, oval, red brown, margin ciliate, otherwise glabrous, deeply notched apically.

Winter. *Twigs* slender, slightly zigzag, reddish brown to gray-brown, either glabrous or slightly hairy but not rough. *Buds* flattened laterally, especially on side of twigs, with 6 to 10 scales, light reddish brown, glabrous or nearly so, often placed a little to one side of the leaf scars; pseudoterminal bud strongly cocked; scales darker-margined, 2-ranked; leaf buds ⅛ to ¼ inch long, ovoid, pointed (but less so than those of the rock elm); flower buds chestnut brown, acute, glabrous or only slightly hairy, with light-colored hairs much larger and more plump than leaf buds. *Bark* becoming a dark ashy gray with irregular longitudinal furrows, separating the broad, flat-topped, and scaly ridges; bark samples showing conspicuous light-dark color pattern when viewed cross-sectionally.

Comparisons. The light-dark, cross-sectional pattern of the bark; the acutely pointed, nearly glabrous, chestnut brown flower buds with few light-colored, rather than dark-colored, hairs; and rather smooth leaf surfaces with no more than 2 or 3 forked veins per leaf help to separate this species from the slippery elm, which has consistently brown bark when viewed cross-sectionally, usually much rougher-surfaced leaves with several to many forked veins per leaf, and more obtuse or blunt, purplish brown, prominently red-hairy flower buds. In winter, the conspicuously cocked pseudo-terminal buds (especially so in this species) help to identify elms from most other genera.

AMERICAN ELM

1. Branch with mature leaves.
2. Flowering branch.
3. Fruiting branch.
4. Winter twig.
5. Detail of bud and leaf scar.
6. Layered cross-section of bark.

The American elm is also known as the white elm, the gray elm, the water elm, or the swamp elm. Its vase-shaped form is so characteristic that even at a distance it is easily recognized. Typically it has a trunk that divides rather low into several large ascending and arching limbs that in turn terminate in a maze of gracefully drooping branches, forming a broadly rounded and very symmetrical crown. The form of the crown is variable, and several types such as the vase, the oak, and the plume forms are commonly recognized. The American elm often attains a height of 75 to 100 feet and a trunk diameter of 2 to 6 feet. It is one of our largest and most handsome trees. It prefers the deep, rich, moist soils of bottomlands and is a common streambank tree, but it also ascends the more moist and fertile slopes. In the swamps it is a common associate of such trees as the red maple, the silver maple, the pin oak, the swamp white oak, and the black ash. The American elm is among the earliest of all the trees to produce flowers in the spring.

The wood is heavy, light-colored (accounting for the common name of white elm) hard, strong, coarse-grained, and rather difficult to split. It is used for furniture, boxes, crates, barrels, and railroad ties. The American elm is highly prized as a shade and ornamental tree. In the early spring, flocks of goldfinches and purple finches are often attracted to the fruiting trees, and both the fruits and buds are an emergency food for the gray squirrel and the fox squirrel. The twigs are sometimes browsed by deer, and the twigs and bark of the smaller trees are eaten by the cottontail rabbit in winter. Its drooping boughs are often chosen by the northern (Baltimore) oriole as nesting sites.

The American elm ranges from southern Newfoundland to eastern Saskatchewan, south to Florida and eastern Texas.

ROCK ELM   *Ulmus thomasii* **Sarg.**

> The branches, which usually develop 1 to 4 parallel, but discontinuous, corky wings the second or third year, and very sharp buds, along with the universally hairy fruits of this species, are most distinctive.

Summer. *Leaves* 2½ to 4½ inches long, 1¼ to 2½ inches wide, alternate, simple, deciduous, oblong-obovate to elliptic, tips long-pointed, base roundish but only slightly lopsided or asymmetrical, margins coarsely, sharply, double-serrate; upper surface dark green, lustrous, rough-hairy to glabrous; lower surface paler and hairy, lateral veins rarely forking. *Flowers* small, racemose, on about 1-inch stalks. *Fruits* (samara) ⅓ inch wide, hairy throughout, with a slight apical notch, ill-defined wings.

Winter. *Twigs* slender, conspicuously ridged with corky outgrowth, slightly zigzag, light reddish brown or yellowish brown; shoots hairy. *Buds* ¼ to ⅜ inch long, sharply acute; bud scales ciliate. *Bark* rough furrows with intersecting ridges, resembles that of the American elm, but is usually darker and much more deeply furrowed.

Comparisons. The unbranched trunk of the rock elm that lacks the traditional vase shape of the American elm; its smaller, nearly symmetrical leaves, which are glabrous above; its hairier fruits; and its winglike branches help separate these two species. The rock elm is similar to the American elm in having very few forking veins per leaf blade. Also, the rock elm can be separated from both the American elm and the slippery elm by its flowers being in racemes, rather than fascicles, by its larger buds, especially those near the twig tips (¼ to ⅜ versus ¹⁄₁₆ to ¼ inches long), which tend to be more sharply pointed and diverging.

––––––––

The rock elm, or cork elm, is a medium-sized to large tree that may attain a height of 100 feet and a trunk diameter of 3 feet or more. In general appearance, it differs from the more V-shaped American elm by having conspicuously drooping lower branches and a narrow oblong crown. Unlike most elms, it often remains unbranched well into the oblong crown. This elm is found most commonly on dry gravelly uplands and rocky slopes, but it attains its best development in the rich soils of bottomlands. The wood is heavy, hard, and tough; the finest, in fact, of all the elm woods. It was from this wood that the tree derived its name of rock elm. Before the ascendancy of steel it was used in the construction of automobile bodies and refrigerators. It is still used in making furniture, agricultural implements, hockey sticks, ax handles, and for other articles requiring wood that will withstand severe strains and shocks.

The range of the rock elm extends from western Vermont, northern New York, southern Ontario, central Michigan, and central Minnesota southwestward to the northern portions of Illinois, Indiana, Missouri, and Kansas.

SLIPPERY ELM   *Ulmus rubra* **Muhl.**

> The very rough leaves, uniformly chocolate-colored bark (when viewed cross-sectionally), very mucilaginous, gluelike, and aromatic inner bark, wingless twigs, and eciliate fruits are distinctive.

Summer. *Leaves* 4 to 7 inches long, 2 to 3 inches wide, alternate, simple, deciduous, oblong obovate to ovate, usually broadest above the middle, tips acuminate, bases asymmetrical or lopsided, margins coarsely and sharply double-serrate; upper surfaces dark green, dull, very rough to the touch (can actually scratch the fingernail surface); with several to many forked veins per leaf; paler, hairy, and somewhat roughish beneath; petioles short, stout, hairy. *Flowers* very small, nearly stalkless, fasciculate, developing in the spring. *Fruits* (samara) ½ inch wide, nearly circular, shallow notches apically, eciliate margined, hairy on the seed portion only.

Winter. *Twigs* slender but stouter than those of the American elm, ashy gray to light brownish gray, harshly rough-hairy, distinctly mucilaginous if chewed. *Buds* very dark brown, more or less rusty-hairy, especially on upper scales where hairs appear to be orange; leaf buds about ¼ inch long, ovoid, blunt-pointed; flower buds about ½ inch long, rounded, densely red-brown-hairy, larger and more plump than leaf buds. *Bark* brown to dark reddish brown; on old trunks, becoming thick, with vertical furrows, separating into broad ridges that eventually break off as large loose plates; inner bark also very mucilaginous (not so in the American elm).

Comparisons. The more reddish outer bark surface (more ash gray in the American elm), uniformly brown color of the bark when viewed cross-sectionally, and uniquely eciliate-margined fruits, which are rounded and larger, will help to separate this species from the American elm and our other elm species. Although the hairy leaves (which appear to be very rough in virtually any direction, due to stiff surface hairs) are said to represent a useful diagnostic character, they provide only limited diagnostic value. Although the smaller leaves of the American elm are usually less rough, or roughened only in one direction, young sprout leaves occasionally produce surfaces as rough as those of slippery elm. The leaves of the slippery elm do, however, have a tendency to produce more forked lateral veins than do those of the American elm. The slippery elm can also be told from the American elm by lacking the characteristic vase-shaped form of the latter species.

Slippery elm is also known as red elm, gray elm, or moose elm. It is a medium-sized tree, usually attaining a height of 40 to 60 feet with a trunk diameter of 1 to 2½ feet. The spreading branches form a rather broad, open, and flat-topped crown. Their trunks are usually clear of branches to a greater height than those of the American elm, and the branches are less drooping than those of the latter species. The slippery elm grows in the bottomlands but also on rich, rocky slopes in a mixed company of other hardwoods. It shows a marked preference for limestone outcrops in the hills.

The wood is heavy, hard, strong, cross-grained, and durable. It is used for much the same purposes as that of the American elm. The mucilaginous, fragrant inner bark, which provides the tree its name, is sometimes chewed (a favorite of country urchins) and is used medicinally for coughs and throat irritations. In some parts of the country it is also used as a poultice for sores. It is somewhat nutritious and was used to some extent by Native Americans as food. The fresh green fruits are eaten by many birds; according to Seton, they were the favorite spring food of the extinct passenger pigeons. In the North, the twigs are often browsed by moose, and so the tree is occasionally called the moose elm.

The slippery elm ranges from Maine and southern Quebec to North Dakota, south to northern Florida and eastern Texas.

WINGED ELM   *Ulmus alata* Michx.

> The branches, or at least those of the second year, usually develop a pair of opposite, lateral, corky wings, often ½ inch wide. The winged elm can also be told from our other elm species by its smaller leaves, and by its smaller, sharply pointed, buds that lack ciliate scales.

Summer. *Leaves* 1½ to 3 inches long, 1 to 1½ inches wide, alternate, simple, deciduous, elliptical or broadly lanceolate, tip sharply pointed, base roundish and lopsided apexes acuminate, margins sharply double-serrate; upper surfaces dark green, glabrous; the lower surfaces paler and hairy; petioles ⅛ to ¼ inch long. *Flowers* perfect, produced in racemes prior to the leaves, appearing from January through March; purple-brown; male and female flowers occurring on the same tree. *Fruits* (samara) ⅜ inch long, elliptical, hairy, with a narrow wing that is notched apically.

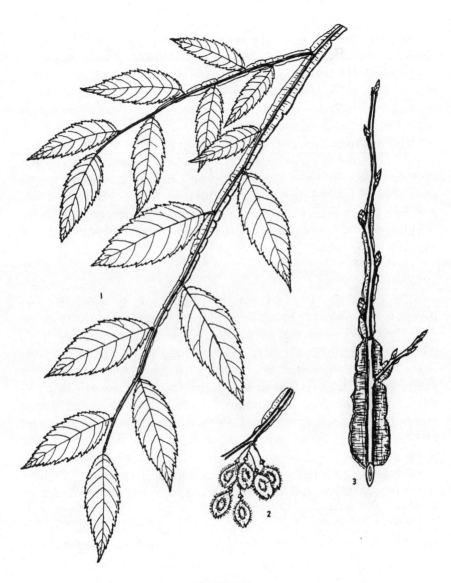

WINGED ELM

1. Branch with mature leaves.
2. Fruits.

3. Winter twig showing winged branch.

Winter. *Twigs* slender, grayish to reddish-brown, slightly zigzag, glabrous or nearly so; branch wings developed at least during the second year, paired, opposite, lateral, corky, often ½ inch wide. *Buds* about ⅛ inch long, ovoid, pointed but not acute, dark brown, glabrous or nearly so; bud scales eciliate-margined. *Bark* grayish brown with furrows separating interlacing, flat-topped ridges.

Comparisons. The racemose rather than fascicled flowers, elliptic to broadly lanceolate leaves and winged twigs help to separate this species from the American elm and the slippery elm. In some cases, however, the winged twigs may be completely absent; the smaller, thinner branches, which produce a more finely branched silhouette than that of the American elm or the slippery elm, will also help to separate those two species from the winged elm.

———

The winged elm, also known as the cork elm and the wahoo, is by far the most common of the southern elms. Its name is derived from the prominent corky wings that are usually present along its branches. It is a round-topped tree, usually 40 to 50 feet in height with a trunk diameter of 1 to 2 feet. Throughout much of the South, except in the mountains, it is a common tree. It grows best on well-drained soils and is not usually present where the soil is excessively wet. The wood is similar to that of most other elms and is simply marketed as elm, although it is not an important timber species. It is frequently planted as a shade tree or street tree in the South. Its leaves are smaller than any of our other native elms.

The range of the winged elm extends from Virginia to southern Indiana, southern Illinois, and Missouri south to Texas and central Florida.

CEDAR ELM   *Ulmus crassifolia* **Nutt.**

> The winged branches, autumnally produced flowers and fruits, and small leaves (the smallest of any native elm) are distinctive. The nonfissured cedarlike bark and shorter, rough-surfaced leaves also help to separate this species from the winged elm and the September elm.

Summer. *Leaves* 1 to 2 inches long, ½ to 1 inch wide, alternate, simple, deciduous, elliptic to oblong or ovate, base asymmetrical or lopsided, apexes acute, margins crenate-serrate, irregularly double serrate, teeth small; upper surfaces dark green, rough, lower surfaces pubescent throughout or along the midvein; petioles pubescent or nearly lacking. *Flowers* green to reddish, developing in the fall. *Fruits* (samara) about ½ inch long, brown to green, short-hairy, apexes notched.

Winter. *Twigs* slender, short-hairy, red-brown, winged or not; wing when present often sporadically produced. *Buds* about ⅛ inch long, brown, broadly ovoid, acute; bud scales shiny, generally somewhat hairy. *Bark* silver gray to brown-gray, not fissured (thus unique among our southern elms), but with flat, interlacing ridges or flat scales.

Comparisons. Like the winged elm, this species has small double-serrate leaves, mostly 2 inches or less long, and winged branches. The leaves of this species, however, are rounded or blunt at the tip and quite rough on the upper surface. Like the September elm, it produces flowers and fruits in the fall instead of early spring; however, that species has considerably larger leaves, which are smooth, rather than rough above, and has somewhat larger fruit hairs.

The cedar elm is a medium-sized tree, 65 to 100 feet in height, occurring along streambanks, low woods, and waste areas. Characteristic of floodplain species, it often develops a buttressed base and strongly fluted bole. The lower branches of the bole often descend while those of the upper bole ascend conspicuously. It can be found with the swamp chestnut oak, overcup oak, Texas oak, water hickory, and sweet-gum. It is found from southwestern Tennessee, Arkansas, Missouri, and southern Oklahoma south to southern Texas, Louisiana, eastern Mississippi, and Florida.

SEPTEMBER ELM   *Ulmus serotina* Sarg.

> The small yellow green leaves; winged branches; deeply notched, silvery hairy fruits; and autumnally produced flowers and fruits are most distinct.

Summer. *Leaves* 2 to 3½ inches long, 1 to 1¾ inches wide, 2-ranked, alternate, simple, deciduous, oblong ovate to elliptical, apically pointed, basally asymmetrical, margins double-serrate; lustrous, yellow-green, glabrous above, paler and slightly hairy below. *Flowers* developing in fall. *Fruits* (samara) ⅜ to ½ inch long, hairy, elliptical with ciliate margins of long, whitish hairs, deeply notched apically, developing in fall.

Winter. *Twigs* with scattered white lenticels; shoots thinly hairy. *Buds* ⅛ to ¼ inch long, obtuse, glabrous or nearly so.

Comparisons. This species, like the rock elm, the cedar elm, and the winged elm, has corky wings on its branches, and like the cedar elm, it flowers and produces its ciliate-margined fruits in the fall. In general appearance the tree resembles the American elm, but has smaller leaves and winged branches. The small leaves also help to separate it from all other elms except the cedar elm.

The September elm, or red elm, is a medium-sized elm ranging from Kentucky and southern Illinois southward to Oklahoma, Arkansas, northern Alabama, and northwestern Georgia. Throughout this range, however, it occurs in scattered and more or less isolated localities.

The Planertree—Planera

PLANERTREE   *Planera aquatica* J. F. Gmel.

> The 2-ranked, single-serrate leaves (with glandular teeth), which are clearly widest below the middle, along with the unusually shaped fruits, and tiny buds help to separate this genus from *Ulmus* (the elms), *Carpinus* (the hornbeams), and *Ostrya* (the hop-hornbeams).

Summer. *Leaves* 1 to 2½ inches long, ½ to 1 inch wide, thick, alternate, simple, deciduous, 2-ranked, ovate, clearly widest below the middle, apically pointed, base asymmetrically rounded, margin sharply but simply crenate-serrate toothed; upper surface dull, dark green; the lower surface paler; both surfaces often roughish; petioles about ¼ inch long. *Flowers* small, borne in dense axillary clusters. *Fruits* (drupe) ⅓ inch long, fleshy, very distinctive, covered with tubular warty projections (burlike), short-stalked.

Winter. *Twigs* slender, slightly zigzag, dark red to reddish brown, often somewhat hairy, dotted with minute white lenticels; leaf scars small, ovate or triangular, with 3 bundle scars. *Buds* all lateral, about ¹⁄₁₆ inch

PLANERTREE

1. Fruit showing corky projections.
2. Branch with mature leaves.
3. Branch with fruits and immature leaves.
4. Detail of bud and leaf scar.
5. Winter twig.

long, ovoid, chestnut brown, somewhat hairy, with several scales arranged in two longitudinal rows. *Bark* grayish brown, flaking off into large, longitudinal, shreddy scales, exposing the reddish brown inner bark.

Comparisons. Aside from the very obvious fruit differences, this genus can be separated from the genus *Ulmus* by its leaves being clearly widest below the middle, rather than at or above the middle.

———

The planertree, or water-elm, is a small tree 20 to 30 feet, or occasionally 40 feet, in height, with a trunk diameter of 1 to 1½ feet. Its trunk typically divides near the ground into several large spreading branches, forming a rather flat-topped, spreading crown. It grows in swamps and along streams where the land is subject to periodic and often prolonged flooding. The weak, soft, light wood has practically no value except as pulpwood.

The range of the planertree extends through the coastal plain from southeastern North Carolina to northern Florida westward to Texas; and northward, in the Mississippi Valley, to southern Illinois.

The Hackberries—Celtis

The hackberries are shrubs or small trees with alternate, simple, deciduous 2-ranked leaves, which are entire or toothed on the margin. They are typically asymmetrical or lopsided at the base, with 3 prominent veins arising from the summit of the short petiole. The twigs are slender, more or less zigzag, and their pith is finely chambered only at the nodes. The very characteristic, dark-colored buds are triangular-shaped, small and tightly appressed to the twigs. The terminal one is lacking, and the lateral ones are placed above the oval- to crescent-shaped leaf scars, which have 3 bundle scars. The flowers are small and inconspicuous, appearing with the leaves, and developing in the spring on wood of the current year (rather than previous year as in the elms). They are followed by the ovoid or rounded fruits that are drupes containing a large stone and a rather thin, dryish, but sugary flesh. The bark of these trees commonly has warty excrescences of a corky nature. Witches' brooms, composed of clusters of small twigs, are frequently observed in the crowns; this disfiguring condition is caused by the mite *Eriophyes*.

SUGAR-BERRY   *Celtis laevigata* **Willd.**

The chambered pith, corky warts on the tree trunk, and the elongated yellow-green leaves (mostly over twice as long as wide) with entire margins, long-tapered tips, and asymmetrical bases, are most distinctive.

Summer. *Leaves* 2 ½ to 5 inches long, 1 to 2 inches wide, alternate, simple, deciduous, usually clearly more than twice as long as wide, broadly lanceolate, margins entire or may have a few teeth toward the elongated tip, bases somewhat heart-shaped or rounded and asymmetrical, light yellow green; glabrous or slightly rough above, glabrous beneath; petioles ¼ to ½ inch long, slender. *Flowers* creamy green, perfect or unisexual; male, female, and perfect flowers occur on the same tree, appearing with the leaves. *Fruits* (drupe) ⅓ to ¼ inch diameter, pea-sized, orange-red, yellowish, or rarely purplish, borne on stalks as long as, or shorter than, the pedicel; beakless.

Winter. *Twigs* greenish to reddish-brown, glabrous to finely hairy, zigzag. *Buds* ¹⁄₁₆ to ⅛ inch long, conspicuously triangular, pointed, tightly appressed to stem, brown, occasionally hairy. *Bark* light gray, smoothish, with prominent warty excrescences.

Comparisons. The yellow-green upper leaves help to separate this species from the dark green upper leaves of our other two *Celtis* species. Also, although the twigs of this species are similar to those of the hackberry, the buds are smaller (¹⁄₁₆ to ⅛ versus ¼ inch long).

———

The sugar-berry is also known as the southern hackberry or Mississippi hackberry. It is a medium-sized tree with a broad crown of spreading or pendulous branches, attaining a height of 60 to 80 feet with a trunk diameter of 2 to 3 feet. Wet, swampy places and the banks of streams are its natural habitats, but it grows well under cultivation and is often planted as a shade or ornamental tree. The wood is neither strong nor hard, but it is used for making furniture, boxes, and baskets. The thin flesh of the fruits is very sweet, resembling a sweetened coffee, and they are eaten by squirrels and many species of birds. This species tends to be resistant to the witches' broom disease commonly found in other species of the genus.

The range of the sugar-berry extends through the coastal plain from southeastern Virginia to Florida west to California; and northward, in the

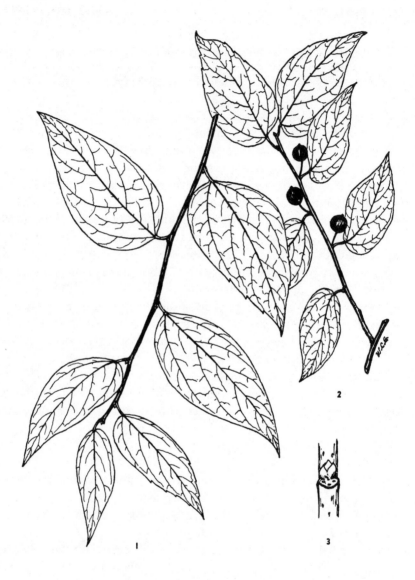

SUGAR-BERRY

1. Branch with mature leaves.
2. Fruiting branch.

3. Detail of winter bud and leaf scar.

Mississippi Valley, to western Oklahoma and the southern portions of Indiana and Illinois.

COMMON HACKBERRY *Celtis occidentalis* **L.**

> The dark green asymmetrical leaves of this species, which are less than twice as long as wide, with serrate margins, along with the warty bark and dark round fruit are distinct.

Summer. *Leaves* 2 to 6 inches long, 1 to 2 inches wide, alternate, simple, deciduous, occasionally slightly more but usually less than twice as long as wide, ovate, long-pointed and often falcate tips, bases oblique, margins coarsely and sharply toothed above but entire toward the base; upper surfaces dark green, glabrous, or slightly rough; paler and glabrous or slightly hairy beneath; petioles short. *Fruits* (drupe) ¼ inch long, ovoid, about pea size, orange red to dark purplish, borne on slender stalks, thick beaked, ripening in September or October, often persisting into the winter; flesh very thin, yellow, sweet with a taste similar to that of dates.

Winter. *Twigs* slender, more or less zigzag, lustrous reddish brown, occasionally slightly hairy, marked with small, pale, longitudinally elongated lenticels; pith white, finely chambered; leaf scars small, semiovate, placed at nearly right angles to the twigs on little projecting cushions; 3 bundle scars often confluent and appearing as one. *Buds* about ⅛ inch long, ovoid, pointed, flattened, appressed, with 3 or 4 light brown, often slightly hairy scales; terminal bud absent. *Bark* grayish brown or ashy gray, at first smooth but becoming roughened with characteristic narrow corky ridges and warty or corky excrescences.

––––––––

The common hackberry is also known as the sugar-berry, nettle-tree, and hoop-ash. It is a small- to medium-sized tree, usually 25 to 40 feet in height with a trunk 1 to 2 feet in diameter. The crown is wide-spreading and round-topped. The branches are often clustered and disfigured by witches' brooms, which are caused by the mite *Eriophes* sp. The common hackberry prefers rich, moist soils, but it often grows on rich, rocky hillsides. It is seldom a common tree, but scattered individuals are often present in hardwood forests.

The wood is rather soft and weak, but heavy and coarse-grained. It is principally used for cheap furniture, boxes, crates, and fencing. The fruits,

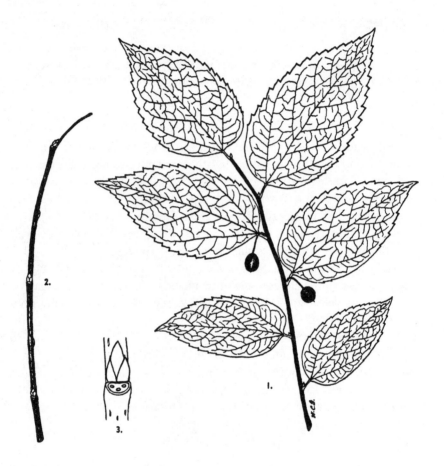

COMMON HACKBERRY

1. Branch with mature leaves and fruits.
2. Winter twig.
3. Details of bud and leaf scar.

while rather dry, are eaten by many kinds of birds, squirrels, chipmunks, and various small rodents. The tree is very seldom planted for ornamental purposes.

The hackberry ranges from New Hampshire and southern Quebec to southern Manitoba and Saskatchewan, south to northern Georgia, Florida, and eastern Texas.

GEORGIA HACKBERRY   *Celtis tenuifolia* **Nutt.**

The small (1 ½ to 2 ½ inches long) rough-surfaced leaves of this species, which are rarely more than 2 inches long, and the light orange-red to reddish brown fruits are most distinct.

Comparisons. Unlike our other two treelike *Celtis* species, the shrubby Georgia hackberry's leaves are leathery, and consistently less than twice as long as wide. Their margins can be entire or toothed, but never toothed toward the base. Some individuals, however, are difficult to separate.

This is a large shrub or sometimes a small, irregularly shaped tree that grows in dry rocky uplands. It has smaller leaves than our other hackberries, usually less than 2 inches long and 1¼ inches wide, which are very rough above and more or less hairy beneath, and has short-stalked, small, dark orange-red to purplish fruits. It occurs from Ontario, Pennsylvania, Indiana, Missouri, and eastern Kansas south to eastern Oklahoma, Louisiana, and northern Florida.

MULBERRY FAMILY—MORACEAE

The Osage-Orange—Maclura

OSAGE-ORANGE *Maclura pomifera* (Raf.) Schneid.

> The thorned twigs and leaf petioles that exude a milky sap when punctured, long-tipped, entire-margined leaves, and huge, knobby, orange- or grapefruit-sized fruits are most distinct.

Summer. *Leaves* 3 to 5 inches long, 2 to 3 inches wide, alternate, simple, ovate, apically acute, bases wedge-shaped, margins entire but wavy; upper surfaces lustrous dark green; paler and glabrous beneath; turning bright yellow in the fall; petioles 1 to 2½ inches long, slender, often clustered from spur shoots. *Flowers* very small, greenish, appearing in late spring, unisexual, male and female flowers borne on separate trees. *Fruits* (an aggregate of nutlets) 3 to 6 inches in diameter, toxic, resembling large pale green oranges, composed of numerous closely packed drupes; when punctured exude a bitter milky juice that turns black on exposure. *Twigs* spiny, a good identifying characteristic in the absence of the fruits.

Winter. *Twigs* rather stout, armed at the nodes with stout spines, greenish brown to orangish brown to yellowish brown, marked with pale but conspicuous lenticels, stipule scars present; leaf scars alternate, broadly inversely triangular to elliptic with several bundle scars often arranged in an ellipse. *Buds* small, depressed, roundish, mostly hidden by bark, with several pale brownish bud scales; terminal bud lacking. *Bark* becoming ashy brown or dark orange-brown, deeply furrowed with irregular longitudinal fissures and scaly ridges; inner bark and roots orange colored.

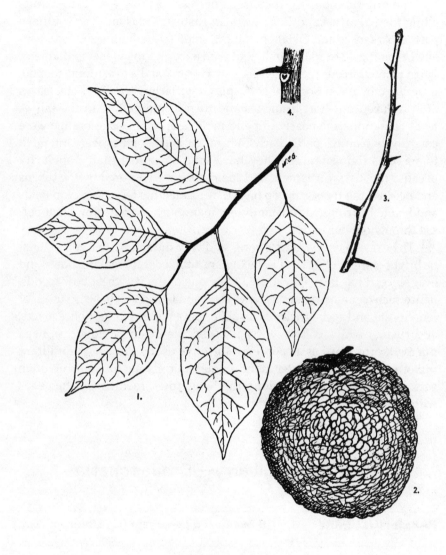

OSAGE-ORANGE

1. Branch with mature leaves.
2. Fruit.
3. Winter twig.
4. Detail of portion of twig.

The original home of the Osage-orange was the rich bottomlands along the Arkansas and Red rivers, in eastern Texas and the southern parts of Arkansas and Oklahoma. It is a small to medium-sized tree, usually becoming 20 to 30 feet in height with a trunk 1 to 1½ feet in diameter when planted in our region. It has a short trunk and a low, round-topped, irregular crown composed of stiff, spiny, interlacing branches. The leaves are produced on short branches and turn bright yellow in the fall. A few generations ago nearly impenetrable hedges of Osage-orange were extensively planted, particularly in rural areas where they were intended to serve as living fences. They have long since lost their popularity because ranchers, cattlemen, and their stock were injured by the thorns and because the trees grew so high they shaded the adjoining crop fields and had to be trimmed constantly, but many such old fencerows still persist throughout our region.

The wood is heavy, hard, strong, and very durable, with a characteristic bright orange color. The Osage Indians utilized it for making bows, and ever since, it has been considered to be one of the very best bow woods, hence such common names as bow-wood and bois d'arc. It is also used for fence posts, and such articles as insulator pins, pulley blocks, police maces, and rustic furniture. The wood also yields a bright yellow dye, used during World War I as a source for the olive drab coloration of military uniforms. During the winter months gray squirrels and fox squirrels often seek the fallen "oranges" along the hedgerows, feeding on the seeds within them.

The Paper-Mulberry—Broussonetia

PAPER-MULBERRY   *Broussonetia papyrifera* (L.) L'Hér ex Vent.

The thin green partition within the pith nodes of the twigs; milky sap of the leaf petioles and twigs; very rough-surfaced, broadly ovate, somewhat aromatic leaves, which are often mitten-shaped, and always 3 main veined from the base, are distinctive.

Summer. *Leaves* alternate or occasionally opposite or whorled, simple, deciduous, blades 3 to 8 inches long, 1½ to 4 inches wide, gray green; usually ovate, rounded to heart-shaped, apically pointed, bases often

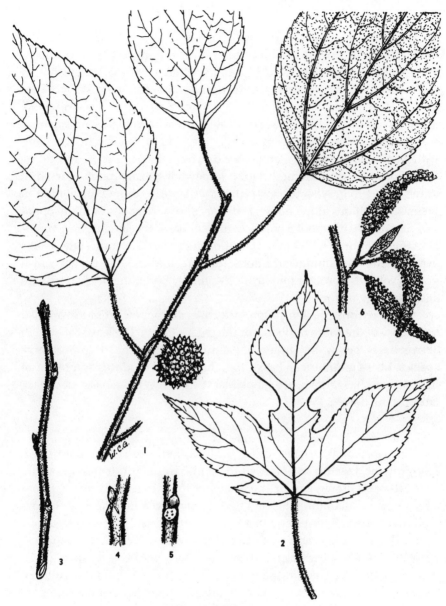

PAPER-MULBERRY

1. Branch with typical leaves and fruit.
2. Lobed leaf from vigorous shoot.
3. Winter twig.

4-5. Details of buds and leaf scars.
6. Staminate flowers.

asymmetrical, palmately veined with 3 main basal veins, margins serrate-dentate except toward the base; blades on the more vigorous shoots mitten-shaped; variously, 3- to 5-lobed leaves are common; roughish with stiff hairs on the upper surfaces, paler and tomentose beneath; petioles mostly 2 to 4 inches long, roughish-hairy. *Flowers* tiny, greenish, unisexual; male flowers in catkins, globose female flowers, developing on separate trees in the spring. *Fruits* in roundish heads about ¾ inch in diameter, with many small, red drupelets protruding from the persistent calyx tubes.

Winter. *Twigs* moderately stout, somewhat zigzag, rough-hairy, dull grayish olive to grayish brown; pith rather large, round, white, with thin greenish partitions at the nodes; leaf scars alternate or occasionally opposite, roundish, with about 5 bundle scars; stipule scars elongate and prominent. *Buds* about ⅛ inch long, conical-ovoid; scales 2 or more, one striate, exposed, showing minute striations; terminal bud lacking. *Bark* greenish gray to yellowish brown, smooth at first, finally becoming finely reticulate and shallowly furrowed.

Comparisons. The long appressed fruits are somewhat more rounded than those of the white mulberry or the red mulberry. The leaves are rough above, hairy below, but otherwise similar to the other two mulberry species. Like the American basswood, this species produces sprouts from its roots and has large heart-shaped leaves; however, the basswoods lack latex production.

———

The paper-mulberry, also called the tapa cloth tree, is a medium-sized, fast-growing tree up to about 40 to 50 feet in height. It has a broadly round-topped crown and brittle branches that are easily broken. In old age, the trunk commonly becomes oddly gnarled and contorted. It does well in hot, dry climates and has few serious pests. It spreads freely by means of root suckers and tends to become weedy. A given tree produces either stamen-bearing or pistil-bearing flowers in the early spring. The staminate or male trees are seen much more frequently in this country. Staminate flowers are produced in nodding catkins; the pistillate ones, in small ball-like heads.

This tree is a native of China and Japan. It was introduced into the warmer parts of this country around 1841 as an ornamental and street tree and is now widely naturalized from southeastern New York, south to Florida and Louisiana in urban or other disturbed areas. In China and Japan the fibrous inner bark of the paper-mulberry is much used in the making of paper, hence the common name. It is also used in making umbrellas and lanterns. A type of cloth called tapa is made from the inner bark by South Pacific Islanders, hence the common and specific names. The tree has no commercial importance in this country.

The Mulberries—Morus

These are trees or shrubs with milky sap and with alternate, simple, deciduous, often lobed leaves with 3 veins emanating from the base. The plants are monoecious or dioecious. The flowers are produced in axillary amentlike spikes with both the staminate and pistallate flowers 4-parted and with 4 stamens. The fruit is a short cylindric syncarp resembling a blackberry.

RED MULBERRY   *Morus rubra* L.

> The large, dark red to black, sweet, juicy, blackberrylike fruits, and the rough-surfaced, dull yellow-green, and variably shaped leaves, which range from being unlobed to having several lobes, along with the zigzag twigs and shiny green buds, are most distinct.

Summer. *Leaves* 3 to 7 inches long, almost as broad, alternate, simple, deciduous, orbicular, ovate, or oblong heart-shaped; dull green, occasionally 2- or 3-lobed, tips abruptly acuminate-pointed, base more or less heart-shaped and palmately veined, margins sharply and coarsely single-serrate; upper surfaces dark green, rough to the touch because of the deep corrugations on the surface due to venation patterns; lower surface paler, often slightly hairy, especially on the veins; petioles exuding a milky sap when cut. *Flowers* appearing before or with the leaves, male and female flowers occurring in separate clusters, but on the same plant. *Fruits* (an aggregate of nutlets) about 1 inch long, sweet, juicy, somewhat resembling those of the blackberry in shape and color, ripening in July.

Winter. *Twigs* fairly slender, somewhat zigzag, greenish brown to dark brown to reddish brown, often tinged with reddish; exuding a milky sap when cut; having a sweetish taste; leaf scars alternate, raised on the swollen nodes, usually sunken or concave, nearly circular, with several scattered bundle scars (elms have 3 bundle scars). *Buds* ¼ to ½ inch long, ovoid, acutely pointed, with 6 to 8 greenish brown to light reddish brown, lustrous scales in two rows; scale margins conspicuously darker; terminal

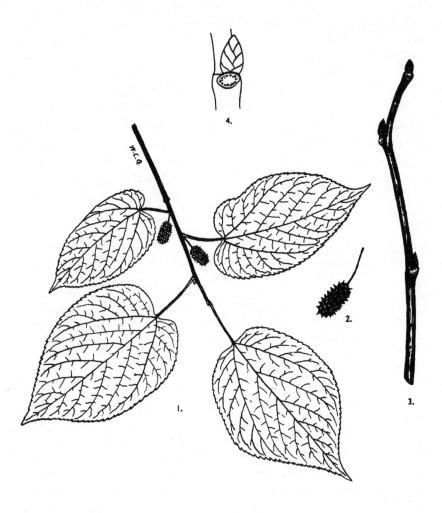

RED MULBERRY

1. Branch with mature leaves and fruits.
2. Fruit.
3. Winter twig.
4. Details of bud and leaf scar.

bud absent. *Bark* rather thin, dark brown, becoming more or less furrowed, often peeling off in rather long, narrow flakes.

Comparisons. This species can be separated from the white mulberry by its larger, juicier, sweeter, more edible black fruits; and by its dull (rather than shiny) leaves (which commonly have 3 or more lobes per leaf) that are more hairy both above and below, and are much rougher on the upper surface. In individuals where the leaves are unlobed, both mulberries can be separated from the basswoods by the presence of white latex found within their leaf petioles, which is lacking in the basswoods.

The red mulberry is a small native tree, usually 20 to 30 feet in height with a trunk diameter of 1 to 1½ feet. The trunk is usually short, and the stout, spreading, and often crooked branches form a dense, broadly round-topped crown. It is seldom a common tree, occurring here and there in stands of other hardwoods. It prefers a rich, moist soil and is most frequently found in bottomland or foothill forests. The tree reaches its maximum development in the Ohio and Mississippi valleys.

The wood is soft but rather tough and very durable in contact with the soil. It is used principally for furniture, fence posts, cooperage, and shipbuilding. The edible fruits are sometimes used for making pies, jellies, and summer drinks. They are rapidly devoured by many species of birds including the American robin, wood thrush, catbird, and cedar waxwing. It is a gala period for the birds when the trees are in fruit! The red mulberry is sometimes planted as an ornamental and to provide bird food.

The red mulberry ranges from Massachusetts and southern Ontario to South Dakota, south to Florida and Texas.

WHITE MULBERRY   *Morus alba* L.

> The shiny, palmately lobed leaves, which are hairy below, coupled with the elongated fruits, along with the reddish brown buds, are most distinct.

Summer. *Leaves* 2½ to 7 inches long, 2 to 5 inches wide, alternate, simple, deciduous, broadly ovate, margins coarsely toothed, unlobed to several lobes, basally rounded to cordate, 3-veined from base; lustrous, dark green, smooth and glabrous above, glabrous or occasionally hairy on the veins and within the axils beneath. *Flowers* minute, greenish, developing in the spring, with male and female flowers borne on the same or separate trees. *Fruits* (an aggregate of nutlets) ⅜ to ¾ inch long, acylindrical to globose, cluster of 1-seeded nutlets; white, pink to purple, insipid at maturity.

Winter. *Twigs* gray to yellowish brown to orangish brown, slender. *Buds* ⅛ to ³⁄₁₆ inch long (somewhat smaller than those of the red mulberry), reddish brown, obtuse, globose to triangular, appressed to the twigs, scale margins not darker. *Bark* light yellowish brown, smooth or furrowed with age.

Comparisons. The fruits of the white mulberry are white, pink, or purple and generally insipid compared with the sweet fruits of the red mulberry. They are also somewhat smaller, more globose, and produced from flowers that develop 2 to 3 weeks earlier than those of the red mulberry. Also, the leaves of the white mulberry are rarely lobed (commonly lobed in the red mulberry) except in stump sprouts, and generally smaller in overall size and glabrous (except occasionally on midveins and their axils) beneath, rather than hairy beneath as in the red mulberry. The winter buds of the white mulberry differ from those of the red mulberry by being smaller, globose to triangular, and closely appressed to the twigs, rather than ovoid and diverging away from the twigs. Moreover, the twigs and bark of the white mulberry tend to be more noticeably orange or yellowish in color compared with grayish brown to reddish brown twigs and bark of the red mulberry.

First cultivated by the Chinese for use in feeding silkworms, the white mulberry of the Orient is an introduced tree with coarser, smaller leaves than our native red mulberry. Although now both species occur in North America, neither has done well in the silk industry here. The leaves of red mulberry apparently are not eaten by silkworms. Nonetheless, the red mulberry does produce strong useful fiber from its inner bark, which was used by the Choctaw Indian tribe in making a coarse cloth.

CORKWOOD FAMILY—LEITNERIACEAE

The Corkwood—Leitneria

CORKWOOD   *Leitneria floridana* **Chapman**

> The lightweight, very brittle, rather thick, reddish brown stems, entire-margined, thick, leathery leaves, which are velvety-hairy beneath, are most distinct. Few other angiosperm tree species are so adapted to water.

Summer. *Leaves* 4 to 6 inches long, 1 to 3 inches wide, alternate, elliptic or lanceolate, pointed at both ends, margins entire, bright green and glabrous above, paler and hairy beneath; petioles 1 to 2 inches long. *Flowers* in catkins, unisexual, appearing before the leaves, male and female flowers borne on separate plants. *Fruits* (drupe) ¾ inch long, ¼ inch wide, dry, brown, wrinkled, flattened.

Winter. *Twigs* rather stout, light purplish to reddish-brown; pith continuous, large, round, and white; leaf scars half-elliptical or somewhat 3-lobed, with 3 bundle scars. *Buds* two kinds usually present—branch buds small, ovoid, pubescent, with about 3 exposed scales; flower buds about ½ inch long, with 12 or more exposed scales, and clustered toward the tip of the twig. *Bark* thin, smooth, reddish brown on young plants, later becoming brownish gray to mottled, with shallow, diamond-shaped fissures separating rounded ridges.

The corkwood is a shrub or small tree, occasionally becoming 20 feet in height, with a trunk diameter of 4 to 5 inches above the swollen base. It occurs rarely and locally along tidewater rivers and in permanently inundated swamps, where it commonly forms thickets, from southeastern

Georgia and western Florida to southeastern Texas; and also in parts of Arkansas and Missouri.

This tree is of particular interest for two reasons: it is the only known representative of its family, and its lemon-yellow wood is the lightest of that of any North American tree, weighing only about 13 pounds per cubic foot. It is thus lighter than cork, with a specific gravity of 0.207 compared with 0.240 of cork *(Quercus suber* L.*)*. The wood is used locally for corks, as well as floats for fishing nets.

CORKWOOD

1. Branch with mature leaves.
2. Fruit.
3. Winter twig with catkins.
4. Detail of winter bud.

WALNUT FAMILY—JUGLANDACEAE

The Walnuts—Juglans

The walnuts are trees with alternate, pinnately compound leaves with 9 to 23 oblong lanceolate leaflets. They have stout, somewhat fragrant twigs with a large, chambered pith; large, more or less 3-lobed or "monkey-faced" leaf scars; and lateral buds, which are commonly superposed. The terminal bud is larger than the lateral ones and has but a few, hairy, visible scales. In late spring the drooping catkins composed of stamen-bearing flowers are conspicuous, but seeing the small pistillate ones in the axils of the developing leaves will require closer scrutiny. The fruits, which develop after wind pollination and fertilization, are sweet-meated nuts with bony shells that are wrinkled or deeply sculptured on the outside. They are enclosed in a semifleshy, nonsplitting husk that eventually rots away, exposing the nut.

The walnuts are important timber trees and are also valuable for the edible nuts that they produce. Two species, the black walnut and the butternut, are native to eastern North America. The English walnuts of commerce are the fruits of an Old World species, *Juglans regia* L.

BUTTERNUT   *Juglans cinerea* L.

> The chocolate-brown-colored pith, a terminal leaflet, which is nearly always present and equally large as the lateral ones, large, pinnately compound leaves, with moustachelike pad on the upper margin of the leaf scar, along with the large, oblong, rather than round, fruits are distinct.

Summer. *Leaves* 15 to 30 inches long, alternate, pinnately compound; leaflets 2 to 4 inches long, about half as broad, 11 to 17, oblong lanceolate,

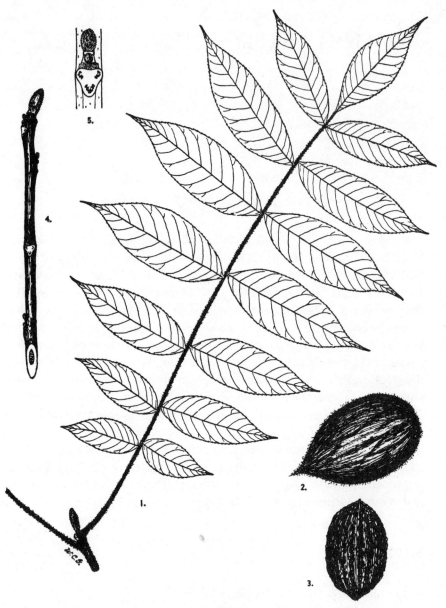

BUTTERNUT

1. Leaf.
2. Fruit with surrounding husk.
3. Nut with husk removed.
4. Winter twig.
5. Detail of bud and leaf scar including "moustache" directly above the leaf scar.

nearly sessile, attached to a stout, viscid-hairy rachis, margins sharply and finely toothed, apically pointed, broadly tapered to rounded bases; yellowish green, hairy, and rough-surfaced above; paler and softly hairy beneath; terminal leaflet as large as the lateral ones; leaf scars on older branches appearing as a moustachelike pad on their upper margins. *Fruits* (nut) about 2 or 2½ inches long, nearly twice as long as wide, oblong ovoid, bony-shelled, deeply sculptured, frequently borne in clusters, ripening in October and soon dropping from the tree; covered with a semifleshy, indehiscent, sticky, hairy husk.

Winter. *Twigs* stout, glabrous or somewhat hairy, greenish gray to buff, dotted with small lenticels; pith large, conspicuously chambered, dark chocolate brown, somewhat fragrant; leaf scars alternate, inversely triangular, 3-lobed, monkey-faced, usually with a convex upper margin, above which there is an elevated hairy pad. *Buds* coated with pale whitish-grayish hair; terminal bud ⅜ to ¾ inch long, irregularly oblong, somewhat flattened, hairy; lateral buds very much smaller, ovoid, commonly superposed. *Bark* on the younger trunks and branches light gray and smooth; on the older trunks becoming roughened by blackish furrows, the flat-topped ridges remaining light gray, whereas the bark of black walnut is dark brown to black.

The butternut is also known as the white walnut and the oilnut. It is a medium-sized tree, commonly attaining a height of 30 to 50 feet with a trunk diameter of 1 to 3 feet, but occasionally it attains a much larger size. It prefers rich, moist soils, commonly occurring in bottomlands, but it often follows the streams far back into the hills. The butternut tolerates cooler climates than the black walnut, ranging much farther northward and occurring at much higher elevations in the mountains than the latter species. It is a more or less common, but minor, associate tree in most of the northeastern hardwood forest associations. Large specimens of the butternut are almost invariably unsound.

The wood of the butternut is light, soft, weak, and close-grained, and is used principally for furniture and interior finish. The inner bark has mild cathartic properties, and it was rather widely used in former years as an orange or yellow dye. In some parts of the country pickles are made from the very young fruits. The nuts have sweet, edible, and very oily kernels. Squirrels of all kinds feed on them, probably providing the chief agency for seed dissemination. The Native Americans made sugar and syrup from the sap of the butternut, and also from that of the black walnut.

ut ranges from New Brunswick to eastern Ontario, south ~~~ansas, and along the Appalachian Mountains to north-~~~ia and Alabama.

BLACK WALNUT   *Juglans nigra* L.

> The pale brown-colored pith, terminal leaflet, if present, conspicuously smaller than the lateral ones, large leaf scars lacking a fuzzy "moustache," and round, rather than oblong, fruits separate the black walnut from the butternut.

Summer. *Leaves* 1 to 2 feet long, alternate, pinnately compound, aromatic when crushed; leaflets 2 to 4 inches long, about half as broad, numbering 13 to 23, short-stalked, ovate-lanceolate, nearly sessile, attached to a stout, hairy, but nonsticky rachis, margins sharply toothed, apically pointed, bases oblique, upper surface yellowish green, paler and usually hairy beneath; terminal leaflet often lacking; if present, conspicuously smaller than lateral ones. *Flowers,* both male and female borne on the same tree. *Fruits* (nut) 1½ to 2 inches in diameter, globular, with a sculptured bony shell; husks surround the shells, semifleshy, indehiscent, fetid or ill smelling; in summer, 2 to 3 inches in diameter, covered with greenish, warty-dotted husks; ripening in October and soon dropping from the trees.

Winter. *Twigs* light brown to orange-brown, somewhat fragrant, dotted with small lenticels; pith large, pale brown, chambered; leaf scars alternate, heart-shaped, 3-lobed, monkey-faced, with a notch along the top margin, a small lateral bud in this notch, and usually another bud directly above it. *Buds* covered with short, grayish, silky hairs; terminal bud ¼ to ⅓ inch long (clearly shorter than those of the butternut), broadly ovoid, gray-hairy, bluntish; lateral buds much smaller, roundish. *Bark* dark brown or nearly black, with deep, roughly diamond-shaped furrows and rounded ridges.

———

The black walnut is a large tree, often 50 to 75 feet or more in height with a trunk from 2 to 4 feet in diameter. It has an open and round-topped crown. When growing in the forest, the trunks are usually free of lateral branches for a considerable distance from the ground. It attains its maxi-

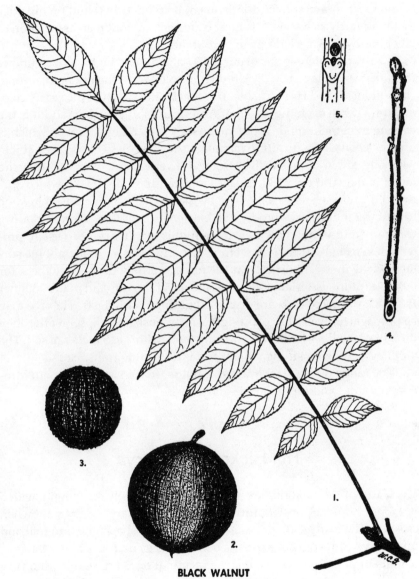

BLACK WALNUT

1. Leaf.
2. Fruit with surrounding husk.
3. Nut with husk removed.
4. Winter twig.
5. Details of winter buds and leaf scar.

mum growth on deep, rich soils, being much smaller on poorer sites. While most common in bottomlands, it is frequently found on hillsides that have fairly rich soils. It is most commonly found in an association of other hardwoods, very rarely in pure stands.

The black walnut is one of our most valuable and highly prized timber trees. The wood is a rich, dark brown in color and is heavy, hard, strong, close-grained, and very durable in contact with the soil. Since early colonial days it has been the queen of American cabinet woods, and it is the leading gunstock wood. Today much of it is made into veneer, which is used extensively by furniture manufacturers. The nuts have sweet, somewhat oily edible kernels with a strong and very distinctive taste. They are much in demand for making cakes and candies. The husks, which surround the nuts, were used as a dye by the pioneers. When boiled in large vats of water, the husks produce an extremely useful metal preservative; trappers would often boil their traps in this manner prior to use to protect them from rusting. This method also produces a gunmetal-blue surface on the metal. Squirrels eat the nuts, and they often bury them for possible future use. Many, of course, are never dug up, and in this manner the black walnut's seeds are dispersed through our forests. The tree may be propagated by simply planting the nuts, husk and all, soon after they drop from the trees in the fall, covering them with 3 to 5 inches of soil. The seedling develops a strong taproot and is difficult to transplant.

The range of the black walnut extends from Massachusetts to Minnesota south to northern Florida and Texas.

The Hickories—Carya

The leaves of the hickories are alternate and pinnately compound, with 5 or more, or rarely 3, leaflets, turn yellow in the fall, and are fragrant when crushed. The leaflets are not uniform in size and shape; the terminal and upper pair of leaflets are conspicuously larger than the lower pairs of leaflets in most species. All but the terminal ones are sessile. The very flexible twigs, which are extremely difficult to break, are usually stout, but sometimes rather slender, with small but conspicuous lenticels and angular or somewhat star-shaped pith, which can be observed by making cross-sectional cuts with a sharp razor blade. The leaf scars are large and conspicuous, heart-shaped or 3-lobed, with numerous bundle scars either scattered or arranged in three distinct groups.

The wind-pollinated flowers of the hickories appear in the spring with the leaves. The staminate flowers are borne in drooping 3-branched aments near the base of the current season's growth; the pistillate ones in inconspicuous, few-flowered, spikelike clusters near the end of the growth. Both kinds of flowers occur on each tree.

The fruits are bony-shelled nuts, which are enclosed within 4-valved husks. In some species the husk is thick, splitting easily to the base at maturity, while others are thin husked, splitting tardily only part way. They ripen in October and soon drop from the trees. Seed dissemination is largely through animals, principally the squirrels, which bury quantities of them in the forest litter as a reserve food supply. Extended periods of wet weather or hard freezes during the flowering period in spring may result in a failure of the nut crop the following fall.

The hickories are typically American trees. The word *hickory* is said to have originated from the American Indian word *powchickora*, first used in English writing by John Smith of Jamestown Colony. Due to the difficulty in both spelling and pronunciation, it is little wonder that it was written no fewer than 17 different ways.

PECAN   *Carya illinoinensis* **(Wangenh.) K. Koch**

The numerous, 11 to 17, asymmetrically falcate-shaped leaflets of this very characteristic vase-shaped tree, with its large, egg-shaped fruits with thin 4-winged husks, and yellow-hairy valvate terminal buds, are distinct.

Summer. *Leaves* 12 to 20 inches long; leaflets 3 to 7 inches long, 1 to 2 inches wide, (9) 11 to 17, sessile or nearly sessile, lanceolate, or more or less sickle-shaped, tip sharply pointed, bases rounded or wedge-shaped, margin sharply toothed; upper surfaces dark yellowish green, lower surfaces paler and often slightly hairy; terminal leaflet smaller than some lateral ones. *Fruits* (nut) 1 to 2 inches long, egg-shaped, usually borne in small clusters of 3 to 11 individuals, oblong, pointed; husk thin, slightly 4-winged; nuts light reddish brown, often with dark spots, glabrous or nearly so, with a thin shell and a sweet kernel, the easiest of all hickories to extract.

Winter. *Twigs* moderately stout, reddish brown, more or less hairy, dotted with prominent orange lenticels; leaf scars obovate, with a number of bundle scars. *Buds* yellowish brown, hairy; terminal bud larger than

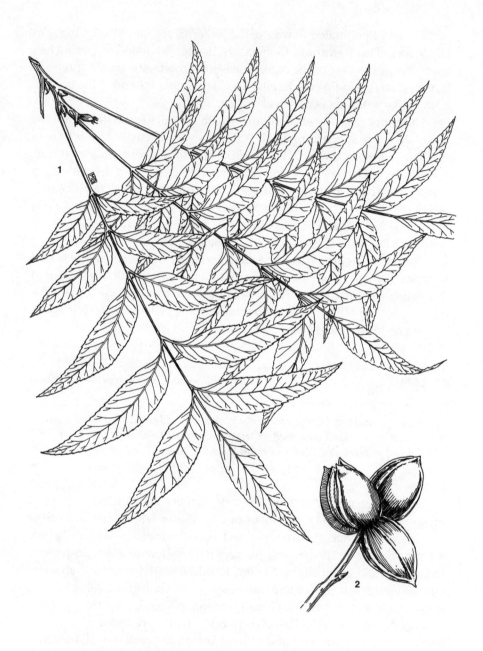

PECAN

1. Branch with mature leaves and falcate-
   shaped leaflets.

2. Multiple fruits with husks.

lateral buds, ¼ to ½ inch long, somewhat 4-angled; bud scales 2, valvate, nonoverlapping; lateral buds often superposed. *Bark* tight, light brown or grayish brown with narrow fissures separating flat, scaly, interlacing ridges.

Comparisons. The pecan is more of an upland species than the similar water hickory, with a more rounded nut and more numerous leaflets.

The pecan, so widely cultivated throughout the South as a shade tree, as well as for its sweet-meated nuts, is a native of the Mississippi Valley region and is the state tree of Texas. It attains a height of 150 feet or more with a trunk diameter of upwards of 3 feet, and in the open it forms a broad rounded crown. It is the largest of our native hickories. Its characteristic vase shape when growing within open, southern plantations is most distinctive. The wood is rather inferior to that of most other hickories, but it is used for boxes and crates, furniture, flooring, and veneer for making baskets. Under a number of cultivated varieties it is commercially important as a nut-producing tree.

The original range of the pecan extended from southern Indiana, Illinois, and Iowa southward and southwestward to western Mississippi, Louisiana, and Texas, the native habitat being rich but well-drained bottomlands. It is now widely cultivated with a number of highly improved fruiting cultivars being produced in the southern states.

This species hybridizes commonly with other hickories such as the bitter-nut hickory, producing *Carya* x *brownii* Sarg., which occurs throughout Missouri, Kansas, and south to Louisiana; with the water hickory, producing *C.* x *lecontei* Little, which extends from Illinois to Texas and South Carolina; with the shell-bark hickory, producing *C.* x *nussbaumeri* Sarg., which occurs throughout Missouri, Iowa, Illinois, Kentucky, and Indiana; and with the mockernut hickory, producing *C.* x *schneckii* Sarg., which occurs in the Illinois and Iowa area.

WATER HICKORY   *Carya aquatica* (Michx. f.) Nutt.

> This is a wetland species, characterized by its 7 to 15 hairy leaflets, dark red-brown, valvate bud scales, and flattened nuts with thin, winged husks.

Summer. *Leaves* 8 to 15 inches long; leaflets 2 to 5 inches long, ½ to 1½ inches wide, (7) 9 to 15, sessile or short-stalked, lanceolate or rather sickle-shaped, apically long-pointed, margins finely but sharply toothed; dark green and glabrous above, brownish-hairy to nearly glabrous beneath. *Fruits* (nut) 1 to 1½ inches long, nearly spherical, with thin and prominently 4-winged husks, splitting nearly but not quite to base; nuts within husks flattened, dark reddish brown, 4-angled or 4-ribbed, with thin, longitudinally wrinkled shells; kernels very bitter.

Winter. *Twigs* slender, reddish brown to grayish brown, glabrous or nearly so, dotted with numerous lenticels; leaf scars ovate. *Buds* dark, reddish brown at maturity, usually hairy, yellow-granular, scales 2, valvate with their edges meeting; terminal bud ⅛ to ¼ inch long, larger than lateral buds. *Bark* light brown or reddish brown, separating into long, loose, shaggy scales.

Comparisons. The water hickory is most often confused with the pecan, from which the former can be told by having hairier leaflets, which have much more symmetrical bases than do those of the pecan, and a cross-sectionally flattened rather than rounded nut.

The water hickory is also called the swamp hickory and bitter pecan. It is usually a medium-sized, narrow crowned tree, but occasionally it attains a height of 80 to 100 feet with a trunk diameter of 2 feet. It is a tree of the deeper swamps and frequently inundated river bottoms. Its wood is not of a high grade and merely finds local usage as posts, props, and fuel. This species hybridizes with the black hickory to produce *C.* x *ludouiciana* (Ashe) Little and with the pecan to produce *C.* x *lecontei* Little.

Water hickory has a range extending through the coastal plain from southeastern Virginia to southern Florida west to eastern Texas; and north, in the Mississippi Valley, to southern Illinois and southeastern Oklahoma.

WATER HICKORY

1. Branch with leaves and fruits.

2. Fruits with surrounding husks.

BITTER-NUT HICKORY   *Carya cordiformis* (Wangenh.) K. Koch

During all seasons, the bitter-nut hickory can be identified from all other native trees by its bright sulfur yellow, glabrous, valvate, granular bud scales. Its 7 to 11 narrow, lanceolate, scythe-shaped leaflets, which are hairy and dotted below, and thin husks on its fruits are also distinct.

Summer. *Leaves* 6 to 10 inches long, alternate, pinnately compound, with (7) 9 to 11 leaflets; terminal and uppermost lateral leaflets 4 to 6 inches long, ¾ to 1¼ inches wide, distinctly narrower than those of the other hickories, lanceolate to lanceolate ovate; upper surfaces bright green and glabrous, lower surfaces paler and usually a little hairy; margins finely to coarsely toothed. *Fruits* (nut) ¾ to 1½ inches long, nearly globular or slightly obovoid; husks thin, 4-winged above the middle, covered with yellow glandular dots, tardily splitting to about the middle; nuts nearly round, often a little broader than long, quite glabrous, pale reddish brown, with comparatively thin shells; intensely bitter and puckery kernels.

Winter. *Twigs* rather slender, buff to grayish brown, glabrous or slightly hairy. *Buds* bright yellow, distinctive; terminal bud ½ to ¾ inch long, slender, flattened, obliquely blunt-pointed, scales valvate, usually with 2 paired scales placed edge to edge; lateral buds smaller, usually superposed. *Bark* close, firm, light grayish, with shallow fissures and interlacing ridges, but never with loose plates.

The bitter-nut hickory, also known as the swamp hickory, is one of the most widely distributed of our hickories. It attains a height of 50 to 75 feet with a trunk diameter of 1 to 2½ feet, but occasional trees are much larger. It prefers wet or moist, rich, loamy or gravelly soils, but it is sometimes found on drier sites well up on the slopes of the hills. It is most common in the bottomlands, in swamps, and along the banks of streams, but it occasionally follows the streams well back into the mountains. Generally the bitternut hickory is found only as a minor species in stands of other hardwoods.

The wood is similar to that of the other hickories, but it is slightly lighter, less stiff, and not quite as strong. It is used for crates and boxes, flooring, furniture, fuel, and for smoking meats. The fruits are too bitter to be edible, and even the squirrels usually ignore them.

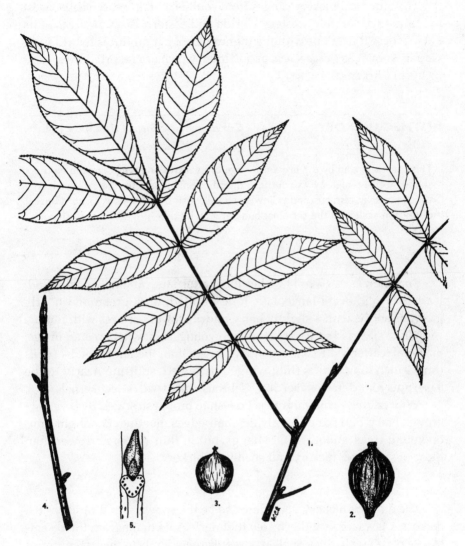

BITTER-NUT HICKORY

1. Branch with leaves.
2. Fruit with surrounding husk.
3. Nut with husk removed.
4. Winter twig.
5. Details of bud and leaf scar.

The bitter-nut hickory ranges from southern Maine and Quebec west to Minnesota, south to western Florida and eastern Texas. In areas of its range where it overlaps with the pignut hickory, it produces hybrid individuals known as *Carya* x *demareei* Palmer, which are reported from Kentucky and Arkansas.

NUTMEG HICKORY   *Carya myristiciformis* (Michx. f.) Nutt.

> This species is told by the brownish tinge of its leaves and twigs, created by the abundance of scales, by its southern distribution, by its 5 to 9 falcate leaflets, which are silky, lustrous, and yellowish to yellowish-brown below, by its valvate outer bud scales on the terminal buds, and by its thin-husked, football-shaped nuts.

Summer. *Leaves* 7 to 14 inches long, alternate, pinnately compound; leaflets 5 to 9, ovate-lanceolate, long-pointed; dark green and nearly glabrous above, with a slightly hairy midrib; lower surfaces with minute whitish to silverish scales at least when young, somewhat greener in age; terminal leaflet 3½ to 6 inches long, larger than the lateral buds. *Fruits* (nut) 1 inch long; husks thin, winged or keeled, splitting nearly to the base; nuts round in cross section, glabrous, thick, with sweet kernels.

Winter. *Twigs* with minute yellowish to brownish scales. *Buds* yellow-brown, hairy, bud scales 2, valvate, their edges meeting. *Bark* light gray, on young trees smooth; later shaggy, but in thin strips, narrower than those of shag-bark hickory and shell-bark hickory.

The nutmeg hickory, considered to be the showiest and rarest of the hickories, is a large southern tree that derives its name from the resemblance of its small, thick-shelled, sweet-kerneled nuts to the true nutmeg. It is a large tree with dark brown, fissured, and scaly bark. It occurs rather rarely along riverbanks, valley floors, bottomland forests, and in swamps of North Carolina and South Carolina; also from central Alabama, Louisiana, and eastern Texas northward to Arkansas and southeastern Oklahoma. Apparently, it is most common in Alabama and southern Arkansas.

SHAG-BARK HICKORY   *Carya ovata* (P. Mill.) K. Koch

The persistent tufts of hairs on or near the teeth apices of five mature leaflets, the long-pointed bud scales, present on at least some of the winter buds, coupled with the conspicuously shaggy bark on trees over 6 inches in diameter, and the large, thick-husked fruits are distinctive.

Summer. *Leaves* 8 to 14 inches long, alternate, pinnately compound; leaflets 5 to 7, usually 5; ovate or obovate, dark yellowish green above, paler and glabrous to lightly hairy beneath; margins finely but sharply toothed, on young leaves densely ciliate, on older leaves producing conspicuous hair tufts at the tips of the teeth; terminal leaflet 5 to 7 inches long, 2 to 3 inches wide; petioles stout, either glabrous or a little hairy. *Flowers* bright green, catkins. *Fruits* (nut) 1 to 2 inches in diameter, nearly spherical, and depressed at the top; husks ⅛ to ½ inch thick, splitting into 4 sections at maturity; nuts white or pale tawny, a little flattened, 4-ridged, with rather thin shells and sweet kernels.

Winter. *Twigs* stout, grayish brown to reddish brown, more or less rough-hairy, covered with numerous small, slightly longitudinally elongated, pale lenticels; leaf scars large, more or less heart-shaped, with numerous scattered bundle scars. *Buds,* terminal bud ½ to ¾ inch long, broadly ovoid, with 3 or 4 pairs of light brown to gray, triangular, and often long-pointed, persistent, loosely spreading outer scales that overlap with the bud; lateral buds much smaller and distinctly divergent. *Bark* dark gray, separating into elongated plates at maturity, ends of which are unattached to bole, creating a shaggy appearance.

Comparisons. The stout twigs and the gray bark, which on mature individuals (mostly 6 inches or more in diameter) exfoliates in long, narrow, shaggy plates, will serve to identify the shag-bark hickory from all other trees, except the Southern shag-bark and the shell-bark hickories. Also, the tufts of hairs on the margins of the leaflets of this species are lacking in the shell-bark hickory.

―――――――――――

The shag-bark hickory is also known as the shell-bark hickory, scaly-bark hickory, or upland hickory. It becomes a large tree, attaining a height of 50 to 80 or more feet and a trunk diameter of 1 to 3 feet, with an open and somewhat narrowly oblong crown. This hickory grows on a variety of soils, but it prefers those that are rich and well drained. While it occurs

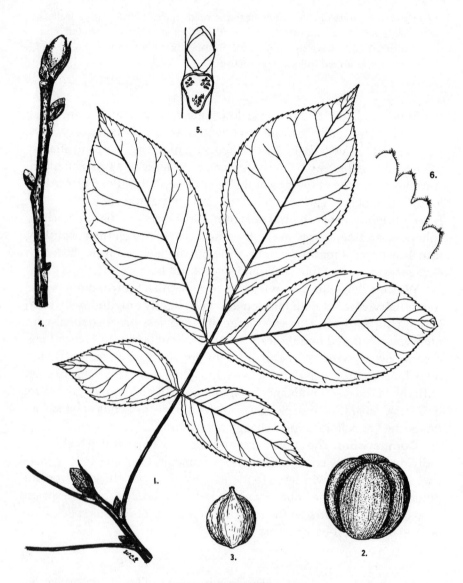

SHAG-BARK HICKORY

1. Leaf.
2. Fruit with surrounding husk.
3. Nut with husk removed.
4. Winter twig.

5. Detail of bud and leaf scar.
6. Detail of leaf margin with dense tufts of marginal hairs.

quite frequently in bottomlands, it is perhaps more common on the hill slopes, and it often occurs on rather dry, rocky hillsides. The wood is very heavy, hard, strong, tough, close-grained, and elastic. Historically, it has been considered as the best of commercial hickories, used as a source of wooden spokes of wagons, carriage carts, and even automobiles. The tree develops a strong taproot, making transplanting difficult, but it is easily propagated by the fruits. The shagbark hickory ranges from Maine and Quebec west to Minnesota, and south to northern Florida and eastern Texas.

SOUTHERN SHAG-BARK HICKORY   *Carya carolinae-septentrionalis* (Ashe) Engl. and Graebn.

The southern shag-bark hickory is also known as the Carolina hickory. It differs from the shag-bark hickory in having a more southern distribution, smaller leaves, narrower lanceolate or inversely lanceolate leaflets; smaller sweet-kerneled nuts, and darker reddish brown to black (rather than tan to brown) terminal buds that are usually glabrous (rather than tomentose); thinner and glabrous (rather than hairy) twigs that turn black when dried. It occurs in rich woods, chiefly in the Piedmont region, from western North Carolina, South Carolina, and Georgia, west to Tennessee, Alabama, and Mississippi.

SHELL-BARK HICKORY   *Carya laciniosa* (Michx. f.) Loud.

The shell-bark may be distinguished from other hickories by its very stout, buff to orange-brown twigs, which are glabrous or nearly so, but covered with small orange-colored lenticels. This, coupled with its large, 7-leaflet leaves, extremely shaggy bark, and large fruits, with the thickest husks of all the hickories, is most distinctive.

Summer. *Leaves*, usually 15 to 24 inches long; leaflets 5 to 9, usually 7; dark green above, paler yellowish green or yellowish brown beneath, lower surfaces usually densely hairy; margins finely and sharply toothed; petioles stout, either glabrous or hairy. *Fruits* (nut) 1¼ to 2¼ inches long, 1½ to 1¾ wide; husk very thick, ⅓ to ½ inch, splitting completely to base

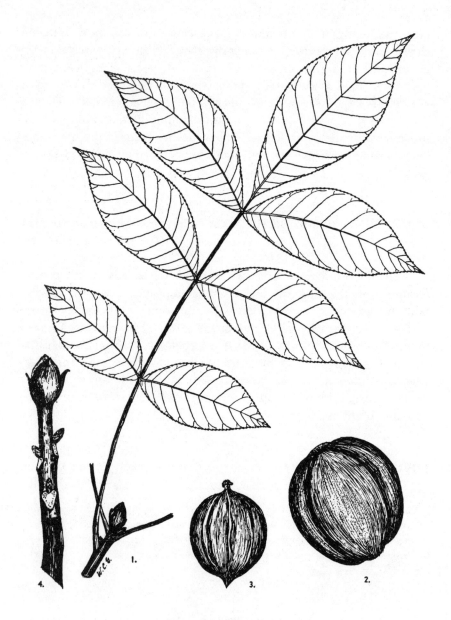

SHELL-BARK HICKORY

1. Leaf.
2. Fruit with surrounding husk.
3. Nut with husk removed.
4. Winter twig.

into 4 sections at maturity; nuts nearly spherical but slightly flattened, 4- to 6-ribbed, with pointed ends, pale yellowish brown to pale reddish brown, with thick shells and sweet kernels.

Winter. *Twigs* very stout, buff to orange brown, glabrous or nearly so, covered with small orange-colored lenticels; leaf scars large, heart-shaped, somewhat 3-lobed, with numerous scattered bundle scars. *Buds* similar to those of the shagbark hickory and southern shagbark hickory but larger and somewhat spreading; the terminal bud ¾ to 1¼ inch long, somewhat hairy. *Bark* dark gray, separating into elongated plates at maturity, ends of which are unattached to bole, creating a very shaggy appearance.

Comparisons. The shell-bark hickory most closely resembles the shag-bark hickory and southern shag-bark hickory. Although their barks are similar, the shell-bark hickory may be identified by its larger leaves, which are hairy below; by its usually 7 leaflets rather than 5; and in some cases by nuts that are 2 to 3 times larger and darker colored. The twigs are also similar, but thicker and slightly more hairy in the shell-bark hickory. Unlike the shag-bark and southern shag-bark hickories, the shell-bark hickory prefers wet bottomlands, even those that are inundated for periods of time. It is often associated with other swamp-loving species such as the American elm, the silver maple, the pin oak, the bur oak, and the swamp white oak. Its wood is essentially the same as that of the shag-bark hickory, and it is utilized in the same ways. Its leaves, however, are clearly larger.

The shell-bark hickory is also known as the big-leaf shag-bark hickory, bottom shell-bark, and kingnut hickory. It has the general appearance of the shag-bark hickory as to form and bark, but it does not attain the height of the latter species.

This is an uncommon to locally rare species that extends from central New York to Nebraska, south to North Carolina, northern Alabama, Mississippi, and Oklahoma.

MOCKERNUT HICKORY   *Carya alba* (L.) Nutt. ex Ell.

The tufted-hairy to woolly leaves, which are very aromatic when crushed, with 7 leaflets, which have tiny yellowish granules on their undersurface, along with their large often cinnamon-hairy winter buds and twigs are distinctive. These characters, along with its rather thick fruit husks, which do not split as easily as those of the shag-bark hickory, will help identify this species.

Summer. *Leaves* 8 to 12 inches long; leaflets lanceolate or obovate, 5 to 9, usually 7, fragrant when crushed; dark lustrous yellowish green above, paler and woolly-hairy beneath; margins coarsely or finely toothed; apical leaflet 5 to 8 inches long, 2½ to 4½ inches wide; petioles stout, also hairy. *Fruits* (nut) 1½ to 2 inches long, obovoid or nearly spherical, deeply 4-channeled from their base to the somewhat depressed top; husks thin to thickish, ⅛ to ¼ inch thick, splitting nearly but not completely to the base at maturity; nuts variable in shape but more or less spherical, light reddish brown, with very hard shells and small, sweet to bitter kernels; inferior in taste to the shag-bark hickory.

Winter. *Twigs* stout, cinnamon to reddish brown to grayish brown, more or less hairy, covered with numerous pale lenticels; leaf scars somewhat heart-shaped, 3-lobed, with the basal lobe rather elongated. *Buds* terminal, ½ to ¾ inch long, nearly globular, broad, blunt; bud scales 10 to 12; outer pair of overlapping bud scales, reddish brown, hairy, shed very early, exposing the yellowish gray, silky inner scales. *Bark* tight, firm, with shallow furrows and rounded, interlacing ridges.

The mockernut hickory is also known as the white heart hickory, big-bud hickory (because of the large winter buds), and bullnut hickory. It becomes a large tree, on better sites attaining a height of 50 to 75 feet with a trunk diameter of 2 to 3 feet. The crown may vary from narrowly oblong to broadly round-topped. The mockernut prefers rich and well-drained soils, but it often occurs on rocky mountain slopes and dry ridges. It occurs in various hardwood forest types, but it is invariably one of the minor species. Of generally southern distribution, it is one of the commonest hickories in the South, but comparatively rare in the northern part of its range.

The wood is very similar to that of the shag-bark hickory and is utilized in the same manner. The name "mockernut" alludes to the fact that

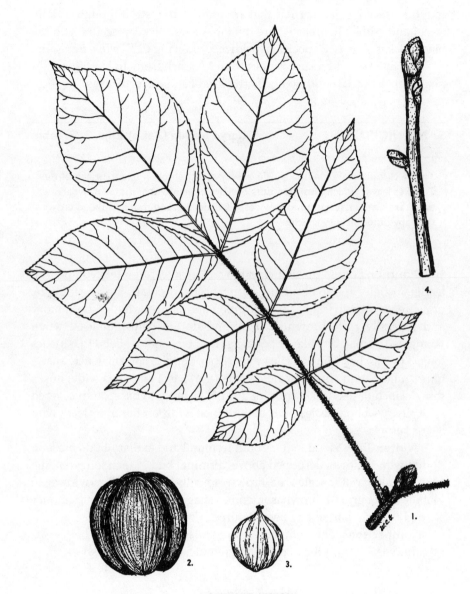

MOCKERNUT HICKORY

1. Leaf.
2. Fruit with surrounding husk.
3. Nut with husk removed.
4. Winter twig.

the nuts, while of a size similar to those of the shag-bark hickory, are very tough-surfaced, small kernels that are inferior in taste, although usually sweet and edible. In areas where the mockernut hickory occurs with the black hickory, the two species hybridize, producing C. x *collina* Laughlin.

The mockernut hickory ranges from Massachusetts to Michigan, Illinois, and Nebraska south to northern Florida and eastern Texas.

SAND HICKORY   *Carya pallida* (Ashe) Engl. & Graebn.

> The thick fruit husks, unusually pale, silvery-scaly, yellowish undersurface of the 7-leaflet leaves, which also have tufts of hairs intermixed, and the fairly narrow twigs are distinct. It has a more widespread, denser, and more rounded crown than any other hickory species.

Summer. *Leaves* 7 to 15 inches long, alternate, pinnately compound; leaflets usually 7, also occurring with 5 or 9, lanceolate, long-acuminate, or acute, asymmetrical base, light green and lustrous above, both hairy and pale silvery-to-brownish scaly and dotted below, at least when young, with small disklike or peltate scales; terminal leaflet 4 to 6 inches long, 1 to 2 inches wide, sessile or nearly so; petioles conspicuously rusty-hairy, mixed with silvery scales. *Fruits* (nut) 1 to 1½ inches wide; husks thin, ⅛ inch or less thick, splitting tardily entirely to base, often covered with silvery-yellow scales; nuts about 1 inch wide, obscurely ridged, with sweet kernels.

Winter. *Twigs* slender. *Buds* both terminal and axillary buds present, dotted with scales as described above; terminal bud ¼ inch long, oblong, 6- to 9-scaled, outer scales red-brown, apically slightly hairy, with resin globules. *Bark* grayish brown, sometimes shaggy, with irregular diamond-shaped ridges separated by deep fissures.

Comparisons. The minutely silvery-scaled fruits and buds help separate this species from the nonscaly pignut hickory and red hickory.

The sand hickory, or pale hickory, is characteristically a medium-sized forest tree, 40 to 50 feet high, of dry upland woods and sandy soils. In the open, it develops a narrow oblong crown with ascending upper branches and drooping lower branches. The small fruits (smaller than most other hickories) have rather thin, tardily opening husks, which are conspicuously dotted with minute, yellow, glandular scales. The ovoid or roundish, angular nuts each contain a sweet kernel.

This species occurs on well-drained slopes, rocky ridges, and sandy plains, most commonly in the Piedmont and upper coastal plain from southern New Jersey south to northwestern Florida, westward to Tennessee and Louisiana.

PIGNUT HICKORY   *Carya glabra* **(P. Mill.) Sweet**

> The unusually bitter, thin-husked, pear-shaped fruit, glabrous leaves with mostly 5 leaflets, and equally glabrous and small winter buds and slender twigs, the latter also being exceptionally slender for a hickory, are most distinct.

Summer. *Leaves* 8 to 12 inches long, alternate, pinnately compound, decidedly glabrous, except with occasional hairs on the veins beneath; leaflets 5 to 7, usually 5, lanceolate, dark green above, paler beneath; terminal leaflet 3 to 6 inches long, 2 to 3 inches wide, sharply serrately toothed. *Fruits* (nut) 1 to 1½ inches long, inversely ovoid with a distinct tapering neck at the base, or a somewhat top-shaped or pear-shaped appearance; husks thin, somewhat 4-winged toward the summit, may remain closed or splitting tardily to or near the middle at maturity; nuts with small, usually bitter kernels.

Winter. *Twigs* under ¼ inch wide, comparatively slender for those of a hickory, decidedly glabrous, reddish brown to grayish brown. *Buds,* terminal bud ¼ to ½ inch long, broadly ovoid to nearly globular, rather bluntly pointed; lateral buds ⅛ to ¼ inch long, somewhat smaller than terminal ones; outer bud scales glabrous, shiny, either greenish or reddish, often shed during the fall or early winter, exposing the grayish, silky-hairy inner scales. *Bark* dark gray, close and firm-looking appearance, shallowly fissured and narrowly ridged; in general having an irregular diamond-shaped pattern.

Comparisons. The pignut hickory and red hickory are the only hickories with consistently glabrous leaves, twigs, and buds.

The pignut hickory is an extremely variable species. It is generally an upland medium- to large-sized tree, usually from 50 to 60 feet in height with a trunk diameter of 1 to 3 feet. Its crown is oblong and rather nar-

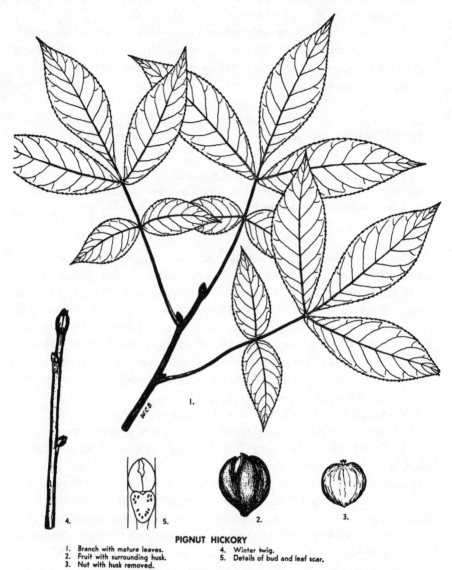

PIGNUT HICKORY

1. Branch with mature leaves.
2. Fruit with surrounding husk.
3. Nut with husk removed.
4. Winter twig.
5. Details of bud and leaf scar.

row, with numerous short and slender branches, the lowermost often with a decided droop. It prefers well-drained to dry, fairly rich soils. In the southern Appalachians, it represents one of the most common of our hickories. The pignut is a characteristic tree of the hillsides and ridges, ranging from Maine to Minnesota, south to Florida and Texas.

The wood is heavy, hard, tough, and strong. It resembles that of the shagbark hickory and is used in the same ways. The pignut makes a very good ornamental tree, but it is difficult to transplant. The nuts are often bitter and are scarcely edible.

The scrub hickory (*C. floridana* Sarg.) of Florida is a similar but smaller species that intergrades with the pignut hickory but has less obvious pear-shaped fruits and bears amber-colored scales on the lower leaves and winter buds. It is also similar to the black hickory, which is not known from Florida, but lacks the reddish hairs on the undersurfaces of the leaflets of that species.

RED HICKORY   *Carya ovalis* (Wangenh.) Sarg.

The red hickory is also known as the sweet pignut hickory and the oval pignut hickory. It usually has 7 yellowish, scaly leaflets, but otherwise glabrous twigs, and its bark is somewhat deeply furrowed or even shaggy. Its smaller, roundish, thin-husked fruits are 4-winged above the middle. The husks split open to the base to release the small but usually sweet-kerneled nuts. Its bark is more deeply furrowed than that of the pignut hickory, becoming somewhat broken into scales or even short loose plates on older individuals. The red hickory occurs throughout much of the range of the pignut hickory, a species with which it is often confused. It can be separated from that species by its 7 rather than 5 leaflets, which are more ovate or obovate in shape, by its thinner rather than thicker shelled fruits that are more rounded rather than pear-shaped and that generally split completely to base rather than about halfway, by its somewhat thicker twigs (¼ inch or more), and by a nut that is 4-ribbed rather than being round, as it is in the pignut hickory. The red hickory also has a shaggier pattern of its bark with sharper ridges than that of the pignut hickory. Some consider red hickory a variety, *C. glabra* var. *odorata* (Marsh.) Little, of the pignut hickory.

BLACK HICKORY   *Carya texana* **Buckl.**

The black hickory is unique among our hickories in that its young branchlets, buds, and developing 7-leaflet leaves are densely coated with rusty-red hairs, some of which persist on the winter twigs and particularly on the buds.

Summer. *Leaves* 6 to 12 inches long, alternate, pinnately compound; leaflets 2½ to 6 inches long, 1¼ to 2½ inches wide, 5 to 7 (mostly 7), oblanceolate to obovate, occasionally diamond-shaped with reddish hairs underneath; margins serrate, ciliate with hair in clusters, apices acuminate, base asymmetrical; upper surface pale with rusty hairs mixed with red to orange glands, with axillary hairs below; petiole ¼ to ½ inch long. *Fruits* (nut) 1¼ to 1⅜ inch long, and nearly as wide, round to obovoid, pear- or egg-shaped; husks 4-valved, rather thin, splitting to the base, covered with rusty hair and occasionally with yellowish branlike scales; nuts slightly 4-angled above the middle to nearly smooth, with coarse network of paler ridges, pale brown to reddish brown; kernels sweet.

Winter. *Twigs* rigid but thin, rusty-red-hairy, scaly, but becoming glabrous in age; pith brown, continuous. *Leaf scars* large, triangular, with 3 bundle scars. *Buds,* terminal buds nearly ½ inch long, about half as wide, obtuse to acute, rusty-hairy, with yellowish scales; lateral buds somewhat smaller. *Bark* thick, black, tight, with blocky ridges at maturity.

Comparisons. This species is similar to the pignut hickory but is easily distinguished by the reddish hairs on the twigs, buds, lower leaf surfaces, and petioles.

BAYBERRY FAMILY—MYRICACEAE

The Bayberries—Morella

SOUTHERN BAYBERRY
Morella cerifera (L.) Small

> The aromatic crushed twigs and evergreen leaves, with tiny, yellow surface resin glands and marginal teeth above the middle, along with small, white fruits, are distinctive.

Leaves 2 to 4 inches long, ½ to 1 inch wide, persistent, evergreen, aromatic, alternate, simple, oblanceolate, usually apically pointed, dotted with small, orange-yellow glands beneath, margins more or less sharply toothed. *Flowers* catkinlike, borne in leaf axils; male and female flowers borne on separate trees. *Fruits* (nut) ⅛ inch wide, in berrylike clusters, small, glaucous (sometimes bluish white) on some plants. *Twigs* aromatic. *Bark* thin, smooth, greenish gray, blotched with gray.

The southern bayberry is also known as the bayberry or the candleberry. It is an evergreen shrub or small tree, sometimes 20 feet or more in height with a trunk up to about 10 inches in diameter, with a narrow to spreading round-topped crown. It grows in damp woodlands and about the borders of swamps and ponds, but only on sandy, never on mucky, soils, often forming large clumps or thickets. Staminate and pistillate flowers are produced on separate plants; thus some plants regularly produce fruits whereas others never do. In early spring the staminate catkins are quite conspicuous while they are shaking their dusty pollen to the winds.

The name candleberry is derived from the use of the waxy coating of the fruits in making the fragrant, greenish white bayberry candles. These

SOUTHERN BAYBERRY

1. Branch with mature leaves.
2. Leaf with entire margin.
3. Winter branch with catkin-like buds.
4. Fruiting branch.
5. Detail of leaf scar and bud.
6. Detail of fruit.

same fruits are eaten by numerous species of wild birds including the bob-white and the wild turkey. The southern bayberry has a range extending through the coastal plain from southern New Jersey to southern Florida, westward to eastern Texas, and northward in the interior to Oklahoma and Arkansas.

BEECH FAMILY—FAGACEAE

The Beeches—Fagus

AMERICAN BEECH   *Fagus grandifolia* **Ehrh.**

During all seasons the American beech may be identified by its smooth, gray bark, which has more or less darker mottling and which is often seen with carved initials. This, coupled with its slender, elongated, golden-brown, cigarlike buds and prickly fruits, and its 9 to 14 pairs of straight parallel leaf veins, is most distinctive.

Summer. *Leaves* 3 to 5 inches long, alternate, 2-ranked, oblong or ovate, tapering apically, wedge-shaped or rounded basally, turning bronzed brown in the autumn; 9 to 14 veins prominent, pinnately parallel, each terminating in a pointed marginal tooth; dark green and glabrous above, paler yellowish green beneath, thin and somewhat papery in texture; petioles short, somewhat silky-hairy. *Flowers* appearing after the leaves unfold; both male and female flowers develop on the same tree, male flowers appearing in tight ball-like clusters, female flower smaller, less tightly congested. *Fruits* (nut) small, light brown, triangular-shaped, borne in pairs in small, 4-valved burs, which have rather soft recurved prickles, maturing in October and dropping from the trees; may often be found on the ground beneath them in winter.

Winter. *Twigs* slender, lustrous brown, more or less zigzag, very often with a few faded and dried leaves persisting on the branches well into spring. *Buds* ¾ to 1 inch long, slender, cigar-shaped, sharp-pointed, pale chestnut brown, distinctive, diverging at an angle of 45 degrees or more from the twigs; bud scales 8 to 18, gray-tipped, arranged in 4 rows.

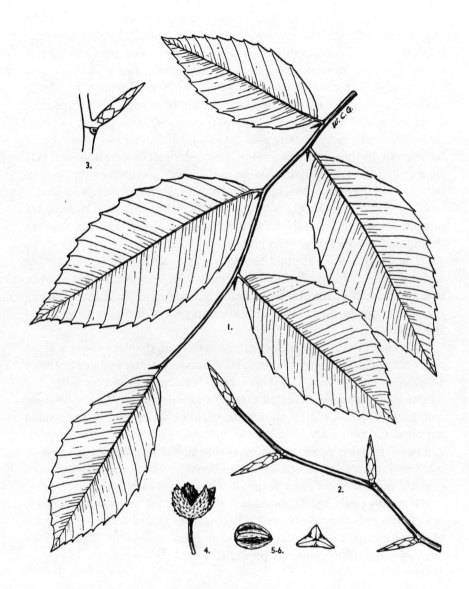

AMERICAN BEECH

1. Branch with mature leaves.
2. Winter twig.
3. Detail of cigar-shaped bud and leaf scar.
4. Opened bur.
5-6. Nuts.

The American beech is a large tree, often attaining a height of 60 to 75 feet and a trunk diameter of 2 to 3 feet. Specimens in virgin forests not infrequently attained heights of more than 100 feet with trunk diameters up to and exceeding 4 feet. The American beech has a shallow root system, and it often sends up suckers from the roots. Consequently large trees are commonly surrounded by a thicket of smaller ones. It prefers deep, fertile, and well-drained soils, but it grows well in a variety of situations. The beech is commonly associated with the sugar maple and other hardwoods in the climax beech-birch-maple forest association, and it is frequently found along with the eastern hemlock and eastern white pine. In the fall, the leaves of this species turn a rich golden yellow and later a coppery brown. The leaves (especially those on the lower branches) are persistent even more so than those of oaks and are retained on the tree throughout much of the winter and early spring.

The wood is close-grained, hard, strong, and tough. It is not durable and it is difficult to season. In former years it was not considered to be of much commercial importance; but now it is commonly utilized for flooring, cooperage, furniture, woodenware, and veneer. It makes an excellent fuel wood.

Although the kernels of beechnuts are small, they are sweet, edible, and nutritious. The nuts are utilized as food by many species of forest wildlife, including white-tailed deer, black bear, raccoon, gray squirrel, red squirrel, flying squirrel, ruffed grouse, and wild turkey. Unfortunately, over most of its range, the American beech does not produce a dependable supply of nuts annually. Deer browse on the coppice growth of the American beech in areas where the more preferred browse species are absent.

The American beech ranges from Nova Scotia to Ontario and Wisconsin, south to Florida and Texas.

The European beech, *Fagus sylvatica* L., is an introduced species, which differs by having fewer leaf veins (5 to 9) and shorter but wider blades with minute, irregular teeth. Some expressions with purple leaves have been described as var. *purpurea* Ait.

The Chestnuts—Castanea

Members of this genus are trees or shrubs with alternate, simple, deciduous leaves that have prominent lateral veins running from the midrib and terminating at one of the marginal teeth. The winter twigs are moderate to slender and have a moderate, continuous, 5-angled or star-shaped pith. Buds are obliquely ovoid with 2 or 3 visible scales, the terminal one lacking and the lateral ones well spaced along the twigs. Leaf scars are half-round with numerous scattered bundle scars. The flowers are whitish, imperfect, and appear in the late spring after the leaves are fully grown. They are borne in ample clusters of catkins 4 to 8 inches long. Staminate flowers occupy most of the length of the catkins; but some in each cluster produce pistillate flowers at the base. The fruits are sweet and edible nuts borne singly or in clusters of 2 or 3 within prickly burs, which open and release the nuts at maturity. The American chestnut, prior to its destruction by the chestnut bark disease, was one of the finest of American forest trees. The more blight-resistant Allegheny-chinkapins are shrubs or small trees.

AMERICAN CHESTNUT   *Castanea dentata* (Marsh.) Borkh.

The large, spiny-burred fruits, small, rounded buds, and the beechlike leaves of this species, which are actually much larger than those of the American beech and have more conspicuously hooked and sharply pointed teeth terminating in a conspicuous spine, are most distinct.

Summer. *Leaves* large, 5 to 11 inches long, 2 to 5 inches wide, large, alternate, simple, deciduous, oblong-lanceolate, thin but firm; dull yellowish green above, paler and glabrous beneath; margins regularly and coarsely toothed with sharp-pointed, somewhat incurved teeth; tips rather long-pointed, bases cuneate, rounded or obtuse; veins prominent, pinnately parallel, each apparently ending or extending beyond the tip of each tooth, creating an upturned bristle-tip in each; petioles stout, short, somewhat hairy. *Flowers* monoecious, apetalous, male and female flowers appearing often with leaves on the same tree; male aments in elongated catkins, 5 to 8 inches long; female flowers 1 to 3 inches long, in a small cluster. *Fruits* when present, are most conspicuous, round, prickly, with branch-spined burs 2 to 3 inches in diameter, containing 2 or 3 ovoid, ¾ to 1 inch long nuts, flat on one side, lustrous brown and pale-hairy toward the tops.

Winter. *Twigs* moderately stout, greenish yellow to reddish brown, glabrous except for numerous small, pale lenticels; may be roundish or slightly angular, rather straight or zigzag; pith stellate in cross section

AMERICAN CHESTNUT

1. Branch with mature leaves.
2. Unopened and open bur showing the nuts.
3. Winter twig.
4. Detail of bud and leaf scar.

(use razor blade to observe); leaf scars alternate, semiovate, slightly elevated, with numerous scattered bundle scars. *Buds* about ¼ inch long, ovoid, bluntly pointed, with 2 to 3 yellowish to greenish brown, glabrous or hairy-tipped scales; terminal bud absent; lateral buds ovoid, often placed a little to one side of the leaf scars. *Bark* on young trunks light brownish, rather smooth; on older trunks becoming dark brown with shallow furrows and broad, rather long flat-topped and oblique ridges.

The American chestnut, once the queen of the eastern American forest trees, is now only a memory. Sometime between 1904 and 1906 a blight, caused by the fungus *Endothia parasitica*, was introduced along the Atlantic seaboard. It caused a fatal bark disease in the American chestnut that spread mercilessly through the forests of the East, the spores being carried from tree to tree by the wind. This fungus, which has an intermediate host (species of the genus *Quercus*), spread over its entire range during the course of a few decades, leaving gaunt skeletons of great trees throughout our forests. There still may be hope for this species. Over the decades, researchers have found a specific fungus that is known to destroy the fungus affecting the American chestnut. If it can be shown to be environmentally safe, and if it can be effectively spread throughout the eastern forests, the American chestnut blight might be a plague of the past.

Historically, the American chestnut was a large tree, sometimes attaining a height of 100 or more feet with trunks 4 to 8 feet in diameter. In the open it developed massive and wide-spreading branches and a deep, broad, rounded crown. It grew everywhere on well-drained soils, from the valleys to the rocky ridges. It sprouted freely from the roots, and today the sprouts are still commonly seen in our forests. Occasionally they grow to 15 or 20 feet, and sometimes even produce a few fruits, but the blight eventually kills them.

The wood of the American chestnut is light, soft, only moderately strong, but very durable in contact with the soil. It was once used for posts and poles, railroad ties, interior finish, and cheap furniture. The bark is rich in tannic acid and formerly was used extensively by tanneries. And last, but not least, this species produced bountiful crops of nuts, which are much superior to the Old World chestnut in both sweetness and flavor. At one time, they were a very important food for forest wildlife of all kinds. The American chestnut was always a dependable source of mast, for it matured a crop of nuts every year. Unlike the American beech and the oaks, whose flowers are often killed by late freezes, the

American chestnut does not put out its flowers until June or early July after the danger of frost is past.

The range of the American chestnut extends from Ontario, Maine to Michigan, south to Delaware, Tennessee, and along the Appalachian Mountains to northern Georgia and Alabama.

ALLEGHENY-CHINKAPIN   *Castanea pumila* (L.) P. Mill.

> The beechlike leaves, which are conspicuously pubescent below; the shrubby nature of this species; and the spiny-burred fruits are most distinctive.

Summer. *Leaves* 3 to 6 inches long, 1½ to 2 inches wide, alternate, simple, deciduous, oblong to elliptic, short-petioled, margin serrate with bristle-tipped teeth; apices acute, bases narrowly oblong, cuneate or rounded, but often asymmetrical; lower leaf surfaces and petioles silvery tomentose. *Flowers* monoecious, apetalous, male and female flowers appearing often with leaves on same tree; male aments in catkins 4 to 6 inches long; female flowers inconspicuous, near base of male catkins. *Fruits* sweet; burs 1 to 1½ inches in diameter.

Winter. *Twigs* slender, reddish brown to dark brown, at first hairy but later becoming nearly glabrous; pith 5-angled, stellate in cross section. *Buds* about ⅛ inch long or a little longer, small, ovoid, blunt-pointed, reddish brown, somewhat hairy, with 2 to 3 scales; terminal bud absent. *Bark* of larger trunks becoming fissured and broken into light red-brown, loose plates.

Comparisons. This species can be told easily from the American chestnut (the only other tree with which the Allegheny-chinkapin could reasonably be confused) by the undersurface of its smaller leaves and leaf petioles, which are covered with a whitish pubescence. Those of the American chestnut are glabrous.

The Allegheny-chinkapin is a thicket-forming shrub or small tree, sometimes 15 to 30 feet in height with a trunk diameter up to 1½ feet. It occurs on rich soils, usually on those containing plenty of humus, from the coastal region to the slopes of the mountains.

Unlike the American chestnut, which is often considered to be the big brother to the Allegheny-chinkapin, this species is highly resistant to the

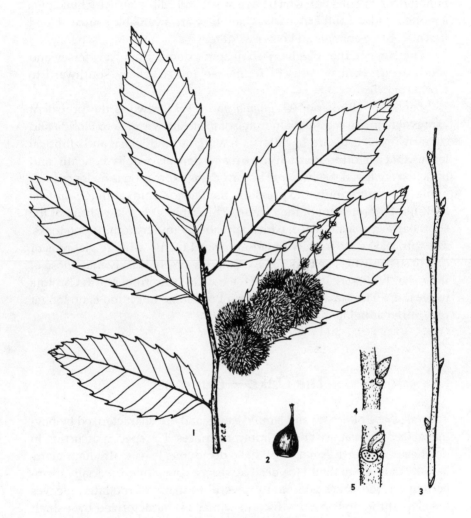

ALLEGHENY-CHINKAPIN

1. Branch with leaves and fruits.
2. Nut.
3. Winter twig.
4-5. Details of leaf scars and winter buds.

blight that has destroyed the great stands of the former. The small fruit burs contain but one nut, which has a sweet and edible kernel. Chinkapins are often sold in southern markets, and they are a valuable source of food for small game animals and other wildlife.

The range of the Allegheny-chinkapin extends from New Jersey and southeastern Pennsylvania to Tennessee and Arkansas, southward to Florida and Texas.

The Ashe chinkapin (*C. pumila* var. *ashei* Sudw.) is the prevalent expression on the coastal plain from southeastern Virginia to Florida and eastern Texas. It is said to differ in having more thickish and elliptical leaves that are often blunt at the tip and densely woolly beneath, and burs that are less densely spiny; however, this expression is no longer recognized. Another minor expression, the Florida chinkapin (*C. alnifolia* Nutt.), is the tree form of the running chinkapin. It is a low shrub of the southeastern coastal plain, which spreads by underground rootstocks. The thin leaves are usually broadest toward the tip and are glabrous or nearly so beneath. The burs are even more sparsely prickly than those of the Ashe chinkapin. It is found on the coastal plain from North Carolina to northern Florida and southeastern Louisiana, but it too is no longer recognized as being distinct.

The Oaks—Quercus

The oaks have alternate and simple leaves and are characterized by having stellate hairs at least on their lower surfaces. The species occurring in northeastern North America all have deciduous leaves, although many have a tendency to retain the dead leaves for some time, especially members of the red oaks. Commonly several to many of the lateral leaves develop at the branch tip, which in winter is characterized by a small cluster of terminal buds. The pith of the twigs is angular or stellate in cross section, which can be observed by making a cross-sectional cut of a twig with a sharp razor blade.

The wind-pollinated flowers of the oaks appear in the early spring when the new branchlets are just developing. The staminate flowers are borne in very slender, drooping aments and arise in clusters from buds on the growth of the previous season. The pistillate flowers are quite small and inconspicuous, being produced in the axils of leaves on the current season's growth. The fruits, called acorns, are nuts that are partially enclosed by scaly cups. Some species of oaks mature the acorns in one growing season, while others do not do so until the autumn of the second year. Acorns provide a staple for many kinds of wildlife including black bears, white-tailed deer, wild turkeys, ruffed grouse, squirrels, chipmunks, and various small rodents. Birds and mammals are responsible for the dissemination of the seeds to a large degree.

The oaks may be divided into two large groups, each of which has distinctive characteristics:

Red oaks: Acorns not maturing until the end of the second growing season, the inner surface of the cups usually being coated with woolly hair, and the kernels usually bitter. The leaves have bristle-tipped teeth or lobes, *or* if entire-margined have a distinct bristle at the tips. The bark is typically dark colored and furrowed, rather hard. The root systems develop from spring seeds.

White oaks: Acorns mature in one growing season; the inner surface of the cup smooth, and the kernels sweet or only slightly bitter. Leaves typically with rounded teeth or lobes, but never bristle-tipped. The bark is typically grayish and usually scaly, rather soft. The root systems develop from fall seeds.

NORTHERN RED OAK   *Quercus rubra* L.

The shallow V-shaped sinused leaves of this species, with the sinuses extending less than halfway to the midrib and the lobes noticeably wider at the base; the red leaf midribs; the acorns, which are nearly totally exposed from the cup; and the conspicuous, long, vertically striate candy-cane-like bark on the bole of the tree are most distinct. Mature and often even immature trees can be easily identified by the peculiar bark pattern, which shows long vertical strips of smooth gray bark adjacent to sections of darker, rougher bark.

Summer. *Leaves* 4 to 9 inches long, 3 to 5 inches wide, alternate, simple, deciduous, ovate or somewhat obovate, apices acute or acuminate, base rounded or cuneate; leaf blades thin, firm, dark dull green and glabrous above, paler and glabrous beneath except for rusty hair tufts within the vein axils; lobes 7 to 11, bristle-tipped, tapering outward, irregularly and coarsely toothed with bristle-tipped teeth, separated by broad usually V-shaped shallow sinuses, which extend less than halfway to the midribs; petioles 1 to 2 inches long, rather stout. *Fruits* (acorn) ¾ to

NORTHERN RED OAK

1. Branch with mature leaves.
2. Acorn with typical shallow cup.
3. Acorn with deep type of cup.
4. Winter twig.
5. Details of bud and leaf scar.

1 inch long or more, sessile or short-stalked; cups shallow, saucerlike to bowl-shaped, lustrous-scaled, enclosing only ⅕ of the basal part of the nut, thus exposing most of the acorns; nuts about 1 inch long, broadly ovoid or occasionally oblong-ovoid, bases broad, chestnut brown, requiring two growing seasons to mature.

Winter. *Twigs* moderately stout, reddish brown, glabrous. *Buds* about ¼ inch long, ovoid, apically sharply pointed, constricted below the middle to a rounded base; scales lustrous chestnut brown, glabrous or nearly so with a few tawny hairs at tip. *Bark* long vertical stripes of smooth gray bark, adjacent to sections of darker, rougher bark; on young trunks and branches, greenish brown to gray, smooth; inner bark of bole light red or pinkish.

Comparisons. See the comparison sections for the scarlet oak, Shumard oak, and black oak.

The northern red oak becomes a large tree, commonly from 70 to 90 feet in height with a trunk diameter of 2 to 4 feet, but occasionally attains a height of 150 feet. Its massive, wide-spreading or ascending branches form a broadly rounded crown in the open; in the forest it usually develops a tall, straight, clean trunk and a relatively narrow crown. The northern red oak grows well on most well-drained soils. In the North it associates with the eastern white pine and northern hardwoods on sandy or gravelly soils; but in the South it is found with other species of oaks, basswood, white ash, and black cherry on the better loams.

The wood is heavy, hard, strong, and close-grained and the species is considered to be the most important lumber tree of the red oak group. Although formerly considered to be much inferior to the white oak as a timber tree, the wood is now commercially valuable and extensively used for furniture, cooperage, general construction, interior finish, railroad ties, and mine props. The northern red oak grows more rapidly than any of our other northern oaks; long-lived, it is a very desirable tree for planting along streets or about the home grounds. The acorns, while not as palatable as those of the white oaks, are eaten by squirrels, deer, and many other forms of wildlife.

The northern red oak ranges from Nova Scotia to Minnesota, south to northern Georgia and Oklahoma.

The variety *ambigua* (Gray) Fern., is distinguished from the typical expression by its deeply bowl-shaped cups, which cover about ⅓ of the acorns, and by the smoother and paler gray bark along its upper bole and branches. This variety is more northern in range than the typical expression, occurring from Quebec to Ontario and southward to Nova Scotia, northern New England, western New York, northwestern Pennsylvania, and in the Appalachians at higher altitudes to North Carolina.

SCARLET OAK   *Quercus coccinea* Muenchh.

> The fuzzy-hairy winter buds, which are hairy about 1/2 their length, the deeply U-shaped leaf sinuses of its shiny-surfaced leaves, pink inner bark, persistent drooping and dead lower lateral branches, buttressing of the trunk base, and deeply seated acorns with concentric rings at the top and with cups that cover nearly half the nut are quite characteristic of the scarlet oak.

Summer. *Leaves* 3 to 7 inches long, 2 1/2 to 5 inches wide, alternate, simple, deciduous, broadly ovate or obovate, broadest above the middle; upper surfaces dark green, lustrous; paler and glabrous beneath except for very small white to rusty hair tufts in the principal vein axils; lobes 5 to 9, but usually 7, long, narrow, sparingly toothed with bristle-tipped teeth; sinuses very deep, more U-shaped than V-shaped; petioles slender, 1 to 2 inches long. *Fruits* (acorn) sessile or nearly so, with deep top-shaped, lustrous brown cups enclosing about 1/2 of the nut; nuts about 1/2 to 7/8 inch long, short-ovoid, light reddish brown, often displaying conspicuous concentric rings at top.

Winter. *Twigs* slender, reddish brown to grayish brown, glabrous. *Buds,* terminal buds 3/16 to 1/4 inch long, broadly ovoid to elliptic, bluntly pointed, coated with pale hair above the middle. *Bark* on young trunks and branches smooth, light greenish brown; on older trunks becoming nearly black, broken by shallow fissures into irregular and somewhat scaly stripes; inner bark pale reddish or pink.

Comparisons. The leaves of the scarlet and northern red oaks are similar; however, those of the former tend to have fewer lobes, are more lustrous above, and have noticeably deeper and more U-shaped sinuses versus the shallower V-shaped sinuses of the northern red oak. Also similar are the leaves of the black oak, but they appear to be more yellow-green in color, with buff-colored rather than whitish to rusty hairs or glabrous below. The leaves of the scarlet oak and the pin oak are also very similar, but those of the latter are smaller and more uniform, and branches and acorns are so distinctly different as to be unmistakable. Furthermore, the

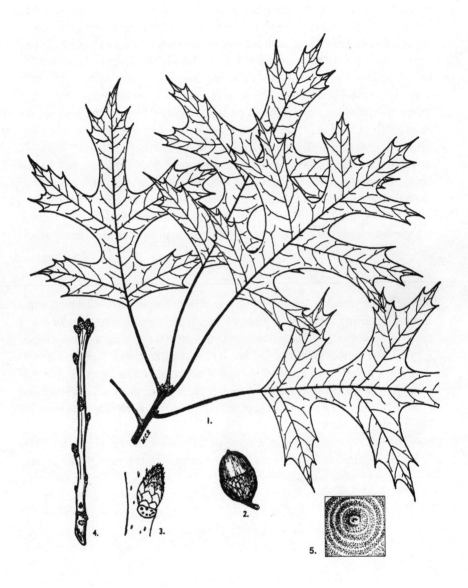

SCARLET OAK

1. Branch with mature leaves.
2. Acorn.
3. Detail of bud and leaf scar.
4. Winter twig.
5. Concentric rings of acorn.

scarlet oak has larger terminal buds than the pin oak—nearly twice as large—which are hairy in the upper half. Moreover, the scarlet oak is typically an upland tree, while the pin oak is found naturally only in wet bottomlands. The bark of the scarlet oak is intermediate between the broadly ridged bark of the northern red oak and the very rough and broken bark of the black oak. The scarlet oak tends to have the somewhat striped bark of the northern red oak, but usually high in the tree, rather than on the lower bole. Unlike the black oak, which has yellow or orange inner bark, that of both the scarlet oak and the northern red oak is pinkish. In winter, the scarlet oak can also be separated from the black oak by the buds of the former being round and white-hairy only near the apex, rather than being angled and woolly. The scarlet oak can be separated from the somewhat similar Shumard oak by its smaller leaves and smaller acorns, which usually have concentric circles near the tips, characters that are lacking in the Shumard oak.

————

The scarlet oak is a medium- to large-sized, open-crowned tree, commonly attaining a height of 60 to 80 feet with a trunk diameter of 1 to 2 feet. It may occasionally reach a height of over 100 feet with a trunk diameter of 3 or 4 feet. When young it has a more or less pyramidal crown with drooping lower branches, but in age it becomes rather broadly round-topped. It is distinctly an upland tree, preferring to grow on dry sandy or gravelly soils and rocky slopes. In such situations it often associates with other oaks and hickories.

The wood is heavy, hard, strong, and coarse-grained. It is often marketed as red oak lumber but is inferior to that of the northern red oak, due in part to the large number of knots in the wood resulting from the dead lateral branches that persist along the upper bole. The scarlet oak makes a very desirable tree for ornamental, shade, or street tree purposes. It grows rapidly and has an attractive form and foliage, the latter becoming a brilliant scarlet in the autumn. Its acorns are also of some value as food for wildlife.

The scarlet oak ranges from Maine to southern Ontario and west to Minnesota, south to northern Georgia and Oklahoma. It is one of the most abundant oaks in the southern Appalachian Mountains.

PIN OAK   *Quercus palustris* **Muenchh.**

At any time of the year, the pin oak, especially when growing in open areas, can be told from all other oak species (save the northern pin oak) by its unusual branching pattern, which is apparent even at a distance; the upper branches ascend, the side branches project horizontally, parallel to the ground, and the lower branches droop or descend at a conspicuous angle toward the ground and remain on the tree even when dead. The small, sharp, pinlike branchlets, leaf lobes that are nearly perpendicular to the midvein, and small acorns with flat cups are also most distinctive. Once understood, the characters of this species should not be confused with those of any other oak. (Also see the northern pin oak.)

Summer. *Leaves* 3 to 6 inches long, 2 to 4 inches wide, alternate, simple, deciduous, ovate, or more rarely obovate; upper surfaces dark green, lustrous, glabrous beneath or rarely with very small hair tufts within the principal vein axils; lobes 5 to 9, but usually 5, narrow, bristle-tipped, sparingly toothed with 3 to 4 bristle-tipped teeth; sinuses deep, wide, broadly U-shaped or rounded; petioles 1 to 2 inches long, slender. *Fruits* (acorn) sharply pointed, sessile or short-stalked, with thin, broad, and shallow saucerlike cups enclosing only the basal part (⅕ to ¼) of the nut; nuts about ⅜ to ½ inch long, roundish, base broad, light brown, usually with fine, dark, longitudinal striations.

Winter. *Twigs* slender, small, painfully sharp, reddish brown to grayish brown, glabrous or with hairy scales, lustrous, dominating the branches, providing a distinctive appearance (giving the tree a most appropriate common name). *Buds* about 1/16 to 1/8 inch long, extremely small, ovoid, sharp-pointed, 5-angled, light brown, nearly glabrous. *Bark* on the younger trunks light reddish brown to grayish brown, smooth, and lustrous; on the older trunks becoming darker and shallowly furrowed, with low, narrow, and somewhat scaly ridges.

Comparisons. This species is similar to the Texas oak, but the latter has wider leaf lobes, smaller leaf sinuses and its acorn cups cover more of its nut (⅓ to ½ versus ⅕ to ¼). It is also similar to the northern red oak, but that species has more vertical, rather than drooping, basal branches with less deeply cut V-shaped rather than U-shaped leaf sinuses, and leaf lobes that are more ascending, rather than perpendicular to the midvein; also, the acorn cups of that species cover more of the nut.

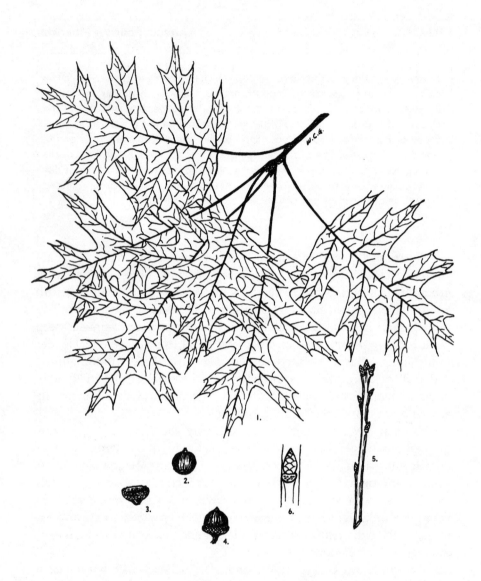

PIN OAK

1. Branch with mature leaves.
2, 3, and 4. Acorns.

5. Winter twig.
6. Details of bud and leaf scar.

The pin oak is also called the swamp oak and the water oak. It is usually a medium-sized tree from 40 to 60 feet in height, with a trunk diameter of 1 to 2 feet, but occasionally it attains a height of over 100 feet. Young specimens have broadly pyramidal crowns with somewhat drooping lower branches, but in age it develops a more round-topped crown. It is characteristically a tree of the wet bottomlands, occurring in nearly pure stands along streams and on river-bottom flats that are periodically flooded.

The wood is heavy, hard, strong, and close-grained, but it warps and checks badly during seasoning. It is principally used for distillation, fuel, and charcoal, but occasionally for cheap construction lumber, cooperage, and railroad ties. The pin oak is probably planted more extensively for ornamental purposes than any other native oak. It has a very attractive form, grows well on almost any soil, is rather tolerant of city smoke, and is relatively immune to damage from storms, insects, and fungi. The small acorns of the pin oak are eaten in some quantities by the wood duck and are utilized as food by many other kinds of wildlife.

The pin oak ranges from Massachusetts to southern Michigan and eastern Kansas, south to North Carolina and Oklahoma.

NORTHERN PIN OAK   *Quercus ellipsoidalis* E. J. Hill

The small, glabrous leaves, with deep sinuses and lobes that are perpendicular to the midvein; yellow inner bark; top-shaped acorns with appressed cup scales; and a branching pattern similar to the pin oak are most characteristic.

Summer. *Leaves* 3 to 7 inches long, 2½ to 4 inches wide, alternate, simple, deciduous, ovate to obovate orbicular, deeply lobed, base cuneate; upper surface dark, shiny green, paler and glabrous beneath or rarely with hair tufts along the midvein; lobes 5 to 7, narrow, bristle-tipped; sinuses wide and rounded. *Fruits* (acorn) elliptic to round, sessile to short-stalked; nuts ½ to ¾ inch long, chestnut brown; become ⅓ to ½ covered by turbinate cups.

Winter. *Twigs* glabrous at maturity, bright reddish brown. *Buds* ³⁄₁₆ to ¼ inch long, glabrous, reddish brown. *Bark* closely ribbed or shallowly furrowed, similar to that of pin oak, but with yellow rather than reddish inner bark.

Comparisons. This is a medium-sized oak, 45 to 70 feet in height, very similar to the pin oak but with a more northern distribution. It is best distinguished from the pin oak by its larger and longer acorns, which are ⅓ to ½ rather than ⅕ to ¼ buried within their deeply bowl-shaped cups, and by its yellowish rather than reddish inner bark. Its habitat also differs from that of the pin oak, occurring principally on dry to well-drained, sandy, and clayey upland soils rather than lowlands and bottom flats. The northern pin oak, however, produces a uniform branching pattern similar to the pin oak, with the upper branches ascending, the side branches horizontal, and the lower branches drooping. The lowermost branches commonly die, yet remain on the tree.

———

Like most species of oak this species has a variety of common names. Locally it is known as the black oak or the jack oak. Sometimes it is called Hill oak after the man who first officially named it. It has a range extending from Michigan and northern Indiana, west to southern Manitoba, southeastern North Dakota, Iowa, and northern Missouri.

SHUMARD OAK   *Quercus shumardii* **Buckl.**

> Unlike most oaks, the leaf shape of the Shumard oak is distinctive in that its lateral lobes are especially broad toward their apices, and the sinuses are very long and deeply U-shaped. The leaves are also much larger than those of most oaks.

Summer. *Leaves* 3 to 8 inches long, 2½ to 6 inches wide, alternate, simple, deciduous, ovate to obovate; leaf blades dark green and lustrous above, paler green and glabrous beneath except for axillary hair tufts along the midrib; lobes 5 to 9, bristle-pointed, coarsely bristle-toothed, separated by very deep, rounded sinuses extending more than halfway to the midrib; petioles slender, about 2 inches long. *Fruits* (acorn) ⅝ to 1¼ inches long, oblong ovoid, seated in shallow to somewhat rounded or bowl-shaped, often somewhat hairy-scaled cups, exposing approximately ¼ to ⅓ of the nut; both cups and nuts grayish or grayish brown and dull.

Winter. *Twigs* moderately stout, yellowish to grayish to grayish brown, glabrous. *Buds* about ¼ inch long, ovoid, pointed, somewhat angled, grayish to yellowish, glabrous. *Bark* grayish brown, thick, smooth,

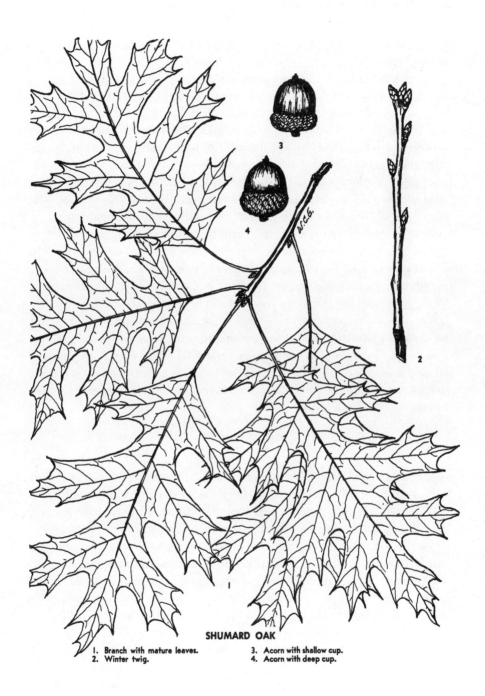

SHUMARD OAK

1. Branch with mature leaves.
2. Winter twig.
3. Acorn with shallow cup.
4. Acorn with deep cup.

with whitish, flat-topped, scaly ridges separated by much deeper and darker furrows.

Comparisons. This species is similar to Texas oak, but differs by having hairier buds, which are reddish brown rather than grayish brown or brownish; by having larger leaves with more lobes (5 to 9 versus 5 to 7); and by having smaller acorns, with more rounded rather than turbinate acorn cups, which cover less of the nut (¼ to ⅓ versus ⅓ to ½). It differs from the scarlet oak by having somewhat larger leaves with more spreading bristle-teeth and larger lobes, with the lateral lobes being especially broad at their apices (much more so than the scarlet oak). The acorns of the Shumard oak also differ from those of the scarlet oak by being finely hairy, enclosing a smaller area of the nut, and by lacking the concentric circles around the apex of the acorn. Furthermore, the Shumard oak is primarily a bottomland species, unlike the scarlet oak, which is a species of drier, poorer upland sites and slopes. The leaves of the Shumard oak are similar to those of both the northern red oak and the black oak, but are usually larger and differ from the former by having their lobes gradually tapered to a narrow tip (broadest at the tip in Shumard oak), as well as having less deeply lobed leaves with fewer bristle-tips and with more wedge-shaped bases, and differ from the latter by having more numerous lobes, deeper sinuses, more truncate (rather than rounded) leaf bases, and also by having broader leaf-lobe tips.

———

The Shumard oak is also known as the Shumard red oak, swamp red oak, and Schneck oak. It is a large tree, one of the largest of our southern oaks, becoming 100 feet or more in height with a trunk diameter of 4 to 5 feet or more, with a broad, open crown composed of stout, spreading branches. It can be usually found in stream bottoms, or about the borders of swamps. In habitat and general appearance it resembles the pin oak, but it has much larger leaves and acorns, and less-drooping branches. In the trade its wood is sold as red oak and used for the same general purposes. The expression known as var. *schneckii* (Britt.) Sarg. generally grows on drier sites and is said to have more uniformly shaped leaves throughout the tree, and deeper and narrower acorn cups.

The range of the Shumard oak extends through the coastal plain and Piedmont from North Carolina to northern Florida west to central Texas; and northward, in the Mississippi Valley, to Oklahoma and the southern portions of Illinois, Indiana, and Ohio. It also occurs locally in West Virginia, southern Pennsylvania, and Maryland.

TURKEY OAK   *Quercus laevis* Walt.

The peculiar manner by which the mostly 3-lobed, triangular-shaped leaves are positioned (perpendicular to the ground) on the crooked branches, and the top-shaped acorn cups are most distinctive.

Summer. *Leaves* 4 to 12 inches long, 1 to 6 inches wide, alternate, simple, deciduous, oblong or obovate, appearing triangular in shape, usually with 3 to 5 long, narrow, often curved, bristle-toothed and bristle-pointed lobes; upper surface lustrous yellowish green; lower surface paler and glabrous except for rusty hair tufts in the principal vein axils; bases pointed; petioles short, usually less than 1 inch long, quite distinctive, usually very twisted permitting the leaves to be held perpendicular to the ground. *Fruits* (acorn) about 1 inch long, ovoid, brown, woolly at the top, with top-shaped, large-scaled cups enclosing about ⅓ to nearly ½ of the nut.

Winter. *Twigs* rather stout, red to dark brown, glabrous or nearly so. *Buds* about ½ inch long, conical, slender, pointed, rusty-hairy at least near the tip. *Bark* dark gray or blackish, irregularly fissured, scaly, often forming black, irregular ridges.

Comparisons. The leaves of this species ought not be confused with the leaves of any other oak species, except possibly the southern red oak, which differs by having universally gray or rusty-hairy, rather than glabrous undersurfaces (or undersurfaces pubescent only in the vein axils) and rounded rather than pointed leaf bases; and possibly the Georgia oak, which has much smaller leaves. The upper scales of the acorn cups of this species, which are rolled inward, also differ from those of the southern red oak.

The turkey oak, so named because of the shape of its leaves, resembling a 3-toed turkey's foot, is a small tree, not more than 20 to 30 feet in height with a trunk up to about a foot in diameter, with an irregular and rather open crown. It occurs on characteristically poor, dry, sandy soils, and is commonly found in the understory of longleaf pine forests with high light intensity. The tree has no commercial importance, but the wood is used locally as fuel and for rough construction. Foresters are prone to consider it a weed tree, and often refer to it by the uncomplimentary name of scrub oak (or bear oak). It is also known as Catesby oak, because

TURKEY OAK

1. Winter twig.
2. Branch with mature leaves.

3. Acorns.
4. Winter bud and leaf-scar.

Michaux named it in honor of Mark Catesby, one of America's earliest naturalists, as *Quercus catesbaei;* but Walter's name has priority.

The range of the turkey oak extends through the coastal plain from southeastern Virginia to central Florida west to southeastern Louisiana.

GEORGIA OAK   *Quercus georgiana* M. A. Curtis

> The 5- to 6-lobed, glabrous leaves of this deep southern species are distinctive.

Summer. *Leaves* 2 to 4 inches long, 1 to 2 inches wide, alternate, simple, deciduous, elliptic, thick, base short-pointed; upper surface lustrous, lower surface paler with hair tufts within the veins; lobes 3 to 5, short-pointed, with 1 to 2 bristles per lobe, larger ones with 1 to 2 small teeth. *Fruits* (acorn) ⅜ to ½ inch long, brown, globose, nearly ¼ to ½ enclosed by its shallow, flat to rounded cup, sessile or short-stalked.

Winter. *Twigs* deep red, glabrous. *Buds*, terminal bud ⅒ to ⅕ inch long, red brown to dark brown, ovoid to narrowly ovoid, glabrous or somewhat ciliate on the scales. *Bark* thin, dark gray to light brown, smooth becoming scaly.

Comparisons. This species resembles the turkey oak but has distinctly smaller leaves (usually less than 4 inches in length) and smaller acorns, with cups that cover ¼ to ½ the nut.

The Georgia oak is a rarely encountered tree or shrub, 35 to 50 feet high and 8 to 12 inches in diameter, commonly found on granite or sandstone mountain slopes, and rocky hills and ridges of the Piedmont of northern Georgia and adjacent South Carolina and Alabama.

TEXAS OAK   *Quercus texana* Buckl.

> The 5- to 7-lobed leaves, which appear to be nearly perpendicular to the midvein and separated by deep C-shaped sinuses, are most distinctive.

Summer. *Leaves* 2 to 5 inches long, 2 to 5 inches wide, alternate, simple, deciduous, ovate, deeply 5- to 7-lobed with bristle-tips, sinuses wide and rounded, dark green and dull above, paler and nearly glabrous beneath, except for hair tufts within the axils of the major veins. *Fruits*

GEORGIA OAK

1. Branch with leaves and acorn.   2. Detail of acorn.

(acorn) ¾ to 1½ inches long, dark longitudinally striped, narrowly ovoid, seated ⅓ to ½ way in top-shaped or turbanlike cups, with a prominent scaly, stalklike base.

Winter. *Twigs* glabrous, brownish gray. *Buds* ⅓ to ½ inch long, gray to brown-gray or brown; bud scales hairy, margin ciliate. *Bark* gray to black or brown, smooth to furrowed.

Comparisons. This species resembles both the scarlet oak and the pin oak in many respects, but has larger, more oblong fruits with deeper cups. It lacks the branching pattern of the pin oak, and the concentrically lined nuts of the scarlet oak. It is also similar to the Shumard oak, but differs by having fewer leaf lobes and by having oblong, striate acorns with deep toplike cups, rather than being oblong in shape with shallow, round or saucer-shaped cups (see the Shumard oak for further comparison).

The Texas oak is a large tree, 60 to 100 feet high and 1 to 3 feet in diameter, with buttressed bases and an open crown of spreading or slightly drooping branches. It is found in wet, poorly drained floodplains on clay soils of the Gulf Coastal Plain and the lower Mississippi Valley. This commercially important species was not distinguished or described until 1927. Its range extends from Alabama westward to eastern Texas, northward to southeastern Oklahoma, Arkansas, southeastern Missouri, and western Tennessee.

BLACK OAK   *Quercus velutina* Lam.

> The strongly reflexed scale tips of the acorn cups that cover ⅓ to ½ of the nut, dark, nearly black bark on older trees, orange inner bark (areas between furrows or where outer bark is removed), and hairy winter buds of this species, which are strongly angled, are distinctive.

Summer. *Leaves* 4 to 9 inches long, 3 to 6 inches wide, alternate, simple, deciduous, usually obovate or ovate; upper surfaces lustrous dark green, with a hairy midrib; lower surfaces yellowish green, paler, more or less coated with powdery buff-colored or yellowish hairs, easily rubbed off, with rusty tufts of hairs in vein axils; very variable, some having deep U-shaped sinuses while others have quite shallow ones; leaf blades rather thick, leathery; lobes 5 to 7, with 3 or more bristle-teeth per lobe; lobes narrow or broad in outline, sinuses U-shaped; petioles 2 to 4 inches long, stout, yellowish. *Fruits* (acorn) short-stalked or sessile; cups deeply top-shaped or turbanlike, finely hairy on the fringe, covering ⅓ to ½ of the nut, with light brown, hairy, loose scales, the upper series with loose and reflexed spreading tips; nuts about ½ to ¾ inch long, ovoid, light brown, often hairy or with fine longitudinal striations.

Winter. *Twigs* rather stout, reddish brown often with gray mottling, usually glabrous. *Buds* ¼ to ⅜ inch long, ovoid or somewhat conical, sharp-pointed, angular, coated with dirty-white tomentose hairs; terminal bud to ½ inch long, larger than lateral buds. *Bark* soon becoming very dark and broken; on the older trunks nearly black, with deep vertical furrows and irregularly broken ridges; inner bark bright yellow or orange.

Comparisons. This species is very similar to the northern red oak. The latter can be separated by its duller leaf surface; more numerous and more oblong leaf lobes; V-shaped rather than U-shaped sinuses; by the lack of hairs on the midribs of its upper leaves; by its acorn scales, which are not recurved; by the candy-cane-striped bark pattern; and to a lesser degree, by its inner bark, which is pink in the northern red oak rather than distinctly orange as in the black oak. Moreover, the terminal buds of the northern red oak are nearly hairless and less angled than the woolly and angled buds of the black oak. Except for the hair condition on the undersurface (see the scarlet oak), the leaves are also very similar and often indistinguishable from those of the scarlet oak. The acorns of this species are much smaller than those of the northern red oak, the scarlet oak, and the Shumard oak, and are easily separated from all of them by the presence of the loose scales of the cup, which appear to be fringed.

The black oak is also known as the yellow oak (due to its yellow inner bark) and as quercitron. It becomes a large-sized tree, commonly from 60 to 80 feet in height with a trunk 2 to 3 feet in diameter. It sometimes attains a height of 150 feet with a trunk 4 or more feet in diameter. Its massive and often crooked branches form a deep, irregular, wide-spreading, or sometimes narrowly rounded crown. The black oak is typically a tree of the dry, rocky, or gravelly slopes and ridges where it commonly associates with the scarlet oak and the chestnut oak, and sometimes the pitch pine.

The wood is heavy, hard, and strong; but it is not tough, and it tends toward checking during the drying process. It is cut and marketed as red oak lumber and used for general construction, interior finish, furniture, and cooperage. Like many oaks the bark is rich in tannic acid and used for tanning leather. The yellow inner bark yields a yellow dye, and it is sometimes used medicinally as an astringent.

The range of the black oak extends from Maine to Minnesota and south to northern Florida and eastern Texas.

SOUTHERN RED OAK   *Quercus falcata* Michx.

The rusty-hairy twigs, very conspicuously bell-shaped or U-shaped leaf bases, and the drooping appearance of the mostly 3-lobed leaves, which are rusty-hairy beneath, are quite distinct.

Summer. *Leaves* 4 to 12 inches long, 3 to 5 inches wide, alternate, simple, deciduous, variable, but of two rather distinct types: one distinctively obovate with broad, shallowly 3-lobed tips, below, which they are contracted and entire; and another ovate with usually 5 or 7 slender, tapering, and often curved or falcate lobes with rather deeply rounded sinuses; lobes all bristle-tipped, terminal leaf lobe commonly much longer than the others, linear or lanceolate, sparingly toothed with bristle-tipped teeth; leaf bases commonly U-shaped, deeply rounded, or occasionally broadly wedge-shaped; upper surfaces lustrous and dark green, lower surfaces usually velvety, grayish or rusty-hairy on the veins; petioles 1 to 2 inches long, rather slender. *Fruits* (acorn) ½ to ⅝ inch long, elliptic to round, short-stalked with shallow, flat, or somewhat top-shaped, slightly hairy cups covering ⅓ to ½ of the nut; nuts about ½ inch long, roundish, broad based, light orange-brown, occasionally striate.

Winter. *Twigs* rather stout, reddish brown to ashy gray, more or less rusty-hairy. *Buds* ⅛ to ¼ inch long, ovoid, sharply pointed, but usually not angled, reddish brown, hairy toward apex. *Bark* on the younger trunks and branches rather smooth, dark reddish brown to gray; on old trunks becoming almost black, closely resembling that of the black oak, but more longitudinally fissured; inner bark pale, not a bright yellow or orange as in the black oak.

Comparisons. The leaves of this species are similar to those of the cherry-bark oak and the turkey oak, but differ by their bases, with the former being bell-shaped and the latter two being long-tapered or wedge-shaped. Moreover, the cherry-bark oak tends to have leaf lobes that are

SOUTHERN RED OAK

1. Leaf with mature leaves.
2. Acorns.
3. Winter twig.
4. Details of bud and leaf scar.

rarely falcate, but are more perpendicular to the midvein than those of the southern red oak, which tend to be more ascending. The cherry-bark oak also has bark that is gray black and scaly or flaky (resembling that of a mature black cherry tree) rather than being deeply longitudinally fissured, as in the southern red oak.

The southern red oak is also known as the Spanish oak, a name reputedly given to this species by the Spaniards due to its similarity to an oak species in Spain. Since it does not resemble any oak from that country, however, it is more likely to have been so named because of its association with the early Spanish colonies. It is a medium- to large-sized tree, commonly attaining a height of 60 to 80 feet with a trunk diameter of 1 to 3 feet, but it may attain a height of about 100 feet. It usually has a short trunk with massive branches forming an open, deep, and broadly rounded crown. The southern red oak is characteristically a tree of dry hills and of poor, sandy, or gravelly soils. It is a common tree in the Piedmont region of the southern United States.

The wood is heavy, hard, strong, and coarse-grained. It warps and checks badly in drying and is generally inferior to that of the northern red oak. The principal uses are for cheap construction lumber and fuel. Tannic acid is obtained from the bark. It makes a rather attractive ornamental tree.

The southern red oak ranges from southern Pennsylvania and New Jersey south to Florida, and west to Texas. In the Mississippi Valley it ranges north to Iowa, southern Illinois, and Indiana.

CHERRY-BARK OAK   *Quercus pagoda* Raf.

> The pagoda-shaped leaves of this species, with their 5 to 11 nearly straight (not curved) lobes, and the black cherry–like bark are most distinctive.

Summer. *Leaves* 5 to 10 inches long, alternate, deciduous, simple, ovate to oblong, bases cuneate, rounded to truncate, 5 to 11 thick-based lobes with falcate tips, shallow U-shaped sinuses, upper surface shiny, dark green, paler tomentose-hairy below with soft, yellow-gray to tan hairs.

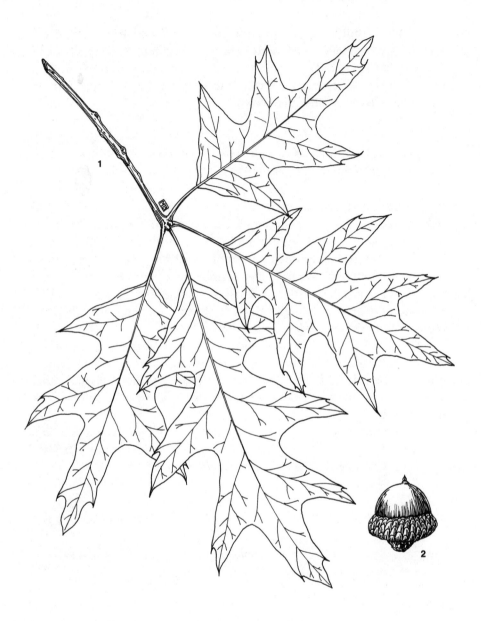

CHERRY-BARK OAK

1. Branch with leaves.   2. Acorn.

Winter. *Twigs* reddish, tomentose-hairy at first. *Buds,* terminal bud ovoid, acute, red brown; bud scales hairy. *Fruits* (acorn) ⅝ inch wide; nuts ⅓ to ½ covered by turbinate, flat, or rounded cups. *Bark* dark gray to nearly black, fissured into narrow ridges and small, firm scales like that of black cherry; on older trees bark of upper trunk appears to be striped horizontally.

Comparisons. The cherry-bark oak is similar to the southern red oak, of which it is often considered to be a variety. The former species can generally be distinguished by its leaves, which lack the U-shaped base of the southern red oak, and which have shallower sinuses between the 5 to 11 lobes, rather than 3 to 5 major lobes. Aside from the leaves being more pointed at the base, they are also lighter-colored beneath than those of the southern red oak, with yellowish gray to light brown rather than rust-colored to gray hairs. Often the leaves of the lower and upper parts of the crown are markedly different in this species, those above being more deeply lobed and often more like the leaves of the southern red oak. The dark gray or blackish scaly bark is very characteristic, somewhat resembling that of the black cherry, hence the common name cherry-bark oak.

This species, also known as the swamp red oak or the swamp Spanish oak, grows to a height of 100 to 135 feet and is considered to be a superior timber species, perhaps the most highly valued of any of the red oaks. It grows in the rich bottomlands and swamps of the coastal plain from New Jersey and Maryland south to Florida and west to eastern Texas, and up the Mississippi River valley to the southern portions of Indiana and Illinois.

BLACKJACK OAK   *Quercus marilandica* **Muenchh.**

> Easily recognized by its leathery, 3-lobed, triangular-shaped leaves, which are conspicuously wider near the tip and rusty-hairy below, by its woolly, somewhat angled bud, and by its nearly black bark and rounded crown.

Summer. *Leaves* 2½ to 8 inches long, 2 to 4 inches wide, alternate, simple, deciduous, triangular to obovate, broadest near the apex, typically broad and shallowly 3- to 5-lobed near the top, contracted about the middle, tapering to the rounded base, somewhat thick and leathery; upper surfaces dark yellowish green, lustrous, lower surfaces paler, with

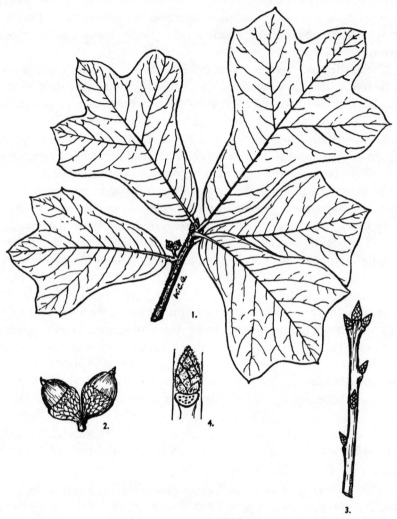

BLACKJACK OAK

1. Branch with mature leaves.
2. Acorns.
3. Winter twig.
4. Detail of bud and leaf scar.

tawny or rust-colored hair; lobes bristle-tipped, occasionally with a few shallow bristle-tipped teeth; becoming scarlet in fall; petioles usually less than ½ inch long, stout. *Fruits* (acorn) ⅝ to ¾ inch long, short-stalked, with deep, more-or-less top- or turban-shaped cups covering about ⅓ to ⅔ of the nut; nuts about ¾ inch long, ovoid, stoutly pointed, finely hairy, yellowish brown, often striate.

Winter. *Twigs* very stout, dark reddish brown, more or less hairy. *Buds* about ¼ inch long, pointed, angular, reddish brown, rather rusty-hairy. *Bark* becoming almost black, roughened by deep fissures and hard, scaly blocks or plates.

Comparisons. This species might be confused with the Arkansas oak, but the latter species has thin rather than leathery leaves, which are shallowly lobed and green rather than rusty-hairy beneath.

———

Blackjack oak is also known as jack oak, black oak, and barren oak. It is a small-sized tree of poor form, usually only 20 to 30 feet in height with a trunk 1 foot or less in diameter. Typically it has a short, nearly black-barked trunk with stout, short, and often contorted branches forming a narrow, compact, round-topped crown. It is a tree of barren, dry, sterile, sandy to clay soils. The blackjack oak is rather southern in its distribution, being one of the commonest and most characteristic trees on the poorer soils throughout the coastal plain and Piedmont regions. In the fall, the scarlet leaves are very attractive.

The wood is heavy, hard, and strong, but of relatively little commercial value. It is sometimes used locally for rough lumber but more commonly for fuel, charcoal, and distillation products.

The range of the blackjack oak extends from southeastern New York to southern Michigan and Nebraska, south to central Florida and eastern Texas.

ARKANSAS OAK   *Quercus arkansana* Sarg.

The conspicuously pear-shaped, completely unlobed or somewhat 3-lobed membranous, rather than leathery leaves, which are clearly widest at the apex, are most distinctive.

Summer. *Leaves* 2 to 5 inches long, 1 to 2½ inches wide, alternate, simple, deciduous, broadly obovate, broadest well above the middle,

ARKANSAS OAK

1. Branch with leaves and acorns.　　　2. Acorn.

3-toothed or remotely 3-lobed with bristle-tips, membranous, with rounded apices, yellow green and glabrous above, paler green below and glabrous or with whitish hairs along the veins only. *Fruits* ½ inch long, green becoming light brown, striate, short-stalked, globose, with less than ¼ of the nut enclosed by the saucer-shaped acorn cup.

Winter. *Twigs* gray brown, stellate-hairy, rarely nearly glabrous. *Buds* red brown, ovoid to acute; bud scale ciliate. *Bark* dark brown to nearly black, thick, deeply furrowed with long scaly ridges.

Comparisons. The leaves of this species are similar to those of the smaller blackjack oak, but are more rounded, more conspicuously tapered toward the base or wedge-shaped basially (rather than concave or rounded at the base in that species), more shallowly lobed, less leathery, and without the rusty hairs on their undersurface. Additionally, the blackjack oak acorns are more enclosed by the cup.

The Arkansas oak, originally described from material collected from the state of Arkansas, grows 40 to 85 feet high, with a crooked trunk up to 3½ feet in diameter. It resembles the blackjack oak, with which it often hybridizes, but attains larger stature. It is found on well-drained sandy soils in hardwood forests, in southwestern Georgia, northern Florida, southeastern Alabama, and southwestern Arkansas.

BEAR OAK   *Quercus ilicifolia* **Wangenh.**

> The bear oak is a small, twisted, thicket-forming species with small, 3- to 7-lobed leaves, which are silvery white beneath and have broad and shallow sinuses, along with diagnostically broadly wedge-shaped leaf bases.

Summer. *Leaves* 2 to 5 inches long, 1½ to 3 inches wide, alternate, simple, deciduous, ovate or obovate, rather thick and leathery; lobes 3 to 7, but usually 5, rather short, broadly triangular, bristle-tipped, often with a few bristle-tipped teeth; sinuses usually broad, shallow; upper surfaces lustrous dark green, lower surfaces whitened with pale gray hair; petioles about 1 inch long, stout, hairy. *Fruits* (acorn) ovoid to rounded, sessile or short-stalked, with deeply bowl-shaped, slightly hairy, pale brown fringed cups enclosing about ¼ to ½ of the nut; nuts about ½ inch long, ovoid, light brown, lustrous, usually brown striate, often clustered, but mostly paired on the twigs.

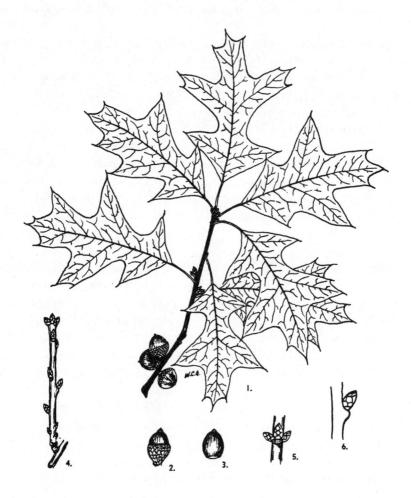

BEAR OAK

1. Branch with mature leaves and acorns.
2-3. Acorns.
4. Winter twig.
5-6. Details of winter buds.

Winter. *Twigs* moderately slender, grayish olive or ashy gray, matted with minutely velvety hairs the first season. *Buds* ⅛ inch or less long, ovoid, sharply or bluntly pointed, chestnut brown, nearly glabrous; commonly three buds above the leaf scars on vigorous twigs, often nearly of the same size; accessory buds mostly much smaller than the usual axillary bud. *Bark* thin, quite smooth, dark greenish brown or grayish brown, only in age developing thin, close scales.

———

The bear oak, or scrub oak, is a conspicuously straggly shrub from 3 to 10 feet in height. It occasionally becomes a small tree, up to 20 feet in height, with a short trunk and stiff, contorted branches. Ordinarily the bear oak occurs in openings in the forest, on barren mountaintops, or on the rockiest slopes, but it often occupies extensive areas following destructive forest fires. Although usually regarded as a weed, it has the ability to thrive on the most inhospitable, dry, and sterile sites, where it often forms a dense protective cover. It is not tolerant of shade, and where fires are not allowed to recur the bear oak is eventually replaced by other trees, such as aspens, maples, and other species of oaks. Bear oak barrens were created by fire, and they are maintained by the same disturbance regime.

The bear oak has no commercial value, but the wood is sometimes used locally as fuel. It provides cover for wildlife in areas that would otherwise be desolate, and its small acorns are utilized as food by the wild turkey, the ruffed grouse, the white-tailed deer, and many small rodents.

The range of the Bear oak extends from Maine to Ohio and southward in the mountains to North Carolina and Kentucky.

WATER OAK   *Quercus nigra* **L.**

> The glossy, conspicuously spatulate-shaped leaves, which have cobwebby hairs within the veins on the undersurface, are most distinctive.

Summer. *Leaves* exceedingly variable in size and shape, but always spatula- or diamond-shaped; typically 2 to 4 inches long, 1 to 2 inches wide, alternate, simple, tardily deciduous, clearly broadest above the middle; rather thin but firm; upper surface dull bluish green, the lower surface paler and glabrous except for hair tufts in the axils of the main veins; mostly with more-or-less 3 bristle-tipped lobes toward the broad

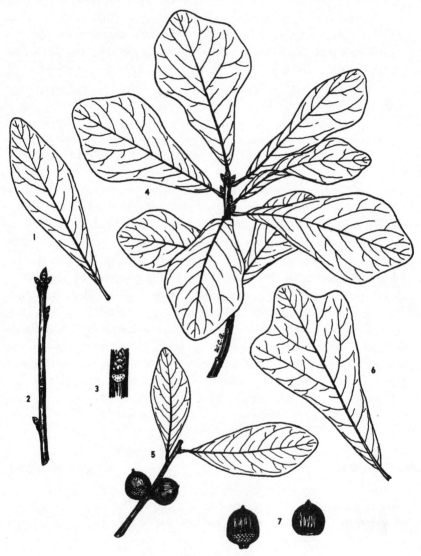

WATER OAK

1. Leaf.
2. Winter twig.
3. Detail of winter bud and leaf-scar.
4. Branch with mature leaves.
5. Branch with acorns.
6. Leaf.
7. Acorns.

summit, but may be variously lobed or even entire. *Fruits* (acorn) about ⅜ to ¾ inch long, striate, roundish, blackish, sessile or short-stalked, shallowly seated in shallow, saucer-shaped cups that cover ⅕ to ⅓ of the acorn.

Winter. *Twigs* slender, conspicuously glabrous, dull red to brown. *Buds* ⅛ to ¼ inch long, ovoid, pointed, prominently angled, glabrous or finely hairy, reddish brown. *Bark* dark gray with fissures separating irregular, scaly ridges.

Comparisons. The leaves of the laurel oak are somewhat similar to those of this species, but unlobed, somewhat larger, and more narrow apically. The acorns of the water oak are very similar to those of the willow oak, but somewhat larger.

The water oak, or possum oak, is a round-topped tree from 50 to 80 feet in height with a trunk diameter of 2 to 3½ feet. It is typically a bottomland species and is widespread and abundant along streams throughout the Southeast, ascending from the coastal plain into the foothills of the mountains. Throughout the same region it is very popular as a shade and street tree. The larger trees are often cut for lumber, which the lumbermen do not differentiate from that of other red oaks. The very numerous small acorns are a valuable food for wild turkeys, squirrels, and various species of wild ducks.

The range of the water oak extends from southern New Jersey south to Florida, west to eastern Texas, and northward in the Mississippi Valley to southeastern Missouri and eastern Oklahoma.

WILLOW OAK *Quercus phellos* L.

The pinlike twigs of this species, smooth gray bark, small acorns, and uncharacteristic willowlike leaves, which are widest near the middle and lack any noticeable marginal lobes or undulations, are most distinctive.

Summer. *Leaves* 2 to 4 inches long, ⅜ to ¾ inch wide, alternate, simple, deciduous, narrowly elliptical or lanceolate, thin or membranous, broadest at the middle, without lobes or undulations; margins entire, tipped with a small bristle; upper surfaces light green and dull to only somewhat lustrous, paler and dull beneath, glabrous, or occasionally a little hairy; petioles about ⅛ inch long, short, slender, glabrous. *Fruits* (acorn) sessile or nearly so, with nearly round, shallow, saucer-shaped, slightly hairy cups covering only the bases (⅕ to ¼) of the nuts; nuts about ⅜ to ½ inch long, roundish, pale yellowish or greenish brown, often minutely hairy or striate.

Winter. *Twigs* slender, glabrous, somewhat lustrous, reddish brown to dark brown. *Buds* chestnut brown; lateral buds about ⅛ inch long, ovoid, sharp-pointed; terminal bud ⅛ to ¼ inch long, pointed, conical, angled, glabrous. *Bark* on the young growth grayish to reddish brown, smooth; on older trunks becoming nearly black, roughened by deep irregular furrows and thick, more or less scaly ridges.

Comparisons. The willowlike leaves of this species can be separated from those of true willow *(Salix)* species by the tiny spine at their apices. They can also be separated from those of the laurel oak by being narrower, more lanceolate, and less rhombic in shape. The leaves of this species are also similar to those of Darlington oak, but differ by being much longer than wide and by usually having hairs within the leaf axils, rather than being completely glabrous beneath.

The willow oak is a medium- to large-sized tree, commonly from 60 to 80 feet in height, with a trunk from 2 to 3 feet in diameter, but it may attain a height of nearly 100 feet and a trunk diameter of about 4 feet. It reaches its maximum development in the South, and is a rather small tree at the northern extremity of its range. Young trees have a pyramidal form, but in age develop an oval or more round-topped crown. The prevalence of short pinlike branchlets reminds one of the pin oak, and this name is sometimes erroneously applied to the willow oak. It is characteristically a bottomland tree, occurring on poorly drained sand or clay soils.

The wood is sometimes marketed as red oak lumber, but it is of a poor quality. It is heavy, strong, and coarse-grained but somewhat softer than that of most other oaks. The tree is very attractive, and it grows well when planted on rather dry upland soils. It has few superiors as a shade, street, or ornamental tree. The small acorns of this, and of related species of oaks, are an important food of the wood duck, the mallard, the black duck, and the wild turkey in the South.

The range of the willow oak extends from southeastern New York to northern Florida, west in the Gulf States to eastern Texas. In the Mississippi Valley it ranges north to southern Illinois.

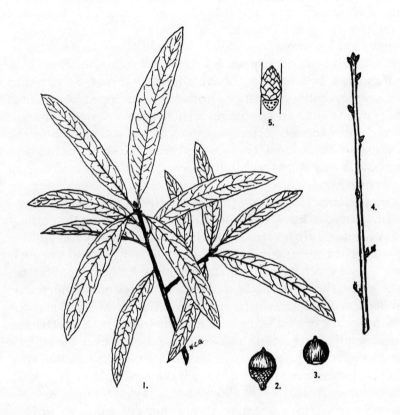

WILLOW OAK

1. Branch with mature leaves.   5. Detail of winter bud and leaf scar.
2-3. Acorns.
4. Winter twig.

DARLINGTON OAK   *Quercus hemisphaerica* Bartr. ex Willd.

> The glabrous, evergreen, lustrous leaves and glabrous twigs are most distinctive.

Leaves 1 to 3½ inches long, ½ to 1 inch wide, alternate, simple, ever-green, leathery, elliptic to lanceolate to oblanceolate, mostly widest at or near the middle, both surfaces glabrous and lustrous, paler beneath than above; margins entire or with few teeth or bristle-tipped lobes, apices acute or obtuse and with or without bristles, base cuneate to rounded; leaves of upper and lower stems morphologically markedly different; petioles short, but evident. *Fruits* (acorn) ⅓ to ½ inch long, tan, hairy throughout or only at the tip; cups flattened or basally rounded, covering ⅕ to ¼ of the nut.

Comparisons. The leaves of this species may be confused with those of the much thicker leaves of the live oak; however, those of the Darling-ton oak are thin, bright green, and lustrous (even below), and entirely glabrous with bristle-tipped apices, while those of the live oak are thick, leathery, gray green beneath, finely tomentose-hairy without bristle-tipped apices. They may also be confused with those of the willow oak, but differ from that species by having at least some of the leaves broadest above the middle (widest at the middle in the willow oak); by retaining its leaves until spring (willow oak leaves are deciduous in the fall); by having broader and hairy leaves, at least along the veins and midvein; and by having undulate or lobed margins (never so in the willow oak). The Darlington oak leaves may also be confused with the more rounded leaves of the laurel oak, but that species has blunt rather than pointed leaf tips, and more obvious reticulate veins (easily seen when held against the light), while those of the Darlington oak are not obvious, are hairy beneath (at least along the midribs), and consistently lack a bristle-tip. The Darlington oak also produces flowers several weeks earlier. Many specimens identified in herberia as laurel oak are actually this species.

———

The Darlington oak is an upland coastal plain species found on dry sandy soils of well-drained woodlands, dunes, and sandhills, where it is commonly found with the slash pine and the long-leaf pine. It is a large tree, 80 to 90 feet high, but becomes dwarfed in drier dune areas. It is often planted as a shade tree or ornamental, but the wood is not consid-ered to be of high quality. The known distribution of this species extends along the coastal plain from Virginia to Florida and westward to Texas.

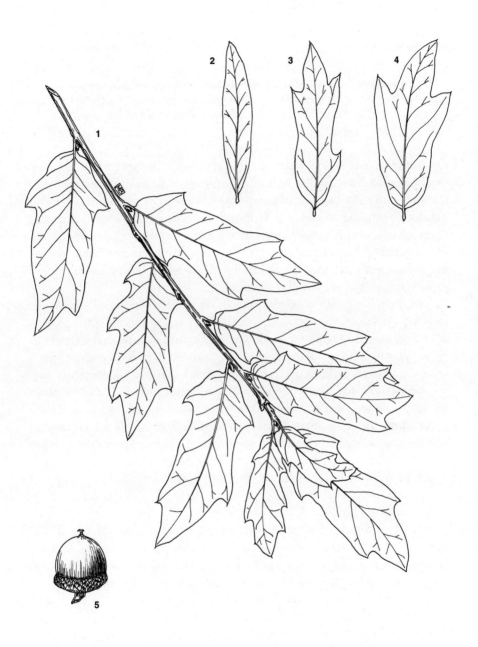

DARLINGTON OAK

1. Branch with leaves.
2–4. Various leaf shapes.

5. Acorn.

LAUREL OAK   *Quercus laurifolia* Michx.

> The diamond-shaped, evergreen, laurel-like leaves of this southern coastal plain oak, which are usually broadest at or near the middle, remain on the branches until early spring, and are glabrous beneath, with entire margins (or nearly so).

Summer. *Leaves* 2 to 5½ inches long, ½ to 1½ inches wide, evergreen or semi-deciduous, usually remaining on the branches until early spring; thickish, dull to lustrous dark green above, somewhat reticulate, paler and glabrous or nearly so beneath, with hair tufts around the vein, elliptical to rhombic or occasionally oblong obovate, apices rounded, bristle-tipped, bases cuneate, broadest at or near the middle; margins entire, unlobed but somewhat wavy and occasionally with a few lobes or teeth; midrib prominent, yellowish; petiole ¼ inch long.

Winter. *Twigs* slender, glabrous, dark reddish brown. *Buds* ovoid, reddish. *Fruits* (acorn) about ½ inch in diameter, roundish, dark brownish black; seated in shallow saucerlike or turbanlike cups that cover ¼ to ⅕ of the nut, with reddish brown, hairy scales. *Bark* dark brown, quite smooth; on old trunks developing flat ridges separated by deep furrows.

Comparisons. The diamond-shaped and rounded, rather than sharply pointed, leaf apex of this species helps to separate it from the more elliptic or lance-shaped leaves of the Darlington oak, which flowers several weeks later and occurs in sandy, drier upland sites rather than in floodplain forest and swamp borders. The leaves are also similar to those of the willow oak, but thinner and much longer and wider.

The laurel oak, so named because of its close resemblance to the Grecian laurel, *Laurus nobilis* L., is a medium- to large-sized tree, usually 50 to 60 feet in height with a trunk diameter of 2 to 3 feet, but at times 100 feet or more in height with a trunk diameter in excess of 4 feet. It develops a broad, round-topped, symmetrical crown when grown in the open, and like the pin oak and the water oak, it produces numerous small, painfully sharp branches. The tree grows naturally in swamps and along floodplain forests, and the banks of streams. It does well, however, in drier upland soils, grows rapidly, and has been widely planted as a street and shade tree in the South under the name of Darlington oak, a name usually applied to *Q. hemisphaerica*. The laurel oak has relatively little importance as a timber tree, but it is occasionally cut and sold as red oak lumber. The

LAUREL OAK

1. Branch with leaves.   2. Acorn.

small acorns are eaten by squirrels, wild turkeys, wild ducks, and other forms of wildlife.

Laurel oak has a range extending through the coastal plain from southern New Jersey to Florida and westward to southeastern Texas.

SHINGLE OAK   *Quercus imbricaria* **Michx.**

> The shiny, leathery leaves with entire margins and bristle-tips, which are broadest at or above the middle, and which have stalked stellate hairs, are most distinctive.

Summer. *Leaves* 3 to 6 inches long, ¾ to 2 inches wide, alternate, simple, deciduous, oblong ovate or oblong obovate, broadest mostly at or above the middle, somewhat thick and leathery, margins entire, often undulate, bristle-tipped; upper surfaces dark green, lustrous, lower surfaces paler, with stalked hairs, prominent midribs; apices acute or obtuse, bases cuneate or rounded; petioles short, rather stout, hairy. *Fruits* (acorn) sessile or nearly so, with deep, bowl-shaped, reddish brown, and slightly hairy cups covering ⅓ to ½ of the nut; nuts about ½ inch long, roundish, dark brown, often striate.

Winter. *Twigs* slender, glabrous, lustrous, dark greenish brown. *Buds* about ⅛ inch long, ovoid, sharp-pointed, brown, often slightly hairy. *Bark* brown, with rather shallow fissures and broad, low, scaly ridges.

Comparisons. The leaves of this species are somewhat similar to those of the more Southern willow oak, but wider and more lustrous above.

The shingle oak is also known as the laurel oak and the water oak, but the latter two names are properly applied to two other species of oaks that are common in the South. It is usually a medium-sized tree attaining a height of 40 to 60 feet and a trunk diameter of 1 to 2 feet, but it sometimes attains a much larger size. The shingle oak develops a broadly pyramidal crown; but it eventually becomes more round-topped, often with drooping lower lateral branches. It occurs most commonly on rich, moist slopes, attaining its maximum development in the lower Ohio Valley.

The wood of this tree was commonly employed for making shingles in pioneer days, hence its common name as well as the specific epithet *imbricaria*, meaning "overlapping." The wood is heavy, hard, and coarse-grained. It checks badly in drying but is used to a limited extent for

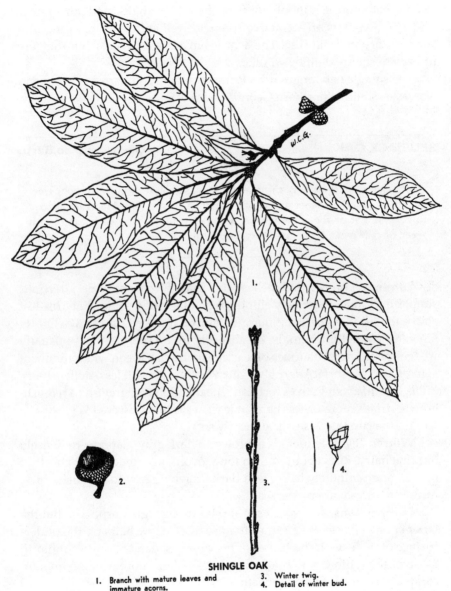

SHINGLE OAK

1. Branch with mature leaves and
   immature acorns.
2. Acorn.
3. Winter twig.
4. Detail of winter bud.

lumber, and more commonly for fuel, charcoal, shingles, and mine props. The shingle oak is an attractive tree and well suited for planting as a shade or ornamental tree. The acorns have bitter kernels, but they are utilized to some extent by wildlife.

The shingle oak ranges from Pennsylvania to southern Michigan and Nebraska, south to northern Georgia and Arkansas.

BLUEJACK OAK   *Quercus incana* Bartr.

> The thicket-forming habit of this sandy-soil, coastal plain shrub or shrubby tree, with its crooked branches and entire-margined, bristle-tipped leaves that tend to be widest at or above the middle, silvery tomentose hairy below, and bluish green or ashy green above, are most distinctive.

Summer. *Leaves* 2 to 5 inches long, ¼ to 1½ inches wide, alternate, simple, deciduous, narrowly elliptic to oblong, often somewhat broadest above the middle, leathery, margins entire, unlobed, or rarely slightly lobed on young individuals, tip abruptly bristle-pointed, base usually wedge-shaped, upper surface blue green or grayish green with prominent veins, the lower surface densely white woolly with stalkless, stellate hairs. *Fruits* (acorn) about ½ to ⅝ inch long, nearly globular, grayish to reddish-brown, striate, more-or-less hairy at least at summits, covered ¼ to ½ of its length by a cup that is sessile or nearly so.

Winter. *Twigs* slender, dark brown to dark gray, glabrous to densely but fine hairy. *Buds* about ¼ inch long, ovoid, pointed, bright chestnut brown, often minutely hairy. *Bark* dark brown or gray to blackish, thick, furrowed into square plates, scaly.

Comparisons. This species is similar to the Oglethorpe oak, but the latter species has stalked rather than sessile yellow hairs on the under-surface of its leaves. The leaves of the bluejack oak are quite similar to those of the willow oak, but somewhat smaller, more gray green, and conspicuously white-hairy beneath.

———

The bluejack is sometimes called the upland willow oak. It is a small, often thicket-forming, scrubby tree, rarely attaining a height of about 30 feet and a trunk diameter of 10 inches. Generally it is a small tree, hardly more than a large shrub with crooked branches. Along with the blackjack

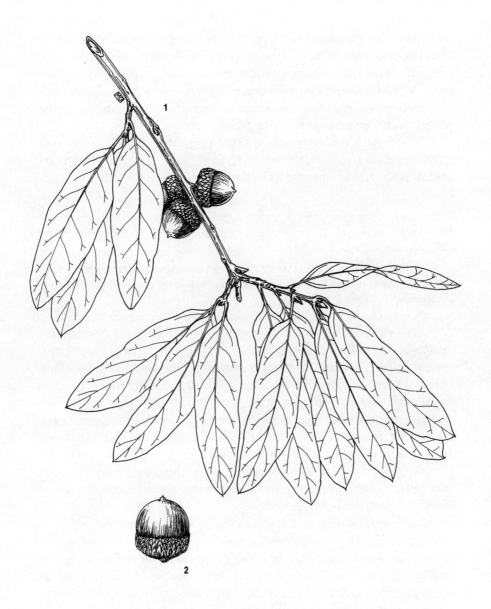

BLUEJACK OAK

1. Branch with leaves and acorns.   2. Acorn.

oak, the turkey oak, and the dwarf chinkapin oak, it occupies the poorer and drier sandy soils of the coastal plain. Its wood makes an excellent fuel but otherwise it has no particular value. The small acorns provide food for wild turkeys, squirrels, and other forms of wildlife. In the early spring the unfolding leaves, which are a delicate seashell pink above and silvery white beneath, are exceedingly attractive.

The bluejack oak has a range extending through the coastal plain from southeastern Virginia to southern Florida, westward to eastern and central Texas and southeastern Oklahoma.

LIVE OAK   *Quercus virginiana* P. Mill.

> Most diagnostic of this species are its evergreen, leathery leaves, which have mostly entire, incurved margins, and which are densely covered with minute, appressed, stellate hairs beneath.

Leaves 2½ to 5 inches long, ⅜ to 2 inches wide, alternate, simple, evergreen, thickish, stiff and leathery, broadest at or above the middle, elliptical to oblong obovate, tips rounded or blunt, occasionally with a tiny tooth, base pointed, margins entire, incurved, or occasionally remotely toothed, especially above the middle on vigorous shoots; upper surface dark green, shiny; lower surface paler, densely covered with tiny stellate hairs that lie flat against the leaf surface. *Fruits* (acorn) ⅝ to 1 inch long, narrow dark brown; cups long-stalked, often clustered, bowl-shaped or turbanlike, cover ¼ to ½ the acorn. *Bark* dark brown, deeply furrowed, somewhat scaly.

Comparisons. This tree species is quite similar to the often thicket-forming and more shrublike sand live oak; however, the former flowers 2 to 3 weeks earlier and differs by its hair types and leaf venation (densely and loosely tomentose hairy on the leaf undersurface of the sand live oak and tightly tomentose hairy on the live oak, which is observable with a lens; also lateral veins less noticeably impressed on the surface of the leaves than those of the sand live oak). Also, the sand live oak leaf margins are revolute and leaf blades tend to roll downward; the live oak has leaf margins that are scarcely revolute and blades that are nearly flat.

LIVE OAK

1. Leaf from vigorous shoot.
2. Typical branch with leaves and acorns.
3. Details of bud and leaf-scar.
4. Acorns.

The live oak, so named because of its evergreen leaves, with its massive trunk and wide-spreading horizontal branches, often festooned with streamers of Spanish moss, is the most typical and majestic tree of the Deep South. Although it seldom attains a height of more than 60 feet, its broad, round-topped crown may have a spread of 100 feet or more, with its lower branches occasionally resting on the ground. The trunk is typically short, buttressed at the base, and divided near the ground into massive spreading limbs. The Middleton Oak in the famous Middleton Gardens near Charleston, South Carolina, has a trunk diameter of almost 9 feet.

In our day the live oak is chiefly prized as a shade or ornamental tree, but in the days of the sailing ships it provided timbers for the ribs and knees of ships. It was considered so important that the United States set aside several large preserves of the tree for the exclusive use of its navy. Timbers for the *USS Constitution*, "Old Ironsides," came from the first such preserve on St. Catherine's Island, Georgia—the state that has adopted the live oak as its state tree.

The range of the live oak extends through the coastal plain from southeastern Virginia to southern Florida and west to southern Texas.

SAND LIVE OAK   *Quercus geminata* Small

This is an evergreen to semievergreen species that is very similar to the live oak, and is often considered to be a variety of that species. It differs, however, by developing its vegetative and floral characters later in the season than that species; by having smaller leaves usually 1–2½ inches long, leaf margins more obviously revolute; by the tendency to have conspicuously downward-rolled leaf blades (rather than being flat as in the live oak); and by having a more noticeable veiny undersurface of its leaves. It often forms impenetrable thickets on dry, sandy soils of woods and coastal dunes, which are commonly subjected to salt spray, from southeastern North Carolina to Florida and west to southeastern Louisiana. It is a smaller and less impressive tree than the live oak, ranging in height from 20 to 30 feet and with a trunk up to about a foot in diameter. Its leaves also differ by being somewhat smaller, usually 1 to 2½ inches long, more veiny in appearance with the lateral veins impressed strongly on the upper surface, and with more strongly revolute margins. Also, the densely and loosely tomentose rather than tightly tomentose hairs on the leaf undersurface of the sand live oak are of two types, many being tightly appressed, but others being clearly erect.

SAND LIVE OAK

1. Branch with leaves and acorns.   2. Acorn.

MYRTLE OAK   *Quercus myrtifolia* **Willd.**

> This southern coastal plain, thicket-forming shrubby tree is characterized by its hairy twigs, and evergreen, leathery, oblong-ovate leaves, which are green on both surfaces and have entire, revolute margins.

Leaves ¾ to 2 inches long, ½ to 2 inches wide, alternate, evergreen, thick and leathery, lustrous and dark green, prominently veiny above; glabrous, duller green beneath with hair tufts within the vein axles, ovate to obovate, broadest at or above the middle, rounded to occasionally pointed apically, sometimes bristle-tipped, gradually tapered to a blunt or rounded base; margins unlobed, but occasionally undulate, revolute and occasionally wavy or toothed; petioles very short, hairy. *Fruits* (acorn) ⅜ to ½ inch long, nearly round, sessile or with a short stalk; nuts enclosed ¼ to ⅓ by the cup. *Bark* light gray, smooth, becoming furrowed in age.

Comparisons. This southern coastal plain species can be distinguished from the other evergreen oaks of the region by its small leaves (¾ to 2 inches long and ½ to 2 inches wide), which are a lustrous, dark green on both surfaces and glabrous beneath except for axillary tufts of hairs and have rolled or revolute margins; and by its small oval or roundish acorns (about ½ inch long), which are seated within saucer-shaped to top-shaped cups. It is similar to the Chapman oak and the sand live oak, but differs from the former species by having leaves that are lustrous, glabrous (at least beneath) rather than sparsely hairy, and dark green rather than dull and yellow green, and from the latter species by not having a hairy leaf undersurface.

———

The myrtle oak is a thicket-forming, much-branched shrub or a small tree, 20 to 30 feet high and 8 to 16 inches in diameter, of little commercial value. It grows among the dunes and on dry sands near the coast, from South Carolina to Florida and west to Mississippi.

BOTTOM-LAND POST OAK   *Quercus similis* Ashe

This is a bottomland species found along the southern coastal plain from Mississippi to Texas and Arkansas and recently found in South Carolina. It is very similar to both the post oak and the sand post oak, differing from the former by having narrower main lobes and by hairs not obscuring the surface of the first-year twigs, and from the latter by lacking basally fused hairs (individual hairs are basally fused in the sand post oak). It is also similar to the overcup oak, but with fewer lobes.

CHAPMAN OAK   *Quercus chapmanii* Sarg.

The deep southern distribution of this entire-margined, evergreen, semi-evergreen, or deciduous oak, with its obovate leaves, which are widest toward the apex and rounded to cordate at the base, along with its gray bark, which exfoliates in a manner similar to that of the white oak, are most diagnostic.

Summer. *Leaves* 2 to 4 inches long, 1 to 1½ inches wide, alternate, simple evergreen to semievergreen or deciduous, persistent, somewhat thickened, obovate to elliptic, tips rounded, base pointed, widest somewhat above the middle; margin entire or undulate to somewhat 3-lobed on the upper half; dull, yellowish green above; paler, yellowish green or silvery green and more or less hairy beneath, especially on the midvein; petioles short. *Fruits* (acorn) about ⅝ to ¾ inch long, ovoid, brown, seated in stalkless bowl-shaped cups, which enclose about ½ of the nut.

Winter. *Twigs* tan to gray, densely stellate-hairy. *Buds* short-oblong to obovoid, chestnut brown. *Bark* thick, gray brown, breaks into irregular strips.

Comparisons. This species is most similar to water oak, but differs from that species by having rounded rather than wedge-shaped leaf bases. It can be separated from the similar myrtle oak by the hairy undersurface of its mature leaves, at least on its veins, and also by lacking a revolute margin.

The Chapman oak is a shrub or small tree, 10 to 30 feet high and 2 to 8 inches in diameter, with a rounded crown of spreading branches. It occurs near the coast from southeastern South Carolina and Georgia to Alabama, and throughout most of Florida in oak-pine forests.

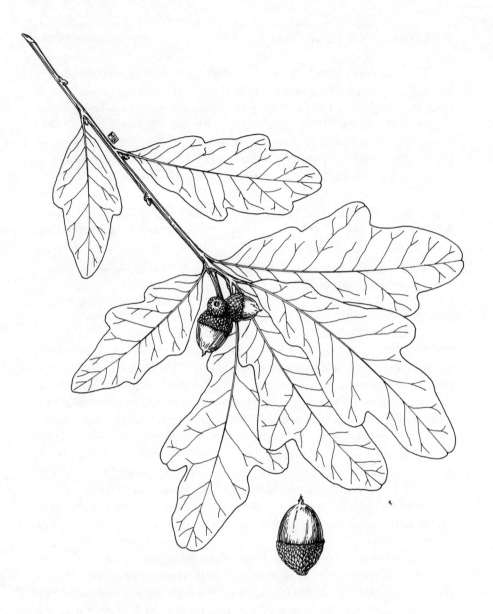

BASTARD OAK

1. Branch with leaves and acorns.　　　　2. Acorn.

BASTARD OAK   *Quercus sinuata* **Walt.**

> The variably shaped, yellowish green, spatulate leaves with entire or 3-lobed
> margins, and woolly undersurfaces, are most distinctive.

Summer. *Leaves* 3 to about 6 inches long, 1 to 3½ inches wide,
alternate, simple, deciduous, obovate or elliptic; entire, unlobed or often
somewhat 3-lobed on the upper half; rounded at the tips, pointed at the
bases, short-petioled; yellowish green above; paler and glabrous or nearly
so beneath. *Fruits* (acorn) ½ to ¾ inch long; narrowly ovoid, pointed, lustrous chestnut brown; seated in a sessile or short-stalked, saucerlike cup.

Winter. *Twigs* glabrous to minutely hairy, gray. *Buds* ¹⁄₁₆ to ⅛ inch
long, reddish brown, glabrous or nearly so. *Bark* light gray, shreddy in
scaly plates.

This is a rather rare tree of the upper coastal plain from southeastern
South Carolina and Georgia westward to southwestern Arkansas and
central Texas. It sometimes attains a height of 60 to 80 feet with a trunk
diameter of 2 to 3 feet.

The expression known as var. *breviloba* (Torr.) C. H. Muller has larger
leaves that are glabrous beneath, tends to be smaller in size, thicket forming, and with acorn cups that are goblet-shaped or shallowly cup-shaped,
rather than saucer-shaped, covering less than ¼ of the nut.

BUR OAK   *Quercus macrocarpa* **Michx.**

> The extremely large acorns (largest of all of the oak species), with a peculiar
> marginal fringe around the edge of the acorn cup, along with the unusual lobing
> pattern of the leaves, which appears to interrupt the margin midway with an
> exceptionally large pair of sinuses, and the corky ridges on the branches, make
> this species easy to identify.

Summer. *Leaves* 4 to 10 inches long, about half as broad, alternate,
simple, deciduous, obovate, broadest above the middle, base cuneate; typically almost divided about the middle by deep, opposing sinuses, usually
with 5 to 7 lobes above and 2 to 3 pairs of shallower sinuses below; lobes

rounded, bristleless, often with irregular, large, wavy teeth, part of marginal lobing appearing to be missing in areas near the middle of the leaf, terminal lobe commonly appearing much larger and broader than the others; upper surfaces dark green, lustrous; lower surfaces paler and hairy. *Fruits* (acorn) very large, sessile or short-stalked, with deeply bowl-shaped cups with gray scales and conspicuously fringed margins; nuts ¾ to 2 inches long and wide, broadly ovoid, hairy, enclosed for ½ to nearly all their length by the cups.

Winter. *Twigs* rather stout, yellowish brown to ashy, glabrous or hairy; developing irregular, narrow, corky ridges after the second season. *Buds* about ⅛ to ¼ inch long, broadly ovoid or conical, reddish brown, more or less pale-hairy, with blunt tips. *Bark* similar to that of the white oak but a darker grayish brown, and usually more definitely ridged.

Comparisons. This species is easily told from the white oak by the unusual lobing pattern of its leaves, which are finely white-hairy beneath (glabrous in the white oak), its larger and peculiar fruits, and by the ridges on its branches.

The bur oak is also known as the mossycup oak or the overcup oak. The scientific name *macrocarpa* means large-fruited and refers to the large acorns. It is a large tree, commonly attaining a height of 60 to 80 feet with a trunk diameter of 2 to 4 feet. The tree reaches its maximum growth in the north-central states, where it often attains a height of 150 feet or more with a trunk 6 or more feet in diameter. Dr. Joseph Illick states that a specimen that grew near Neff's Mill, Huntingdon County, Pennsylvania, had a trunk diameter of 7 feet at breast height. It was destroyed during a storm in 1924.

The bur oak prefers a rich, moist soil, and it is most often found growing in bottomlands, frequently along streams. It makes a very attractive ornamental tree and in cultivation succeeds very well even in dry, clay soils. It is more tolerant of city smoke conditions than most other species of oaks. The wood is very similar to that of the white oak, from which it is seldom distinguished commercially.

Bur oak ranges from Nova Scotia to Manitoba, south to Pennsylvania, Tennessee, Oklahoma, and Texas.

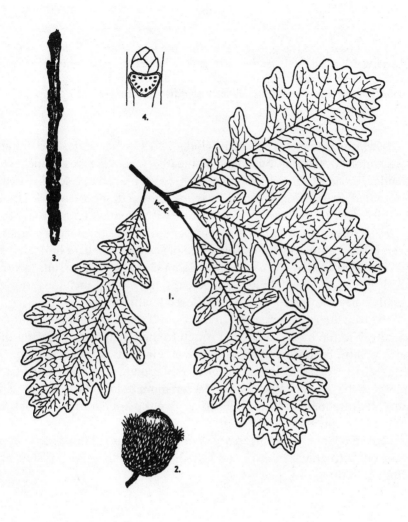

BUR OAK

1. Branch with mature leaves.
2. Acorn.
3. Winter twig.
4. Details of bud and leaf scar.

POST OAK   *Quercus stellata* Wangenh.

> The crucifix-shaped leaves with a squarish main lobe, along with the first-year twigs, which are densely matted with gray to tan hairs, and commonly mixed with black granules that often obscure the twig surface, especially toward its apex, will help to separate this oak from all other species.

Summer. *Leaves* 3½ to 6 inches long, 2 to 4 inches wide, thick, alternate, simple, deciduous, but somewhat leathery, obovate, base cuneate to rounded, broadest above the middle, clustered at branch tips; lobes usually 5, rounded, bristleless, two middle lobes arranged opposite each other, conspicuously larger than the other lobes, with squarish ends, giving the leaves a cross-shaped appearance; upper surfaces lustrous dark green, often feeling rough due to the presence of scattered stellate hairs; lower surfaces paler, coated with a tawny or somewhat rusty hair. *Fruits* (acorn) sessile or nearly so, with bowl-shaped cups; nuts ½ to 1 inch long, ovoid, usually hairy above, about ⅓ to ½ enclosed by the cups.

Winter. *Twigs* rather stout; first season light orange brown, matted with gray to tan hairs, somewhat rough to the touch and obscuring the surface; later becoming very dark brown, glabrous, shiny. *Buds* ⅛ inch long, broadly ovoid, bluntish, bright rusty brown, sparingly hairy. *Bark* similar to that of the white oak but darker, more reddish brown, and with more definite longitudinal ridges that give the appearance of twisting along the length of the bole.

Comparisons. The bark pattern of this species is similar to that of white oak, but grayer in color and less scaly. Leaf lobing is unmistakably different in these two species.

The post oak is also known as the box white oak and the iron oak. It is a small- or medium-sized tree, sometimes attaining a height of 60 feet with a trunk diameter of 1 to 2 feet, but commonly much smaller. Trees growing in the open have a dense, round-topped crown with stout, spreading branches and conspicuously clustered leaves, which are said to represent or resemble stars at the branch tips, hence the scientific name. It is typically a tree of poorer dry, rocky, or sandy soils. The wood is heavy, hard, strong, and very durable in contact with the soil. It is used principally for posts, railroad ties, mine props, and fuel, although the larger trees are sometimes sawed into lumber and marketed with the white oak.

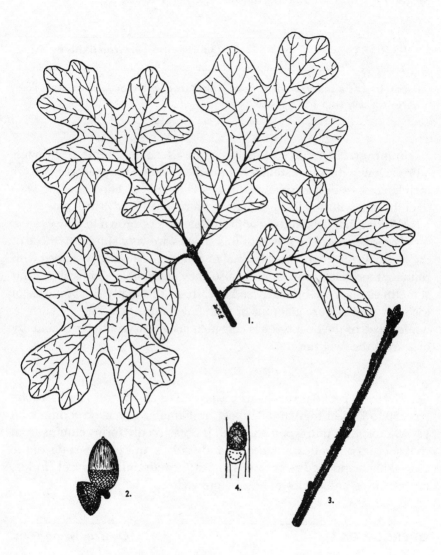

POST OAK

1. Branch with cross-shaped mature leaves.
2. Acorn.
3. Winter twig.
4. Detail of bud and leaf scar.

The post oak ranges from Massachusetts to southern Pennsylvania, west to Iowa and south to northern Florida and Texas.

SAND POST OAK   *Quercus margarettae* Ashe ex Small

Recognized as a small southern coastal plain tree with cruciform or crosslike leaves, typically with 3 to 5 round lobes.

Summer. *Leaves* 1¼ to 4 inches wide, alternate, simple, deciduous, hairy below with 4 to 9 stellately branched hairs. *Fruits* (acorn) ⅜ to ⅞ inch long, sessile or on short peduncles ⅜ inch long, cups covering ¼ to ⅓ of the nut, with small scales that are hairy; nuts ⅜ to ⅞ inch long.

Winter. *Twigs* glabrous or with scattered hairs, brown to gray.

Comparisons. The leaves of this species are very similar to those of the post oak, but are noticeably smaller and more irregularly shaped with round rather than squarish lobes; also, they are more glabrous above and sometimes glabrous or nearly so beneath. Additionally, the branches of the sand post oak are glabrous or with few hairs, not hiding the surface, while those of the post oak are conspicuously hairy, with hairs actually obscuring the twig surface.

The sand post oak, or dwarf post oak, is a shrub or a small scrubby tree, 50 to 75 feet high and 3½ feet in diameter. It has no commercial value, except for pulpwood and fuel. It occasionally forms clumps from root suckers on well-drained dry sandy ridges and pine barrens of the coastal plain and Piedmont from southeastern Virginia to central Florida, central Texas, and the lower Mississippi Valley.

OVERCUP OAK   *Quercus lyrata* Walt.

Aside from the long, 5- to 9-lobed leaves, one of the most diagnostic characters of this wetland species is its acorns, which are nearly completely enclosed by the spherical, ragged-edged cups, leaving only the tips protruding. This coupled with the numerous epicormic branches from the frequently twisted and but-tressed bole are distinctive.

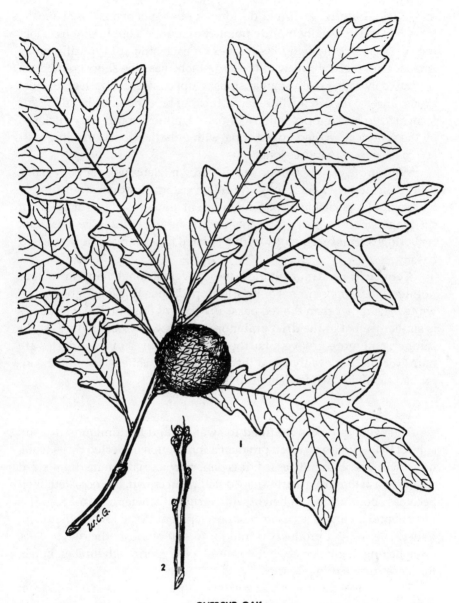

OVERCUP OAK

1. Branch with leaves and acorn. 2. Winter twig.

Summer. *Leaves* very variable, typically 6 to 10 inches long, 1 to 4 inches wide, alternate, simple, deciduous, oblong obovate, base cuneate; lobes 5 to 9 (11), usually bluntly pointed to rounded but bristle free; lobing variable, but the two lowest lobes on each side are typically much smaller than those above, with the largest lobe near the short-pointed tip, separated by rather deep angular sinuses; upper surfaces dark green, glabrous; lower pale, often white-hairy; turning bright scarlet in fall. *Fruits* (acorn) ½ to 1 inch long, solitary or paired, almost completely enclosed by the spherical, ragged-edged cups, with only the tips protruding; sessile or on stalks 1½ inches long.

Winter. *Twigs* rather stout, grayish brown, glabrous to slightly hairy, dull. *Buds* about ⅛ inch long, roundish ovoid, light chestnut brown, hairy; stipules persistent, frequently present among the buds at the tip of the twig. *Bark* brownish gray, separated by fissures into large, irregular, scaly ridges. *Trunk* frequently with a twisted appearance and buttressed basally.

Comparisons. Although the leaves may occasionally appear to have pointed lobes, they are never bristle-tipped; thus it is a member of the white oaks rather than the red oaks. The bark of this bottomland species is similar to that of the drier and more upland white oak, but less scaly, thinner, and more grooved. Furthermore, the leaves of this species are narrower and less evenly lobed than those of the white oak, and the winter buds are hairy, while glabrous in the white oak.

———

The overcup oak is confined to swamps and bottomlands that are subject to frequent and often prolonged inundation, reflected by its trunk base, which is often buttressed. It is generally a small- to medium-sized tree with a rather irregularly shaped and open crown, but occasionally it becomes about 100 feet in height with a trunk diameter of 3 to 4 feet. It is most abundant and reaches its best development in the lower Mississippi Valley. The wood it produces is inferior to that of most other white oaks, often having many defects, but it is used locally for rough lumber. In fall, the leaves turn a bright scarlet.

The range of the overcup oak extends through the coastal plain from southern New Jersey and Maryland to northwestern Florida and west to eastern Texas; and northward, in the Mississippi Valley, to southeastern Oklahoma, southern Illinois, and southwestern Indiana.

WHITE OAK   *Quercus alba* L.

> The completely glabrous, round-lobed leaves, which are whitish beneath, along with the very warty or knobby-cupped acorns, and the light gray, flaky bark, are distinctive.

Summer. *Leaves* 5 to 9 inches long, about half as broad, alternate, simple, deciduous, elliptic, usually obovate, broadest above the middle, entirely glabrous; bright green above, usually somewhat whitish glaucous beneath; bases wedge-shaped, lobes (5) 7 to 11, but usually 7, more or less ascending and rounded, without bristles; sinuses rather shallow and lobes broad on some leaves, while others have deep sinuses and long and narrow lobes. *Fruits* (acorn) sessile or short-stalked; nuts about ½ to ¾ inch long, ovoid, light brown, shiny; enclosed for about ¼ of their length by the warty, shallow, knobby, bowl-shaped cups.

Winter. *Twigs* moderately stout, reddish green to purplish gray, very glabrous, glaucous, usually having a polished or pearly appearance. *Buds* broadly ovoid or almost rounded, glabrous, reddish brown or purplish brown; terminal bud about ⅛ to ¼ inch long. *Bark* light ashy gray, variable: shallowly fissured with long, irregular scales and very flaky in appearance on some trees, while on others more deeply furrowed with distinct ridges broken into oblong blocks, and scarcely scaly.

Comparisons. This species is similar to the bluff oak, but has white rather than green leaf undersurfaces. Also, the white oak has a greater number of regular (rather than irregular) lobes on its leaf margins, and the lobes are generally much longer with deeper sinuses; this is especially so on leaves of the upper crown. In winter, the white oak can be easily distinguished from the bur oak by its diverging rather than appressed lateral buds, bud scales that are all broad (some bud scales of the bur oak are narrow), lack of corky outgrowths on its branches, and light gray and thin-scaled bark rather than dark gray and thick-scaled bark.

———

The white oak is one of our largest and most valuable forest trees and clearly the most important lumber species of the white oak group. Average specimens will be from 60 to 80 feet in height with a trunk diameter of 1 to 2 feet, but it often attains a much larger size. Occasionally we still see old giants from the virgin forest that are often well over 100 feet in height with trunks from 3 to 5 feet in diameter. Freshly cut stumps of such large specimens reveal that they are from three to five centuries old,

WHITE OAK

1. Branch with mature leaves.
2-3. Acorns.
4. Winter twig.
5. Details of bud and leaf scar.

by actual ring count. The white oak grows slowly but it attains a good age. It often requires 50 or more years to produce fruits. With age, trees grown in the open develop a broadly rounded crown composed of many massive branches, which are often gnarled and twisted. It is tolerant of most soils except those that are very wet, and is found in bottomlands and dry ridges alike. In some areas it is the dominant tree on the wind-swept, rounded, soil-covered hilltops.

The wood is very heavy, hard, strong, tough, and close-grained; a very high-grade, all-purpose wood. It is one of the best woods known for tight cooperage, and one of the finest for furniture and hardwood floor-ing. Other uses were for shipbuilding, the manufacturing of wagons and agricultural implements, railroad ties, posts, and for fuel. The acorns of the white oak are quite sweet and edible (reputed to be the sweetest of all the oaks), and they were made into flour by Native Americans for use in bread making. They are a very important source of mast and are utilized as food by many kinds of wild birds and mammals.

The range of the white oak extends from Maine and Quebec west to Minnesota, south to northern Florida and eastern Texas.

BLUFF OAK   *Quercus austrina* Small

> The scaly, gray bark and small white oak–like leaves, which are green rather than white beneath, are most distinctive.

Summer. *Leaves* 2 to 6 inches long, 1 to 3½ inches wide, alternate, simple, deciduous, obovate, pointed basally, widest above the middle; usually with 5 (3 to 6) rounded, bristleless lobes separated by shallow sinuses; dark green and lustrous above, paler green and smooth beneath. *Fruits* (acorn) ½ to ¾ inch long, ovoid, seated in sessile or short-stalked, bowl-shaped cups covering about ½ of the nut.

Winter. *Twigs* reddish brown, turning gray, brittle jointed; glabrous during the first year. *Buds* ovoid to conic, reddish brown, somewhat hairy, middle and upper buds consistently long hairy. *Bark* gray, furrowed, scaly.

Comparisons. Although similar in bark character, this species differs from the white oak by having leaf sinuses more shallowly cut; consistently smaller, fewer, and more irregularly spaced lobes (3 to 6 versus usually 7 to 11); smaller-sized leaves, which are greenish, rather than whitish beneath; and much thinner scales of the acorn cups (those of white oak being thick and knobby).

The bluff oak, or bastard white oak, is a fairly large tree, 50 to 70 feet high and 30 inches in diameter. It occurs within mixed hardwood forests or on well-drained wooded upland slopes of the coastal plain from southeastern South Carolina to central Florida and westward to Mississippi.

OGLETHORPE OAK   *Quercus oglethorpensis* Duncan

> The entire-margined leaves of this somewhat rare southern species, which are conspicuously yellowish-hairy below, widest at or near the middle, and lack an apical bristle-tip, are most distinctive.

Summer. *Leaves* 1½ to 5 inches long, ¾ to 1½ inches wide, alternate, simple, deciduous, nonleathery, narrowly elliptic to obovate, broadest at or above the middle, margins entire or slightly wavy, bristle-tipped, thin; green and glabrous above; paler and yellow beneath with stalked, velvety hairs. *Fruits* (acorn) about ⅜ inch long, ovoid or elliptic, brown, sessile or stalked (to ¼ inch), ⅓ covered by top- or turban-shaped cups.

Winter. *Twigs* reddish to purplish, glabrous or with stalked, stellate hairs. *Buds* ⅛ inch long, with noticeably hairy scales on upper half of bud only. *Bark* light gray, scaly or becoming furrowed.

Comparisons. This species is similar to the bluejack oak, but that species has a bristle-tipped leaf apex and has non-yellow sessile, stellate hairs on the undersurface of the leaves. It is also similar to the shingle oak, but that species has somewhat larger, bristle-tipped leaves and brown, rather than gray, bark.

The Oglethorpe oak was described by Dr. Wilbur H. Duncan of the University of Georgia in 1940. It is 50 to 80 feet high and 20 to 30 inches in diameter, with scaly bark similar to that of white oak. It grows in low grounds, or flatwoods, on poorly drained soil along streams of the southern Piedmont and is known to occur only in a limited area in South Carolina (Edgewood, Greenwood, McCormick, and Saluda counties), Georgia (Elbert, Green, Oglethorpe, and Wilkes counties), Mississippi, and adjacent Louisiana.

SWAMP WHITE OAK   *Quercus bicolor* Willd.

The dark brownish bark of the branches, which peels or exfoliates in sycamore fashion into large, ragged, papery curls, exposing the lighter-colored inner bark, is most distinctive. No other oak has this characteristic. This coupled with the pale undersurfaces of its leaves, which have very shallow leaf sinuses, short lobes that are widest below the middle, and acorns that are borne on conspicuously long (1 to 3 inches) stalks (longer than the leaf petioles) makes this species easy to identify.

Summer. *Leaves* 4 to 9 inches long, 2 to 4 inches wide, alternate, simple, deciduous, distinctly obovate, broadest above the center, abruptly pointed at base and apex, margins with large and irregular wavy teeth, 5 to 8 per side, bristleless, shallowly rounded; upper surfaces lustrous dark green; lower surfaces decidedly paler, being more or less densely covered with whitish hairs. *Fruits* (acorn) ¾ to 3 inches long, typically borne in pairs on conspicuous, long stalks 1 to 3 inches long; nuts about 1 inch long, ovoid, light brown; cups enclosing about ⅓ of the length of acorn, deeply bowl-shaped, with a thin marginal fringe.

Winter. *Twigs* medium stout, glabrous to slightly hairy, dull, greenish yellow to light reddish brown. *Buds* about ⅛ inch long, ovoid or globular, blunt-pointed, light chestnut brown, nearly glabrous or loosely hairy above the middle. *Bark* grayish brown with deep longitudinal fissures separating the long, rather flat-topped scaly ridges.

———

The swamp white oak, as its scientific name suggests, is a species with leaves that are lighter colored beneath than above; as its common name suggests, it is a tree of low-lying and more or less swampy habitats, often occurring in swamp bottomlands and along the banks of streams. It is a medium- to large-sized tree, commonly attaining a height of 60 to 80 feet and a trunk diameter of 2 to 3 feet. In the open it develops an irregularly rounded, broad, and rather open crown with tortuous branches, the lowermost ones very often drooping. The swamp white oak is a relatively rare tree, usually occurring as a minor associate in forests of river-bottom hardwoods with the silver maple, the red maple, the American elm, the American sycamore, and the pin oak.

The wood of the swamp white oak is similar to that of the white oak, from which it is not distinguished commercially. The lateral branches of

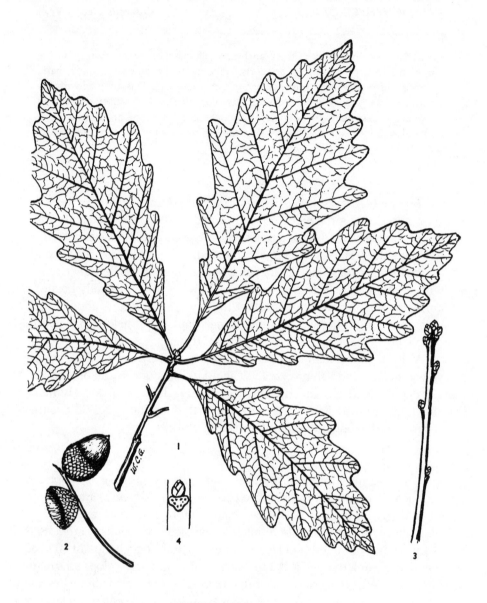

SWAMP WHITE OAK

1. Branch with mature leaves.
2. Acorn.
3. Winter twig.
4. Detail of bud and leaf-scar.

the swamp white oak have a tendency to persist, and its lumber is usually knotty and of poor quality.

The swamp white oak ranges from Quebec and southern Maine west to Minnesota, south to northern Georgia and Oklahoma.

SWAMP CHESTNUT OAK   *Quercus michauxii* **Nutt.**

> The light, silvery-white bark, which is not deeply corrugated; the silvery-hairy undersurface of the leaves, with hairs that tend to be short and stout rather than elongated and narrow; and the bottomland habitat will help separate this species from the chestnut oak.

Summer. *Leaves* 4 to 9 inches long, 2 to 6 inches wide, alternate, simple, deciduous, obovate, widest above the middle, coarsely and sharply toothed, bases wedge-shaped, margins coarsely wavy toothed, with 9 to 14 bristleless teeth per side, abruptly pointed apically; dark green, glabrous, and lustrous above; pale and whitish-hairy beneath. *Fruits* (acorn) 1 to 1⅔ inches long, oblong ovoid, lustrous brown; cups short-stalked or sessile, deeply bowl-shaped, enclosing about ⅓ of the acorn, with hairy scales that are free nearly to their bases.

Winter. *Twigs* moderately stout, reddish to orange brown, glabrous. *Buds* about ¼ inch long, ovoid, sharply pointed, dark red, minutely hairy at the apex. *Bark* silvery white, thick, irregularly furrowed, separated into thin red-tinged scales.

Comparisons. This bottomland or floodplain species, which has bark of the white oak, is similar to the drier upland chestnut oak. The latter, however, has a tighter and darker, nearly black, much more deeply furrowed or corrugated bark pattern, and has fewer individual stellate hairs per cluster (2 to 5 versus 2 to 8) on the undersurface of the leaves. The swamp chestnut oak leaves are also somewhat similar to those of the chinkapin oak, but are slightly larger, more crenate or round lobed, while those of the latter are usually sharply pointed. Additionally, the leaf undersurface of the chinkapin oak has sparsely scattered short hairs, while that of the swamp chestnut oak is covered with densely appressed hairs, and tends to have more simple hairs than does the chinkapin oak.

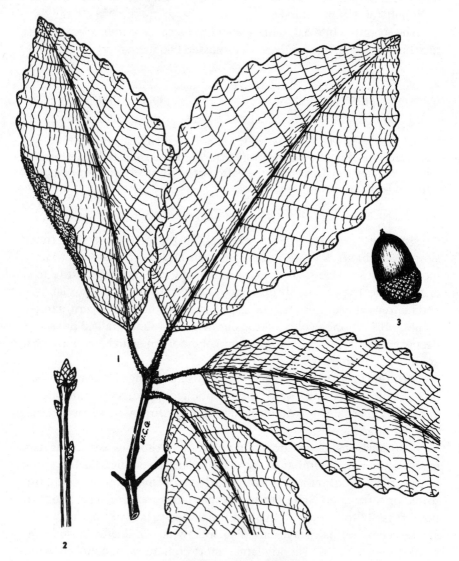

SWAMP CHESTNUT OAK

1. Mature branch with leaves.   3. Acorn.
2. Winter twig.

The swamp chestnut oak is also known as the cow oak or the basket oak. It is a moderate-sized tree that attains a height of 60 to 80 feet and a trunk diameter of 2 to 3 feet or more; with a compact, rather narrow crown. It inhabits bottomlands that are periodically inundated for short periods, rather than permanently flooded swamps. Usually it occurs as a scattered tree but locally it is sometimes quite abundant. The wood is similar to that of the white oak and is not usually differentiated by lumbermen. The use of its wood for making basket splints is responsible for the common name of basket oak.

The range of the swamp chestnut oak extends through the coastal plain from New Jersey southward to central Florida and westward to eastern Texas; and northward, in the Mississippi Valley, to central Illinois and southeastern Ohio.

CHESTNUT OAK   *Quercus prinus* L.

> The chestnutlike leaves with rounded lobes of this species, the orange brown twigs, and the deeply vertically furrowed or corrugated washboardlike bark, which is very dark in color and very rough in appearance, broken into long, irregular, V-shaped ridges, with deep intervening furrows, are quite characteristic.

Summer. *Leaves* 4 to 9 inches long, 2 to 4 inches wide, alternate, simple, deciduous, usually obovate but occasionally elliptical, rather thick; upper surfaces dark, lustrous yellowish green; paler beneath, finely hairy or glabrous; tips bluntly pointed, bases broadly wedge-shaped, margins with 9 to 16 pairs of rounded, bristleless, coarsely rounded teeth per side. *Fruits* (acorn) short-stalked; cups deeply bowl-shaped or somewhat top-shaped, warty-scaled, fringeless, enclosing about ⅓ of the nut; nuts ¾ to 1½ inches long, oblong ovate, lustrous chestnut brown; sweet and edible kernels.

Winter. *Twigs* rather stout, varying from light orange brown to reddish brown, quite glabrous. *Buds*, lateral buds about ¼ inch long, conical, sharp-pointed, often angled, light chestnut brown, often a little hairy toward the tips; terminal bud somewhat larger, up to ½ inch long. *Bark* tight, dark brown to nearly black, deeply furrowed with vertical grooves that appear as corrugated steel sheets covering the trunk.

Comparisons. The leaves of chestnut oak are similar to those of chinkapin oak, differing by having more rounded rather than pointed

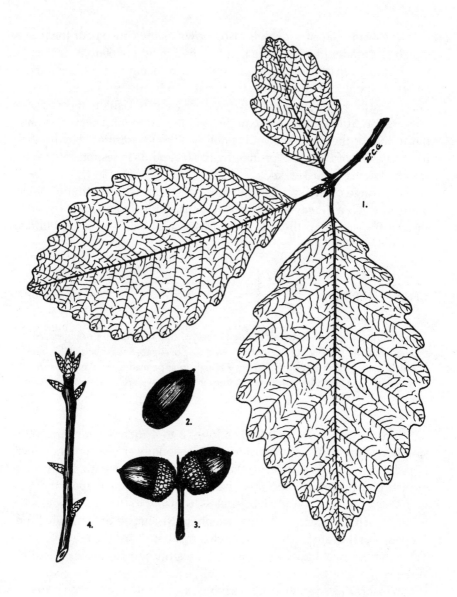

CHESTNUT OAK

1. Branch with mature leaves.
2-3. Acorns.

4. Winter twig.

lobes and sinuses. The unique bark will help separate it from all of its relatives.

———

The chestnut oak is also known as the rock oak and the rock chestnut oak. Although chestnut oak has come to be its generally accepted common name, rock oak is certainly a far more appropriate one. It is predominantly a tree of rocky places. On the dry, rock-strewn mountain ridges, it associates with the pitch pine and the mountain-laurel, but it often mingles with the scarlet oak and the black oak on the rocky slopes of the mountains and on outlying rocky hilltops. The chestnut oak is usually only a medium-sized tree, attaining a height of 50 to 70 feet and a trunk diameter of 1 to 2 feet.

The wood is heavy, hard, strong, close-grained, and durable in contact with the soil. It is sometimes marketed as white oak lumber but is principally used for general construction lumber, railroad ties, posts, and as fuel. The bark is valuable, being richer in tannin content than that of any other species of oak, and it is extensively utilized in the tanning of leather. With the loss of the American chestnut, which formerly was one of its principal associates, the sweet-kerneled nuts of the chestnut oak have become the most important source of mast along our mountain ridges, and a most valuable food for gray squirrels, black bears, white-tailed deer, wild turkeys, and many other forms of wildlife.

The chestnut oak ranges from southern Maine and southern Ontario southwest to the Ohio Valley and Tennessee, and along the Appalachian Mountains to northern Georgia and Alabama.

CHINKAPIN OAK   *Quercus muehlenbergii* Engelm.

Although the shiny, dark green leaves of this species are quite similar to those of the chestnut oak, the bark is conspicuously different, more closely resembling that of the white oak.

Summer. *Leaves* 4 to 6 inches long, 1 to 4 inches wide, alternate, simple, deciduous, usually broadly lanceolate but occasionally a little broader above the middle, tips taper-pointed, bases broadly wedge-shaped; marginal teeth large, 9 to 15 pairs, coarse, quite regular, somewhat pointed, but without bristles, often slightly incurved; upper surfaces

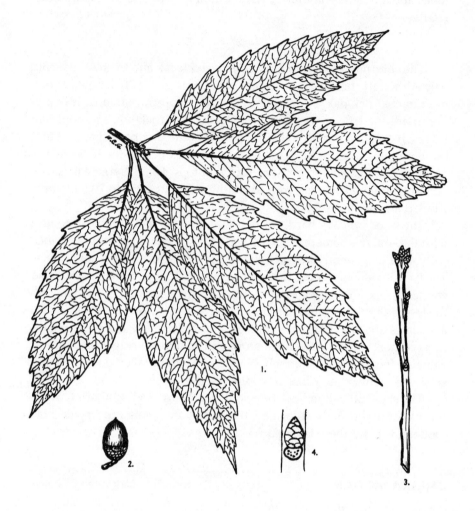

CHINKAPIN OAK

1. Branch with mature leaves.
2. Acorn.

3. Winter twig.
4. Detail of bud and leaf scar.

dark, lustrous yellowish green; lower surfaces paler green, often minutely hairy, but occasionally nearly glabrous. *Fruits* (acorn) ½ to 1 inch long, sessile or short-stalked, with rather shallow bowl-like cups enclosing ⅓ to ½ of the nut; nuts ½ to ¾ inch long, ovoid, light to dark brown.

Winter. *Twigs* rather slender, light orange brown to ashy brown, glabrous. *Buds* about ⅛ to 3/16 inch long, ovoid or conical, mostly glabrous, rather sharp-pointed, light chestnut brown. *Bark* characteristically light gray, noticeably flaky, very similar to that of the white oak.

Comparisons. Although the leaves of the chinkapin oak are similar to those of the more southern swamp chestnut oak, they have more sharply pointed rather than rounded teeth, and have blades that are more narrowly lenceolate to elliptic rather than broadly obovate. Moreover, the swamp chestnut oak occupies river bottoms and other wet areas, whereas the chinkapin oak grows on drier, calcareous slopes and sandy ridges and bluffs. Also, the acorns of the chinkapin oak are mostly ⅓ to 1 inch long, while those of the swamp chestnut oak extend to 1⅔ inches long. The acorn cups scales are free only at their apices in the chinkapin oak, while free to nearly their bases in the swamp chestnut oak. The leaves of the chinkapin oak are similar to those of the swamp chestnut and chestnut oaks but have more sharply pointed lobes. The dwarf chinkapin oak is also somewhat similar in leaf morphology, but is a shrubby species.

The chinkapin oak is also known as the yellow oak, and incorrectly as the chestnut oak. It is a medium-sized tree 40 to 50 feet in height with a trunk from 1 to 3 feet in diameter. It attains its maximum development in the lower Ohio Valley, where it often becomes a rather large tree. The chinkapin oak evidently prefers the rich soils of the bottomlands, and there attains its greatest size, but farther east it commonly occupies dry hillsides, particularly in the vicinity of limestone outcroppings.

The wood is heavy, hard, strong, close-grained, and durable, but it checks badly in drying and is of no value for use in tight cooperage or cabinetwork. It is used principally for railroad ties, fuel, and construction lumber. The chinkapin oak is an attractive tree and suitable for planting as a shade or ornamental tree, although it grows rather slowly.

The range of the chinkapin oak extends from Ontario west to Minnesota and Nebraska, south to Delaware, western Florida, and Texas.

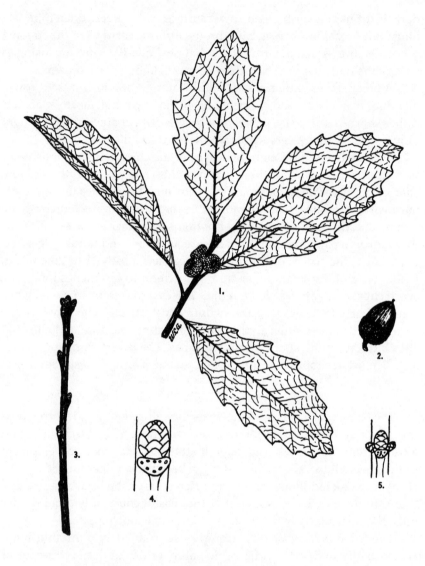

DWARF CHINKAPIN OAK

1. Branch with mature leaves and immature acorns.
2. Acorns.
3. Winter twig.
4. Detail of bud and leaf scar.
5. Detail of lateral accessory buds.

DWARF CHINKAPIN OAK   *Quercus prinoides* **Willd.**

> The shrubby habit of this species, with few lobes (3 to 7) per leaf side, and knobby-scaled acorn cups, are most distinct.

Summer. *Leaves* 3 to 5 inches long, 1½ to 2½ inches wide, alternate, simple, deciduous, usually obovate, margins with 3 to 7 pairs of coarse, bristleless, rounded or slightly pointed teeth per side; dark yellowish green above, paler and gray hairy beneath; tips usually rather bluntly pointed, bases wedge-shaped. *Fruits* (acorn) sessile or short-stalked, with deeply bowl-shaped, pale-hairy cups enclosing ½ or more of the nut; nuts about ¾ inch long, ovate, shiny light brown.

Winter. *Twigs* less than ⅛ inch in diameter, slender, light orange brown to reddish brown, usually glabrous. *Buds* less than ⅛ inch long, ovoid, blunt-pointed, light brown, often 3 at a node. *Bark* thin, light brown, definitely scaly on trunks.

Comparisons. This species can be separated from chestnut oak, swamp chestnut oak, and swamp white oak by its fewer-lobed leaves, which have tiny, stellate hairs on their undersurfaces (hairs larger on the other species), and by its more shrubby habit.

—————

The dwarf chinkapin oak, also known as the scrub chestnut oak, usually occurs as a low, spreading, and thicket-forming shrub, from 2 to 4 feet in height, but it occasionally attains a height of 12 to 15 feet with a diameter of about 4 inches. This scrubby oak grows on rather dry rocky or sandy soils, along roadsides, on barren slopes, and in hillside pastures. The wood is of no commercial value but is sometimes used as fuel. It is usually regarded as a weed tree but it may have some real value as a soil binder along roadsides and on rocky slopes. Furthermore, as it is a prolific producer of sweet-kerneled acorns, it is of definite value to wildlife.

The dwarf chinkapin oak ranges from Maine to Nebraska and south to North Carolina and Texas.

BIRCH FAMILY—BETULACEAE

The Birches—Betula

The birches have alternate, simple leaves with double-serrate and some-times lobed margins. On the second-year twigs the leaves are characteris-tically arranged in pairs on short spurlike branches. The twigs are slender, usually with conspicuous lenticels, and are marked by the semioval to crescent-shaped leaf scars, which have 3 bundle scars. Terminal buds are not present. Catkins, the partially developed staminate flowers, are often present and conspicuous. The bark on the young trunks and branches is smooth, more or less resinous, and prominently marked with horizon-tally elongated lenticels.

The wind-pollinated flowers of the birches appear in the early spring before the leaves. The staminate ones occur in slender and drooping aments, the pistillate ones in smaller and more or less erect aments on growth of the previous season. Both staminate and pistillate flowers occur on the same tree. The fruits are little conelike structures, technically called strobili, consisting of central axes to which numerous scales are attached. The scales are 3-lobed and resemble little fleurs-de-lis. The seeds have a pair of semirounded, thin lateral wings and are dispersed by the wind.

SWEET BIRCH *Betula lenta* **L.**

> The sweet birch may be identified by its close-fitting, reddish brown, cherrylike bark, and by its twigs, which have a pronounced odor when broken and taste of wintergreen.

Summer. *Leaves* 2 to 5 inches long, alternate, simple, ovate to oblong, apically acute to acuminate, cordate or rounded at base; dark dull green above, paler yellowish green beneath; glabrous or nearly so when mature, may be white hairy within the 9 to 12 vein axils, margins irregularly and finely toothed with sharp-pointed teeth, blades with an odor and taste of wintergreen when bruised. *Flowers,* male aments drooping, 1 inch or less long, extending to 3 to 4 inches long at maturity in spring; female aments ½ to 1 inch long. *Fruits* (nutlet) tiny, compressed, glabrous, produced in elongated, erect strobili, 1 to 1½ inches long, ½ inch wide; seed wing narrower than seed; fruiting bracts glabrous or sparingly ciliate and slightly hairy near the base; appearing like tiny bird's-footprints, with 3 ascending lobes, the 2 lateral scale lobes attaching somewhat above or very near the middle.

Winter. *Twigs* slender, glabrous, lustrous, reddish brown with scattered, small, pale lenticels, with a very pronounced odor and taste of wintergreen. *Buds* ¼ inch long, glabrous, ovate, all sharply tipped with red-brown scales, divergent, axillary except those on lateral spur shoots. *Bark* on old trunks becoming nearly black, broken into large, thick, irregular plates, with a smooth surface; resembles that of black cherry.

Comparisons. The sweet birch can be told from the yellow birch by its overall smaller size; its larger and generally more hairy fruit scales; its dark brown to black rather than yellowish bark, which is tight rather than curled and fringed; and also by its buds that diverge from, rather than are appressed to, the twigs; by the twigs and buds, which are glabrous rather than hairy; and by the less consistently hairy leaves, which have fewer unbranched side veins.

The sweet birch is also known as the black birch or the cherry birch. It is a small- to medium-sized tree, commonly attaining a height of 50 to 60 feet and a trunk diameter of 2 to 3 feet, but occasional specimens may be much larger. The trunks of young trees are more or less continuous, with ascending branches forming a somewhat pyramidal crown. Older trees often have forking trunks and spreading or drooping branches forming a rather wide, open, round-topped crown. The sweet birch prefers moist, rich, and more or less rocky soils, but it often occurs on rather dry mountain slopes. It is one of the principal associates of the American beech and the sugar maple in the climax forest type.

The wood of the sweet birch is heavy, hard, close-grained, and strong. It is used principally for furniture and for hardwood flooring, but also for millwork, boxes, crates, baskets, and various small wooden articles. It is an excellent firewood, burning with a clear, hot flame. Oil of wintergreen,

Black
Locust →

SWEET BIRCH

1. Branch with mature leaves and fruits.
2. Mature strobiles.
3. Winter twig with catkins.
4. Details of bud and leaf scar.
5. Scale from strobile.
6. Winged nutlet.

which is used medicinally and as a flavoring in candies and chewing gum, is distilled from twigs, bark, and wood. Birch beer is made by fermenting the sap obtained by tapping the trees in the early spring. Country children invariably find the twigs to be pleasant chewing. The sweet birch makes good deer browse, and its bark and twigs are eaten by both the snowshoe hare and the cottontail rabbit. The ruffed grouse utilizes its buds for food during the winter season, and the seeds are eaten by many of the small seed-eating birds and mammals.

The range of the sweet birch extends from southern Maine to Ohio, south to Delaware and along the Appalachian Mountains to northern Georgia and Alabama.

YELLOW BIRCH   *Betula alleghaniensis* **Britt.**

> At all seasons mature yellow birch may be identified by its more or less lustrous, amber yellow to silvery yellowish-gray bark that peels in thin, filmlike curls. This, coupled with the hairy twigs, hairy, ciliate fruit bract, and the faint wintergreen odor and taste of the twigs (less so than the twigs of sweet birch), is most distinct. In the winter, the 2-toned brown bud scales and odor of the broken twigs provide easy identification.

Summer. *Leaves* 2 to 5 inches long, alternate, doubly serrate, ovate, gradually tapering to an acuminate or acute apex, bases cordate, hairy below, especially within axils of the 9 to 12 veins; very closely resemble leaves of the sweet birch. *Twigs* dull and more inclined to remain hairy, while those of the sweet birch soon become lustrous. *Flowers*, male aments drooping, ¾ to 1 inch long in winter, extend to 3 to 3½ inches long when fully developed; female aments ½ to ¾ inch long, more erect. *Fruits* (nutlet) tiny, hairy at apex, produced in elongated, erect strobili, 1 to 1½ inches long, ⅝ inch wide; seed wings narrower than seed; fruiting bracts hairy on their back, appearing as tiny bird's-footprints, with the 3 narrowly ascending scale lobes attached somewhat above the middle. *Bark* more or less lustrous, amber yellow to silvery yellowish gray, peeling off in thin, filmlike curls.

Winter. *Twigs* slender, dull light yellowish brown, slightly hairy (while those of the sweet birch are glabrous, lustrous, reddish brown), with a rather faint odor and taste of wintergreen. *Buds* chestnut, slightly hairy, appressed to twig, apices acute. *Bark* with a rather faint odor and

YELLOW BIRCH

1. Branch with mature leaves.
2. Flowering branch.
3. Fruit.
4. Winter twig with catkins.
5. Winter twig.
6. Detail of bud and leaf scar.
7. Scale from strobilus.
8. Winged nutlet.

taste of wintergreen; on the lower part of very old trunks becoming red-dish brown, broken into irregular plates.

Comparisons. This is one of the three eastern birch species with aromatic twigs, the others being the sweet birch and the Virginia round-leaf birch. The latter can be easily separated by its limited distribution and by its very round leaves with blunt apices and only 3 to 6 veins per leaf side (the yellow and the sweet birches both have 9 to 12 veins per leaf side). The sweet birch can be separated from the yellow birch by its cherrylike bark.

———

The yellow birch is also known as the silver birch and the gray birch, but the latter name is properly applied to *Betula populifolia*. The yellow birch is one of the largest of eastern hardwoods, usually attaining a height of 60 to 80 feet, or occasionally nearly 100 feet, with a trunk diameter of 2 to 4 feet. The trunk of trees grown in the open commonly branches low, and the spreading or somewhat drooping branches form a broad, open crown. Trees growing in the forest usually have their trunks clear of lateral branches for some distance from the ground.

This birch requires a cool, moist habitat and rich soil for its best development; but it often grows in swampy and exceedingly rocky areas. Frequently seedlings will begin to grow on old, mossy logs or on the tops of decaying tree stumps, sending roots down over them into the soil. Thus one often sees even fair-sized yellow birches that seem to be perched above the ground on several sturdy supporting roots, long after the log or stump on which they started to grow has completely decayed and disappeared. The yellow birch is one of the principal members of the climax beech-birch-maple forest association.

The yellow birch is the most valuable of all of our birches from the commercial standpoint. The wood is heavy, hard, strong, and close-grained. It is used for furniture, flooring, interior finish, woodenware, handles, spools, boxes, veneer, and plywood. It is an excellent fuelwood and also much in demand for chemical distillation. Like the paper birch, the thin films of bark are highly flammable, even when wet, and are often used by campers for starting fires. It is said that a palatable tea can be brewed from the leaves, and birch beer can be produced from the sap. Of the two major aromatic birches, the other being sweet birch, this one clearly yields the highest content of oil of wintergreen. Yellow birch is one of the preferred browse species for the white-tailed deer. The bark is eaten by the varying hare, the cottontail, and the beaver. The buds are utilized as food by the ruffed grouse during the winter season.

The range of the yellow birch extends from Newfoundland to Manitoba, south to Pennsylvania and Minnesota, and along the Appalachian Mountains to northern Georgia.

The Virginia round-leaf birch, *Betula uber* (Ashe) Fern., is a very rare species (or perhaps hybrid) of birch found only in a small area in southwestern Virginia, and is now considered to be endangered. This birch is easily recognized by its small, orbicular, heart-shaped leaves; rounded apices; 3 to 6 pairs of lateral veins; and dark brownish black bark with prominent lenticels and a strong odor of wintergreen. It was first collected by W. W. Ashe of the U.S. Forest Service in 1914, but was considered to be extinct until rediscovered in 1975.

RIVER BIRCH   *Betula nigra* L.

> The river birch may be identified by its light reddish brown, pinkish- to cinnamon-colored, exfoliating bark, which peels off into thin, papery layers. This, along with the sharply wedge-shaped, rhombic or nearly 4-sided leaves, and bottomland habitat, is most distinct.

Summer. *Leaves* 1½ to 4 inches long, 1½ to 2½ inches wide, alternate, rhombic ovate, tips acutely short-pointed, bases broadly wedge-shaped; dark green above, paler yellowish green to grayish or whitish beneath, lower surfaces often somewhat tomentose, at least along the 8 to 9 pairs of veins; margins sharply and doubly serrate. *Flowers,* male and female flowers borne on the same tree; male aments drooping, 1 inch or less long, extending to 2 to 3 inches at maturity; female aments more erect, ⅕ to ½ inch long. *Fruits* (nutlet) tiny, compressed, produced in strobili 1 to 1½ inches long; seed wings somewhat narrower than seed; fruiting bracts 3-lobed, hairy, with the ascending lobes attached at or below the midpoint.

Winter. *Twigs* slender, reddish brown, more or less thickly covered with pale lenticels, usually glabrous but occasionally slightly hairy. *Buds* ¼ inch long, ovate, pointed, light chestnut brown, often slightly hairy. *Bark* exfoliating; on the younger trunks and branches resembles that of the yellow birch except in color; on old trunks, especially at base, becoming reddish brown, deeply furrowed, broken into irregular, platelike scales.

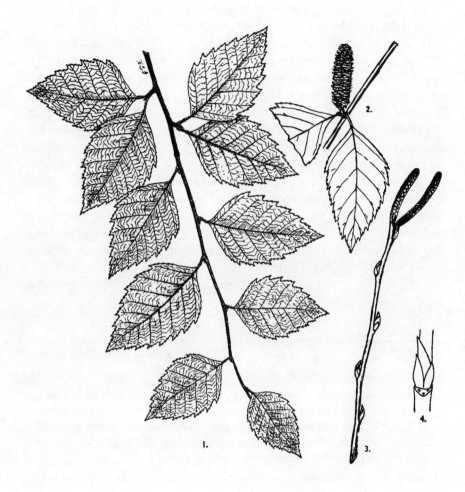

RIVER BIRCH

1. Branch with mature leaves.
2. Portion of branch with fruit.
3. Winter twig.
4. Detail of bud and leaf scar.

The river birch, or red birch, is the most common birch of the South. It is a medium- to large-sized tree, often 30 to 50 feet in height with a trunk diameter of 1 to 2 feet, but it may attain a height of nearly 100 feet with trunks 3 to 4 feet in diameter. The trunks are often short, dividing close to their bases into a few large ascending or slightly spreading limbs, which have numerous slender and often drooping branches, forming an irregular oblong crown. The river birch is primarily a southern species, and in the North it rarely attains a large size. It is typically a tree of streambanks and of swampy bottomlands, which are periodically flooded. It is unique among the birches in that the fruits do not mature until the spring, following flowering.

The wood of the river birch is light but rather hard, strong, and close-grained. It is not of great commercial importance, but it is used to some extent for furniture, woodenware, boxes, and in turnery. The river birch makes a very attractive ornamental tree. It will adapt itself to even fairly dry situations under cultivation. It is unquestionably of much value in preventing the erosion of streambanks.

The river birch ranges from Massachusetts west to Minnesota, and south to northern Florida and eastern Texas.

GRAY BIRCH   *Betula populifolia* **Marsh.**

The larger trunks of this species are very characteristic with their close-fitting, chalky-white bark, and the conspicuous dark, chevron-shaped blotches below the branches. This, coupled with its triangular leaves, which are basally truncate, apically long-tapered, and supported by black glandular-dotted petioles, and the single terminal staminate catkin, is most distinctive.

Summer. *Leaves* 2 to 3½ inches long, 1½ to 2½ inches wide, distinctly triangular ovate, tips long acuminate, bases truncate, obtuse, or cordate, on elongated black glandular-dotted petioles; quite glabrous, dark green and lustrous above, paler and glabrous beneath; margins sharply and doubly serrate with glandular teeth, at times almost appearing to be shallowly lobed. *Flowers* developed with the leaves; male aments drooping, about 1 inch long or less in winter, extending to 2 to 3½ inches long at full maturity; female aments more erect, about ⅖ to ⅗ inch long. *Fruits* (nutlet) tiny, compressed, produced in elongated, semierect to pendent, cylindrical strobili, ¾ inch long, and ¼ to ⅓ inch thick; seed wings much

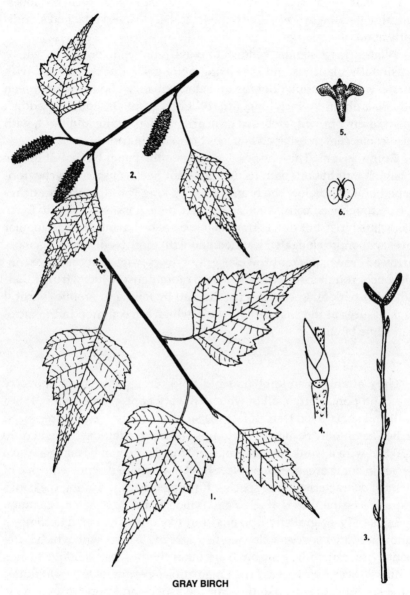

GRAY BIRCH

1. Branch with mature leaves.
2. Branch with leaves and fruits (strobili).
3. Winter twig.
4. Detail of bud and leaf scar.
5. Scale from strobilus.
6. Winged nutlet.

broader than seed; fruiting bracts with hairy somewhat recurved lobes; central scale-lobe tip very short, the lateral scale lobes attached significantly above the middle.

Winter. *Twigs* slender, reddish to grayish-brown to orange brown, or occasionally glaucous and appearing quite gray; thickly covered with minute, warty, glandular dots as to feel roughish, without a wintergreen odor. *Buds* about ³⁄₁₆ inch long, often slightly resinous, pointed, reddish brown to gray brown, glabrous or nearly so. *Bark* white and tight, with conspicuous chevron-shaped blotches below the branches.

Comparisons. This species is similar to the paper birch, but differs by having a tight bark pattern that does not peel; conspicuous chevron-shaped blotches below the branches; very long leaf tips; and branches that are roughened conspicuously by resin dots. It is also similar to European white birch, but differs from that species by having more triangular leaves with more elongated leaf tips, and with more teeth per side, a more narrowed crown, darker brown or gray-brown twigs that are more conspicuously roughened with resin dots, more densely hairy fruit scales, and duller bark that peels less readily, and by failing to produce vertical black fissures at the base of the trunk, which are common in the European white birch.

———————

Gray birch is also known as old field birch, white birch, poverty birch, and poplar birch, all of which are very appropriate names. It is a small and short-lived tree, in fact the smallest of our Eastern tree-sized birches, commonly occurring in clumps and often attaining a height of 20 to 30 feet with a trunk diameter of 6 to 12 inches. It can be an aggressive species in some areas, such as New England, where it represents one of the most characteristic tree species. It frequently grows along the banks of streams or the shores of lakes and ponds, but it is often very common on dry, sandy, or gravelly uplands, and like quaking aspen becomes a common invader species following fire. Like the aspens, with which it frequently associates, the gray birch aggressively invades abandoned fields or burned-over forest areas. The long petioles permit its leaves to flutter in the slightest breeze, like those of the aspens and poplars, hence the name poplar birch.

The wood of the gray birch is light, soft, and neither strong nor durable. It is of little commercial importance but used to some extent for spools, toothpicks, barrel hoops, paper pulp, and for fuel. The gray birch makes a very attractive ornamental tree, but it is not planted extensively because it is so short-lived. It is a valuable cover tree on badly abused areas, eventually being succeeded by a forest of more valuable trees if fire is kept out. It is apparently only casually browsed by the white-tailed deer. In some localities the trees are cut by the beaver, but its bark is evidently not a preferred item on the beaver's bill of fare. The buds are sometimes eaten by the ruffed grouse during the winter season.

The gray birch ranges from Nova Scotia to Lake Ontario, southwestward to Delaware and southern Pennsylvania.

EUROPEAN WHITE BIRCH   *Betula pendula* Roth

This species, the most commonly planted birch in North America, is a graceful tree that grows to a height of about 60 feet. Its white outer bark is separable into thin papery layers but it is not inclined to peel as freely as that of our native paper birch. The bark at the base of the trunk becomes deeply furrowed, exposing the blackish inner bark. The forms of this birch most commonly planted in this country can be distinguished by their triangular leaves, which are usually deeply lobed or cut, and by their gracefully drooping branches with small glandular dots.

PAPER BIRCH   *Betula papyrifera* Marsh.

At all seasons the paper birch may be identified by its chalky-white to creamy-white bark, which peels off in thin papery layers, exposing the orange-colored inner bark. This, coupled with the leaf blades being doubly serrate and broadest below the middle, is often the most diagnostic feature.

Summer. *Leaves* ovate, 2 to 4 inches long, 1½ to 2 inches wide, alternate, simple, rather thick and firm, glabrous or nearly so; dark green above, paler beneath with hairs in the 5 to 9 veins and with black glands; tips sharply pointed, acute to acuminate, base usually rounded, margins sharply and somewhat doubly serrate; petioles rather long, stout, yellowish. *Flowers,* male aments drooping, ¾ to 1¼ inches long, extending to 3 to 4 inches long at maturity; female aments more erect, 1 to 1½ inches long. *Fruits* (nutlet) tiny, compressed, produced in elongated, pendent strobili 1 to 1½ inches long, ¼ inch wide; seed wings wider than seed; fruiting bracts slightly hairy on their backs, cross-shaped, with two of the three scale lobes attached at the center of the bracts, pointing directly outward from the middle of the fruit.

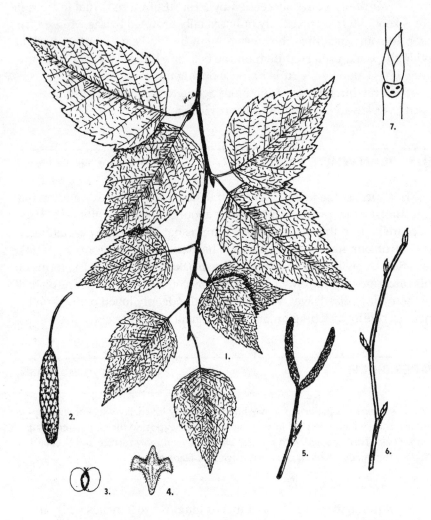

PAPER BIRCH

1. Branch with mature leaves.
2. Strobilus.
3. Winged nutlet.
4. Scale from strobilus.
5. Winter twig with catkins.
6. Winter twig.
7. Detail of bud and leaf scar.

Winter. *Twigs* stouter than those of our other birches, glabrous or slightly hairy, reddish brown to orange brown, with conspicuous lenticels, and without a wintergreen odor. *Buds* blunt to pointed, gummy, green brown. *Bark* becoming blackish and furrowed near the ground on old trunks.

Comparisons. The paper birch, like the river birch, develops a conspicuous ragged-looking bark, and both have fewer leaf veins than the sweet or yellow birches. However, all four species can be easily separated by their bark characters. Although three of the species have bark that peels, the bark of the river birch is more reddish or cinnamon in color, whereas that of the paper birch is chalky white and that of the yellow birch is more yellow and appears ragged or fringed.

————

The paper birch is also known as the canoe birch, the white birch, or the silver birch. In the minds of most of us, it is inseparably associated with the North Country and with Native Americans. It becomes a large tree, from 50 to 75 feet in height, with a trunk diameter of 1 to 3 feet; developing an open, irregularly rounded crown composed of numerous nearly horizontal to ascending branches. The paper birch grows along the banks of streams or the shores of lakes and ascends the rich, moist slopes of the hills. It is most frequently scattered in stands of coniferous trees or other northern hardwoods and is quick to reforest after fire.

The wood of the paper birch is light, strong, hard, and very close-grained. It is principally used for spools and other turned articles, toothpicks, wood pulp, and fuel. The tough, resinous, waterproof, and durable bark was used by the northern Native Americans for canoes, wigwams, and various kinds of utensils. Practical articles such as drinking cups, dishes, and even containers for heating water can be made from the sheets of bark. The resin-filled bark is very flammable, even when wet, and is often used by campers in kindling fires. The northern American Indians used the sap as a sweet drink and sometimes evaporated it to make sugar. The buds are an important winter food of the ruffed grouse in the North, and the seeds are eaten by various species of finches, sparrows, and small rodents. The bark is eaten by the snowshoe hare, but the twigs are only casually browsed by the white-tailed deer. The paper birch makes a very attractive ornamental tree.

The range of the paper birch extends from Labrador to Alaska, north as far as the limit of tree growth, south to Pennsylvania and the region of the Great Lakes, and west to the Rocky Mountains and the state of Washington.

MOUNTAIN PAPER BIRCH *Betula papyrifera* var. *cordifolia*
(Regel) Fern.

This eastern variety of the much wider ranging paper birch is distinguished by its minutely resin-dotted rather than undotted upper leaf blades, its usually heart-shaped leaf bases, which may occasionally be rounded to truncate (mostly wedge-shaped to rounded in the paper birch), its more heavily glandular twigs, slightly larger fruits, larger stigmas, larger and more rounded middle fruit lobe, more ragged bark, longer lenticels, and its more horizontal rather than ascending branches. It occurs occasionally throughout the general range of the paper birch in the Northeast, but in more moist sites, and at higher elevations in the mountains of North Carolina, such as the Black Mountains and Mount Mitchell.

The Hornbeam—Carpinus

AMERICAN HORNBEAM *Carpinus caroliniana* Walt.

> The American hornbeam may be identified by its contorted, very musclelike, vertically fluted trunk, which has smooth, dark bluish gray bark. This, coupled with the conspicuous lenticels on the branches, unusual fruits, and double-serrate leaves, is distinctive.

Summer. *Leaves* 2 to 4 inches long, 1 to 1¾ inches wide, alternate, simple, more or less elliptical to ovate oblong, thin but firm; dark green above, glabrous, paler beneath, quite glabrous except for tufts of hair in the axils; tips rather long-pointed, bases rounded, margins finely and sharply double serrate, veins not forked, blades turning scarlet or brilliant orange in autumn. *Flowers,* male and female flowers develop in separate clusters on the same tree; male aments 1 to 1½ inches long; female aments ½ to ¾ inch long. *Fruits* (nutlet) ⅛ inch long, characteristic and very distinctive; small, ovoid, each one enclosed within the base of a 3-lobed, leaflike bract, 1 to 1½ inches long, borne in pairs in rather loose and drooping clusters.

Winter. *Twigs* slender, zigzag, somewhat lustrous, reddish brown, marked with numerous small, pale lenticels; leaf scars quite small, with three bundle scars. *Buds* all lateral, about ⅛ to ⅕ inch long, acute and

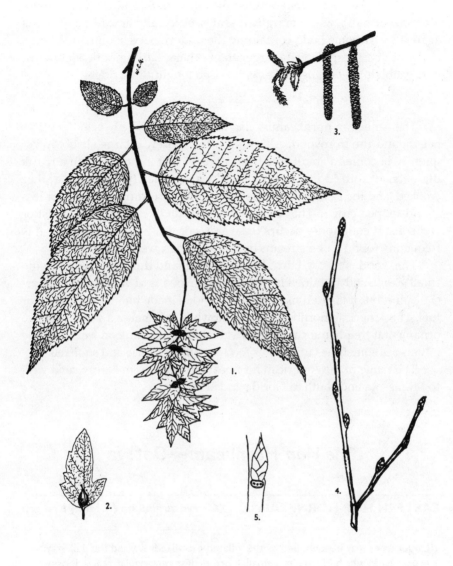

AMERICAN HORNBEAM

1. Branch with mature leaves and cluster
   of fruits.
2. Single bract with nutlet at its base.
3. Flowering branch.
4. Winter twig.
5. Detail of bud and leaf scar.

somewhat incurved, ovoid, angled or not, with 8 to 12 reddish brown, glabrous or hairy, white-margined scales, especially apically, appressed against twigs; some buds, containing the undeveloped staminate flowers, appear to be conspicuously larger than others. *Bark* smooth, slate gray, noticeably fluted or musclelike, with raised longitudinal ridges.

The American hornbeam is also known as the blue beech, the water beech, and the ironwood. Although often merely a large shrub, it frequently becomes a small tree from 10 to 30 feet in height with a trunk diameter of 8 to 12 inches. The trunks are typically short and rather crooked, and the slender branches form a low, spreading, but more or less round-topped crown. The American hornbeam likes deep, rich, moist or wet soils. It commonly occurs in swamps or wet bottomlands, and it is frequently found along streams or about springs, well up in the hills.

The wood is heavy, hard, tough, strong, and durable. Owing to the small size usually attained by the tree, the wood is of very little commercial value, but it is often used for levers, homemade tool handles, and for fuel. The American hornbeam grows slowly, but it makes a very attractive ornamental tree, being particularly valuable for planting on wet sites. The nutlets are sometimes utilized as food by ruffed grouse and squirrels.

The range of the American hornbeam extends from Nova Scotia west to Minnesota and south to Florida and Texas.

The Hop-Hornbeam—Ostrya

EASTERN HOP-HORNBEAM   *Ostrya virginiana* (P. Mill.) K. Koch

Larger trees may be identified by the inflated-sack-like fruits and the dull, grayish brown bark, which breaks into small, more or less rectangular scales, loosened at both ends, giving the trunk a characteristic shreddy appearance.

Summer. *Leaves* 2½ to 5 inches long, 1½ to 2 inches wide, alternate, simple, oblong ovate, thin but tough, apically acuminate, basally rounded or somewhat heart-shaped and asymmetrical; upper surfaces dull yellowish green, paler and often slightly hairy beneath, especially the vein

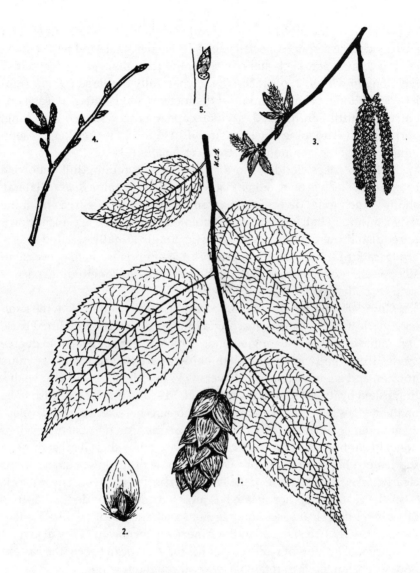

EASTERN HOP-HORNBEAM

1. Branch with mature leaves and cluster of fruits.
2. Bract which is opened to show the nutlet.
3. Flowering branch.
4. Winter twig with catkins.
5. Detail of bud and leaf scar.

axils and along the midrib; lower lateral veins folded; margins finely and sharply double serrate, especially apically. *Flowers*, male and female flowers borne in separate clusters on the same tree; male aments about ½ inch long in winter, 2 to 3 inches long when fully developed. *Fruits* (nutlet) ¼ inch long, peculiar and most distinctive; small, flattened, each one enclosed within an inflated, saclike, papery bract about ¾ inch long, borne in little drooping clusters (strobili) 1½ to 2½ inches long, resembling fruits of the common hop *(Humulus lupulus* L.).

Winter. *Twigs* slender, more or less zigzag, tough, dull yellowish brown to reddish brown, either glabrous or slightly hairy. *Buds* all lateral, about ¼ inch long, diverging at an angle of about 45 degrees from the twigs, minutely hairy, ovoid, sharp-pointed, with 6 to 8 greenish brown to reddish brown, with very diagnostic, longitudinally striated scales. *Fruits* (catkin) small, usually in groups of 3, often present, may occasionally persist into the winter. *Bark* shreddy, broken into longitudinal narrow strips at both ends.

Comparisons. In winter, this species can be separated from the similar American hornbeam by its shreddy rather than tight and fluted bark, and rounded rather than angled buds, which diverge at nearly 45 degree angles from the twigs rather than being appressed to them, are more gummy, and somewhat larger (¼ versus ⅛ to ⅕ inch). It can also be distinguished by its longitudinally striated bud scales that lack whitish hairs on their edges. Also, the eastern hop-hornbeam characteristically develops an abundance of winter catkins, while the American hornbeam develops none. In summer the two trees can be separated by their leaves; those of the eastern hop-hornbeam have at least some of the lower lateral veins clearly forked, unlike those of the American hornbeam, which do not fork. Also, the eastern hop-hornbeam has more narrowly rounded rather than broadly rounded leaf bases and marginal teeth that are indistinctly rather than distinctly two sizes, as in the American hornbeam. They also have conspicuously different fruit types. Like the American beech, the eastern hop-hornbeam tends to retain its leaves throughout winter.

The eastern hop-hornbeam, so named because of the close resemblance of its fruit clusters to that of the common hop, is also known as the ironwood, the leverwood, and the deerwood. It is usually a small tree, from 20 to 30 feet in height with a trunk 1 foot or less in diameter, but occasionally it attains a height of around 60 feet. The slender branches form an irregularly oblong or broadly round-topped crown. The eastern hop-hornbeam is scattered throughout the hardwood forests of the northeastern states, commonly occurring as a small understory tree. It seems to prefer the rather dry and gravelly or rocky slopes and ridges to bottomlands.

The wood is strong, hard, tough, and durable; hence the tree's common name of ironwood. It is useful for fence posts, levers, and tool handles, and is often made into mallets and other small tools. The nutlets are frequently eaten by ruffed grouse during the fall and winter months, and they are occasionally eaten by the gray squirrel and the fox squirrel. The cottontail rabbit sometimes eats the bark and the twigs, and it is occasionally browsed by the white-tailed deer.

The range of the eastern hop-hornbeam extends from Nova Scotia to Minnesota and south to central Florida and eastern Texas.

TEA FAMILY—THEACEAE

The Franklintree—Franklinia

FRANKLINTREE   *Franklinia alatamaha* **Bartr. ex. Marsh.**

> Bark dark to nearly black, with conspicuous vertical white lines. Flowers very showy, white, and fragrant.

Summer. *Leaves* 2½ to 6 inches long, 1½ to 2 inches wide, alternate, simple, deciduous, clustered at the ends of the twigs; broadest above the middle, apices acute or obtuse, gradually tapered to the base, margins finely but sharply toothed, especially above the middle; dark green, glabrous above except for a slightly hairy midvein, paler and hairy below, turning red in the autumn; petioles ⅓ to ⅔ inch long, hairy. *Flowers* 2½ to 3⅔ inches across, large, showy, white, produced singly in the leaf axils, fragrant; petals 5, broadest above the middle, rounded apically; sepals 5; stamens numerous, bright yellow. *Fruits* (capsule) ½ to ¾ inch wide, globose, woody, splitting lengthwise from apex to base from both ends along alternating suture lines into 5 sections, each with 6 to 8 wingless seeds.

Winter. *Twigs* slender, slightly angled, dark reddish brown; bundle scar 1; stipule scars lacking; pith large, continuous, coffee colored. *Buds*, terminal bud present, with tan hairs. *Bark* on trunk and large branches black with vertical stripes.

Comparisons. The deciduous rather than evergreen leaves, sessile flowers, and globular capsules that split from both ends along alternating suture lines can help to separate this species from its relative, the loblolly-bay.

374

The Franklintree is undoubtedly one of the rarest trees in the world regarding its wild populations. The species is thought to be extirpated in the wild and is now known only in cultivation.

All of the horticultural material in existence was propagated from a single plant collected by John Bartram and his son William. The original collection was made along the banks of the Altamaha River near Fort Barrington, Georgia. Since then, it has been relocated at least twice, once in 1773 by William Bartram and again in 1790 by Dr. Moses. It has been reported that the plant may have been susceptible to a cotton blight, which could have destroyed the original population. Fortunately, it is easily propagated by both seed and cuttings and now is used extensively in horticulture. The large, fragrant flowers, resembling those of a camellia, are quite spectacular and thus prized. The scientific name of this tree was intended to honor both Benjamin Franklin and the river in Georgia where it was originally found.

The Loblolly-Bay—Gordonia

LOBLOLLY-BAY   *Gordonia lasianthus* (L.) Ellis

The large, evergreen, finely toothed leaves (mostly toothed above the middle), which are not aromatic when crushed, and the large, showy, fragrant flowers, with hairy petals, are most distinctive.

Leaves 3 to 6 inches long, ½ to 2 inches wide, thick, leathery, evergreen, narrowly elliptic to oblanceolate, tips acute, obtuse or acuminate, bases cuneate, margins shallowly and rather finely toothed only above the middle with small blunt teeth; upper surfaces dark green and lustrous, the lower surfaces paler and glabrous or nearly so; petioles about ½ inch long, stout. *Flowers* 2 to 2½ inches across, perfect, solitary, fragrant, exteriorly hairy, flowering throughout the summer; petals 1¼ to 1½ inches long, 5, white, fringed, waxy; stamens yellow, numerous. *Fruits* (capsule) about ½ to ¾ inch long, long-stalked, ovoid, woody, silky on the surface, seated in the persistent calyx, splitting into 5 sections, each containing 2 to 8 square, winged seeds. *Bark* dark reddish brown, thick, with deep furrows separating flat-topped narrow ridges.

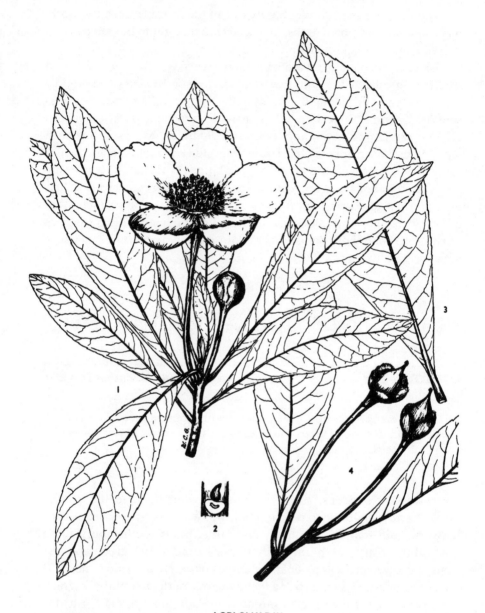

LOBLOLLY-BAY

1. Branch with leaves and flowers.
2. Detail of bud and leaf scar.
3. Typical leaf.
4. Fruiting branch.

Comparisons. The large evergreen leaves of this species may be confused with those of the sweetbay, but that species has aromatic entire-margined leaves that are hairy rather than glabrous and often (but not consistently) whitish beneath. Also, the loblolly-bay may be confused with the swampbay and red bay, but those species have aromatic foliage and entire, rather than toothed, margins.

———

The loblolly-bay is a small but beautiful tree, occasionally 60 to 70 feet in height with a trunk 1 to 1½ feet in diameter. Its crown is narrowly oblong with conspicuous upward-pointing branches, and in midsummer the loblolly-bay displays handsome, 5-petaled white flowers about 2½ inches in width. If it were less demanding, it would make a splendid subject for cultivation; it thrives, however, only in the deep, damp peat of bogs and the borders of swamps, where its beauty is so often hidden. As a timber tree it must be relegated to a position of minor importance, although the pinkish wood is used locally for veneer and cabinetmaking. Although somewhat difficult to grow, the loblolly-bay has recently made its way into cultivation in the Southeast, with variegated-leaf cultivars being much sought after, but difficult to obtain.

Loblolly-bay is a close kin of the camellias and of the lost Franklintree. The range of the loblolly-bay extends through the coastal plain from southeastern Virginia to central Florida, westward to southern Mississippi.

LINDEN FAMILY—TILIACEAE

The Basswoods and the Lindens—Tilia

A very useful character of the genus *Tilia* is the unusual development of multiple sprouts from the trunk base. In 1891, Sargent, in his *Silva of North America,* recognized three native species of *Tilia,* which are now considered to represent a single species with three varieties. Identification of these varietal expressions (or "species") is somewhat difficult, although it is relatively easy to identify the species itself. The varietal expressions have been segregated primarily on the degree of hairiness of leaves and twigs. As far as basswood is concerned, there is often a great deal of variation in such characters as leaf size, shape, and degree of hairiness among the leaves of the same tree. The name basswood originates from a type of cloth, called bass cloth, made from the inner bark of the tree. The bark can also be made into excellent-quality ropes, mats, cordage, strings, and even shoes.

AMERICAN BASSWOOD   *Tilia americana* **L.**

This species is easily told by its large, asymmetrically heart-shaped leaves, reddish twigs, fragrant flowers, hooded buds (which are edible), unusually shaped fruit bracts, and sucker sprouts around the trunk base.

Summer. *Leaves* 4 to 10 inches long, 3 to 8 inches wide, alternate, simple, deciduous, 2-ranked, broadly ovate, asymmetrical, tips rather abruptly long-acuminately pointed, bases heart-shaped or very nearly straight but slanting; margins coarsely but sharply and singly serrate with glandular tipped teeth; at maturity firm, dark green and glabrous above,

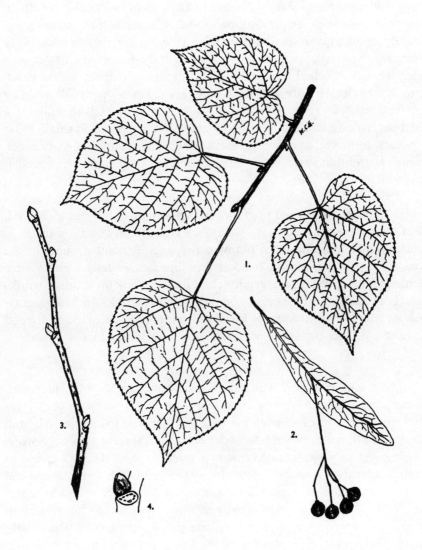

AMERICAN BASSWOOD

1. Branch with mature leaves.
2. Fruit.
3. Zigzagging winter twig.
4. Detail of bud and leaf scar.

paler beneath, palmately veined and developing secondary veins visible only from the ventral side, glabrous or hairy except for small hair tufts in the vein axils; stipules present; petioles 2 to 3 inches long, rather long, slender, round, glabrous. *Flowers* ½ inch wide, perfect, creamy white, very fragrant, 5-parted, borne in loose, few- to many-flowered clusters on a slender stalk attached for about half its length to a narrow, leaflike bract, produced in June or July after the leaves are fully developed; pollinated by insects, chiefly by bees. *Fruits* (nut) ¼ to ⅜ inch wide, each about the size of a pea, woody, ball-like, brown- or grayish-hairy, borne in small, loose clusters at the end of a slender stalk attached to a straplike leafy bract, which is useful in wind dispersal; maturing in October and often persisting well into the winter.

Winter. *Twigs* glabrous, slender to moderately stout, more or less zigzag, tough, bright red to green, somewhat mucilaginous if chewed; leaf scars elevated, semiovate, with several scattered bundle scars. *Buds* about ¼ inch long, alternate, plump ovoid, slightly pointed, shiny, bright red, divergent, conspicuously hooded or lopsided, usually with 2 visible scales, one atop the other; terminal bud lacking. *Bark* on younger trunks and branches gray or greenish gray; on the older trunks thick, dark grayish and deeply longitudinally furrowed, with long flat- to round-topped ridges, which are transversely broken into short oblong blocks.

———

American basswood is also known as American linden, whitewood, linn, lime, or beetree. It is a large tree attaining a height of 60 to over 100 feet, with a trunk diameter from 2 to 4 feet. The trunk is usually tall and straight, with numerous slender branches forming a broadly ovate, oblong, or somewhat rounded crown. Sometimes there are 3 or 4 trunks in a clump, for the basswood sprouts freely when it is cut, and often several of the more vigorous sprouts develop into trunks. The preferred habitat is bottomland, where the soils are deep, moist, and fertile, but it is often found on the slopes of hills, even in places that are quite rocky. It associates with other species of hardwoods in the forest and very rarely forms even small-sized pure stands.

The wood is light, soft, moderately strong, close-grained, and quite tough. Native American tribes, such as the Iroquois, use the wood for carving false-face masks. It is also used for cheap furniture, boxes, cooperage, woodenware, apiary supplies, veneer, wood pulp, and excelsior. Basswood is the best wood available for food containers, particularly for butter tubs, as it imparts no odor or taste to the contents.

The basswoods are among the most important of American honey trees, and the honey is famous for its excellence. Occasionally the flowers are used in making a tea. The American basswood is often planted as a shade or street tree, possessing among its many excellent qualities a fairly rapid rate of growth. The fruits are sometimes eaten by squirrels, chipmunks, and other small rodents. It is an excellent and apparently palatable browse for the white-tailed deer, and cottontails frequently eat the bark and sprouts during the winter. Old basswoods are very frequently hollow, making excellent nesting and den sites for many kinds of wild birds and mammals.

The American basswood ranges from New Brunswick to Manitoba, south to Delaware and eastern Kansas, and along the Appalachian Mountains to North Carolina.

WHITE BASSWOOD *Tilia americana* var. *heterophylla* (Vent.) Loud.

The white basswood, or mountain basswood, is similar in most respects to the American basswood. It is distinguished principally by the undersurfaces of the leaves, which are more or less densely coated with white to pale-tawny stellate hairs that can be seen even at a significant distance. Its flowers and fruits are borne in larger clusters than are those of the American basswood, commonly with 10 to 20 flowers in a cluster. It is most abundant in the southern Appalachian Mountains, but it ranges from New York and eastern Canada west to Iowa and southern Illinois and south to northwestern Florida and northern Arkansas.

CAROLINA BASSWOOD *Tilia americana* var. *caroliniana* (P. Mill.) Castigl.

Comparisons. Although the large leaves of this varietal expression may be confused with those of the mulberries, unlike those plants, the basswoods in general have hooded bud scales and lack the production of latex from the stem and leaf base.

The Carolina basswood, which is also known as the Florida basswood, is a small- to medium-sized tree found chiefly in the coastal plain and

Piedmont regions of the Southeast. It ranges from North Carolina south to central Florida and west to Texas, southeastern Oklahoma, and central Arkansas. Its leaves are 3 to 5 inches long and about as broad. They are dark green above and vary from densely to sparsely stellate hairy on the lower surface. These hairs may be pale or rusty brown. Sometimes the leaves become quite glabrous at maturity or may be glaucous. Often the leafstalks and the twigs are likewise hairy. This is the prevalent basswood expression in all but the mountainous regions of the Southeast.

Campanula am.

CACAO FAMILY—STERCULIACEAE

The Parasol-tree—Firmiana

CHINESE PARASOL-TREE   *Firmiana simplex* **(L.) W. Wight**

> The large maplelike leaves, thick, clubby, green branches and bark, and elongated inflorescences are most distinctive.

Summer. *Leaves* 4 to 15 inches long, nearly as wide, alternate, simple, deciduous, rounded in outline, palmately lobed and veined with 3 to 5 lobes, margins entire, bases strongly cordate; green and glabrous above, glabrous to white tomentose below; petioles large, up to 20 inches long. *Flowers* numerous, apetalous, bell-shaped, greenish yellow to lemon yellow, perfect or unisexual, produced in elongated paniculate clusters up to 4 feet long; calyx ⅓ to ½ inch long, straplike, yellowish at first, then reddish; stamens numerous, up to 15 or more. *Fruits* (capsule) 2½ to 3⅔ inches long, spoonlike, wrinkled, 5-parted, containing 1 to 3 large, rounded seeds (from which a tea can be made).

Winter. *Twigs* thick and clubby, conspicuously green; pith large, white. *Buds* large, hairy, velvety red brown. *Bark* gray green, glaucous.

———

The Chinese parasol-tree is another Asian introduction, brought into the United States in 1757 and now naturalized in certain areas. It is a fast-growing though rather short-lived species, 30 to 70 feet high, and tolerant of nearly any soil type. It is often used as a shade or street tree because of its large leaves. Although it is most commonly seen in the South from Florida to Texas, it is hardy to Washington, D.C.

CHINESE PARASOL-TREE

1. Branch with palmately lobed leaves.
2. Flowering branch.
3. Large, nearly circular leaf scars and clubby branch.

TAMARISK FAMILY—TAMARICACEAE

The Salt-Cedar—Tamarix

SALT-CEDAR	*Tamarix ramosissima* Ledeb.

> The tiny, scalelike leaves, which resemble those of junipers, and the numerous tiny pinkish flowers are most distinctive.

Summer. *Leaves* less than ¹⁄₁₆ inch long, alternate, simple, deciduous (at least in the northern areas), somewhat persistent in the South, scale-like, often clasping or sheathing the long slender stems. *Flowers* about ¹⁄₁₆ inch long, pink to whitish, racemose, blooming nearly the entire summer season; petals 4 to 5. *Fruits* (capsule) about ³⁄₁₆ inch long, small, dry.

Winter. *Twigs* thin, often drooping and deciduous with the leaves; pith white; leaf scars lacking. *Buds* small, sessile, rounded, 1 to 3 in small groups; bud scales 2 to 3.

———

The salt-cedars collectively are flowering tree species that most superficially resemble junipers or other conifers vegetatively. They produce open crowns with drooping branches and grow along waterways and old homesites, especially in areas of moist, saline soils. Like many members of this genus, the salt-cedar was originally introduced for erosion control, dune stabilization, and windbreaks, but has invaded much of the country, especially the western United States, where its deep and highly aggressive, water-absorbing root system often enables it to outcompete native species. The fallen leaves contain a high salt concentration, which further precludes native species from growing, creating a nearly sterile environ-

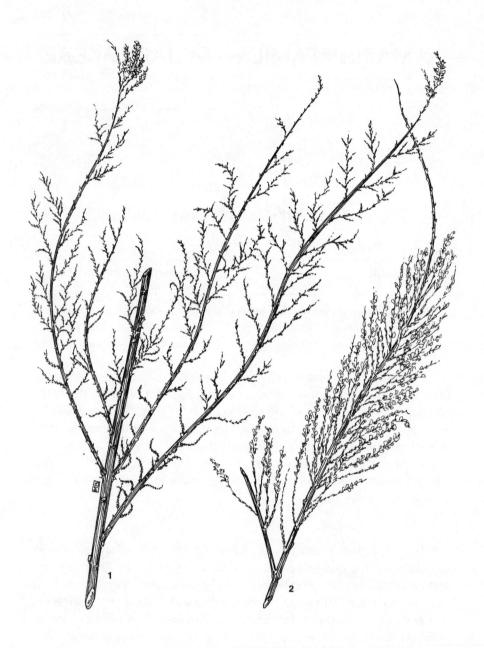

SALT-CEDAR

1. Branch with scalelike leaves. 2. Flowering branch.

ment. Like other members of the genus, once established, this species is difficult to eradicate; however, biological control methods are now being used.

There are some nine species of *Tamarix* in eastern North America that are now escaping to various degrees. Their identifications are rather difficult, based primarily upon petal morphology and stamen numbers. Because of their invasive behavior, tamarisk species are not recommended for planting.

WILLOW FAMILY—SALICACEAE

The Aspens and the Poplars—Populus

The aspens and the poplars have alternate, simple, deciduous leaves with toothed and occasionally lobed margins. The petioles are long and slender, sometimes decidedly flattened. The branches are typically brittle and easily separated at their point of attachment. Many species reproduce freely by the means of root suckers, and cuttings may be rooted with comparative ease. Winter twigs have conspicuous leaf scars, which show three distinct simple, or compound groups, of bundle scars. A very diagnostic character of this genus is that the lateral buds have their lowermost or outer scale centered directly above a leaf scar.

The flowers appear on the branches in early spring before the leaves unfold. Trees bear either staminate or pistillate flowers, which are arranged in drooping aments. The pollen is carried by the wind. The fruits are small, narrowly conical, 2-valved capsules borne in drooping aments. When mature they split open and release the small seeds, which have a mat of long silky hairs to assure their dispersal by the winds. The cottony appearance of the massed seeds is responsible for the name cottonwood, which is applied to some species.

WHITE POPLAR   *Populus alba* **L.**

> The conspicuously white-hairy, feltlike undersurfaces of the maplelike leaves, along with the whitish bark with dark blotches, are most distinctive.

Summer. *Leaves* 2 to 4 inches long, almost as wide, alternate, simple, deciduous, apices acute or obtuse, bases truncate or cordate, dark green above and silvery white beneath, with lower surfaces usually coated with

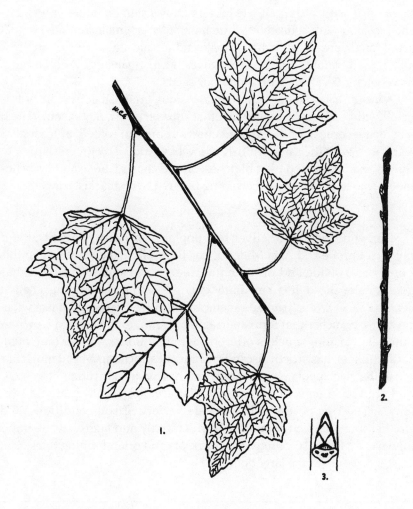

WHITE POPLAR

1. Branch with mature leaves.
2. Winter twig.
3. Details of winter bud and leaf scar.

a matted, white wool; blades thickish, ovate to roundish, margins irregularly and coarsely toothed, with wavy teeth; often lobed and maplelike in appearance, with 3 to 5 palmate lobes; petioles slender, more or less flattened, coated with cobwebby white hairs. *Flowers,* male aments 1½ to 3 inches long, densely white hairy; male and female aments borne on separate trees, developing before the leaves. *Fruits* (capsule) ³⁄₁₆ inch long, ovoid oblong, 2-valved, with numerous seeds.

Winter. *Twigs* slender to moderately stout, greenish gray, more or less coated with a cobwebby white wool that rubs off easily. *Buds* about ¼ inch long, ovate conical, pointed, light chestnut brown; coated, at least near their bases, with the same whitish, cobwebby wool. *Bark* greenish gray to whitish, marked with darker blotches; on the young trunks and branches smooth; bases of old trunks becoming fissured, with blackish ridges.

––––––

The white poplar, or silver-leaf poplar, is a native of central and southern Europe and Asia Minor. It has been planted extensively in this country as a shade and ornamental tree, and in some localities it has become naturalized. It is a medium- to large-sized tree, attaining a height of 40 to 75 feet with a trunk diameter of 2 to 4 feet. Typically it has wide-spreading branches that form an irregular, broad, round-topped crown. A minor expression, which is often recognized, Bolles' Poplar (var. *pyramidalis* Bunge), has strictly ascending branches, forming a head much like that of the black poplar, but it is only rarely seen in cultivation.

Large specimens of the white poplar are often seen about old residences. The tree is adapted to a wide variety of soil conditions, and is rather tolerant of city smoke. It grows rapidly and aggressively, and is quite weedy, freely sprouting from the roots and often forming thickets of smaller trees about the larger ones.

QUAKING ASPEN   *Populus tremuloides* Michx.

The nearly round leaf blades supported by exceptionally flat, long petioles (longer than the leaf blade), finely toothed leaf margins, small, glabrous, varnished-looking winter buds, and whitish bark are most distinctive. The flattened petioles of the quaking aspen restricts the movement of the leaves to shake or quake in even the slightest breeze. In some languages the common name translates to "woman's tongue," or in the language of the Onondaga Indians, the phrase *Nut-ki-e,* meaning "noisy-leaf."

Summer. *Leaves* alternate, simple, roundish to slightly ovate, margins ciliate, finely and regularly toothed, with 20 or more teeth per side, moving, or quaking, in even the slightest breeze; leaf blades 1 to 2 inches long and wide, nearly circular, thin but firm, lustrous and bright green above, paler, glabrous, and dull beneath; petioles usually longer than the blades, slender, laterally flattened, often with two apical nectariferous glands. *Fruits* (capsule) ¼ inch long, glabrous, 2-valved, cone-shaped.

Winter. *Twigs* rather slender, round, glabrous, lustrous, reddish brown, with scarious margins, glaucous to a varying degree. *Buds* narrowly conical, sharp-pointed, reddish brown, lustrous, glabrous; terminal bud about ¼ inch long; lateral buds similar, but slightly smaller than terminal bud, more or less appressed to the twigs, and curved inward. *Bark* on young trees and branches smooth, light yellowish green to greenish white to nearly white, with darker horizontal ridges and dusky blotches beneath the branches; on older trunks becoming thick, furrowed, nearly black, especially near the base.

Comparisons. In winter, this species is most often confused with the big-tooth aspen; however, they can be separated by their buds, with quaking aspen having glabrous, shining (appearing varnished) red buds, which are often slightly sticky and closely appressed to the twigs, while those of big-tooth aspen are somewhat hairy, dull gray looking, plumper, and divergent from the twig. Bark coloration can also be useful in separating these two species, in that the bark of quaking aspen is whiter in color, indeed nearly pure white at times, and more deeply roughened at the tree base, while that of big-tooth aspen tends to be yellow or yellow green, especially on the limbs, with the trunk bark being less deeply furrowed. In summer, they can be told easily by their leaf blades. In spring, the leaves of quaking aspen develop 7 to 10 days earlier than those of the big-tooth aspen and are smaller than the petioles, while those of big-tooth aspen are larger than the petioles. The number of teeth per leaf side is also helpful in separating the two, with 5 to 18 present in big-tooth aspen, and 20 or more present in quaking aspen.

———

Quaking aspen is also known as American aspen, trembling aspen, small-tooth aspen, or simply as aspen or poplar. It is ordinarily a small tree from 30 to 40 feet in height, with a trunk diameter of 8 to 15 inches, but occasionally much larger specimens may occur. The trunk is tapering and continuous, with slender, brittle, ascending branches forming a rather narrow, round-topped crown. It spreads vegetatively and freely by means of root suckers, often establishing huge colonies of identically cloned indi-

platinus
occidentalis

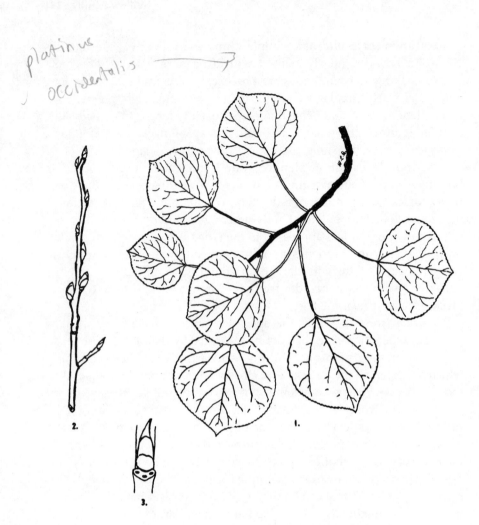

QUAKING ASPEN

1. Branch with mature leaves.
2. Winter twig.

3. Detail of winter bud and leaf scar.

viduals. Quaking aspen is apparently indifferent to soil conditions, growing almost everywhere except in the wettest swamps. It is a common pioneer tree, quickly establishing itself on denuded or burned-over forest
land and in abandoned fields. It is short-lived and of temporary status,
being crowded out and succeeded by other trees in the forest succession.

Quaking aspen is one of the leading American pulpwood trees. Its
wood is soft, light, weak, and close-grained, but it decays rapidly. It is
used to some extent for boxes, pails, kegs, wooden dishes, and for excelsior. The bark of the quaking aspen is one of the preferred foods of the
beaver, and its trunks and branches are utilized in the construction of
their houses and dams. The bark is also one of the important winter
foods of the snowshoe hare. The twigs are often browsed by the white-
tailed deer, and the buds are a winter food of the ruffed grouse.

The quaking aspen, the most widely distributed North American
tree, ranges across the continent from Newfoundland and Labrador to
Alaska, south to New Jersey, Pennsylvania, and the states bordering the
Great Lakes, Iowa, and Minnesota; south along the Appalachian Moun-
tains to Kentucky; also in the region of the Rocky Mountains west to the
Pacific Coast and south to Mexico.

BIG-TOOTH ASPEN   *Populus grandidentata* **Michx.**

> The combination of coarsely toothed leaf margins with curved teeth, flattened
> petioles, and apically hairy buds helps to separate this species from other poplars.

Summer. *Leaves* alternate, simple, more often broadly ovate, less commonly roundish, short-pointed; leaf blades 2½ to 5 inches long, 2 to 2½
inches wide, thin but firm, dark green above, paler beneath, glabrous on
both surfaces when mature, with 15 to 18 very large, coarse, somewhat
irregular teeth on the ciliate margins; mostly whitish-hairy when young,
remaining whitish-hairy beneath; petioles somewhat shorter or about as
long as the leaf blades, laterally flattened, with two apical nectariferous
glands. *Fruits* (capsule) ⅛ to ¼ inch long, 2-valved, cone-shaped.

Winter. *Twigs* moderately stout, varying from yellowish brown to
reddish brown or grayish brown, always dull, commonly hoary-hairy
when leaves are developing and occasionally retaining some hair in age.
Buds, terminal bud ¼ to ⅜ inch long, ovate to conical and pointed, usually
divergent from the twigs; lateral buds similar, curved inward; bud scales

BIG-TOOTH ASPEN

1. Branch with mature leaves.
2. Leaf.
3. Winter twig.
4. Detail of winter bud and leaf scar.

6 or 7, chestnut brown, with a dull and dusty appearance, covered with a fine grayish tomentum. *Bark* resembles that of the quaking aspen in general, but usually more orange yellowish or olive greenish, and never as light or whitish as the bark of that species.

———————

The big-tooth aspen is also known as the large-tooth aspen, and as the popple, or the poplar. It is ordinarily a small- or medium-sized tree up to 30 or 40 feet in height, with a trunk diameter of 1 to 2 feet. The trunk is continuous and tapering; the more or less spreading lateral branches forming an irregularly rounded crown. It propagates freely from root suckers. Like the quaking aspen, it frequently pioneers in burned-over areas or in abandoned fields, but it shows a more marked preference for richer and moister soils than that species. In many places both aspen species may be seen growing together. It is short-lived and eventually becomes crowded out by other trees as the forest becomes reestablished.

The wood of the big-tooth aspen is very similar to that of the quaking aspen, from which it is not distinguished commercially. Utilization by wildlife is also similar wherever it occurs.

The big-tooth aspen has a more limited range than does the quaking aspen. It occurs from Nova Scotia west to Ontario, south to Delaware, Pennsylvania, and Minnesota, and southward along the Appalachian Mountains to North Carolina and Tennessee.

BALSAM POPLAR   *Populus balsamifera* L.

> The very fragrant crushed leaves and fragrant long-pointed buds (the latter of which exude a sticky yellow-amber-colored resin), round petioles, and rounded or heart-shaped leaf bases are most diagnostic.

Summer. *Leaves* 3 to 6 inches long, 2 to 4 inches wide, ovate to broadly lanceolate, apically pointed, base wedge-shaped, rounded, or heart-shaped, with finely and bluntly incurved teeth on ciliate margins; dark green and lustrous above, paler and glabrous or nearly so beneath, often stained with resin blotches; petioles 1½ to 3 inches long, slender, glabrous or hairy, round, often with nectariferous apical glands. *Fruits* (capsule) ¼ to ⅓ inch long, ovoid oblong, glabrous, 2-valved.

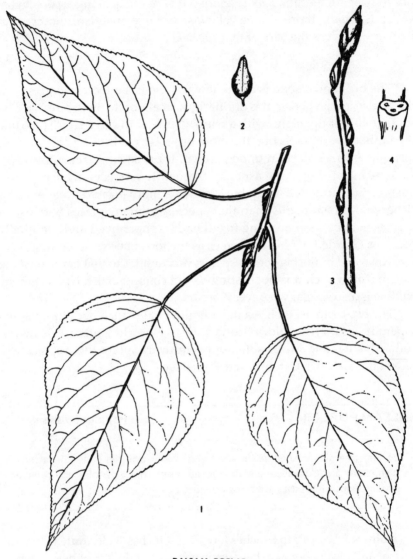

BALSAM POPLAR

1. Branch with leaves.
2. Fruit.
3. Winter twig.
4. Detail of leaf-scar.

Winter. *Twigs* moderately stout, round, reddish brown to dark orange, glabrous, lustrous. *Buds* large, red-brown, very resinous, fragrant; terminal bud about ¾ to 1 inch long, long-pointed, with about 5 visible scales; lateral ones smaller, appressed, with 2 to 4 visible scales. *Bark* greenish gray on younger stems; on older trunks becoming dark gray, with V-shaped furrows, with flat, scaly ridges.

———

The northernmost hardwood tree species in North America, the balsam poplar, the balm of Gilead, the hackmatack, or the tacamahac is of medium size, 60 to 80 feet in height, with a trunk diameter of 1 to 3 feet, and a rather narrow, open, pyramidal crown. It grows in alluvial bottomlands, along streambanks, and about the borders of swamps, reaching its maximum development in the northwestern part of Canada. It grows rapidly, spreads extensively from the roots, and often occurs in pure or nearly pure stands. The tree is easily transplanted, propagates from cuttings, and is frequently used for shelter belts. The wood is used for making boxes and crates and as pulpwood, and the fragrant resin from its buds has been used in cough medicine.

The range of the balsam poplar extends across Canada from Newfoundland and Labrador to Alaska, southward in the Rocky Mountains to Colorado, and south to eastern North Dakota, Minnesota, the region of the Great Lakes, New York, and northern New England.

The hairy balm of Gilead, var. *subcordata* Hyl., is no longer considered to be a distinct taxon. It was said to differ by having more broadly heart-shaped leaves, which are more or less hairy beneath, with hairy petioles, and occurring from Newfoundland, Quebec, and Ontario southward to Maine and the northern portions of New York and Michigan. The balm of Gilead, var. *candicans* (Ait.) A. Gray, widely planted in the northeastern United States and southeastern Canada, appears to be a sterile clone of var. *subcordata*, producing only pistillate flowers. It too is no longer recognized as being distinct.

BLACK POPLAR   *Populus nigra* **L.**

> Flattened petioles, diamond- or rhombic-shaped leaves, and narrow, spirelike crown are most distinctive.

Summer. *Leaves*, leaf blades 1½ to 3 inches wide, usually a little broader than long, broadly rhomboid- (4-sided) or diamond-shaped triangular ovate or deltoid, tips abruptly pointed; thickish, dark green and lustrous above, paler beneath; margins finely and regularly toothed with bluntish gland-tipped teeth; petioles slender, laterally compressed, almost as long as the leaf blades, lacking glands at the apex. *Flowers*, male aments 1½ to 2 inches long, drooping, with numerous male flowers developing before the leaves; no female flowers are produced.

Winter. *Twigs* slender, lustrous; yellowish brown to orange the first year, becoming grayish the second year. *Buds* ¼ to ⅜ inch long, conical, pointed, greenish brown, rather lustrous, resinous; lateral buds appressed. *Bark* on older trunks grayish brown, deeply furrowed.

Comparisons. The truncate leaf bases of this species are somewhat similar to those of the eastern cottonwood, but the leaves are more rhomboid or 4-sided than triangular, and they lack the basal glands and large, coarse teeth. The leaf margins are similar to those of the trembling aspen, but are more coarsely toothed than in that species.

––––––––

The typical expression of the black poplar is not often seen in North America; however, our common expression, cv *italica* (Lombardy poplar), which is thought to have arisen in Italy, was introduced into North America in 1784. The black poplar can be a tall, columnar-shaped tree or open-crowned tree without the spirelike shape, attaining a height from 70 to 100 feet. Their often tall, narrow, and spirelike crowns, which are familiar to most people, can be seen planted throughout the United States as windbreaks. In some areas in western North America, it is known as Mormon tree because it is quickly upright and was commonly planted in early Mormon settlements. Since its introduction into this country from colonial times, it has since been extensively planted as an ornamental tree. It is prone, however, to a European canker that often kills the branches. Large specimens are often seen about old residences, or bordering the lanes which lead to them. The tree is comparatively short-lived. Since all plants are male (neither female flowers nor fruits are produced), all reproduction

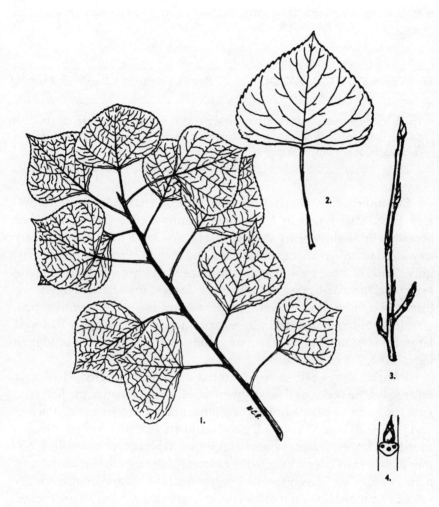

BLACK POPLAR

1. Branch with mature leaves.
2. Leaf.
3. Winter twig.
4. Detail of winter bud and leaf scar.

is vegetative. It suckers freely from the roots and may be easily propagated from cuttings.

EASTERN COTTONWOOD   *Populus deltoides* Bartr. ex Marsh.

> The strongly truncate leaf base; narrowly translucent leaf margins; apical glands on the flattened petiole; yellowish, somewhat angled summer twigs; and shiny resinous buds are most distinctive.

Summer. *Leaves* alternate, simple, broadly triangular ovate, or deltoid, broad based, usually truncate or slightly wedge-shaped, rarely or occasionally slightly heart-shaped; leaf blades 3 to 5 inches long, nearly as wide, dark green and lustrous above, paler and glabrous beneath, margins ciliate, narrow, translucent, with somewhat inwardly hooked teeth, serrate, glandular-tipped, rather coarse, largest toward the base of the leaves, becoming progressively smaller toward the usually pointed tips; petioles about as long as leaf blades, or a little longer, decidedly flattened laterally, with apical nectariferous glands. *Fruits* (capsule) ¼ to ⅓ inch long, ovoid, 2- to 4-valved.

Winter. *Twigs* rather stout, round or slightly angled, distinctly enlarged at the nodes, yellowish green to yellowish brown in the first year, with conspicuous paler lenticels, becoming grayish brown during the second year. *Buds* conical, pointed, glabrous, lustrous, with 6 to 7 olive brown to reddish brown scales, somewhat resinous, fragrant when crushed; terminal buds ½ to ¾ inch long, yellow brown, glabrous, angled; lateral ones a little smaller and divergent. *Bark* on younger trunks and branches fairly smooth, greenish gray; on older trunks becoming ashy gray, roughened by long, deep, longitudinal, and interconnecting furrows, with broadly rounded ridges.

Comparisons. The stout, yellow summer twigs of this species will help separate it from the slender, reddish brown twigs of the quaking aspen, as well as the stout, but reddish brown to orangish twigs of the balsam poplar.

––––––––

The eastern cottonwood is also known as the poplar and as the whitewood. It is a large tree, the largest of the poplars, attaining a height of 50 to 100 feet with a trunk diameter of 2 to 5 feet. It is typically a tree of rich, moist alluvial bottoms, swamps, and the shores of lakes; but it will thrive

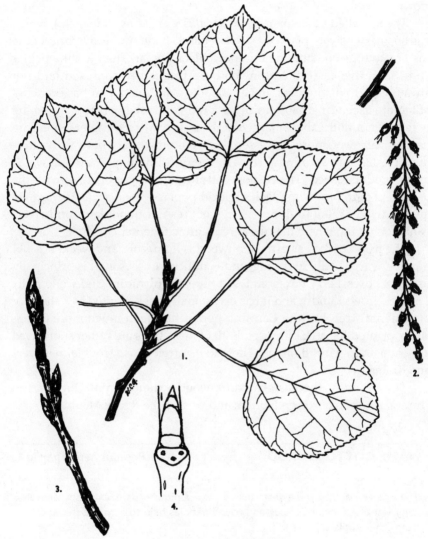

EASTERN COTTONWOOD

1. Branch with mature leaves.
2. Fruits.
3. Winter twig.
4. Details of winter bud and leaf scar.

when planted on rather dry soils. It has a tapering and continuous trunk and spreading branches, typically forming a broadly rounded and open crown.

The so-called Carolina poplar (*Populus* x *canadensis* Moench.), which has been extensively planted as a street and shade tree, is a hybrid of the eastern cottonwood and the European black poplar. The Carolina poplar and the native eastern cottonwood are frequently confused and not always easy to distinguish. In general, the Carolina poplar has branches of a more ascending habit, forming a more narrowly oblong crown. Its twigs are not noticeably enlarged at the nodes, while the lateral buds are usually narrower, more appressed, and commonly have outwardly curving tips. As only staminate trees of the Carolina poplar are known, it never produces seed. The eastern cottonwood also hybridizes with the balsam poplar, producing Jack's hybrid poplar (*Populus* x *jackii* Sarg.), a medium-size tree found mostly in wet areas of floodplains and riverbanks, occurring where the two parents grow together.

The wood of the eastern cottonwood is light, soft, and weak. It is not durable, warps badly in drying, and is difficult to season. It is principally used for boxes, berry boxes, crates, tubs, pails, furniture, and wood pulp. The tree grows rapidly, and it has occasionally been planted as a shade or ornamental tree, but the Carolina poplar has been much more extensively planted for such purposes. Both of these trees are rather short-lived and subject to wind damage. Their roots often cause trouble in sewers and drains.

The range of the eastern cottonwood extends from Quebec and Ontario south to northern Florida, and west to the Rocky Mountains.

SWAMP COTTONWOOD   *Populus heterophylla* L.

The orange-colored somewhat stellate-shaped pith, cordate leaf bases, densely hairy leaf blade undersurfaces, and round petioles help to separate this species from other poplars.

Summer. *Leaves* alternate, simple, large ovate, tip rounded or blunt, base rounded or heart-shaped; blades 4 to 8 inches long, 3 to 6 inches wide, margins ciliate, rather regularly but finely and bluntly toothed, lower surfaces densely coated with tawny or whitish wool when young, tending to become glabrous, although pale beneath at maturity; upper

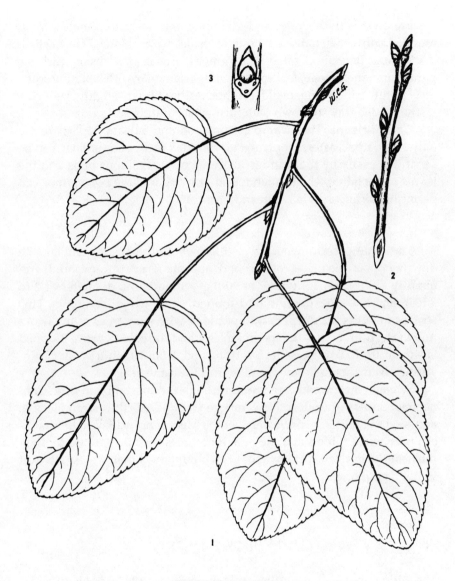

SWAMP COTTONWOOD

1. Branch with leaves.
2. Winter twig.
3. Detail of bud and leaf-scar.

surface always dark green and glabrous; petioles 2 to 3 inches long, rounded rather than flattened. *Fruits* (capsule) ovoid oblong, 2- to 4-celled.

Winter. *Twigs* moderately stout, grayish brown, glabrous or nearly so; pith prominent, orange; leaf scars broadly triangular with 3 bundle scars. *Buds* about ½ inch long, ovoid, bright chestnut brown, slightly resinous, lustrous. *Bark* grayish brown with furrows separating scaly ridges.

Comparisons. The swamp cottonwood and balsam poplar are the only two native eastern poplars with rounded leaf petioles. They can be separated easily by the wonderful aroma of the resinous buds and the leaves of the latter, which when found growing in large populations can permeate the air, especially after a rainstorm.

The swamp cottonwood is also known as the swamp poplar, the downy poplar, the black cottonwood, and the river cottonwood. It frequently attains a height of 70 to 90 feet with a trunk diameter of 2 to 3 feet; and has a narrowly round-topped, often irregular, crown. This species inhabits the deeper swamps along with such trees as the water tupelo, the overcup oak, the pumpkin ash, and the bald-cypress. Its wood is similar to that of the eastern cottonwood, from which it is not distinguished by most lumbermen, and it finds the same usage.

Swamp cottonwoods are found through the coastal plain from Connecticut and southeastern New York to Georgia, northwestern Florida, and west to Louisiana; northward, in the Mississippi Valley, to the southern portions of Illinois and Indiana. It occupies sites that are wetter than those of the eastern cottonwood, growing in areas that are usually wet throughout the year.

The Willows—Salix

The willows have alternate, or rarely opposite, simple leaves with entire or toothed margins. Most species have long and narrow, or oblong, lanceolate leaves with short petioles. Some have persistent and often foliaceous stipules, while in others, the stipules are small and often deciduous. The twigs are round, slender, flexible, and often brittle at the base. The leaf scars are small and have 3 bundle scars. The buds are usually very flat on the side next to the twig and convex on the outer side, commonly appressed, and covered with a solitary bud scale. The majority of the willows are shrubby, but a few become small- or even large-sized trees.

Cuttings made from the branches root rapidly when placed in water or moist soil. The bark of many species contains salicin, which is the active organic compound found in aspirin.

The flowers of the willows appear in the early spring, either before or with the developing leaves. Staminate and pistillate flowers are produced on different trees. Both are borne in aments, or catkins. Each flower has a gland that secretes nectar. The pollen is carried from the staminate to the pistillate flowers by insects, usually by bees. The fruits are 2-valved capsules, borne in usually drooping aments and containing several silky-haired seeds. The seeds are disseminated by the wind.

It is not difficult for the average person to tell a willow from other trees, but it is quite an achievement to be able to distinguish the various species of willows. This is a task for only those experienced in plant taxonomy. Hybrids and sports are quite common. The keys presented here are merely intended to give the distinguishing characteristics of the seven tree-sized willows.

BLACK WILLOW   *Salix nigra* Marsh.

> The large treelike habit, dark shaggy bark, brittle branches, glabrous capsules, lanceolate-linear leaf blades (which are nearly equally green on both surfaces), and reddish glandular teeth on the leaf margin are most characteristic.

Summer. *Leaves* 3 to 6 inches long, ¼ to ⅝ an inch wide, alternate, simple, narrowly lanceolate, falcate, tips long-tapering, bases broadly wedge-shaped or rounded; light green and somewhat lustrous on both surfaces, margins finely serrately toothed; petioles glandless. *Sepals* rather large, persistent, foliaceous on some individuals, or small and soon shed on others. *Fruits* (capsule) ⅛ to ¼ inch long, glabrous, red brown.

Winter. *Twigs* slender, glabrous, reddish brown, lustrous, quite brittle at the base. *Buds* about ⅛ inch long, narrowly conical, short-pointed, lustrous, reddish brown. *Bark* on large trunks becomes thick and blackish brown, roughened by deep furrows and broad, interlacing, scaly-topped ridges.

————

The black willow is the largest of our native tree willows and the most common in the South. It is the big willow so often seen in bottomlands and along the banks of streams. It commonly attains a height of 30

BLACK WILLOW

1. Branch with mature leaves.
2. Staminate flowers.
3. Branch with mature fruits.
4. Open fruit.
5. Winter twig.
6-7. Winter buds.

to 50 feet, or occasionally 80 feet, with a trunk diameter of 1 to 2 feet, or occasionally 3 feet. The trunks are generally crooked, often in clumps of 3 to 5, and usually inclined. The crown is more or less irregular, open, and round topped.

The black willow is of very little commercial value. Its wood is light, soft, weak, and lacking in durability. It is used principally for fuel and making charcoal. The bark is said to make a good substitute for quinine. It contains a glucoside, salicin, which is used as a drug. The tree is seldom planted for shade. The brittle branches of the black willow are often carried downstream, where they become lodged and grow. Its greatest value may be the part it plays in holding streambanks in place.

The range of the black willow extends from southern New Brunswick to Ontario and North Dakota, south to Georgia, Oklahoma, and Texas.

CAROLINA WILLOW   *Salix caroliniana* Michx.

> The glabrous capsules, very large, round stipules, conspicuously glaucous undersurface of the leaves, yellowish glandular teeth on the leaf margins, and small fruit are distinctive.

Summer. *Leaves* 2½ to 6 inches long, ⅜ to 1¼ inches wide, narrowly to broadly lanceolate, often somewhat curved or falcate, tip narrowly pointed, base rounded to broadly pointed, margin finely glandular-toothed; upper surface dark green and glabrous, lower surface glabrous or hairy at midrib and paler or distinctly whitened; petioles ¼ to ½ inch long, often somewhat hairy, frequently with minute glands at the summit; large stipules generally present on the leaves of more vigorous shoots. *Fruits* (capsule) ³⁄₁₆ to ⅜ inch long, glabrous.

Winter. *Twigs* slender, yellowish brown to reddish brown, glabrous or somewhat hairy, more or less brittle at the base. *Buds* about ⅛ inch long, ovoid, sharply pointed, yellowish brown to greenish brown and often reddish at the tip, glabrous or nearly so; bud scales free at margin and overlapping. *Bark* dark gray, ridged.

Carolina willow is also known as Harbison willow or coastal plain willow. It is often merely a large shrub but on occasions may become a tree to about 30 feet in height. It grows in low swampy places and along

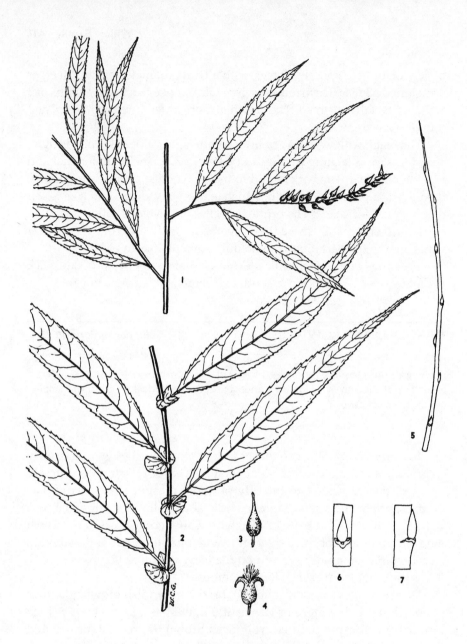

CAROLINA WILLOW

1. Branch with leaves and fruits.
2. Branch with leaves from vigorous shoot.
3-4. Fruits.

5. Winter twig.
6-7. Details of winter buds.

Ship To:
John Mobley
990 N WOODLAWN AVE
Saint Louis, MO 631222802 USA

Ship From:

TEXTBOOKSNOW-AMAZON
8950 W PALMER ST
RIVER GROVE, IL 60171

Date: 06/06/2011

(Attn: Returns)

Order #: 002-2089581-1947462

SKU	Qty	Condition	Title	Price	Total
4846887U	1	Used	Illustrated Book of Trees	$ 10.24	$ 10.24
			9780811728119 Refund Eligible Through= 7/8/2011		

Sub Total	$	10.24
Shipping & Handling	$	3.99
Sales Tax	$	0.00
Order Total	**$**	**14.23**

Order #: 002-2089581-1947462

Refund Policy: All items must be returned within 30 days of receipt. Pack your book securely, so it will arrive back to us in its original condition. To avoid delays, please use the return section and label provided with your original packing slip to identify your return. Be sure to include a return reason. For your protection, we suggest using a traceable, insured shipping service (UPS or Insured Parcel Post). We are not responsible for lost or damaged returns. Item(s) returned must be received in the original condition as sold and including all additional materials such as CDs, workbooks, etc. We will initiate a refund of your purchase price including applicable taxes within 5 business days of receipt. Shipping charges will not be refunded unless we have committed an error with your order. If there is an error with your order or the item is not received in the condition as purchased, please contact us immediately for return assistance.

Reason for Refund/Return:

Condition   Incorrect Item Received   Incorrect Item Ordered   Dropped Class   Purchased Elsewhere   Other

Contact Us: For customer service, email us at customerservice@textbooksNow.com.

Page 1 of 1

the banks of streams from Maryland southward to Florida and westward to southern Illinois, and the eastern portions of Kansas and Texas. The Carolina willow is too small to be of any commercial importance, but like so many of our willow species it plays an important role in preventing streambank erosion.

SHINING WILLOW   *Salix lucida* **Muhl.**

> This willow may be easily recognized by its glabrous capsules, shiny, long-pointed leaves, which are definitely green on both surfaces, and by the glands at the apex of its petioles.

Summer. *Leaves* 3 to 5 inches long, ¾ to 1½ inches wide, broadly lanceolate, extremely long tapering tips, bases either rounded or broadly wedge-shaped, margins finely and regularly toothed; upper surfaces lustrous dark green, only slightly paler beneath, midribs prominent, yellow; petioles stout, yellowish, with more or less conspicuous glands near the summits; often with foliaceous and persistent stipules. *Fruits* (capsule) ³⁄₁₆ to ¼ inch long, brown, glabrous.

Winter. *Twigs* bluntly pointed, lustrous, yellowish brown to orange brown during the first season. *Buds* about ¼ inch long, narrowly ovoid, yellowish brown, lustrous. *Bark* smooth, thin, light brown, often tinged with reddish.

———

The shining willow is often merely a large shrub, but it may become a small tree up to 30 feet in height with a trunk diameter of 6 to 8 inches. The trunk is short, and the ascending branches form a rather symmetrical, broadly round-topped crown. Streambanks and swamps are its natural habitat.

The wood is of no commercial importance. Ernest Thompson Seton says that the inner bark makes the best native material for fish lines and fish nets to be found in the North. Its tough, pliant branches are sometimes used in the country as cordage. The shining willow is one of the most attractive of all of our native willows, and it is very suitable for ornamental planting. It is also of value in preventing the erosion of streambanks.

The shining willow ranges from Newfoundland to Manitoba, south to Pennsylvania and Nebraska.

SHINING WILLOW

1. Branch with mature leaves.
2. Staminate flowers.
3. Mature fruits.
4. Mature fruit which has opened
5. Mature closed fruit.

CRACK WILLOW   *Salix fragilis* **L.**

This is the common, large, eastern tree willow with yellowish branchlets, exceptionally fragile twigs that can be broken with the fingers, and long-tapered leaf blades, which have two basal glands near the apex of the petioles.

Summer. *Leaves* 3 to 6 inches long, ½ to 1½ inches wide, alternate, simple, deciduous, lanceolate, tips long-pointed; lustrous dark green above and paler beneath; margins with rather fine serrations, and glandular teeth; petioles short, with a pair of glands at their summits. *Flowers*, catkins 1 to 2¼ inches long, yellowish or greenish, stamens 2, developing in the spring. *Fruits* (capsule) 3/16 inch long, brown.

Winter. *Twigs* slender, yellowish green to yellowish brown, bases very brittle. *Buds* about ¼ inch long, long conical, obtuse, glabrous, bright yellowish brown; bud scale margins fused. *Bark* on the older trunks becoming gray brown, thick, deeply fissured, with irregular and scaly ridges.

Comparisons. Crack willow can be easily separated from the black willow by having more whitish leaf undersurfaces; more irregular teeth; smaller stipules; glands at the leaf base; 2 rather than 4 to 6 stamens; more elongated and falcate leaf tips; larger buds, and gray rather than dark brown on black bark with narrow rather than flat-topped ridges.

The crack willow is a native of Europe and western Asia, where it is of some value as a timber tree. It is one of our largest willows, often 35 to 85 feet in height with a trunk diameter of 2 to 4 feet. The trunk is typically short, sometimes quite massive, and the spreading branches form a broad, rounded, open crown. Since it was first introduced into the United States about 1800, it has become naturalized in many locations.

Although the wood of the crack willow is of little or no commercial importance, it has been planted as a shade or ornamental tree, and it is commonly found as an escapee along streams. It grows rapidly but the exceptionally fragile branches are easily damaged by storms.

CRACK WILLOW

1. Branch with mature leaves.
2. Margin of leaf (enlarged).
3. Winter twig.
4. Winter bud.

WEEPING WILLOW

Salix x *pendulina* **Wenderoth**
and *Salix* x *sepulcralis* **Simonkai**

During all seasons, the weeping willow can be distinguished by its long and gracefully drooping branchlets.

Summer. *Leaves* 3 to 6 inches long, ¼ to ½ inch wide, very narrowly lanceolate, apically long taper-pointed, glabrous; dark green above and a paler grayish green beneath; margins finely and regularly toothed; petioles short, occasionally with very minute glands. *Fruits* (capsule) ³⁄₁₆ to ¼ inch long.

Winter. *Twigs* olive green to yellowish brown, glabrous, very slender, much elongated and pendulous. *Buds* about ⅛ inch long, narrowly conical, pointed, brownish. *Bark* on older trunks grayish, irregularly and shallowly fissured.

The true weeping willow (*S. babylonica* L.) is a native of China. Instead, what we have in North America are various hybrids, including *S.* x *pendulina*, which is a hybrid between *S. fragilis* and some other species or hybrid; and *S.* x *sepulcralis*, which is a hybrid between *S. alba* and perhaps *S. pendulina*. True *S. babylonica* is a doubtful occurrence as a naturalized tree for North America. These hybrids were introduced into this country during colonial days, and planted more extensively for shade and ornamental purposes than any other willow. They are usually medium-sized trees, attaining a height of 40 to 50 feet, with a rounded or fountainlike crown and pendulous branches, often many feet in length. They grow rapidly but are comparatively short-lived, and are propagated by cuttings that root quickly. In the North, the wood of the branchlets frequently does not harden before the advent of cold weather, and they are winter-killed.

GRAY WILLOW

Salix bebbiana **Sarg.**

This species can be told by its hairy, long-beaked capsules and hairy twigs, and somewhat leathery, short-acuminate, obovate or ovate leaves, which are whitish to gray beneath, net-veined, and often with a dark gland present at the end of each marginal tooth.

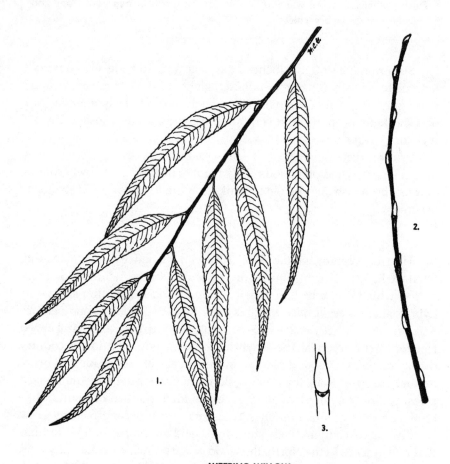

WEEPING WILLOW

1. Branch with mature leaves.   3. Winter bud.
2. Winter twig.

GRAY WILLOW

1. Branch with mature leaves.   3. Fruit.
2. Mature fruits.

Summer. *Leaves* 1 to 3 inches long, ½ to 1 inch wide, ovate to oblong obovate, apically pointed, bases wedge-shaped or rounded, margins entire or sparingly glandular toothed; thickish in texture, dull dark green above, wrinkled or rough looking, paler and grayish-hairy beneath, with prominent veins; petioles ¼ to ½ inch long, rather slender, often hairy, reddish. *Fruits* (capsule) ¼ to ⅜ inch long, long-beaked, slightly hairy.

Winter. *Twigs* slender, hairy or quite glabrous, purplish to dark orange brown. *Buds* about ¼ inch long or less, narrowly oblong, apically rounded, bright chestnut brown. *Bark* reddish green to grayish, with shallow fissures and appressed scales.

The gray willow, Bebb willow, or beaked willow is a large shrub or a small bushy tree from 5 to 20 feet in height with a trunk up to about 8 inches in diameter. It is a common weedy species, especially in burned-over areas. The trunk is typically short, often twisted, and more or less inclined, with a broadly rounded crown. It grows in a wide variety of sites from swamps and bottomlands to rather dry, rocky slopes.

This willow is of no commercial importance. It may be very useful in soil conservation work as it seems to be able to thrive on soils of widely varied character, and it tends to form thickets.

The gray willow ranges from Newfoundland to Alaska, and south to New Jersey, Pennsylvania, and Iowa.

PUSSY WILLOW   *Salix discolor* Muhl.

The large flower buds, which are larger than the leaf buds that appear early in the spring; large, hairy capsules; and leaves which are shiny green above, lightly glaucous underneath, and often appearing with undulate margins are most distinctive.

Summer. *Leaves* 1½ to 4 inches long, ½ to 1½ inches wide, alternate, simple, rather broadly lanceolate to elliptical, gradually narrowed toward both ends; bright green above, more or less whitish and occasionally somewhat hairy beneath; leaf blades conspicuously veiny, usually with a rather wrinkled appearance, margins almost entire, with merely a few remote, shallow, and bluntish teeth, often undulate.

Winter. *Twigs* flexible but rather stout for a willow, usually a dark reddish purple, but occasionally greenish, tinged with purple, hairy at first,

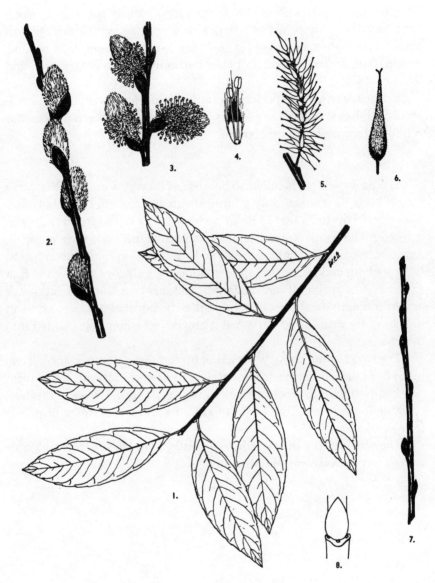

PUSSY WILLOW

1. Branch with mature leaves.
2. Twig with opening flower buds.
3. Staminate flowers.
4. Detail of staminate flower.
5. Fruits.
6. Fruit.
7. Winter twig.
8. Winter bud.

later become glabrous. *Buds* ¼ to ⅜ inch long, closely appressed, ovoid, pointed, rather plump, lustrous, dark reddish purple, occasionally almost black; flower buds somewhat larger than leaf buds. *Bark* light reddish brown, thin, at first smooth but later becoming shallowly fissured and somewhat scaly.

Comparisons. This species is commonly confused with the gray willow, which has smaller, hairy leaves, grayish green rather than glaucous below and somewhat more obovate.

The pussy willow is called so because of its very soft pussylike furry flower buds. It is often only a large shrub, but it sometimes becomes a small tree up to 25 feet in height with a trunk from 6 to 10 inches in diameter. The trunk is short, and the ascending branches form an open, round-topped head. The pussy willow is well known for its silvery-gray, furry-looking catkins, which appear along the branches during the first warm days of spring. It has the largest and most conspicuous catkins of any of the native willows. Streambanks, the borders of lakes, and wet meadows are its usual habitats, but it grows well when transplanted into drier soils.

The wood of the pussy willow is of no commercial importance. It has often been planted as an ornamental tree because of its attractive form and handsome bright green foliage as well as its vernal flowers. It is also of value in protecting the banks of streams and the margins of ponds from erosion.

The range of the pussy willow extends from Nova Scotia to Manitoba, south to Delaware and Missouri.

TITI FAMILY—CYRILLACEAE

The Buckwheat-Tree—Cliftonia

BUCKWHEAT-TREE   *Cliftonia monophylla* (Lam.) Britt. ex Sarg.

> Easily identified by the 4-winged fruit, and by the conspicuous, yet tiny notch at the apex of its evergreen leaves. So diagnostic is the apical notch that the apex from a single leaf should separate this species from all eastern North American trees!

Leaves 1 to 2 inches long and ½ to ¾ inch wide, alternate, simple, evergreen, entire, narrowly elliptic or obovate, tip rounded and notched, base wedge-shaped; upper surface shiny green, lower surface pale, dull, glabrous; stipule lacking; petioles very short or lacking. *Flowers* ¼ inch wide, perfect, fragrant, borne in terminal racemes in the spring; petals 5 to 8, white. *Fruits* (capsule) about ¼ inch long, strongly 2- to 4-angled or winged, light brown, borne in terminal racemes. *Twigs* slender, reddish brown, glabrous, somewhat glaucous, commonly somewhat 3-angled. *Bark* on larger trunks thin, dark reddish brown to black, breaking into small elongate scales.

———

The buckwheat-tree is also known as the black titi and the ironwood. It is often only a large shrub but becomes a small tree, sometimes 30 feet in height with a trunk 6 to 12 inches in diameter. Its common name of buckwheat-tree is derived from the fancied resemblance of its fruits to those of the cultivated buckwheat plant. The small, fragrant, white to pinkish flowers appear in terminal racemes in early spring. They are laden with nectar, and the flowering plants attract hordes of bees and

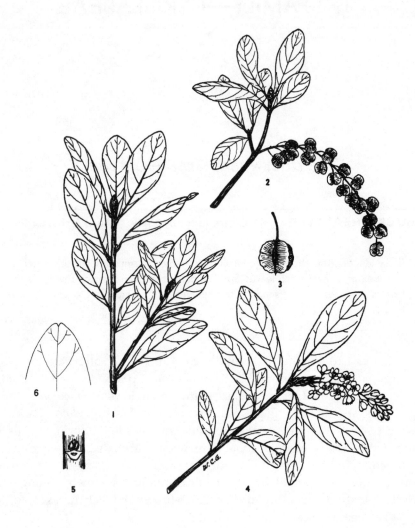

BUCKWHEAT-TREE

1. Branch with mature leaves.
2. Branch with fruits.
3. Detail of fruit.
4. Flowering branch.
5. Detail of bud and leaf scar.
6. Detail of apically notched leaf tip.

other insects. It is an important honey plant, a prime source of the titi honey so prized by the natives within the plant's range.

The buckwheat-tree often forms dense thickets about the borders of swamps and in low ground along streams of the coastal plain from southeastern South Carolina to Georgia and northwestern Florida, westward to Louisiana.

The Tities—Cyrilla

SWAMP TITI   *Cyrilla racemiflora* L.

> This is a thicket-forming, coastal plain species with entire, evergreen or semievergreen leaves that cluster at the branch tips.

Summer. *Leaves* 2 to 4 inches long, ½ to 1 inch wide, alternate, simple, evergreen or semievergreen, shiny, entire, narrowly elliptic or narrowly obovate, tip rather bluntly pointed or minutely notched, base wedge-shaped, more or less clustered at the ends of the branchlets; upper surface dark green and lustrous, lower surface pale and glabrous; stipule lacking; petioles ¼ to ½ inch long. *Flowers* about ⅛ to ¼ inch long, small, perfect, fragrant, occurring in spreading or drooping racemes on wood of previous year; petals 5, white. *Fruits* (capsule) about ⅛ inch long, arranged in narrow, often clustered, persisting, lateral racemes, 2-seeded.

Winter. *Leaves* often persist, turning red in the fall. *Twigs* slender, lustrous, glabrous, reddish brown, often somewhat 3-angled; leaf scars alternate, fringed apically, shield-shaped with a solitary bundle scar. *Buds* ovoid; terminal bud ¼ inch long, with several imbricated scales; lateral buds ⅛ inch or less long, occasionally some superposed; scales several, glabrous, chestnut brown. *Bark* thin, grayish brown, eventually breaking into shreddy scales.

Swamp titi is also known as American cyrilla, white titi, swamp cyrilla, leatherwood, and ironwood. It is a large shrub or a small tree, often not over 15 feet high but sometimes 25 to 30 feet high with a trunk diameter of 10 to 14 inches. The swamp titi often forms dense thickets

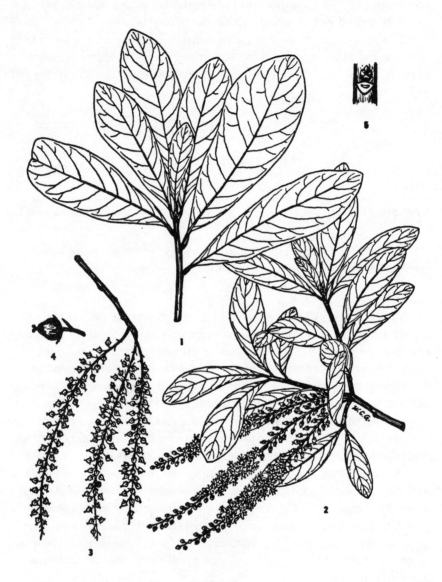

SWAMP TITI

1. Branch with leaves.
2. Flowering branch.
3. Fruit clusters.
4. Detail of fruit.
5. Detail of winter bud and leaf scar.

about the borders of swamps and pine-barren ponds. In the Gulf states it also occupies exposed sandy ridges rising above the banks of streams. When growing in water, the bark at the base becomes very thick, spongy, and felted with fine roots. Such bark is said to possess astringent and absorbent properties. It is an important honey plant, a source of the nectar that bees use in making titi honey.

The range of the swamp titi extends through the coastal plain from southeastern Virginia to northern Florida and westward to eastern Texas.

A similar species, *C. parvifolia* Raf. (little-leaf titi), with smaller (less than 2 inches long) and more leathery leaves, smaller flowers, smaller inflorescences, and more globose fruits, also occurs in the southeast, from Georgia to Florida. Since some of these characters, however, appear to blend with the swamp titi, some scientists consider the latter species to be a variety of the former (*C. racemiflora* var. *parvifolia* Sarg.).

HEATH FAMILY—ERICACEAE

The Rhododendrons—Rhododendron

These are branching trees or shrubs with alternate, simple, deciduous or (as in our tree species) evergreen, coriaceous leaves with entire margins. The flowers are large, various colored (purple to white in our tree species), corymbose or umbellate, with 5 to 10 stamens and a superior ovary. The corollas are campanulate or funnelform, irregular or somewhat regular. All members of this genus have a dry capsule as a fruit type with numerous seeds.

GREAT-LAUREL   *Rhododendron maximum* **L.**

> Easily distinguished by its large, leathery, evergreen leaves with entire, inrolled margins, thicket-forming habit, large flower buds, white to pink flowers, and persistent woody capsules.

Leaves 4 to 10 inches long, 1½ to 3 inches wide, alternate, simple, evergreen, thick, leathery, persisting for 2 or 3 years; ovate or oblong lanceolate, apically pointed, bases wedge-shaped or rounded, margins entire; dark green and lustrous above, paler and glabrous or nearly so beneath, clustered toward the tips of the branches; petioles about 1 inch long, stout. *Buds,* at most seasons terminal flower buds are quite conspicuous, very large, light yellowish green, ovoid. *Flowers* bell-shaped, 10 to 24 in terminal umbels, 4 to 5 inches across; petals 1 to 1½ inches wide, 5-lobed, rose purple to white, upper lobe greenish yellow spotted. *Fruits* (capsule) ⅜ to ½ inch long, long-stalked, red brown, glandular hairy, elongated, many-seeded, sticky-hairy when young, borne in open terminal clusters, often persisting on the branches for a year or more.

GREAT-LAUREL

1. Leaf.
2. Flowering branch.
3. Fruiting branch.
4. Portion of branch showing terminal flower bud.

The great-laurel, or the rosebay rhododendron, is usually only a large shrub in the northern portion of its range, attaining a height of 5 to 12 feet, but in the southern Appalachians it often becomes a bushy tree, sometimes 25 feet in height with a trunk up to 10 inches in diameter. It often forms extensive and impenetrable thickets in the understory of mountain forests, particularly along the banks of streams.

The rhododendrons are extremely popular as ornamental plants, and this species is extensively planted. It is one of our most attractive native woody plants, retaining its handsome foliage throughout the year, and producing large, terminal, ball-like clusters of white or pale pink flowers in late June or early July. Those who would grow rhododendrons of any kind in the garden should bear in mind that they are acid-soil plants that will not thrive on limestone soils. Peat moss and aluminum sulphate are often mixed with the soil to maintain the degree of acidity that these plants require.

In the southern mountains the wood is sometimes used for tool handles, engravers' blocks, and for fuel. In the northern mountains the dense thickets of rhododendron are favorite winter yarding areas for the white-tailed deer; in many localities the plant is heavily browsed, although it has little if any actual food value. Sheep are known to have been fatally poisoned by eating the leaves, and in excessive quantities they may also be somewhat toxic to deer.

The great-laurel ranges from Nova Scotia southward, chiefly along the mountains, to northern Georgia.

CATAWBA ROSEBAY   *Rhododendron catawbiense* **Michx.**

The catawba rosebay, more southern in distribution than the great-laurel, has noticeably smaller leaves that are whitish beneath; leaf bases and apices that are rounded rather than tapered; flowers that are deep lilac purple rather than rose-colored to white; buds lacking the long, thin bracts found in the great-laurel; and capsules that are rusty-hairy rather than glabrous. It ranges from Virginia to Georgia, west to Kentucky and Tennessee.

The Mountain-Laurel—Kalmia

MOUNTAIN-LAUREL   *Kalmia latifolia* L.

> The terminally clustered, thick, evergreen leaves of this thicket-forming species, and its white to pink flowers are distinctive.

Leaves 2 to 4 inches long, ¾ to 1¼ inches wide, alternate (rarely sub-opposite) or 3-whorled, simple, evergreen, thick, leathery, persisting on the branches for 2 or 3 years; narrowly elliptic lanceolate to ovate, acute at both ends, margins entire; dark green and lustrous above, yellowish green, glabrous and glaucous beneath; petioles ½ to ¾ inch long, rather stout; both the petioles and midribs yellowish, and frequently tinged with red. *Flowers* about ¾ inch in diameter, saucer-shaped, pinkish to white, borne in rather dense terminal corymbs with up to 75 or more individual flowers, appearing in late May or early June; petals 5-lobed, provided with peculiar little pockets in which the anthers fit (once jarred, the pollen is released by the stamen springing forward, dislodging the anthers). *Fruits* (capsule) ¼ inch wide, small, roundish, 5-lobed, rusty-glandular-hairy, tipped with a persistent style, borne in loose terminal clusters, often persisting on the branches for a year or more.

The mountain-laurel, the ivy, or the calico bush is usually a shrub in the northern portion of its range, commonly only from 2 to 10 feet in height, but in the southern Appalachians it is often a small tree up to about 40 feet in height, with a trunk diameter of a foot or more. A gigantic specimen in the Great Smoky Mountains National Park measures 6 feet 10 inches in diameter at its base, and one of its limbs is more than 2½ feet in diameter. In our mountain forests the mountain-laurel is often a very common to abundant understory plant. It grows rather profusely on the dry, rocky ridges beneath the pitch pines and the oaks.

In its native habitats the mountain-laurel is a strikingly beautiful shrub or small tree, but it is not as extensively cultivated as the great-laurel or the catawba rosebay. Where it attains a large size its wood is frequently used for such small articles as tobacco pipes, tool handles, bucket handles, and also as fuel. The leaves are known to be poisonous to livestock. They are frequently eaten by the white-tailed deer, although

MOUNTAIN-LAUREL

1. Branch with leaves and flowers.
2. Branch with leaves and fruits.
3. Winter branch with leaves and flower buds.
4. Detail of fruit.

the leaves apparently have little or no real food value. The honey derived from the flowers is said to be poisonous.

The mountain-laurel ranges from New Brunswick and Ontario to Ohio and Tennessee, southward in the Appalachian Mountain region to Georgia and western Florida.

The Sourwood—Oxydendrum

SOURWOOD   *Oxydendrum arboreum* (L.) DC.

> This species can be easily identified by the strongly disagreeable odor of its reddish or greenish twigs, by its fragrant lily-of-the-valley–like flowers that give rise to conspicuous capsular fruits that persist into winter, by its extremely crooked growth habit, and by its finely toothed, alternate, sour-tasting leaves that turn bright red in the autumn, which are so symmetrical that when folded widthwise, the apex and the base overlap nearly exactly.

Summer. *Leaves* 4 to 7 inches long, 1 to 2 inches wide, alternate, simple, deciduous, oblong lanceolate, tips taper-pointed, bases broadly wedge-shaped, margins finely but sharply toothed; rather thin, dark green and lustrous above, pale beneath; lateral veins meeting the midvein nearly perpendicularly, sour tasting, turning bright red in the autumn; petioles glandless. *Flowers* ¼ inch long, small, cream white, urn-shaped, 5-lobed, borne in compound, 1-sided racemes at branch tips; having a marked resemblance to those of the lily of the valley. *Fruits* (capsule) ⅜ inch long, small, oblong, 5-angled, woody, tipped with a short persistent style; seeds small, numerous.

Winter. *Twigs* rather slender, light orange brown to reddish brown, glabrous, marked with small but conspicuous lenticels, disagreeably odored; leaf scars alternate, semiround or inversely triangular; bundle scar solitary, uniquely U-shaped, stipule scar lacking. *Buds* about ¹⁄₁₆ inch long, small, rather blunt-pointed, partially hidden within the bark, with about 3 visible, reddish brown, obtuse scales; terminal bud lacking. *Bark* of the trunks gray, thick, deeply furrowed, with rather scaly ridges, appearing nearly furlike from a short distance.

Comparisons. In shape, the leaves resemble those of the black cherry, but they lack the distinctive odor, have glandless petioles, and have a

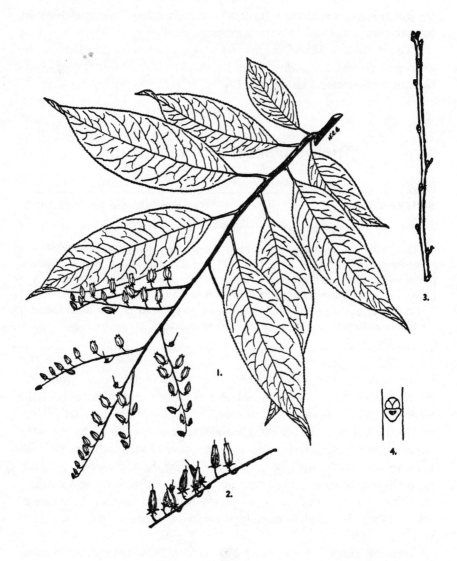

SOURWOOD

1. Branch with leaves and flower cluster.
2. Portion of fruit cluster.
3. Winter twig.
4. Detail of bud and leaf scar.

decidedly sour taste. They also resemble those of the common persimmon, but lack the dark blemishes of that species and are finely toothed along the margin. The conspicuously symmetrical leaves, which are as wide above the middle as below, are useful in separating the sourwood from these other species.

———

The sourwood, the sorrel tree, or the lily-of-the-valley tree is a small, weedy tree that occasionally attains a height of 40 to 60 feet in the southern Appalachian Mountains, where it reaches its largest size and maximum abundance. It generally grows on slopes that have a light, well-drained, acid soil containing a large amount of humus. Occasionally it occurs in bottomlands. Its growth habit is usually gnarled, with crooked trunks.

Although it is a very attractive tree, it is rather difficult to transplant and is not common in cultivation. Like the rhododendrons and the mountain-laurel it will not thrive on any but acid soils. Its wood is of little commercial value, but it is used locally for tool handles and small turned articles. Sourwood honey is much esteemed in the southern mountains.

The sourwood ranges from southwestern Pennsylvania west to southern Indiana and Illinois, south to northern Florida and western Louisiana.

The Blueberries—Vaccinium

TREE SPARKLE-BERRY   *Vaccinium arboreum* **Marsh.**

> Our only blueberry that reaches tree size, this species can be easily identified by its scaly exfoliating bark, crooked trunk, black, berrylike fruit, and lustrous leaves.

Summer. *Leaves* 1 to 2½ inches long, ½ to 1 inch wide, alternate, simple, deciduous or persisting; elliptic to oblong or obovate to nearly circular, tips rounded to somewhat short-pointed, bases pointed, margins entire or minutely toothed and somewhat revolute; thickish and firm, dark green and lustrous above, paler and often somewhat hairy beneath. *Flowers* ⅕ to ⅓ inch across, white, in racemes; petals 5, bell-shaped, with reflexed tips. *Fruits* (berry) about ¼ inch in diameter, rather dry, lustrous, black, many-seeded, ripening in late autumn.

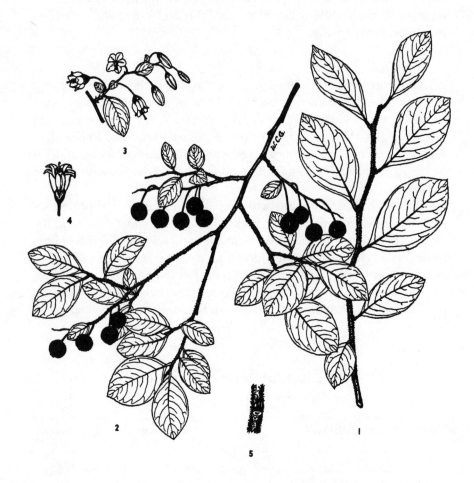

TREE SPARKLE-BERRY

1. Branch with leaves.
2. Branch with leaves and fruits.
3. Flowers.
4. Detail of flower.
5. Detail of winter bud and leaf scar.

Winter. *Fruits* (berry) often remain well into the winter. *Leaves* persistent southward. *Twigs* very slender, zigzag, brownish, red to reddish brown, glabrous or somewhat hairy when young; leaf scars broadly crescent-shaped, with a solitary bundle scar, stipule scar lacking. *Buds* small, roundish, with about 4 exposed reddish to purplish acute scales; terminal bud lacking. *Bark* thin, brown to purplish brown, fine scaly, ultimately becoming shreddy and exfoliating.

––––––

The tree sparkle-berry, also known as the farkle-berry or the tree huckleberry, is the largest of the blueberries. It is usually a large shrub but in favorable situations it becomes a tree up to 30 feet in height with a trunk up to 10 inches in diameter, the twisted branches forming a rather dense, rounded crown. It grows on moist to well-drained soils, usually near ponds or streams, from the coast to the lower slopes of the mountains. The bell-shaped white flowers are borne in leafy-bracted axillary racemes. While by human standards the fruits are scarcely edible, they are frequently eaten by several species of wild birds.

The range of the tree sparkle-berry extends from southeastern Virginia south to Florida and west to southern Indiana, Illinois, Missouri, Oklahoma, Kansas, and Texas.

ROSE FAMILY—ROSACEAE

The Peaches, the Plums, and the Cherries—Prunus

The leaves are alternate, simple, with toothed margins, and commonly with glandular petioles. In many species the twigs, the bark, and sometimes even the leaves have a characteristic rank odor of bitter almonds. The leaves of some species, and particularly the wilted leaves of our native wild cherries, are known to poison livestock eating them, the poisonous principle being hydrocyanic or prussic acid, which is produced in the leaves by the decomposition of the glucoside amygdalin. Many species have short lateral fruit spurs, and sometimes these lateral spurs are spiny. The fruits are technically known as drupes. They have an inner bony portion (commonly called the stone or pit), which encloses the seed, and this is surrounded by a fleshy layer.

Some taxonomists divide the genus into two separate genera. Those species producing flowers and fruits in lateral umbel-like clusters from buds of the previous season's growth are placed in the genus *Prunus;* those producing flowers and fruits in elongated clusters, or racemes, at the ends of branches of the current season are placed in the genus *Padus.*

The cherries can be separated from the plums by the former having true terminal buds, lacking thornlike branches, and also lacking a glaucous coating on the fruits. Interestingly, no hybridization is known to exist between the cherries and plums.

PEACH   *Prunus persica* (L.) Batsch

> The lustrous, long-acuminate leaves, reddish upper branches (green beneath), sessile (or nearly so), rather than pedicellate, pink and white flowers produced early in the spring, and the very characteristic large, fleshy fruits are distinctive.

Summer. *Leaves* 3 to 9 inches long, ¾ to 1½ inches wide, alternate, simple, deciduous, lanceolate to narrowly oblong, lustrous above, paler beneath, odoriferous when crushed, margins finely serrate with small glandular teeth, upwardly curving from the midrib toward the margin, apices long acuminate; petioles short, glandular, with 2 conspicuous glands at the summit. *Flowers* 1 to 1½ inches wide, showy, produced in early spring before the leaves; petals 5, pink, more deeply colored at base, rarely white. *Fruits* (drupe) 2 to 3 inches in diameter, yellow to pink, globose, grooved, finely hairy, sweet, edible; seed large, elliptical.

Winter. *Twigs* slender, glabrous, lustrous reddish brown on the uppersides, usually greenish beneath. *Buds,* terminal bud present, gray to tan, woolly. *Bark* smooth on young individuals, becoming scaly in age with conspicuous horizontal lenticels.

Comparisons. This species differs from the wild plums by producing large hairy fruits and by having pink rather than white flowers.

This is a small deciduous tree, up to 35 feet, originally introduced from China. The specific name *persica* was derived from *malus persicum* (apple of Persia) in Greek and Roman, suggesting its introduction into Europe from Iran (Persia). It was perhaps originally brought into the United States through Florida by early Spaniards or French travelers in the late 1500s. It has now escaped from cultivation in many areas and can be seen along roadsides and near old homesites. It is generally a short-lived tree subject to numerous problems involving leaf curl. In open sunny areas, it generally will fruit when only three years old. Although the flowers are generally pink, some of the 2,000 or more cultivars are white and reddish flowered; the flowers are produced well before the leaves. In many areas, the early development of flowers creates severe problems for growers. Flowers are very sensitive to frost damage and entire crops can be lost if unseasonable springtime temperatures are followed by a single killing frost. A beautiful double-flowered cultivar was produced as early as 1776 and is still available.

PEACH

1. Branch with leaves and fruit.

AMERICAN PLUM

Prunus americana **Marsh.**

The thicket-forming nature of this species, along with the double-serrate leaves with glandless marginal teeth; flattened fruit pits; somewhat unpleasantly odored white flowers that open as the leaves expand; sharp, spine-tipped spur shoots; twigs that lack terminal buds; and platelike or shaggy bark, is most distinctive.

Summer. *Leaves* 1 to 5 inches long, up to 1 to 1½ inches wide, alternate, simple, deciduous, narrowly lanceolate to obovate, broadest at or below (very rarely above) the middle, tips acuminate to long-acuminate (long-pointed), bases rounded or broadly wedge-shaped, margins sharply, finely, and doubly or singly serrate with glandless teeth; blades firm, dark green, rather conspicuously veiny, slightly roughened above by reticulate veins, paler and glabrous or occasionally slightly hairy beneath, blades flat; petioles ½ to ¾ inch long, slender, lacking glands at their summits. *Flowers* about 1 inch wide, perfect, unpleasantly odored, occurring in umbellate inflorescences of 2 to 5 flowers, appearing before the leaves; petals ⅓ to ½ inch long, 5, white, with red claws. *Fruits* (drupe) ¾ to 1¼ inches in diameter, roundish or slightly ovate-shaped, with thick, yellow or partially red glaucous skins, juicy, but sour; with large, flat, ovate stones, borne in small lateral clusters, ripening from August to October.

Winter. *Twigs* moderately slender, glabrous (hairy in bigtree plum), gray to reddish brown, more or less glaucous, with rather small but conspicuous scattered lenticels; spinelike lateral spur shoots developing during the second year; leaf scars half-rounded or U-shaped, with hairy fringe on upper margins, bundle scars 3. *Buds,* lateral buds ⅛ to 3⁄16 inch long, ovoid or conical, sharp-pointed, appressed; scales light red gray, hairy-margined; terminal bud lacking. *Bark* on the young growth grayish brown, glabrous; on the older trunks shaggy, breaking or exfoliating into large, thin, and persistent plates.

Comparisons. This species can be separated from both the chickasaw plum and the Mexican plum by its shaggy bark, large flowers (about 1 inch versus ⅓ to ¾ inch wide), and larger leaves with acuminate (rather than acute) leaf tips. The larger, rather unpleasantly scented flowers develop with or before the leaves (flowers develop before the leaves begin to appear in the chickasaw plum). It can be further separated from the Mexican plum by the fact that the latter species generally has densely hairy (rather than thinly hairy) leaf undersurfaces, has consistently hairy rather than glabrous twigs, has more conspicuously rugose leaves, and has somewhat

AMERICAN PLUM

1. Branch with mature leaves and fruits.
2. Winter twig.
3. Detail of bud and leaf scar.

larger and deeper purple (rather than red or purple) fruits, which are more densely glaucous.

The American plum is also known as the wild red plum or the yellow plum. It is a shrub or a small tree from 10 to 30 feet in height with a trunk diameter of 5 to 12 inches. The trunk is typically short, dividing a few feet above the ground into many slender, spreading, or slightly drooping spiny branches, and forming a deep and rather broad crown. The plum prefers deep, rich, and moist soils, and is most commonly found in bottomlands. It frequently forms thickets along streambanks, fencerows, or the borders of woods and swamps.

The wood is of no commercial value. Several varieties of cultivated plums have been derived from this native wild species, and it makes excellent stock on which to graft cultivated plums. Its fruits are succulent but almost too sour to be eaten raw. They do, however, make excellent jelly and preserves.

The American plum ranges from Maine, Ontario, and Massachusetts to Manitoba and Saskatchewan, south to Florida, New Mexico, and Utah.

BIGTREE PLUM   *Prunus mexicana* S. Wats.

> The deeply rugose and hairy leaves, hairy twigs, and large flowers help to distinguish this species from all other native plums.

Summer. *Leaves* 2½ to 4 inches long, 1 to 2 inches wide, thick, ovate, broadly ovate to obovate, margins serrate to double serrate with glandless teeth, base rounded, apices acute to short acuminate, upper surface dull green, rugose with noticeably sunken veins, lower surfaces yellow green, hairy, conspicuously veiny. *Flowers* ½ to ¾ inch across, longer than wide, with a fetid odor, appearing with or before the leaves, solitary or in clusters of 2 to 4; petals mostly ⅓ inch long, 5, white. *Fruits* (drupe) 1 to 1½ inches wide, slightly elongated, red to purple red, glaucous, pulp sweet, developing in August to September.

Winter. *Twigs* hairy, stiff, moderately slender, red brown to grayish; leaf scars oval, with hairy fringe on upper margin; bundle scars 3. *Buds,* lateral buds ⅛ to ¼ inch long, ovoid; terminal bud lacking. *Bark* dark, exfoliating into scales when young, deeply furrowed at maturity.

Comparisons. This species is similar to the American plum, but has larger fruits (generally over 1 inch long); 1 to 2 glands near the petiole apex (glands lacking in the latter species); usually lacks root suckers (root suckering common in following species); has hairy (rather than glabrous) twigs; conspicuously hairy (rather than thinly hairy) leaf undersurfaces, petioles, and sepals; and slightly larger and more rugose-surfaced leaves.

The largest of our native plums, the bigtree or Mexican plum is a simple-stemmed tree, up to 30 feet or more high and 6 to 12 inches in diameter. It is found in dry woodlands or in the moist soil of valleys, where it does not form thickets as do some of our other native plums. It extends from South Dakota to Texas, eastward to the Carolinas and north to Wisconsin.

CANADA PLUM   *Prunus nigra* Ait.

> The large, acuminate leaf blades, red-glandular petioles, thornlike branches, and white flowers that appear before the leaves are most distinctive.

Summer. *Leaves* 2 to 5 inches long, 1¼ to 2½ inches wide, alternate, simple, deciduous, oblong ovate or obovate, widest above the middle, tips abruptly acuminate, bases obtuse, cordate to widely cuneate, margins finely and doubly crenate, with glandular teeth occurring on spinelike spur shoots; blades obovate to ovate, dull dark green above, paler beneath; petioles stout, glandular at the apex, with 2 dark glands. *Flowers* 1¼ inches wide, on ½- to ¾-inch-long pedicels, in umbellate clusters of 2 to 5 flowers, slightly fragrant, developing before the leaves; petals 5, white turning pink with age. *Fruits* (drupe) 1 to 1¼ inches long, elliptic, red to yellowish, developing in late summer.

Winter. *Twigs* slender, zigzag, red brown to black, thornlike, spur shoots present. *Buds* ⅛ to ¼ inch long, gray brown, tightly appressed, acute, glabrous; scales thin, margins frayed and paler than the scale body; terminal bud lacking. *Bark* black, splitting vertically and exposing inner bark on the crooked trunks.

Comparisons. This species differs from the more southern American plum by having oblong to ovate to obovate (rather than lanceolate) leaf blades that are widest above rather than at or below the middle; abruptly acuminate (rather than acute or long acuminate) leaf tips; crenate to double-crenate (more rounded), rather than sharply pointed, serrate or double-serrate (more sharply pointed) teeth, the smaller of which have tiny glands on the tips (the teeth of the American wild plum lack glands altogether.) The flowers also differ in that those of the Canada plum generally open before the leaves rather than with the leaves and have ciliate sepal tips, while those of the American plum are glabrous. Also, the two conspicuous dark glands on the petiole apex (lacking on the American wild plum) help to separate this species. Canada plum differs from the choke cherry by having larger fruits that occur in umbels (rather than racemes); double-crenate (rather than single-serrate) margins; and spiny twigs and spur shoots. It differs from the fire cherry by lacking the brightly red-colored twigs and horizontally peeling red bark, and having both larger fruits and spiny twigs.

The Canada plum is a small tree, 20 or 25 feet high, with twisted branches. The fruits are oblong ovoid, orange red, and about 1 inch long. It usually occurs along streams from New England to the Great Lakes states northward to Iowa, into southern Canada.

ALLEGHENY PLUM   *Prunus alleghaniensis* Porter

A thicket-forming habit and occasionally thorny branches are most distinctive.

Summer. *Leaves* 2 to 3 inches long, ⅔ to 1¼ inches wide, obovate elliptic to lanceolate, widest near the middle, tips acuminate, bases rounded, dark green above, somewhat hairy on the veins beneath, margins with simple, sharp, serrate, glandular teeth; petioles hairy, slender, with 2 large glands at their summits. *Flowers* about ½ inch across, 2 to 4 per umbel, petals 5, white turning pink, appearing with the leaves. *Fruits* rarely more than ½ inch in diameter, roundish or somewhat ovate, dark purplish, glaucous. *Bark* scaly.

Winter. *Twigs* hairy, slender, occasionally spiny at tip, reddish brown. *Bark* dark brown or grayish, scaly.

Comparisons. This species is very similar to the flatwoods plum, but is more northern in distribution, and much rarer.

Allegheny plum, also known as the Porter plum or the sloe, is a straggling shrub or intricately branched small tree, 8 feet high, occasionally to 20 feet, which often forms extensive thickets. It is a species that ranges from Michigan, Pennsylvania, and southern Connecticut, south in the Appalachian Mountains to North Carolina occurring on well-drained slopes in areas with low moisture content. It is the most geographically restricted of any of our treelike plums, perhaps reaching its greatest development in the area of Huntingdon, Clearfield, and Elk counties in Pennsylvania.

CHICKASAW PLUM   *Prunus angustifolia* **Marsh.**

> The nearly impenetrable thicket-forming habit, and troughlike lustrous leaves with small red-glandular marginal teeth are diagnostic.

Summer. *Leaves* 1 to 2½ inches long, up to ⅔ inch wide, alternate, simple, deciduous, glabrous, lanceolate, often clustered on spur shoots, apices acute to apiculate, margins sharply but finely serrate with rounded teeth; lustrous, bright green, and glabrous above, paler below, leaf sides conspicuously upward curved (troughlike) from midvein; petioles glandular with 2 red glands near the apex. *Flowers* small, ⅓ to ½ inch across, fragrant, perfect, borne in one 2- to 4-flowered umbel, developing before the leaves; petals 5, white. *Fruits* (drupe) ½ to ¾ to about 1 inch in diameter, red or yellow, noticeably glaucous, nearly globular, sweet and edible, ripening in early summer.

Winter. *Twigs* bright red to reddish, hairless, zigzag, slender, with short twigs terminating in a spine. *Buds* less than ⅛ inch long, nearly as long as wide; terminal bud lacking. *Bark* dark reddish brown, scaly.

Comparisons. This species can be separated from the flatwoods and the American plums by the presence of red-glandular marginal teeth on the leaves (absent in these other two species), and by its more consistent thicket-forming nature (usually more single stemmed in the other species unless their terminal buds are damaged by fire). Also, the developing leaves of this species unfold by a troughlike fold, rather than in a flat plane as in the other two species.

The Chickasaw plum (named for the Chickasaw Indians, who made great use of the fruits and who were responsible for bringing the species

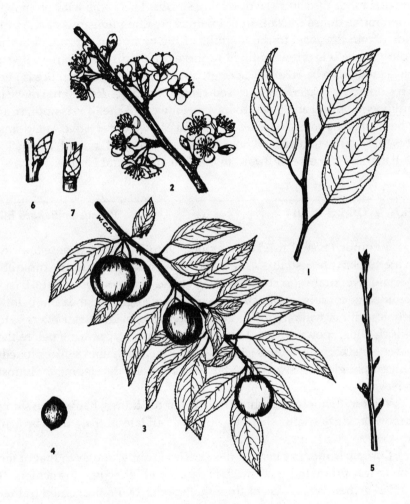

CHICKASAW PLUM

1. Branch with mature leaves.
2. Flowering branch.
3. Branch with leaves and fruits.
4. Stone from fruit.
5. Winter twig.
6-7. Details of winter buds.

into the East from the Southwest) is a thicket-forming shrub or a small tree, 10 to 25 feet high, with trunk up to 10 inches in diameter. It is one of the earliest of the southern flowering shrubs. This is the wild plum that often forms dense thickets in old fields and along fencerows and road-sides, from the coast to the foothills of the mountains, throughout the South. Since it is often confined to these highly disturbed areas, it was once thought to be an exotic species, but its restricted occurrence is per-haps due to its intolerance of closed-canopy woodlots. Its original range is unknown, but it is believed to have been west of the Mississippi, from whence it is supposed to have been spread eastward by Native Americans. It is thoroughly naturalized now from New Jersey, Maryland, Kentucky, Indiana, and Illinois southward to the Gulf and central Florida.

FLATWOODS PLUM   *Prunus umbellata* Ell.

Summer. *Leaves* 1 to 2¾ inches long, ½ to 1¼ inches wide, elliptic to ovate to obovate, usually widest above the middle, margins minutely crenate to crenate serrate, glandless, apices acute or acuminate, bases rounded to cordate, upper surfaces glabrous, slightly pubescent below; petioles with or without glands at their summits, blades flat. *Flowers* ⅜ to ⅔ inch wide, showy, unscented, 2 to 5 per cluster, appearing before the leaves, petals 5, white. *Fruits* (drupe) ¼ to ⅝ inch in diameter, black to red-dish purple, globose, sweet or bitter, very glaucous, developing in August to November.

Winter. *Twigs* slender, shiny, red gray or red brown, hairy, often shiny, somewhat zigzag, spur shoot thorny. *Buds* all lateral. *Bark* dark brown, scaly.

Comparisons. The bark of this species is quite similar to that of the Chickasaw plum, but with more lustrous and less spiny branchlets. It can be further distinguished from that species by its unscented (rather than fragrant) flowers and by its glandless marginal teeth (those of the Chickasaw plum are conspicuously red glandular).

The flatwoods plum is also known as the black sloe and the hog plum. The epithet *umbellata* refers to the umbellate or umbrellalike inflo-rescence. This is a small- to medium-size spreading tree, rounded or umbrella-shaped. The fruits are scarcely edible when raw, but make very good jelly or preserves. It occurs chiefly in the coastal plain from southern

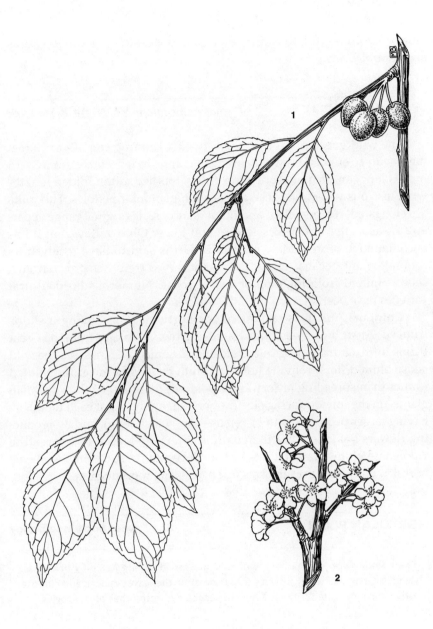

FLATWOODS PLUM

1. Branch with leaves and fruits. 2. Flowering branch.

North Carolina south to central Florida and west to southern Arkansas and central Texas.

WILD GOOSE PLUM   *Prunus munsoniana* **W. Wight & Hedrick**

The wild goose plum is a small, thicket-forming tree, 15 to 20 feet high, with a rounded crown. Leaves are elliptic to lanceolate, from 3 to 5 inches long, an inch or more wide, finely toothed, often folded length-wise, lustrous yellowish green above, with glandular petioles. The fruits are elongated, red or yellow, and often glaucous. Its original range apparently was in the upper Mississippi and lower Ohio valleys, but it has become much more widely naturalized. It is said to have received its common name because one of the first observed trees was grown from a seed obtained from the crop of a wild goose. Numerous horticultural varieties have been derived from this species.

Comparisons. It is similar to the hortulan plum, being a short-trunked, 2-foot high tree with a rounded crown. It ranges from the Great Plains to Texas, extending into Ohio and Virginia to Tennessee. The wild goose plum differs from the hortulan plum by having inwardly pointed (rather than spreading or forwardly pointed) marginal teeth, with small glands on the inward-facing side (rather than on the tip of each tooth), by having larger pedicels (⅜ to ½ versus ½ to ¾ inch long), and by producing flowers before (rather than with or after) the leaves. Moreover, the wild goose plum forms thickets by way of vegetative suckering, while the hortulan plum produces thickets through sexual reproduction.

HORTULAN PLUM   *Prunus hortulana* **Bailey**

The combination of characters of this species including its spiny branches, glandular marginal teeth, flowers that form after the leaves appear, and globose rather than elongated fruits will help to separate it from other plum species.

Summer. *Leaves* 3 to 6 inches long, 2 to 3 inches wide, alternate, simple, deciduous, ovate to ovate lanceolate, broadest near the base, apices long-acuminate, bases round to cuneate; dark green above, lustrous and paler beneath, hairy on the veins; margins finely serrated, teeth with glands at the tips; petioles ⅜ to ⅔ inch long, often reddish-hairy at least

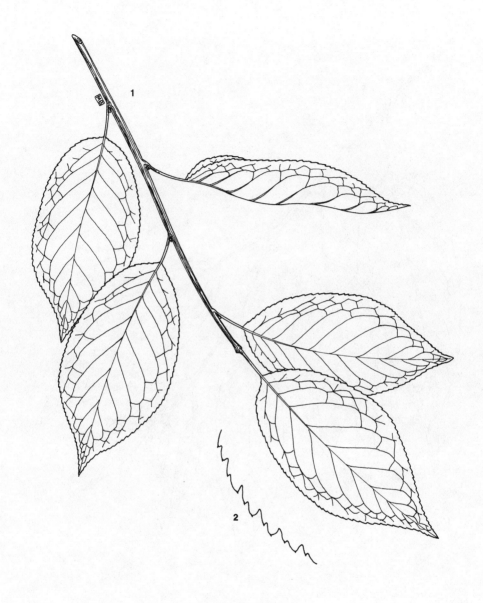

WILD GOOSE PLUM

1. Branch with leaves.

2. Detail of leaf margin

HORTULAN PLUM

1. Branch with leaves.

2. Detail of leaf margin and terminal tooth glands.

above, usually with 2 glands at the summit. *Flowers* ½ to ¾ inch across, white, perfect, clustered, produced in April to May with or after the leaves; petals ¼ to ⅜ inch long, 5, ovate, apices rounded or notched; stamens about 30. *Fruits* (drupe) ¾ to 1¼ inches across, globose to ovate, dark red to yellow, sweet and juicy, with or without a bloom.

Winter. *Twigs* thin, glabrous, reddish brown, often glaucous; leaf scars ovate; bundle scars 3; pith brown, continuous. *Buds* ⅛ to 3⁄16 inch long, brown; bud scales slightly ciliate. *Bark* red brown, thin at first, becoming laterally curly in age, exposing a lighter brown inner bark.

Comparisons. This species is similar to the wildgoose plum, but has larger leaves that are flat rather than folded lengthwise, are dark green (rather than yellow green), and marginal teeth that point forward (rather than curve inward), with glands present at the exact top of each tooth (rather than between the teeth or toward one side), and flowers that appear with or after rather than before the leaves. Their fruits also differ in that those of the wild goose plum are globose to subglobose, while those of the hortulan plum are clearly elongated.

The hortulan plum is a large thicket-forming shrub or small tree, 6½ to 13 feet high, which also grows as a single individual. It is found in rich bottomlands, roadsides, and woodland margins from Nebraska to Texas, extending eastward to Virginia, West Virginia, and Maryland.

FIRE CHERRY   *Prunus pensylvanica* **L. f.**

> This high-elevation or far-northern species is characterized by its bright red fruits; lustrous red bark, which peels in horizontal strips; long-pointed, narrow leaves; umbel-like flower clusters; brown pith; and clustered buds at the ends of the twigs.

Summer. *Leaves* 3 to 5 inches long, ¾ to 1¼ inches wide, alternate, simple, deciduous, oblong, lanceolate, broadest below the middle, often falcate, tips acute to acuminate, bases rounded or wedge-shaped, margins finely and sharply toothed; blades rather thin, glabrous, lustrous, bright yellowish green on both surfaces but slightly paler beneath; petioles ½ to 1 inch long, slender, with a pair of glands at their summits. *Flowers* about

FIRE CHERRY

1. Branch with mature leaves and fruits.
2. Flowering branch.
3. Winter twig.
4-5. Details of buds and leaf scars.

½ inch wide, small, perfect, borne 3 to 7 per umbellate inflorescence, appearing with the leaves; petals 5, white. *Fruits* (drupe) about ¼ inch in diameter, bright red, translucent; flesh thin, very sour; borne in small, lateral, umbel-like clusters; ripen during July and August.

Winter. *Twigs* slender, with fetid odor, glabrous, often lustrous, reddish brown, more or less glaucous; pith orangish. *Buds* 1⁄16 to ⅛ inch long, ovoid, apically blunt, dark reddish brown, characteristically clustered at the tips of the twigs; lateral buds commonly with accessory buds alongside them; terminal bud present. *Bark* of the young trunks and branches very lustrous, bright reddish brown, conspicuously marked with the horizontally elongated lenticels; frequently peeling in horizontal strips; inner bark green, aromatic, very bitter.

Comparisons. Our four native deciduous cherries can be separated by their leaf shape alone: fire cherry is broadest below the middle, choke cherry and Alabama cherry are broadest above the middle, and black cherry is broadest mostly at the middle. The red twigs, shiny red bark, completely glabrous, yellow-green (rather than dark green) leaves, and umbellate rather than racemose inflorescence help to separate this species from the Alabama cherry, the black cherry, and the choke cherry.

―――――――

The fire cherry is also known as the wild red cherry, the pin cherry, or the bird cherry. It is a small, short-lived tree occasionally attaining a height of around 30 feet with a trunk up to 1 foot in diameter. It commonly occurs in clearings and along fencerows or roadsides. Along with our aspen species it forms a pioneer association on cutover or burned-over forest lands (hence its common name), particularly those formerly dominated by eastern white pine, eastern hemlock, or other northern hardwoods, such as gray birch. The fire cherry cannot withstand shading, and it soon dies when it is overtopped by the crowns of other trees.

The wood of the fire cherry is of no commercial value. The fruits are eaten by many species of wild birds, including the ruffed grouse, and birds are almost wholly responsible for the dissemination of its seeds. Chipmunks and deer mice eat the pits, or seeds, and the fruits are eaten by several other species of mammals. Deer apparently are not fond of the fire cherry as browse. The bark is sometimes eaten by beavers when more preferred food species are not available.

The fire cherry ranges from Labrador west to British Columbia and south to Colorado and North Carolina and Georgia.

PERFUMED CHERRY   *Prunus mahaleb* L.

> The hairy twigs, spur shoots, nearly circular leaves, and pleasantly aromatic bark
> and wood are most distinctive.

Summer. *Leaves* 1 to 2 inches long, nearly as wide, alternate, simple, deciduous, ovate to nearly round, apices sharply acuminately pointed, bases cordate to rounded, margins finely crenate serrate; blades pale green on both surfaces, glabrous or with few hairs along the midrib; petioles ¼ to ⅜ inch long, glabrous with 1 to 2 glands near the summit. *Flowers* ⅜ to ⅔ inch across, white, very fragrant, perfect, borne in narrow elongate corymbose-racemose clusters of 4 to 10 individuals, produced from April to May, once the leaves have partially emerged; petals 5, oval to obovate; stamens 20. *Fruits* (drupe) ¼ to ⅓ inch across, round to oblong, black to reddish black, very bitter.

Winter. *Twigs* thin, velvety hairy, becoming glabrous, pale green at first, thereafter red brown to gray, aromatic, spur shoots present; leaf scars narrow, half round; bundle scars 3; pith green to brown, continuous. *Buds* 1/16 to ⅛ inch long, acute; bud scales red brown, hairy at tips. *Bark* smooth and gray brown at first, becoming darker in color and scaly with age, with large conspicuous lenticels.

Comparisons. The combination of fragrant, hairy, gray (rather than red) twigs, accompanying spur shoots, nearly circular leaves, and flowers that are produced after the leaves appear help to separate this species from others within the genus.

The perfumed cherry is a 20- to 35-foot-high, occasionally thicket-forming, tree or shrub introduced from Europe in the 1850s and now rarely escaping and naturalized in the East. It has a short, often clustered, contorted trunk; thick twigs; and conspicuous spur shoots. Nearly all parts of this tree are pleasantly aromatic and used for pipes and walking sticks. Although inedible, its fruits have been used in liquer and dye making and its seeds used to fix perfumes. It is found along roadsides, old homesites, farms, and fencerows. In cultivation, it tends to be short-lived and very intolerant of wet or heavy soils, but more cold hardy and drought tolerant than the sweet cherry.

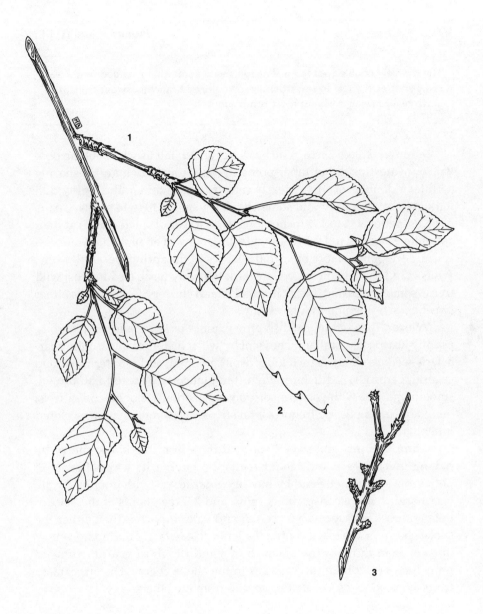

PERFUMED CHERRY

1. Branch with leaves.
2. Detail of leaf margin with marginal glandular teeth.
3. Winter twig with spur shoots.

SWEET CHERRY   *Prunus avium (L.) L.*

The coarsely double-toothed leaf margins with somewhat rounded teeth, two red glands at the leaf bases, stout, lightly colored branches, sweet fruits, and horizontally peeling bark, are most conspicuous.

Summer. *Leaves* 2 to 6⅓ inches long, about half as wide, oblong obovate or ovate, tips rather taper-pointed, bases rounded, margins sharply serrate or doubly serrate to nearly cerrate; blades thin, rather veiny, dull dark green above, paler and somewhat hairy on the 10 to 14 primary pairs of veins; petioles ¾ to 1½ inches long, with a pair of small glands at their summits. *Flowers* 1 to 1¼ inches wide, 1 to many in an umbellate inflorescence, developing before or with the leaves in the spring; petals 5, white. *Fruits* ⅞ to 1 inch diameter, yellow dark to nearly black (red in most wild trees), somewhat ovoid, borne in small lateral clusters; flesh may be either sweet or tart; ripening in June or July.

Winter. *Twigs* stout, reddish brown, more or less glaucous, glabrous, usually lustrous; lateral branches stubby, with clusters of buds, quite characteristic. *Buds* about ½ inch long, ovoid, pointed; scales of terminal bud several, glabrous, reddish brown, often glaucous. *Bark* reddish brown, smooth, marked with very conspicuous horizontally elongated lenticels; on older trunks peeling in horizontal strips, exposing the lighter-colored inner bark.

Comparisons. The sweet cherry differs from the black cherry by having much larger and tastier fruits; by having its leaves borne on noticeable spur shoots; and by having wider leaves with double-serrate leaf margins, more conspicuous veins, and 2 large glands at the apex of the petioles. This species has stouter and paler branches than either the choke cherry or the black cherry, the lenticels are larger and more yellow in color than those of the black cherry, and the flowers and fruits are umbellate rather than racemose as in the choke cherry. The large, tasty fruits alone should separate this species from the others.

––––––––

The sweet cherry is also known as the mazzard or the European bird cherry. It becomes a large tree, up to 75 feet in height with a trunk diameter of 2 to 3 feet, with a very distinctive pyramidal form. This is the commonest of the domestic cherries now found in the wild. It occurs very commonly along fencerows and roadsides, and is occasionally found

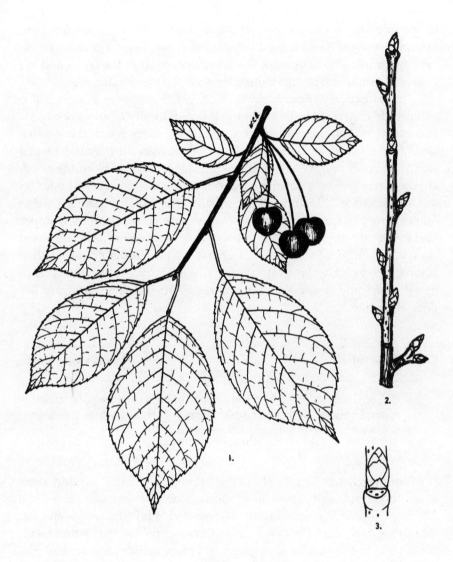

SWEET CHERRY

1. Branch with mature leaves and fruits.
2. Winter twig.
3. Detail of bud and leaf scar.

in open woods. Several varieties of this tree are common in cultivation. In Europe the wood is often used for interior finish, and for making furniture and musical instruments. Birds are very fond of the fruits and are chiefly instrumental in distributing the tree over the countryside.

The sour cherry (*Prunus cerasus* L.) is also a native of Europe and is extensively cultivated in this country. It occurs locally as an escape but is less common than the sweet cherry and rarely naturalized. It is a much smaller tree (20 to 30 feet versus 50 to 75 feet) with a low, round-topped crown, grayish rough bark, and lacking the central trunk of the sweet cherry. It tends to be a hardier species than the sweet cherry. The leaves are thickish in texture, more rigid, smaller (2 to 4 inches versus 3 to 6⅓ inches long), narrowly obovate to ovate, quite lustrous on their upper surfaces, and with fewer vein pairs (6 to 9 versus 10 to 14). The sweet cherry also differs from the sour cherry by having hairy rather than glabrous lower leaves (at least in vein axils), glandular rather than glandless petioles, and larger, sweeter, and tastier fruits (also see winter key differences).

CHOKE CHERRY   *Prunus virginiana* **L.**

> This species is characterized by the fetid odor of its broken twigs, by its dull, thin, obovate (thicker near the tip) leaf blades, which have sharp, divergent, spreading teeth, and by its racemose inflorescence.

Summer. *Leaves* 2 to 4 inches long, approximately half as wide, alternate, simple, oblong obovate, nearly always noticeably widest above the middle, tips acuminate-pointed, bases rounded or broadly wedge-shaped, margins sharply and finely serrate with rather narrowly pointed teeth; blades thin but firm, dull dark green and glabrous above, paler and glabrous beneath, except for occasional hair tufts in the vein axils of the 8 to 11 pairs of veins; petioles ⅜ to ¾ inch long, with a pair of glands at their summits. *Flowers* ¼ to ⅓ inch across, small, in very densely flowered racemes at branch tips, developing after the leaves; petals 5, white. *Fruits* (drupe) ⅓ to ½ inch in diameter, dark reddish or purplish-red, borne in loose, drooping clusters, ripen in July or August, harshly astringent.

Winter. *Twigs* rather stout, glabrous, light brown to gray brown, with a rank or very disagreeable odor, more so than the black cherry. *Buds* about ⅓ inch long, narrowly ovoid, glabrous, sharply pointed, scales

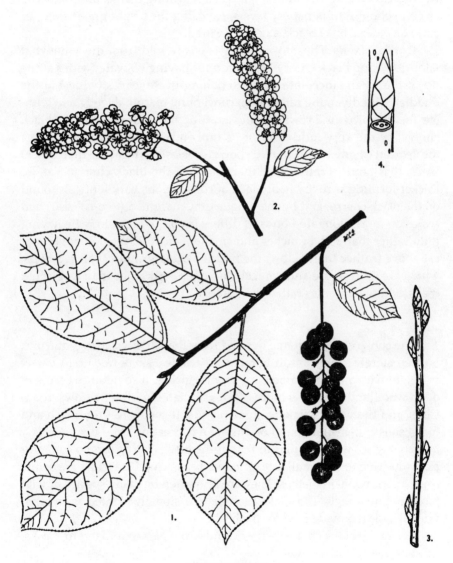

CHOKE CHERRY

1. Branch with mature leaves and fruits.
2. Flowering branch.
3. Winter twig.
4. Detail of bud and leaf scar.

obtusely pointed, 6 or more, light brownish, with paler grayish to light brown margins; terminal bud present. *Bark* smooth, dull grayish brown, with conspicuous buff-colored lenticels; on young trunks and branches often peeling in thin, papery layers, exposing the bright greenish inner bark; on older trunks black, slightly fissured.

Comparisons. The choke cherry is easily told from the somewhat later flowering black cherry by the former having obovate (wider at the tip) rather than lanceolate-ovate to oblong-ovate leaves (widest at the middle), with diverging rather than converging marginal teeth, and without the conspicuous 2 rows of hairs abutting the midvein as in the black cherry; by the very fetid odor of its broken twigs and buds (the most unpleasant of any of our native cherry species); red (rather than black) fruits that tend to fall earlier than those of the black cherry; a more thicket-forming shrubby habit; lack of conspicuous bark lenticels found on the black cherry; and by the unique gray-margined (two-colored) bud scales on more elongated buds. It differs from the fire cherry by having gray, rather than red, branches and smaller, wider leaves that are broadest above (rather than below) the middle; brown rather than red buds, which are more acute and conical; and deep red rather than bright red fruits, borne in racemes rather than umbels.

————

The choke cherry, a name derived from the harshly astringent fruits, is often merely a large shrub, but it may become a small tree up to 25 feet in height with a trunk diameter of about 8 inches. It sometimes occurs in open woodlands, but it is more often associated with fencerows, roadsides, and the waste thickets of farmlands. It seems to prefer rich and moist soils, but is often found on soils of a poorer and drier type.

The wood, while similar to that of the black cherry, has no commercial value due to the small size attained by the tree. The fruits are sometimes used in making jellies. They are also eaten by many species of wild birds and mammals. The choke cherry is occasionally planted as an ornamental and to provide food for the birds.

The range of the choke cherry extends from Newfoundland to Alaska, south to Georgia and Texas.

BLACK CHERRY   *Prunus serotina* **Ehrh.**

The thin, lustrous, lanceolate (widest near the middle) leaves, inward-pointed marginal teeth, the unusual potato-chip-like flaking bark, glandular petioles, racemose inflorescence, and conspicuous concentration of brown hairs (initially white) abutting against both sides of the midrib on the undersurface of the leaves are most distinctive.

Summer. *Leaves* 2 to 5 inches long, ¾ to 1½ inches wide, alternate, simple, deciduous, narrowly ovate to oblong lanceolate, tips acute, bases broadly wedge-shaped or rounded, margins finely serrate with incurved and somewhat callous-pointed teeth, resembling tiny bird heads when viewed individually and magnified, with teeth representing the bill or mandible (choke cherry has larger, coarser, upward-pointed teeth ending in a spine tip); blades thickish and firm, dark green and lustrous above, paler and glabrous beneath, with conspicuous concentration of brown hairs adjacent to each side of the midrib on undersurface; veins 12 to 15 pairs; petioles ½ to 1 inch long, with a pair of reddish glands at their summits. *Flowers* ¼ inch wide, white, 5-petaled, borne in terminal, drooping, numerous-flowered racemes, 4 to 6 inches across. *Fruits* (drupe) ⅓ to ½ inch in diameter, dark purplish black, with a juicy bittersweet pulp, borne in loose drooping clusters, ripening in August or September.

Winter. *Twigs* slender, glabrous, reddish brown or olive brown, glaucous, thickly dotted with small, pale lenticels, with a very pronounced, but not disagreeable, odor of bitter almonds. *Buds* about ⅕ inch long, ovoid, blunt, or sharp-pointed (less pointed than the choke cherry); scales sharply pointed, 4 or 5, glabrous, lustrous, reddish brown with greenish touches; terminal bud present. *Bark* on the young trunks and branches olive brown or reddish brown, smooth, conspicuously marked with horizontally elongated lenticels; on the older trunks becoming nearly black, much roughened with thick, irregular, scaly plates, which are somewhat upturned along the edges, resembling burnt potato chips.

Comparisons. This species is easily separated from the choke cherry by its leaves, which are broadest at rather than above the middle, by its finely incurved rather than spreading teeth, and most notably by the less fetid odor of its broken twigs. Even in the winter, this species can be easily distinguished from the choke cherry by the milder almond odor of the broken twigs, by its more upright treelike habit (more shrublike in the

BLACK CHERRY

1. Branch with mature leaves and fruits.
2. Flowering branch.
3. Winter twig.

4. Detail of bud and leaf scar.
5. Detail of hairs on leaf undersurface.

choke cherry), and by the darker-colored buds, which have dark, rather than light gray or brownish scale margins that are sharply pointed rather than rounded as in the choke cherry.

———

The black cherry is also known as the wild cherry, the wild black cherry, the rum cherry, and the cabinet cherry. It is a medium-sized to large tree, commonly 50 to 60 feet in height with a trunk diameter of 1½ to 3 feet, but old specimens often attain a height of 100 feet or more with trunks 4 or 5 feet in diameter. It has an irregularly oblong crown, but in the forest it develops a tall, straight, clean trunk with a relatively small, lofty crown. The tree makes its best growth on deep, moist, fertile soils, but it is often found growing on rather dry, gravelly, or sandy soils in the uplands. It is a common associate in the more southern oak forest types, but it is not uncommon as an associate of the eastern white pine, eastern hemlock, and northern hardwoods. The most magnificent specimens of the black cherry (the most highly valued of any of our cherries) occur in the virgin Tionesta Tract in the Allegheny National Forest and surrounding forests.

The valuable wood is moderately heavy, hard, strong, and close-grained. It is used principally for interior finish and furniture (both solid lumber and as a veneer), and for various tools and implements. The inner bark is used medicinally as a tonic, sedative, and expectorant. The fruits have a pleasantly bittersweet and winy flavor and are often used for making wine and jelly. The black cherry produces its fruits prolifically, and it is a singularly dependable source of food for wildlife. The cherries are eaten by many species of wild birds, including the ruffed grouse, and by such mammals as the black bear, the raccoon, the skunk, and the fox. The pits are a favorite food of the chipmunk and the deer mouse, the former often storing large quantities for its winter food supply. Like some other members of the genus, a hydrocyanic toxin builds in the leaves and has been known to poison browsing livestock.

The black cherry ranges from Nova Scotia to Minnesota, south to central Florida and eastern Texas.

ALABAMA CHERRY   *Prunus alabamensis* Mohr

> The thick, ovate leaves, with glandular-dotted leaf margins, and hairy twigs and leaf undersurface are most distinctive.

Comparisons. The hairy branches and leaf petioles, more whitish, rather than pale undersurface of its leaves, along with the obovate (rather than lanceolate to ovate) leaves with blunt rather than acute leaf apices, help to separate this species from the similar, but glabrous, black cherry.

The Alabama cherry is a much smaller and infrequent-to-rare tree species found from eastern Georgia west to northeastern Alabama and Mississippi, and locally in North Carolina and South Carolina, south to northwestern Florida. Its leaves are blunt or roundish and sometimes slightly notched at the tip, and more or less hairy or woolly on the lower surface. The stalks of the flower clusters and the young branchlets are similarly hairy.

CAROLINA LAUREL CHERRY   *Prunus caroliniana* (P. Mill.) Ait.

> The evergreen, entire or sparingly toothed leaves, with tiny bristles on the apex and marginal teeth, and the racemose flowers are most distinctive.

Leaves 2 to 4½ inches long and ¾ to 1½ inches wide, alternate, simple, evergreen, with a pleasant cherrylike odor when crushed; oblong lanceolate, pointed at both ends, margins entire or sparingly toothed, slightly revolute; thickish, lustrous dark green above, paler beneath, entirely glabrous; petioles about ¼ inch long, glandless, stout, orange-red. *Flowers* small, less than ¼ inch wide, fragrant, borne within leaf axils, racemose, opening in late March or early April while fruits of the previous year may still be present on the branches; petals 5, white. *Fruits* (drupe) about ½ inch long, leathery and inedible, oblong to roundish, black, ripening in the fall, unusual in persisting well into the following spring. *Bark* smooth, grayish, with horizontally elongated lenticels; in age becoming irregularly roughened.

ALABAMA BLACK CHERRY

1. Branch with leaves and fruits.

CAROLINA LAUREL CHERRY

1. Branch with leaves, flowers, and fruits.
2. Detail of leaf scar.
3. Detail of winter buds.
4. Stone from fruit.

The Carolina laurel cherry is also known as the laurel cherry, the Carolina cherry, the mock orange, and the wild orange. It is a handsome small tree with a more or less oblong, open crown and is used widely in the south in the horticultural trade. Occasionally it attains a height of 30 to 40 feet with a trunk diameter of almost a foot. The fruits are dry-fleshed and inedible by human standards, but they are eaten by many birds. The laurel cherry grows naturally on well-drained soils, often on the bluffs and banks bordering streams. Along the southeastern coast it sometimes forms dense thickets among the sand dunes. It is widely planted as an ornamental tree in the south. The wilted leaves contain prussic acid and may cause fatal poisoning if browsed by livestock.

The Carolina laurel cherry occurs in the coastal plain from southeastern North Carolina to central Florida and eastern Texas.

The Pears—Pyrus

COMMON PEAR *Pyrus communis* L.

Easily recognized by its short, thornlike spur shoots, uniformly shaped fruits, white flowers, and a more strict crown than that of the common apple.

Summer. *Leaves* 1½ to 4 inches long, 1 to 2 inches wide, alternate, simple, ovate to broadly ovate, tips rather short-pointed, bases rounded or broadly wedge-shaped, margins wavy and finely serrate and regularly toothed, elliptical, rather thick and firm, dark green and lustrous above, paler and glabrous beneath; petioles ¾ to 2 inches long, slender, glabrous. *Flowers* 1 to 1¼ inches across, clustered; petals 5, white, developing in the spring. *Fruits* of wild trees usually small, seldom more than 2 inches long, greenish, rather dry, and very gritty.

Winter. *Twigs* moderately stout, glabrous or nearly so, ranging from olive brown to reddish brown, with scattered pale lenticels; spur shoots present, leaf scars narrow, crescent-shaped, somewhat elevated, with 3 bundle scars; stipule scar present. *Buds* about ¼ inch long, ovoid or conical, sharp-pointed; terminal bud with 4 or more scales, rather glabrous, chestnut brown or somewhat grayish. *Bark* grayish brown, at first smooth; on older trunks broken by shallow longitudinal fissures into irregular, flat-

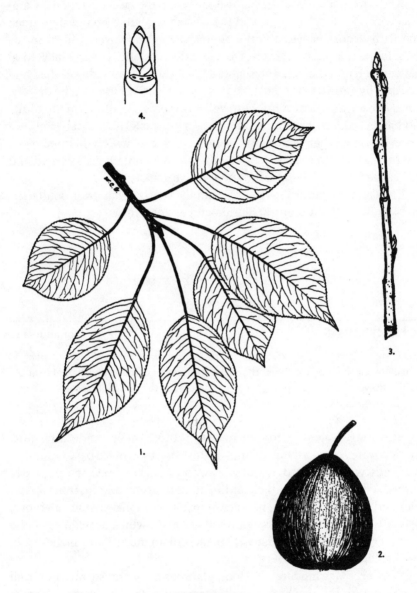

COMMON PEAR

1. Branch with mature leaves.
2. Fruit.
3. Winter twig.
4. Detail of bud and leaf scar.

topped, more or less scaly ridges; spinelike lateral spurs common on the branches.

Comparisons. The common pear can be separated from the common apple by the silhouette of the former being more strict or pointed rather than spreading, by having less-hairy twigs and leaves, and by having more thorny branches.

The common pear is a native of Europe and western Asia. Since the early 1600s, it has been cultivated in this country for its edible fruits, and many horticultural varieties are known. Occasionally the pear is found growing wild, but volunteer trees are not as widespread and common as those of the apple. The pear is a slow-growing, long-lived tree. It has an erect and more or less continuous trunk with ascending branches forming a pyramidal crown. The wood is sometimes used for tool handles, knife handles, drawing instruments, and in wood engraving.

BRADFORD PEAR   *Pyrus calleryana* Dcne.

> The nearly perfectly pyramidal shape, showy display of spring flowers, and dark, glossy leaves with conspicuously undulating or wavy margins are most distinctive.

Summer. *Leaves* 1 to 3 inches long, broadly ovate to ovate, lustrous and glabrous above and below, turning scarlet in the autumn; apices short-acuminate, bases rounded to broadly cuneate, margins conspicuously undulate, with cuneate teeth; petioles 7/8 to 1 5/8 inches long. *Flowers* 7/8 to 1 inch long, 1 inch across, white, produced in 3-inch corymbs, developing in early spring; stamens 20. *Fruits* 1/4 to 1/2 inch across, globose, russet-colored and dotted, generally rarely produced.

Winter. *Twigs* glabrous. *Buds* finely pubescent.

The Bradford pear, which grows 30 to 50 feet tall, is an Asian introduction, native to China, and highly prized for its horticultural values. Its attractive pyramidal shape, dark lustrous leaves, and showy spring flowers, in addition to its tolerance of high levels of pollution make it extremely popular in plantings. It should be noted, however, that once mature, the branches tend to die back and break, severely altering its pyramidal shape. Occasionally the short branches can be sharp and thorn-

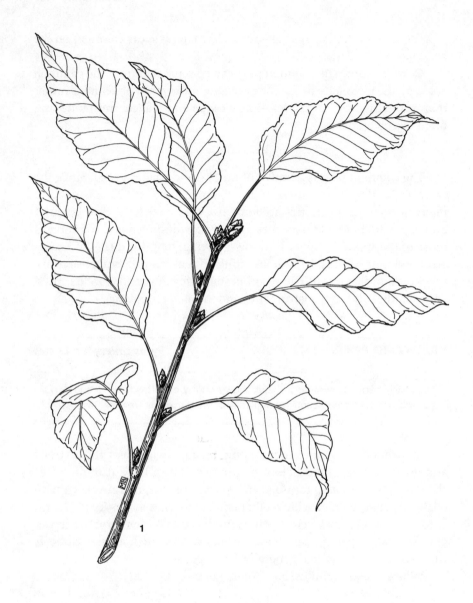

BRADFORD PEAR

1. Branch with leaves (with wavy leaf margins) and buds.

like, but this is only a minor annoyance. (Thornless expressions are also available.) It is unique among pears in that it is quite resistant to fire blight. It was introduced into the United States around 1908, with the Bradford selection being named in 1963 after Frederick Charles Bradford, former director of the USDA Plant Introduction Station in Glenn Dale, Maryland.

The Apples and the Crabapples—Malus

The crabapples are small trees with alternate, simple, pinnately veined leaves with toothed and sometimes lobed margins. The lateral branches are commonly short, spurlike, and slow growing. Occasionally, they are tipped with a short, stiff, spinelike point. The flowers and fruits are borne on some of these spurlike lateral branches, which are commonly known as the fruit spurs. The leaf scars are usually crescent-shaped and have 3 more-or-less indistinct bundle scars.

The flowers are showy and fragrant, appearing in the early spring with the newly developing leaves. They are perfect, with 5 pale to deep pink petals, and have numerous stamens. The fruits are small apples, technically known as pomes. The 5 carpels, which are closely united and cartilaginous in texture, form the core. This is surrounded by the enlarged and more or less fleshy calyx and receptacle, which form the edible portion of the apple. Our native species all produce greenish apples, which are small, hard, and very tart.

Aside from the obvious difference in fruits, the crabapples differ from the hawthorns by producing leafy thorns with leaf scars on the thorns rather than the naked, axillary spines of the hawthorns, which lack leaf scars.

SWEET CRABAPPLE   *Malus coronaria* (L.) P. Mill.

> The pink, exceedingly fragrant flowers, sharp-spiny spur shoot branches, and glabrous mature leaves with serrate margins and acute or acuminate apices are most distinctive.

Summer. *Leaves* 1½ to 5 inches long, ½ to 2½ inches wide, alternate, simple, deciduous, variable, ovate to broadly ovate or triangular, widest

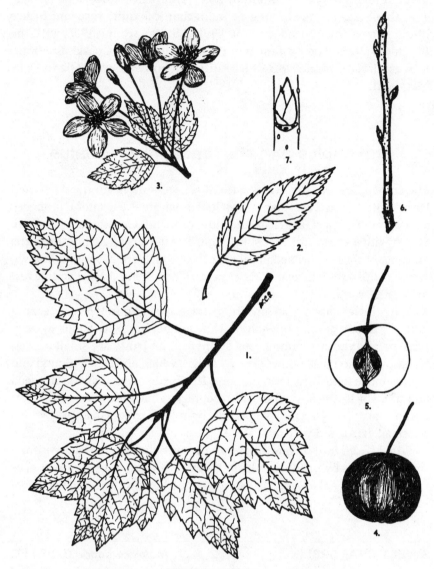

SWEET CRABAPPLE

1. Branch with mature leaves.
2. Narrow type of leaf.
3. Flowering branch.
4. Fruit.

5. Fruit in longitudinal section.
6. Winter twig.
7. Detail of bud and leaf scar.

toward base; on some trees lanceolate, apically acute to acuminate, bases usually rounded or, rarely, heart-shaped; margins sharply singly or doubly serrate or, in the case of the broader ones, with several short triangular lobes, dark green at maturity and often a bit glossy above, quite glabrous and paler beneath; petioles ½ to about 1 inch long, slender, round. *Flowers* ¾ to 2 inches wide, perfect, very fragrant, unisexual, in 3 to 6 flowered clusters, appearing with the leaves; petals 5, rose white, often streaked with pink, with externally glabrous sepals. *Fruits* (pome) mostly 1¼ to 2 or rarely 2 inches in diameter, small, roundish or somewhat depressed, yellowish green, fragrant, very sour, with a hard and very acidic flesh, surface feeling greasy to the touch, borne on long, slender stalks about 1½ inches in length.

Winter. *Twigs* slightly stout, reddish brown, densely hairy at first, becoming quite glabrous; developing very sharp spine-tipped, spurlike lateral branches during the second year. *Buds,* terminal bud ⅛ to ¼ inch long, ovoid, bluntish; scales 4 to 8, bright red, margins minutely hairy, but otherwise glabrous and lustrous; lateral buds smaller, appressed, conical. *Bark* dark reddish brown to grayish brown with shallow longitudinal fissures and low scaly topped ridges.

Comparisons. This species can be separated from the southern crabapple by the leaf bases of the former being rounded rather than tapered or cuneate and by the acuminate rather than blunt or broadly tapered leaf tips.

The sweet crabapple is also known as the American crabapple or the wild crabapple. It is a small thicket-forming shrub or small tree that occasionally attains a height of 20 to 25 feet, with a short trunk up to about 1 foot in diameter, and crooked branches that develop into a low, open, and broadly round-topped crown. It often forms dense thickets in abandoned fields and pastures, or along fencerows and roadsides. Less commonly it occurs as a small understory tree in woodlands.

Sweet indeed is the delightful perfume broadcast by the sweet crabapple's flowers, borne in the spring, at which time few trees are more beautiful. The bright pink flowers are laden with nectar and there is a constant hum from the horde of bees about the flowering trees.

Gather some of the little apples after the first frosts of autumn, and their delightful fragrance will rub off on your hands. Although they are hard and intensely sour, they make a pleasantly tart jelly, which is crystal clear and orange red in color. It is said that no jelly made from the red cultivated apples comes anywhere near matching it. In the fall and winter the fallen fruits are eaten by deer, raccoons, skunks, and foxes. Squirrels discard the fleshy portion but are apparently quite fond of the seeds.

The sweet crabapple produces no wood of commercial value. It is heavy, hard, and close-grained and is sometimes used for wood carving, tool handles, or small turned articles.

The sweet crabapple extends from central New York west to southern Ontario; south to southeastern Virginia, western North Carolina, and the northern portions of Georgia, Alabama, and Arkansas.

SOUTHERN CRABAPPLE *Malus angustifolia* (Ait.) Michx.

> The mostly crenate to crenate-serrate leaf margins, blunt leaf apices, externally glabrous sepals, thorny branches, scaly bark, and thickish leaves of this thicket-forming species are distinctive.

Summer. *Leaves* 1 to 3 inches long, ½ to 1 inch wide, alternate, simple, deciduous, persistent, apically clustered, oblong to oblong lanceolate to elliptic, thickish, tips bluntly acute to rounded, bases cuneate to tapered; glabrous on both surfaces; dull green above and paler beneath, margins rather sparingly and cuneate-serrate to practically entire. *Flowers* about 1 inch across, in clusters of 3 to 5, terminating the spur shoots, exceptionally fragrant; petals 5, white to pink, opening in March or April; similar to those of the sweet crabapple. *Fruits* (pome) 1 to 1½ inches in diameter, bitter or exceptionally sour, also similar to those of the sweet crabapple.

Winter. *Twigs* glabrous, reddish brown, hairy when young, becoming glabrous in age, slender to thick, dotted with orangish lenticels; leaf scars linear with 3 bundle traces; stipule scars present; pith continuous. *Buds* small, hairy, dark brown, obtuse with 4 scales; terminal bud about ⅛ inch long, blunt. *Bark* red brown, deeply divided by longitudinal fissures and scaly ridges, exposing a reddish brown inner bark.

Comparisons. The southern crabapple is readily distinguished from the sweet crabapple by its thick, nearly evergreen, glabrous adult leaves, which are more oblong or lanceolate to narrowly elliptic (rather than ovate), with bluntly toothed or crenate (rather than sharply serrate) margins, and are more cuneately tapered, with rather blunt apices and bases.

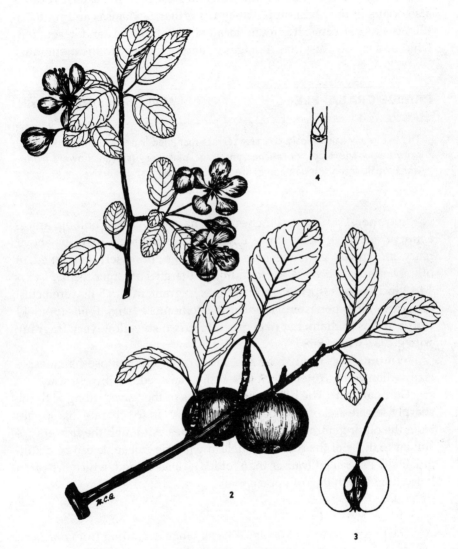

SOUTHERN CRABAPPLE

1. Branch with immature leaves and flowers.
2. Branch with mature leaves and fruits.
3. Cross-section of fruit.
4. Detail of winter bud and leaf scar.

This is the common wild crabapple of the coastal plain from southern New Jersey south to northern Florida and west to southeastern Texas. It also occurs in the Mississippi Valley to northern Arkansas and southern Illinois along streams. It is found locally in West Virginia and in southern Ohio, and in the Carolinas it ranges inland practically to the mountains.

PRAIRIE CRABAPPLE   *Malus ioensis* (Wood) Britt.

The externally hairy sepals, coarsely serrate-margined leaves, which are densely hairy below, short, spiny branches, and large, pink, very fragrant flowers from which small, green, fragrant apples are produced are most distinctive.

Summer. *Leaves* 2 to 4 inches long, narrow, ovate to oblong, apices acute or rounded, bases cuneate to round, dark green, lustrous above, hairy and grayish green beneath, leaf margins entire, serrate-toothed, or often variously lobed, veins extending to margins of larger teeth. *Flowers* 1 to 2 inches across, perfect, pink to rose, fragrant, in 2 to 5 flowered clusters; calyx lobes persistent, more or less tomentose-hairy. *Fruits* (pome) 1 to 1½ inches in diameter, pale green to greenish yellow, very fragrant, with greasy, waxy skin.

Winter. *Twigs* reddish brown, more or less tomentose-hairy, especially when young, often thorny. *Bark* thin, dark reddish brown, scaly.

Comparisons. The hairy undersurfaces of the leaves, along with the sharply serrate and often lobed leaf margins, help to separate this species from the other glabrous-leaved *Malus* species. Although the flowers are similar to those of the common apple, the prairie crabapple can be distinguished by its rolled (rather than folded) leaves in bud, which are often lobed (unlobed in the common apple).

———

The prairie, or Iowa, crabapple has a range extending from northern Indiana to southeastern Minnesota, south to southeastern Nebraska, eastern Kansas, Arkansas, Texas, and Louisiana. The flowers are similar to those of the cultivated apples. Many consider this species to be the most beautiful and fragrant of all our wild crabapples. The cultivated Bechtel crabapple, with large and double rose-colored flowers, has been derived from this species.

COMMON APPLE   *Malus pumila* P. Mill.

> Easily recognized by its large, edible fruits that develop in the autumn, by its large, showy, white to pink flowers, by its conspicuous spur shoots that support both the leaves and flowers, and by its spreading crown, which is distinct even at a distance.

Summer. *Leaves* 2 to 4 inches long, 1¼ to 2½ inches wide, ovate to broadly ovate, tips short-pointed, bases rounded to broadly wedge-shaped, margins rather finely and round-toothed; upper surfaces bright green and glabrous, lower surfaces paler and more or less covered with felted white hairs, veins not extending to margins. *Flowers* 1¼ inches across, large; petals 5, white or pink, appearing in early spring. *Fruits* 2 to 3½ inches in diameter, the familiar apples; greenish, yellowish, or red, with either sweet or sour taste; usually small, and often knobby or "crippled" on wild trees.

Winter. *Twigs* moderately stout, reddish brown or yellowish brown, hairy (especially so when young); bundle scars 3; stipules lacking. *Buds* ¼ inch or less long, ovoid or roundish, blunt, reddish brown, more or less coated with a whitish wool; terminal bud obtuse, hairy, much larger than lateral ones. *Bark* grayish brown, eventually scaling off in thin, brittle flakes.

Comparisons. Unique among our apple species in lacking thorny branches or sharp buds and in having round rather than pointed teeth on the leaf margins.

––––––––

The common apple is a small- or medium-sized tree that sometimes attains a height of 30 to 40 feet. The trunk is characteristically short with wide-spreading branches forming a broadly round-topped crown. The apple is of European origin, having been brought to this country by the early colonists. Numerous varieties are found in cultivation. Wild or volunteer apple trees are frequent in old fields, along the roadsides and fencerows, and even in remote forested areas. The wild apple trees so often seen in the mountains undoubtedly grew from cores discarded by lumberjacks and teamsters. Wild apples are particularly common about old sawmill or camp sites and along the old tram roads.

The wood of the common apple tree is heavy, hard, tough, and close-grained. It makes a good fuel, and in many country districts it is com-

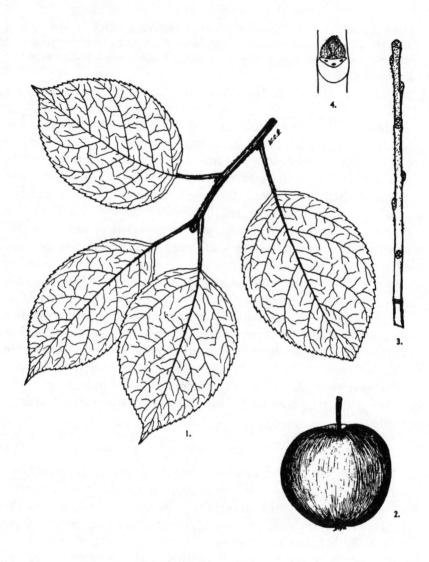

COMMON APPLE

1. Branch with mature leaves.
2. Fruit.

3. Winter twig.
4. Detail of bud and leaf scar.

monly employed for smoking meats. It is used to some extent in cabinet-making and also for tool handles and shoemakers' lasts. The fruits and their domestic utilization are familiar to everyone. They are utilized as food by many kinds of wildlife including white-tailed deer, black bears, raccoons, and foxes. The wild trees, and those in orchards as well, are often browsed by the deer during the winter months; the apple buds are also a favorite winter food of the ruffed grouse—both result in damage to the trees by forcing excessive budding to occur. Many unknown Johnny Appleseeds unwittingly provided wildlife with a good food supply when they threw their apple cores into the brush in the backwoods.

The Mountain-Ashes—Sorbus

These are trees or shrubs with alternate, deciduous, odd pinnately compound leaves and serrated leaflets. The white flowers are perfect and regular, borne in terminal cymes, with 5 obovate petals, which are short-clawed and spreading. Each flower has 15 to 20 stamens and an inferior ovary. At least in our native species, the buds are sticky and the leaf-scars are narrow and crescent-shaped. The fruits are small, orange red, berry-like pomes. Mountain-ashes, as the name suggests, are trees of high elevation areas or of northern latitudes. Their fruits and leaves are generally quite colorful in autumn, adding brilliance to the fall foliage.

AMERICAN MOUNTAIN-ASH   *Sorbus americana* **Marsh.**

A high mountain or far northern species of acid soil swamplands with orange-red fruits; alternate, pinnately compound leaves with red petioles; long-pointed or acuminate leaflets; clubby, glabrous branches; and flat, white-flowered inflorescences, this species ought not be confused with any other (see other mountain-ash species for comparisons).

Summer. *Leaves* 6 to 10 inches long, alternate, odd pinnately compound, deciduous; leaflets 1 to 3 ¼ inches long, from ½ to ¾ inch wide, 9 to 17 per leaf, all but the terminal one sessile, lanceolate to oblong-lanceolate, broadest below middle, commonly more than three times as long as wide, tips tapering acute to acuminate, bases asymmetrically

AMERICAN MOUNTAIN-ASH

1. Branch with mature leaves and fruits.
2. Winter twig.
3. Detail of bud and leaf scar.

rounded, margins finely and sharply serrately toothed, often to base; upper surfaces dark yellowish green, glabrous, and more or less lustrous; paler and glabrous beneath; petioles and rachis usually reddish. *Flowers* ⅛ to ¼ inch across, small, perfect, flat-topped, in terminal cymose clusters, 3 to 6 inches across, appearing often with the leaves; petals 5, white. *Fruits* (pome) ¼ inch in diameter, berrylike, borne in large flat-topped clusters; brilliant orange red at maturity.

Winter. *Twigs* stout, glabrous, grayish to reddish brown, marked with conspicuous, scattered, large, pale lenticels, spur shoots often present; leaf scars large, rather narrow, crescent-shaped or broadly U-shaped, with 5 to 7 distinct bundle scars. *Buds* glabrous, dark purplish red, somewhat gummy, with 2 or 3 visible bud scales; terminal bud about ½ inch long, conical, acute, resinous, curved, shiny, slightly hairy; lateral buds much smaller, ¼ inch long, conspicuously appressed to the twigs. *Bark* light grayish brown, usually smooth, but somewhat slightly roughened on the older trunks, aromatic when bruised.

The American mountain-ash is also called the rowantree, for which Roan Mountain in North Carolina was named. The word roan is actually derived from a Scandinavian word meaning red, indicating the color of the fruits of the related European mountain-ash. The American mountain-ash is a small tree, rarely exceeding a height of 20 feet or a trunk diameter of more than 1 foot. It is distinctly a northern species, growing along the borders of cold swamps and bogs, or on rocky mountain ridges. In some places it associates with the red spruce, the eastern white pine, and the eastern hemlock; in others with the rock-loving yellow birch. There are few localities where it is at all common. It does not grow very rapidly and is comparatively short-lived.

The wood of the mountain-ash is of no commercial value. It is a very attractive ornamental tree, producing large, flat-topped clusters of white flowers in May or June and brilliant orange-red fruits in the fall. The fruits are very acid and unpleasant to the taste, but they are evidently eaten with great relish by many species of birds.

The American mountain-ash ranges from Newfoundland to Manitoba, south to the northern portions of the United States and along the Appalachian Mountains to North Carolina and Georgia.

NORTHERN MOUNTAIN-ASH   *Sorbus decora* (Sarg.) Schneid.

A large boreal shrub or small tree, 15 to 75 feet high, is much like the American mountain-ash, with wider leaflets, larger flowers, and larger and darker fruits. Both of our native mountain-ash species have glabrous buds, which separate them from the European mountain-ash.

Summer. *Leaves* 5 to 8½ inches long, alternately pinnately compound, deciduous; leaflets 2 to 3½ inches long, ½ to 1 inch wide, 7 to 17, only 2 to 3 times as long as broad, oblong to narrowly oblong ovate to ovate lanceolate to elliptic, broadest near the middle, of a firmer texture than the American mountain-ash; margins scarcely tapered, sharply and finely serrate to middle or slightly below, tip rounded to a short point, bases asymmetrical; blue green above, not lustrous, whitened and hairy beneath; stipules early deciduous; petioles long, reddish. *Flowers* ⅜ to ½ inch wide, on hairy pedicels in flat-topped terminal cluster, appearing in June or early July after the leaves; larger and opening about 1 or 2 weeks later than those of the American mountain-ash, in a more open cluster. *Fruits* (pome) about ½ inch across, bright red, glaucous, larger than those of the American mountain-ash.

Winter. *Twigs* stout, red brown to gray, glabrous, hairy when young. *Buds* shiny, gummy, slightly hairy, dark red brown, cone-shaped; terminal bud ½ inch long, curved apically; lateral buds similar, but smaller. *Bark* smooth or scaly, silvery gray to gray green.

Comparisons. This species is similar to the American mountain-ash, but with much larger fruits (about twice as large); larger and showier flowers that bloom a week or two later, wider, shorter leaves that appear to be horizontally positioned rather than arching, and broader, more obtusely narrowly elliptic rather than lanceolate leaflets; red-hairy inner bud scales (nearly hairless in those of the American mountain-ash); and a more rounded form.

Sargent, in his *Silva of North America*, originally described this tree as a variety of the American mountain-ash, but it is now considered to be specifically distinct. Viewed by many to be the most beautiful of our native mountain-ashes, it is a tree 15 to 30 feet high with a trunk 12 inches in diameter, with silvery-gray, smooth bark. It is found in woodlands and on rocky shores and slopes from southern Greenland, Labrador, and

Newfoundland westward to northern Ontario, Saskatchewan, and Minnesota, and southward to Maine, New York, Ohio, northern Indiana, and Iowa.

EUROPEAN MOUNTAIN-ASH   *Sorbus aucuparia* L.

Summer. *Leaves* 4 to 8 inches long, 1 to 2 inches wide, alternate, odd pinnately compound deciduous; leaflets 1 to 2 inches long, ½ to ¾ inch wide, 9 to 17 in number, oblong to lanceolate, obtuse, sessile except for the terminal one; margins serrate to just above base; dull green above, white-hairy below. *Flowers* small, ⅜ inch wide, borne in cymose clusters of 3 to 6 after the leaves; petals 5, white. *Fruits* (pome) ⅜ to ⁵⁄₁₆ inch wide, berry-like or small applelike, orange to scarlet red.

Winter. *Twigs* stout, densely white hairy especially when young, reddish brown; leaf scars linear to crescent, with 3 to 7 bundle scars. *Buds* reddish purple, ovoid; terminal bud ⅜ to ¾ inch long, hairy, much larger than lateral buds. *Bark* gray, smooth, and bronze-colored when young, becoming slightly rough at maturity.

Comparisons. The blunt rather than acutely pointed leaflets, which are hairy rather than glabrous above and below, clearly rounded or short-pointed basally, and the large fruits, consistently hairy twigs, and woolly-hairy rather than slightly hairy buds, which are not as sticky (only slightly hairy in the American mountain-ash), separate this species from the American mountain-ash. Both the American mountain-ash and the northern mountain-ash can be distinguished from the European species by their sticky terminal buds.

This is a fairly small tree, 20 to 40 feet high, producing an oval or rounded crown. It is an introduced species that is often praised in horticulture for its brightly colored fruits and showy inflorescences. According to E. L. Little Jr. (1980), this is the only tree naturalized in Alaska, where it was introduced in the southeastern part of the state.

The Hawthorns—Crataegus

The hawthorns, or thorn-apples, are shrubs or small trees with alternate, simple, toothed or lobed leaves. They characteristically have stiff and sharply pointed thorns on their stems and branches. The showy, white (or rarely pinkish) flowers are usually borne in terminal, cymelike clusters, and are perfect with 5 sepals and petals, and numerous stamens. They have a compound pistil composed of 1 to 5 carpels, and as many separate styles. The fruits are small, applelike pomes, tipped with the conspicuous remains of the calyx, and containing 1 to 5 bony, 1-seeded nutlets.

Hawthorns evidently occurred as suppressed understory plants in the virgin forests of America; and with the clearing of the dominant trees they were released and ran rampant. Today they are often abundant in clearings, in abandoned fields, and along fencerows. Several species have been more or less widely cultivated for their showy spring flowers and attractive fruits. They are not usually particular as to soils but like sunny situations. The fruits of the hawthorns furnish food for wildlife, being an important fall and winter food of ruffed grouse, white-tailed deer, cottontail rabbits, raccoons, foxes, squirrels, and many small rodents. Some species possess a fairly palatable flesh, and the fruits are sometimes utilized for making jelly. Owing to the density of their crowns, which are rendered almost impregnable by thorns, they afford excellent nesting sites for many kinds of songbirds.

This is a large and very complicated genus. Although readily distinguished as a genus, the various species are extremely difficult to determine. There is much disagreement among the taxonomists as to the number of species and their characterization, with some suggesting in excess of a hundred species recorded from Pennsylvania alone. The characteristics of many, perhaps most, species are rather unstable, and hybrids are quite numerous. Those who desire to attempt a classification of the various species should consult some of the technical manuals or seek assistance from specialists. Most of us will have to rest content with knowing simply that they are hawthorns. Only a few of the commoner species are described and illustrated in this manual, and owing to the difficulty of determining the species, the usual keys have been omitted.

The hawthorns may be readily distinguished even in the winter, inasmuch as the long thorns, straight or sometimes slightly curved, are not shared by many of our other native trees or shrubs. The twigs are moderate or slender, round, more or less zigzag, and often appear rather lustrous. The leaf scars are narrowly crescent-shaped and show 3 bundle scars. The buds are rather small, roundish or slightly obovoid, generally glabrous and reddish or bright chestnut in color, and have several to about a half dozen exposed bud scales.

COCK'S-SPUR HAWTHORN   *Crataegus crus-galli* L.

> This is a shrub or small tree with dark grayish or brownish, scaly bark, numerous, slender, mostly straight thorns from 2 to 4 inches in length, and large, shiny leaves.

Summer. *Leaves* 2 to 4 inches long, 1 to 2 inches wide, alternate, simple, deciduous, obovate, tip rounded to pointed, base wedge-shaped, margins sharply toothed above the middle; blades thickish and somewhat leathery, dark green and lustrous above, paler and glabrous or nearly so beneath; petioles ½ to ¾ inch long, slightly winged. *Flowers* ⅜ to ½ inch wide; petals 5, white. *Fruits* (pome) about ⅜ inch in diameter, roundish or ovoid, greenish to dull red, with a hard, dryish flesh, usually containing 2 nutlets.

Winter. Since winter characters of most hawthorns are not useful for separating individual species, they are not provided here.

Comparisons. This species differs from the little-hip hawthorn (*C. spathulata* Michx.) by the leaf veins terminating at both leaf sinuses and teeth.

———

The cock's-spur hawthorn is one of our best known and more easily recognized species of hawthorn. It is typical of the *crus-galli* group. Its stout, rigid, and spreading branches form a broadly round-topped head. The flowers appear in great abundance in May or June; the fruits, which ripen in October, often persist well into the winter season. The leaves turn orange and scarlet in the fall. This hawthorn occurs quite commonly in thickets and old pastures on fairly fertile or sandy soils.

In eastern and northern Europe the cock's-spur hawthorn is a favorite hedge plant, and it is planted extensively for ornamental purposes in this country. It is a very satisfactory and quite attractive shrub.

The range of the cock's-spur hawthorn extends from Quebec to Ontario and Minnesota southward to Florida, Georgia, Kansas, and eastern Texas.

COCK'S-SPUR HAWTHORN

1. Branch with mature leaves and fruits.
2. Fruit with portion removed to show seeds.
3. Winter twig.
4-5. Details of winter buds and leaf scars.

DOTTED HAWTHORN   *Crataegus punctata* Jacq.

A small, flat-topped tree or shrub with roughish, gray-brown bark and scattered, stout, mostly straight thorns from 2 to 3 inches in length.

Summer. *Leaves* 2 to 3 inches long, 1½ to 2 inches wide, alternate, simple, obovate, tip rounded to pointed, base wedge-shaped, margins sharply and doubly serrate above the middle; blades firm, upper surfaces dull grayish green, impressed-veiny, glabrous, paler and more or less hairy beneath; petioles ¼ to ½ inch long, slightly winged, more or less hairy. *Fruits* (pome) ½ to ¾ inch in diameter, short-oblong to roundish, yellow to red, prominently dotted, with a thick, mealy, and rather dry flesh, containing 3 to 5 nutlets.

Winter. Since winter characters of most hawthorns are not useful for separating individual species, they are not provided here.

The dotted or large-fruit hawthorn is typical of the *Punctatae* group. In May or June it produces a profuse display of white flowers. The fruits ripen in October and soon fall. The common name is derived from the small but conspicuous dark dots on the fruits. Like most of the hawthorns, this species has inconstant characteristics, and several varieties have been described. It is often found on fertile soils, both in the stream bottoms and on the slopes.

The range of the dotted hawthorn extends from Quebec to Ontario and southward to North Carolina and Kentucky to as far as Mississippi and Georgia.

FAN-LEAF HAWTHORN   *Crataegus flabellata* (Spach) Kirchn.

A shrub or a small tree with ascending branches, and pale brown, scaly bark.

Summer. *Leaves* 1 to 2¾ inches long, ¾ to 2½ inches wide, alternate, simple, ovate to broadly ovate, apically pointed, base usually rounded or truncate, margins with about 5 pairs of broadly triangular, sharply toothed lateral lobes; blades thin, dark yellowish green above, slightly paler beneath, glabrous or nearly so on both surfaces; petioles ¾ to 1¼ inches long, slender, often slightly winged toward the summits, occasionally slightly glandular. *Fruits* (pome) ⅜ to ⅝ inch in diameter, oblong or

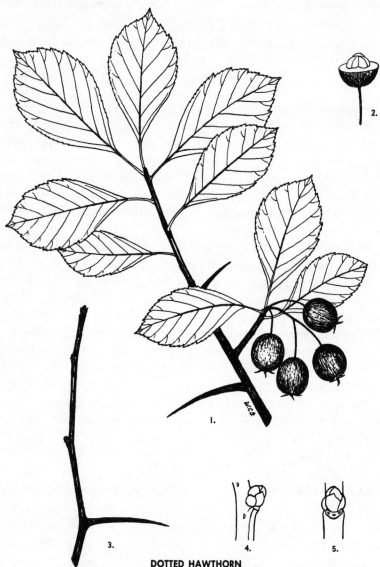

DOTTED HAWTHORN

1. Branch with mature leaves and fruits.
2. Fruit with portion removed to show seeds.
3. Winter twig.
4-5. Details of buds and leaf scars.

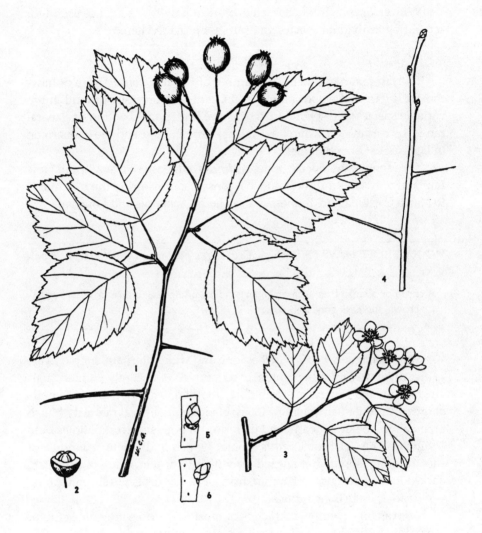

FAN-LEAF HAWTHORN

1. Branch with leaves and fruits.
2. Section of fruit.
3. Flowering branch.

4. Winter twig.
5-6. Details of winter buds.

slightly obovoid, bright red, with thick, mellow, or succulent flesh; containing from 3 to 5 bony nutlets.

Winter. Since winter characters of most hawthorns are not useful for separating individual species, they are not provided here.

The fan-leaf hawthorn, an example of the *Tenuifoliae* group of hawthorns, is found in woods and thickets, generally on stony ground. It is a variable species, and several varieties have been named within its general range. Its corymbs of white flowers are borne in May, and the fruits ripen in late August or September.

The range of this species extends from southeastern Canada and New England to northern Illinois and Wisconsin, southward in the mountains to North Carolina and Tennessee to as far as Arkansas and Louisiana.

WAXY-FRUIT HAWTHORN   *Crataegus pruinosa* (Wendl. f.) K. Koch

A shrub or a small tree with ascending, thorny branches, a more or less irregular crown, and dark gray, scaly bark.

Summer. *Leaves* 1 to 2½ inches long and wide, alternate, simple, ovate to broadly ovate, apically pointed, base rounded or abruptly pointed, margin sharply and somewhat irregularly toothed, usually with 3 or 4 pairs of broadly pointed and shallow lobes; blades quite firm at maturity, bluish green above, paler beneath, and glabrous on both surfaces; petioles ¾ to 1¼ inches long, glabrous. *Fruits* (pome) ½ inch in diameter, roundish or short-oblong, somewhat angled, greenish to dull crimson or purplish, dark-dotted, glaucous, with a thin, firm, or rather dryish flesh, containing 4 or 5 rather large bony nutlets.

Winter. Since winter characters of most hawthorns are not useful for separating individual species, they are not provided here.

The waxy-fruit hawthorn, a typical member of the *Pruinosae* group, occurs in woods and thickets chiefly on rocky ground. It is a variable species, and several varieties of it have been described. The corymbs of white flowers appear in May. The fruits, however, do not ripen until about October, frequently remaining hard and green until late in the season.

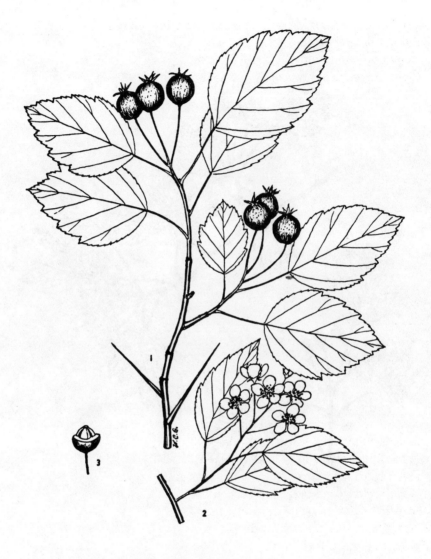

WAXY-FRUIT HAWTHORN

1. Branch with leaves and fruits.
2. Flowering branch.

3. Section of fruit.

PARSLEY HAWTHORN

1. Branch with flowers.　　　　2. Branch with fruits.

The range of this species of hawthorn extends from southeastern Canada to Michigan and Wisconsin, southward to North Carolina, Kentucky, Arkansas, and Louisiana.

PARSLEY HAWTHORN   *Crataegus marshallii* **Eggle.**

> This conspicuously small tree, 15 or 20 feet in height, with thorny, spreading branches, forms a broad, irregular, open crown and has deeply incised leaves with truncate bases.

Summer. *Leaves* 1½ to 2½ inches long, ¾ to 1½ inches wide, alternate, simple, deciduous, broadly ovate to roundish; blades triangular-shaped, deeply 5- to 7-cleft, the narrow divisions prominently and irregularly sharply toothed above the middle, margins also toothed; at maturity glabrous or nearly so, bright green and lustrous above, paler beneath; petioles 1 to 1½ inches long, slender. *Flowers* ½ to ¾ inch wide, pink to white; anthers red. *Fruits* (pome) about ⅓ inch long, short-oblong, bright red, containing from 1 to 3 large bony nutlets; ripen about October.

Winter. *Bark* brown to gray, often exfoliating on large individuals, exposing a brown or orange inner bark.

The parsley hawthorn, or parsley haw, is a good example of the *Microcarpae* group of hawthorns. It is one of the most handsome of our native species, and makes a very beautiful specimen tree under cultivation. It is also one of the easiest hawthorns to identify, for its foliage is quite unique. It may be found growing along streams and about the borders of swamps in the coastal plain, but farther inland it also occurs on the slopes of the hills. In many areas of the South, this species represents the earliest-flowering member of the genus.

The range of this species extends from Virginia, Missouri, and Oklahoma southward to Florida and Texas.

The Service-berries—Amelanchier

The service-berries, also called sarvice-berries, Juneberries, or shadbushes, are shrubs or small trees with deciduous, alternate, simple leaves, which in our tree species have finely and sharply toothed margins. The twigs are slender, slightly zigzag, and have a somewhat 5-angled, continuous, pale pith. The buds are narrowly conical, often slightly twisted, and have about a half dozen greenish or reddish-tinged scales. A terminal bud is present but not much larger than the lateral ones. The buds of service-berries have hairs scattered along the scale edges, which differ from glabrous scale edges of beech species. The leaf scars are narrowly crescent-shaped and show 3 bundle scars. The bark of the trunks is usually smooth and gray, with characteristic darker longitudinal streaks. The flowers, which appear with the leaves in the spring, are borne in showy drooping clusters. They are perfect and have 5 narrow white petals. The fruits are globular, edible, mostly juicy but occasionally dry and tasteless berrylike pomes. Winter characters of our tree species are not distinctive enough to permit certain identification.

The fact that the major lateral leaf veins run parallel, and indeed appear to be appressed to the midvein for a short distance and then quickly curve outward toward the leaf margin (use lens), helps to separate this genus from *Prunus*. Vegetatively, the two genera can also be separated by the conspicuous black vertical striping of the lower bark present in the former, but lacking in the latter.

DOWNY SERVICE-BERRY   *Amelanchier arborea* **(Michx. f.) Fern.**

> The smooth and light gray bark, which has longitudinal dark stripes, large, conical, beechlike buds, and white flowers that appear before the leaves are quite distinctive.

Summer. *Leaves* 2 to 4 inches long, from 1 to 2 inches wide, apically clustered, alternate, simple, deciduous, broadly ovate or somewhat obovate, tips short-pointed, bases rounded or heart-shaped, margins rather finely and sharply serrate; upper surfaces bright green, glabrous at maturity; paler beneath, glabrous or with a few silky hairs; petioles about 1 inch long, slender, usually retaining some silky hairs. *Flowers* 1 to 1¼ inches wide, perfect, erect, in racemose clusters, appearing before the leaves; petals 5, white, linear, strap-shaped, clawed at base. *Fruits* (pome) ¼ to ⅓

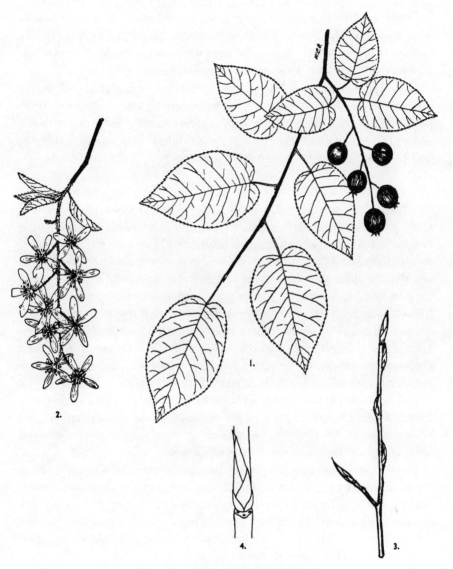

DOWNY SERVICE-BERRY

1. Branch with mature leaves and fruits.
2. Flowering branch.
3. Winter twig.
4. Details of bud and leaf scar.

inch long, small, berrylike; ripening in early summer, at first red, but becoming dark purplish and glaucous when fully ripe, dry and tasteless.

Winter. *Twigs* slender, slightly zigzag, glabrous, reddish brown or olive green, more or less glaucous; leaf scars alternate, very narrowly crescent-shaped, with 3 bundle scars; pith continuous, slightly stellate. *Buds* ¼ to ½ inch long, long-conical; terminal bud ¾ inch long.

Comparisons. The buds of this species are somewhat suggestive of those of the American beech, being narrower and perhaps sharply pointed, but smaller; often curved, scarcely divergent. Bud scales are olive green to reddish brown rather than light brown to tan; glabrous; and considerably fewer than in American beech.

———

The downy service-berry is also known as the Juneberry, the shad-bush, or the servicetree. It is a small tree, commonly only 15 to 25 feet in height, but occasionally attaining a height of 40 feet with a trunk 1 to 1½ feet in diameter. Although most commonly associated with the borders of woodlands, streambanks, and the fencerows in open country, the downy service-berry is commonly scattered through our forests, particularly on hillsides and on the mountain slopes. Its common name of shadbush was given to the tree by early settlers who associated its blooming with the runs of shad, which formerly occurred in many of our eastern creeks and rivers. Additionally, the common name, service-berry, comes from early settler doctors who offered their services to expectant mothers, many of whom delivered in the spring, which coincided with the tree's flowering. (Sarvice-berry is a corruption of the common name.) This event is most conspicuous in April, when the downy service-berry becomes covered with drooping clusters of snowy-white flowers.

The wood is heavy, hard, and strong, but it tends to warp and check badly during drying. It is occasionally used for tool handles and for small turned articles. The fruits are somewhat dry and insipid, but are rapidly devoured by a host of wild birds, including the ruffed grouse. They are also eagerly sought by such mammals as the black bear, the white-tailed deer, the raccoon, the opossum, and the fox.

The downy service-berry ranges from Maine to Iowa and Nebraska, south to northern Florida, Louisiana, and Texas.

This species is similar to the more shrubby Canadian service-berry (*A. canadensis* (L.) Medik.), but differs from that species by its mature leaves being hairy rather than glabrous beneath, with more acute rather than acuminate apices, and with more upright rather than drooping or spreading racemes.

ALLEGHENY SERVICE-BERRY   *Amelanchier laevis* Wieg.

This is a large shrub or small tree very similar to the preceding species. It may be distinguished from the downy service-berry by its leaves, which are essentially glabrous at all stages.

Leaves at flowering time, about half-grown, with distinct reddish or purplish-bronze cast; mature leaves 1½ to about 2½ inches long, 1 to 1½ inches wide, ovate or obovate, tips short-pointed, bases rounded to somewhat heart-shaped, margins rather finely and sharply toothed; dark green above, paler and often slightly whitened beneath; entirely glabrous on both surfaces. *Flowers* in drooping clusters. *Fruits* somewhat larger than those of the preceding species, dark purplish black, often glaucous, sweet, juicy.

Comparisons. The glabrous, rather than hairy, leaves (only slightly hairy in bud), which are nearly half developed at anthesis, and the showier, larger flowers that give rise to more juicy fruits, with large pedicels (1 to 2 inches versus ⅜ to ½ inch long), help to separate this species from the downy serviceberry.

The Allegheny service-berry, or smooth service-berry, is small but quite showy in the early spring, when its clusters of snow-white flowers are produced in great abundance. Southward, the fruits ripen about June, although it may be August before they ripen in the northern part of its range. They are sweet and juicy, of a much better quality than those of the downy service-berry, and well known to most country folk. It is said that they were among the preferred wild fruits of many of the Native American tribes. Wild birds, including the ruffed grouse, are very fond of them. They are also eagerly sought by the black bear, the white-tailed deer, the raccoon, the opossum, the red fox, and the gray fox.

The range of the Allegheny service-berry extends from Newfoundland west to southern Quebec, Ontario, and Minnesota and southward to Maine, Delaware, Ohio, Indiana, and Missouri. In the mountains it extends as far south as northern Georgia and Alabama.

The expression known as var. *nitida* (Wieg.) Fern. occurs in Newfoundland and Nova Scotia. It is thought to be distinguishable by its leaves, which are lustrous above and have coarser marginal teeth drawn out into more prolonged points. These differences, however, are too variable to be recognized.

SAPOTE FAMILY—SAPOTACEAE

The Bullies—Sideroxylon

The bullies are shrubs or small trees with alternate, simple, evergreen or deciduous leaves, commonly clustered on short lateral spurs. The twigs are usually armed with short, straight or curved thorns, which themselves often bear leaves. When cut or broken, the twigs exude a milky sap. The flowers are minute, whitish, perfect, and are borne in more or less dense axillary clusters. The fruits are roundish to oblong black drupes that contain a large stone. Although most bullies produce an exceedingly hard wood, they are so small that they have no commercial value as timber trees.

BUCKTHORN BULLY   *Sideroxylon lycioides* L.

> The milky sap of freshly cut twigs, spiny branches, white flowers, and fetid odor of the peeled bark are distinctive.

Summer. *Leaves* 2 to 6 inches long, ½ to 1¼ inches wide, alternate, simple, deciduous or persisting; elliptical to narrowly obovate, widest above the middle, shiny above, paler below, glabrous or nearly so on both surfaces at maturity; tips more or less pointed, bases wedge-shaped, often clustered on sides of twigs; margins entire. *Flowers* ⅛ inch wide, small, bell-shaped, in clusters; petals 5-lobed, white; calyx covered with rust-colored hairs. *Fruits* ½ inch long, elliptic to ovoid or obovoid.

Winter. *Twigs* flexible, reddish brown, slender, usually with sharply pointed thorns up to ¾ inch in length; spur branches present; sap slightly milky. *Buds* ¹⁄₁₆ to ⅛ inch long, globose. *Bark* reddish gray, thin, scaly or smooth.

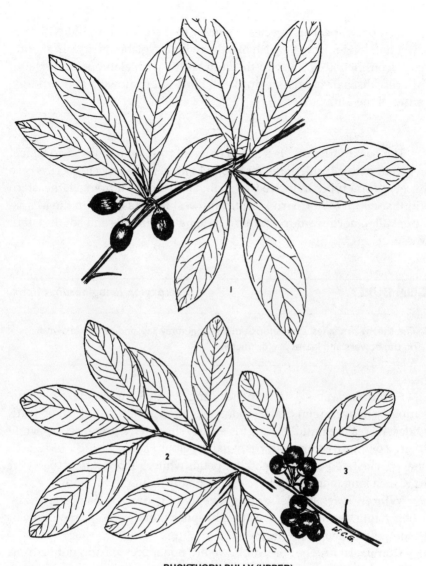

BUCKTHORN BULLY (UPPER)

1. Branch with mature leaves and fruits.

GUM BULLY (LOWER)

2. Branch with mature leaves.   3. Portion of fruiting branch.

Comparisons. This species is similar to the gum bully, but with narrower and longer leaves, which like the twigs are glabrous or only slightly hairy (conspicuously hairy in the gum bully), with glabrous flowers and inflorescenses or nearly so, unlike the pubescent flowers and inflorescenses of the gum bully.

The buckthorn bully is a shrub or small tree, sometimes 25 to 50 feet in height with a trunk diameter of 6 to 12 inches. This species occurs on a variety of soil types in the coastal plain and Piedmont from southeastern Virginia, south to northern Florida and west to Texas; and, in the Mississippi Valley, northward to southern Indiana and Illinois and southeastern Missouri.

GUM BULLY   *Sideroxylon lanuginosum* **Michx.**

> The thorny branches, spur shoots, milky or gummy sap, and tan or brown hairs on the flowers and leaves are distinctive.

Summer. *Leaves* 1 to 3 inches long, ³⁄₈ to 1 inch wide, alternate, simple, semievergreen or deciduous, clustered at tips; elliptic to obovate, widest above the middle, margins entire; shiny dark green above, white to gray or, more commonly, rusty-hairy below. *Flowers* ⅛ inch wide, bell-shaped, clustered on slender stalks; petals white, 5-lobed. *Fruits* (berry) ³⁄₈ to ½ inch long, purple black; 1-seeded, maturing in the autumn.

Winter. *Twigs* slender, zigzag, deeply gray or rusty-hairy, especially when young, terminating in a straight spike; bundle scars 3; sap milky or gummy. *Buds* small, ball-like, woolly.

Comparisons. The spreading, woolly, nonappressed and nonlustrous hairs on the undersurfaces of the leaves of the gum bully help to separate it from the tough bully, which has tightly appressed and shiny hairs that tend to lie parallel to the lateral veins on its leaf undersurfaces, rather than in various directions.

The gum bully is also known as the gum elastic, the gum bumelia, the woolly buckthorn, and the chittamwood. It is a shrub or small tree, sometimes 40 feet in height, with a narrowly oblong crown. It can be distinguished from the other bullies by the densely woolly lower leaf surfaces. The wool is usually a reddish brown but varies to silvery white in the subspecies *albicans* (Sarg.) Kartesz & Gandhi.

The gum bully occurs both in moist lowlands and on the drier, rocky or sandy soils of uplands. Its range extends through the coastal plain from South Carolina, southern Georgia, and northern Florida west to Texas; and northward, in the Mississippi Valley, to southern Illinois, central Missouri, and Kansas.

TOUGH BULLY   *Sideroxylon tenax* L.

The thorny branches, milky latex from the leaf petioles, and dense, closely appressed, shiny hairs that lie parallel to the lateral veins on the undersurfaces of the leaves help to identify this species.

Leaves ¾ to 2½ inches long, up to 1¼ inches wide, evergreen to semievergreen, clustered on short twigs, obovate, elliptic to oblanceolate, clearly widest above the middle, margins entire, tips round or blunt pointed, bases cuneate; upper surfaces dark, lustrous, and glabrous at maturity, lower surfaces, with tightly appressed, shiny, conspicuously densely tomentose hairs that lie parallel to the lateral veins. *Flowers* ⅛ inch wide, bell-shaped; petals 5-lobed; calyx covered silky-hairy. *Fruits* (berry) ⅜ to ½ inch long, round to elliptic, 1-seeded.

Comparisons. This species is similar to the gum bully, but has smaller and more persistent, evergreen to semievergreen leaves with lustrous yellow or golden silky, appressed hairs that lie parallel to the lateral veins, rather than nonlustrous, rusty-brown, tan, or whitish hairs that tend to lie in various directions toward the lateral veins.

This species is also known as the tough buckthorn, tough bumelia, or the ironwood. It is a small tree found only on the drier sands near the coast from southeastern South Carolina to southern Florida. It is readily distinguished from the other true bullies by the combination of small, narrowly obovate to oblanceolate lustrous leaves, which are ¾ to 2½ inches long, pointed at the base, rounded or notched at the tip, and coated beneath with coppery or golden-brown silky, shiny, appressed hairs. The tough bully has brown-gray bark with firm ridges. Both the common and scientific names allude to the flexible but exceedingly tough branches, which are usually armed with thorns.

EBONY FAMILY—EBENACEAE

The Persimmon—Diospyros

COMMON PERSIMMON   *Diospyros virginiana* **L.**

A very nondescript, alternate-leaved species that can be identified by its black leaf spots, which commonly form on the undersurfaces of its entire margined leaves, by its thick, usually hairy petioles, by its nearly black, alligator hide bark, by its small black buds, and by its unusually shaped fruits.

Summer. *Leaves* 4 to 6 inches long, 1½ to 3 inches wide, alternate, simple, deciduous, thick and firm; ovate or oblong ovate to elliptic, tips rather acuminate-pointed, bases rounded, margins wavy but entire; upper surfaces dark green, lustrous, lower surfaces paler, often whitish, hairy, nearly always black-spotted; petioles ½ to 1 inch long, rather slender, usually hairy. *Flowers* bell-shaped, male and female flowers developing on separate trees; petals 4-lobed; male flowers about ½ to ¾ inch long, tubular, cream to white to greenish; female flowers ¾ inch long, wider than the male flowers. *Fruits* (berry) about 1 to 1½ inches in diameter, almost round, glaucous, tipped with a short persistent style, with a 4-lobed persistent calyx at its base; ripening about October; orange and often tinged with purplish when ripe; juicy, sweet, edible; unripened fruits very astringent; often conspicuous on the tree during autumn and winter after leaves have fallen.

Winter. *Twigs* moderately slender, zigzag, grayish to reddish brown, with conspicuous, scattered orange lenticels; may be either glabrous or slightly hairy; pith large, greenish to white, often chambered with lacelike partitions; leaf scars alternate, broadly crescent-shaped to semiround, with a solitary bundle scar, stipule scar lacking. *Buds* broadly ovoid,

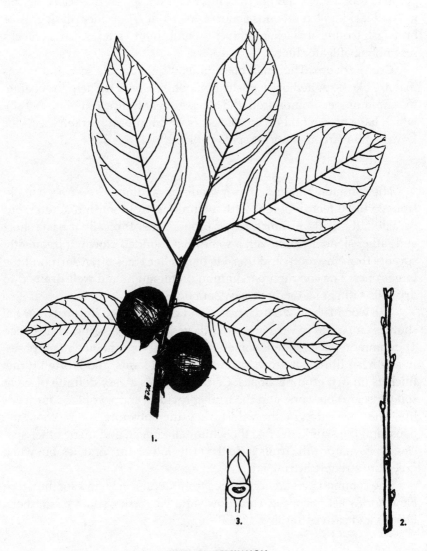

COMMON PERSIMMON

1. Branch with mature leaves and fruit.   3. Detail of bud and leaf scar.
2. Winter twig.

pointed, dark brown and lustrous, more or less appressed, 2-scaled; terminal bud lacking; lateral buds about ⅛ inch long. *Bark* thick, dark gray or brownish to almost black, prominently broken into scaly, squarish blocks resembling alligator hide.

Comparisons. The small black buds, single bundle scar, and leaves that are black-spotted or blemished but whitish beneath help to separate the common persimmon from the black gum and tupelos (genus *Nyssa*), which have brown buds, 3 bundle scars, and uniformly green leaves, or leaves with maroon or purple spots or blemishes.

The common persimmon is a small- or medium-sized tree, usually from 25 to 50 feet in height with a trunk up to 1 foot in diameter, but occasionally it attains much larger proportions. Typically it has a short and rather slender trunk with a somewhat rounded crown. It frequently sprouts from the roots, and thickets of smaller trees often surround the larger ones. The common persimmon prefers light and well-drained to dry soils, either of a sandy or clay-loam type.

The wood is heavy, hard, strong, and close-grained. It is used for the shuttles employed in weaving, billiard cues, mallets, flooring, and veneer. The common persimmon is sometimes planted for ornamental purposes. In southern Illinois it grows on coal-stripped lands, and it often forms thickets on dry, eroding slopes. Certainly it has a very definite place in soil conservation work, and the fruits provide a supply of food for wildlife. They are eaten by the wild turkey, the bobwhite, the raccoon, the opossum, the skunk, the fox, the white-tailed deer, and many other species. Once mature, the fruits have the taste and texture of dates, but when green are strongly astringent.

The common persimmon ranges from Connecticut and southeastern New York west to southeastern Iowa and Nebraska, south to southern Florida and eastern Texas.

SNOWBELL FAMILY—STYRACACEAE

The Silverbells—Halesia

These are small trees or shrubs with alternate, deciduous, simple leaves, most of which are covered with stellate hairs and have toothed margins. The flowers are large, white, bell-shaped, drooping in umbel-like lateral clusters or short racemes, appearing with or before the leaves. Each flower has 8 to 16 stamens and an inferior ovary. The corolla comprises 4 to 5 petals separate to the base or nearly so, and the fruits are dry, oblong, and indehiscent, with 2 to 4 longitudinal wings. Like the service-berries, the bark of the trunk and the branches are often striped, but once cut, the small branches and the twigs reveal a distinct chambered pith, which is lacking in the service-berries.

MOUNTAIN SILVERBELL   *Halesia tetraptera* Ellis

The vertically striated bark, showy, drooping, white, bell-shaped flowers, and chambered pith are distinctive.

Summer. *Leaves* 3 to 6 inches long, 1½ to 3 inches wide, simple, deciduous, ovate or elliptical to oblong, tips sharply long-pointed, bases pointed, margins very finely but sharply serrately toothed, upper surfaces dark yellowish green, lower surfaces paler and more or less hairy with stellate hairs; petioles ¼ to ½ inch long. *Flowers* ½ to 1 inch long, white or rarely pinkish, bell-shaped, borne on long stalks, in clusters of 2 to 5, developing in the spring; petals 4, lobes short, extending less than the length of the tube. *Fruits* (pod) 1¼ to 2 inches long, elliptical, dry, with 4 broad wings.

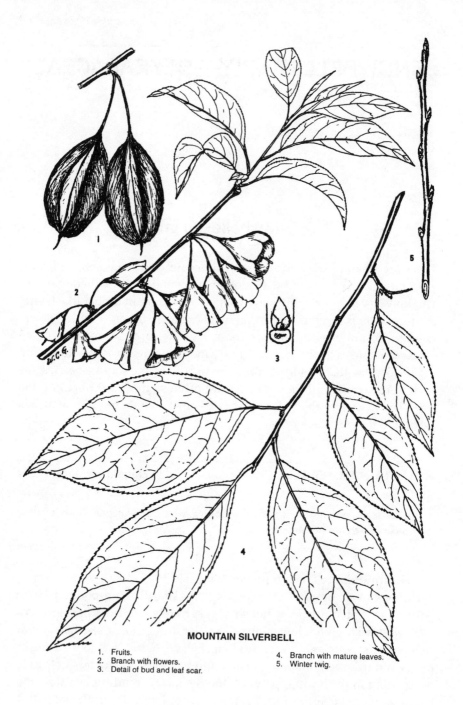

MOUNTAIN SILVERBELL

1. Fruits.
2. Branch with flowers.
3. Detail of bud and leaf scar.
4. Branch with mature leaves.
5. Winter twig.

Winter. *Fruits* persistent, very useful in winter identification. *Twigs* slender, orange brown to reddish brown, glabrous or with stellate hairs; pith white, chambered; leaf scars crescent-shaped, with a solitary bundle scar. *Buds* about ⅛ inch long, superposed, ovoid, pointed, with about 4 reddish scales; terminal bud present or appearing so; lateral buds of various sizes, scales 2 to 4. *Bark* on young branches reddish brown with white streaks; on older trunks becoming broken into thin, flat scales.

———

The mountain silverbell, or opossum-wood, is a medium- to small-sized tree or shrub rarely attaining a height of 35 feet and a trunk diameter of about a foot. Commonly the trunk divides near the ground into several spreading branches, forming a broad, rounded crown. It generally occurs as an understory tree on the slopes of the mountains, particularly along streams, and may descend into the upper portion of the Piedmont. In late April or early May the branches of this little tree become bedecked with drooping bell-shaped flowers up to an inch in length, snow white or flushed with pink. It has considerable merit as an ornamental tree, because of its showy white flowers and yellow autumn foliage.

The range of the mountain silverbell extends from New York and Michigan to Texas and Oklahoma, eastward to Georgia and the Carolinas.

The var. *monticola* (Rehd.) Reveal & Seldin, is said to occur at higher elevations in the mountains of North Carolina, Kentucky, Tennessee, and Georgia. It is supposed to be a larger tree with larger leaves, flowers, and fruits than the mountain silverbell.

Another species, the Carolina silverbell (*Halesia carolina* L.) is a shrub or small tree growing in dry soils of the coastal plain from South Carolina, southern Georgia, and northern Florida westward to eastern Mississippi. Its twigs, leaf stalks, and lower leaf surfaces are hairy. The flowers are small, not over ½ inch long, and the fruits are club-shaped and have narrow wings.

TWO-WING SILVERBELL　　　　　　　　　*Halesia diptera* Ellis

Summer. *Leaves* 2½ to 4½ inches long, 1½ to 2½ inches wide, broadly obovate to nearly round, long-pointed, margins finely serrately toothed; upper surfaces light green, nearly glabrous, lower surfaces paler, stellate-hairy; petioles ¼ to ½ inch long. *Flowers* ⅝ to 1¼ inches long, bell-shaped, borne in clusters of 3 to 6, developing in the spring; petals white, somewhat hairy, 4-lobed, elongated beyond the size of the tube. *Fruits* 1½ to 2 inches long, oblong, dry, dark brown, with 2 broad wings, persisting in the winter.

Winter. *Twigs* light green, slender, hairy when young. *Buds,* terminal bud lacking; lateral buds all similar in size; scales 3 to 4.

Comparisons. The fruits, which persist in the winter, are useful in separating this species from the other silverbells.

———

The two-wing silverbell is a shrub or small tree of floodplain swamps. It ranges from South Carolina to Florida, west to Texas and Arkansas. It is a species of wet soil and bottomlands.

SWEETLEAF FAMILY— SYMPLOCACEAE

The Sweetleaf—Symplocos

COMMON SWEETLEAF   *Symplocos tinctoria* (L.) L'Hér.

> This southern tree species, with its yellow leaf midribs and conspicuous, showy yellow flowers that appear before the leaves (at least in higher elevations), is so striking in the springtime as not to be confused with any other southern tree. The flowers, along with the chambered pith and sweet taste of the leaves (especially the midvein), are most distinctive.

Summer. *Leaves* 2 to 6 inches long, 1 to 2 inches wide, alternate, simple, deciduous or semievergreen, thickish and somewhat leathery, terminally clustered; oblong, obovate to narrowly elliptic, pointed at both ends, margins entire below the middle or obscurely, serrately toothed; dark yellowish green, glabrous and somewhat lustrous above, paler and glabrous or somewhat hairy beneath, with yellow midribs; petioles about ¼ inch long, stout, yellow. *Flowers* ⅜ to ½ inch long, small, nearly sessile, perfect, somewhat fragrant, yellow to creamy white, borne in axillary clusters in early spring. *Fruits* (drupe) ⅓ to ½ inch long, orange brown, ovoid, dry, hairy, with 5 apical teeth.

Winter. *Leaves* tardily deciduous in the South. *Twigs* somewhat thickened or stout, light green to grayish or reddish brown, glabrous or somewhat hairy; pith chambered; leaf scars alternate, half-round, with a single bundle scar. *Buds,* terminal leaf bud ¼ inch long, broadly ovoid, somewhat pointed, angular; scales 4, brown to greenish, usually glabrous, but with hairy margins, with two opposite scales overlapping the third; lateral buds stand out from the twigs. *Bark* grayish, smooth or often with small warty excrescences and shallow fissures.

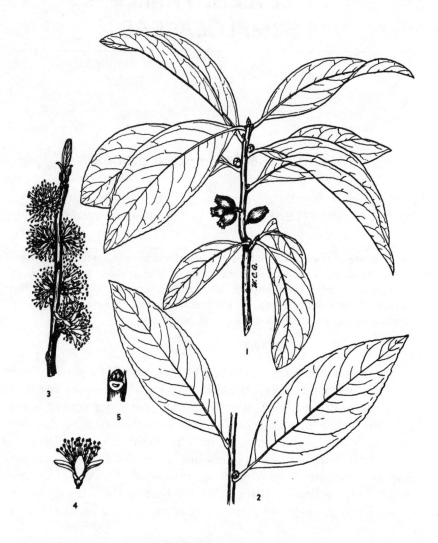

COMMON SWEETLEAF

1. Branch with leaves and fruits.
2. Portion of branch with leaves.
3. Twig with flowers.
4. Detail of flower.
5. Winter bud and leaf scar.

Comparisons. The common sweetleaf might be confused with the silverbells, but differs by having a yellow rather than green leaf midrib and brown to greenish rather than reddish buds, and by lacking the vertically striped bark on the trunk that is common in the silverbells. It might also be confused with the common persimmon, but that species has blemished or spotted leaves and darker buds with only 2 rather than 4 scales.

The sweetleaf, the horse-sugar, or the yellow-wood is a large shrub or a small tree sometimes 25 feet in height with a trunk diameter of about 6 inches. It is most conspicuous in early spring, when the clusters of creamy-white flowers open up along its branchlets. The sweetish taste of the leaves, especially the midrib, coupled with the fact that the leaves are eaten with great relish by horses and cattle, suggests the tree's common names. The common name yellow-wood is derived from the use of the leaves and bark in making a yellow dye in pioneer days. The tubular, glaucous drupe fruit develops in the autumn. The sweetleaf grows in rich, moist soils from the coast to altitudes of over 3,000 feet in the mountains.

The range of the sweetleaf extends from Delaware to northern Florida west to eastern Texas, and north to southeastern Oklahoma, southern Arkansas, southeastern Tennessee, and North Carolina.

PEA FAMILY—FABACEAE

The Silktree—Albizia

SILKTREE *Albizia julibrissin* **Durazz.**

The sensitivity of the very fernlike, bipinnately compound leaves, which close upon handling, the pink, very fragrant, pincushion-like flowers, and long, podlike fruits are distinctive. Even in winter, this species can be easily identified at a distance by its exceptionally broad, umbrella-like crown and erect branches.

Summer. *Leaves* 6 to 15 inches long, alternate, deciduous, twice compound; each of the 10 to 24 divisions with 30 to 60 leaflets; leaflets small, oblong, pointed, 1-sided. *Flowers* 1 to 2 inches in diameter, tawny pink to bright pink, crowded into ball-like clusters, with numerous pink stamens. *Fruits* (legume) 4 to 8 inches long, brown to yellowish brown, flattened, much wrinkled between the flat and ovate beanlike seeds.

Winter. *Twigs* glabrous, moderately stout to stout, zigzag and somewhat angled, greenish brown, dotted with numerous conspicuous pale lenticels; leaf scars alternate, somewhat 3-lobed, showing 3 bundle scars. *Buds* small, roundish, occasionally superposed, partially embedded, with about 3 exposed scales, no terminal bud. *Bark* smooth, light brown, on the younger trunks marked with conspicuous lenticels, becoming a darker brownish to nearly black on older ones.

The silktree (not to be confused with the white mulberry that feeds the silkworms), or mimosa-tree (not to be confused with the true *Mimosa* genus of the Fabaceae family) as it is commonly called in the South, is a fast-growing, short-lived, umbrella-shaped tree that attains a height of 10

SILKTREE

1. Branch with leaves and flowers.
2. Detail of leaflets.
3. Fruit.
4. Seed.
5. Winter twig.

to 40 feet but is usually much smaller. A native of Asia, it has been exten-sively planted as an ornamental tree in the warmer parts of this country, where it was introduced in 1785 by André Michaux.

The Mesquite—Prosopis

HONEY MESQUITE   *Prosopis glandulosa* **Torr.**

> The unusual bipinnately compound leaves with 2 pinnae, along with the thorny branches, bright red elongated fruits, and multiple crooked trunks are most distinctive.

Summer. *Leaves* alternate, bipinnately compound with 2 or occasion-ally 4 pinnae, which are 2½ to 6⅓ inches long; deciduous, clustered at branch tips, sessile, yellow green, glabrous; leaflets ⅞ to 1½ inches long, ¹⁄₁₆ to ⅛ inch wide, 12 to 40 per leaf; margins entire, apices acute, mucro-nate, terminal pair curved inward; petioles long, slender. *Flowers* ⅛ to ¼ inch long, borne in axillary spikes 2⅞ to 3⅔ inches long, yellow green, tinged reddish, very fragrant, perfect, sessile; petals ¹⁄₁₆ to ⅛ inch long, 5, quite small; stamens 10. *Fruits* (legume) 2⅞ to 8 inches long, ⅜ inch wide, 1 to 3 per cluster, yellowish, elongated, indehiscent, with obvious con-strictions between the 2 to 10 seeded fruit.

Winter. *Twigs* thin, zigzag, rigid, glabrous, red brown to gray brown, armed with straight, hairy spines to 2 inches long at the swollen nodes; leaf scars oval, very small, hidden by petiole base; pith white, continuous. *Buds* ⅛ to ³⁄₁₆ inch long, small, ovoid, globular; bud scales brown with elongated tips. *Bark* dark gray brown, thin, rough, furrowed with short ridges.

The honey mesquite is a very invasive small tree or shrub, 10 to 35 feet high with a rounded crown and multiple crooked trunks. It has been introduced into the Southeast, but occurs naturally from Texas to Kansas to Colorado, where it grows in dry plains, sandy valleys, and uplands. Although the wood is of little importance, the ribbed legumes are used as a livestock and a wildlife food and the fragrant flowers are an important

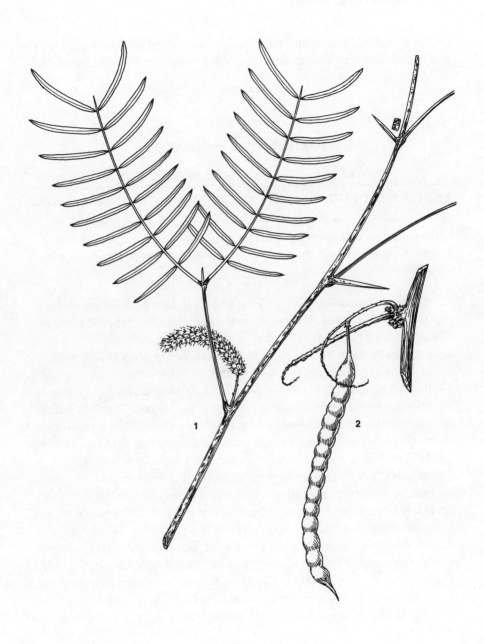

HONEY MESQUITE

1. Branch with bipinnate (having two pinnae) leaves and flower.

2. Fruit.

source of honey. Native Americans in the Southwest use the legumes by grinding them into a meal and preparing them into various foods and drinks.

The Redbud—Cercis

EASTERN REDBUD   *Cercis canadensis* L.

> The broadly rounded, deeply cordate leaves with entire margins and 5 to 7 palmate veins, along with the purple to pink spring flowers, are most distinctive.

Summer. *Leaves* 3 to 5 inches long and wide, alternate, simple, deciduous, 2-ranked, conspicuously heart-shaped, rather abruptly pointed, slightly thickish, palmately veined, glabrous or nearly so; dark green above, paler beneath, margins entire, undulate and slightly rolled; petioles 2 to 4 inches long, slender, round, glabrous, with a very characteristic swelling just below the blade of the leaf and another swelling at its attachment on the twig. *Flowers* about ½ inch long, perfect, deep pink to purple, in 4- to 8-flowered umbellate clusters, developing before the leaves. *Fruits* (legume) 2 to 4 inches long, ½ inch wide, thin, flattened, light rose to light brown, containing about a half dozen flattened, light brown seeds.

Winter. *Twigs* slender, zigzag, light to dark brown, lustrous, with numerous, minute, pale lenticels; pith often streaked with red; leaf scars inversely triangular, fringed on their upper margin, decurrently ridged from the corners, with 3 conspicuous bundle scars; stipule scar lacking. *Buds* ⅛ inch or less long, dark red, ovoid, blunt, somewhat flattened, appressed; scales 2 or 3, visible, dark purplish red, may be slightly hairy along the edges; terminal bud lacking; lateral buds often superposed, with flowering buds above the leaf buds. *Bark* reddish brown to blackish, thin, shallowly fissured, with somewhat scaly ridges.

The eastern redbud, or Judas tree, so named because its flowers "blushed pink for shame" (a similar Asian species—supposedly the tree species selected by Judas to hang himself—has flowers that were thought to be white prior to that horrific event!), is a small tree from 15 to 30 feet in height, with a short trunk and upright or spreading branches that form

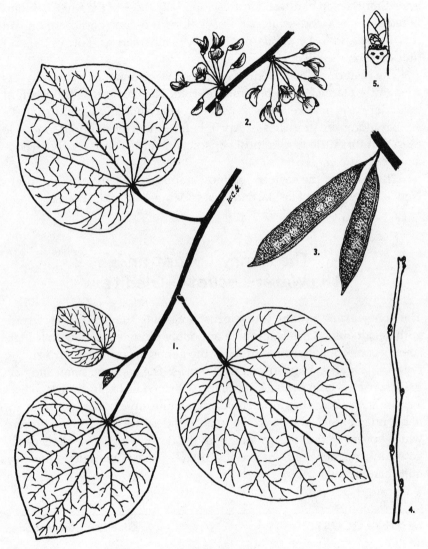

EASTERN REDBUD

1. Branch with mature leaves.
2. Flowering branch.
3. Fruits.
4. Winter twig.
5. Details of bud and leaf scar.

a low, broad, and rather irregular crown. It is principally found as an understory tree in hardwood forests, especially those of the white oak, and of red oak–basswood–white ash associations. It occurs most commonly in rich, moist, and rocky woods, particularly where there are outcroppings of limestone on the hillsides.

The eastern redbud produces no wood of commercial value, but it is frequently planted as an ornamental tree. The clusters of 4 to 8 bright lavender-rose, pealike flowers, which are occasionally eaten in salads, appear along the branches in April, before the leaves unfold, and it is then that this little tree is most conspicuous either in its native woodlands or in the garden.

The range of the eastern redbud extends from southern Ontario to New Jersey, south to Florida, and west to Minnesota and Arkansas.

The Honey-Locust and the Water-Locust—Gleditsia

The honey-locust and the water-locust are small- to medium-sized trees with deciduous, alternate, pinnate or doubly pinnate leaves with leaflets conspicuously smaller than those of the genus *Robinia*, and with zigzag twigs, which are usually armed with thorns. The buds are small and partially sunken within the bark above the U-shaped leaf scars, which show 3 bundle scars. Branches and trunks are commonly studded with formidable, often branched thorns. The small, odorless, yellowish green flowers, which appear in the spring along with the developing leaves, may easily go unnoticed, but the flattened beanlike legumes that follow them are quite conspicuous.

HONEY-LOCUST   *Gleditsia triacanthos* **L.**

The double-pinnate, alternate leaves, huge branched thorns, and elongated, twisted fruits are most distinctive. The trunks and larger branches are usually thickly beset with stout branched spines, but a spineless expression occurs rather rarely.

Summer. *Leaves* 7 to 12 inches long, alternate, evenly or oddly pinnate or bipinnately compound on the same tree; deciduous; leaflets ½ to 1¼

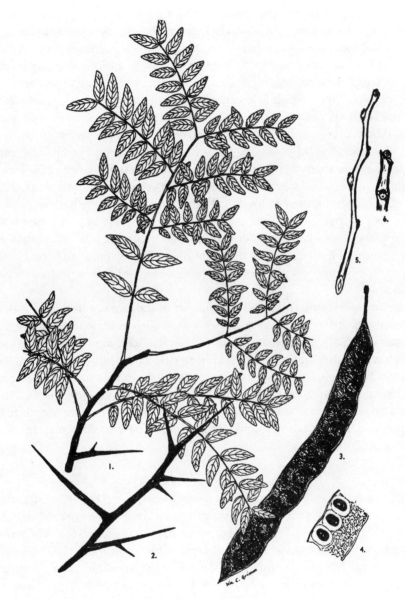

HONEY-LOCUST

1. Branch with mature leaves.
2. Branched thorn from trunk.
3. Fruit.

4. Section of fruit showing seeds.
5. Winter twig.
6. Detail of winter twig.

inches long, 18 or more in number, oblong lanceolate, tips rounded or blunt, bases rounded; glabrous, dark green above, paler beneath, margins with inconspicuous roundish teeth, usually sessile; petioles and rachises hairy. *Flowers* racemose, about ¼ to ⅜ inch wide, perfect and imperfect, appearing after the leaves, male and female flowers borne on separate branches or trees; petals 5, green white, finely hairy. *Fruits* (legume) 10 to 18 inches long, 1 to 1½ inches wide, thin, flattened, straplike, twisted, purplish brown, containing numerous flat, ovate, brownish seeds.

Winter. *Fruits* persistent. *Twigs* moderately stout, zigzag, glabrous, lustrous, greenish brown to reddish brown, usually with a few large, simple or branched thorns; leaf scars U-shaped, with 3 bundle scars. *Buds* indistinct, superposed in a vertical row, buried within the bark with only the tips exposed; terminal bud lacking. *Bark* grayish brown, often with conspicuous lenticels; on older trunks often becoming blackish with deep longitudinal fissures, ridges broad, scaly, with projecting and somewhat recurved edges; very characteristic large branched spines up to 8 inches long.

Comparisons. This species is similar to the more bottomland water-locust, but differs by having larger leaves with more leaflets and more commonly with multiple divisions (rather than commonly once pinnate); by having hairy petioles and leaflet midribs (use lens); and by having larger fruits with many seeds. The spines of the honey-locust differ from those of the water-locust by being larger (4 to 8 inches long versus 2 to 5 inches); simple to 3-branched to many branched versus simple to 1- to 2-branched; and by being round, rather than somewhat flattened, in basal cross section.

———

Honey-locust is also known as sweet locust, thorn tree, three-thorned acacia, or honey shucks. It is a medium- or large-sized tree attaining a height of 50 to over 100 feet, and a trunk diameter of 2 to 6 feet. The trunk is generally short, dividing into several slightly spreading limbs, which in turn subdivide into numerous somewhat horizontal branches, forming a broadly obovate or rounded crown. It can often be seen with numerous large branched spines emanating from the bole. A popular thornless horticultural expression, forma *inermis* (L.) Zab., can often be seen in gardens. A cultivar called Sunburst is an expression with bright yellowish foliage, which is also used extensively in horticulture. The honey-locust grows naturally in rich bottomlands or on slopes where the soils are mostly of limestone origin.

The wood is heavy, hard, strong, and durable in contact with the soil. It is used for posts, rails, railroad ties, hubs of wheels, furniture, and sometimes for general construction. The honey-locust is often planted as a shade or ornamental tree, and in the West, it has been extensively used in shelterbelt plantings. Several of the tree's common names have been derived from the fact that the thin pulp of the legumes has a very sweetish taste. Unlike the showy flowers of the black locust, those of the honey-locust are quite inconspicuous, small, and greenish in color. The stamens and pistils occur in different flowers and often on separate trees.

The original range of the honey-locust extended from Ontario to western Pennsylvania to southeastern Minnesota, south to northwestern Georgia and eastern Texas, but it has become naturalized over a more extensive area.

WATER-LOCUST   *Gleditsia aquatica* Marsh.

Summer. *Leaves* 5 to 10 inches long, alternate, deciduous, occasionally doubly pinnate but usually only once pinnate, commonly paired on lateral knobby spurs; leaflets ½ to 1 inch long by ¼ to ½ inch wide, sessile, numbering 12 to about 20, oblong ovate or elliptic, margin cuneate serrate, tips roundish; wider, duller, and more yellowish green above than those of the honey-locust; petioles and rachises usually glabrous. *Fruits* (legume) 1 to 3 inches long, about an inch wide, bright brown, flat, ovate, usually 1- to 3-seeded, long-stalked, occasionally solitary but more often in clusters.

Winter. *Twigs* orange brown to grayish brown, rather slender, more or less zigzag, often with a few simple, or occasionally branched, slender thorns. *Bark* dull dark gray to nearly black, separated by shallow fissures into vertical plates; thorns more slender, smaller (up to 4 to 5 inches long), and less frequently branched than those of the honey-locust.

Comparisons. The much shorter fruits with 1 or rarely 3 seeds (many seeds in the honey-locust) and glabrous leaves help to separate this species from the honey-locust.

The water-locust is usually a moderate-sized tree found in swamps and river bottoms that are subject to frequent flooding. At times, it may attain a height of 50 to 60 feet and have a trunk diameter of 1 to 2 feet. It has a rather wide, irregular, more-or-less flat-topped crown composed of stout, crooked, spreading branches, which often arise close to the ground.

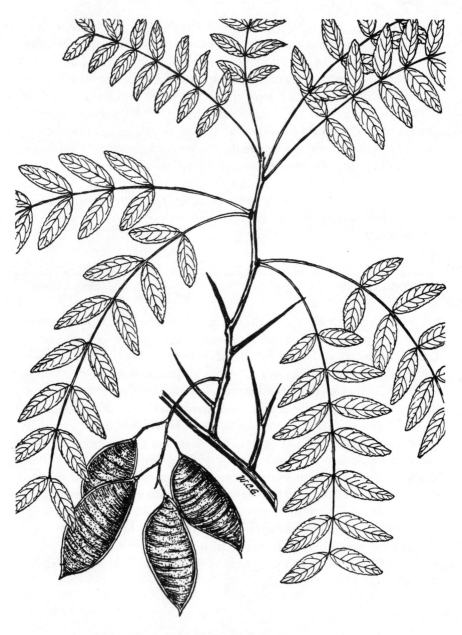

WATER-LOCUST

1. Branch with leaves and fruits.

Commonly the trunk is well armed with thorns. The tree is of practically no commercial value, but its wood is used locally for cabinetwork and interior finish.

The range of the water-locust extends through the coastal plain from South Carolina to central Florida and west to eastern Texas; northward, in the Mississippi Valley, to southern Illinois and southwestern Indiana.

The Coffeetree—Gymnocladus

KENTUCKY COFFEETREE   *Gymnocladus dioicus* **(L.) K. Koch**

> The thick, contorted, clubby, and often thorny branches, with orange pith and large leaf scars, along with the very large, twice compound, alternate leaves, and peculiar winter twigs that appear to lack buds are most distinctive.

Summer. *Leaves* 1 to 3 feet long, 2 feet wide, alternate, bipinnately or tripinnately compound; leaflets 2 to 2½ inches long, 1 to 1½ inches wide, often numbering 40 or more, ovate, broadest below the middle, apically pointed, bases rounded or broadly wedge-shaped, margins entire, individually short-stalked; blades thin but firm, dark green and glabrous above, paler and glabrous or nearly so beneath. *Flowers* perfect, male and female flowers borne on separate trees, appearing after the leaves, borne in long terminal racemes of 15 to 20 individuals; petals 5, obovate, ³⁄₁₆ inch long, green white. *Fruits* (legume) 4 to 10 inches long, 1 to 2 inches wide, thick, flattened, reddish brown, short-stalked, containing 6 or more large, flat, rounded, dark brown, poisonous seeds.

Winter. *Twigs* very stout and clumsy looking, somewhat crooked, glabrous or slightly hairy, greenish brown, often glaucous; lenticels rather large, conspicuous; pith large, salmon pink to orange; leaf scars large, broadly heart-shaped, with 3 to 5 conspicuous, raised bundle scars. *Buds* small, with scarcely visible hairs, black, often superposed, imbedded in and surrounded by an incurved hairy rim of the bark; terminal bud absent; lateral buds superposed, larger above the axillary buds. *Bark* dark grayish brown with shallow and irregular longitudinal fissures separating narrow, low, hard, recurved-scaly ridges, very similar to that of the mature black cherry.

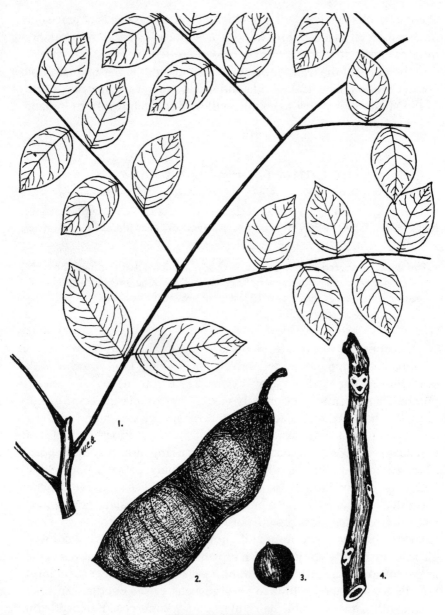

KENTUCKY COFFEETREE

1. Branch and portion of a compound leaf.
2. Fruit.
3. Seed.
4. Winter twig.

The Kentucky coffeetree is usually a medium-sized tree attaining a height of 40 to 75 feet and a trunk diameter of 1 to 2 feet. Its trunk commonly divides a few feet above the ground into 3 or 4 almost vertically ascending limbs, which form a narrowly obovate crown. The tree's generic name *Gymnocladus* means naked branch, alluding to the stout and clumsy-looking branches, which are devoid of foliage for almost half of the year, as well as the winter buds, which are nearly or completely buried within the bark. This is most peculiar in light of the fact that leaves of this tree are some of the largest of any of our forest species. The common name likely comes from the very dark coffeelike seeds found within the large fruits, rather than from the reputed fact that the very bitter fruits were used as coffee substitutes by the early pioneers. Rarely common anywhere within its range, and decidedly local in its occurrence, the Kentucky coffeetree grows in the bottomlands, where the soils are deep, moist, and fertile.

The wood is rather heavy but soft, strong, and coarse-grained. It is sometimes used in cabinetwork, for fence posts, and in construction. The Kentucky coffeetree is hardy as far north as New England, and it is rather extensively planted as an ornamental tree.

It ranges from central New York and Ontario to southern Minnesota, south to Tennessee and Oklahoma.

The Yellow-wood—Cladrastis

YELLOW-WOOD   *Cladrastis kentukea* (Dum.-Cours.) Rudd

The smooth, beechlike bark; naked buds; bright yellow wood; and alternate, compound leaves on petioles that enclose the leaf bud are distinctive.

Summer. *Leaves* 8 to 12 inches long, alternate, deciduous, odd pinnately compound; leaflets 3 to 4 inches long, 1 to 2 inches wide, 5 to 11, arranged subalternately along the rachis, elliptic to obovate, pointed at the ends, margins entire; dark yellowish green above, paler and glabrous beneath; petiole enclosing buds. *Flowers* 1 to 1¼ inches long, perfect, fragrant, arranged at branch tips, appearing rarely (once or twice per decade), after the leaves, on 12- to 14-inch-long terminal panicles; petals 5, white with pale yellow center. *Fruits* (legume) 2 to 4 inches long, short-stalked, flattened, beanlike, containing 2 to 6 dark brown seeds.

YELLOW-WOOD

1. Branch with leaves and fruits.
2. Side view of buds and leaf scar.
3. Portion of winter twig.

Winter. *Twigs* moderately stout, zigzag, brown to gray, glabrous; pith continuous, white; wood bright yellow; stipule scar lacking. *Buds,* terminal bud lacking; lateral buds naked, brown, woolly, superposed, hidden beneath a hollow petiole or surrounded by a U-shaped leaf scar containing 3 to 5 bundle scars. *Bark* dark gray or brownish, smooth, resembling that of the American beech.

———

The yellow-wood is one of our rarer and most beautiful native trees. It is reported to be rare in 7 of the 20 or so states where it occurs. It is singularly attractive and is often planted beyond its natural range as a shade or ornamental tree, often under the name of Virgilia. It becomes a tree of medium size, 30 to 50 feet in height with a trunk diameter of 1½ to 2½ feet, and a spreading round-topped crown. Where it occurs naturally, one can look for it in moist coves among the mountains, or on the slopes and cliffs bordering streams. Both its common and scientific names allude to the tree's bright yellow wood, which in former years, yielded a yellow dye. In May or June its drooping clusters of white, wisterialike flowers scent the surrounding air.

Yellow-wood occurs locally from Kentucky and western North Carolina to northern Georgia, west to southern Illinois, southwestern Missouri, central Arkansas, and northeastern Oklahoma.

The Necklacepod—Sophora

EVE'S NECKLACEPOD *Sophora affinis* Torr. & Gray

The odd pinnately compound leaves with entire-margined leaflets, necklacelike fruits, and pink, wisteria-like, finely hairy flowers are most distinctive.

Summer. *Leaves* 6 to 10 inches long, alternate, odd pinnately compound, deciduous; leaflets mostly 1 to 1½ inches long, ½ inch wide, 13 to 19, borne on a narrow, hairy rachis; terminal leaflets much longer than wide, margins entire, apices acute to mucronate, bases rounded, yellow green above, lighter and hairy below. *Flowers* ½ inch long, pink or occasionally yellow, finely hairy, perfect, borne in drooping, axillary racemes,

EVE'S NECKLACEPOD

1. Branch with leaves and fruits.

3 to 5 inches long, produced in April to June; stamens 10, 9 united and 1 free. *Fruits* (legume) ½ to 3 inches long, black, strongly constricted between the 1 to 8 globose, black seeds, appearing as individual beads on a string, similar to a necklace.

Winter. *Twigs* somewhat zigzag, slender to moderately thick, green at first, turning orange brown to dark brown, swollen at nodes; leaf scars alternate, somewhat elevated, nearly circular to shield-shaped, becoming U-shaped; bundle scars 3; stipule scars present but small; pith pale to greenish, continuous. *Buds* all lateral, woolly, covered with a netlike membrane, superposed, sessile. *Bark* thin, reddish brown, scaly, furrowed with age.

Eve's necklacepod is a small, moderately fast-growing tree or large shrub, 15 to 25 feet high and 5 to 10 inches in diameter. In the wild, it is an understory tree that forms small colonies or thickets on hillsides along streams, in ravines, and in moist areas on limestone soils. The wood is hard and dense, light red to reddish brown, and produces a yellow dye; the seeds contain a poisonous alkaloid. Because of its drought tolerance and showy flowers, it is used occasionally in horticulture, but occurs naturally from southern Oklahoma to Texas, extending eastward into Arkansas and Louisiana.

The Locust—Robinia

BLACK LOCUST   *Robinia pseudoacacia* L.

> The painfully sharp thorns, odd pinnately compound leaves, and exceptionally fragrant, white flowers are distinctive. The glabrous twigs usually have a pair of stout thorns (modified stipules) at the nodes that persists on the branches; however, a thornless expression (cv *inermis*) occurs rather uncommonly.

Summer. *Leaves* 8 to 14 inches long, alternate, deciduous, odd pinnate; leaflets 1 to 2 inches long, ½ to ¾ inch wide, 7 to 19 per leaf, ovate or oblong ovate, short-stalked, bases rounded, apices rounded with a small bristle-tip, margin entire; thin, dull, dark bluish green above, paler

BLACK LOCUST

1. Branch with mature leaves.
2. Cluster of flowers.
3. Fruits.
4. Winter twig.
5. Detail of leaf scar and imbedded buds.

beneath, glabrous or nearly so. *Flowers* ¾ to 1 inch long, fragrant, perfect, borne in 3- to 5-inch racemes; petals 5, cream white, with a yellow spot on the lower petal. *Fruits* (legume) 2 to 4 inches long, about ½ inch wide, thin, flattened, brown, persisting through winter, containing 3 to 15 small, flattened, brownish seeds, which are often mottled.

Winter. *Twigs* moderately stout, brittle, more or less zigzag, somewhat angular, glabrous or nearly so, greenish brown to light reddish brown; marked with scattered pale lenticels; usually with a pair of broad-based, somewhat triangular thorns at the nodes; leaf scars located between these thorns, rather variable in shape but commonly inversely triangular, somewhat 3-lobed, with 3 bundle scars. *Buds* inconspicuous, superposed, small, imbedded within the bark beneath the leaf scars, not visible until spring; terminal bud absent. *Bark* dark reddish brown to nearly black, soon becoming roughened with deep furrows and interlacing, rounded, and somewhat fibrous ridges.

Comparisons. The black locust can be told from all other members of the genus by its white flowers and glabrous twigs. It can be easily separated from the honey-locust and water-locust by its consistently single, rather than multiple, pinnate leaves and by its unbranched spines.

––––––––––

The black locust is also known as the acacia, the common locust, the yellow locust, or the white locust. It is generally a small- to medium-sized tree from 30 to 70 feet in height with a trunk diameter of from 1 to 2½ feet. The crown is irregularly oblong and rather open, composed of numerous, slender, scraggly branches. Sprouts from the roots often form thickets of smaller trees about the larger ones. The black locust makes its best growth in the deep, rich, moist soils of bottomlands, but it is often abundant on drier limestone soils, and at times not uncommon on rocky, sterile ridges. It, along with other members of the genus, has a peculiar characteristic of folding its leaflets at dark or prior to rainfall.

The wood is heavy, very hard and strong, and durable in contact with the soil. It is extensively used for erosion control, posts, railroad ties, mine props, insulator pins, and formerly, at least, was much in demand for shipbuilding. Although sometimes planted as a shade or ornamental tree, it is often subject to the attacks of the locust borer, which damage and weaken the trunks, and by the locust leaf miner, which causes the premature browning and death of the foliage. In May the drooping clusters of 1-inch-long, white, pealike, and very fragrant flowers are quite attractive. The inner bark of the black locust contains a poisonous compound, which is likely to be responsible for the severe pain induced by being pricked by the large thorns. Livestock have been fatally poisoned by eating the young shoots or browsing on the bark. The bark, however, is often eaten by cottontail rabbits during the winter months, and the seeds are sometimes eaten by birds, including the mourning dove and the bobwhite.

The black locust originally ranged from southern Pennsylvania south in the Appalachian Mountains to northern Georgia, and likely in the Ozark Mountains of Missouri and Arkansas. It is now naturalized over much of the United States.

OLEASTER FAMILY—ELAEAGNACEAE

The Russian-Olive—Elaeagnus

RUSSIAN-OLIVE   *Elaeagnus angustifolia* **L.**

> The silvery-scaly and brown-dotted twigs and lower leaves, thorny branches, and fragrant flowers are most distinctive.

Summer. *Leaves* 1½ to 3¼ inches long, ⅜ to ⅔ inches wide, alternate, simple, deciduous, ovate lanceolate to oblong lanceolate, widest at or above the middle, margins entire, often undulate, light green above, silvery scaly and brown dotted below, apices acute or obtuse, bases slightly narrowed, petioles ³⁄₁₆ to ⅓ inch long. *Flowers* apetalous, very fragrant, perfect or plants polygamous, borne singly or in clusters of 2 to 4 in leaf axils, produced in May to June; calyx about ⅜ inch long, ⅓ to ⅜ inch wide, 4-lobed, silvery without, yellow within; stamens 4. *Fruits* (drupe) ⅜ to ⅔ inch long, yellow brown, somewhat elliptic, silvery gray, scaly.

Winter. *Twigs* flexible, silvery scaly at first, becoming glabrous and green-brown, commonly terminating in a spine; leaf scars semicircular, tiny, somewhat elevated; bundle scars 1; pith salmon colored, continuous. *Buds* small, round to conical, gray brown, silvery scaly; bud scales 2 to 4. *Bark* gray brown, thin, shed in vertical strips.

Comparisons. The 2 to 4 bud scales and silvery-scaly twigs immediately separate the Russian-olive from the members of the willow genus, *Salix*, which lack such scales and have but a single bud scale.

The Russian-olive is a small tree or shrub, 17 to 55 feet high, often with thorny, twisted, and contorted branches. A European introduction

RUSSIAN-OLIVE

1. Branch with leaves and flowers.

that is hardy in our northern states, it is now thoroughly naturalized from central Canada to Texas and from coast to coast. It is often planted as a windbreak; for its fruits, which are valuable to wildlife; and for the horticultural value of its silvery-scaly vegetation and fragrant flowers. It is tolerant of salt and poor soils, exceptionally resistant to drought, and thrives in the Piedmont of the Southeast. Although it grows quickly and will do well in numerous soil types, it is rather invasive and therefore not recommended for planting.

LOOSESTRIFE FAMILY—LYTHRACEAE

The Crape-Myrtle—Lagerstroemia

CRAPE-MYRTLE   *Lagerstroemia indica* **L.**

Aside from the peculiar crinkled flowers, the strongly angled, often winged branches, retuse leaf blades, and smooth bark will readily identify this species.

Summer. *Leaves* 1 to 3 inches long, ½ to 1½ inches wide, alternate (or occasionally opposite), simple, deciduous, broadest at or above the middle, apices often retuse or broadly notched, bases tapered and rounded; petioles absent or very short. *Flowers* pink to purple or white, very showy, produced in terminal clusters, in June to October; petals 6, each on a large slender and fringed claw; sepals 6 to 9; stamens numerous. *Fruits* a dry capsule, ½ to ⅔ inch long, ovate to elliptic.

Winter. *Twigs* thin, conspicuously 4-angled, often winged; bundle scar 1, crescent-shaped; stipule scars lacking; pith small, continuous. *Buds* small, several times longer than wide, all lateral, sessile, conspicuously elongated; bud scales 2, ciliate. *Bark* somewhat fluted, quite smooth due to exfoliation, leaving a green inner bark exposed.

The crape-myrtle is an Asian introduction, brought to the United States in the late 1780s and now commonly planted in the Southeast, where it escapes in woodlots and around homesites. It is a small tree, 10 to 25 feet high, spreading by seeds and by suckering, occasionally forming colonies. It is extremely heat tolerant and thus used extensively in sunny horticultural plantings from Florida to Virginia, and is quite popular because of its long-lasting and numerous flowers. In autumn, the

CRAPE-MYRTLE

1. Branch with leaves and fruits.   2. Detail of fruit.

leaves turn a gold to red color. If protected, it will grow northward as far as Baltimore, Washington, D.C., and Wilmington, Delaware, but it usually succumbs to freezing temperatures that persist for more than a 24-hour period. Numerous cultivars have been developed, but many of these are susceptible to powdery mildew.

DOGWOOD FAMILY—CORNACEAE

The Dogwoods—Cornus

The dogwoods are shrubs or small trees with opposite (or rarely alternate), simple, oval or roundish leaves in which the pinnate veins curve and tend to parallel the leaf margins. The twigs are slender and have a continuous pith. Leaf scars are commonly crescent-shaped and often raised on the persistent bases of the petioles. There are 3 bundle scars. The buds are variable but commonly have 2 to 4 exposed scales, and the lateral ones are sometimes hidden by the persistent petiole bases. The flowers are small and perfect, and are borne in either open flat-topped clusters or in dense heads. In the latter case they are often surrounded by 2 or 3 pairs of conspicuous petal-like bracts, which are actually modified leaves. The fruits are drupes that have a solitary bony "seed" surrounded by more or less pulpy flesh.

FLOWERING DOGWOOD   *Cornus florida* L.

> The opposite, entire-margined leaves; biscuitlike flowering buds; alligator-hide bark; and large, white, showy flowering bracts are most distinct.

Summer. *Leaves* 3 to 5 inches long, 2 to 3 inches wide, opposite, simple, deciduous, ovate, apically acuminate, bases broadly wedge-shaped to almost rounded, margins entire or with tiny teeth, but more or less wavy, clustered at twig apices; veins 6 to 7 pairs, pinnately parallel, strongly curved, tend to parallel the margins of the leaves; blades rather thick and firm, bright dark green above, paler or somewhat whitened and often somewhat hairy beneath; petioles ½ to ¾ inch long, stout, grooved. *Flowers* ⅛ inch wide, tiny, perfect, greenish yellow, very inconspicuous,

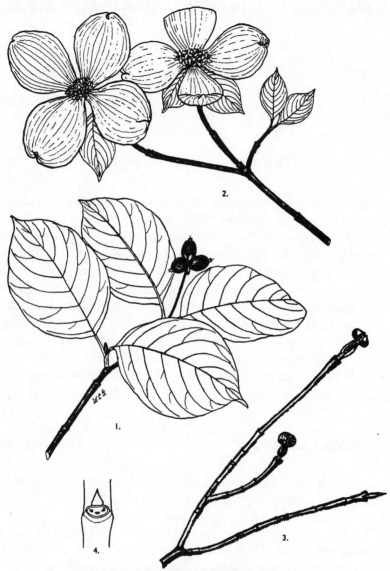

FLOWERING DOGWOOD

1. Branch with leaves and fruits.
2. Flowering branch.
3. Winter twig.
4. Detail of leaf scar and bud after base of petiole is removed.

appearing in May before the leaves, clustered in small heads surrounded by 4 showy, petal-like bracts; bracts very conspicuous, white or sometimes pinkish, apically notched. *Fruits* (drupe) ⅓ to ⅝ inch long, ovoid, prominently tipped with the persistent styles, borne in compact clusters of 3 to 5, brilliant scarlet at maturity.

Winter. *Twigs* slender, flexible, glabrous or somewhat hoary with minute appressed white hairs, greenish to purplish-red, often more or less bicolored. *Petioles,* bases persistent, concealing the leaf scars and the small lateral buds. *Buds,* terminal buds larger, exposed, with 2 hairy scales; flower buds most conspicuous and characteristically turbanlike or biscuit-like, about ½ inch in diameter, stalked, gray white, somewhat spherical, transversely flattened, rather mealy or hoary with a dense coating of minute appressed hairs; nonflowering buds about ¼ inch long, narrowly conical, purplish to greenish, with some minute appressed hairs, 2-scaled. *Bark* of the trunks very dark brown, almost black, distinctly broken into small, squarish blocks, resembling alligator hide on mature trees.

Comparisons. Although the alligator-hide bark pattern is also present in the sourwood, the black gum, the common persimmon, and the blackhaw, this characteristic, in combination with the opposite leaves with parallel veins and green to purplish twigs, will help identify this species.

———

The flowering dogwood is a very spectacular tree, especially in the spring when the showy floral bracts adorn its branches. In October, it is equally attractive when the leaves turn a deep purplish red and the branches are tipped with the clusters of scarlet fruits. It is a small tree, usually 10 to 20 feet in height with a trunk from 4 to 6 inches in diameter, but it occasionally attains a height of about 40 feet and a trunk diameter up to about 12 inches. The trunk is short and the numerous, long, slender, horizontally spreading branches form a low, rather dense, more or less flat-topped crown. The flowering dogwood thrives on almost any well-drained, fairly fertile soil. It is a very common understory tree in forests of oaks and other hardwood trees, and frequently common on wooded hillsides, in old abandoned fields, and along fencerows and roadsides.

The wood is very heavy, hard, strong, durable, and tough. It is the principal wood used for the shuttles that are employed in weaving; and is also used for various turned articles, tool handles, mallet heads, golf-club heads, and jewelers' and engravers' blocks. The inner bark and twigs are very bitter and have a property similar to the cinchona. It was once used medicinally in tonics as a substitute for quinine in combating fevers. A red dye was also made from the bark of the roots. The flowering dogwood is extensively planted as an ornamental, and it certainly is one of the most beautiful and attractive of our smaller native trees. The fruits and berries are eaten by many wild birds including the ruffed grouse, the bobwhite, and the wild turkey. The seeds are often eaten by squirrels, chipmunks, and other rodents.

The flowering dogwood ranges from southern Maine to southern Michigan and Illinois, south to Florida and Texas.

STIFF DOGWOOD   *Cornus foemina* P. Mill.

The stiff dogwood is usually a shrub but occasionally becomes a small tree to 15 feet. Its glabrous, opposite leaves are ovate or narrowly ovate, 1½ to 5 inches long, and have tapering tips. They are dull dark green above and slightly paler beneath. The roundish light-blue fruits develop in open flat-topped clusters. Winter twigs are reddish brown to purplish brown, slender, glabrous, lustrous, and have a white pith. It is a species of swamps and wet bottomlands from eastern Virginia south to Florida and Texas, and extending north in the Mississippi Valley to Missouri and southern Indiana.

ALTERNATE-LEAF DOGWOOD   *Cornus alternifolia* L. f.

This is our only alternate-leaved dogwood with leaves produced on conspicuously thin and elongated petioles, which are terminally clustered and appear to be whorled, and ill-scented broken twigs.

Summer. *Leaves* 3 to 5 inches long, 2½ to 3½ inches wide, usually alternate, simple, deciduous, but often clustered at the twig tips, ovate to broadly ovate, tips long, slender, and pointed, bases rounded or broadly wedge-shaped, margins entire or with tiny teeth, but more or less wavy; leaf blades thin, dark green and nearly glabrous above, pale or whitened beneath, more or less coated with minute appressed hairs; veins 5 to 6 pairs, strongly curved, tending to parallel the leaf margins; petioles 1 to 2 inches long, slender, grooved; both petioles and midribs often tinged with a reddish color. *Flowers* ¼ inch across, quite small, produced in large,

ALTERNATE-LEAF DOGWOOD

1. Branch with mature leaves and fruits.
2. Winter twig.
3. Detail of bud and leaf scar (enlarged).
4. Detail of terminal portion of twig.

flat-topped cymes; petals 4, cream colored. *Fruits* (drupe) about ⅜ inch in diameter, roundish, dark bluish black; borne in loose, flat-topped, red-stemmed clusters; ripening in September to October.

Winter. *Twigs* rather slender, flexible, glabrous, lustrous, reddish, greenish, red brown to purple, with a fetid odor when crushed; pith white; leaf scars mostly alternate, crescent-shaped, with 3 distinct bundle scars. *Buds* small, ovoid, pointed, glabrous, dark purplish red, with 2 or 3 visible scales; terminal bud about ¼ inch long; lateral buds somewhat smaller. *Bark* on the young trunks and branches usually dark green, often streaked with a whitish color; on the older trunks becoming reddish brown with shallow longitudinal fissures.

Comparisons. The alternate rather than opposite leaves and imbricated rather than valvate or naked buds will help separate this species from all other dogwoods at any time of the year.

———

The alternate-leaf dogwood is also known as the blue dogwood, the pagoda dogwood, and the green osier. It is a large shrub or a small tree, usually from 10 to 15 feet in height, although it occasionally attains a height of about 30 feet with a trunk diameter of nearly 8 inches. The trunk is generally short, and the almost horizontal, slender branches form a rather irregular flat-topped or pagoda-like crown. The alternate-leaf dogwood is found principally in the understory of cool, moist woods, and is often common in ravines, along the wooded banks of streams, and in the borders of swamps. It is seldom abundant anywhere, but it occurs in the understories of various forest types.

The wood of the alternate-leaf dogwood is not used commercially, as the tree is usually very small. In its native habitat the species is very attractive, and it is occasionally used for ornamental planting. The leaves turn scarlet in the autumn. The bitter fruits are eaten by many species of wild birds.

The alternate-leaf dogwood ranges from New Brunswick to Minnesota, south to northern Georgia, Alabama, and Florida.

The Black Gum and the Tupelos—Nyssa

The black gum and the tupelos are small- to large-sized trees (plus one shrub species) with alternate, simple, deciduous leaves that are usually entire but occasionally have a few large marginal teeth. The twigs are slender to moderately stout, very tough, and have a round white pith that is interrupted by transverse woody plates. A terminal bud is present and is usually somewhat larger than the lateral ones, which commonly have about 4 exposed scales. Leaf scars are crescent-shaped to semicircular and show 3 distinct bundle scars that appear like a tiny Halloween mask complete with two eyes and a nose. Short lateral spurlike branches are often present, with leaves more or less crowded toward their tips. The flowers may appear before or with the developing leaves, being small and greenish white and not always perfect. They contain an abundance of nectar and are pollinated chiefly by bees. The fruits are drupes that contain a ridged or somewhat winged pit and a pulpy, acid flesh. Some species are timber trees of commercial importance.

BLACK GUM   *Nyssa sylvatica* **Marsh.**

> The terminally clustered, shiny dark green leaves with acuminate leaf tips, entire leaf margins, 3 very distinct bundle traces within the leaf scars (appearing as a tiny Halloween mask) that are recognizable even on older branches, the alligator-hide bark, and the distinct lateral or pendent habit of the branches are all diagnostic.

Summer. *Leaves* 2 to 6 inches long, 1 to 3 inches wide, alternate, simple, deciduous, elliptic to ovate, appearing to be widest at or above the middle; tips acute or acuminate, bases wedge-shaped, margins entire but wavy, rarely with 1 to 3 irregular teeth; thick and firm, dark green and lustrous above, paler and glabrous or slightly hairy beneath; petioles ¼ to 1 inch long, rather slender, often slightly winged. *Flowers* about ⅛ inch long, small, with small petals, green white, developing on long stalks and appearing with the leaves; male and female flowers (2 to 6) produced on the same or separate trees. *Fruits* (drupe) ⅜ to ½ inch long, ovoid, bluish black; borne 2 or 6 together on a long stalk; stony pits only slightly ribbed, ripening in October.

Winter. *Twigs* slender, glabrous or nearly so, ashy to light reddish brown; pith diaphragmatic; leaf scars alternate, broadly crescent-shaped

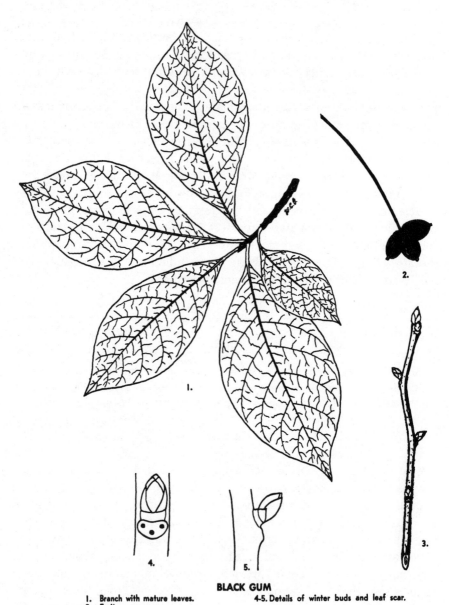

BLACK GUM

1. Branch with mature leaves.
2. Fruits.
3. Winter twig.

4-5. Details of winter buds and leaf scar.

to semiround, with 3 distinct bundle scars that resemble a tiny Hallow-een mask. *Buds* ⅛ to ¼ inch long, ovoid, curved, dark reddish brown, turning bright red in the spring, frequently minutely hairy but appearing glabrous or nearly so, with about 5 visible scales; terminal bud somewhat larger than the divergent lateral buds. *Bark* on the younger trunks gray-ish, smooth or scaly; on the older trunks becoming rather dark, thick, deeply fissured, and with irregular blocklike ridges.

Comparisons. The green undersurfaces of the occasionally toothed leaves of this species can be separated from those of the common persim-mon, which are whitish beneath and have the tendency to produce black spots or dots (versus the dark maroon spots on the black gum). The com-mon persimmon can also be told by its single (rather than three) bundle scar, pseudo-terminal rather than terminal bud, and continuous rather than diaphragmatic pith.

———

The black gum is also known as the black tupelo, the sour gum, and the pepperidge. The generic name *Nyssa* originates from the Greek word for water nymphs of river and lakes. It is usually a medium-sized tree, 30 to 40 feet in height with a trunk diameter of 1 to 2 feet. Occasionally it attains a height of nearly 100 feet with a trunk diameter of 3 to 4 feet. The exceedingly numerous spreading and often horizontal branches form an irregularly rounded or flat-topped crown in older trees, although young specimens may be very nearly pyramidal. The black gum usually attains its best development in rich, moist bottomlands, but it is often common on dry mountain ridges, on burned-over forest land or abandoned fields, and in cold mountain swamps.

The wood of this tree is of exceptionally poor quality, one of the poor-est in the region. It is heavy, moderately strong, stiff, and tough, but rather soft, not resistant to moisture or fungal infection, and very difficult to season for working or splitting. It is used for furniture, cooperage, boxes and crates, railroad ties, baskets, chopping bowls, rolling pins, ironing boards, broom handles, and excelsior. The black gum is a rather attractive tree; usually among the first of our native trees to assume its autumn coloration, the leaves often become a brilliant red early in Sep-tember. The fruits are eaten by many species of wild birds, including the ruffed grouse and the wild turkey, and also by many species of mammals.

The black gum ranges from Maine and southern Ontario to Michi-gan, south to northern Florida and eastern Texas.

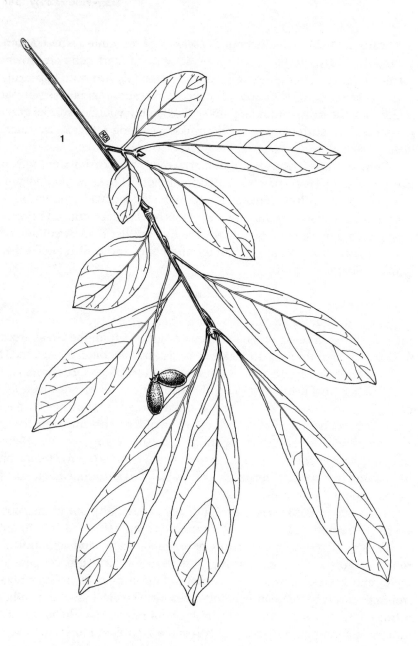

SWAMP TUPELO

1. Branch with leaves and fruits.

SWAMP TUPELO   *Nyssa biflora* Walt.

Leaves 1½ to 4 inches long, ½ to 1½ inches wide, alternate, simple, deciduous, narrowly oblong or obovate, blade clearly widest above the middle, apices acute, obtuse, or rarely short-acuminate, margins entire, bases cuneate; lustrous above, paler beneath. *Flowers* regularly borne in pairs, opening after leaves. *Fruits* (drupe) ⅓ to ½ inch long, bluish black, borne in pairs or occasionally solitary; seeds distinctly flattened; stony pits have very prominent longitudinal ribs. *Trunk* usually prominently swollen or buttressed at the base.

Comparisons. This species is similar to the black gum, but has narrower, oblong (rather than elliptic) leaves that are broadest above the middle, with more obtuse (rather than acute or acuminate) apices, and has fewer fruits per cluster. Additionally, it grows in wetter habitats than the black gum.

The swamp black tupelo, or swamp tupelo, occurs in coastal plain swamps and ponds from Delaware and eastern Maryland south to Florida, west to eastern Texas, and north to western and southern Tennessee.

WATER TUPELO   *Nyssa aquatica* L.

> The swampy habitat of this species, diaphragmatic pith, swollen bases on mature trees, large, lustrous leaves, often with a few teeth, and clustered, long-stemmed, plumlike, glaucous fruits are distinctive.

Summer. *Leaves* 5 to 10 inches long, 2 to 4 inches wide, alternate, simple, deciduous, large, ovate or oblong ovate, tips acuminate, bases broadly pointed or rounded, margins entire or with one or more large teeth; upper surfaces dark lustrous green, lower surfaces paler and hairy; petioles 1 to 3 inches long, stout, grooved, hairy. *Flowers* tiny, greenish, male and female flowers usually borne on separate trees; male flowers ½ to ⅝ inch wide, numerous in heads; female flowers ⅜ inch long, commonly solitary single fruit. *Fruits* (drupe) about 1 inch long, oblong, dark purple, acid-fleshed; borne on stalks an inch or more long.

Winter. *Twigs* moderately stout, reddish to reddish brown, hairy when young, soon becoming glabrous, dotted with small lenticels; pith

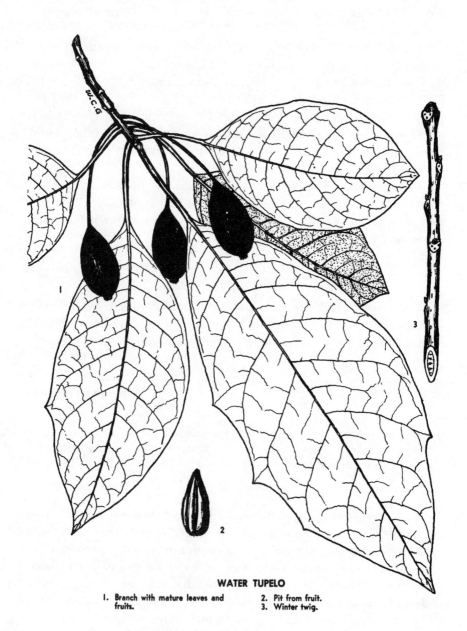

WATER TUPELO

1. Branch with mature leaves and fruits.
2. Pit from fruit.
3. Winter twig.

diaphragmatic; leaf scars nearly round, with 3 bundle scars. *Buds*, terminal bud about ⅛ inch long, roundish, blunt, glabrous to only slightly-hairy; lateral buds very small. *Bark* thin, dark brown, with rough and scaly ridges.

Comparisons. The water tupelo and Ogeechee tupelo differ from the black gum and the swamp tupelo by having larger leaves and fruits, and by having consistently single rather than multiple fruits per stalk. The former two tupelos can be separated from each other by water tupelo's single straight trunk, marginal teeth to the leaves, and acuminate leaf apices, versus the one or more trunks of the Ogeechee tupelo and its mostly entire leaf margins and broadly rounded or short-pointed leaf apices. Also, the hairy rather than glabrous twigs and more rounded rather than ovoid buds help to separate the water tupelo from the black gum.

The water tupelo is also known as the tupelo gum, the cotton gum, and the two-flower tupelo. It is a large tree, up to 100 feet or more in height and 3 feet or more in diameter above the conspicuously swollen base, with a tapering trunk and rather narrow oblong crown. As its name suggests, it is a tree of the deeper swamps and of frequently inundated bottomlands. An important timber species, its wood is used for furniture, cooperage, boxes, crates, baskets, railroad ties, and as pulpwood. Wood from the swollen bases of the trunks is lighter and more spongy and is often used locally for making fishnet floats and bottle corks. From the flowers, bees obtain a nectar that makes an excellent honey.

The range of the water tupelo extends through the coastal plain from southeastern Virginia to northern Florida west to southeastern Texas, and northward, in the Mississippi Valley, to southern Illinois.

OGEECHEE TUPELO   *Nyssa ogeche* **Bartr. ex Marsh.**

> The hairy leaves and twigs, blunt leaf tips, and red fruits on stalks that are shorter than the individual fruits are diagnostic.

Summer. *Leaves* 3 to 6 inches long, 1½ to 2½ inches wide, elliptic or oblong, tips mucronate, rather broadly rounded or abruptly short-pointed, bases rounded or broadly pointed, margins entire but often wavy; blades thick but deciduous, dark green and shiny above, paler and hairy beneath

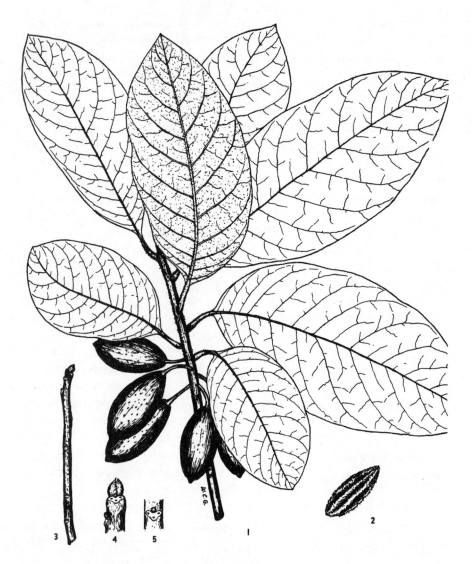

OGEECHEE TUPELO

1. Branch with leaves and fruits.
2. Stone from fruit.
3. Winter twig.
4. Detail of tip of winter twig.
5. Detail of lateral bud and leaf-scar.

especially on the vein, short-petioled. *Flowers* tiny, greenish, hairy, male and female flowers usually borne on separate trees; male flowers ½ to ⅝ inch wide, numerous in heads, female flowers ⅜ inch long, commonly solitary, rarely in 2s. *Fruits* 1 to 1½ inches long, oblong, red, acid-fleshed, occurring singly on stalks ¼ to ½ inch long.

Winter. *Twigs* moderately stout, light greenish brown to reddish brown, more or less rusty-hairy. *Buds*, terminal bud about ⅛ inch long, rounded, with usually 2 (3) visible and minutely hairy scales; lateral buds very small; leaf scars broadly crescent-shaped or somewhat 3-lobed, showing 3 bundle scars. *Bark* thin, dark brown, irregularly fissured.

Comparisons. This crooked-stemmed and often multiple-stemmed South Carolina, Georgia, and Florida endemic can be separated from our other more widespread straight and single-boled species of the genus by its leaves, which have a tiny needlelike projection at the tip of each (lacking in the water tupelo); by its hairy rather than glabrous leaf undersurfaces; and by its larger fruits, which at maturity are red rather than blue or purple, suspended on shorter stalks.

———

The Ogeechee tupelo is also known as the sour tupelo, the Ogeechee gum, or the Ogeechee lime, referring to the Ogeechee River in Georgia, where it was first discovered. It is a small, more or less round-topped, often bushy tree, 30 to 40 feet high, which grows about the borders of swamps, pineland ponds, and inundated riverbanks from southeastern South Carolina to northern Florida. Like the previous species, the word tupelo comes from the Cree Indian word meaning swamp tree. It was first discovered by John and William Bartram, the famous Philadelphia Quaker botanists, in 1765. The Bartrams referred to the use of the fruits in making punch; they are now often used in making preserves. The little tree yields no wood of value, but its flowers provide a flow of nectar from which bees make excellent tupelo honey.

HOLLY FAMILY—AQUIFOLICEAE

The Hollies—Ilex

The hollies are shrubs or small trees with alternate, simple, deciduous or evergreen leaves, with coal-black hairs, if present, and tiny yet distinct stipule scars. The slender twigs have small crescent-shaped leaf scars containing a solitary bundle scar, and small, often superposed, buds. The small greenish white flowers have from 4 to 6 petals and as many stamens. Usually the stamen-bearing and pistil-bearing flowers are on separate plants. Pollination is accomplished by insects, principally bees, which are attracted by the heavy aroma and the abundance of nectar. The hollies are excellent honey plants and the fruits are eaten by birds and other wildlife. The fruits are berrylike drupes with a rather dry mealy or pulpy flesh and from 4 to 6 bony nutlets that fit together like the sections of an orange. In our holly tree species the fruits are bright red, or occasionally yellow. Several of our native species are used in ornamental planting, and those with evergreen leaves are widely used as Christmas greens.

AMERICAN HOLLY *Ilex opaca* **Ait.**

> Easily identified by being the only native evergreen tree that has thick, leathery, alternate leaves with multiple-spined margins.

Leaves 2 to 4 inches long, 1 to 2½ inches wide, evergreen, alternate, simple, ovate, coarsely undulating and yellow spiny-toothed (rarely spineless); stiff and leathery, glabrous, lustrous dark green above and yellowish green beneath; petioles ¼ to ½ inch long, stout. *Flowers* small, ¼ inch wide, male and female flowers borne on separate trees in the spring; petals 4 to 6, greenish or cream white. *Fruits* (drupe) ¼ to ⅜ inch in diameter,

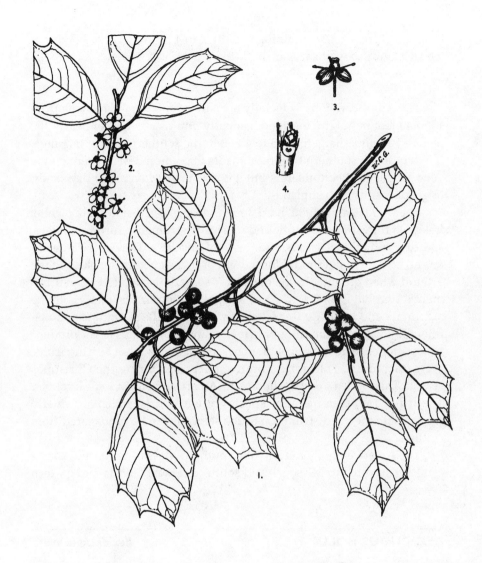

AMERICAN HOLLY

1. Branch with mature leaves and fruits.
2. Flowering branch.
3. Detail of pistillate flower.
4. Detail of bud and leaf scar.

berrylike, bright red, containing usually 2 to 4 prominently ribbed nut-lets. *Bark* gray to whitish, splotchy.

———

The American holly is usually a small- or medium-sized tree from 15 to 40 feet in height, but it occasionally attains a height of nearly 100 feet and a trunk diameter of 3 to 4 feet in the southern part of its range. It is typically a southern tree, reaching its maximum development on the deep, rich soils of bottomlands, but it is able to grow on rather dry, sandy, or gravelly soils in the uplands.

The wood is fairly light, hard, tough, close-grained, and chalky white. It is used for various scientific and musical instruments, furniture inlays, sporting and athletic goods, and toys and novelties. The American holly has an attractive pyramidal form, with branches persisting close to the ground when growing in the open. It is sometimes planted as an orna-mental tree, but grows slowly, and will not produce fruits unless both the staminate and pistillate trees are planted. Since the staminate and pis-tillate flowers occur on different trees, many individuals never produce fruits. Immense quantities of branches, particularly those bearing fruits, are gathered and sold for decorative purposes during the Christmas season. This has led to extirpation of the American holly in some localities. The fruits are eaten by many species of wild birds, which are chiefly responsible for the distribution of the seeds. It can be propagated from cuttings.

The American holly ranges from southern Massachusetts and south-ern Pennsylvania to Missouri, and south to central Florida and eastern Texas.

DECIDUOUS HOLLY   *Ilex decidua* **Walt.**

> The deciduous leaves, crenate leaf margins, numerous spur shoots, and short fruit stalks separate this holly from our other native species.

Summer. *Leaves* 1 to 3 inches long, ½ to 1¼ inches wide, alternate, simple, deciduous, membranous, often clustered at tips of spur shoots, narrowly ovate, lance obovate to spatulate, mostly broadest above the middle, tip broadly pointed, obtuse or emarginate, base wedge-shaped, margins bluntly crenately toothed chiefly above the middle, each tooth with a gland in the sinus or on the apical side; light green and glabrous above, paler and glabrous or nearly so beneath, except on the midrib; petioles ⅛ to ¼ inch long, often a bit hairy. *Flowers* ⅜ to ½ inch long, whitish green, male and female flowers borne on separate trees. *Fruits* (drupe) about ¼ inch in diameter, berrylike, bright red, yellow, or orange.

Winter. *Twigs* slender, rather straight, stiff, glabrous, light gray, developing short lateral spurlike branches the second year; leaf scars semiround, with a solitary bundle scar. *Buds* quite small, ovoid or roundish, apically blunt, showing 2 or 3 visible scales. *Bark* of the larger branches and trunks grayish to gray brown, thin, rather smooth, mottled.

Comparisons. The deciduous leaves of this species separate it from the evergreen yaupon, and the crenate leaf margins separate it from the entire- to serrate-leaved sarvis holly (*I. amelanchier* M. A. Curtis ex Chapman), which is a rare but locally abundant small tree or shrub of the southeastern coastal plain of North Carolina to Louisiana. It can be distinguished from the Carolina holly (*I. ambigua* (Michx.) Torr.), another small shrub or occasional small tree of the southeastern coastal plain, by its glabrous or minutely hairy, rather than hairy, leaves, by its 4- rather than 5-parted flowers, and by its crenate rather than mostly coarsely serrate leaf margins. This species might also be confused with the long-stalk holly (*I. collina* Alexander), but that species can be separated by its elongated fruit stalks and by being nearly exclusively shrubby.

The deciduous holly, or possum-haw, is a large shrub or small tree about 25 feet in height. It occurs along streams and about the borders of swamps in the southern coastal plain, but farther inland it occupies the understory of hardwood forests on the moister slopes. In the southern Appalachians it grows on the lower slopes, while the mountain winterberry occurs at the highest elevations. The fruits usually persist throughout the winter season and some may even remain when the plant blooms again the following spring.

The deciduous holly ranges from Virginia, southern Illinois, Missouri, and Oklahoma southward to northern Florida and central Texas.

DAHOON

5. Branch with leaves and fruit.

6. Detail of bud and leaf scar.

DAHOON   *Ilex cassine* **L.**

> The bristle-tipped, alternate, evergreen leaves and bottomland habitat are most distinctive.

Leaves 1½ to about 3½ inches long, ¼ to 1¼ inches wide, usually more than twice as long as wide, alternate, simple, evergreen, oblanceolate to obovate or oblong ovate, margins either slightly revolute or flat, entire or with a few small sharply serrate teeth above the middle; blade thickish, and leathery, tips obtuse or acute to emarginate, base cuneate, dark green and lustrous above, paler beneath, glabrous or nearly so on both blade surfaces; petioles short, stout, more or less hairy. *Flowers* ⅜ to ½ inch across, in axillary clusters; petals 4, white, similar to those of the American holly. *Fruits* (drupe) ⅜ to ⅝ inch long, about the same in diameter, berrylike, red or occasionally orange to yellow. *Bark* smooth, light gray.

Comparisons. This species, although similar to the myrtle dahoon, is easily identified by its consistently larger leaves with nearly flat or only occasionally slightly revolute margins (very strongly revolute margins in the myrtle dahoon). It is also similar to the yaupon, with which it commonly occurs, but that species has conspicuously scalloped leaf margins. The dahoon differs from the American holly by having leaves that are less stiff and lacking the sharply spined leaf margins (including the spine at leaf apex).

The dahoon is a large shrub or a small tree that rises to about 25 feet in height. It grows about the borders of swamps and on the damper sand ridges in the coastal plain from North Carolina, south to Florida and west to Texas, reaching its greatest size from Alabama to Florida.

MYRTLE DAHOON   *Ilex myrtifolia* **Walt.**

> The stiffly spiky branchlets, studded with stiff, short, and narrow (nearly linear) evergreen leaves with revolute margins are characteristic.

Leaves ½ to 1½ inches long, ⅛ to ⅜ inch wide, usually twice as long as wide, alternate, simple, evergreen, lustrous, linear to narrowly elliptic, thick, leathery, very rigid, abruptly tipped with a small spine, margin rolled inward, entire or with a few inconspicuous sharp teeth near the tip; petioles very short. *Flowers* small, ³⁄₁₆ inch wide, borne in leaf axils; petals white. *Fruits* (drupe) about ¼ inch in diameter, berrylike, bright red or occasionally yellow.

Comparisons. The fruits of this species are similar to those of the dahoon (a tree of wetter sites with richer soil), but the leaves are clearly smaller and narrower than in that species.

————

The myrtle dahoon is a small, straggling, crooked tree, inhabiting low swampy woods and the shallow waters of the cypress ponds in the southeastern coastal plain. It ranges from North Carolina southward to central Florida and westward to southeastern Louisiana and Texas.

YAUPON   *Ilex vomitoria* Ait.

Easily told by its dark green, blunt-tipped, evergreen, alternate leaves, with distinctly scalloped margins.

Leaves ½ to 2 inches long, ¼ to ¾ inch wide, alternate, simple, evergreen, lustrous, ovate, elliptic to oblong, margins regularly crenate toothed or scalloped with conspicuously rounded or blunt teeth; thickish and leathery, glabrous, green on both surfaces, dark green above, obtuse at both ends; petioles short, stout. *Flowers* small, ³⁄₁₆ inch wide, axillary in glabrous cymes; petals white. *Fruits* (drupe) about ¼ inch in diameter, berrylike, bright red. *Twigs* straight, rather stiff, somewhat angled, gray, usually perpendicular to the main branches.

————

The yaupon, also known as the cassine and the Christmas-berry, is a shrub or a small, slender tree to about 20 to 30 feet in height. It often forms dense thickets immediately behind the sand dunes along our southern coast. The leaves contain an appreciable caffeine content and were once used by the Indians in concocting a kind of ceremonial drink called the black drink, strong enough to induce vomiting; hence the scientific name. The young leaves are sometimes dried and used as a substitute for tea to the present day. A closely related South American plant is the source of

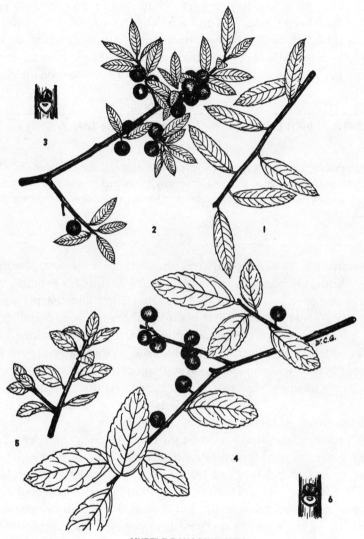

MYRTLE DAHOON (UPPER)

1. Branch with mature leaves.
2. Fruiting branch.

3. Detail of bud and leaf scar.

YAUPON (LOWER)

4. Branch with mature leaves and fruits.
5. Branch with leaves.

6. Detail of bud and leaf scar.

the drink *maté*, which is popular there. The yaupon is a very attractive plant and it is widely cultivated as an ornamental. A number of creeping cultivars have been propagated and can be seen throughout the South.

The range of the yaupon extends through the coastal plain from southeastern Virginia south to central Florida and west to south central Texas. In the Mississippi Valley it extends north to Arkansas and Oklahoma.

MOUNTAIN HOLLY   *Ilex montana* Torr. & Gray ex Gray

An Appalachian Mountains species, with conspicuous spur shoots, large red fruits that persist into winter, and large (for a holly), thin deciduous leaves with conspicuous marginal teeth that more closely resemble those of a cherry or a plum than a holly.

Summer. *Leaves* 2½ to 6 inches long, simple, alternate, deciduous; ovate, elliptic, or oblong lanceolate, thin; tips acuminate to acute, bases broadly wedge-shaped to rounded, margins finely and sharply serrate; blades dark green, lustrous and glabrous above, paler and glabrous or slightly hairy beneath on the veins; petioles from ⅜ to ¾ inch long, rather slender, usually glabrous, frequently clustered on short lateral spurs. *Flowers* about ¼ inch wide, in cymes on spur shoots; petals 4 (sometimes 5), white. *Fruits* (drupe) ⅓ to ½ inch in diameter, berrylike, subglobose, scarlet, roundish, contain 3 to 5 ribbed nutlets, borne on slender stalks ⅛ to ¼ inch long, either solitary or in lateral clusters of 2 or 3.

Winter. *Fruits* seldom persist on the branches. *Twigs* slender, slightly zigzag, glabrous, olive green to reddish brown, more or less glaucous, becoming dark gray during the second year and developing short lateral spurs; leaf scars semiround with a solitary bundle scar. *Buds* about ⅛ inch long, ovoid or roundish, usually blunt, with 3 or 4 dull brown, visible scales; lateral buds often superposed, uppermost bud decidedly largest. *Bark* thin, light brown or grayish brown, roughened with numerous enlarged, rather warty lenticels.

Comparisons. In the Southeast, this species is often confused with the deciduous holly, which probably accounts for the reports from Florida, Louisiana, Mississippi, and Texas. Although similar, the mountain holly has larger fruits (nearly twice as large as those of the deciduous holly), much larger leaves with more conspicuous marginal teeth, and smaller veins on the upper leaf surface. It may also be confused with the

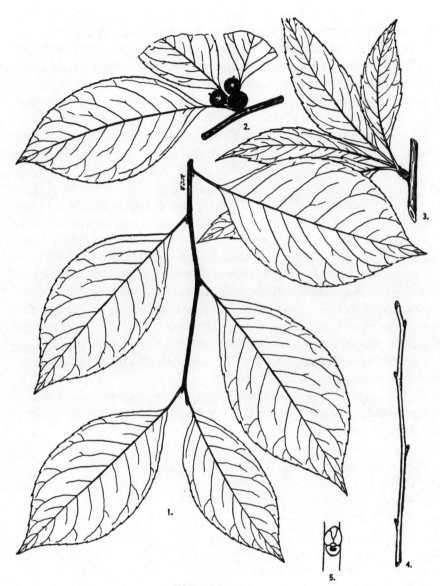

MOUNTAIN HOLLY

1. Branch with mature leaves.
2. Portion of branch bearing fruits.
3. Cluster of leaves on short spurlike lateral branch.
4. Winter twig.
5. Detail of bud and leaf scar.

shrubby Carolina holly (*I. ambigua* (Michx.) Torr.); however, the latter species has shorter leaves (less than 4 inches long), which are long-acuminate, rather than obtuse or short acuminate. The Carolina holly is a southern, mostly coastal plain species, smaller in nearly all respects, with small, usually inconspicuous teeth on the leaf margins; and smaller fruits. Mountain holly is also somewhat similar to the common winter-berry (*I. verticillata* (L.) Gray); however, that species is more shrublike, with noticeably thicker leaves, which are more conspicuously veiny on the lower leaf surface.

The mountain holly is sometimes called the large-leaf holly or mountain winter-berry. As its name suggests, it is a mountain species with large leaves produced on conspicuous spur shoots, with prominent marginal teeth and large fruits. The mountain holly is usually a mere shrub, but it occasionally becomes a tree from 5 to 20 feet in height with a trunk usually less than 6 inches in diameter. This holly is commonly found in the understory of cool, moist forests. It is very tolerant of shade and prefers a rich, more-or-less rocky soil. It is of no commercial importance and is only rarely cultivated as an ornamental, but is strikingly beautiful when seen in fruit in its native habitats. The staminate and pistillate flowers are usually produced on different plants.

The mountain holly ranges from western and central New York southward, principally along the Appalachian Mountains, to northern Georgia, and Alabama.

SPURGE FAMILY—EUPHORBIACEAE

The Tung-Oiltree—Vernicia

TUNG-OILTREE   *Vernicia fordii* (Hemsl.) Airy-shaw

> The large, palmately veined and occasionally lobed leaves with red-glandular petioles, thick branches that exude a milky sap, and large, showy spring flowers are most distinctive.

Summer. *Leaves* alternate, simple, deciduous, dark green above, paler below, broadly ovate, appressed hairy on both surfaces, apices short-acuminate, bases cordate to truncate, palmately veined with 5 major veins from base; margins entire, but some blades, especially those on vigorous shoots, 2- to 3-lobed, with red glands within the sinuses; petioles long, with bright red glands at their summits. *Flowers* large, 1 to 2¾ inches across, white with red veins within, borne in terminal cymes, produced before the leaves, unisexual, plants monoecious; petals 5 (6 to 8), all separate, oblong obovate, tips recurved. *Fruits* (drupe) 1½ to 3 inches across, ovoid to globose, 3- to 5-valved, producing 3 to 7 large seeds.

Winter. *Twigs* stout, glabrous, dark gray to brown, occasionally swollen at the nodes, with milky sap; leaf scars circular to semicircular to oblong. *Bark* light gray.

————

The tung-oiltree, which grows to only 35 feet, is an Asian introduction (native to China), which has become established in Alabama, Florida, Georgia, Louisiana, and Mississippi. The common name refers to the fact that its seeds, which are highly poisonous if eaten, yield an oil used in the

TUNG-OILTREE

1. Branch with leaves and fruit.

production of paints and varnishes. Because of its large, showy spring flowers, it is often used in cultivation, creating a beautiful sight wherever planted.

The Tallowtree—Triadica

CHINESE TALLOWTREE
Triadica sebifera (L.) **Small**

> The unusual poplarlike leaves with entire margins and milky sap are most distinctive.

Leaves 1½ to 3 inches long, 1¼ to 2¾ inches wide, alternate, simple, deciduous; blades ovate or roundish, tips abruptly long-pointed, bases broadly pointed, margins entire; both surfaces glabrous; petioles 1 to 2 inches long, slender. *Flowers*, both male and female flowers borne on the same tree; male flowers small, yellow, in an erect cluster, female flowers borne at base of the male flowers. *Fruits* (capsule) about ½ inch in diameter, roundish, 3-lobed; at maturity the outer part splits and falls away, leaving the 3 white and glaucous seeds hanging from a central column.

This is a moderate-sized tree that bears a marked resemblance to the genus *Populus*, especially aspens, but with entire-margined leaves. It is both heat and drought tolerant and does well on a variety of soil types. It grows to a height of about 30 to 40 feet. The flowers are borne in erect terminal spikes, with the greenish yellow staminate ones above and the pistillate ones toward the base. The leaves in some trees turn a bright red or yellow in the autumn, while those of others remain greenish until shed.

The milky sap of the tree is poisonous. In China, the white wax that coats the seeds is used to obtain vegetable tallow for making candles and soap and as a dressing for cloth. Some of the close relatives of this tree are good sources of rubber.

The Chinese tallowtree is a native of China and Japan. It has been introduced as an ornamental tree in the warmer portions of the Southeast and is now naturalized in the coastal plain from South Carolina to Florida and westward to Louisiana and Texas.

CHINESE TALLOWTREE

1. Branch with leaves and fruits.
2. Fruits splitting to expose seeds.

3. Winter bud.

BUCKTHORN FAMILY—RHAMNACEAE

The False Buckthorns—Frangula

CAROLINA FALSE BUCKTHORN	*Frangula caroliniana* **(Walt.) Gray**

Easily recognized by its strongly fetid, lustrous, but deciduous, alternate leaves with unusually straight parallel veins, angled twigs, and naked buds.

Summer. *Leaves* 2 to 6 inches long, 1 to 2 inches wide, alternate, simple, elliptic to broadly elliptic, apically pointed, bases rounded or pointed, margins obscurely toothed and undulate; lustrous yellow green above, paler and glabrous or occasionally rusty-hairy beneath, especially when young; veins prominently parallel; petioles ½ to 1 inch long, producing an offensive, skunklike odor when crushed. *Flowers* 3/16 inch wide, tiny, borne in small clusters at leaf base, very fetid odored; sepals 5, yellow green, bell-shaped. *Fruits* (drupe) 3/8 inch wide, nearly globular, black at maturity, with a sweet but dryish flesh and 2 to 4 bony pits.

Winter. *Twigs* slender, glabrous or nearly so, with a fetid odor; angled; at first reddish brown, often glaucous but ultimately dark gray; leaf scars crescent-shaped, with 3 bundle scars. *Buds,* terminal bud elongate, naked, densely woolly-hairy; lateral buds ovate, smaller. *Bark* quite smooth, grayish or ashy, with characteristically blackish patches.

Comparisons. This species and the yellow-flowered glossy false buckthorn (*Frangula alnus* P. Mill.) are our only two treelike species with long, stalkless, naked buds, 3 bundle scars, and alternate, simple leaves. The native Carolina false buckthorn is similar to the glossy false buckthorn, but taller, with toothed (rather than entire) leaf margins and larger leaves (2 to 6 inches versus 1 to 3 inches long). Although possibly confused with some of our hollies, the black fruits and unusually straightly parallel-veined leaves of the Carolina false buckthorn help to separate it from the hollies, which have red fruits and lack the unusual pattern of venation.

––––––

The Carolina false buckthorn is also known as the Carolina buckthorn, the Indian cherry, the yellow buckthorn, and the polecat tree (due to the unpleasant odor of its twigs and flowers). It is a shrub or small tree, occasionally growing to 30 or 40 feet in height with a trunk up to 10 inches in diameter. It occurs most commonly along streambanks but is also found on hillsides and ridges, generally on limestone soils. The umbellate flowers, which appear in the axils of the leaves in early summer, are not very conspicuous. It is, nevertheless, an attractive tree and is occasionally planted as an ornamental.

The range of the Carolina false buckthorn extends from southwestern Virginia, West Virginia, the Ohio Valley, and Nebraska southward to Florida, Missouri, Oklahoma, and Texas.

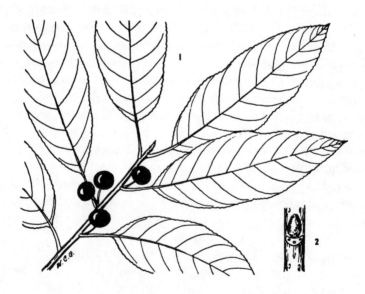

CAROLINA FALSE BUCKTHORN

1.   Branch with leaves and fruit.   2.   Detail of lateral winter bud.

HORSE-CHESTNUT FAMILY— HIPPOCASTANACEAE

The Buckeyes and the Horse-Chestnut—Aesculus

Buckeye and horse-chestnut leaves are opposite and palmately compound with 5 to 9 short-stalked, rather large leaflets. The twigs are stout, with a large pith, and are marked by conspicuous opposite, heart-shaped or inversely triangular leaf scars. The leaf scars contain several bundle scars that are arranged in a curved line or in 3 definite groups. The buds are opposite, ovoid, pointed, with several exposed scales. The terminal buds are particularly large and very conspicuous. The flowers are produced in the spring when the leaves are well developed, and are borne in erect terminal clusters. They are usually perfect, very showy, and insect pollinated. The fruits are large, thick, leathery pods, often spiny, containing from 1 to 3 large, lustrous brown seeds (the buckeyes) that are marked with a conspicuous lighter-colored scar.

The fruits contain poisonous glucosides and should never be eaten. Cases of fatal poisoning in livestock have been known to result from eating the young shoots and leaves of our native buckeyes.

HORSE-CHESTNUT   *Aesculus hippocastanum* L.

> The very large, dark, sticky terminal buds, 7 to 9 leaflets of palmately compound leaves with leaflets widest near the apex and tapered towards the base, the spiny husks of the fruits, and the claw of the upper petal being shorter than the calyx distinguish this tree from our native buckeyes.

Summer. *Leaves* opposite, palmately compound, deciduous, usually 7- to 9-foliate (rarely 5-foliate); leaflets 4 to 6 inches long, oblong obovate,

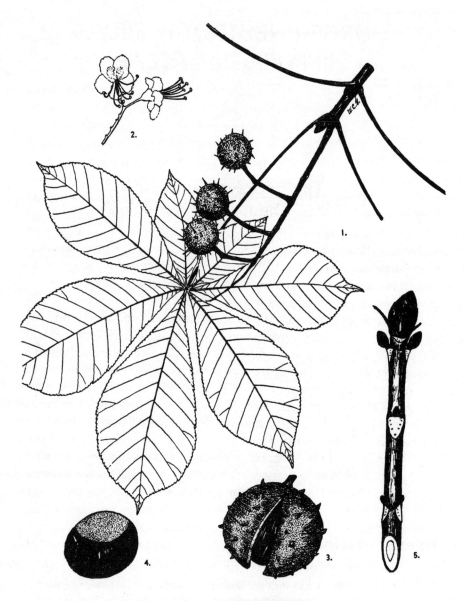

HORSE-CHESTNUT

1. Branch with leaf and immature fruits.
2. Portion of flower cluster.
3. Fruit.
4. Seed.
5. Winter twig.

distinctly broadest above the middle, bases cuneate, tips abruptly pointed, margins irregularly toothed; dark green above and pale beneath, glabrous or nearly so; petioles 4 to 6 inches long, stout. *Flowers* about 1 inch long, bell-shaped, appearing in the spring; petals white, upper 3 spotted with yellow and purple at base; stamens exserted. *Fruits* (capsule) 2 to 3 inches in diameter, thick, leathery, rather round, spiny; containing 1 to 3 large, glabrous, lustrous brown nuts.

Winter. *Twigs* stout, glabrous, light reddish brown or ashy, without disagreeable odor; leaf scars large, inversely triangular with 3 to 9 (generally 7) bundle scars arranged in a curved line; stipule scar lacking. *Buds* large, ovoid, pointed, dark brown, coated with a sticky and gummy resin, appearing varnished; terminal buds from ¾ to 1 inch long, much larger than the lateral buds, with 5 pairs of bud scales. *Bark* dull brown, thin; on the trunks becoming roughened by shallow furrows and low ridges covered with thin scaly plates, similar to that of the common apple.

The horse-chestnut is the buckeye with which most persons are familiar, for the tree is widely planted in our cities as a street and shade tree. It occasionally attains a height of 40 to 70 feet with a trunk diameter of 1 to 2 feet, with a handsome, broadly pyramidal or oblong and rounded-topped crown. It represents the largest species of the genus. In May or June the showy, erect clusters of white flowers are most conspicuous.

This tree is a native of the Balkan Peninsula. In Europe, its wood is much used by wood-carvers and turners. Some superstitious people believe that attacks of rheumatism may be prevented by carrying the nuts in one's pockets. The seeds have been reported to be used in tonics to stop horses from coughing, hence the common name. Like those of the native buckeyes, the seeds are rather poisonous if eaten; if made into a paste, they will repel insects. They should never be confused with the edible nuts of the true chestnuts (*Castanea*). A skin-protectant extract known as esculin is obtained from the bark and leaves.

BOTTLEBRUSH BUCKEYE   *Aesculus parviflora* **Walt.**

> The exceptionally long flower spikes, longer than any of our native buckeyes, spineless fruits, small shrubby tree habit, and restricted geographic range are most distinctive.

Summer. *Leaves* palmately 5-foliate, alternate, simple, deciduous; leaflets up to 8 inches long; turning bright golden yellow in the autumn. *Flowers* in a columnar cluster up to 20 inches long; petals white, nearly equal in length; stamens exserted, 3 to 4 times longer than petals. *Fruits* 1 to 2 inches long, round or nearly so, spineless, 1- to 2-seeded.

Winter. *Twigs* without a rank odor. *Buds,* terminal bud about ¼ inch long, without keeled scales.

———

The bottlebrush buckeye is a shrub or small tree, rising to 15 feet high, found in rich wooded bottomlands in South Carolina, Georgia, and Alabama. Because of its very beautifully elongated inflorescences with numerous white flowers and leaves that turn a bright golden yellow in the autumn, this species is used extensively in the nursery trade.

OHIO BUCKEYE   *Aesculus glabra* **Willd.**

> Our only native buckeye with this combination of spiny fruits and pronounced disagreeably odored twigs and leaves.

Summer. *Leaves* opposite, deciduous, palmately 5-foliate (rarely 7-foliate), with a pronounced fetid odor when crushed; leaflets 3 to 6 inches long, ovate or oblong obovate, broadest about the middle and gradually narrowed to the pointed bases and acuminate tips; margins finely and irregularly toothed, light green above, paler beneath and glabrous or nearly so, hairy on the veins; petioles 4 to 6 inches long, rather stout. *Flowers* ¾ inch long, unpleasantly odored, bell-shaped in large, upright, broadly pyramidal clusters, 4 to 6 inches long; petals 4, yellow to green yellow, all nearly equal in size; stamens exserted far beyond the petals, twice their length. *Fruits* (capsule) about 1 to 2 inches in diameter, and almost round; thick, leathery, nearly always prickly or spiny, borne on a

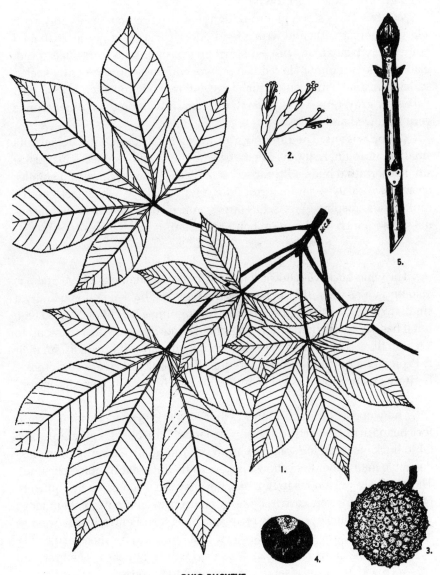

OHIO BUCKEYE

1. Branch with mature leaves.
2. Portion of flower cluster.
3. Fruit.
4. Seed.
5. Winter twig.

stout stalk, splitting along 2 to 3 sutures; usually containing a solitary, large, glabrous, lustrous brown nut.

Winter. *Twigs* stout, glabrous, light reddish brown to ashy gray, with a large greenish pith, and with a fetid odor; leaf scars large, heart-shaped or inversely triangular, with 3 distinct groups of bundle scars. *Buds* ovoid, glabrous, not gummy, pale reddish brown, with rather prominently keeled scales; terminal bud about ⅝ inch long, lateral buds considerably smaller. *Bark* ashy gray, rather corky-warty, unpleasantly odorous; on older trunks very furrowed and scaly.

Comparisons. The rank odor of the twigs of the Ohio buckeye; its smaller, more finely toothed leaflets; smooth, weakly spined fruit husks; smaller terminal buds with conspicuously keeled bud scales; and smaller overall size easily separate it from the yellow buckeye, which lacks both a rank odor and spined husks, has larger, unkeeled or weakly keeled terminal buds (¾ inch long), and in habit represents a much larger tree.

———————

The Ohio buckeye (Ohio's state tree, hence the name Buckeye State) is also known as the fetid buckeye or the stinking buckeye. It is usually a small- to medium-sized tree, frequently attaining a height of 20 to 40 feet, but it has been known to attain a height of about 90 feet with a trunk up to 2 feet in diameter. In the northern portion of its range it is usually small. It is typically a bottomland tree, frequenting banks of rivers and creeks. It attains its best development in the lower Ohio and upper Mississippi river valleys.

The wood is light, soft, and rather weak. It is used to some extent for cheap furniture, artificial limbs, woodenware, boxes, and crates. The Ohio buckeye is seldom planted as an ornamental tree, being much less desirable than either the yellow buckeye or the introduced horse-chestnut. The seeds are poisonous to humans, but they are often eaten by squirrels. Historically, they were carried by early pioneers to eliminate joint ailments.

The Ohio buckeye ranges from southwestern Pennsylvania west to Nebraska, south to Georgia, northern Alabama, and northeastern Texas.

Two expressions have been described within our area. The first, var. *arguta* (Buckl.) Robins., is a plant having 7 to 11 narrow leaflets, ⅜ to 2 inches wide. It occurs from Iowa to Arkansas and west from Wyoming to Texas. The second, var. *glabra,* has somewhat fewer (5 to 7) and wider (1⅓ to 2½ inches) leaflets. It is the more eastern expression, found from Massachusetts through Pennsylvania, south to Georgia, extending west to Texas and the southern Great Plains.

YELLOW BUCKEYE   *Aesculus flava* **Ait.**

> This is a large Appalachian Mountain tree species, characterized by its yellow flowers on glandular hairy stalks and nonspiny fruits.

Summer. *Leaves* opposite, palmately 5-foliate (rarely 7-foliate), deciduous; leaflets 4 to 8 inches long, ovate obovate or oblong ovate, broadest about the middle, gradually narrowed to the pointed bases and acuminate tips, margins finely and irregularly serrate, dark green above, yellowish green and usually somewhat hairy beneath, especially in the leaf axils; petioles 4 to 6 inches long, stout. *Flowers* yellow; 1½ inches long, borne in clusters 4 to 6 inches long; petals 4, noticeably unequal in length; stamens inserted. *Fruits* (capsule) 2 to 3 inches long, thick, leathery, somewhat oblong or pear-shaped, glabrous; borne on a stout stalk, splitting along 2 or 3 sutures; usually containing 2 large, glabrous, lustrous brown, poisonous nuts.

Winter. *Twigs* stout, glabrous, light reddish brown to ashy gray, often hairy, with a large greenish pith; leaf scars look like tiny horseshoes complete with nail holes. *Buds* ovoid, glabrous, not gummy, pale reddish brown, scales slightly keeled; terminal bud about ¾ inch long; lateral buds considerably smaller. *Bark* smooth, grayish brown, becoming furrowed on the trunks, and with thin scales on the low ridges.

Comparisons. Leaves and twigs may best be distinguished from those of the Ohio buckeye by the absence of a pronounced fetid odor.

The yellow buckeye is also known as the sweet buckeye or the large buckeye. It is a medium- to large-sized tree (largest of our buckeyes), usually attaining a height of 40 to 60 feet and a trunk diameter of 1 to 2 feet, though it is sometimes much larger. In the northern part of its range it usually occurs in stream valleys, occasionally ascending the lower slopes of river hills, but in the South it is common in the mountains. It reaches its maximum development in the Great Smoky Mountains of western North Carolina and eastern Tennessee.

The wood is light, soft, and rather weak. It is principally used for cheap furniture, artificial limbs, woodenware, boxes, and crates. The yellow buckeye is often planted as a shade or ornamental tree, and it is very attractive. The nuts are poisonous to humans if eaten raw, but they are frequently eaten by the gray squirrel and the fox squirrel.

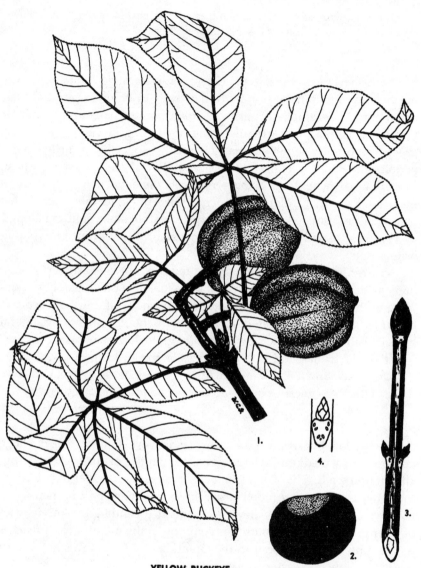

YELLOW BUCKEYE

1. Branch with mature leaves and fruits.
2. Seed.
3. Winter twig.
4. Details of bud and leaf scar.

The yellow buckeye ranges from southwestern Pennsylvania and central Ohio south along the Appalachian Mountains to northern Georgia and Alabama.

RED BUCKEYE   *Aesculus pavia* L.

> This is a coastal plain shrub or small tree species, with spectacularly showy red flowers (occasionally yellow in Texas populations), with their individual petals of different lengths and with nonspiny fruits.

Summer. *Leaves* opposite, palmately compound, deciduous; leaflets 4 to 6 inches long, 1½ to 2½ inches wide, usually 5 (rarely 7), obovate to elliptic, apically pointed, bases wedge-shaped, margins sharply and doubly serrate; at maturity dark green and glabrous above, paler and glabrous, or with axillary hair tufts, beneath; petioles 4 to 6 inches long. *Flowers* 1¼ inches long, borne in showy, oblong clusters, 4 to 8 inches long; petals unequal, 4, with glandular-hairy, lateral margins, red (or yellow in Texas populations); stamens somewhat exserted. *Fruits* (capsule) 1 to 2 inches in diameter, glabrous, globular, spineless, splitting along 2 to 3 sutures, containing 1 to 3 lustrous, dark chestnut-brown seeds about 1 inch in diameter.

Winter. *Twigs* stout, glabrous, greenish gray to grayish brown or reddish brown, with prominent scattered lenticels. *Buds* ovoid, pointed, light brown to grayish brown, glabrous; terminal bud ¼ to ½ inch long, bud scales not prominently keeled. *Bark* grayish brown, smooth, eventually flaking off in irregular patches.

Comparisons. The bright red flowers separate at once this species from all other buckeyes. The scarlet flowers, twigs that do not have a rank odor, spineless fruits, and small terminal buds help to separate this species from the Ohio buckeye, which is our only other buckeye with keeled bud scales.

The red buckeye is a shrub or occasionally an irregularly shaped tree growing up to about 30 feet in height, with a trunk diameter of about 8 inches. Some of our other species of buckeyes at times have red-tinted or partially reddish flowers, but all parts of the flowers of this one, including the slightly protruding stamens, are a bright fiery red (yellow in Texas

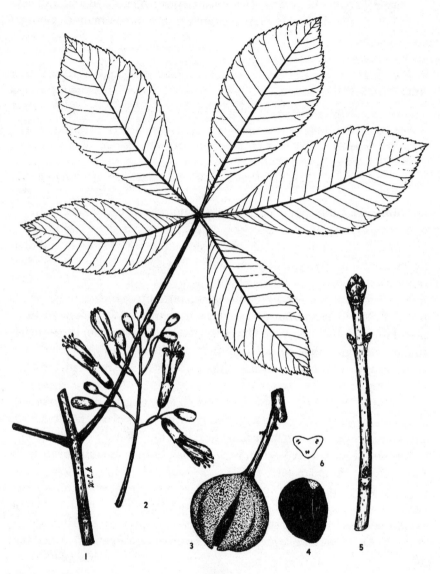

RED BUCKEYE

1. Branch with mature leaf.
2. Cluster of flowers.
3. Fruit.
4. Nut removed from husk.
5. Winter twig.
6. Detail of leaf-scar.

populations). Often, in early spring, one catches a glimpse of them on the little trees in the understory of the coastal hardwoods and pines. The red buckeye is too small to produce wood of any value, but it makes an excellent subject for ornamental planting.

The range of the red buckeye extends through the coastal plain, from southeastern Virginia to Florida and west to central Texas; and northward, in the Mississippi Valley, to southeastern Oklahoma and southern Illinois.

PAINTED BUCKEYE   *Aesculus sylvatica* **Bartr.**

> This Piedmont shrub or small tree is characterized by its relatively long leaflet stalks (more than 1/8 inch long) and by its unequal, yellow to cream petals, included stamens, and spineless fruits.

Summer. *Leaves* opposite, palmately compound; leaflets 3 to 8 inches long, 1½ to 2½ inches wide; usually 5 leaflets, slender, narrowly elliptic, margins sharply double-serrate, yellow green above, hairy and green beneath; petioles 4 to 6 inches long. *Flowers* 1 to 1¼ inches long, oblong to pyramidal, borne in clusters 4 to 6 inches long; petals unequal, 4, yellow green to bright yellow or occasionally tinged reddish; stamens included. *Fruits* (capsule) 1 to 1½ inches long, nearly round, spineless, lustrous brown, glabrous, splitting along 3 sutures, containing a solitary, poisonous, light brown seed.

Winter. *Twigs* light reddish brown, stout, glabrous. *Buds*, terminal bud less than ½ inch long, bud scales not keeled.

The painted buckeye, which is also known as the Georgia buckeye or the dwarf buckeye, is usually a shrub, spreading by extensive underground runners, but occasionally it becomes a tree up to about 30 feet in height. It occurs on well-drained hillsides and slopes. This is a species of the southern Piedmont through Georgia, Alabama, and northwestern Florida. It is used in horticulture in some areas of the South and is prized for its showy flowers.

MAPLE FAMILY—ACERACEAE

The Maples—Acer

The maples have opposite, simple, palmately compound leaves, or more rarely, leaves that are pinnately compound. The chiefly insect-pollinated flowers are variable, but usually the stamens and the pistils occur in different flowers, and very often the staminate and the pistillate flowers are on separate trees. The flowers of the red maple and the silver maple occur in lateral clusters, developing in early spring, before the leaves appear, from buds that were on twigs throughout the winter. Those of our other maples appear either with the leaves or after the leaves are fully developed; both often developing from the same buds. The wind-dispersed fruits are very characteristic, consisting of a pair of wings with the seed enclosed in the base, and joined together to form the familiar maple "keys." The buds are quite variable and afford an important means of identifying the species during the winter season. The leaf scars are crescent-shaped or V-shaped with 3 rather conspicuous bundle scars that are sometimes compounded. In the timber industry, the hard and soft maples can be separated by applying a chemical solution of ferric salt, which produces different colored stains on the sapwood; blue stain indicates soft maple, green stain indicates hard maple. The two groups can also be separated by their leaf morphology, with the hard maples having rounded, U-shaped leaf sinuses and green leaf undersurfaces, while those of the soft maples have V-shaped margins and whitish undersurfaces.

NORWAY MAPLE   *Acer platanoides* L.

> The milky sap of the leaf petioles and the 5- to 7-lobed leaves (more lobes than any other eastern maple) are most distinctive.

Summer. *Leaves* 4 to 7 inches long and wide, opposite, simple, deciduous, usually 5- to 7-lobed, margins with irregular, coarse, sharply pointed teeth; bases heart-shaped; blades thin but very firm, glabrous, conspicuously dark green above, only slightly paler and bright green beneath; petioles 3 to 4 inches long, slender, glabrous, exuding milky sap when broken. *Flowers* ¼ to ⁵⁄₁₆ inch wide, male and female flowers borne on separate trees, developing in the spring; petals 5, green yellow. *Fruits* with very divergent wings; wings about 2 inches long, each pair borne on a slender stalk in loose terminal clusters; maturing in the early autumn.

Winter. *Twigs* moderately stout, glabrous, more or less lustrous, greenish to brown; leaf scars V-shaped, opposing tips meeting (this helps to separate the Norway maple from similar species such as the sycamore maple). *Buds* large, terminal buds about ¼ inch long, very broadly ovoid, short-stalked, reddish, or greenish purple toward their base, with 2 to 4 more-or-less keeled visible scales, occasionally superposed; lateral buds smaller and appressed; all buds exuding a white sap when cut. *Bark* dark gray, close, firm, roughened by shallow fissures and narrow, more or less interconnected ridges.

Comparisons. The leaves quite closely resemble those of the sugar maple, from which they may be readily distinguished by the milky sap that exudes from broken leaf petioles, as well as by their deeper green color rather than yellowish green color and more numerous, sharper, lobes (5 to 7 versus 3 to 5); by their wider and more obtuse terminal buds with 3 to 4 rather than 4 to 8 pairs of scales that appear to be reddish to purple, but are intermixed with green; and by their more broadly diverging winged fruits. It can be separated from the sycamore maple by the leaf scar differences stated above.

The Norway maple is a native of Europe, where it is an important timber tree, often attaining a height of around 100 feet. In this country it is usually a medium-sized tree, sometimes 40 to 60 feet in height, with a trunk diameter from 1 to 2 feet. It has a beautifully symmetrical, dense, rounded crown and handsome dark green foliage that turns pale yellow in

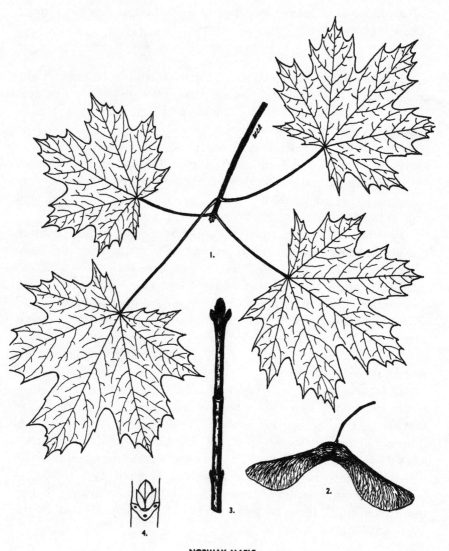

NORWAY MAPLE

1. Branch with mature leaves.
2. Fruit.
3. Winter twig.
4. Details of bud and leaf scar.

the autumn and thus represents one of the most widely cultivated trees in our northern states. This is one of the five eastern maples (others are the chalk maple, the black maple, the sugar maple, and the Florida maple) that have lobed but entire-margined leaves, lacking the serrated teeth found on our other maple species such as the red maple, the sycamore maple, the silver maple, the mountain maple, and the striped maple. The milky sap within the leaf petioles makes the Norway maple easy to identify.

The Norway maple has been extensively planted in North America as a street and shade tree, for which purposes it is most admirably adapted. It grows quite rapidly, is very tolerant of city smoke and dust, and is relatively free of insect pests and fungus diseases. In the autumn it holds its foliage at least two weeks longer than do any of our native maples.

A minor expression, which is no longer recognized as a distinct taxon, the Schwedler maple (var. *schwedleri* Nichols.), has leaves that are a bright red while they are young, turning a deep green at maturity. It is less commonly planted than the typical Norway maple.

MOUNTAIN MAPLE   *Acer spicatum* Lam.

> The mountain maple can be separated from all other maples by this combination of characters: shrubby habit, 2-valve bud scales, stalked buds, hairy twigs, 3-lobed leaves with ciliate leaf margins, and erect inflorescences, which appear after the leaves are fully formed. This is our only maple with ciliate leaf margins; thus even a small portion of a leaf margin is identifiable.

Summer. *Leaves* 2¾ to 5 inches long and wide, roundish, opposite, simple, deciduous, distinctly 3-lobed above the middle or occasionally slightly 5-lobed; lobes rather broad, short, gradually pointed, long tipped margins with rather coarsely and sharply singly serrate teeth; sinuses shallow, rather broadly V-shaped; blades thin, base cordate to truncate; dark yellowish green and glabrous above, paler beneath, covered with short grayish hairs; petioles 2 to 3 inches long, slender, usually red. *Flowers* ¼ inch across, small, pale yellow green, in erect inflorescences on branch tips, often appearing after the leaves, male and female flowers borne in separate bracts on the same tree. *Fruits* (samara) ¾ to 1 inch long, red in the fall, borne in drooping, racemose clusters, with more or less divergent wings about ½ inch long.

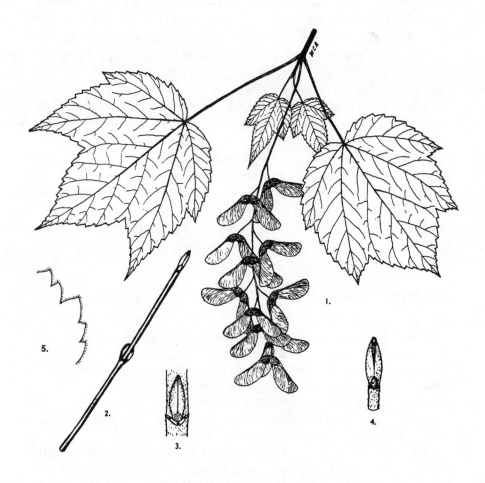

MOUNTAIN MAPLE

1. Branch with mature leaves and fruits.
2. Winter twig.
3. Detail of bud and leaf scar.
4. Detail of terminal bud.
5. Detail of ciliate leaf margin.

Winter. *Twigs* slender, purplish red, or often yellow green on one side, minutely hairy with short, appressed, grayish hairs, particularly about the nodes and toward the tips; leaf scars narrowly crescent-shaped, tips not quite meeting. *Buds* usually less than ¼ inch long, 2 to 3 times long as wide, slender, nearly always stalked or rarely sessile, oblong ovoid, pointed, red but dull with minute, appressed, grayish hairs, and 2 visible scales meeting along the edges without overlapping. *Bark* thin, brownish or grayish-brown, smooth, eventually becoming slightly furrowed or warty, occasionally blotched.

The mountain maple is a large shrub or a small tree that attains a height of 20 to 30 feet and a trunk diameter of 4 to 8 inches. The trunk is short, with short, slender, upright branches forming a rather small, rounded crown. The mountain maple, as its name implies, is usually found in the cool, shady, moist, and rocky mountain forests. In both habit and habitat, it closely resembles the striped maple, but differs substantially morphologically. The specific epithet, *spicatum*, refers to the elongated flowering spikes produced in early summer.

The wood of the mountain maple is not used commercially. Like the striped maple, it makes very good browse for the white-tailed deer. It is an attractive small tree or shrub, and is occasionally used in ornamental plantings. In the autumn the leaves turn orange or scarlet.

The mountain maple ranges from Nova Scotia and Newfoundland to Saskatchewan, southward to the northern portions of the eastern United States, and along the Appalachian Mountains to northern Georgia.

STRIPED MAPLE   *Acer pensylvanicum* L.

> The greenish to reddish-brown striated bark with prominent longitudinal whitish streaks is distinctive at any season. This, along with its long-acuminate, 3-lobed leaves and racemose inflorescences with large yellow petals, is most distinct.

Summer. *Leaves*, 5 to 7 inches long, nearly as broad, opposite, distinctly 3-lobed above the middle; lobes short, broad, contracted into long-acuminate tips, bases rounded or heart-shaped; margins inwardly curved, with sharp, double serrate teeth; sinuses very broadly rounded; blades thin, bright yellowish green, glabrous above, paler and glabrous or nearly

Wm. C. Grimm.

STRIPED MAPLE

1. Branch with mature leaves and fruits.　　3. Detail of bud and leaf scar.
2. Winter twig.

so beneath; petioles 1½ to 2 inches long, stout, grooved, often red. *Flowers* ¼ to ⅜ inch wide, petals yellow, appearing after the leaves, male and female flowers borne in separate, terminal, drooping racemes on the same tree. *Fruits* (samara) 1 to 1¼ inches long, borne in long, drooping, racemose clusters; wings about ¾ to 1 inch long, divergent; seed portion pitted on the side.

Winter. *Twigs* moderately stout, glabrous, lustrous, greenish to red brown; leaf scars crescent-shaped, tips not quite meeting; pith pale brown. *Buds* about ½ inch long, 2 to 3 times long as wide, bright red, glabrous, stalked, oblong ovate, apically blunt; scales 2, visible, more or less keeled, meeting at their edges, but not overlapping; terminal bud somewhat larger than the lateral buds, which are appressed to the twigs.

Comparisons. In winter, this species, along with the mountain maple, can be told from all other maple species by the stalked winter buds. The two species, however, are easily separated by the leaf margins being eciliate in the striped maple, rather than ciliate, and by the bark being conspicuously green and white-striped in the former and nonstriped and brown to brownish gray in the latter.

Striped maple is also known as moosewood, whistle-wood, and goosefoot maple. It is a large shrub or a small, short-trunked tree from 10 to 30 feet in height and from 4 to 8 inches in diameter, found in cool, moist, rocky woods in the shaded understory of the forest. It occurs most commonly in forests of the northern hardwood type, but it is also found in mixed stands of hardwoods and conifers. In the Great Smoky Mountains of North Carolina and Tennessee it reaches its maximum development.

The striped maple produces no wood of commercial value. It provides excellent browse for the white-tailed deer, however, and in the north woods it is extensively utilized by the moose, hence one of its common names. The bark is also eaten by rabbits and by beavers. The resemblance of its large leaves to the outline of a goose's foot is responsible for the name of goosefoot maple. In its native habitats this shrub or small tree is strikingly beautiful. In autumn its leaves turn a pale yellow.

The striped maple ranges from Nova Scotia to Minnesota, south to the region of the Great Lakes and New England, and along the Appalachian Mountains to northern Georgia.

SUGAR MAPLE   *Acer saccharum* **Marsh.**

The sugar maple may be distinguished by its palmately lobed leaves, which are apically squarish, by its glabrous leaves and twigs, narrowly conical sharp-pointed buds with 6 to 16 pale, somewhat hairy brownish scales, and by its paired samaras that form nearly parallel sides.

Summer. *Leaves* rigid, opposite, simple, deciduous, 5-lobed; lobes sparingly and irregularly toothed, teeth and lobes with long acuminate tips, the terminal lobe square with nearly parallel sides; sinuses between the lobes rounded or U-shaped at the base; leaf blades 3 to 6 inches long, 5 to 7 inches wide, thin but firm, dark green to yellowish green above, paler and glabrous beneath; becoming golden yellow, often more or less suffused with red in the autumn; petioles long, slender. *Flowers* small, ³/₁₆ inch long, apetalous, borne in fascicles, appearing with the leaves. *Fruits* (samara) 1¼ to 1½ inches long, borne on stalks generally longer than the fruits, may persist occasionally into the winter; with slightly divergent wings, a typical maple key.

Winter. *Twigs* slender, glabrous, shiny, varying from pale reddish brown to buffy brown, with numerous pale lenticels. *Buds* narrowly conical, sharp-pointed; scales 6 to 16, pale brownish, somewhat hairy; terminal bud about ½ inch long; lateral buds ¼ inch long, more or less appressed to the twigs. *Bark* on older trunks becoming dark gray, deeply furrowed into long thick plates, which are often loose along one edge.

Comparisons. This species can be separated from the black maple by its glabrous rather than hairy leaves and twigs and by its flat rather than conspicuously drooping 5-lobed rather than 3- to 5-lobed leaves, which lack stipules at the petiole base, by its brown rather than yellowish brown to ashy gray twigs, and by its grayish to light brown bark, rather than dark brown to blackish bark on the mature trees.

———

The sugar maple, or rock maple, is a handsome tree, often attaining a height of 60 to nearly 100 feet, and a trunk diameter of 3 or 4 feet. Open-grown specimens have broadly rounded crowns. Although it prefers fertile and well-drained soils, it succeeds quite well on many of the poorer and rocky soil types. Sugar maple is a prominent member of the climax beech-birch-maple forest association.

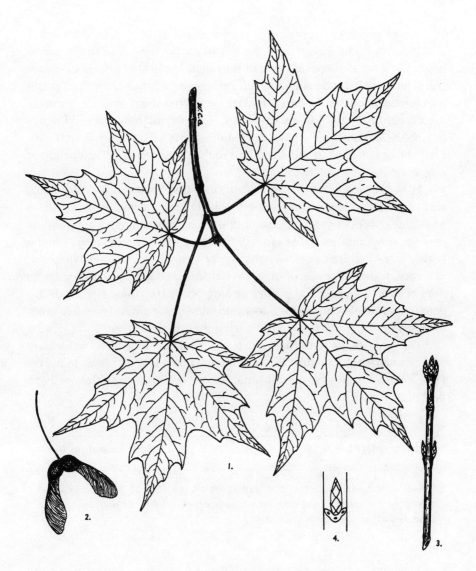

SUGAR MAPLE

1. Branch with mature leaves.
2. Fruit.
3. Winter twig.
4. Detail of bud and leaf scar.

From the Native Americans, our pioneer forefathers learned the art of making syrup and sugar from the sap of native trees, the sugar maple being the principal species. Today the sugar bushes, or groves of maple trees, with their rustic sugaring-off houses are a familiar sight in many parts of the country. The trees are tapped during the late winter or early spring, before the buds begin to swell. Cold frosty nights, with mild thaws during the daytime, seem to be the requirements for good sap flow. It generally takes between 30 and 40 gallons of the crude sap to make a gallon of maple syrup.

The sugar maple ranks high as a timber tree. Its wood is heavy, hard, and very close-grained. It is used extensively for flooring, furniture, boxes and crates, woodenware, spools and bobbins, wooden novelties, and as veneer. Abnormalities in the grain of the wood of some trees results in the highly prized cabinet woods known as curly maple or bird's-eye maple. It is a very desirable shade or ornamental tree, and many fine specimens may be seen around rural homes or along country lanes. The seeds are eaten by squirrels, chipmunks, deer mice, and some birds. Twigs are often browsed by the white-tailed deer during the winter season.

The range of the sugar maple extends from Newfoundland to Ontario and Minnesota, southward through the northern United States to northern Georgia and northern Louisiana. It is most abundant in the northern part of its range.

FLORIDA MAPLE   *Acer barbatum* Michx.

> The whitish undersurface of the leaves, the elongated type of leaf lobes, and the unusually smooth, light gray, American beech–like bark of the trunk and the branches of younger trees are distinctive.

The Florida maple is a tall, straight, single-stemmed tree and a close southern dwarf relative of the sugar maple, but with smaller, hairy leaves; leaf blades 1½ to 3 inches long, more blue green in color, with noticeably smaller petioles; 3 to 5 rounded or acute lobes (the sugar maple has 5) and wavy margins, which are scarcely if ever toothed. The teeth of the sugar maple leaf are much more pronounced, with very sharply acute or acuminate tips. The leaves of the Florida maple are similar to those of the crooked, often multistemmed chalk maple, but differ by the undersurfaces of the leaves being whitish glaucous rather than greenish. The bark of the

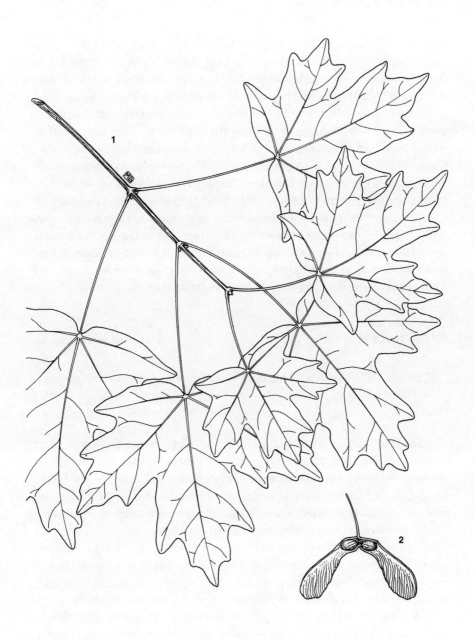

FLORIDA MAPLE

1. Branch with mature leaves (lobed but entire margins).
2. Fruit.

Florida maple, especially on old trees, has the same tendency as that of the sugar maple to produce characteristic long, flat, often smooth plates. The fruits, however, are smaller, about half the size of the sugar maple, and the bark is lighter in color. The wavy leaf margin of the Florida maple suggests that of the black maple, but the latter has consistently hairy leaf undersurfaces with drooping leaves that appear to have a somewhat wilted appearance, and is more northern in range. The Florida maple also has leaves that are dark green above and paler or slightly whitened (both leaf surfaces are green in the black maple) and glabrous, or somewhat hairy beneath. The male flowers of the Florida maple are short-stalked, ⅝ to 1 inch long, compared with those of the sugar maple or the black maple, with its 1- to 2-inch-long stalks. The Florida maple occurs in the coastal plain from southeastern Virginia to central Florida west to eastern Texas; and northward, in the Mississippi Valley, to southeastern Missouri and Illinois. It is also known as the southern sugar maple.

SYCAMORE MAPLE   *Acer pseudoplatanus* L.

> The bright green winter buds and the 5-lobed leaves with serrated margins are distinctive.

Summer. *Leaves* 3 to 6 inches long and wide, rather thick and firm; upper surfaces dark green and glabrous, with a wrinkled or roughish appearance, lower surfaces paler or slightly whitened, more or less hairy; lobes usually 5 (more rarely 3), bases rather broad and gradually tapering, margins coarsely toothed, sinuses rather narrow, V-shaped, extending about midway to the midribs, bases heart-shaped; petioles 3 to 4 inches long, rather stout. *Flowers* ³⁄₁₆ to ¼ inch wide, in long pendent clusters; petals 5, greenish yellow, developing in early spring. *Fruits* about 1¼ to 2 inches long, with wings diverging at nearly a 45° angle; borne in drooping, racemose, terminal clusters; maturing in summer to early autumn.

Winter. *Twigs* rather stout, glabrous, somewhat lustrous, greenish to brownish or gray; opposing tips of leaf scars do not meet (see the Norway maple for comparison). *Buds* bright greenish, occasionally tinged with pink or red, with 4 or 5 more-or-less visible keeled scales; terminal bud ¼ to ½ inch long, often appearing double, broadly ovoid or roundish, bluntly pointed; lateral buds smaller, somewhat divergent. *Bark* grayish brown to reddish brown, on the larger trunks breaking into short-oblong scales.

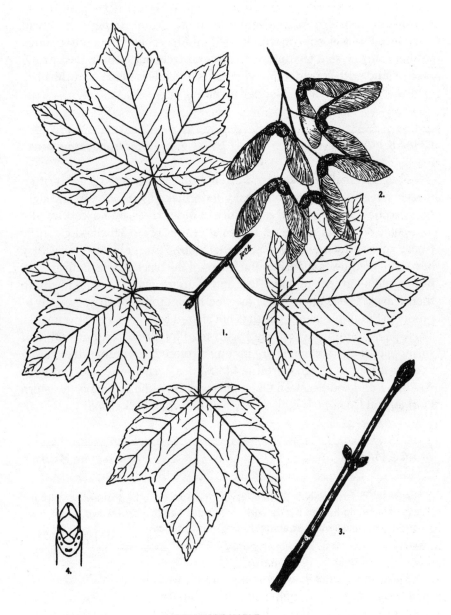

SYCAMORE MAPLE

1. Branch with mature leaves.
2. Cluster of fruits.
3. Winter twig.
4. Detail of bud and leaf scar.

The sycamore maple, which grows 60 to 70 feet high, is native to Europe and western Asia, where it is an important timber tree. It was introduced into North America in 1803 and has been frequently planted in this country as a shade or ornamental tree, and although it grows rapidly and with considerable vigor, it is much less hardy and thus less extensively used than the Norway maple.

CHALK MAPLE   *Acer leucoderme* Small

This is a small, crooked, and often multiple-stemmed tree, or often merely a large shrub, which is easily recognized by its smooth and light gray to chalky-white bark, especially in older trees, and exceptionally noticeable on the upper stems. The small leaves, 1½ to 3 inches long, have from 3 to occasionally 5 long, acuminate lobes; except for their size, they have a marked resemblance to the leaves of the black maple. Both species have a yellow-green and hairy leaf undersurface, and both tend to clump their leaves. The chalk maple, however, has an unusual characteristic of producing multiple stems, which is not shared by any other native maple. This species might be confused with the Florida maple, but both leaf surfaces of the chalk maple are greenish colored. It occurs rather rarely and locally from North Carolina to southeastern Tennessee, southern Arkansas, and southeastern Oklahoma, south to Louisiana, northeastern Florida, and Georgia. It is also known as the white-bark maple.

BLACK MAPLE   *Acer nigrum* Michx. f.

The 3- (or occasionally 5-) lobed leaves that appear to be somewhat wilted, resembling limp human hands, with their sides bending downward, and hairy petioles, leaf undersurfaces, and twigs are most distinctive.

Summer. *Leaves* 4 to 6 inches long, 5 to 7 inches wide, opposite, simple, deciduous, tips long-acuminate; usually distinctly 3-lobed (occasionally 5), but otherwise margins entire or with a few wavy teeth, terminal lobe square with nearly parallel sides; blades typically having a marked tendency to droop on the sides; upper surfaces darker green than those of the sugar maple, lower surfaces paler yellowish green, more or less distinctly hairy, with tan, velvety hairs extending along the leaf

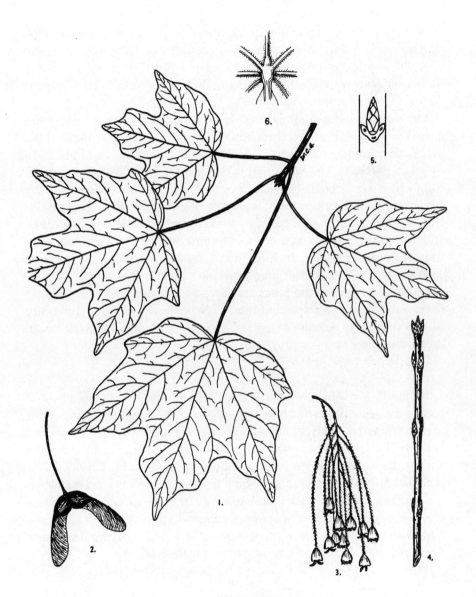

BLACK MAPLE

1. Branch with mature leaves.
2. Fruit.
3. Cluster of flowers.
4. Winter twig.
5. Detail of bud and leaf scar.
6. Detail of hair on leaf undersurface.

stalk; very often with prominent stipules at the bases of the leaf stalks. *Flowers* small, ³⁄₁₆ inch long, yellow green, appearing with leaves, in sessile corymbs, similar to those of the sugar maple. *Fruits* (samara) similar to those of the sugar maple but tending to have somewhat more divergent wings.

Winter. *Twigs* moderately stout, hairy, dull yellow brown. *Buds* small, hairy, ovoid, dark brown, acute; bud scales 8 to 16. *Bark* on older trunks deeply furrowed, usually rough, darker, often tending toward blackish.

Comparisons. The black maple closely resembles the sugar maple, from which it may be distinguished by its leaf blades, which appear to be somewhat wilted, but propped-up by the petioles; by its more rounded leaf lobes, which lack serrations; by the hairy undersurface of the leaves, with the hairs not being confined to the veins; with stipules present at the base of the leaf petioles (lacking in the sugar maple); and by having a darker, nearly black (rather than gray) bark, which is more furrowed or corrugated. In general the twigs and buds of the black maple are similar to those of the sugar maple, but tend to be somewhat stouter, dull buffy brown, with more prominent lenticels, and the buds are somewhat larger, duller, and more or less hairy.

The black maple is sometimes called the black sugar maple, and by some authorities it has been considered to be a variety of the sugar maple. While the two trees are quite similar, there are obvious differences between them, and the black maple is now generally regarded as a distinct species. Its wood is very much like that of the sugar maple, and lumbermen do not make any distinction, both being marketed as hard maple.

The range of the black maple extends from Vermont and southern Quebec westward to southern Minnesota and southward to New Jersey, and mostly in the mountains of North Carolina, Georgia, Tennessee, Kentucky, and Missouri, extending to northeastern Kansas.

SILVER MAPLE
Acer saccharinum **L.**

> Unlike most maples that have parallel or converging sides on the terminal lobe, this species has divergent sides, sloping outwards. The silvery undersurface of the leaves, very long fruits (the largest of any eastern native maple), and strongly fetid odor of the twigs (the only native maple with this condition) help to separate the silver maple from all of our other maples.

Summer. *Leaves* 3 to 6 inches long and wide, opposite, simple, deciduous, bright green above and silvery-white beneath, 5-lobed, terminal lobe with divergent sides sloping outwards, having a distinctive keystone appearance; sinuses deeply cut and sharply pointed or slightly rounded; leaf margins coarsely toothed, often with smaller lobes; petioles 3 to 5 inches long, slender, often bright red, at least above, drooping. *Flowers* small, ¼ inch long, green yellow to pale red, produced in early spring before the leaves, male and female flowers borne on same or different trees. *Fruits* (samara), the largest produced by any of our native eastern maples, with divergent wings 1½ to 2½ inches long, borne in small lateral clusters, maturing in May, persisting but a short time.

Winter. *Twigs* glabrous, shiny, more of a chestnut brown to gray brown, emitting a fetid odor when bruised or broken. *Buds,* leaf buds fewer than twice as long as wide, blunt, with fewer than 6 scales; flower buds numerous, produced in a ring of clusters around most twigs in late winter. *Bark* on the young trunks and branches smooth, gray; on older trunks becoming shaggy, more reddish brown, separating into long, thin scales, which are loosened at the ends.

Comparisons. The twigs and buds are very similar to those of the red maple. The silver maple differs from the red maple in the more silvery, rather than white, undersurface of the leaves; deeper-cut sinuses, especially between the terminal and the second lobes; the convex rather than concave shape of the terminal lobe, which is greater than half the leaf-blade length (less than half the leaf-blade length in the red maple); the fetid, rather than pleasant, odor of the twigs; and by its apetalous flowers.

The silver maple is also known as the soft maple or the river maple. It is a medium- to large-sized tree, usually 60 to 80 feet in height but occasionally rising to around 100 feet, with a trunk diameter of 2 to 4 feet. The trunk is usually short, dividing low into several ascending subtrunks,

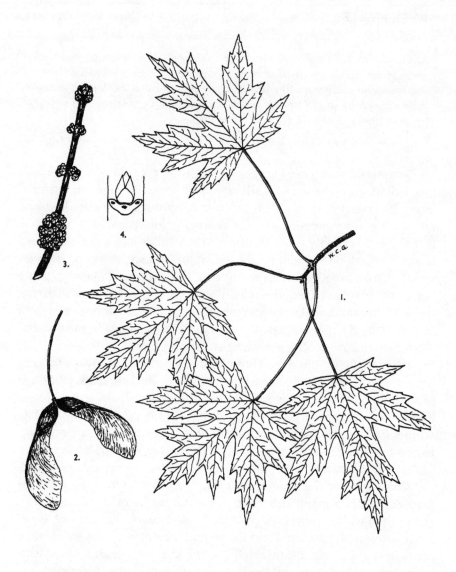

SILVER MAPLE

1. Branch with mature leaves.
2. Fruit.
3. Winter twig with clusters of flower buds.
4. Details of bud and leaf scar.

which again subdivide into numerous smaller branches, forming a very broad-topped and rounded crown. The long, slender lateral branches, which sweep downwards and then gracefully curve upwards at their tips, are decidedly characteristic. The silver maple is typically a tree of streambanks and low, moist, rich bottomlands that are periodically inundated by flood waters. It attains its maximum development in the Ohio River valley.

The wood is quite hard but brittle, and is neither strong nor durable. It is used for flooring, cheap furniture, railroad ties, woodenware, novelties, pulpwood, boxes, and crates. The silver maple has been extensively planted as a street tree and shade tree. It grows rapidly, has an attractive form, and is readily adapted to a variety of soil conditions, but its brittle branches are easily damaged by storms, and the trunks and larger branches are prone to develop weakening cavities. Syrup and sugar are sometimes made from the sap, but the yield is much less than that from an equivalent quantity of sap from the sugar maple.

The silver maple ranges from New Brunswick west to South Dakota and Saskatchewan, south to Georgia and Oklahoma.

RED MAPLE   *Acer rubrum* L.

The shallowly lobed leaves, small, paired samaras, with wings that are slightly divergent from each other and with their wing tips pointing outward, along with the bright red buds, red petioles, and red flowers (the earliest of our native tree species to flower) help to separate this species from our other native maples. The red winter twigs, serrate leaf margins, and glaucous lower leaf surface are also distinct.

Summer. *Leaves* 2½ to 6 inches long and wide, opposite, simple, deciduous; lobes often 5 but occasionally 3 (rarely, lobes lacking in populations along the coastal plain); the primary lobes often with smaller lobes and with coarse, irregular, singly or doubly serrate teeth on their margins; sides of the terminal lobe parallel or sloping outward, resulting in a square shape; sinuses V-shaped, much less deeply cut than those of the silver maple, which has somewhat U-shaped sinuses; upper surfaces dark green, glaucous, and glabrous; the lower surfaces light green to glaucous, glabrous or nearly so; petioles 2 to 4 inches long, slender, usually red. *Flowers* tiny, ⅛ inch long, bright red, orange or yellowish, appearing very

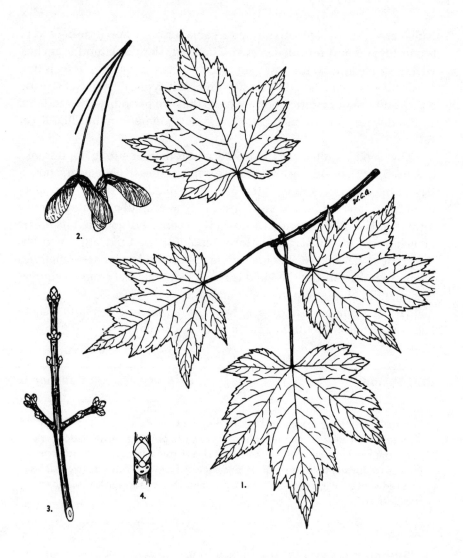

RED MAPLE

1. Branch with mature leaves.
2. Fruits.
3. Winter twig.
4. Detail of bud and leaf scar.

early in spring before the leaves; male flowers sessile; female flowers long-stalked, deeper red than the male flowers. *Fruits* (samara) ⅔ to 1 inch long; having slightly divergent wings about ¾ inch long; bright red, borne on slender drooping stems in small lateral clusters; maturing in May or June.

Winter. *Twigs* slender, lustrous, bright to dark red, glabrous but dotted with small pale lenticels; leaf scars crescent-shaped, tips of the opposing scars not meeting. *Buds* about ⅛ inch in length, bright red, broadly ovate or ovoid, with 4 or fewer pairs of visible scales with woolly margins; flower buds roundish, clustered at the nodes. *Bark* on the young trunks and branches light gray, smooth; on the older trunks becoming darker gray, shallowly fissured, with long, scaly or shaggy ridges.

Comparisons. The brightly colored red (rather than brown) winter twigs; leaves that lack a silver undersurface, with converging (rather than diverging) terminal leaf lobes; and deeply cut sinuses that do not extend near the midrib help to separate this species from the silver maple. Although the paired samara wings are divergent, as in the silver maple, they are much smaller in the red maple, and the wing tips point outward rather than inward.

The red maple is also known as the swamp maple, the scarlet maple, the white maple, the water maple, or the soft maple. It is a medium- or large-sized tree usually 40 to 70 feet in height, but occasionally reaching a height of 100 feet or more, with a trunk diameter of 2 to 4 feet. When growing in the open it has a short trunk and a rather narrowly oblong but dense crown. In the forest the trunks are usually clean for some distance from the ground. The red maple occupies a variety of habitats ranging from wet bottomlands and swamps to mountain ridges and cold northern bogs. It frequently follows the aspens into old clearings and burned-over areas, usually being one of the first forest trees to become established therein. The red maple is an important member in the developmental stages of many forest types.

The wood is moderately heavy, soft, and neither strong nor durable. It is utilized for furniture, woodenware, boxes, crates, wood pulp, and distillation products. The red maple is frequently planted as an ornamental or shade tree. It is one of the very first trees to flower in the spring. In the autumn the foliage turns a brilliant red as a rule, although in some trees the autumn coloration is regularly yellow. Sugar and syrup are sometimes made from the sap. The red maple furnishes large quantities of palatable and nutritious browse for white-tailed deer, and is frequently utilized as food by cottontail rabbits, varying hares, and beavers.

The red maple ranges from Nova Scotia west to Manitoba, south to Florida and eastern Texas.

CAROLINA RED MAPLE

Acer rubrum var. *trilobum*
Torr. & Gray ex K. Koch

This is a rather striking varietal expression of the red maple, prevalent throughout the coastal plain and Piedmont of the South Atlantic and Gulf states, and in the Mississippi Valley as far north as southern Illinois. It can be recognized by its small, thickish, roundish leaf blades, from 1½ to 3 inches in length; by its yellowish flowers; and by its smaller fruits. The leaves are usually shallowly 3-lobed near the summit, dark green above, and are more or less densely coated beneath with a white to rusty wool. In all other respects it is practically identical to the typical expression of the red maple.

DRUMMOND RED MAPLE

Acer rubrum var. *drummondii*
(Hook. & Arn. ex Nutt.) Sarg.

The Drummond red maple, or swamp red maple, is a northern variety of the red maple. It was named for its discoverer, Thomas Drummond, a Scotch nurseryman and botanical explorer, who collected it in the Allegheny Mountains in 1832. The 5-lobed leaves are very similar to those of the typical expression of the red maple except that they are densely woolly beneath, especially along the vein and the petioles, and are usually broader than long. The bright red fruits are substantially larger than those of the typical red maple (about twice as long), with convergent to divergent wings 1½ to 2½ inches long. It is primarily a swamp-inhabiting tree, often found growing in standing water, with a range extending from New Jersey to southern Illinois, and southeastern Missouri south to eastern Texas, Louisiana, Mississippi, Alabama, and Florida.

ASH-LEAF MAPLE (Box Elder) *Acer negundo* L.

> The opposite, pinnately compound leaves, coarsely toothed leaflets, and green twigs are most distinctive. This is our only native maple with bright green to green-purple branches and pinnately compound leaves.

Summer. *Leaves* 6 to 15 inches long, opposite, pinnately compound; leaflets 2 to 4 inches long, 1½ to 3 inches wide, numbering 3 or 5 (more rarely 7 or 9); short-stalked, ovate to obovate, apically pointed, bases sub-cordate to rounded or wedge-shaped, margins coarsely serrate or slightly lobed; light green and glabrous above, paler and either glabrous or slightly hairy beneath, especially in the veins; petioles 2 to 8 inches long, moderately stout, quite glabrous. *Flowers* small, yellow green, apetalous, appearing just before the leaves, male and female flowers borne on separate trees with the male flowers in small clusters and female flowers in drooping racemes. *Fruits* (samara) 1 to 1½ inches long, the typical maple keys, scarcely divergent and often incurved wings in V-shaped pairs; borne on slender stems in drooping, racemose clusters; maturing in late summer to fall.

Winter. *Twigs* rather stout, shiny, green to purplish green, glabrous, lustrous, or often glaucous (easily rubbed off), marked with prominent pale lenticels; leaf scars V-shaped, opposing tips meeting at a sharp angle. *Buds* reddish; terminal bud slightly larger than lateral buds, rather broadly ovoid, tips blunt, white-woolly or hairy, with 2 to 4 visible scales; lateral buds ⅛ to ¼ inch long, unusually beadlike, somewhat short-stalked to sessile, lateral buds appressed. *Bark* on young trunks and branches grayish or grayish-brown, rather smooth; on older trunks becoming roughened with shallow fissures and numerous, very narrow, and somewhat confluent ridges.

The ash-leaf maple is also known as the box-elder maple and the three-leaf maple. It is a small- or medium-sized tree often attaining a height of 30 to 50 feet, with a trunk diameter of 1 to 2 feet. The trunk commonly divides into several stout and wide-spreading branches forming a rather open, asymmetrical, rounded crown. The ash-leaf maple's native habitats are the banks of bottomland streams and the margins of ponds and swamps. It attains its best development in the lower Ohio and Mississippi valleys.

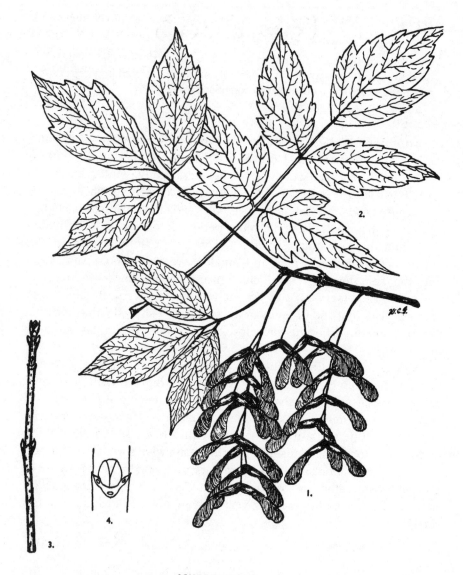

ASH-LEAF MAPLE

1. Branch with mature leaves and fruits.
2. Leaf.
3. Winter twig.
4. Detail of bud and leaf scar.

The wood is light, soft, weak, and close-grained. It is similar to the wood of the soft maple species and is used for cheap furniture, woodenware, boxes, crates, pulpwood, and for chemical distillation. The tree is frequently planted as a street or shade tree. It grows rapidly, but it is comparatively short-lived and rather inferior in decorative qualities. Small quantities of sugar and syrup are locally made from the sap. The sugar is said to be white and of very good quality.

The ash-leaf maple's native range may have been from Maine to Ontario, south to northern Florida and eastern Texas, but it now ranges from coast to coast.

In our area, four expressions have been described based upon twig color and vestiture. In the var. *interius* (Britton) Sarg., the twigs tend to be hairy, while the fruits and petioles are glabrous. This differs from the var. *violaceum* (Kirchn.) Jaeger, which has purple-gray and glaucous twigs. Both the twigs and fruits of the var. *texanum* Pax are hairy, but the petioles are glabrous. The typical expression has green glabrous twigs.

CASHEW FAMILY—ANACARDIACEAE

The Smoketree—Cotinus

AMERICAN SMOKETREE   *Cotinus obovatus* **Raf.**

> The small notch at the apex of the nearly rounded, simple, alternate long-petioled leaves and large, smokelike clusters of fruit are distinctive.

Summer. *Leaves* usually 2 to 5 inches long, 1 to 3 inches wide, alternate, simple, deciduous, mostly rounded to ovate or obovate, tips rounded or notched, bases somewhat pointed, margins entire, somewhat revolute; dark green and glabrous above, paler and glabrous or somewhat hairy beneath; petioles ½ to 4 inches long. *Flowers* ⅛ inch wide, small, unisexual, borne in large, pyramidal, terminal panicles 5 to 6 inches long, very dense, resembling plumes of smoke, male and female flowers borne on separate trees; petals 5, greenish yellow; stamens 5. *Fruits* (drupe) about ⅛ to ¼ inch long, somewhat compressed, single, seeded.

Winter. *Twigs* slender, greenish or purplish to pale reddish brown, glabrous, with prominent whitish lenticels; aromatic, exuding a gummy sap if broken; leaf scars crescent-shaped or somewhat 3-lobed, elevated, showing 3 bundle scars; pith yellow to orangish brown. *Buds,* terminal bud about ¼ inch long, ovoid, reddish brown, with several exposed scales; lateral buds smaller, crowded near twig tips, acute, with 2 to 4 visible scales; bud scales acuminate and sharply pointed. *Bark* thin, grayish brown or gray, ultimately very rough and imbricate, scaly.

The American smoketree, or chittamwood, is a small tree 30 to 55 feet in height with a trunk up to about a foot in diameter. It typically has a short trunk and a wide-spreading crown. The large clusters of slender, hairy, smoky pink, and usually sterile flower stalks persist for a long time. From a distance they look very much like puffs of smoke, hence the tree's common name. The smoketree makes a very handsome ornamental tree, the leaves turning a brilliant scarlet or orange in the fall. The wood is durable in contact with the soil and yields an orange-brown dye. It occurs rather sparingly on rocky limestone ridges and bluffs from eastern Tennessee and Alabama westward to Missouri, Arkansas, Oklahoma, and Texas.

Poison-Sumac—Toxicodendron

POISON-SUMAC   *Toxicodendron vernix* (L.) Kuntze

> The alternate, odd pinnately compound leaves with entire margins, the white, berrylike fruits that droop in lateral clusters, the glabrous and speckled branches (lenticels), and the swampy or wet habitat are distinctive.

Summer. *Leaves* 7 to 24 inches long, alternate, odd pinnately compound; leaflets 2 to 4 inches long, 1 to 2 inches wide, 7 to 13, short-stalked, conspicuously ascending on the rachis, terminal leaflet stalked, often with 2 to 3 lobes, ovate to oblong obovate, tips acuminate, bases asymmetrically wedge-shaped, margins entire and revolute; glabrous, blades lustrous dark green above, and paler beneath; petioles and rachises bright red or reddish, stout. *Flowers* about ⅛ to ⅜ inch wide, usually unisexual, male and female flowers borne on the same or separate trees in long axillary panicles; petals 5, yellow green. *Fruits* (drupe) about ⅕ to ¼ inch in diameter, glaucous, glabrous, ivory white, berrylike; borne in loose, drooping clusters 4 to 8 inches long, persisting throughout winter.

Winter. *Twigs* glabrous, rather stout, light orange brown, reddish to grayish-brown, often mottled, with numerous, raised, scattered, elongated pale lenticels but otherwise glabrous, sap clear, turning black upon exposure; leaf scars numerous, large, inversely triangular or shieldlike, almost straight on the upper margin, not surrounding the bud, with numerous bundle scars either scattered or arranged in a curved line. *Buds* ⅛ to ½ inch long, small, short-conical; scales few, purplish gray, somewhat hairy;

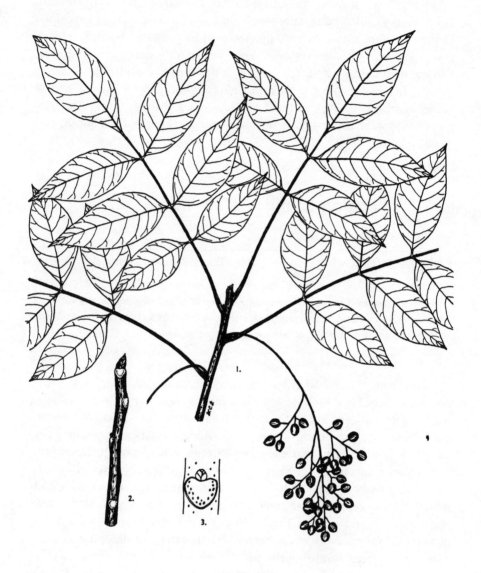

POISON-SUMAC

1. Branch with mature leaves and fruits.
2. Winter twig.
3. Detail of bud and leaf scar.

terminal bud ¼ inch long, somewhat larger than lateral buds, with 2 purplish bud scales. *Bark* thin, grayish or ashy, smooth or slightly roughened by the somewhat horizontally elongated lenticels.

———

The poison-sumac is also known as the swamp sumac, the poison dogwood, or the poison elder. It is a shrub or small tree from 5 to 20 feet in height, with a short trunk and low, open, rounded crown. Swamps, bogs, and low wet grounds are the habitats of the poison-sumac. All parts of the plant, at all seasons of the year, contain a nonvolatile oil, a rather violent skin irritant, that is even worse than that of poison ivy. Some persons are more susceptible to the poison than others, but it is always advisable to thoroughly wash all exposed surfaces of the skin with strong soap or alcohol as soon as possible after contact. Protective solutions of ferric chloride (5g), water (50cc), and glycerine (50cc) to be applied to the skin before contact have been used to reduce the severity of skin irritation.

The poison-sumac has no commercial value. A lustrous, black varnish (*vernix* means varnish) is made from the sap of this species as well as a related species native to the Orient. The presence of this black sap can be seen by applying the juice from crushed leaves on a sheet of white paper (be careful not to touch the leaf or the juice with your hands) and allowing the juice to set for 12 to 24 hours. The juice will turn brown and ultimately black. Cases of severe poisoning have been known to result from handling articles that were covered with this varnish, or from inhaling the smoke from burning leaves or branches. The poisonous principle in both of these trees, and also in the poison ivy, is urushiol. In the fall the brilliant red leaves and attractive clusters of white fruits look alluring, but they are dangerous. Many species of wild birds, however, feast on the fruits without apparent harm.

The poison-sumac ranges from southern Ontario to Minnesota, south to Florida and Texas.

The Sumacs—Rhus

The sumacs are clubby-branched, root-suckering shrubs or small trees with alternate, deciduous, pinnately compound leaves. They have small, 5-parted, greenish white to yellowish flowers borne in compact, conical, upright clusters. The fruits are small dryish drupes covered with a very thin pulp and more or less densely covered with bright red hairs. Winter twigs are moderate to stout, round or indistinctly 3-angled, and have a large pith. The buds are rather small, roundish or ovoid and without visible scales; the end bud is lacking. The leaf scars are crescent-shaped to C-shaped and have a number of bundle scars, sometimes arranged in 3 groups.

Sumacs belong to the cashew family, most of whose members are found in the tropics. The familiar cashew nut of commerce is a tropical American member of the family, now grown extensively in tropical countries. None of our red-fruited sumacs are poisonous.

STAG-HORN SUMAC   *Rhus typhina* L.

> The clubby, densely velvety twigs that resemble deer antlers in velvet and once broken secrete a white latex help in distinguishing the stag-horn sumac at any season of the year.

Summer. *Leaves* 14 to 24 inches long, alternate, odd pinnately compound; leaflets 2 to 5 inches long, 11 to 31 per leaf, upper and lower leaflets shorter than those in the middle, sessile or nearly so, oblong lanceolate, tips taper-pointed, bases rounded or heart-shaped, margins sharply toothed; dark green and glabrous above, distinctly whitened and occasionally somewhat hairy beneath; petioles and rachises velvety hairy and reddish, exuding a milky sap when cut. *Flowers* 1/8 to 3/16 inch wide, borne in terminal compound panicles, male and female flowers generally on separate trees, appearing after the leaves; male flower cluster 8 to 12 inches long; female flower cluster shorter; petals 5, yellow green, strap-shaped. *Fruits* (drupe) 1/8 to 3/16 inch in diameter, with a very thin pulp, densely covered with bright red hairs; borne in compact, erect, conical clusters 5 to 8 inches in length, persisting throughout the winter.

Winter. *Twigs* stout, densely velvety with black holes, exuding a milky sap when cut; pith very large, composing nearly half the twig diameter, yellowish brown; terminal portion often dying back for several inches; leaf scars large, narrowly horseshoe-shaped, nearly encircling the buds; with several bundle scars either scattered or arranged in 3 groups. *Buds* about 1/8 to 1/4 inch long, covered with rusty, velvety hairs, conical, hidden by petiole base; terminal bud lacking. *Bark* thin, dark brown; on the branches and younger trunks often roughened with corky dots (enlarged lenticels) but otherwise smooth; on old trunks becoming somewhat scaly.

STAG-HORN SUMAC

1. Branch with mature leaf and cluster of fruit.
2. Fruit.
3. Winter twig.
4. Detail of bud and leaf scar.

Comparisons. The smooth sumac (*Rhus glabra* L.) is a lower, more shrubby species, which closely resembles the stag-horn sumac except that its branches are entirely glabrous, with glaucous stout twigs.

———

The stag-horn sumac, the largest of our native sumacs, is a shrub or small tree from 10 to 20 feet in height, which often sprouts from the roots and forms thickets. Its common name has been derived from a fancied resemblance of its stout and velvety twigs to the antlers of the male deer, or stag, when they are in velvet. The tree has a straggling habit of growth, the forking and often crooked branches forming an irregular, broad-topped crown. It is commonly found on well-drained to dry, rather fertile sites, but it often occurs on rocky, somewhat sterile slopes. Occasionally one will find it in open woodlands, but it is most abundant in clearings or abandoned fields, and along fencerows and roadsides.

The wood is soft and brittle with a satiny appearance, orange to greenish in color. It is seldom used commercially, but sometimes small articles such as napkin rings, picture frames, and darners are manufactured from it. The fruits are sometimes used to make a pleasantly acidic summer drink, which is often called Indian lemonade, and they are frequently eaten by the ruffed grouse; most birds, however, seem to regard them as an emergency ration, probably because of their dryness. White-tailed deer and flying squirrels frequently eat them. The bark and the twigs are often eaten by the deer and the cottontail rabbit during the winter months. The bark, particularly that of the roots, is rich in tannic acid. The stag-horn sumacs are very attractive in the fall when their foliage becomes a flaming red.

The stag-horn sumac ranges from Nova Scotia to Minnesota, south to Georgia and west to Missouri and Kansas.

WINGED SUMAC   *Rhus copallina* L.

> The small, but conspicuously numerous raised lenticels on the twigs, the red fruits, and the winged rachises of the alternate, odd pinnately compound leaves are most distinctive.

Summer. *Leaves* 6 to 12 inches long, alternate, deciduous, odd pinnate, with peculiar winglike projections along the rachis between the leaflets (wings rarely lacking); leaflets 1½ to 3 inches long, ¾ to 1 inch wide, 7 to 21 per leaf, sessile, ovate or oblong lanceolate, apically acute or acuminate, bases wedge-shaped, margins nearly entire but often somewhat revolute, slightly thickened; lustrous and dark green above, paler green and hairy beneath; petioles glabrous to hairy, rounded. *Flowers* about ⅛ inch across, male and female borne on separate trees, in terminal panicles 4 to 6 inches long; petals 5, green yellow. *Fruits* (drupe) about ⅛ inch in diameter, small, rather dry, with a thin red coat, covered with reddish, glandular hairs; borne in fairly compact, pyramidal, and somewhat drooping clusters.

Winter. *Twigs* only moderately stout, somewhat zigzag, light reddish brown or ashy brown, minutely but finely hairy, marked with small but numerous raised lenticels; leaf scars broadly crescent-shaped, with several bundle scars either scattered or arranged in 3 distinct groups; pith yellow brown, nonmilky. *Buds* very small, roundish to conical, tawny to rusty-hairy, terminal bud lacking. *Bark* light brown, often tinged with red; smooth on the younger trunks; on the older trunks becoming roughened with conspicuous projections, or peeling off in papery layers.

Comparisons. This species can be confused with the somewhat larger smooth sumac (*R. glabra* L.). It differs from that species as well as from the stag-horn sumac, however, by having thinner and more numerous branches; winged (rather than wingless) leaf rachises; dark lustrous leaves; broadly crescent-shaped, rather than horseshoe-shaped leaf scars that extend perhaps to the top of the bud but not completely around it; and drooping, rather than erect, fruiting heads. The hairy fruits and leaves, and more numerous leaflets, help to separate this species from the glabrous Brazilian peppertree (*Schinus terebinthifolius* Raddi), which has been introduced into Florida.

The winged sumac is also known as the dwarf sumac, the shining sumac, and the mountain sumac. It is a root-suckering shrub or small tree;

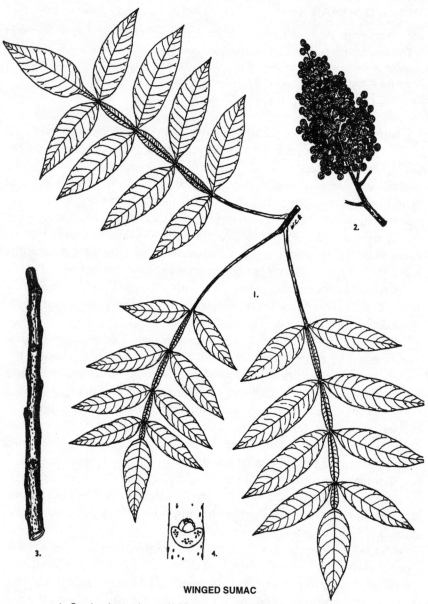

WINGED SUMAC

1. Branch and mature leaves with winged rachis.
2. Cluster of fruits.
3. Winter twig.
4. Detail of bud and leaf scar.

in our region it seldom attains a height of more than 8 feet, with trunks only a few inches in diameter. The winged sumac grows most commonly on the dry hills and rocky ridges, where it frequently invades clearings or abandoned fields. It is the common species of sumac on the sandy soils of the coastal plain in the southeastern United States.

The leaves and twigs are rich in tannic acid. They are sometimes gathered for use in tanneries and for use as a dye. In autumn the lustrous green foliage turns a deep purplish red; thus, the tree is sometimes planted as an ornamental. White-tailed deer often browse on the twigs during the winter, and the bark and twigs are eaten by the cottontail rabbit in the same season.

The winged sumac ranges from Maine and southern Ontario to Minnesota, south to Florida and Texas.

The species itself is somewhat variable, with several expressions found within our area. The typical expression, which occurs more easterly from New York through Pennsylvania, southward to Florida and Alabama, differs from the more widespread var. *latifolia* Engl. by its leaflets being narrower (³⁄₈ to ⁷⁄₈ inch versus 1 to 1 ⁵⁄₈ inches wide) and more numerous (11 to 23 versus 9 to 15) and by being entirely eastern in distribution, occurring along Atlantic and Gulf states rather than throughout the range of the species. Variety *leucantha* (Jacq.) DC. is an expression found chiefly in the coastal plain from Virginia south to Florida and west to southern Mississippi.

QUASSIA FAMILY—SIMAROUBACEAE

The Tree-of-Heaven—Ailanthus

TREE-OF-HEAVEN   *Ailanthus altissima* (P. Mill.) Swingle

> The alternate, pinnately compound leaves with 1 or 2 pairs of tiny basal glandular teeth on each leaflet, the fetid odor of the flowers and twigs, the erect, clubby branches, and the smooth bark are most distinctive.

Summer. *Leaves* 1½ to 3 feet long, alternate, pinnately compound; leaflets 2 to 6 inches long, 1 to 2 inches wide, 11 to 41, short-stalked, ovate lanceolate, tips taper-pointed, bases somewhat rounded but asymmetrical, margins entire except for a few coarse, glandular teeth toward the base; dark green and glabrous above, paler and glabrous beneath; petioles stout, glabrous. *Flowers* ¼ inch long, small, perfect, clustered, male and female flowers usually borne on separate trees, developing in spring and early summer; petals yellow green. *Fruits* 1½ to 2½ inches long, winged, with a solitary centrally placed seed, more or less twisted, reddish or yellowish-green; borne in large and conspicuous clusters.

Winter. *Fruits* clusters persistent. *Twigs* stout, slightly crooked, pointed upward, very ill scented, yellowish to reddish brown, finely velvety-hairy, with conspicuous lenticels, large light yellow to yellow-brown pith; leaf scars large, heart-shaped, with numerous bundle scars arranged in a curved line. *Buds* about ⅛ inch long, small, globular, brown, hairy, found within notch of the upper part of leaf scar; terminal bud lacking. *Bark* smooth, grayish; old trunks have shallow, interlacing, longitudinal fissures, conspicuously lighter in color than the irregular low ridges.

Comparisons. This tree is often confused with the sumacs, from which it may be readily distinguished by the rank odor of its twigs and

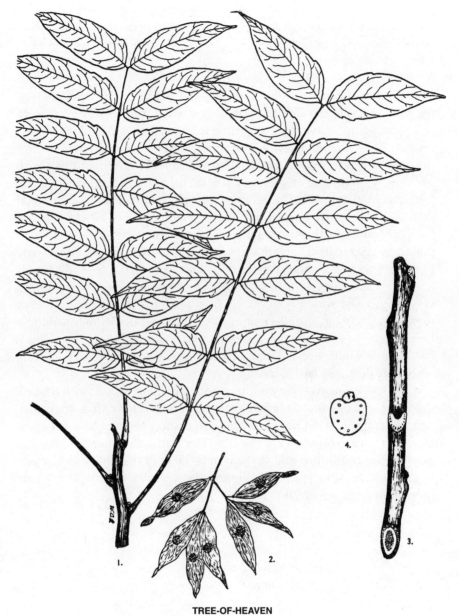

TREE-OF-HEAVEN

1. Branch with mature leaves.
2. Portion of fruit cluster.
3. Winter twig.
4. Detail of leaf scar.

flowers and by the conspicuous 1 or 2 basal teeth occurring on the otherwise entire-margined leaflets.

————

The tree-of-heaven is also known as the ailanthus, the paradise tree, the stink tree, and the Chinese sumac. The name tree-of-heaven refers to its upward-pointed twigs or, according to some, the twigs and male flowers that "stink to high heaven." An immigrant from China, it was introduced into North America in 1784 by William Hamilton and has been extensively planted in this country, particularly in the larger cities, and is frequently naturalized. The yellow-green to green-white staminate and pistillate flowers are borne on different trees. When in blossom, about June, the staminate trees emit a most disagreeable stench and their pollen is said to aggravate a catarrhal condition in sensitive individuals; the pistillate ones bear bountiful crops of wind-borne seeds. Tree-of-heaven is known to cause dermatitis in some people who handle the leaves. It grows very rapidly and sprouts extensively from the roots (suckering 150 feet or more from the main trunk), creating large colonial populations, making it very difficult to eradicate once it has become established. In many places it has become a nuisance, a veritable forest weed, aggressively competing with more desirable native trees.

The tree-of-heaven may attain a height of 50 to 80 feet with a trunk diameter of 2 to 3 feet. It is fast growing and develops an open, broad, and more or less flat-topped crown with clumsy-looking branches that are often bare except toward the tips. The tree is extremely tolerant of adverse city conditions and very often is the only tree that can be made to grow on certain sites. It should never be tolerated in any place where more desirable trees are able to grow.

MAHOGANY FAMILY—MELIACEAE

The China-berry—Melia

CHINA-BERRY   *Melia azedarach* **L.**

> The strongly scented, bi- or tripinnately compound leaves with leaflet margins that are coarsely toothed or lobed, the fragrant, lavender flowers, and the yellowish, round fruits, which remain on the tree through the winter, are most distinctive.

Summer. *Leaves* 10 to 20 inches long, alternate, twice or thrice pinnately divided into many leaflets; leaflets 1½ to 2½ inches long, ovate, tips long-pointed, margins toothed or occasionally lobed; glabrous or nearly so on both surfaces. *Flowers* pale purple to lavender, with a strongly disagreeable odor, appearing after leaves. *Fruits* (drupe) about ½ inch or slightly more in diameter, roundish, pale yellow; borne in open, drooping clusters; smooth at first, becoming wrinkled in autumn and winter.

Winter. *Twigs* olive green to brownish, rather stout, with a continuous white pith; leaf scars large, often numerous, 3-lobed, with 3 prominent C-shaped groups of bundle scars. *Buds*, terminal bud lacking; lateral buds small, roundish, hairy, with about 3 exposed scales. *Bark* dark brownish, furrowed.

The china-berry is a conspicuous tree in the Piedmont and coastal plains of our southeastern states. A native of the Himalaya region of Asia, it has been extensively planted and naturalized as a shade or ornamental tree in the South. It is often reported that almost every small cabin in the pinelands has one or more china-berry trees planted in its dooryard. The

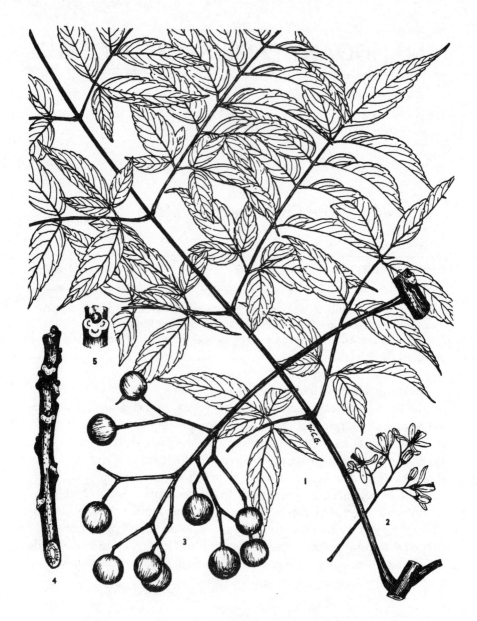

CHINA-BERRY

1. Portion of mature leaf.
2. Portion of flower cluster.
3. Fruits.

4. Winter twig.
5. Detail of leaf scar and bud.

tree is also known as the chinatree, the pride-of-India, or the pride-of-China.

In early summer the china-berry displays ample clusters of ½-inch, fragrant, lilac-colored flowers. The fruits should never be eaten, as their pulp contains a poisonous narcotic substance called azadirachtim. It is said that the fruits are poisonous to pigs and poultry, and children have been known to be poisoned by eating them. Others claim that the "berries" are a good vermifuge and an efficient repellent of insect pests. They are often eaten by wintering flocks of robins, waxwings, and other birds. There are, however, reliable accounts of birds being found in a stupor and apparently intoxicated by feasting upon them. An expression of the tree with a low, dense, and flattened crown, commonly called the umbrella-tree, originated in Texas and is now a popular ornamental tree.

RUE FAMILY—RUTACEAE

The Hercules'-Club—Zanthoxylum

HERCULES'-CLUB

Zanthoxylum clava-herculis **L.**

> The trunks and clubby branches of this coastal plain species are amply armed with stout thorns, which become elevated on conical cushions of cork. Twigs, bark, and, to some extent, the glandular-dotted leaves have a pungently aromatic lemon fragrance.

Summer. *Leaves* 5 to 15 inches long, alternate, pinnately compound, deciduous; leaflets 1 to 2½ inches long, 7 to 19 per leaf, sessile or nearly sessile, ovate lanceolate or often somewhat sickle-shaped; somewhat leathery, apically pointed, bases asymmetrically wedge-shaped or rounded, margin bluntly crenate serrate and somewhat undulate; upper surface lustrous bright green, glabrous to slightly hairy, the lower surface paler; rachises stout, somewhat hairy, usually armed with a few, sharp prickles. *Flowers* in large terminal cymes, appearing after the leaves, male and female flowers borne on separate trees; petals ⅛ to ¼ inch long, 5, greenish. *Fruits* (capsule) ¼ inch long, brown, ovoid, roughish, containing a solitary black seed that often remains hanging by a slender thread.

Winter. *Leaves* often persist well into the winter, in some instances remaining until spring. *Twigs* stout, aromatic when crushed, grayish brown to yellowish brown, more or less hairy, with straight spines ½ inch or more in length; leaf scars heart-shaped or triangular, with 3 bundle scars. *Buds* small, glabrous, dark colored, with indistinct scales. *Bark* ashy gray, smooth except for the corky excrescences mentioned above.

The Hercules'-club is also known as the southern prickly-ash, the sting-tongue, and the toothachetree. It is a shrub or small tree becoming 15 to 50 feet in height with a trunk diameter of about a foot. One may look for it on the sandy soils along the coast or in alluvial bottoms farther inland. Although it has no commercial importance, the pungent inner bark was formerly used as a remedy for toothache; hence some of the common names for this species. This bark, as well as the leaves and fruits, contains tiny, stinging crystals that cause a numbing sensation in the mouth when chewed.

Hercules'-club has a range extending through the coastal plain from southeastern Virginia to southern Florida, west to eastern Texas, and north to southeastern Oklahoma and southern Arkansas.

The Hoptree—Ptelea

COMMON HOPTREE   *Ptelea trifoliata* L.

> The ternately compound, alternate (3 leaflets) leaves, which are fragrant when crushed and glandular-dotted beneath, along with the bark and slender twigs, which are ill scented, with a lemonlike odor when bruised, and the winged fruit are distinctive.
>
> Aside from poison ivy, which occasionally reaches tree size, this is the only ternately compound, alternate-leaved native species occurring within our area.

Summer. *Leaves* alternate, deciduous, divided into three ovate leaflets, fragrant when crushed; leaflets 2 to 6 inches long, 1 to 3½ inches wide, ovate to elliptic, the side two leaflets sessile, terminal one short-stalked, pointed at both ends, bases cuneate, margins entire or nearly so; dark green and lustrous above, paler, tiny glandular-dotted and glabrous to densely hairy beneath; leafstalks 2½ to 4 inches long. *Flowers* small, ⅜ inch wide, ill scented, in terminal cluster, appearing after the leaves; petals 4, green white. *Fruits* (samara) ¾ to 1¼ inches in diameter, flat and circular or disk-shaped, 2-seeded, with numerous translucent dots, visible when held against a light source, completely surrounded by a thin, yellowish, veiny wing; borne in rather dense clusters.

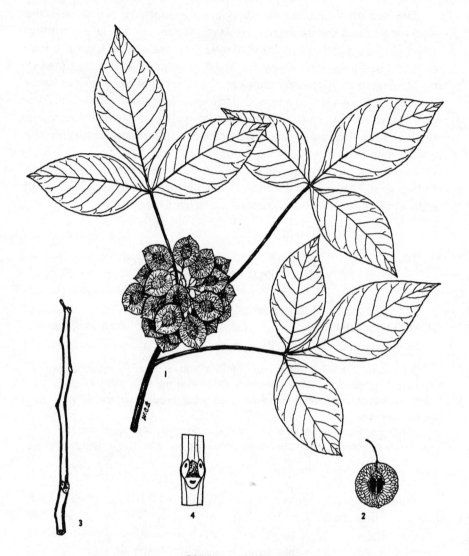

COMMON HOPTREE

1. Branch with leaves and fruits.
2. Fruit (sectioned).
3. Winter twig.
4. Detail of bud and leaf scar.

Winter. *Twigs* moderately slender, brittle, glabrous, yellowish brown to reddish brown, warty-dotted, with a fetid odor; pith large, continuous, white; leaf scars U-shaped, with 3 bundle scars. *Buds* small, yellow, superposed, partially sunken into bark, without distinct scales, silvery silky; terminal bud absent. *Bark* dark gray, smooth except for warty excrescences.

Comparisons. This species differs from the American bladdernut (*Staphylea trifolia* L.) by having alternate rather than opposite leaves. The small seedlings and even saplings of the common hoptree may also be confused with poison ivy, but the terminal leaflets of that species are always stalked, not dotted, and are nearly as large as the lateral leaflets. Moreover, the 2-seeded rather than single-seeded fruits help to separate the common hoptree from those of the genus *Ulmus*.

The common hoptree is also known as the wafer ash or the stinking ash. It is a large shrub or a small tree, occasionally to about 20 feet in height with a trunk from 6 to 12 inches in diameter. It grows in dry sandy or rocky situations and often in river valleys. The conspicuous fruits, which mature in the early fall, and the bark both contain a bitter substance. The fruits have been used as a substitute for hops, hence the common name of hoptree. The bark has been utilized in medicinal preparations, often as a substitute for quinine, although it is doubtful that it has any of the properties of the latter other than bitterness. It is occasionally planted as an ornamental.

The range of the common hoptree extends from Connecticut, New York, southern Ontario, Michigan, Illinois, and Missouri southward to Arizona, southern Texas and the Gulf States, and northern Florida.

GINSENG FAMILY—ARALIACEAE

The Aralia—Aralia

DEVIL'S-WALKINGSTICK   *Aralia spinosa* **L.**

At all seasons of the year the devil's-walkingstick may be recognized by its very stout, clubby twigs, which are about ¾ to I inch or more in diameter and armed with stout, scattered prickles. This, coupled with its huge, compound leaves (up to 3 ½ feet long) and massive flower-clusters, is most distinctive.

Summer. *Leaves* often 3 feet long, 2 to 2½ feet wide, very large, alternate, or bi- or tripinnately compound, clustered at the ends of the twigs; leaflets 2 to 3 inches long, numerous, short-stalked, ovate, apically acute or acuminate, bases rounded or wedged-shaped, margins sharply toothed; petioles stout, often prickly; rachises may also have scattered prickles. *Flowers* ¹⁄₁₆ to ⅛ inch across, tiny, perfect, developing in midsummer; borne in huge, 3- to 4-foot-long, many-flowered terminal panicle-umbel-type inflorescences; petals 5, white to green white. *Fruits* (berry) ⅛ inch across, aromatic, ovoid, black, 5-angled, tipped with persistent styles; borne in numerous small clusters (umbels); umbels arranged in ample, pyramidal clusters.

Winter. *Twigs* ¾ to 1 inch or more in diameter, clublike, with hollow pith; very stout, armed with stout scattered prickles; leaf scars alternate, U-shaped, narrow, about half encircling the twigs, with several bundle scars arranged in a curved line. *Buds* lateral buds about ¼ inch long, rather triangular, flattened, chestnut brown; terminal bud sometimes as much as 1 inch long, conical, covered with chestnut-colored scales. *Bark* thin, light brown or ashy, rather smooth, only on the old trunks becoming slightly furrowed and ridged; inner bark very yellow.

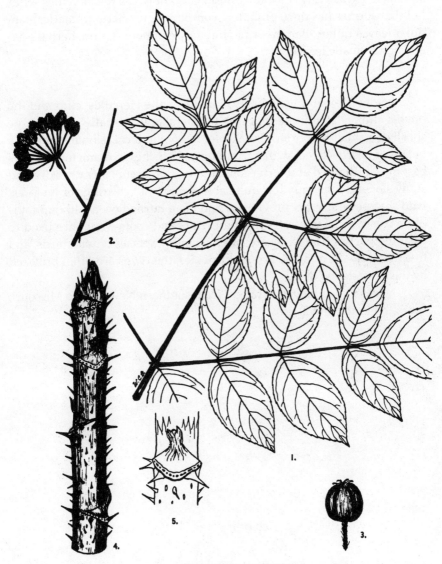

DEVIL'S-WALKINGSTICK

1. Portion of a compound leaf.
2. Portion of a fruit cluster.
3. Fruit.

4. Winter twig.
5. Detail of bud and leaf scar.

Comparisons. This species might be confused with the very thick-stemmed, exclusively coastal plain species known as the Hercules'-club, but that species has once pinnately compound, leathery, aromatic, glandular leaves rather than bi- or tripinnately compound, thin, herbaceous, and nonaromatic leaves.

————

The devil's-walkingstick, also known as the Hercules' club and the devil's club, is so unique that it is unmistakable. Usually only a large shrub or a small tree from 10 to 20 feet in height, it occasionally attains a height of nearly 40 feet with a trunk up to 12 inches in diameter. It grows best in well-drained and fertile soils, but it often occurs on rather dry and stony slopes. Frequently it is quite abundant in old clearings or on forest land that, several years previously, had been burned over. Although it is of no commercial value, its fragrant fruits and roots were once used to treat toothaches. The fruits are eaten by many species of wild birds, and in spite of the formidable array of prickles, the twigs are often browsed by the white-tailed deer.

The devil's-walkingstick ranges from southern New York to Missouri, south to Florida and Texas.

VERBENA FAMILY—VERBENACEAE

The Black Mangrove—Avicennia

BLACK MANGROVE *Avicennia germinans* **(L.) L.**

The opposite, evergreen leaves of this deeply southern, tidal zone species with its numerous, conspicuous aerial roots that are elevated above water level are most distinctive.

Summer. *Leaves* 2 to 4 inches long, ¾ to 1½ inches wide, opposite, simple, evergreen, leathery, oblong to elliptic, widest at or near the middle, apices acute or obtuse, bases cuneate; yellow green and lustrous above, gray finely hairy below, often covered with salt crystals; margins entire, somewhat revolute; petioles about 1½ inch long, grooved above, basally swollen. *Flowers* white, perfect, produced in midsummer, in short spikelike clusters; corolla about ½ inch wide, tubular, 4-lobed; stamens 4, attached to the corolla. *Fruits* (capsule) 1 to 1½ inches long, about 1 inch wide, elliptic, finely hairy, 1-seeded.

Winter. *Twigs* slender, tough, somewhat 4-angled, finely pubescent, orange brown in age and glabrous, swollen at the nodes and ringed; pith continuous, leaf scars U-shaped. *Buds* tiny. *Bark* dark brown, thick, blocky, often longitudinally fissured, outer bark when removed revealing an orange-red inner bark.

The black mangrove, hardiest of the mangroves, is most readily identified by its numerous unbranched aerial roots, or pneumatophores, which extend above the water level. It is a thicket-forming, shrubby tree with a round, spreading crown, growing 15 to 30 feet in height in the United

BLACK MANGROVE

1. Branch with leaves and flowers.　　　　2. Mature fruit.

States, but in the tropics it becomes a substantial tree, 60 to 70 feet high and 18 to 24 inches in diameter. It is found in the coastal tidal areas and mangrove swamps of Florida to Louisiana and Texas.

The wood of the black-mangrove is dark brown to nearly black, exceptionally hard, and used in a variety of ways for construction, posts, and fuel. The fragrant flowers are a very important source of honey.

OLIVE FAMILY—OLEACEAE

The Wild-Olive—Osmanthus

DEVILWOOD   *Osmanthus americanus* **(L.) Benth. & Hook. f. ex Gray**

> This is our only native interior tree with consistently opposite, evergreen, thick, leathery leaves.

Leaves 2½ to 4½ inches long, 1 to 2½ inches wide, opposite, simple, evergreen, thick, leathery, lustrous, narrowly elliptic or occasionally obovate, tips pointed or rounded, bases pointed, margins entire, flat or revolute; bright green and lustrous above, paler beneath, entirely glabrous; petioles ½ to ¾ inch long, stout. *Twigs* glabrous, stout, red brown, glaucous, often somewhat angled. *Flowers* 3/16 inch wide, bell-shaped, very fragrant, in many-flowered clusters, appearing in early spring, occasionally bisexual, male and female flowers generally borne on separate trees; petals 4, whitish to yellow. *Fruits* (drupe) ⅜ to ¾ inch long, elliptic, olive-like, becoming dark bluish purple when ripe. *Bark* thin, grayish brown; scales small, breaking away and exposing the reddish inner bark.

The devilwood, or wild-olive, is a small tree, at times attaining a height of 50 to 70 feet and a trunk diameter of about a foot, with a rather narrowly oblong crown. It grows among the sand dunes along the coast and in the borders of the great coastal swamps, following the swampy stream bottoms for a considerable distance into the flat pinelands. Under cultivation it makes a very handsome ornamental tree and it succeeds quite well on well-drained soils. Its tough wood, which gives the woodcutter a "devil of a hard time" to split, is of no particular commercial value.

DEVILWOOD

1. Branch with mature leaves, fruits, and flower buds.
2. Portion of flowering branch.
3. Leaf.
4-5. Flowers.

The small, fragrant, creamy-white flowers appear in axillary clusters in early spring before the new leaves unfold; often, at the same time, mature fruits of the previous year are still present on the branchlets.

The range of the devilwood extends through the coastal plain from southeastern Virginia to central Florida and westward to southeastern Louisiana and east Texas.

The Flowering-Ash—Chionanthus

FRINGETREE   *Chionanthus virginicus* **L.**

> The opposite, simple, entire-margined leaves on purple petioles that appear very late in the spring, the conspicuously warty twigs with sharply pointed and sharply keeled buds, the unusual straplike white petals, the fragrant flowers, and the loosely clustered olivelike or grapelike fruits are diagnostic.

Summer. *Leaves* 4 to 8 inches long, 1 to 4 inches wide, opposite, simple, deciduous, thick, firm; elliptic, ovate or obovate, tips pointed or blunt, bases wedge-shaped, margins entire, glabrous or nearly so; dark green and somewhat lustrous above and paler beneath, clustered mostly near the branch tips; petioles ½ to 1 inch long, purplish, stout, often minutely hairy. *Flowers* fragrant, drooping, perfect or functionally unisexual, male and female flowers usually borne on separate plants; petals 4, white, straplike, very slender. *Fruits* (drupe) ¼ to ¾ inch long, elliptic, olivelike, dark bluish black, often glaucous at maturity; borne in loose, drooping clusters, on stalks with conspicuous leaflike bracts.

Winter. *Twigs* moderately stout, light greenish brown, slightly angled, glabrous or slightly hairy, with conspicuous warty lenticels; leaf scars opposite, semiround, with a solitary bundle scar, stipule scar lacking. *Buds* ⅛ to ¼ inch long, ovoid, pointed, sharply 4-angled or keeled, light brown; scales 6 to 8, covering the buds, hairy-margined. *Bark* of the younger stems light orange brown, smooth; on older trunks becoming darker and scaly.

Comparisons. In the winter, the fringetree can be easily identified by its somewhat clubby, opposite branches, conspicuous warty lenticels on its branches, and by the 6 to 8 bud scales on its terminal buds. All of our native ashes and most of our arrow-woods and blackhaws also have deciduous leaves, but their branches do not have such conspicuously warty

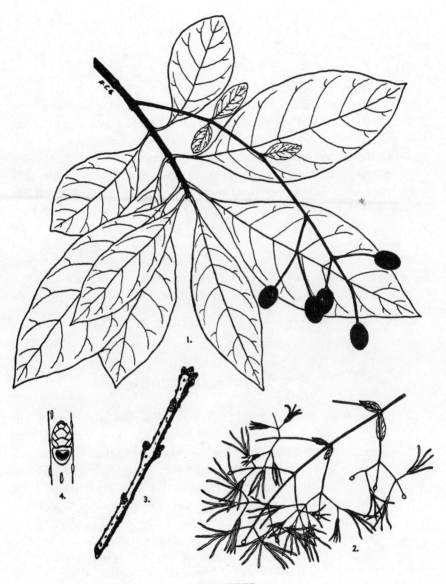

FRINGETREE

1. Branch with mature leaves and fruits.
2. Flower cluster.
3. Winter twig.
4. Detail of bud and leaf scar.

lenticels; also, our few treelike arrow-wood species all have 2, rather than 6 to 8, bud scales.

———

The fringetree is also known as the flowering ash or the old man's beard. It is a large shrub or a small tree often reaching a height of 10 to 20 feet, but occasionally attaining 40 feet in height and 1 foot in trunk diameter. It prefers deep, moist, and fertile soils, and is most commonly found along streambanks or the borders of swamps.

This small tree produces no wood of commercial value, but it is very attractive and makes an excellent specimen or ornamental tree. In late May or June it produces drooping clusters of fragrant flowers, which have very narrow white petals. En masse, they look filmy and fringelike, hence its common name of fringetree. In the autumn the foliage turns a clear yellow, but it is shed rather early. English horticulturists consider this to be one of the finest American introductions into their gardens.

The fringetree ranges from southern New Jersey and southeastern Pennsylvania, south to Florida and Texas.

The Ashes—Fraxinus

Like those of the maples and the buckeyes, ash leaves are opposite, but differ by being odd pinnately compound (except for ash-leaf maple), with toothed to nearly entire-margined leaflets. Also, unlike the maples, which have thin twigs, ash twigs are rather stout, somewhat enlarged and flattened at the nodes, and have rather conspicuous lenticels. The leaf scars are opposite, large and conspicuous, broadly crescent-shaped to semi-round, and have several bundle scars, which are arranged in more or less U-shaped lines. The buds have 2 or 3 pairs of opposite, visible scales. The terminal buds are broad and considerably larger than the lateral ones. The wind-pollinated flowers usually appear in the early spring, before the leaves, from buds on the previous season's growth. The staminate and pistillate flowers, except in a few species, always occur on separate trees. They have no corolla and only a diminutive, ringlike calyx, and are arranged in compound clusters. The fruits are 1-seeded, cylindrical samaras, with elongated, flat, terminal, paperlike wings, borne in compound, drooping clusters. They mature in the autumn and often persist throughout the winter. Wind is the principal agent of seed dispersal.

BLUE ASH   *Fraxinus quadrangulata* Michx.

The very broad 4-angled and more or less 4-winged twigs that continue through the internodes, the opposite leaves, the somewhat shaggy bark, and the exposed inner bark that turns blue upon exposure to the air help to identify this species at any season. This is one of our two eastern ashes (the black ash being the other one) that lacks a calyx.

Summer. *Leaves* 8 to 12 inches long, opposite, deciduous, pinnately compound; leaflets 2½ to 5 inches long, 1 to 2 inches wide, 5 to 11 on short stalks; broadly lanceolate to ovate or lanceolate, apically pointed, bases pointed to roundish, margins coarsely serrately toothed, upper surfaces dark yellowish green, lower surfaces paler, glabrous, with small tufts of hair within vein axils. *Flowers* ⅛ inch or less long, small, purplish, lacking both petals and sepals, clustered, male and female flowers borne on separate trees, developing before the leaves. *Fruits* (samara) 1 to 2 inches long, ¼ to ½ inch wide, brown to tan; wing broad, often twisted, tips broad and squarish, often notched apically, extending nearly to the base of the flat seed portion and surrounding it. *Bark* gray, with fissures separating shaggy and scaly plates.

Winter. *Twigs* stout, gray brown, 4-angled or with 4 distinct vertical ridges; leaf scars shield-shaped. *Buds* dark brown, hairy; two uppermost lateral buds about the same level as the terminal bud; terminal bud with 3 pairs of scales.

Comparisons. The squarish broad fruit tip, the inner bark that turns blue upon exposure to the air, the flat seed portion of the fruit, and the 4-angled and 4-lined or somewhat winged twigs separate this species from all other ashes.

The blue ash is a medium- to large-sized tree, sometimes attaining a height of 60 to 100 feet with a trunk diameter of 3 feet, with a small and slender crown composed of spreading branches. In pioneer days a blue dye was obtained from the tree's inner bark, which contains a mucilaginous substance that turns blue upon exposure to the air, and when crushed will turn water a blue color; hence the tree's common name. Its wood is usually cut and marketed as white ash, although it is heavier and somewhat more brittle. The blue ash occurs less commonly than the white ash over most of its range, and the two are often found together on the better soils. The blue ash, however, is more frequent on the poorer, drier, limestone soils of the uplands.

The range of the blue ash extends from southern Ontario and Michigan to southern Wisconsin and southeastern Iowa; south to West Virginia, Alabama, Arkansas, and northeastern Oklahoma.

WHITE ASH   *Fraxinus americana* L.

> The stalked leaflets with pale or whitish undersurfaces that are covered with microscopic projections, the tiny canoe-paddle-shaped fruits, the diamond-shaped bark pattern, and the somewhat shreddy mature twigs are most distinctive.

Summer. *Leaves* 8 to 15 inches long, opposite, deciduous, pinnately compound; leaflet 2½ to 5 inches long, 1 to 2½ inches wide, 5 to 9 but usually 7, slender-stalked, appearing opposite, ovate or oblong-lanceolate, apically pointed, bases broadly wedge-shaped to rounded, margins entire or obscurely serrately round toothed; dark green and glabrous above, paler or somewhat whitened beneath, purplish in autumn, usually glabrous but occasionally hairy beneath; petiole and rachis usually glabrous but occasionally hairy in the expression known as the Biltmore ash. *Flowers* ¼ inch long, small, purplish, apetalous, in small clusters, perfect or as separate types on the same or different trees, appearing in the spring before the leaves. *Fruits* (samara) 1 to 2 inches long, light brown to tan, appearing as a tiny canoe paddle, with a plump seed portion and a wing that scarcely extends down its sides.

Winter. *Twigs* stout, round, greenish gray to ashy brown, epidermis on mature twigs flaking or peeling, usually glabrous with a polished appearance or glaucous, but hairy in the expression known as Biltmore ash; leaf scars broadly crescent-shaped or semiovate, with a deep apical notch on the upper margin partially surrounding the bud. *Buds* rusty brown; terminal bud ¼ inch long, broadly ovoid, broader than long, blunt, angled, with 4 to 6 exposed scales; two uppermost lateral buds abutted tightly against the nearly identical terminal bud, with no space between the three buds, making them appear as one multiheaded bud. *Bark* ashy gray, with deep diamond-shaped furrows and rather narrow interlacing ridges.

Comparisons. This species can be separated from other native ashes by its white or pale leaf undersurfaces, which are covered with microscopic, rounded projections. The white ash is not at all easily separated

5.

1.

3.

2.

4.

WHITE ASH

1. Portion of branch with mature leaves.
2. Portion of fruit cluster.
3. Winter twig.
4. Detail of bud and leaf scar.
5. Detail of terminal bud.

from the green ash. They are quite similar morphologically and quite variable in leaflet size and shape. Aside from the undersurfaces of the leaves being whitish and covered with small projections, and twigs being glabrous (rather than hairy to glabrous) in the white ash, however, the seed portion of the fruit is large and cylindrical, thick-cigar-shaped, nearly twice as thick as the thin-cigar-shaped seed of the green ash! The long, narrow seed portion of the winged fruit of the green ash (with the wing portion extending to about the middle of the seed) versus the plump cylindrical seed portion of the white ash (with the wing portion extending to just a little below the seed top) provides one of the best means of differentiation. Also, the buds of the green ash are smaller than those of the white ash, with the first pair of lateral buds of the green ash appearing to be set below the plane of the terminal bud. In the white ash the first pair of lateral buds appears to be at the same level as the terminal one. For comparison, the first two lateral buds of the black ash are set dramatically below the terminal bud, thus creating a stalked terminal bud appearance. Additionally, the mature twigs of the green ash do not shred or peel as in the white ash, and the leaf scars of the green ash are semicircular, not at all or only slightly concave apically, while those of the white ash are deeply notched apically. The green ash is a low-elevation species often found on poorly drained soils, while the white ash is an upland species found on well-drained soil. Also, the somewhat larger toothed leaflets of the green ash tend to be narrower than those of the white ash, and occur on slightly larger stalks.

The white ash is a large tree commonly 70 to 80 feet in height, sometimes attaining a height of more than 100 feet, with a breast-high diameter of 2 to 3 feet, and sometimes as much as 5 feet. The trunk is usually long and straight and, in the forest, free of lower branches, but in the open it develops an open and rather round-topped crown with branches extending quite close to the ground. White ash prefers deep, rich, well-drained to moist soils. It is commonly found in bottomlands but it also ascends slopes where the soil is not excessively dry and stony.

White ash is the largest and most valuable of our native ashes from a timber standpoint. Its wood is heavy, hard, strong, tough, and elastic. It is used for furniture, interior finish, wagons, agricultural implements, tool handles, athletic equipment, baskets, boxes, crates, railroad ties, and as fuel. It is often planted as a street or shade tree. As a source of firewood, white ash is considered to be the best. It provides very little smoke and burns hot. The fruits are eaten by a few species of wild birds such as the purple finch and the evening grosbeak.

The white ash ranges from Newfoundland and Nova Scotia west to Minnesota, and south to northern Florida and eastern Texas.

PUMPKIN ASH   *Fraxinus profunda* (Bush) Bush

> This is a large swamp tree with very large, often leathery, pinnately compound leaves, with hairy veins on the undersurfaces of the leaflets, with densely hairy twigs, with a prominently swollen trunk base, and with light gray, shallowly fissured bark.

Summer. *Leaves* 8 to 18 inches long, opposite, pinnately compound, deciduous; leaflets 4 to 10 inches long, 1½ to 3 inches wide, usually 7, but occasionally 9; elliptic to lanceolate, apically pointed, bases asymmetrically cuneate to rounded, margins entire or slightly serrately toothed; dark green above, glabrous; light green and hairy below, northern trees usually having rachises and lower surfaces of the leaflets more or less densely woolly; southern ones entirely glabrous. *Flowers* ¼ inch long, small, male and female flowers borne on different trees, in clusters, appearing before the leaves in the spring. *Fruits* (samara) 2 to 3 inches long, about ½ inch wide, yellowish to tan, with a wing extending to about the middle of the seed portion.

Winter. *Twigs* stout, grayish brown, glabrous to rather densely velvet-hairy in northern trees; leaf scars broadly U-shaped, apically deeply notched. *Buds* light reddish brown, set in the upper margin; terminal bud with 3 pairs of scales, outer pair of bud scales with truncated tips. *Bark* gray, furrowed, diamond patterned.

Comparisons. This species is quite similar to the green ash, but has larger fruits and leaves. It is also similar to the Carolina ash, which is more southern in distribution and has more membranous leaves and conspicuously wider fruits.

The pumpkin ash is strictly a large tree of deeper swamps and inundated river bottoms. It may attain a height of 100 to 120 feet with a trunk diameter of 2 to 3½ feet, and has a narrow, open crown composed of small spreading branches. Although its wood is inferior to that of the

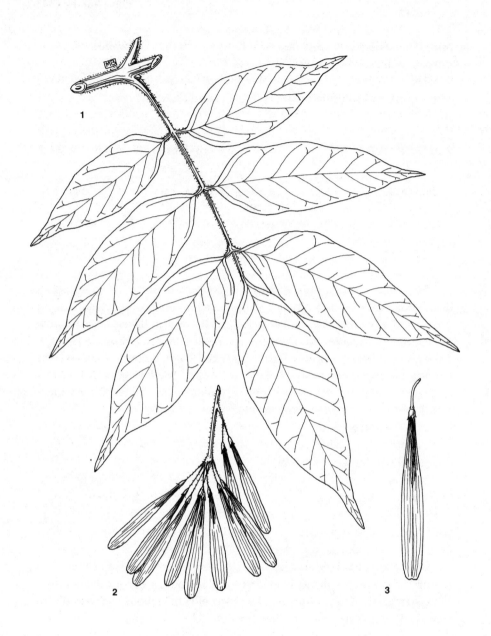

PUMPKIN ASH

1. Branch with mature leaf.
2. Fruits.

3. Detail of mature fruit.

white ash, it is used for boxes, crates, railroad ties, veneer, pulpwood, and fuel. The buttressed base of this species and the epithet *profunda* (thick or dense) suggest that it is expansive. This provides additional support and anchorage in wetlands where it grows.

The range of the pumpkin ash extends chiefly through the coastal plain, from southeastern New York to Florida west to Louisiana; and northward, in the Mississippi Valley, to the southern parts of Ohio, Indiana, and Illinois.

A very minor expression, var. *ashei* Palmer, with glabrous foliage and southern distribution, has been occasionally recognized as being distinct.

GREEN ASH   *Fraxinus pennsylvanica* Marsh.

The conspicuous wing stalk of the basal leaflet, the velvet or woolly surface of the twigs and undersurfaces of the leaflets, and the peculiar leaf scar, which is nearly straight across or only slightly notched on its upper edge, are distinctive. In the expression known as the red ash (var. *pennsylvanica*), the twigs and leaves are hairy. In the expression commonly referred to as the northern red ash (var. *austinii* Fern.), the leaves are prominently toothed, while in the expression known as the green ash (var. *subintegerrima* (Vahl.) Fern.), leaves, flower stalks, and fruit stalks are nearly or completely glabrous.

Summer. *Leaves* 9 to 12 inches long, pinnately compound; leaflets 2 to 5 inches long, 1 to 2 inches wide, 7 to 9, usually 7; lustrous, short-stalked, oblong lanceolate or narrowly ovate, apically pointed, bases broadly wedge-shaped or rounded, margins shallowly or finely serrate (especially above the middle) to entire; thin but firm, bright green above, slightly paler beneath, glabrous on both surfaces or more or less silky hairy beneath in the expression known as the red ash; petiole, rachis, and branchlets also hairy in the expression known as the red ash. *Flowers* ⅛ inch long, greenish, apetalous, clustered, developing in early spring before the leaves, male and female flowers borne on separate trees. *Fruits* (samara) 1 to 2 inches long, yellow to light tan, with narrow wings; wings ¼ inch or less wide, extending less than halfway down the sides of the plump seed portion.

Winter. *Twigs* similar to those of the white ash; generally grayish, more slender, more or less densely hairy in the expression known as the red ash; leaf scars semiround, with a straight or, rarely, slightly concave upper margin (leaf scars of the white ash are always deeply notched on the upper margin). *Buds* rusty-brown, hairy, similar to those of the white

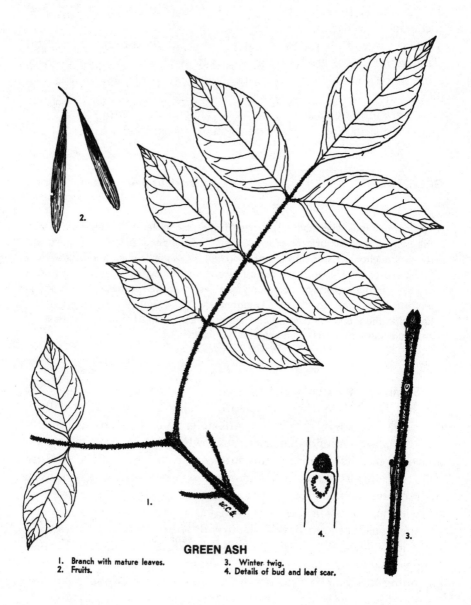

GREEN ASH

1. Branch with mature leaves.
2. Fruits.
3. Winter twig.
4. Details of bud and leaf scar.

ash but a bit smaller; outermost lateral bud smaller and positioned adjacent to the terminal bud; terminal bud with 3 pairs of scales. *Bark* also similar to that of the white ash, but somewhat less deeply furrowed.

Comparisons. Green ash is quite similar to white ash, but it lacks the whitish coloration and tiny projections on the undersurfaces of its leaves. Also, when the bark of green ash twigs is scraped with a knife blade, it produces red-orange-colored bark flakes, while white ash produces pale brown-colored to tan-colored flakes. Like the Carolina ash, the leaf scar of the green ash is virtually straight across its apex or only shallowly notched, certainly not like the deeply notched leaf scars of the white ash or the pumpkin ash. The somewhat winged basal leaflets also help to separate this species from our other eastern ashes.

The green ash (or the red ash, as the expression with hairy leaves and twigs is often called) is a medium-sized tree usually attaining a height of 30 to 60 feet with a trunk diameter of 1 to 3 feet, but occasionally it is somewhat larger. The numerous more or less upright branches form a rather irregular, broad, compact crown. Unlike white ash, which occurs throughout eastern deciduous forests, green ash is typically a tree of deep, rich, moist soils of bottomlands and banks of streams, rather rarely ascending drier slopes.

The wood of the green ash is heavy, hard, strong, coarse-grained, and brittle. It is inferior to that of the white ash but the two are not usually distinguished by lumbermen.

The green ash ranges from Nova Scotia west to Saskatchewan, south to northern Florida and eastern Texas.

CAROLINA ASH   *Fraxinus caroliniana* P. Mill.

> The conspicuously wide wings of the fruits of this species, which often occur in 3s and remain wide to the fruit base, help to separate it from our other ash species.

Summer. *Leaves* 4 to 10 inches long, opposite, deciduous, pinnately compound; leaflets 1 to 4 inches long, ¾ to 2 inches wide, usually 5 or 7, more or less thick and leathery; elliptic to broadly lanceolate, pointed at both ends, margins entire or somewhat coarsely serrately toothed; dark green above, paler and glabrous or nearly so beneath. *Flowers* ⅛ inch

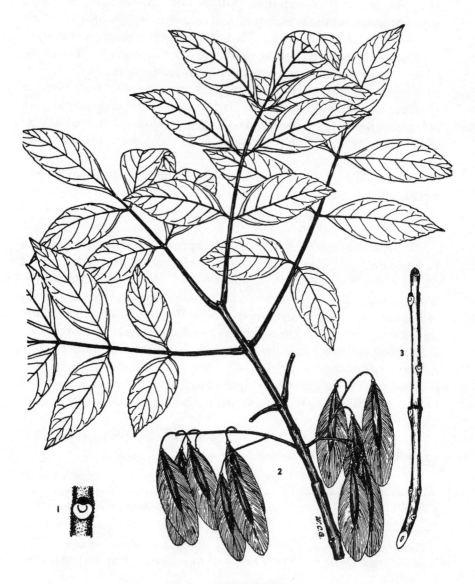

CAROLINA ASH

1. Detail of bud and leaf scar.
2. Branch with leaves and fruits.
3. Winter twig.

long, apetalous, clustered, developing in early spring before the leaves, male and female flowers borne on separate trees. *Fruits* (samara) 1½ to 2 inches long, ¾ to 1 inch wide, broadly elliptical and often 3-winged; wings extending to the base of the flattened seed portion, yellow to tan or often bright violet.

Winter. *Twigs* rather slender, glabrous, light orange brown to reddish brown; leaf scars semicircular, with a chestnut-brown bud placed above them. *Bark* thin, grayish, irregularly scaly.

Comparisons. The leaves of this species are similar to those of the white ash, but are not whitish below, and the fruits are dramatically different.

Carolina ash, also known as water ash, swamp ash, and pop ash, is the southernmost of our eastern ashes. It is a small tree, usually no more than 25 to 50 feet in height with a trunk diameter of 6 to 8 inches, but occasionally larger. It grows in deep swamps and in frequently inundated bottomlands along streams near the South Atlantic and Gulf coasts. Its small size, multitrunked habit, and weak, light wood make it of practically no value as a timber tree, but its logs, no doubt, go indiscriminately along with those of other trees to the pulp mills of the region.

The Carolina ash occurs in the coastal plain from southeastern Virginia to southern Florida, west to Arkansas and eastern Texas.

BLACK ASH   *Fraxinus nigra* Marsh.

The cold, swampy habitat where this species occurs, the sessile lateral leaflets that are distinctly toothed, the unusual, corky, scaly, grayish trunk bark, the nearly circular leaf scars, and the exceptionally dark brown to black buds, with the first two lateral buds positioned somewhat below the base of the terminal bud, creating a stalked appearance, are distinctive. Equally distinctive are the exceptionally flattened seed cavities, which are the widest of any native ash species (others are cigar-shaped).

Summer. *Leaves* 10 to 16 inches long, opposite, deciduous, pinnately compound; leaflets 3 to 5 inches long, 1 to 1½ inches wide, 7 to 11 (usually 9), all but the terminal one decidedly stalkless; broadly lanceolate, tips taper-pointed, bases obliquely rounded or broadly wedge-shaped, margins finely but distinctly and sharply serrately toothed; thin but firm, dark green and glabrous above, paler and glabrous or nearly so beneath;

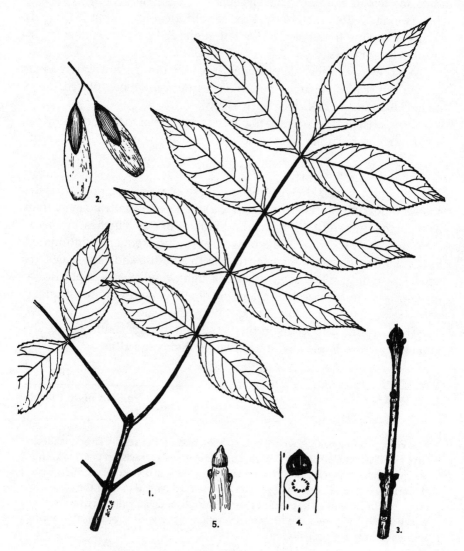

BLACK ASH

1. Branch with mature leaves.
2. Fruits.
3. Winter twig.
4. Detail of bud and leaf scar.
5. Detail of terminal bud.

petiole and rachis also glabrous except for the tufts of hairs where leaflets attach to the leaf rachis. *Flowers* ⅛ inch long, purplish, lacking both petals and sepals, formed in small clusters, usually perfect, appearing in April or May before the leaves, male and female flowers produced on the same or different trees. *Fruits* (samara) 1 to 1½ inches long, often twisted, unusually blunt at both ends, often notched apically, with a winged portion about ⅜ inch wide, extending to the base of the seed; seed extremely wide, wider than any other native ash.

Winter. *Twigs* rather stout, pale ashy olive to gray, dull, glabrous; leaf scars ovate to semiovate or nearly circular. *Buds* very dark brownish black; terminal bud ¼ inch long or more, broadly ovoid, decidedly apically pointed; the two uppermost lateral buds positioned well below the terminal bud, exposing a small section of bark between the terminal and lateral buds. *Bark* smoother than that of our other ashes, ashy gray, scaly, somewhat corky, ridged, may be easily powdered by rubbing.

Comparisons. The shallowly ridged and flaky bark of the black ash is similar to that of the blue ash, but both of these are quite different from the diamond-shaped bark pattern of the white ash or the green ash. Also, the leaflet margins of the black ash are more conspicuously toothed than those of the white ash or the green ash. The fruits of the black ash are similar to those of the blue ash and the Carolina ash in that the wing extends all the way to the base of the seed, whereas it extends from just a little below the top of the seed portion in the white ash and to about the middle of the seed portion in both the green ash and the pumpkin ash.

The black ash, also known as the hoop ash, the basket ash, the brown ash, or the swamp ash, is our most northern ash species. It is a small- to medium-sized tree usually attaining a height of 40 to 60 feet with a trunk diameter of 1 to 2 feet. The trunk is usually tall, rather slender, and of very uniform diameter up to the rather narrow and open crown. The black ash is strictly a tree of wet places: low wet woods, cold swamps, and river bottoms that are periodically inundated. In such places it commonly associates with the red maple, the American elm, the swamp white oak, and other swamp trees.

The wood is moderately heavy, rather soft, weak, coarse-grained, and rather durable. It is easily separated into thin layers and is commonly used for making baskets, barrel hoops, chair bottoms, and for interior finish.

The black ash ranges from Newfoundland to Manitoba, south to Delaware, Virginia, and Iowa.

FIGWORT FAMILY— SCROPHULARIACEAE

The Princesstree—Paulownia

PRINCESSTREE

Paulownia tomentosa
(Thunb.) Sieb. & Zucc. ex Steud.

> The huge, palmately veined, heart-shaped leaves, the large, conspicuous flowers that appear before the leaves, the ill-scented hollow twigs (except at the nodes), and the conspicuously ugly clusters of small, walnut-sized fruits that remain on the trees in both autumn and winter are most distinctive.

Summer. *Leaves* opposite, simple, deciduous, occasionally whorled; blades usually 5 to 15 inches long, about as wide, broadly ovate, heart-shaped, abruptly pointed, margins entire or slightly 3-lobed; slightly hairy above and densely soft-hairy beneath, palmately veined; petioles 3 to 8 inches long. *Flowers* about 2 inches long, erect, bell-shaped; petals blue to purple with yellow interior stripes, very fragrant, appearing before the leaves. *Fruits* (capsule) 1 to 1¾ inches long, egg-shaped, nutlike, apically pointed, containing a large number of very small winged seeds persisting long after splitting and discharging the seeds.

Winter. *Twigs* stout, olive brown to dark brown, densely soft-hairy, at least when young, ill-scented, dotted with prominent pale brownish lenticels, with chambered or hollow pith (except at nodes); leaf scars opposite, somewhat elevated, ovate, more or less notched at the top, with a number of bundle scars arranged in a circle. *Buds,* lateral buds small, sunken within the bark, often superposed, with but a few exposed scales; terminal bud lacking; flower buds tawny, velvety-hairy, in erect terminal clusters. *Bark* somewhat fissured, gray to brown.

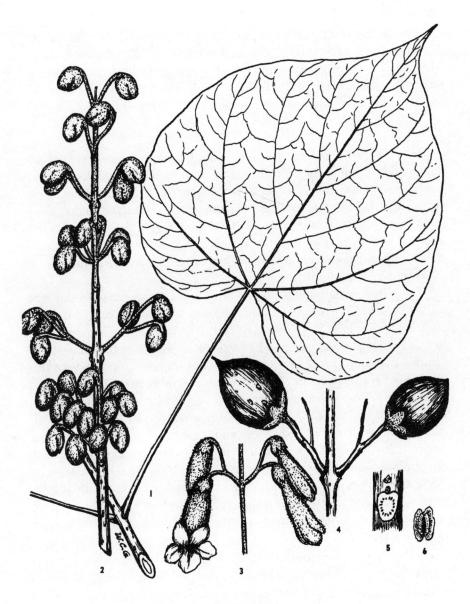

PRINCESSTREE

1. Portion of branch with typical leaf.
2. Portion of cluster of flower buds.
3. Portion of flower cluster.
4. Portion of fruit cluster.
5. Detail of leaf scar and buds.
6. Winged seed (much enlarged).

Comparisons. The leaves resemble those of the catalpas. This species differs from our native catalpas by having larger, more cordate leaf blades which are opposite rather than whorled and are less tapered; by having blue rather than mostly white flowers; by its pith, which is chambered or hollow rather than solid; and by having wholly different fruits.

————

In early spring, before the leaves unfold, the princesstree is resplendent with its large upright clusters of fragrant violet-colored flowers that last but a few days. Each tubular flower is from 1½ to 2 inches long, hairy on the outside, with 5 spreading and somewhat unequally rounded lobes at the summit. The flower buds are developed during the previous summer and are present on the tree all through the winter. Because these flower buds are usually killed by low winter temperatures in the North, the trees do not bloom there.

The princesstree, named after Princess Anna Paulowna (1795–1865) of the Netherlands, is a native of China. Seeds of this species were sent to the United States in 1830. Since then it has been planted as an ornamental tree in the South and does quite well as far north as New York City and southern Indiana and Illinois. In some places it has become thoroughly naturalized and is a veritable forest weed; it is quite common in areas along the Blue Ridge Parkway. A botanist once counted 2,000 seeds in one pod and estimated that over 21 million seeds were produced by the tree. He calculated that if all of the seeds grew, and if each tree produced the same number of seeds, the offspring of this one tree would, in the third generation, produce enough plants to cover 20,442 worlds the size of ours! The tree grows very rapidly, and indeed is considered to be one of the fastest-growing trees in eastern North America. Sprouts are known to have grown 15 feet and more during a single growing season in the southern Appalachian region.

TRUMPET CREEPER FAMILY— BIGNONIACEAE

The Catalpas—Catalpa

The leaves are opposite or in whorls of 3, simple, heart-shaped, and long petioled. The twigs are stout, glabrous or hairy, with a large white pith, and very conspicuous opposite or whorled leaf scars, which are oval-shaped, depressed in the center, and contain several bundle scars arranged in the form of an oval. The buds are small and quite inconspicuous, being partially embedded within the bark. The terminal bud is lacking. The flowers appear after the leaves are fully developed, in June or July, and are borne in rather large, showy, somewhat pyramidal terminal clusters. They are perfect, with short tubular corollas expanded above into a 5-lobed, somewhat 2-lipped, ragged-margined border; flowers are white with inconspicuous purplish spots, and with yellow dots in the open throat. The fruits are very long, cylindrical, drooping pods, familiarly known as Indian tobies or Indian beans, which contain numerous flattened seeds having fringed wings.

The catalpas are trees of the South and the Midwest, but they are very commonly planted as street, shade, or ornamental trees and so are familiar to most persons.

SOUTHERN CATALPA   *Catalpa bignonioides* **Walt.**

> This species, like the northern catalpa, is easily identified by its large, heart-shaped, whorled or opposite leaves, large, clustered flowers, and long, beanlike fruits.

Summer. *Leaves* 4 to 10 inches long, 3 to 7 inches wide, heart-shaped, ovate, tips rather abruptly pointed, barely if at all acuminate, margins

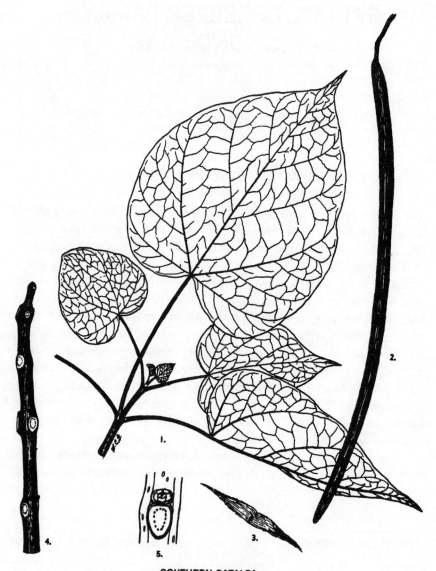

SOUTHERN CATALPA

1. Branch with leaves.
2. Fruit.
3. Seed.
4. Winter twig.
5. Details of bud and leaf scar.

entire but wavy; blades rather thin-textured, light green above, paler and hairy beneath, emitting a rather unpleasant odor when crushed; lobes occasionally short, on either or both sides toward the base; petioles 3 to 6 inches long. *Flowers* 1 to 1⅝ inches long, bell-shaped, perfect, bilabiate, borne after the leaves; petals white, but spotted with lavender-purple and flecked with yellow, lower petal not notched. *Fruits* (capsule) ⅓ to ½ inch in diameter, 6 to 15 inches long, cigar-shaped, thin-walled, containing numerous seeds with wings pointed at the tips.

Winter. *Twigs* thick, clubby, green at first, turning brown, glabrous or nearly so; bark furrowed, light brown to reddish.

Comparisons. This species is best distinguished from the northern catalpa by its smaller pods, which have thinner walls and more apically pointed seeds. It also has shorter pointed leaves, smaller, more densely spotted flowers that appear several weeks later than those of the northern catalpa, and reddish brown rather than dark brown bark that is somewhat thinner than that of the northern catalpa.

———

The southern, or common, catalpa ranges from southwestern Georgia and western Florida west to Mississippi. Its common and generic names come from the Cherokee Indians. It is usually a small- or medium-sized tree, smaller in size than the northern catalpa, from 20 to 40 feet in height with a trunk 1 to 2 feet in diameter. The trunk is typically short and crooked, with a rather broad but irregular crown composed of short, crooked branches. It is extensively planted as a shade or ornamental tree, but it is less hardy in the North than the northern catalpa. The expression cv. *nana*, which has a very dense, broad, umbrella-like head, is very common in cultivation. In the South the wood is sometimes used for posts and railroad ties. The large caterpillars that feed on the foliage are considered to be a very excellent fish bait.

NORTHERN CATALPA

Catalpa speciosa
(Warder) Warder ex Engelm.

> Very similar to the southern catalpa but somewhat larger, with furrowed rather than scaly bark, long-acuminate leaf apices, larger flowers, and leaves lacking an unpleasant odor.

Summer. *Leaves* 6 to 12 inches long, 4 to 8 inches wide, heart-shaped, closely resembling those of the southern catalpa, but usually larger, thicker-textured, tips longer-pointed, odorless when crushed. *Flowers* 1⅜ to 2 inches long, not yellow spotted, lower petal notched. *Fruits* 8 to 23 inches long, about ⅔ to ⅝ inch in diameter, thick-walled; containing numerous seeds with broad and apically squarish wings.

Winter. *Bark* thick, reddish brown, with flat, thick-scaled ridges.

Comparisons. Similar to the southern catalpa, northern catalpa is best distinguished by its thick-walled fruits and seeds with obtuse or squarish-tipped wings. It tends to be hardier than the southern catalpa, flowers somewhat earlier, and has larger flowers. Even in winter, catalpas can be separated from the princesstree by having a continuous rather than hollow pith. In the summer, the elongated cigarlike (rather than egg-shaped) fruits of the catalpas easily separate these two genera.

Although only weakly differing from the southern catalpa, the northern catalpa, or hardy catalpa, ranges from southern Indiana and Illinois, south to western Tennessee and northeastern Arkansas. It is usually a medium-sized tree 40 to 75 feet in height and from 1 to 2 feet in diameter, but occasionally it reaches much larger proportions. The trunk is usually short and often crooked, with a rather narrowly oblong crown. Since this species is hardier than the southern catalpa, it is rather commonly planted as a street or shade tree in the North. Its wood is light, soft, rather weak, and coarse-grained, but it is durable in contact with the soil. It is used for fence posts, railroad ties, interior finish, and for cheap furniture.

The similar Chinese catalpa (*Catalpa ovata* G. Don) is a shrub or small tree, but with short-acute to short-acuminate glabrous leaves and with yellow flowers marked with orange and purple.

MADDER FAMILY—RUBIACEAE

The Fevertree—Pinckneya

FEVERTREE   *Pinckneya bracteata* **(Bartr.) Raf.**

> The hairy surfaces of the opposite leaves, the hairy twigs, the connecting stipule scars, and the conspicuous, but beautiful, pink- to cream-colored, petal-like sepals that develop on some of the flowers are most distinct.

Summer. *Leaves* 5 to 8 inches long, 3 to 4 inches wide, opposite, simple, deciduous, ovate or elliptical, margins entire; blades apically pointed, bases roundish; upper surfaces dark green and somewhat hairy, lower surfaces paler and densely hairy; stipules prominent; petioles about 1 inch long, stout. *Flowers* 1 to 1½ inches long, perfect, with a single sepal developing into a large 2- to 3-inch bractlike structure, pink to cream colored; petals green yellow, red spotted within, tubular. *Fruits* (capsule) about ¾ inch in diameter, persistent, light brown, globular. *Bark* light brown; on older trunks becoming minutely scaly.

Winter. *Twigs* slender to moderately stout, reddish brown, more or less tawny to gray hairy; leaf scars opposite, crescent-shaped, with a solitary C-shaped bundle scar; stipules present, connecting bases of opposite leaf petioles. *Buds,* terminal bud about ½ inch long, conical, with 2 to 4 reddish brown scales; lateral buds small, ovoid, indistinct.

The fevertree is a small tree sometimes 25 feet high with a trunk 6 to 8 inches across, but most often it is much smaller, and frequently shrublike with multiple trunks. It grows rather sporadically from southeastern South Carolina to the northern part of Florida, along streams and about

FEVERTREE

1. Branch with leaves and flowers.
2. Detail of flower.
3. Cluster of fruits.
4. Winter twig.
5. Detail of leaf scar and bud.

the borders of swamps. When the plant flowers in the spring it is very showy, but actually it is the rosy pink to nearly white, peculiarly leaflike expanded tips of some of the calyx lobes, instead of petals, which put on the show. The greenish yellow, red-spotted corolla is relatively inconspicuous.

The name fevertree (also known as Georgiabark) suggests the fact that the bitter inner bark of the little tree has been used successfully in the treatment of malaria. Actually, it is a close relative of the cinchona tree of Peru, which is the source of the official quinine. It is also known as the pinckneya, for Charles Coatesworth Pinckney of South Carolina, statesman and Revolutionary War general who was also interested in the subject of botany. Today fevertree is grown extensively in the Southeast as an ornamental.

HONEYSUCKLE FAMILY— CAPRIFOLIACEAE

The Arrow-woods and the Blackhaws—Viburnum

The arrow-woods and the blackhaws are shrubs or small trees with opposite, simple, deciduous leaves, which in our native arborescent species are pinnately veined. The lithe or sometimes spikelike twigs have opposite, crescent-shaped leaf scars with 3 bundle scars, and a terminal bud that is somewhat larger than the appressed lateral ones. In our tree species, the buds have but a single pair of visible scales. The small, insect-pollinated, creamy-white flowers are perfect and have a 5-lobed corolla with protruding stamens. They are borne in flat-topped terminal clusters after the leaves are fairly well developed. The fruits are drupes with a large flattened stone and a thin flesh. These small trees have no commercial importance, but they have ornamental possibilities and furnish food for birds and other wildlife.

NANNY-BERRY   *Viburnum lentago* **L.**

> The tiny dark glands on the undersurfaces of the opposite leaves, the winged petioles, the naked buds, and the disagreeable odor of the twigs of this northern tree or shrub when broken are distinctive.

Summer. *Leaves* 2 to 5 inches long, 1 to 3 inches wide, opposite, simple, deciduous, ovate to elliptic, tips abruptly long-pointed, bases rounded or slightly wedge-shaped, margins finely serrately toothed; blades firm, glabrous and dark green above, paler yellow green and glabrous with tiny black glands beneath; petioles ½ to 1 inch long, grooved, and distinctly winged; petioles and midribs occasionally a little rusty scurfy. *Flowers* ¼ inch wide, in convex cymose clusters, on short peduncles less than ⅜ inch

w.c.4.

1.

2.

3.

4.

5.

NANNY-BERRY

1. Branch with mature leaves and fruits.
2-3. Winter twigs.
4. Detail of bud and leaf scar.
5. Detail of winged petiole.

long or sessile, slightly fragrant, developing in the spring; petals 5. *Fruits* (drupe) about ½ inch long, ovate to elliptic, dark bluish black, often glaucous; borne in loose, terminal, red-stemmed clusters; ripening in September.

Winter. *Twigs* slender, flexible, pale orange brown to ashy brown, glabrous, ill scented when crushed; leaf scars crescent-shaped, opposite, with 3 bundle scars. *Buds* lateral buds ½ to ¾ inch long, narrow, often slightly curved, with 2 grayish-scurfy scales; terminal bud larger; flower buds with conspicuously swollen bases. *Bark* reddish brown to gray brown, divided into scaly plates, often with a fetid odor.

Comparisons. The nanny-berry is very similar to both the blackhaw and the possumhaw (*Viburnum nudum* L.). The latter species is smaller and shrubby. It has indistinctly toothed leaves, and flower rays and fruit clusters with a short common stalk. Those of the nanny-berry, and also the blackhaw, are apparently stalkless. Also, unlike nanny-berry, neither the crushed twigs of the possumhaw nor the blackhaw produce a disagreeable odor.

———

The nanny-berry is also known as the sweet viburnum (because of its fruits), the stinking viburnum, or the sheepberry (because of the fetid odor that suggests dirty sheep or goats). It is commonly a large shrub or a small tree 10 to 15 feet in height, but it occasionally attains a height of nearly 30 feet with a trunk up to 10 inches in diameter. The trunk is typically short with a low, bushy, round-topped crown. The nanny-berry prefers the deep, moist, rich soils that occur along the banks of streams, the borders of swamps, and bottomlands.

The wood of the nanny-berry is not used commercially. The fruits have a thin and sugary flesh, which is often relished by country children, but the stones are disagreeably large. The fruits are eaten by several species of wild birds, including the ruffed grouse, and also by a number of species of wild mammals. Birds are undoubtedly most instrumental in distributing the seeds. The nanny-berry is occasionally cultivated as an ornamental. Like the other arrow-woods, it produces flat-topped clusters of small white or creamy-white flowers in May.

The nanny-berry ranges from Quebec to Saskatchewan, south to Georgia and Missouri.

BLACKHAW

Viburnum prunifolium L.

> The peculiar and numerous pinlike or spinelike branchlets and alligator-hide bark are distinctive and observable even at a distance.

Summer. *Leaves* 1 to 3 inches long, ¼ to 2 inches wide, opposite, simple, deciduous, elliptic, ovate, tips abruptly short-pointed, bases rounded or slightly wedge-shaped, margins finely serrately toothed; firm, quite glabrous, dark dull green above and paler beneath; petioles ⅜ to ⅝ inch long, grooved but wingless. *Flowers* ¼ inch wide, in flat-topped cymes; petals white. *Fruits* (drupe) about ⅜ to ½ inch long, elliptical to ovate, dark bluish black, occasionally glaucous; borne in loose, terminal, red-stemmed clusters; ripening in September.

Winter. *Twigs* slender, stiff, spiny in appearance, ashy brown to grayish, quite glabrous; leaf scars crescent- or U-shaped, opposite, with 3 bundle scars. *Buds,* lateral buds about ¼ inch long, narrow and appressed, rather blunt-pointed, somewhat hairy, grayish brown or lead colored, with 2 visible scales; terminal bud larger; flower buds with conspicuously swollen bases. *Bark* dark reddish brown; on the older trunks or stems becoming very rough and broken into small, scaly blocks.

Comparisons. The blackhaw is very similar to the nanny-berry, but has leaf petioles lacking wings and smaller leaves lacking the dark glands on their undersurfaces. It also lacks the fetid odor of the nanny-berry. Moreover, the nanny-berry lacks the dense, spurlike branching pattern of the blackhaw and also has mostly convex rather than flat-topped inflorescences. The blackhaw is also similar to the possumhaw (*Viburnum nudum* L.), which very seldom attains tree size. The latter has indistinctly toothed leaves, and flower rays and fruit clusters with a short common stalk. Those of the blackhaw and also the nanny-berry are apparently stalkless. The rough bark on the mature individuals resembles that of the flowering dogwood.

The blackhaw is commonly a large shrub or a small tree up to 10 or 15 feet in height, but sometimes it attains a height of nearly 30 feet with a trunk up to 10 inches in diameter. The trunk is typically short and often crooked, and the stiff, more-or-less crooked branches form a low and rather broad, round-topped crown. The blackhaw usually occurs on drier

BLACKHAW

1. Branch with mature leaves.
2. Fruiting branch.

3-4. Winter twigs.
5. Detail of bud and leaf scar.

soils than the nanny-berry. It is often common on dry, rocky hillsides, and sometimes forms thickets along old fencerows and roads.

The wood is quite similar to that of the nanny-berry and is not used commercially. The bark and particularly the roots are used medicinally in tonics. The fruits, like those of the nanny-berry, have a thin and sugary flesh and very large stones. They are eaten by various wild birds and mammals. The blackhaw is sometimes planted as an ornamental and to provide food for birds.

The blackhaw ranges from Connecticut to Michigan, south to Florida and Texas.

RUSTY BLACKHAW   *Viburnum rufidulum* **Raf.**

> The alligator-hide bark, leathery, lustrous leaf uppersurfaces, along with the red rusty-hairy buds, leaf petioles (which are winged), midribs of the leaves, and fruit stalks are conspicuous.

Summer. *Leaves* 1½ to 3½ inches long, 1 to 2 inches wide, opposite, simple, deciduous, leathery, ovate to obovate; tips rounded or abruptly sharp-pointed, bases usually pointed, margins finely serrately toothed; blades thick, dark green and lustrous above, paler and more or less rusty-hairy beneath; petioles ¼ to ½ inch long, stout, grooved, somewhat winged, rusty-hairy. *Flowers* ¼ inch wide, small, clustered on short peduncles or sessile; petals 5, white. *Fruits* (drupe) about ½ inch long, elliptical oblong ovoid, bright blue, often glaucous.

Winter. *Twigs* slender, dull reddish brown to ashy, glabrous or more or less rusty-woolly. *Buds* ovoid, reddish, rather densely rusty-woolly; terminal bud up to ½ inch long, largest of the buds, much swollen. *Bark* nearly black, fissured into small blocks, resembling alligator hide.

Comparisons. This species is easily separated from the blackhaw by its larger red-hairy leaves and buds, paler blue fruits, and stout winged petioles.

The rusty blackhaw is also called the southern blackhaw, the rusty nanny-berry, and the bluehaw. It is a large shrub or a small tree sometimes 25 feet in height and 5 or 6 inches in diameter. While it occurs on a wide variety of soil types, it attains its best development in rich, moist bottomlands. It is common throughout much of the South from the coast to the lower slopes of the mountains. The fruits are quite fleshy and are greedily eaten by various birds.

The range of the rusty blackhaw extends from Virginia, Kentucky, southern Ohio, southern Illinois, Missouri, and northeastern Kansas, south to central Florida, the Gulf States, Oklahoma, and central Texas.

SMALL-LEAF ARROW-WOOD   *Viburnum obovatum* Walt.

> The blunt-tipped, sessile or short-petioled (less than ¼ inch long) obovate leaves, with crenate-dentate margins from only above the middle of the leaf blades, are the most distinctive characteristics of this strictly southern coastal plain species.

Summer. *Leaves* usually ¾ to 1½ inches long, ¼ to about ½ inch wide, opposite, simple, evergreen, leathery; obovate, apically rounded, bases pointed, sessile or nearly so, margins entire or somewhat obscurely and bluntly toothed; blades dark green and lustrous above, paler and with minute red hairs beneath. *Flowers* ¼ inch wide, small, clustered on short peduncles or sessile; petals white. *Fruits* (drupe) about ¼ to 5/16 inch long, ovoid to elliptical, slightly flattened, blackish.

Winter. *Twigs* slender, flexible, glabrous or nearly so, reddish brown to grayish. *Buds* small, narrow, reddish brown, hairy; terminal bud about ¼ inch long, larger than lateral buds. *Bark* nearly black, fissured into angular blocks.

———

The small-leaf arrow-wood is also known as the Walter viburnum. It is a small tree (smallest of our tree-sized arrow-woods), attaining a height of about 20 feet and a trunk diameter of 5 or 6 inches. It grows in swamps and in low moist woodlands, or along the banks of streams. All parts of the plant emit a strong odor when crushed or broken, more so, perhaps, than is the case in other arrow-wood species. The fruits have a very thin mealy flesh, but they seem to be relished by many kinds of birds.

This arrow-wood has a range through the coastal plain from South Carolina to the central and northwestern portions of Florida, west to Alabama.

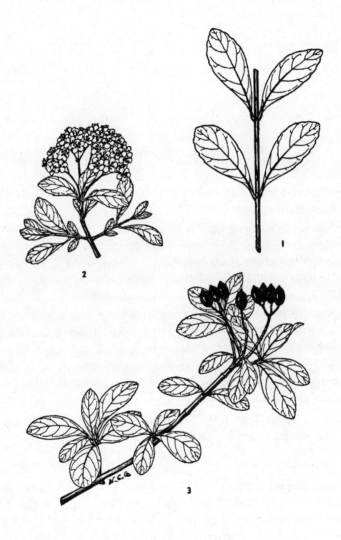

SMALL-LEAF ARROW-WOOD

1. Leaves on vigorous shoot.
2. Flowering branch.

3. Branch with leaves and fruits.

PALM FAMILY—ARECACEAE

The Palmettos—Sabal

The members of the palm family (Arecaceae), to which the palmettos belong, have stems covered by a thick rind. They are usually marked with ringlike scars left by fallen leafstalks, and often, toward the top, retain their persistent sheaths. These trees grow by means of a solitary terminal bud and their leaves are characteristically clustered at the top of the stem. The stems have no true cambium layer and do not show annual growth rings such as are found in the stems of our other trees.

The only native tree palms found north of semitropical southern Florida are those of the genus *Sabal*. These have long-petioled, fan-shaped leaves, which are deeply folded toward the middle and outwardly divided into numerous, often drooping segments edged with threadlike fibers. The 3-parted flowers, which appear about June, are small and fragrant and arranged in rather large drooping clusters. The fruits are small, 1-seeded berries, which ripen late in the fall. Two species of tree-sized palmettos occur in the southeastern United States.

CABBAGE PALMETTO   *Sabal palmetto*
(Walt.) Lodd. ex J. A. & J. H. Schultes

> This semitropical palm species, 15 to 80 feet in height, with its large, clustered, fan-shaped leaves that terminate the nearly straight trunk, is the only treelike palm within our area.

Leaves 4 to 6 feet long and nearly as wide, evergreen, much folded and divided into narrow segments with threadlike fibers hanging between them. *Leafstalks* 5 to 7 feet long, stiff, flat above, rounded beneath, unarmed.

CABBAGE PALMETTO

1. Leaf (very much reduced). 2. Portion of fruit cluster.

Flowers ¼ inch wide, yellow. *Fruits* about ⅓ inch in diameter, nearly black, roundish, 1-seeded, borne in much branched, drooping clusters, 5 or 6 feet long.

————

The cabbage palmetto (from the Spanish word *palmito*, meaning little palm) is a 20- to 50-foot-high tree that grows in a narrow coastal strip from southeastern North Carolina to Georgia, and throughout Florida, where it is by far the most common palm. It is widely planted as a street or ornamental tree throughout the lower part of the South.

Long before the advent of the first Spanish and English colonists, the big white terminal buds of this palm were relished as a food item by the Native American tribes; from them, the first conquistadors and settlers learned about the delicacy hidden in the heart of the swamp cabbage, as the tree came to be known. The disbudding practice, of course, ruins the beauty of the tree and causes its death. Subsequently the white man learned that the palmetto trunks made excellent docks and wharf pilings. During the American Revolution, British cannonballs bounced harmlessly off the tough palmetto logs used in the walls of Fort Moultrie, which guarded Charleston Harbor. Many uses are made of the cabbage palmetto. Fibers from leafstalks are made into brushes and whiskbrooms. The leaves are used as thatch and for making hats, baskets, and mats. The flowers are an excellent source of nectar from which bees make honey. It is the state tree of both South Carolina and Florida.

DWARF PALMETTO   *Sabal minor* (Jacq.) Pers.

The dwarf palmetto, also known as the Louisiana palmetto, has leaves only up to about 3 feet wide, which differ from those of the cabbage palmetto in that the segments do not have threadlike filaments on the margin. It is the northernmost of New World palms, growing in latitude 36° north on the coast of northeastern North Carolina. Northward it is merely a shrub, the main stem being a rootstock. Only along the Gulf Coast, from Florida westward to southeastern Texas, and northward in the lower Mississippi Valley to southern Arkansas, does it become the size of a small tree, up to 6 or 8 feet tall.

Glossary

Abscission. Act or process of cutting off.

Accessory buds. Buds that are at or near the nodes but not in the axils of the leaves.

Achene. A small, dry, 1-seeded, unwinged fruit.

Achlorophyllus. Devoid of chlorophyll or appearing to be so.

Acorn. The fruit of the oaks, which consists of a nut partly enclosed by a scale-covered cup.

Acuminate. Gradually tapering to a diminishing point and with the margin bowing inward; long-pointed.

Acute. Sharp-pointed, but less tapering than acuminate.

Alternate. Leaves, branches, buds, etc., which are scattered singly along the stem; not opposite.

Ament. A catkin.

Angiosperm. A plant in which the seeds are enclosed in the ovary.

Anther. The part of the stamen that bears the pollen.

Anthesis. Strictly, the time of expansion of the flower, but also used for the period during which the flower is open and functional.

Apex. The top or tip of a leaf or bud.

Appressed. Lying close and flat against; a bud that lies close and flat against the twig.

Aromatic. Fragrant or with a pleasing odor.

Awl-like. Shaped like an awl; small and tapering to a slender point.

Axil. The upper angle formed by the junction of a leaf with the stem, or a similar angle formed by the principal veins of a leaf with the midrib.

Axillary. Occurring in an axil; buds that occur in the axils of leaves, or tufts of down that occur in the axils of the veins of the leaves.

Bark. The outer covering of the trunks or branches of trees and shrubs.

Base. The bottom of the blade of the leaf.

Berry. A fruit that is fleshy or pulpy throughout.

Bilabiate. Two-lipped (calyx or corolla).

Bladderlike. Shaped like a sac or bag that is inflated.

Blade. The flat or expanded portion of a leaf.

Bloom. A powdery or waxy substance that is easily rubbed off.

Bract. A more or less modified leaf that subtends a flower or an inflorescence.

Branch. A secondary division of a tree trunk.

Branchlet. A small branch.

Bud. An undeveloped stem or branch, flower, or inflorescence.

Bud scales. Reduced or modified leaves that cover a bud.

Bundle. A cluster, such as a cluster of pine needles.

Bundle-scars. Scars on the surfaces of leaf scars, which represent the broken ends of the fibrovascular bundles that run through the petioles into the blades of the leaves.

Bur. A dry fruit that is covered with prickles or spines.

Calyx. The outer series of modified leaves in a flower, which are usually green in color.

Cambium. A layer of living cells between the inner bark and the sapwood where growth takes place, resulting in the increase in diameter of the trunk and the branches.

Campanulate. Bell-shaped.

Capsule. A dry fruit composed of more than one carpel that splits open at maturity to release the seeds.

Carpel. A simple pistil or one of the sections of a compound pistil.

Catkin. An elongated cluster of unisexual flowers, which are subtended by scalelike bracts.

Chambered. Pith that is interrupted by hollow spaces.

Chlorophyll. The green coloring matter found in plants.

Chloroplasts. The microscopic bodies that contain chlorophyll.

Ciliate. Fringed with hairs on the margin.

Claw. The long, narrow base of a petal or sepal.

Cluster. A group of two or more occurring close together.

Compound. A leaf that is divided into several more or less similar parts, or smaller leaflike portions.

Concave. Depressed or hollowed out.

Cone. A fruit with closely overlapping woody scales, such as those of the pines.

Confluent. Appearing as if flowing together.

Conical. Cone-shaped; largest at the base and tapering to the apex.

Conifer. A cone-bearing tree.

Continuous. Said of pith that is not interrupted with hollow spaces.

Convex. Arched.

Coppice. Thicket of trees that originated from shoots or root suckers, not seeds.

Cordate. Heart-shaped.

Coriaceous. Leathery in texture; tough.

Corolla. The inner series of modified leaves of a flower, which are usually brightly colored and showy.

Corymb. An inflorescence or flower cluster with a flat-topped appearance, in which the outermost flowers bloom first.

Corymbose. Arranged in corymbs.

Crenate. Having the margin cut with rounded teeth; scalloped.

Crown. The upper part of the tree, composed of the branches and foliage.

Cuneate. Wedge-shaped; triangular, with the narrow part at the point of attachment.

Cup. The cuplike or bowl-like involucre surrounding the nut in oaks.

Cylindrical. Round in cross section but much elongated.

Cyme. An inflorescence or flower cluster with a flat-topped appearance, in which the central flowers bloom first.

Deciduous. Not persistent; falling away, as the leaves of many trees do in autumn.

Decurrent. Extending downward; ridges that extend down from leaf scars, for example.

Dehiscent. Splitting open.

Deltoid. Shaped like a delta of a river, or broadly triangular.

Depressed. Somewhat flattened from above.

Dioecious. Having staminate and pistillate flowers in different plants.

Divergent. Buds, etc., which point away from the twig.

Double-serrate. Doubly toothed.

Doubly toothed. A margin that has larger teeth that in turn have smaller teeth on them.

Downy. Covered with fine hairs.

Drupe. A fruit in which the seed is enclosed in a bony or stony inner portion, and with a fleshy or pulpy outer portion surrounding it.

Eciliate. Without hairs on the margins.

E-, Ex-. Latin prefix meaning without, out of, from.

Egg-shaped. Shaped like an egg, with the broadest portion below the middle.

Elliptical. Oblong with rounded ends.

Elongate. Much longer than broad.

Entire. Without divisions, lobes, or teeth.

Epi-. Prefix meaning "upon" or "above."

Erose. Jagged, or appearing as if gnawed.

Evergreen. With green leaves during the winter season.

Exfoliate. To peel off or shed, as the layers of bark.

Falcate. Sickle-shaped.

Fascicle. A close cluster or bundle of flowers, leaves, stems, or roots.

Fasciculate. In a fascicle.

Fibrovascular bundle. The strands of tissues engaged in transporting fluids throughout a plant; these extend through the petioles and into the veins of the leaves.

Filament. The stalklike part of a stamen, which supports the anther.

Flaky. Bark with loose scales that are easily rubbed off.

Fleshy. Succulent or juicy.

Flocculent. With small tufts of soft woolly hair.

Flower. A branch with modified leaves, such as sepals or petals, and the sexual organs.

Flower bud. A bud that contains a flower or a cluster of flowers.

Fluted. With rounded ridges.

Foliaceous. Leaflike.

Foliage. The leaves taken collectively.

Follicle. A podlike fruit derived from a single carpel and splitting open along one side.

Fruit. The seed-bearing portion of a plant.

Glabrate. Almost glabrous; tending to be glabrous.

Glabrescent. Becoming glabrous.

Glabrous. Without hairs.

Gland. A small protuberance or structure with a secreting surface.

Glandular. Bearing glands.

Glaucous. Covered or whitened with a bloom, as a cabbage leaf; bluish white or bluish gray.

Globular. Spherical or nearly so.

Gymnosperm. A tree of the pine family that bears naked seeds on the upper surfaces of the cone scales.

Habit. The general appearance of a tree as seen from a distance.

Habitat. The place where a tree grows naturally, such as in a swamp, a river floodplain, or a dry ridge.

Hairy. With long hairs.

Hardwood. A term applied to broad-leaved trees as opposed to the conifers.

Head. The crown of a tree.

Heartwood. The dead interior wood of the trunks and larger branches of a tree.

Hoary. Grayish white with a fine down.

Hybrid. A cross between two closely related species.

Imbricate. Overlapping as shingles on a roof.

Imperfect. A term applied to a flower that contains only one set of sexual organs, either stamens or pistils.

Indehiscent. Not splitting open.

Inflorescence. The flowering portion of a plant.

Involucre. The bracts that surround a flower cluster.

Keeled. With a central ridge like the keel of a boat.

Key. A winged fruit, particularly that of the maples.

Lanceolate. Lance-shaped; much longer than broad, tapering from below the middle to the apex and (more abruptly) to the base.

Lateral. Situated along the side of a twig.

Leaf. The green expansions borne by the branches of a tree.

Leaf bud. A bud that contains undeveloped leaves but not flowers.

Leaf cushion. The individual decurrent swelling of stems from which the leaves are attached.

Leaflet. One of the small leaflike portions of a compound leaf.

Leaf scar. The scar left on a twig by the fall of a leaf.

Legume. A podlike fruit composed of a solitary carpel, which usually splits into two halves at maturity.

Lenticels. Corky spots on the surfaces of twigs, which sometimes persist on the bark of branches, to admit air into the interior.

Linear. Very long and narrow with parallel edges.

Lobe. A more or less rounded division of an organ.

Lobed. Provided with lobes; leaves that have deep indentations, often extending halfway or more to the midrib.

Longitudinal. Lengthwise.
Lustrous. Glossy; shining.

Membranous. Of the nature of a membrane; thin, soft, and pliable.
Midrib. The central vein of a leaf.
Monoecious. Having staminate and pistillate flowers on the same plant, but not perfect ones.
Mucilaginous. Slimy when chewed.
Mucronate. With a small and short abrupt tip of an organ, as the projection of the midrib of a leaf.

Naked bud. A bud that lacks bud scales.
Nectar. A sweet secretion of glands in many kinds of flowers.
Nectariferous. Nectar bearing; having a nectary, or an organ that secrets nectar.
Needle. A very narrow leaf of such trees as pines and spruces.
Needlelike. Very long, narrow, and pointed at the tip; shaped like a needle.
Node. The point on a stem where one or more leaves are attached.
Nut. A hard-shelled, 1-seeded, indehiscent fruit.
Nutlet. A diminutive nut.

Oblanceolate. Inversely lanceolate.
Oblique. Slanted, or with unequal sides.
Oblong. Longer than broad and of fairly uniform diameter.
Obovate. Egg-shaped, with the broadest part above the middle.
Obovoid. An egg-shaped solid, with the broadest part above the middle.
Opposite. Leaves, branches, buds, etc., which occur on opposite sides of the stem at a node.
Oval. Broadly elliptical.
Ovary. The portion of the pistil that contains the ovules.
Ovate. Egg-shaped, with the broadest part below the middle.
Ovoid. An egg-shaped solid, with the broadest part below the middle.
Ovule. The part of a flower that, after fertilization, becomes the seed.

Palmate. Radiately lobed or compounded; also applied to leaf venation where the primary veins radiate from the summit of the petiole.
Panicle. A loose, irregularly compounded inflorescence of pediceled flowers.
Pedicel. The stalk of a single flower in an inflorescence.
Peduncle. The stalk of either a solitary flower or of an inflorescence.

Peltate. Shield-shaped; a flat body having the stalk attached to the lower surface instead of at the base or margin.

Pendent. Hanging downward.

Pendulous. More or less pendent or hanging.

Perfect. A term applied to a flower that contains both sexual organs (stamens and pistils).

Persistent. Existing for a long or continuous time; e.g., fruits that remain on the branches throughout the winter, calyxes that remain on the fruits, etc.

Petal. One of the divisions of the corolla.

Petiole. The stalk of a leaf.

Pinnate. Pinnately compound.

Pinnately compound. A compound leaf in which the leaflets are arranged along a common rachis.

Pistil. The female sexual organ of flowers.

Pistillate. Flowers that have one or more pistils but no stamens.

Pith. The softer central portion of a twig or stem.

Pneumatophore. Negatively geotropic extensions of the root systems of some trees growing in swampy habitats; they grow upward and out of the water to assure adequate aeration.

Pollen. The male sexual cells, which are produced in the anthers.

Pollination. The act of transferring the pollen from the stamens to the receptive part of the pistils.

Pome. A fleshy fruit such as the apple, in which the receptacle is joined to the pistils and develops into a part of the fruit.

Prickle. A small spine that grows from the bark.

Puberulent. Minutely pubescent.

Pubescence. Covered with short, soft hairs; downy.

Raceme. A simple inflorescence in which the flowers are arranged along an elongated axis or stalk.

Racemose. Resembling a raceme.

Rachis (pl. *rachises*). The extension of the petiole of a compound leaf corresponding to the midrib; the central axis of an inflorescence such as a spike or a raceme.

Receptacle. The portion of a flower to which the various organs are attached.

Recurved. Bent backward or downward.

Resinous. Coated with a sticky gum or resin.

Reticulate. With a network; net-veined.

Retuse. Notched shallowly at a rounded apex.

Revolute. Turned or rolled backward.

Rosette. A short stem or branch bearing a cluster of leaves.

Rugose. Wrinkled.

Samara. An indehiscent, 1-seeded, winged fruit.

Sapwood. The younger, living, outer layer of wood in the trunk and the branches of trees.

Scale. A small modified leaf of a bud or cone; a flake into which the outer bark often divides.

Scalelike. Resembling scales.

Scaly. Provided with scales; flaky.

Scarious. Thin, dry, and membranous, not green.

Scurfy. Covered with small, branlike scales.

Seed. A ripened ovule.

Sepal. One of the divisions of the calyx.

Serrate. Toothed, with sharp teeth pointing forward like those of a saw.

Serrulate. Finely serrate.

Sessile. Without a stalk.

Sheath. A tubular envelope, such as occurs at the base of the clusters of needles in most species of pines.

Shrub. A low, woody plant, which commonly divides close to the ground into many stems.

Simple. Consisting of one piece; leaves in which the blade is in one piece, not compound.

Sinuous. Wavy, like the path of a snake.

Sinus. The cleft or the space between two lobes.

Softwood. A term applied to conifers as opposed to the broad-leaved trees, or hardwoods.

Spherical. Nearly round.

Spike. A simple inflorescence of sessile flowers arranged on a common and elongated stalk or axis.

Spine. A sharp, woody outgrowth from a stem.

Spring wood. Wood that is formed during the period of rapid growth in the spring, appearing lighter in color than the wood formed later as the growth slows down.

Spur shoot. A short, slow-growing branchlet.

Stalked. Provided with a stalk.

Stamen. The male sexual organ of flowers.

Staminate. Flowers that contain only stamens.

Stellate. Star-shaped; a hair that is short-stalked and has numerous radially arranged divisions.

Sterigmata. Small woody stalks to which the leaves of spruces and hemlocks are attached, which persist on the twigs after the leaves fall.

Sterile. Not producing seed; also applied to soils that are unproductive.

Stigma. The part of the pistil that receives the pollen.

Stipule. A leaflike appendage, which occurs at the base of the petiole of a leaf.

Stipule-scar. The scar left on a twig by the fall of a stipule.

Striate. Marked with fine, longitudinal lines or ridges.

Strobilus (pl. *strobili*). Conelike structure(s).

Style. A portion of the pistil that connects the stigma and the ovary.

Subglobose. Somewhat spherical or rounded.

Subtend. To lie under or opposite to.

Summer wood. Wood produced late in the growing season when growth is slow.

Superposed. Accessory buds that occur above the axillary buds.

Syncarp. A multiple or fleshy aggregate fruit.

Terminal bud. A bud that is formed at the tip of a twig or branchlet.

Thorn. A stiff, woody, sharp-pointed projection.

Tomentose. With tomentum; covered with rather short, densely matted, soft white woolly hairs.

Tomentum. Densely matted or woolly hairs.

Toothed. Provided with teeth or small projections.

Translucent. Semiclear.

Truncate. Appearing as if cut off; square.

Trunk. The main stem of a tree.

Turbinate. Top-shaped; inversely conical.

Twig. A young shoot; a term generally applied to the growth of the past season.

Two-ranked. In two vertical rows.

Umbel. A simple inflorescence in which the flowers radiate from the same point.

Umbellate. Borne in an umbel.

Undulate. With a wavy margin.

Unisexual. Not perfect; a flower that contains only stamens or pistils.

Veins. The strands of fibrovascular tissue in a leaf.

Vestiture. That which covers the surface, as hair, scales, and so on.

Viscid. Sticky.

Whorl. An arrangement of three or more leaves or branches in a circle about a common axis.

Wing. A thin, flat appendage.

Wood. The hard or firm portion of a stem lying between the pith and the bark.

Woody. Of the consistency of wood.

Woolly. Covered with tangled or matted hairs.

Selected References

Argus, G. W. *The Genus Salix (Salicaceae) in the Southeastern United States.* Systematic Botany Monographs vol. 9. American Society of Plant Taxonomists, 1986.

Barnes, B. V., and W. H. Wagner, Jr. *Michigan Trees.* Ann Arbor: University of Michigan Press, 1981.

Blackburn, B. *Trees and Shrubs in Eastern North America.* New York: Oxford University Press, 1952.

Blakeslee, A. F., and C. D. Jarvis. *Trees in Winter.* New York: Macmillan, 1931.

Britton, N. L., and J. A. Shafer. *North American Trees.* New York: Henry Holt, 1908.

Brockman, C. F. *Trees of North America.* New York: Golden Press, 1968.

Brooks, A. B. *West Virginia Trees.* Morgantown, W.Va.: Agricultural Experiment Station, College of Agriculture, 1920.

Brown, C. A. *Louisiana Trees and Shrubs.* Baton Rouge: Louisiana Forestry Commission, 1945.

Brown C. L., and L. K. Kirkman. *Trees of Georgia and Adjacent States.* Portland, Oreg.: Timber Press, Inc., 1990.

Brown, H. P. *Trees of New York State, Native and Naturalized.* Syracuse, N.Y.: N.Y. State College of Forestry, 1921

Burns, C. P., and C. H. Otis. *The Trees of Vermont.* Burlington: Vermont Agricultural Experiment Station, 1916.

Canada Forest Service. *Native Trees of Canada.* Ottawa: 1939.

Coker, W. C., and H. R. Totten. *Trees of the Southeastern United States.* Chapel Hill: University of North Carolina Press, 1945.

Collingwood, G. H. *Knowing Your Trees.* Washington, D.C.: American Forestry Association.

Core, E. L., and N. Ammons. *Woody Plants of West Virginia in Winter Condition.* Morgantown: West Virginia University, 1947.

Cox, P. W., and P. Leslie. *Texas Trees: A Friendly Guide.* San Antonio: Corona Publishing Co., 1997.

Curtis, C. C., and S. C. Bausor. *The Complete Guide to North American Trees.* Philadelphia: Blakiston Co., 1943.

Duncan, W. H. *Guide to Georgia Trees.* Athens: University of Georgia Press, 1941.

Duncan, W. H., and M. B. Duncan. *Trees of the Southeastern United States.* Athens: University of Georgia Press, 1988.

Elias, T. S. *The Complete Trees of North America: Field Guide and Natural History.* New York: Times Mirror Magazines, Inc., 1980.

Farrar, J. L. *Trees of the Northern United States and Canada.* Ames: Iowa State University Press, 1995.

Fernald, M. L. *Gray's Manual of Botany.* 8th ed. New York: American Book Co., 1950.

Fernald, M. L., and A. C. Kinsey. *Edible Wild Plants of Eastern North America.* Cornwall-on-Hudson, N.Y.: Idlewild Press, 1943.

Godfrey, R. K. *Trees, Shrubs, and Woody Vines of Northern Florida and Adjacent Georgia and Alabama.* Athens: University of Georgia Press, 1988.

Graves, A. H. *Illustrated Guide to Trees and Shrubs.* Rev. ed. New York: Harper and Brothers, Publisher, 1956.

Green, C. H. *Trees of the South.* Chapel Hill: University of North Carolina Press, 1939.

Grimm, W. C. *The Illustrated Book of Wildflowers and Shrubs.* Rev. ed. Mechanicsburg, Pa.: Stackpole Books, 1993.

———. *The Trees of Pennsylvania.* Harrisburg, Pa.: Stackpole Company, 1950.

Harlow, W. M., and E. S. Harrar. *Textbook of Dendrology.* New York: McGraw-Hill, 1941.

Harrar, E. S., and J. G. Harrar. *Guide to Southern Trees.* New York: McGraw-Hill, 1946.

Hosie, R. C. *Native Trees of Canada.* Ottawa: Department of the Environment, 1969.

Hough, R. B. *Handbook of Trees of the Northern States and Canada East of the Rocky Mountains.* New York: Macmillan, 1947.

Hunter, C. G. *Trees, Shrubs and Vines of Arkansas.* Little Rock, Ark.: Ozark Society Foundation, 1989.

Illick, J. S. *Pennsylvania Trees.* Harrisburg: Pennsylvania Department of Forests and Waters, 1925.

Jacobson, A. L. *North American Landscape Trees.* Berkeley, Calif.: Ten Speed Press, 1996.

Kartesz, J. T. (Biota of North America Program). *A Synonymized Checklist of the Vascular Flora of the United States, Canada, and Greenland.* vols. 1-2. 2d ed. Portland, Or.: Timber Press, 1994.

————. J. T. A Synonymized Checklist and Atlas with Biological Attributes for the Vascular Flora of the United States, Canada, and Greenland. 1st ed. In: Kartesz, J. T., and C. A. Meacham. Synthesis of the North American Flora, version 1.0. Chapel Hill: North Carolina Botanical Garden, 1999.

Kurz, H., and R. K. Godfrey. *Trees of Northern Florida.* Gainesville: University of Florida Press, 1962.

Lance, R. *Woody Plants of the Southeastern U.S.* Unpublished manuscript.

Little, E. L., Jr. *Checklist of United States Trees (Native and Naturalized).* Agriculture Handbook No. 541. Washington, D.C.: Forest Service, USDA, 1979.

————. *National Audubon Society Field Guide to North American Trees: Eastern Region.* New York: Chanticleer Press, 1980.

Martin, A. C., H. S. Zim, and A. L. Nelson. *American Wildlife and Plants.* New York: McGraw-Hill, 1951.

Matthews, F. S. *Field Book of American Trees and Shrubs.* New York: G. P. Putnam's Sons, 1915.

Miller, R. B., and L. R. Tehon. *The Native and Naturalized Trees of Illinois.* Urbana, Ill.: Natural History Survey, 1929.

Muenscher, W. C. *Keys to Woody Plants.* Ithaca, N.Y.: Comstock, 1950.

Nelson, G. *The Trees of Florida.* Sarasota: Pineapple Press, Inc., 1994.

Otis, C. H. *Michigan Trees.* Ann Arbor: University of Michigan, 1923.

Peattie, D. C. *A Natural History of Trees of Eastern and Central North America.* Boston: Houghton Mifflin, 1950.

Petrides, G. A. *A Field Guide to Trees and Shrubs.* Boston: Houghton Mifflin Co., 1958.

————. *Eastern Trees: Peterson Field Guides.* Illustrated by J. Wehr. 1st ed. Boston: Houghton Mifflin Co., 1998.

Preston, R. I., Jr. *North American Trees.* Ames: Iowa State University Press, 1961.

Radford, A. E., H. E. Ahles, and C. R. Bell. *Manual of the Vascular Flora of the Carolinas.* Chapel Hill: University of North Carolina Press, 1968.

Rosendahl, C. O. *Trees and Shrubs of the Upper Midwest.* Minneapolis: University of Minnesota Press, 1955.

Sargent, C. S. *The Silva of North America*. Boston: Houghton Mifflin, 1891–1902.

———. *Manual of the Trees of North America*. Boston: Houghton Mifflin, 1922.

Scoggan, H. J. *The Flora of Canada*. 4 vols. Ottawa: Natural Museum of Natural Sciences, Natural Museum of Canada, 1978.

Small, J. K. *Manual of the Southeastern Flora*. Lancaster, Pa.: Press of the Science Press, 1933.

Society of American Foresters. *Forest Cover Types of the Eastern United States*. Washington, D.C.: 1932.

Stephens, H. A. *Woody Plants of the North Central Plains*. Lawrence: University Press of Kansas, 1973.

Stupka, A. *Trees, Shrubs, and Woody Vines of Great Smoky Mountains National Park*. Knoxville: University of Tennessee Press, 1964.

Swanson, R. E. *A Field Guide to the Trees and Shrubs of the Southern Appalachians*. Baltimore: Johns Hopkins University Press, 1994.

Taber, W. S. *Delaware Trees*. 2d ed. Dover: Delaware State Forestry Department, 1960.

Treleuse, W. *Winter Botany: An Identification Guide to Native Trees and Shrubs*. 3d ed. New York: Dover Publications, Inc., 1931.

Van der Linden, P. J., and D. R. Farrar. *Forest and Shade Trees of Iowa*. 2d ed. Ames: Iowa State University Press, 1993.

Van Dersal, W. R. *Native Woody Plants of the United States—Their Erosion-Control and Wildlife Values*. Washington, D.C.: USDA, 1938.

West, E., and L. E. Arnold. *The Native Trees of Florida*. Gainesville: University of Florida Press, 1952.

Wildman, E. E. *Penn's Woods*. Philadelphia: Christopher Sower, 1933.

Index

Page numbers in italics refer to illustrations.

William Carey Grimm was a botanist and illustrator who wrote extensively on tree and plant identification. His books include *The Illustrated Book of Wildflowers and Shrubs, Familiar Trees of America, Recognizing Native Shrubs, Recognizing Flowering Wild Plants, The Wondrous World of Seedless Plants,* and *The Study of Flowers Made Simple.* Grimm was a science educator and member of the Pennsylvania Game Commission. He died in 1992.

Dr. John T. Kartesz is the director of the Biota of North America Program of the North Carolina Botanical Garden. He is the author of scores of books and papers on the North American flora and serves on both the Management and Editorial Committees of Flora North America.